Juniper® and Cisco™ Routing

Policy and Protocols for Multivendor IP Networks

Juniper® and Cisco™ Routing

Policy and Protocols for Multivendor IP Networks

Walter J. Goralski

Wiley Publishing, Inc.

Publisher: Robert Ipsen
Editor: Carol Long
Developmental Editor: Scott Amerman
Associate Managing Editor: John Atkins
Text Design & Composition: Wiley Composition Services

Designations used by companies to distinguish their products are often claimed as trademarks. In all instances where Wiley Publishing, Inc. is aware of a claim, the product names appear in initial capital or ALL CAPITAL LETTERS. Readers, however, should contact the appropriate companies for more complete information regarding trademarks and registration.

This book is printed on acid-free paper. ∞

For general information on our other products and services please contact our Customer Care Department within the United States at (800) 762-2974, outside the United States at (317) 572-3993 or fax (317) 572-4002.

Wiley also publishes its books in a variety of electronic formats. Some content that appears in print may not be available in electronic books.

Library of Congress Cataloging-in-Publication Data:
ISBN: 0-471-21592-9

Printed in the United States of America

10 9 8 7 6 5 4 3 2 1

Contents

Acknowledgments

At this point in my career, I find myself working with an incredible array of people of pure genius and inspiration. My employer, Juniper Networks, has provided me with a home unlike any I have found in a career spanning more than 30 years. I feel truly lucky to be here.

I would like to thank my employer, Juniper Networks, and especially Scott Kriens and Pradeep Sindhu, for creating the type of intellectual work environment where personal growth is always encouraged and for nurturing a climate that creates a quest for knowledge. I owe special thanks to Matt Kolon, who brought me on board, Todd Warble, my manager, and Scott Edwards for respecting my ideas and never failing to support my efforts.

I owe a great deal to individuals I have had contact with over the years who took time to show me their work and correct my numerous misunderstandings of what at times seemed beyond my comprehension. I must especially mention some of my fellow developers, instructors, and associates: Tim Brown, Jeff Doyle, Paul Goyette, Alan Gravett, Hannes Gredler, Pete Moyer, Harry Reynolds, Scott Robohn, Jason Rogan, Derek Rogillio, Chris Summers, and Tom Van Meter. All took the time to answer my frequent questions and provide me with key sources of information when I needed it. And Matt Kolon even provided a router when I needed it (but I got the upgrade!).

Some others helped directly with the book. Patrick Ames had the vision to propose this series in the first place, Aviva Garrett looked at the early drafts and pronounced them up to Juniper Networks standards (a judgment I seriously worried about), Peter Lundquist shared key findings of his own on Cisco/Juniper Networks router interoperability and configurations, Joe Soricelli wrote a whole course on routing policy that I contributed to and formed the basis for the later chapters in this book, and Richard Salaiz read the first draft and reviewed the content. Outside of Juniper Networks, William Caban-Babilonia was a key source of support and information, and Tony Martin provided a close reading of the first draft.

On the publishing side at Wiley, Margaret Eldridge has been a great supporter and editor. The production editor, John Atkins, supported the process from start to finish with efficiency.

Finally, my family and inner circle continue to provide support as well. Camille Obert, the love of my life, has stood by me throughout the writing effort. Sometimes she sensed my distress and suggested a late night of writing or a Saturday of router lab time without me even having to ask (is she a keeper, or what?). Clay Obert has become the "one more child" I always wanted. Kay Obert welcomed me into the fold and made me feel right at home. Camille's sister and husband, Kim and Iako Tsoukalas, have provided welcome relief from the stress and strain of the writing grind. My children, Christopher, Alexander, and Arianna, are now used to having a writer for a father. Thank you all.

Introduction

It seems appropriate to launch this initial volume in this series of texts on the multivendor aspects of routing and the Internet with a more comprehensive introduction than might be expected in later volumes in the series. This will establish the general philosophy and approach of the texts and provide the reader with a context for determining the purpose of each of the volumes. For instance, this volume on routing policy is not just about routing protocols, but how routers use various configurable *policies* to determine precisely which routes are accepted by the router or *advertised* to (shared with) other routers. In keeping with the multivendor theme of the series, once the role of a particular routing policy is established in a chapter, the actual syntax used to implement that routing policy in the configuration languages of both Cisco and Juniper Networks routers is presented. So a chapter and section on prepending AS Path information with the BGP AS Path attribute is followed by sections on prepending AS Path information in both the Cisco and Juniper Networks router environment.

This brief section has already introduced some key terms such as *policies* and *advertised*. Several other key terms are used over and over again in this book. All of these terms are more fully explained when first introduced. Be aware that this is not a book about routing *protocol*. Nevertheless, enough of the operational details of all the major routing protocols such as OSPF, IS-IS, and BGP are given to allow the reader to appreciate what is being done to the routing protocols through the use of routing policies. The emphasis throughout this book is on the routing *policy* and in particular those features of the routing policy that add to, delete from, or modify the routing information normally shared by routers when no routing policies are in place.

Sometimes routing policy is treated as having almost the same meaning as *policy-based routing*, but in this book we distinguish the two terms. There are no real official definitions of these terms, so this is the place, right up front, to be clear about how the terms are used in this book. Policy-based routing, as normally defined and used, means *the local application of additional packet information, such as the source address, to influence how a packet is routed to the next-hop router*. This might be done, for instance, to selectively forward a particular customer's packets to one transit ISP or another, depending on circumstances, or for quality of service (QoS) considerations, such as finding and setting some packet's type of service (TOS) header bits for preferential treatment downstream, or for potential cost savings by routing bulk or interactive traffic over certain links. There might even be more reasons to base routing on one policy or another.

Whatever the reason, the key is that *policy-based* routing usually concerns how a packet is handled *locally*, in conformance to a locally defined policy. In contrast, in this book, *routing policy* applies not so much to how packets are routed locally (although that is the end result, of course), but how routing information is distributed and used by the routing protocols beyond the local router. So policy-based routing has a more restricted, local scope, and routing policy has a more general, wider scope than just the local router. In fact, routing policy is most effective when formulated and enforced over as wide a scope and among as many routers as possible, whether an OSPF area, an IS-IS level, a whole AS, or even between ISP peers.

All of these terms and ideas are fully discussed in this book. The point here is that every router vendor today has a *routing policy framework* (a set of tools) in place for configuration purposes that enables the construction and use of a *routing policy* that can be used for, among other things, *policy-based routing* of packets through the collection of routers. This is how these terms are defined for the purposes of this book and how the concepts relate to each other. The emphasis here is on the routing policy itself, although the related concepts will play a role as well.

Overview of the Book and Technology

Books about Internet routing protocols and the role that these routing protocols play on the Internet have been around for a while. But other books tend to play up the nuts-and-bolts aspects of the routing protocols such as message exchanges and protocol packet structures. So there are long chapters on the low-level functioning of OSPF Link-State Advertisements (LSAs), IS-IS Type-Length-Value (TLV) extensions, and BGP attributes, but little information about *how* network administrators use these routing protocols on the Internet today. A key aspect of the way these routing protocols interoperate and interact today is the concept of a *routing policy*. A routing policy is just a set of rules that establish the ways that a route (today most often called a *prefix*) is used when learned by the router and then passed on (advertised) to other routers. Yet information about the formulation and use of these routing policies is quite hard to come by.

For example, the index to a major and standard book on BGP references only four pages concerning routing policies out of a total page count of almost 500. A well-known and standard text on OSPF is no better: eight pages listed in the index out of almost 350 in the book. And these texts can be considered as treating routing policy very well when it comes to some other texts. One standard treatment of IS-IS is typical of these books: one solitary page on policy routing out of about 500.

Now, it is true enough that routing policy plays little role in IGP routing protocols such as OSPF and IS-IS, especially when each IGP is considered in isolation. But routing policy has an absolutely crucial role in BGP, and considering that on the Internet today no IGP is ever used in isolation without at least some interaction with BGP, routing policy should still be a topic even when IGPs are the focus of the discussion.

In fairness, the goal of many of these books is not routing policy or use of the routing protocols, but just a detailed (and often *very* detailed) examination of the role of every byte and every bit in every packet and every message type in the routing protocol. But even one huge book that explores the operational aspects of the routing protocols, a book that emphasizes the actual use of the routing protocols, devotes little more than 20 pages to routing policy out of more than 1,000. Many of the other books in this field are written by academics or router vendor gurus that apparently have little time to spend in a lab actually configuring routers and seeing how they behave when distributing routing information, or finding out how the ISPs actually use routing protocols and routing policy. Most of these other books also seem to be embedded in "Cisco-speak," the assumption being that the reader will only be using a Cisco router to implement any of these protocols. For instance, one BGP book's section on route stability makes certain Cisco-specific actions seem like key features of the BGP specification. When many authors say "BGP," they often mean "Cisco's implementation of BGP," although this is rarely made clear to the reader.

This book corrects these situations in several ways. First, the emphasis is not so much on how the routing protocols exchange messages or the format of the protocol message fields, although that information is, of course, present. The emphasis in this book (and series) is on configuring the routing protocols to do what needs to be done, either to attach a site to an ISP, to allow a router to participate in an ISP backbone, or to connect the router to other ISPs' routers.

There is more than enough information in this book on IS-IS and OSPF in general, but the emphasis is on BGP as the most important routing protocol on the Internet today. Second, there are numerous real-world examples showing the configuration parameters in action in a vendor-independent fashion. For instance, when we discuss a BGP feature such as route damping, the general topic is followed by a section on how to configure the key damping parameters on a Cisco router. Then there is a section on how to configure the same behavior on a Juniper Networks router. At each step, comparisons are made, but not in a judgmental fashion. Including information on only Cisco and Juniper Networks routers is in no way intended as a critical judgment on other vendor's products or methods. The exclusion of router vendors other than Cisco and Juniper Networks is a decision forced by the demands of time, resources, and sheer magnitude of the task.

How This Book Is Organized

This book about routing protocols and routing policy addresses not only IGPs such as IS-IS and OSPF but also the key EGP known as BGPv4. Also addressed are Cisco implementations of routing policies as well as implementations for Juniper Networks routers as well. All aspects of routing policy are fully covered. Despite the recent industry doldrums, the Internet remains a key part of life around the world. The time for such a volume is clearly here.

This book also demystifies the operation of all routing protocols in general and BGP in particular. Full attention is paid to details of operation at the lower levels of the protocols, such as what happens when two BGP routers first interact. But the whole idea is to present a framework for understanding how routers are gathered into ISP networks and how these networks are combined into the Internet. It is at this point of creating an *internetwork* that routing policy plays a key role.

No other books are available that explain how routing policy works in nontechnical detail and at the same time explain why routing policy technologies are so important to the Internet today. So far, most of the latest ideas in the routing policy field have been discussed only in vendor white papers and technical journals. This book is state-of-the-art subject matter with a multivendor approach. This is a fresh approach to the entire field of routing policy.

This routing policy book is organized as a readable, practical guide rather than a reference manual. The structure offers a balance between the extreme technical detail of the vendor reference materials and the high-level overviews found in the trade press and magazine articles dedicated to other subjects. By working through the numerous real-world applications and examples, especially in the later portions of the work, this book reaches readers with a variety of backgrounds and experience.

This book has no computations to speak of, other than a few algebraic formulas to illustrate topics like route damping. And these are represented graphically as well as in formal mathematical notation.

One final note is needed regarding the scope of the chapters on the routing protocols and the example networks used to illustrate the main routing protocol principles. None of the example networks are intended to exhaustively explore every aspect of each routing protocol and all of the routing policy possibilities. To do so would require a book at least twice as large as the present volume. So there is no mention or configuration of more obscure (but worthwhile) features such as ignoring the attach bit, creating virtual links, or multiple hops for border routers. All of the routing protocol and routing policy basics are covered, but the size of the book limited the depth to which each protocol and policy could be explored.

Part 1: The Internet and the Router. These six chapters set the tone for the rest of the book and series. This part of the book positions the Internet, Web, the IP packet, and the role of the router (both Cisco and Juniper Networks routers) so that readers can appreciate the importance of later topics in the book.

Chapter 1: A Brief History of the Internet and Router. This chapter sets the stage not only for the whole work but for the whole series. This is a historical overview of the Internet, with the emphasis on what has happened since the Web hit town in the 1990s. The emphasis, naturally, is on the role of the ISPs and the use of the router today as the network node of the Internet. The Internet history presented here is an overview, focusing on the growth of the Internet since around 1983 rather than the details of the roots of early Internet as ARPANET. Then the history of the Internet almost merges around 1993 with the history and growth of the Web (then the World Wide Web). The growth of the Internet and Web spurred the currently continuing evolution of the router as the key component and network node of the Internet. Finally, the role of the Internet service providers (ISPs) themselves is introduced, again in historical perspective.

Chapter 2: TCP/IP Survivor's Guide. This chapter offers an overview of the Internet protocol suite, more commonly known as the TCP/IP stack. The intent is to provide basic information and knowledge that is assumed in the later chapters. The approach treats the TCP/IP protocol stack's lower layers first, meaning the basic frame structures and transports used for IP packet and routing protocol information transfer. Next come the Internet protocol suite upper layers, meaning transport protocols TCP and UDP, as well as the applications that rely on these and other lower layers to perform their roles. Several adjunct IP functions such as DNS and ARP are also discussed here. Finally, the basic structure of the IP version 4 (IPv4) packet header is examined. Although the emphasis throughout most of this book is on IPv4 (simply called IP in this book), the next chapter takes a close look at the newer IP version 6 (IPv6).

Chapter 3: IP Addressing and Routing.   This chapter explores the key topic of the IP address space. Routers in a very real sense do little more when they receive a packet than figure out just what to do with an IP address. The differences between direct routing and indirect routing are investigated. This chapter also looks at IPv6 addressing and headers. The main topics here are the original *classful* IP address space, IPv4 as currently implemented using *classless* IP addressing, and IPv6 addressing.

Chapter 4: Subnets and Supernets.   This chapter puts all of the concepts from the previous chapters together. The chapter introduces the idea of the IP masking to create subnets and supernets and how routers deal with IP addresses with variable-length network *prefixes*. All of the necessary terminology and practices regarding subnets and supernets are explored, as well as the key topic of variable-length subnet masking (VLSM). Various forms of IP prefix notation are also covered in full, especially with regard to IPv6.

Chapter 5: Cisco Router Configuration.   This chapter begins with a discussion of Cisco router architectures, using generic Cisco memory components as examples. This chapter then introduces the notation used for the configuration and routing policy examples used in the rest of the book. The examples in this book assume the simplest case of router access for configuration purposes: direct terminal console connection to the router. Other methods of access are briefly discussed, but not in detail. The normal look and feel of the configuration files and command-line interfaces for Cisco routers is also shown in this chapter. The chapter ends with the configuration of a Cisco router for global and interface parameters, and then a loopback address, some static routes, and an aggregate route.

Chapter 6: Juniper Networks Router Configuration.   This chapter begins with a discussion of Juniper Networks router architectures and products, emphasizing Juniper Networks routers' distinct hardware-based approach to routing. Access methods for Juniper Networks routers are discussed, but the examples in this book assume the simplest case of router access for configuration purposes: direct terminal console connection to the router. Other methods of access are briefly discussed, but not in detail. The normal look and feel of the configuration files and command-line interfaces for Juniper Networks routers is also shown in this chapter. The chapter ends with the configuration of a Juniper Networks router for global and interface parameters, and then a loopback address, some static routes, and an aggregate route.

Part 2: Interior Routing Protocols.   These six chapters show the operation of the leading IGP routing protocols OSPF and IS-IS. Even RIP is covered, but mostly to show the shortcomings of RIP with regard to current thinking about what an IGP should and could do. The intent here is to avoid getting bogged down in the operational details of protocols like OSPF and IS-IS during the later discussions of IGP routing policies.

Chapter 7: Routing Information Protocol (RIP).   This is a chapter about the first standardized IGP routing protocol, RIP. The chapter also explains why RIP is not often used today for "serious" Internet routing. The whole point is to explain why RIP is not used much in this book, despite the continued use of RIP. The chapter starts with a look at how RIP functions, and then proceeds to specifically detail the reasons that RIP should probably be avoided today.

Chapter 8: Configuring RIP.   This chapter includes a look at how to configure RIP and RIPv2 on a Cisco and Juniper Networks routers. This is done mostly to prepare the reader for the OSPF and IS-IS configurations given later in this part of the book. There is a section on the use of RIPng for IPv6. Finally, because they are specific to Cisco, the chapter only includes a note on IGRP/EIGRP, and there is no detailed treatment of the Cisco IGRP and EIGRP routing protocols at all in this multivendor book.

Chapter 9: Open Shortest Path First (OSPF).   This chapter details the architecture and operation of OSPF. All aspects of OSPF are explored, from updates to handshakes, and from areas to subareas. After an introduction to the origins of OSPF, the chapter investigates the key concept of OSPF areas, and all aspects of using OSPF as an IGP today. A short section considers extensions to OSPF for IPv6 use.

Chapter 10: Configuring OSPF.   All the details on how to configure OSPF on Cisco and Juniper Networks routers are examined in this chapter. First, general configuration steps are given, and then several specific examples of a Cisco OSPF configuration and a Juniper Networks OSPF configuration, both using the same reference network.

Chapter 11: Intermediate System.   Intermediate System (IS-IS). This chapter details the operation of the key components of the IS-IS routing protocol. The treatment is at the same depth as that for OSPF. So after an introduction to the origins of IS-IS, the chapter investigates the concepts of IS-IS level, and all other aspects of using IS-IS as an IGP today. The chapter is mainly presented as a helpful list of the differences between the OSPF and IS-IS routing protocol.

Chapter 12: Configuring IS-IS.   This chapter provides all the details on how to configure IS-IS on Cisco and Juniper Networks routers. As with OSPF, there are first general configuration steps, and then several specific examples of a Cisco IS-IS configuration and a Juniper Networks IS-IS configuration, both using the same reference network.

Part 3: Exterior Routing Protocols.   These two chapters explore how the Internet relies on EGPs (almost exclusively BGP) for connectivity between ISPs. The emphasis here is on the different needs of EGPs as opposed to IGPs and how BGPv4 fills these needs admirably.

Chapter 13: Border Gateway Protocol (BGP).   This chapter investigates the BGP routing protocol in detail. From the basics of BGP, such as message formats and attributes, the chapter moves on the consider EBGP and IBGP (and a bit about CBGP). All of the roles of BGP are investigated, including route reflectors and confederations. The chapter closes with a look at the interactions between BGP and the IGP, since BGP cannot bootstrap itself into existence the way that an IGP can. Some simple policies to distribute BGP routes and address *next-hop self* solutions to BGP reachability problems are given as well.

Chapter 14: Configuring BGP.   In this chapter, all the details on how to configure BGP on Cisco and Juniper Networks routers are provided. As with the IGPs, there are first general configuration steps using defaults, and then many specific examples of a Cisco BGP configuration and a Juniper Networks BGP configuration, both using the same reference network. Both IBGP and EBGP are fully explored. Even router reflector and confederation configurations are included.

Part 4: IGP Routing Policies.   To this point, the emphasis in the book has been on just getting the routing protocols up and running. Now the emphasis shifts in these two chapters to creating and implementing the routing policies needed to make the routing protocols interact in the way necessary to shuttle traffic as needed around the network.

Chapter 15: Routing Policy.   This chapter is primarily a background and terminology chapter. This chapter introduces concepts such as *regular expressions*, the differences between an input policy and an output policy, and so on. This chapter explores just why routing policies are needed and introduces the key idea of a *default policy* for each routing protocol. Some typical example input policies for an IGP are given, and then some example output policies. The routing policy "language" for both Cisco and Juniper Networks routers is covered.

The Cisco examples include the use of route map, several types of access list, prefix lists, and distribution lists.

Chapter 16: IGP Routing Policies.   This chapter details the operation of the routing policies normally used in OSPF and IS-IS. Again, complete configuration sections are added in this chapter. There are first general configuration steps using defaults, and then a specific example of a Cisco OSPF policy configuration and a Juniper Networks OSPF policy configuration, both using the same reference network. Then a method of converting from an OSPF to an IS-IS network is considered (with a few words about converting IS-IS to OSPF). The chapter ends with a detailed look at IS-IS route leaking and how routing policies are used to implement this very important IS-IS feature.

Part 5: EGP Routing Policies.   These final three chapters apply the concepts regarding routing policy introduced in the earlier IGP policy chapters to BGP, which is perhaps the most important goal of the book. Despite the title, this part of the book exclusively examines BGP, which is the only standard EGP in widespread use on the Internet today.

Chapter 17: Basic BGP Routing Policies.   This chapter explores the various ways that routing policy influences BGP operation. This chapter examines IP address space aggregation in more detail, and the two most fundamental BGP attributes used for BGP route selection, the Origin and Multi-Exit Discriminator (MED) attribute. MED is the closest thing that BGP has to a pure IGP metric, but it is used between ASs rather than inside an AS.

Chapter 18: AS Path and Local Preference.   This chapter covers the use of AS Path and Local Preference attributes in BGP routing policies. More than any other attributes, the AS Path and Local Preference control the flow of packets through the Internet from ISP to ISP. AS Path regular expressions are covered here as well. Several real examples are used to illustrate the use of the AS Path and Local Preference.

Chapter 19: BGP Community and Route Damping.   The final chapter in this book deals with the BGP Community attribute and BGP route damping. The Juniper Networks regular expressions for BGP Communities are fully discussed. Routing policies to adjust Community strings and Community use are presented, with a real-world example, and the book closes with a look at how routing policies can control route damping for different links between different categories of ASs and ISPs.

From start to finish, this book is designed to build concept upon concept, from the simplest ideas about IP prefixes to the most complex BGP routing policies used between ISP peers on the Internet.

A Note on the Configurations

Almost all of the configurations and show command output presented were captured directly from console terminal connections to the routers themselves. There were very few exceptions, mostly along the lines of configuration fragments to add a certain feature (knob) to an existing configuration. In other words, the networks or lab setups created in this book are real networks, with real results, and are not simply taken from other sources or vendor documentation.

Every effort has been made to accurately represent the behavior of a routing protocol or routing policy. The only compromise is that in many cases the Juniper Networks routers used were running JUNOS software on a UNIX platform in a kind of *router emulation* package. This is not a supported configuration, but often used internally at Juniper Networks for quick investigations into router behavior. The only real differences in behavior from M-series routers are with regard to certain chassis-related commands and firewall filters, neither of which are used in this book at all. For purposes of realism, the interface names were edited to reflect Fast Ethernet M-series interface naming, however.

A total of 22 routers were used to configure the example networks used in this book, but no more than 12 in any one network. There was a core network consisting of nine UNIX-based PCs running JUNOS software. This was a home-lab setup, but frequently nine real M-5 routers were available for the preparation of this book.

In addition to these 18 Juniper Networks routers, 4 Cisco routers were used. Two were older AGS+ routers running IOS 10.4, but these were mostly used as traffic sources and external BGP peers. Most of the real work was done on a Cisco MGS running IOS 11.3, which remains the most common IOS in use. This 1 router went a long way, and creative use of addressing made this single router appear to be two in some cases. For newer features, or when Cisco-to-Cisco checking was needed, a small 2610 running IOS 12.2 was used as well. For consistency, these configurations were edited to appear as Fast Ethernet as well.

Finally, it should be pointed out that the configurations presented are intended to highlight one routing protocol or policy feature or another and therefore should not be considered realistic examples of a total configuration on a real production network. In the real world, production configurations would be much more robust and have many features (mostly regarding security) that are not present in these configurations because of space limitations. But none of these extras would alter the behavior of the routing protocols or policies themselves.

Who Should Read This Book

Routing protocols and the rules that form routing policies are key technologies to equipment vendors, service providers, and customers today. These areas include, but are not limited to, IS-IS, OSPF, BGP, route filtering, changing route attributes, and so on. Anyone with an interest in any of the areas and technologies should find this book rewarding.

The multivendor aspect of this approach to these protocols and technologies is one of the main attractions of this book and other forthcoming titles in the series.

The primary audience for this book is ISP personnel. There just are not any books they can read today that address the whole idea of routing protocols and routing policies adequately. ISP personnel working with customers and users need to understand routing protocols, and routing policies especially, to provide guidance for the potential users of ISP services.

A secondary audience is the large field of the certification and training activities undertaken by networking companies, telephone companies, ISPs, and industry employees. It is hoped that this text will provide all the knowledge needed to become proficient with regard to just how routing policies play a role in, and are implemented by, network services offered through the Internet. Another secondary audience for this book is the technical IT or IS professional interested in how the global Internet functions between client and server.

The third audience for this routing book is educators and consultants. Because of the lack of nontechnical information in a full-length work, there is a tremendous need for educating professionals regarding routing policy.

Tools You Will Need

Only minimal working knowledge of networks, both local and wide, is assumed here. If a reader has successfully exchanged email, seen a Web page, or downloaded a file over the Internet, that is all that is really expected in terms of expertise. You need not know the details of 10Base-T Ethernet, but it is a bonus if you realize that there is often a hub between workstation, PC, or laptop and the router linking the user to the Internet.

The early chapters are not intended as a rigorous tutorial. There are many other books that form much more detailed sources for topics like TCP/IP or LANs. There should be something here for the more experienced as well. Even those familiar with the early days of the Internet, Web, or router industry should enjoy some of the stories and lore of events in the past often forgotten in the rush toward the future.

All that is really needed to get the most out of this book is an interest in the topics covered.

Summary

From here, Part 1 of this book introduces and details the Internet, IP and routers, IP addresses old and new, and the key concept of the variable-length IP prefix. This will be new material to some and simply a review for others. But even those who work with these concepts every day might enjoy a new perspective on even familiar territory.

By the end of this book, readers should have a complete idea of how routing protocols and routing policies fit together to make the Internet what it is today.

PART

One

The Internet
and the Router

It is impossible to write about routing protocols and the routing policies that affect the behavior of these routing protocols without a firm grasp of just what these twin tools are trying to accomplish. Routing *protocols* establish the global connectivity between routers that in turn establish the global connectivity that makes the Internet what it is today. Routing *policies* adjust and tune the behavior of the routing protocols so that this connectivity is made more effective and efficient.

Routers are the *network nodes* of the global public Internet, passing IP address information back and forth as needed so that every router that needs to knows when a new network (IP prefix) has been added anywhere in the world, or when a link or router has failed and so other networks might now be (temporarily) unreachable. Routers can dynamically route around failed links and routers in many cases, unless the destination network happens to be right there on the local router itself. Routers are network nodes in the sense that there are no users on the router itself that originate or read email (for example), although routers routinely take on a client or a server role (or both) for administrative purposes. Routers almost always just pass IP packet traffic through from one interface to another, input port to output port, all the while trying to make sure that the traffic is making progress through the network and moving one step closer to its destination.

The network that a great many routers find themselves attached to is, of course, the global, public Internet. This is not always the case, however, and there are still plenty of private router networks with no links to the Internet at all, sometimes for the sake of security, often just because connectivity to the Internet for this network is simply not needed or desired. Often local area networks (LANs) used in private organizations use routers to link departments, usually within the same building or office complex. This book will mention such private router networks only in passing, not because these networks are unimportant, but mainly because the role of routing policy is more critical when the global public Internet is involved than when connectivity between the Sales and the Marketing departments are the only issue. The emphasis on this book is on the global, public Internet.

The situation in the router world and on the modern Internet is complicated by considerations of dynamic host addresses, IP network address translation (NAT), and other features often used now for security purposes. The emphasis in this book will be on router use of publicly assigned IP address spaces. Again, the intent is not to downplay the significant role that dynamic host address configuration or NAT play in modern router networks, but just to make the main topics of routing protocol and routing policy behavior more understandable and less complex than they already are.

So this book starts off with a look at the role of the router as the platform of the routing protocols, and the history of the Internet that forms the context within which the routing policies operate.

A Brief History of the Internet and Router

The days of conceiving the Internet as something to be mapped, grasped, understood, controlled, and so on are quite frankly gone. What exists instead in today's world of interconnected computers is a kind of *ISP grid net*, a haphazard, interconnected mesh of Internet service providers (ISPs) and related Internet-connected entities such as governments and learning institutions. But why introduce a new term when *Internet* is much more common and perfectly fine for most discussions of routers? Because only with an appreciation of the Internet as an ISP grid net can the important role of routing protocols and routing policies in today's Internet be understood. Talk of peers and aggregate summaries and backbones and access points and points of presence (POPs) make much more sense in the ISP grid net context than in the older context of a monolithic Internet.

The idea of the Internet as ISP grid net is shown in Figure 1.1. Large national ISPs, smaller regional ISPs, and even tiny local ISPs make up the grid net. In addition, pieces of the Internet act as exchange points for traffic such as CIX (Commercial Internet Exchange), FIX (Federal Internet Exchange), and NAPs (network access points). The precise role of the NAPs, CIX (now officially obsolete), and FIX will be explained later on in this chapter. They are included in the discussion to point out the overall and varied structure over time of what appears to be a unified Internet.

These Internet pieces are all chained together by a haphazard series of links with only a few rules, mostly of local scope (although there are important exceptions). NAPs, which are collections of routers where different ISPs can exchange traffic, are meshed with very high-speed links, and *Tier 1 ISPs* must have high-speed links to two (or more) NAPs. The smallest ISP can link to another ISP and thus allow their users to participate in the global, public Internet. Increasingly, linking between these ISPs is governed by a series of agreements known as *peering arrangements*. National ISPs may be peers to each other, but they view smaller ISPs as just another type of customer. Peering arrangements detail the reciprocal way that traffic is handed off from one ISP to another. Peers might agree to deliver each other's packets for no charge but bill non-peer ISPs for this privilege, since presumably the national ISP's backbone will be shuttling a large number of the smaller ISP's packets around but using the smaller ISP for the same purpose to a lesser degree. A few examples of Tier 1 ISPs, peer ISPs, and customer ISPs are shown in the figure.

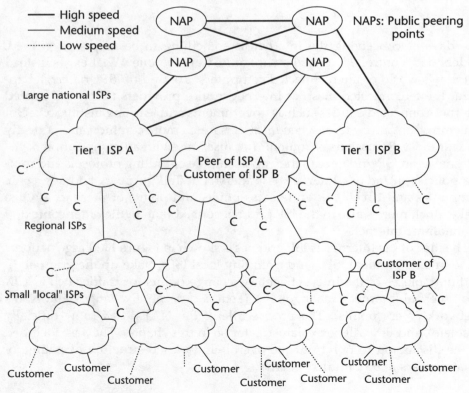

Figure 1.1   The ISP grid net.

At the bottom of Figure 1.1, millions of personal computers (PCs), minicomputers, and mainframes act as either clients, servers, or both on the Internet. These hosts—anything running Transmission Control Protocol/Internet Protocol (TCP/IP)—are usually attached by LANs and linked by routers to the Internet. These LANs are just shown as customers to the ISPs. Although all attached computers conform to this client/server architecture, many of them are strictly Web clients (that is, browsers) or Web servers (that is, Web sites) as the Web continues to take over more of the form and function of the Internet at large. Only at this bottom level is the term *customer* spelled out. At the other levels, members of each ISP's network are represented by just a *C*. For the sake of simplicity, Figure 1.1 ignores important details of the grid net such as the LANs and routers. However, it is important to realize that the clients and servers are on LANs and that routers are the network nodes of the Internet. The number of clients actually exceeds the number of servers many times over, but this is not apparent from the figure.

Moving up one level, the figure shows the thousands of ISPs that have emerged in the 1990s, especially since the Web explosion of 1993 to 1994. Usually, the link from the client user to the ISP is by way of a simple modem-attached, dial-up telephone line. In contrast, the link from a server to the ISP is most likely a leased private line, but there are important exceptions to this simplistic view. Although also not shown in the figure, a variety of Web servers may be within the ISP's own cloud network. For instance, the Web server on which an ISP's members may create and maintain their own Web pages would be located here.

A common practice in the networking field is to represent an ISP's (or any other type of service provider's) network as a cloud or oval. Sometimes the graphic actually *looks* like a cloud, but this practice only detracts from the figure's message in many cases, and networks are anything but light and fluffy. The use of the network cloud goes back to a telephony service provider data network known as the X.25 public packet-switching network, which shares many features with the Internet. The reason for the X.25 cloud was twofold. First, customers and users did not have to concern themselves with the details of the network in any way. Packets went into the cloud and emerged from the other side. Second, the cloud hid the fact that what was inside it was really exactly the same types of things that customers had on their own networks: network devices and links between them. There was no magic at all, just a network. X.25 was simply a public version of a private network, but with hidden details, packets, and economies of scale. In the same way today, ISPs condense their networks into clouds to hide the details of their actual network structures from customers (who do not need to know), competitors (who almost all want to know but should not), and hackers (who definitely should not know). Moving up again to a higher cloud layer, the smaller ISPs link into the large backbone of the national ISPs. Some may link in directly, whereas others are forced for technical or financial reasons to link in daisy-chain fashion to other ISPs, which link to other ISPs, and so on until an ISP with direct access to a NAP is reached. Note that direct links between ISPs, especially those with older Internet roots, are possible and sometimes common. In fact, the NAPs were once so congested that most major ISPs prefer to link to each other directly today, and so are peering directly to one another, bypassing the need to use the NAP hierarchy to deliver traffic.

The NAPs themselves are fully mesh-connected—that is, they all link directly to all other NAPs. Figure 1.1 shows only the general structure of the U.S. portion of the Internet. However, a large percentage of all inter-European traffic passes through the U.S. NAPs. Most other countries obtain Internet connectivity by linking to a NAP in the United States. Large ISPs routinely link to more than one NAP for redundancy. The same is true of individual ISPs, except for the truly small ones, which rarely link to more than one ISP, usually for cost reasons. Note also that peer ISPs often have multiple, redundant links between them.

Speeds vary greatly in different parts of the Internet. For the most part, client access is by way of low-speed dial-up telephone lines, typically at a speed 33.6 to 56 kilobits per second (Kbps). Servers are connected by medium-speed private leased lines, typically in the range of 64 Kbps to 1.5 megabits per second (Mbps). The high-speed backbone links between national ISPs run at higher speeds still, sometimes up to 45 Mbps. On a few, and between the NAPs themselves, speeds of 155 Mbps (known as OC-3c), 622 Mbps (OC-12c), 2.4 gigabits per second (Gbps) (OC-48c), and now even 10 Gbps (OC-192c) are not unheard of. Higher speeds are needed both to minimize large Web site page transfer latency times and to concentrate and aggregate traffic from millions of clients and servers onto one network.

Where did the ISP grid net come from? What happened to the Internet along the way? How did the routers and the protocols that run on these routers become so important to the Internet and Web? To answer these questions, we need to start at the beginning.

The Pre-Web Internet

A popular television commercial in the United States once switched back and forth between images of 1960s-era rock concerts and peace rallies and a small group of white-shirted, pocket-protected, glasses-wearing nerds trying to make a computer the size of a small car power up properly. The nerds consulted their slide rules, which were devices used by engineers to make calculations before there were electronic calculators, and finally managed to make the computer flash green lights in a satisfying manner. The commercial then ended in the present, and as the gray-haired and paunchy nerds labored with new equipment, a youthful engineer gazed in wonder at the slide rule that was found in a drawer. The point was, of course, that in 1969, while many people frolicked through the carefree 1960s, a few dedicated engineers were putting together the first sites for what would become the Internet. The commercial was full of obvious improbabilities, such as the stereotyped appearance of the group and the presence of a slide rule in a modern computer lab. Even by 1969, many engineers had already embraced the expensive and bulky laptop-sized electronic calculators that could only add, subtract, multiply and divide but were starting to appear on the market. But the Internet and computer networking in general are not all that old, and many network pioneers are still productively involved in all aspects of modern research and development. Despite the relative newness of the technology, the networking variations from the late twentieth century seem antiquated today. The Internet of 1990, for example, is in some ways as different from the modern Internet as an old World War I vintage biplane is from a modern jet fighter.

Of course, it is just as wrong, and just as right, to call the network built in 1969 the Internet as it is to call the contemporary ISP grid net the Internet. What the nerds had wrought, at the same time almost to the day that many other college students were happily rolling in the mud in upstate New York at the Woodstock Music and Arts Festival, was a U.S. government network called (in true federal government acronym fashion) the ARPANET, or Advanced Research Project Agency Network. ARPANET was funded in 1968 to perform research into packet-switching networks, and the network nodes were to be built by a company called Bolt, Beranek, and Newman (BBN). These network nodes were not called routers, or even gateways (the older Internet term for router). They were called interface message processors, or IMPs. Not everyone in government, even those who know about the BBN contract, was quite sure what was going on or even just what an "interface" was. The story goes that Senator Edward Kennedy, in whose home state of Massachusetts BBN was headquartered, sent a congratulatory message to BBN thanking them for the efforts to bridge religious differences with their new *interfaith* message processor.

ARPA itself had been created under the U.S. Department of Defense (DoD) to combat the perceived gap between the U.S. and Russian space programs. This gap was made painfully obvious to some when the Russians launched Sputnik, the first earth-orbiting satellite in 1957. The possibility of spying or even bombing from orbit became a real concern, and interservice rivalry between the Army and Navy over their own satellite plans slowed the U.S. response even further. Research into rocketry and related systems such as in-flight guidance at U.S. colleges and universities was slowed by a lack of communications between staff efforts to address problems. The answer, ARPA soon decided, to all these scattered efforts was closer coordination among agencies and institutions receiving ARPA funds under the DoD banner for research. Since many of the engineering issues that had been raised by then-current research were being addressed graphically on computers, it seemed plain to many that some form of computer network was needed to bring some semblance of order to these efforts.

The problem was that no one at the time had the slightest idea how a network for computers, as opposed to, say, telephones, should look and act. The early 1960s saw progress on this basic problem in the form of a series of papers. From 1961 to 1964, three crucial papers outlined the basic concepts. Leonard Kleinrock, at the Massachusetts Institute of Technology (MIT), examined packet switching using small parcels of data that came to be called datagrams; J.C.R. Licklider and W. Clark at MIT, explored the idea that computer communication could take place "online" in real time; and Paul Baran, at RAND, an important think tank, investigated the absolutely key concept that a network intended for national defense should have no central point of failure, or even a place where everything was controlled.

Implementation of these ideas started slowly. In 1965, two computers were linked with a 1,200 bits per second (bps) telephone line, pretty much state-of-the-art speed for the time. At least telephone giant AT&T had already invented the modulator-demodulator, or modem, for analog-digital conversion at Bell Laboratories sometime during World War II so that digital computer bits could flow over a standard analog telephone line. One story about the modem has it that Bell Labs wanted to demonstrate a new telephone system computer at a conference at Dartmouth College in New Hampshire. But in the early 1940s, the threat of sabotage and spying was considered too great to actually risk shipping the computer by truck from New Jersey. So the engineers devised the modem as a way for an engineer to sit at a teletype machine keyboard (those had been around since the early 1900s) at Dartmouth, type a command for the computer in New Jersey, and then see the output as it scrolled on the teletype machine's paper output. Its purpose served, the modems apparently went into a closet somewhere until they were needed again 20 or so years later.

Various plans for a full ARPANET were circulated over the next few years, until by December of 1969, four nodes were up and running. These were at the University of California at Los Angeles (UCLA, whose IMP was installed on August 30), Stanford Research Institute (SRI, whose IMP was connected on October 1), the University of California at Santa Barbara (UCSB, whose IMP was connected on November 1), and the University of Utah (linked soon after). A logical map of the initial four-node Internet appears in Figure 1.2. The computers linked were an IBM 360, a DEC PDP 10, an SDS Sigma 7, and an SDS 940. Ironically, the ARPANET was all ready to go after the space race was over, having been won by the United States in July of 1969 with the initial lunar landing.

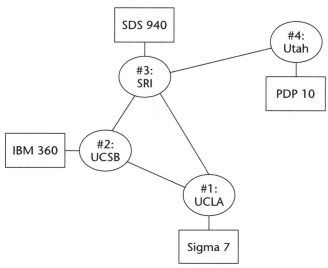

Figure 1.2 The original four-node ARPANET in 1969.

Note that the SRI IMP not only had to deliver packets to the attached SRI host but pass packets on to Utah. This forwarding aspect of traffic not for itself is the essence of network node and router operation. One of the most important features of this initial ARPANET was that the computers linked were from different vendors, as shown in Figure 1.2. So all four nodes used different operating systems, internal representations of data, and low-level languages. The function of the IMPs was to take the vendor-specific internals of the source data and translate them to a common "protocol" as the information flowed between the IMPs. Thus, each IMP only had to convert between two formats: the internal format of the host computer and the network format. This was much more important then than it is now. By the late 1970s, there were at least 10 major computer vendors in the United States alone, all with their own architectures and internals. An IMP, even with a whopping (for the time) 12 kilobytes (KB) of memory, could hardly be expected to understand and translate among them all. The format used on the network complied with the ARPANET Host-Host Protocol, which was soon replaced with the more robust Network Control Protocol (NCP), and later still by TCP/IP.

The early network pioneers, called the Network Working Group, were not even sure they were always doing what was expected of them. They had a mandate from Washington to create a computer network; that much was clear. But with the planners all the way back on the East Coast, the implementers were not taking any chances that they were somehow exceeding their authority of going beyond the strict terms of the contract between ARPA and BBN.

So right from the start, in April 1969, Stephen Crocker at UCLA decided to document implementation issues and Network Working Group decisions on how to solve them. Since many were convinced that some "pro from the East" would appear at some point and tell them exactly what to do, these messages back to the East Coast were titled "requests for comments." This practice gave birth to the famous series of Internet specifications, the RFCs, but unfortunately (or fortunately), no one ever showed up to take charge.

The newly born network spent many years more or less inventing itself. ARPANET was a hit from the start, but only among the groups under the ARPA umbrella. Digital lines (rare at the time) running at 56 Kbps came in 1970 to link BBN to UCLA, and MIT to Utah. Fifteen nodes were operational by the end of 1971, which was the planned target size, and the familiar email @ sign made its debut. International links came in 1973, to England by way of Norway, and in 1976 Elizabeth II, Queen of the United Kingdom, sent out an email from the first head of state at the Royal Signal and Radar Establishment.

This is not to say that the ARPANET did not have problems. In 1973, there was a famous lockup on Christmas Day when the Harvard IMP decided to tell all the other IMPs that it was zero hops away from every destination on the ARPANET. Naturally, all packets converged on Harvard, creating the first *black hole* in Internet history. And right from the start, it became obvious that pure packet streams could arrive out of sequence or not at all. Independent routing was robust and reliable when it came to reachability (if there's a way for a packet to get there, it will), but error-prone and "unreliable" when it came to basic service quality (no errors, then many packets missing; in sequence, then not . . .). So in 1974, these and other problems were addressed in a paper from Kahn and Vinton Cerf proposing an additional protocol layer to add some simple reliability to the packet shuffling through the IMPs on the ARPANET. This was to be called the *Transmission Control Program* (TCP).

ARPANET provided three key services to its users: email, remote computer access (to become Telnet), and file transfer (actually, file copy) across the network. In 1973, the most important use of the ARPANET appeared to be email: a study done that year showed that fully 75 percent of the traffic on the ARPANET was email. ARPANET quickly grew far beyond its initial 15-node vision, and by 1983 comprised 113 nodes.

The term *Internet* appears to have been introduced in 1982, once TCP (now Transmission Control Protocol) and IP (Internet Protocol) became the standard protocols for ARPANET. TCP and IP were originally intended to be meshed as one protocol layer, but during the development cycle in 1978, the decision was made to try to make TCP and IP independent. However, in many features the split was just not practical, so the designation TCP/IP reflected the close relationship between the two functions. Any collection of networks linked by TCP/IP formed an internet. Those that linked networks on the ARPANET formed the Internet according to some documents released around that time, although the ARPANET did not disappear officially until 1990.

However, the initial networks linked by the IMPs were just isolated mini-computers and mainframes with their associated terminals. It was not until the LAN came along in the early 1980s that the idea of a "network of networks" or internet was used in the modern sense of the word. So "network of networks" came to mean "a wide area network of local area networks," although there was and is no reason that wide area networks (WANs) could not form an internet in addition to LANs. In fact, this was done in 1982 when what was now the Internet was linked to another packet WAN. LANs came along when Bob Metcalf linked Xerox Alto computers (early PCs) with a coaxial cable snaking through the Xerox's Palo Alto Research Center (PARC) in the late 1970s. This network was soon standardized as *Ethernet,* although technically the standard version should be called an IEEE 802.3 LAN.

The first *exterior gateway protocol*, called without a sense of irony the Exterior Gateway Protocol (EGP), was used to link other WANs to the Internet through what was called a *gateway*. These gateways were another step along the evolutionary path to the modern router. Originally, all routing information was distributed using a single algorithm to each and every device on the Internet. So all network nodes knew every detail of the network. Even by the mid-1980s, this degree of housekeeping was proving to be beyond the capabilities of even high-end processors. Thus, the gateways allowed for interconnection of separate *routing domains* to the core Internet, and each piece of the Internet would run an interior gateway protocol (IGP) to provide full connectivity information within a specific routing domain. Between routing domains, however, only basic reachability information was needed so that each portion of the total Internet knew generally where things were. A driver leaving Chicago only needs to know that San Diego is in southern California somewhere. Only once across the California border are more precise directions needed.

Several other key developments and experiments matured during 1983 and 1984 and changed the world of networking forever. First and foremost, the cutover to TCP/IP from NCP began. Then the University of Wisconsin developed the concept of a *name server* so that users no longer had to look up the network address of computers and email recipients in bulky books. This work lead directly the Domain Name System (DNS) that could translate something like an email addressed to walterg@juniper.net to the proper IP address without user intervention. But beyond a doubt the most important development during that time period was the incorporation of TCP/IP into an open, standard, supported, powerful, inexpensive, multi-user operating system: UNIX. Once linking a computer to the Internet no longer required specialized hardware or software (almost every UNIX workstation had an Ethernet interface built in), the entire research community began to use UNIX and the Internet as an indispensable part of their work.

Now LAN interconnection over the Internet began in earnest, fueled by the ready availability of Berkeley UNIX (4.2 BSD) on desktop workstations. BSD took the BBN TCP/IP code and first merged it, and later essentially rewrote the code, into UNIX. BSD had the TCP/IP protocol preinstalled and instantly usable. In contrast, the "official" UNIX developed and distributed by AT&T Bell Labs had no integrated networking capability at all. But because of restrictions on AT&T as a regulated telephone company, UNIX could not be sold for profit by AT&T and was available to anyone who paid Bell Labs to ship it out. And these users in turn were free to add, subtract, or modify anything they wanted in UNIX, and even redistribute the result. BSD was a true distribution of UNIX independent of the official AT&T channels. It is important to realize that these new networking capabilities were at this time more or less restricted to UNIX users. The common IBM-architecture PC was in this timeframe marketed and sold as a standalone device that networking users tended to sneer at. And Apple computer users were always proud of their independence from standards or trends outside their own world.

UNIX today forms the core operating system for many types of computers, workstations, and even routers. Hardware vendors now had a choice. They could spend a lot of time and effort developing a new operating system from scratch, and then marketing it and teaching people to use the new commands and interface. Or they could just get a version of UNIX for practically nothing, adapt it for their own architecture, and then provide their users with a familiar command set and interface. Figure 1.3 traces the evolution of UNIX from its origins in 1969 to the many slightly different, yet always familiar, versions available today. Many users today encounter UNIX as Linux or FreeBSD. Even Mac OS 10 has strong elements of UNIX in it, to the extent that Mac OS 10 must spawn a Mac OS 9 process to run older, non-UNIX-oriented applications.

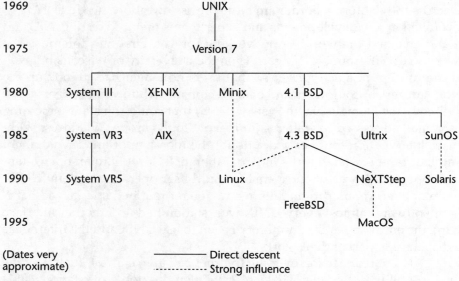

Figure 1.3 The evolution of UNIX.

In the same timeframe, ARPANET linked through a gateway to CSNET, another large network. All this linking made the U.S. Department of Defense nervous, since many military bases were now on the network as well. So in 1983, ARPANET split off the military bases on the network as MILNET, leaving only 45 of the 113 nodes behind. DNS registration began when symbolics.com was registered on March 15, 1985.

In 1986, the National Science Foundation (NSF) built a backbone for the Internet (NSFNET) with 56-Kbps lines to link supercomputer centers at universities. This began a new surge of universities and colleges onto the Internet, this time with no apparent government research ties. The routers of the day did a great job of routing around link failures just as planned—when they could. On December 12, 1986, an AT&T cable was broken between Newark, New Jersey, and White Plains, New York. All seven ARPANET trunk lines running to New England happened to run through that single cable, so that the region was effectively isolated from the rest of the world.

Early in the following year, NSF signed an agreement to manage the NSFNET backbone with Merit Network, Inc. Merit brought computer giant IBM and telephone company MCI on board, and together they founded Advanced Network Systems (ANS). The ANS dial-up network later became the basis for the America Online (AOL) network for PC modem users. ANS was the closest thing that the Internet ever had to a location the Internet was run from operationally. ANS was headquartered for years in Elmsford, New York, a tiny village about 30 miles north of New York City. And Senator Al Gore did indeed "invent" the Internet in a sense when he officially requested a national network for research and education. Why build something new when the Internet was lying around? After all, RFCs had reached 1,000, and attached hosts now topped 10,000.

The Internet was truly becoming global by 1988. NSFNET had links to Canada, Denmark, Finland, France, Iceland, Norway, and Sweden.

By the late 1980s, most of the major pieces of the Internet were in place. There were plenty of college students sending email, LANs, WAN links, routers (gateways), routing protocols, routing domains, the basic name service (DNS), and workstations running UNIX with TCP/IP built in. All that was missing was the ordinary people without a high degree of computer or network sophistication. With the Web, the people would come. And they would come in a rush.

The Web Comes to Town

Most people encountered the Internet in college. Internet links were usually subsidized and paid for by grants, so no one had to worry about paying for Internet access or connection time. The first commercial ISP came in 1990, when The World began charging customers to dial in to the Internet with a modem. Those without UNIX and TCP/IP (almost everyone with a PC or Mac) could use a terminal emulation application to communicate with a real host attached to the Internet. This caused some consternation at first, since the acceptable use policy (AUP) in place at the time mandated Internet use for research and education, not commercial purposes. But as government subsidies began to dry up, NSF lifted commercial restrictions on the Internet in March 1991. Now there was a scramble to figure out how to make money, or at least not go broke, linking pieces of the Internet together. Anybody with a router and a link could find a way to hook up to the Internet. But routers were very expensive.

The evolution of the Internet and the evolution of the router cannot be considered in isolation. As the Internet grew, routers had to evolve to keep up with the growth of traffic and routing table size. And more powerful routers in turn encouraged more Internet links, more networked applications, and so forth. When the Web explosion came, the router industry was ready, and one company even more so than others. That router company was Cisco.

As important as the University of California at Berkeley was for UNIX (BSD UNIX), Stanford University in nearby Palo Alto was even more important where the Internet was concerned. One Stanford engineering building, Margaret Jacks Hall, was the birthplace of industry leaders Silicon Graphics Incorporated (SGI), Sun Microsystems (Sun stands for Stanford University Network), and router "inventor" Cisco Systems. While Cisco did not really invent the router any more than anyone "invented" the Internet, Cisco did popularize the name *router* instead of gateway and basically defined what a router for the Internet should do. Routers at the time were also called *firewalls*, since routers could prevent many of the problems that surfaced when linking many LANs together with bridges. Bridging created one big LAN at the frame layer, and this meant that any problem on one LAN at one site could easily take down all of the sites linked by the bridge. Routers created one big network (or *internetwork*) at the packet layer, but all of the LANs were still separate at the frame layer. So LAN problems could be stopped by the packet-handling firewall created by the router.

By the early 1990s, there were 11 vendors of networking equipment that sold devices that had at least some routing capabilities. Some of these products were positioned as *enhanced bridges*, since most LAN administrators were more familiar and comfortable with the bridging features of these products and not all worried about full implementations of all routing protocols. But all dealt with IP packets at least at some level. These vendors were 3Com, Alantec, Bay (Wellfleet), Cabletron, Cisco, DEC, Hewlett-Packard, IBM, Proteon, Retix, and SMC. The most successful of these was to be Cisco, although when the Web hit town, the most powerful backbone IP routers were made by Wellfleet (soon to become, with Synoptics, Bay Networks). One dollar invested in Cisco in 1995 became eight dollars in 1998. By 1999, Cisco was the eighth most valuable company in the United States.

The Cisco AGS+ router was a marvel of engineering at the time, and yet today that fact is hard to believe. The CPU ran at 25 or 30 MHz and typically routed packets between four LAN and two serial WAN ports, although much larger numbers of ports were supported. A hard drive with a couple hundred megabytes was included as well. The AGS usually had about 4 MB of RAM, depending on configuration and position in the network, but 16 MB could be used as well. A single megabyte of RAM cost up to $250 at the time. But for the Internet of the day, the router worked: Packets went in and packets went out.

The Internet was not the only game in town. There were online services and bulletin board systems for ordinary citizens with PCs and Macs that were totally independent of the Internet. But these "proprietary" services such as CompuServe, Prodigy, and AOL were more concerned with keeping their users satisfied with their own content rather than unleashing them on the Internet. Besides, what was there on a government research network that everyday people would want? And pay for?

In the early 1990s, there were some other very good reasons why most people, even people with personal computers at work or at home, had no good reason to think about joining the Internet. People with PCs were just getting used to pointing and clicking at things with Windows (Mac users did not suffer from this sudden shock). The almost totally UNIX command-driven Internet was too different even from DOS to feel comfortable for most people. Computers did not come with modems built in, and external analog modems, which now ran at 9,600 bps, cost about $700 (the computer itself at the time could cost upwards of $6,000 for current technology, and early double-speed CD-ROM drives cost $1,000 or more). Most affordable modems ran at only 1,200 bps. And since there were few places to dial in for Internet access, the phone call itself was often long distance. Demand could quickly drive down the price for the hardware, but what could drive the demand for modems and computers, and routers?

The answer, of course, turned out to be the Web.

The Birth of the Web

Imagine life on the pre-Web Internet. UNIX systems ran TCP/IP and hooked up to a router. Server processes waited for client processes, run by users, to talk to them, usually when a user sat down at a monitor and keyboard and typed in a command like "mail." Perhaps the user was a scientist at a research institution using the Internet to check his email. Today, there might be a response from a colleague who might be able to recommend a paper requested to advance a current research project. The email scrolls across the screen, and the colleague thinks there might be something on a computer on the Internet, but in another country. And the colleague cannot remember exactly where it was on the computer. No matter, the scientist can type in and run "telnet" as a client and log in as "guest" on the remote computer. Now the UNIX commands are run on the remote computer as if the scientist were a local user. Directories are listed and probed with Telnet commands. What luck! The title of one paper seems to be just the thing. Now the scientist can type in and run "ftp" as an "anonymous" user and again list the contents of the directory (however, the commands to list files in a directory with Telnet are different than those used in FTP). Assuming the scientist knows these commands, the scientist can get a copy of the paper transferred to his or her own machine. Unfortunately, the paper title was misleading and is of no help to the scientist at all.

What's wrong with this picture? Well, for one thing, this is a lot of work just to fetch a paper. The three programs are separate clients, and only Windows or a Mac or UNIX can actually run them all at once. Because the clients are three separate tools, the commands are different and they do not work with each other. The paper was found with Telnet, but Telnet cannot directly transfer the file (actually, there are other UNIX programs accessible through Telnet that could do this, but this is just an example).

The whole point is that with the Web site (server) and Web browser (client) in place, everything changes. The browser is a type of *universal client* that allows users to send email, access other computers, transfer files, view content, and so on all with the same familiar pointing and clicking instead of needing to remember arcane commands. Information at the Web site is organized according to what are still called *hypertext* links, although the links can lead to pictures, movies, or music.

In retrospect, the Web seems so obvious that it's a wonder it took so long to be invented. But in a world of expensive computers and slow link speeds, the Web seemed like a luxury rather than a necessity. Nevertheless, the reaction the first time people, especially people without a technical background in networks and computers, saw the Web was "I need that *now*!"

Not that inventing the Web was easy or fast.

The idea of hypertext was first used in 1981 in a book called *Literary Machines* by computer scientist Ted Nelson. Hypertext is the idea of following a nonlinear path through data and documents through a series of linked "nodes" of information.

This nonlinear concept can be traced back to 1945 to Vannevar Bush, who wanted to design a computer information database he called a *memex*. Memex computer users would be able to read data on a subject and from within that document be able to link to related information throughout the database. The user would follow a trail of links throughout the database that was not limited to a specific topic but allowed for connections across boundaries of classification. Information about "Wall Street" is just as likely to lead to "New York City" as "Stock Exchange." This whole concept became the basis for the Web. The very "web" structure sometimes makes for a frustrating experience, because following links can be confusing. If the objective of a "Wall Street" search is to find stock prices, "New York City" is not helpful. What does "New York City" have to do with all this?

Although many associate Web-like linking with the Internet, the idea would eventually have its first real application not on the Internet, but inside a computer. In 1987 Apple Computers released a software package called Hyper-Card that came bundled free with the Macintosh and its operating system. HyperCard not only allowed the linking of documents; it enabled users to create links to sounds and images within those documents. HyperCard restricted the links to the same system, but in some sense, the Web is just the old Mac HyperCard system (or Windows Help system) with links allowed to other computers.

The attempt to bring the concept of hypertext to the Internet began in the late 1980s when Tim Berners-Lee was employed as a software engineer at CERN, the European Particle Physics Institute, in Geneva, Switzerland. The high-energy physics community was spread throughout various universities and industries in Europe. The information and the research data this community of scientists produced spread over many computers and networks.

In March 1989, Berners-Lee proposed a way of linking text documents with other documents using *networked hypertext*. Working with Robert Cailliau, they eventually produced a design document in November 1990 that was a proposal for developing a system based on their idea of networked hypertext. "Hypertext is a way to link and access information of various kinds as a web of nodes in which the user can browse at will," the document stated. "Potentially, hypertext provides a single user-interface to many large classes of stored information, such as reports, notes, databases, computer documents, and online systems help."

This paper used the term *world wide web* without the capitals. After passing a few documents among computers, the pair quickly found that the documents needed a standard format that could be interpreted by each computer and still convey the information. So they developed a new language called the *Hypertext Markup Language (HTML)*, modeled after, and a subset of, a much more complex formatting language called the *Standard Generalized Markup Language (SGML)*. Today, HTML and SGML have been both essentially merged into a new tool called the *Extensible Markup Language (XML)*.

The resulting Web software would be a mixture of Web servers (even a large group of Web servers was now just called a Web site) and Web browsers (the universal client terminology has become the Web browser). The browser is software that runs on the user's client computer and talks to the software running on the Web server to request certain files. These files could be any type representing the various resources a user needs to access. If written in HTML, the files can contain information the browser can display in addition to the names of files of related resources and their locations (the hypertext links).

The World Wide Web was used successfully at CERN by May 1991. The first browser developed was a *line-mode browser* that was really just an advanced version of a Telnet session, as shown in Figure 1.4. The term *line-mode* refers to the line-by-line output of this first browser. Berners-Lee then presented the World Wide Web to the world in December 1991 at the Hypertext '91 conference in San Antonio, Texas, where it caused somewhat of a sensation among the crowd, which included some influential Internet people. In January 1992, the line-mode browser was made available for downloading to anyone with an Internet connection.

Word of the World Wide Web quickly spread and was propagated through Internet discussion groups and conferences. In July 1992, the University of California at Berkeley became the birthplace of the first modern-looking browser. This graphical browser was developed by a postgraduate associate named Pei Wei. The browser, named Viola, was available on UNIX systems using X Windows, which is roughly the UNIX equivalent of Microsoft Windows. It was the first browser to introduce familiar and distinctive browser features such as distinguishing hypertext links by colors and underscoring. Viola's other key feature was the capability to allow simple mouse pointing-and-clicking to activate the hypertext links. But Viola remained only an interesting experiment, because Pei Wei had no interest in developing Viola further as an experiment or as a commercial product.

```
Welcome to the World-Wide Web
THE WORLD-WIDE WEB

For more information, select by number:
A list of available W3 client programs   [1]
Everything about the W3 project  [2]
Places to start exploring [3]
The first International WWW Conference  [4]

This telnet service is provided by the WWW team
at CERN [5]
1-5 Up, Quit, or Help
```

Figure 1.4 The original Web "browser."

The Web Explodes

Others, however, were extremely interested in the Web browser potential. They realized that as computing power grew, graphical Web browsers would not need the powerful UNIX operating system and X Windows to perform adequately. Even Macintoshes and Windows-based PCs would do just as well.

And so in February 1993, a new Web browser called Mosaic was released by the National Center for Supercomputing Applications (NCSA), part of the University of Illinois at Urbana-Champaign. Marc Andreessen, a graduate student at the University of Illinois at Urbana-Champaign, with the help of Eric Bina, a programmer at the NCSA, developed the new Web browser. It was originally designed to run in a UNIX environment (with X Windows). But because of its popularity, the Windows and Macintosh versions of Mosaic browser were released in the fall of 1993. This date can truly be thought of as the real beginning of the Web.

Mosaic was not just an innovative Internet application; it was *the* tool, the universal client that opened the portal to the Internet for ordinary people. Once exposed to the Web, many realized that HTML was not a complicated computer language, but rather a relatively simple formatting tool that even those who had previously only used a word processor could master in a short time. Today many word processors allow users to build pages within them and will generate the HTML code so that the users never even have to learn HTML at all. Users just keep using the word processor as they have all along.

Marc Andreessen left the NCSA to cofound a company called Mosaic Communications, which eventually became Netscape Communications Corporation with the release of the Netscape browser, a new redesign of Mosaic. Andreessen jokingly called Netscape a "combination of Godzilla and Mosaic," leading to the merged code name of "Mozilla."

The popularity of the Web caught many by surprise. Microsoft even held off the release of the Windows 95 operating system software so that it could incorporate its Internet Explorer Web browser into the package. To keep ahead of the pack, Netscape offered extensions to the HTML standards to enhance the interaction and function of its Web browser.

What was all the excitement about? Was the Web experience so different that people actually got excited about the Internet, or more specifically, the Web servers attached to the Internet that made up the Web? Well, yes. Without the Web the average PC or Macintosh user people would be unable to go online and buy a car, order a book, obtain hard-to-find forms, pay their bills, bid on goods and services, get software upgrades, find directions to out-of-the-way places, and many other everyday tasks that they now do.

The commercial potential of the Web was apparent very early. Even before the Web browser made its way onto the Macintosh and PC platforms, at least a few people could order pizza over the Internet using the Web.

By the end of 1994 there were several thousand Web sites scattered around the Internet world. You could listen to the Japanese national anthem, download sales information from a few high-tech companies who saw the promising future of this new tool, and (even then) see pictures that no one should show their mother. But there was one Web site that was so distinctive that many people went there just to look and marvel. This was arguably the first commercial Web site: www.pizzahut.com.

Legend has it that the software and hardware engineers working at SCO UNIX (Santa Cruz Operation, a leader in developing UNIX server software) in California had a real hunger for Pizza Hut pizza. Working long and late hours meant missed meals, and sending someone out for pizza meant juggling or stalled tasks while the rest of the teams worked. One of the key projects involved the World Wide Web. So the story goes that SCO got together with Pizza Hut and put a Web server into the local Pizza Hut store.

Now the software team could use their Web browser at SCO to access the www.pizzahut.com Web site by entering that URL (this used to be called "pointing your browser at . . ."). Once there, they filled in name, street address, and voice phone number (apparently, even software types were tempted to order deliveries to vacant lots). Note the use of the term *voice phone number* to prevent confusion with modem links. After a few more entries on other pages, the pizza would arrive. Oddly, this Santa Cruz Pizza Hut page could be accessed, and pizza could be ordered from anywhere in the Internet universe, but deliveries ordered outside of the local area were quite cold if and when they arrived.

Figure 1.5 shows the electronic storefront Pizza Hut Web page as it looked in 1994. Despite its rudimentary appearance today, which would be laughable if not for the page's pioneering status, there are many features that have become indispensable for e-commerce sites. First, note that the company logo is prominently displayed (the original has a glorious and then startling red roof). Note also the careful respect for trademarks (the ® signs) and the use of the company name in the URL. This was the first common use of the term "webmaster" (but with no capital W), and clicking on the link allowed users to send email to the Webmaster. Then there is the form to fill out, a feature that took many Web sites much longer to offer on their own pages. Of course, there is a hypertext link to SCO as well. How many people who went to look at Pizza Hut went to SCO as well? Probably plenty, and this directly lead to the kind of banner and sidebar advertising overkill seen today at many Web sites.

Other business-oriented Web sites were also around in 1994. For example, the Internet Shopping Network, at URL www.internet.net, offered lots of things for sale—among them clothes, kitchenware, and small appliances. But after some initial interest, most of these early efforts failed because of one simple thing: People knew that the Internet offered no security or privacy whatsoever. Anyone with a network monitor or the right software could see everything that went by, especially on the local LANs at each end, which just happened to be where all the clients and servers were.

Sending your credit card information over the Internet without any security features at all was deemed as irresponsible as leaving a credit card on your desk at work while you went to lunch. To be sure, there were people who routinely did both, and they thought nothing of it. These folks were variously called "trusting" or "suckers," depending on who was doing the talking.

For offerings like Pizza Hut, these considerations mattered little. You paid for the pizza on delivery. The stakes were relatively low. But for operations like the Internet Shopping Network, the stakes were potentially higher. How can you sell to people if they won't give you their credit card information over the Internet? You can't push cash money down the wire.

The Internet Shopping Network handled this by establishing a membership code for everyone who wanted to shop. Prospective shoppers had to call up by phone to give their names, addresses, and payment method information before they were allowed to buy at the Web site. Then at the site, they just entered their membership code and shopped till they dropped.

Unfortunately, there were many drawbacks to this plan. It struck many as odd that they had to call by phone to use the network. Why not just call in a catalogue order instead? It was hard to sent gifts also, since the only address shipped to was the member's address on file. There was no allowance for alternate payment methods, either, such as a second credit card. Naturally, all of these issues had to be addressed (and they were) before the Web became more attractive for general business use.

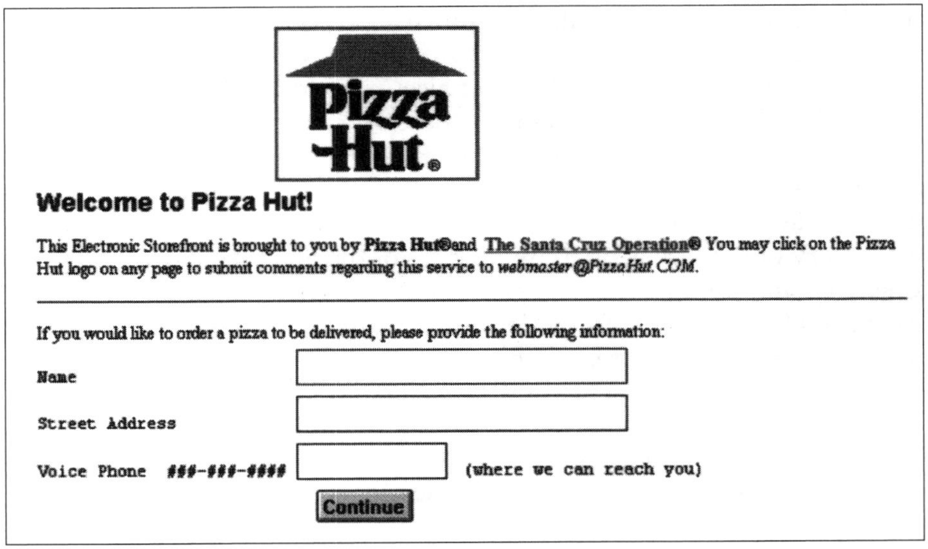

Figure 1.5 Web page from www.pizzahut.com, from 1994.

The Birth of the ISPs

In 1994, as the Web was having a huge impact on what the Internet meant to people, the federal support dollars for the NSFNET were phased out as planned. In 1993, the NSF deemed the then-experimental high-speed NSFNET network begun in 1984 a success, but stated that it was not the type of research network needed for the future. The NSF invested in a newer study of high-speed computing and networking and announced that "the Internet" would have to eventually fund itself commercially without government subsidies. The NSF continued funding for portions of the Internet, cutting funds 20 percent per year from 1994 until 1998 when they disappeared entirely.

The idea that the U.S. government should provide taxpayer dollars to encourage new technologies that might improve the life of citizens is outlined in the Constitution. The Internet did not set a precedent in this regard. For example, Samuel F. B. Morse, inventor of the telegraph, was an art professor, not a professional inventor (although he did explore more than the telegraph in this regard). Federal money was used to run the first telegraph line between Washington, DC, and Baltimore, Maryland. As a result, initial use of this line was free, but by the time the money ran out, it was obvious that the people had embraced the telegraph and money from users would support the new industry.

By the 1990s, it was also obvious that the Internet formed an important part of university and college life. Withdrawing the NSFNET subsidy just meant that funds for continued operations had to be gathered from the users of the network. To face this challenge, the Internet was restructured into a small number of network access points (NAPs) run for the most part by major telephone companies. Any part of the Internet could reach any other part of the Internet through these NAPs if the separate parts did not have direct peer connections to each other.

In addition to the NAPs, the Internet also came to include other types of peering points. The most important of these were the Commercial Internet Exchange (CIX) and the Federal Internet Exchange (FIX). The CIX and FIX were independent of the NAPs but also provide places for the ISPs that link to them to exchange traffic.

The history of the CIX is brief. In the days of the acceptable use policy, the Internet was supposed to be for "research and education" only. Use of the free Internet to make money was forbidden. As companies began to use the Internet for sales, marketing, and more, the line between what was acceptable and unacceptable became blurred. Is sending a sales brochure blatant commercial use of the Internet or still educational ("educating" people about the product?). Maybe to be safe, a company should send such commercial information over separate links and keep this traffic off of the global public Internet whenever possible.

So the CIX was formed to allow companies and service providers to send commercial content back and forth without worrying about violating the Internet spirit of research and education. ISPs or companies could exchange traffic at one of several CIX sites on the Internet, as long as they maintained links there, of course. CIX was disbanded in January 2002, its purpose obsolete in these days of the wide-open Internet. Today, going to www.cix.org (the old Web site) pops up the page for the U.S. Internet Service Providers Association. The new emphasis of the organization is on privacy, content restrictions, and intellectual property.

U.S. government networks exchanged traffic at two FIX points located on the east and west coasts of the United States. Government agencies such as NASA or the Department of Energy used these peering points in a fashion similar to the early days of the Internet. Today, peering points like CIX and FIX are mainly of historical interest.

Of course, any network entity providing Internet service (really just access to servers on the Internet) had to pay for the lines running to the NAPs and other charges as well. How would they get the money needed to pay for NAP connections? These organizations in many cases reached out beyond the university and college community and went public. Now calling themselves Internet service providers (ISPs), the smaller, regional portions of the Internet began advertising and signing up as many people as they could for Internet access. Some organizations were so successful that they grew into national ISPs very quickly, while others either accepted their smaller, regional role or at least were content with it.

It helped that there was already a precedent for such online services. In the 1980s, the availability of PCs and the appearance of these PCs in people's homes, as well as on their desktops at work, led to the appearance of various specialized networking companies or bulletin board services.

The popularity of the IBM PC in the early 1980s caused a revolution not only in business computer use but also in home computer use. For the first time, ordinary people at home had access to the enormous computing power previously available only to a select few with home computer terminals. And these select few had no real computing power in their homes. The computing power was still in the office mainframe or minicomputer; the terminal only provided access to the office computer over a telephone line. A person with a home PC could run applications and programs such as spreadsheets and word processors formerly restricted to a corporate environment. And when it came to word processing, spreadsheets, and even simple graphics, the humble PC often outperformed many mainframes and minicomputers, because of the rapid advances in technology. All that was missing was a network to tie together all of these new PC users, isolated in their homes in front of their screens.

By the mid-1980s, the PC community had a way to network their isolated PCs together. It appeared in the form of a variety of online services, some large, some small. The smaller ones consisted of a single PC running special "server" software similar in nature to Internet server software, but not based on the same protocols in most cases. A few telephone lines connected to modems allowed others to simply dial in with their terminal emulation software packages to become *clients*. This simple but powerful arrangement launched a cottage industry of bulletin board systems (BBSs) that lasted well into the 1990s and that still linger in some portions of the networking world. These small electronic bulletin boards usually addressed the needs of a small, contained group (a factory workers union local, for example) and offered meager features, such as email among users, as well as a common point to post files and messages. Many BBSs were staffed on a voluntary basis, and there was no charge to users beyond telephone calling time charges, which were usually minimal, except for users outside the local calling area.

The larger systems addressed the needs of the public at large for such services. Generally, the services were much the same, with the addition of some special user groups for those with shared interests, such as military history or houseplants. These larger online services benefited from special rules that the federal government laid down in the United States in 1984, specifically to encourage the growth of such services. The larger services had many points of presence (POPs) throughout the United States so that local users did not have to constantly dial long-distance numbers and pay high rates and the consequent high bills for access to these systems. Membership was typically based on a flat monthly rate and usage charges, although some offered totally flat-rate services, which users embraced wholeheartedly. Naturally, these online service providers were concentrated in major metropolitan areas, but there were some in almost every state in one place or another.

By the time the Web exploded onto the world in 1993 and 1994, the world of the large online service providers was filled by three companies: CompuServe (CSi), America Online (AOL), and Prodigy, arranged in order of their first public service offerings.

CompuServe began in 1982, virtually at the beginning of the PC industry itself. CompuServe quickly gained a reputation as the service of choice for technology-oriented PC enthusiasts. The more users cared about things such as operating system optimization, writing their own utility programs, or adding their own hard drive to their system, the more the users liked CompuServe. Oddly, for all its reputed sophistication, CompuServe was one of the last to realize that the Internet and Web were important to its users and lagged behind in offering easy and integrated Internet and Web access to its members.

America Online began offering services to the public at large in 1985. Their reputation was that their members did not need a great deal of PC sophistication or have to be a computer science wizard to access their various chat rooms and sample their offerings. AOL's aggressive marketing techniques turned some people off but certainly raised the consciousness of average PC users who at least tried the online service to see whether they would like it. Many did. AOL was among the first to see the Internet and Web as an adjunct service to their bulletin-board-based system, but not as a replacement to their "keyword" services.

Prodigy began as a joint effort between IBM and Sears in 1984 to encourage PC users to communicate online. Public service was launched in the United States in 1988, and Prodigy seemed determined to "out-AOL AOL" in terms of user-friendliness and services, such as home shopping and electronic newspapers. However, Prodigy alienated some with insistent advertising from sponsors (virtually absent on other service providers' systems) and suffered from some early negative publicity. While Prodigy saw that the long-term future of networking for ordinary people would revolve around advertising, sales, and marketing, CompuServe and AOL people at the time tended to treat these key aspects of the Internet today with disdain.

By the early 1990s, PC users in the United States were comfortable with the idea that an online service could put them in touch with other users with similar interests and offer them access to information that would otherwise be difficult to obtain. When the ISPs were faced with a loss of government funds, many of them saw a solution in simple repositioning. Rather than provide Internet access to colleges and universities, why not offer Internet access to anyone willing to pay the price? This involved installing TCP/IP client software on the user's PC, but software installation by this time was not the headache it once had been, and Windows 95 solved that problem by integrating TCP/IP into the operating system.

In the mid-1990s, three separate threads came together to encourage the expansion of Internet and Web access in the United States. The first was the idea that anyone with a PC could benefit from networking with other PC users through an online service. The second thread was that the ISPs were faced with having to make their operations financially self-supporting. The last thread was the Web itself, with its colorful graphics and multimedia in place of the stodgy commands of the recent past. The big online service providers, especially the Big Three of CSi, AOL, and Prodigy, were not slow to react. When the Web broke onto the world, Prodigy became the first of the Big Three to offer a Web browser as an integral part of its client software package in January of 1995. AOL quickly followed and went Prodigy one better. In 1995, AOL went out and bought the assets of ANS, the principal operations arm of the NSFNET Internet backbone. ANS got money and AOL got Web access for their users. CompuServe soon also realized that their members might want access to the Internet and the Web, but many had already decided not to wait and signed up with AOL or another ISP.

Today, there are still thousands of mostly small ISPs around the world. Only about 20 or 30 have an extensive national backbone of their own (the uncertainty is due to the lack of a standard definition of "national," "backbone," and "own" when it comes to ISPs). The others basically simply link to other ISPs, which might link to other ISPs, and eventually everything is linked together at the major NAPs. So the Internet is not one network but more like thousands of interconnected ISP networks, each with a large or small number of Web servers (Web sites) maintained by their individual members (customers) or members' organizations.

The Router's Role

So far, all well and good. The Internet took off when the Web hit town. The ISPs were right there to provide Internet (and Web) access for a steadily falling price. What has all this to do with routers, routing protocols, and routing policies?

As already mentioned, once the number of routes and routers reached a critical point, it was impossible for all routers to know all of the details of the Internet. So the Internet today consists of an increasing number of *routing domains*. Each routing domain has its own internal and external routing policies. The sizes of routing domains vary greatly, from only one IP address space to thousands. Each domain is called an autonomous system (AS). In many cases, an ISP has only one AS, but national or global ISPs might have several. For example, a global ISP might have one AS for North America, another for Europe, and a third for the rest of the world. Each AS must have a uniquely assigned AS number, although there can be various, logical "sub-ASs" called *confederations* or *subconfederations* (both terms are used) inside a single AS.

An AS forms a group of IP networks sharing a unified *routing policy framework*. A routing policy framework is a series of rules and guidelines used by the ISP to formulate the actual routing policies that are configured on the routers. Between different ASs, which are often administered by different ISPs, things are trickier. Careful coordination of routing frameworks and routing policies between ASs is needed to communicate complicated policies between different ASs.

Routes not only need to be advertised to another AS, but need to be accepted by the receiving AS. The decision on which routes to advertise and which routes to accept is determined by routing policy, of course. The situation is summarized in Figure 1.6, which shows the extremely simple exchange of routing information between two ASs that are peers. The routing information is transferred by the routing protocol running between the routers, usually BGP (Border Gateway Protocol, another reflection of the router as gateway).

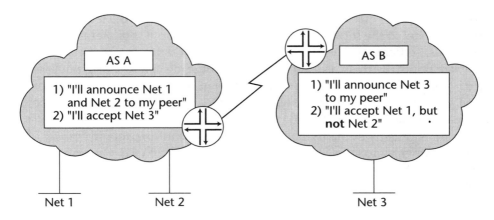

No host on Net 2 can be reached by directly from AS B!

Figure 1.6 The effects of routing policy.

Usually, the exchange of routing information is bidirectional, but this is not always a given. In some cases, the routing policy might completely stifle the flow of routing information in one direction, either because of the routing policy of the sender (suppress the advertising of a route or routes) or the receiver (ignore the routing information from the sender). If routing information is not sent or accepted between ASs, peers or not, then hosts (clients or servers) in one AS cannot reach other hosts on the networks represented by that routing information in the other AS. This situation is shown in Figure 1.6 as well.

Financial considerations often play a role in routing policies. In the "old days" of federal subsidies this was not much of an issue, and there were always grants available for continuing support for the research and educational network. Now the ISP grid net has raised issues as ISPs installed POPs in many regions and countries. ISPs can have their own customers, but they can also be customers of other ISPs as well. Who pays whom, and how much?

Telephony solved this problem with a concept called *settlements*, where one telephone company usually bills the call originator and shares a portion of the amount with other telephone companies as an *access charge*. Access charges compensate the other telephone companies that carry the call for the loss of the use of their own facilities for the duration of the call. On the Internet, the issue becomes how should one ISP compensate (if at all) another ISP for delivering packets that originate on the other ISP. The issue is complicated by the fact that the call is now a stream of packets, and an ISP might just be a transit ISP for packets originating in one ISP's AS and destined for a third ISP's AS.

Nevertheless, ISP peers have tried three ways to translate the telephony settlements model to the Internet. First, there are very popular bilateral (between two parties) settlements based on the "call," usually defined as some aspect of IP packet flows. In this case, the first ISP, where the packet originates at a client, gets all of the revenue from the customer, but the first ISP shares some of this money with the other ISP where the server is located. Second, there is the idea of *sender keeps all* (SKA), where the flow of packets from client to server one way is presumably balanced by the flow of packets from client to server the other way, so each might as well just keep all of the customer revenue. Finally, there is the idea of *transit fees*, which are just settlements between one ISP to another, usually from smaller ISPs to larger (since this traffic flow is seldom symmetrical).

None of these methods have worked out well on the Internet. There are often many more than just two or three ISPs involved between client and server. There is no easy way to track and account for the packets that should constitute a call, and even TCP sessions leave a lot to be desired because a simple Web page load might involved many rapid TCP connections between client and server. It is often hard to determine the "origin," and packets do not follow stable network paths. Packets are often dropped, and it seems hardly fair to bill someone else for re-sent packets replacing those that might have been counted but not delivered in the first place. Finally, dynamic routing might not be symmetric: so-called hot-potato routing seeks to pass packets off to another ISP as soon as possible. So the path from client to server might pass through different ISPs than server-to-client replies.

The drawbacks of the telephony settlements model have resulted in a movement to more simplistic arrangements between ISP peers, which just means ISPs of roughly equal size. These are often called *peering arrangements* or just *peering*. But another issue has arisen because there is no strict definition of what a peer is or is not. In this book, *peering* will just mean that two ISPs are directly connected and have instituted some routing policies between them. Financially, there is often also a sender-keeps-all arrangement in place, so no money changes hands. However, this applies only to peers. An ISP that is not a peer of the others is in a sense just a *customer* of the other ISPs. And customers must pay for services rendered. Since there are typically no financial arrangements for peer ISPs providing transit services to a third peer, however, peer ISPs do not provide transit to a third peer ISP (unless, of course, the third peer ISP is willing to pay and become a customer of one of the other ISPs). This situation is shown in Figure 1.7.

All three ISPs are peers in the sense that they are roughly equal in terms of network resources. They might all be small or regional or national ISPs, but the point is the same. ISP A is peering with ISP B and ISP B is peering with ISP C, but ISP A has no peering arrangement (or direct link) with ISP C. So packet deliveries from hosts in ISP A to ISP B (and back) are allowed, as are packet deliveries from hosts in ISP C to and from ISP B. But ISP B has routing policies in place to prevent transit traffic from ISP A to and from ISP C through ISP B. Unless ISP A and ISP C are willing to peer with each other, or ISP A or ISP C is willing to become a customer of ISP B, there will be no routing information sent to ISP A or ISP B to allow these ISPs to reach each other through ISP B. The routing policies enforced on the routers in ISP B will make sure of this.

The ISP grid net, without a clearly defined hierarchy of natural peers, complicates this simplistic application of peering drastically. Peering is often a political issue. The politics of peering more or less began in 1997, when a large ISP informed about 15 other ISPs that their current easy-going peering arrangements would be terminated. New agreements for transit traffic were now required, the ISP said, and the former peers were effectively transformed into customers. As the trend spread among the larger ISPs, direct connections were favored over public peering points such as the NAPs or CIX. The ISPs with multiple, high-speed links to NAPs (Tier 1 ISPs) peered only with each other.

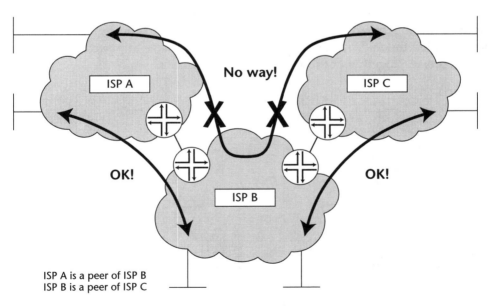

ISP A is a peer of ISP B
ISP B is a peer of ISP C

But there is no direct connection between ISP A and ISP C.
Therefore, no financial arrangement covers the transit traffic,
and routing policy can block it.

Figure 1.7 Peer ISPs do not provide free transit services.

Naturally, no ISP wants to be a customer of another ISP. All ISPs want to be peers, and peers of the biggest ISPs around. When it comes to peering, bigger is definitely better, so a series of mergers and acquisitions (although it is often claimed that there are really no mergers, only acquisitions) among the ISPs took place as each ISP sought to become a bigger peer than another. This consolidation has decreased the number of Tier 1 ISPs and reduced the number of potential peers considerably.

Today, potential partners for peering arrangements are closely scrutinized in several key areas. ISPs being considered for potential peerage must have high-capacity backbones, be of roughly the same size, cover key areas, have a good network operations center (NOC), have about the same quality of service (QoS) in terms of delay and dropped packets, and most importantly, exchange traffic roughly symmetrically. Because the work of the Internet routers is done delivering packets, nobody wants to peer with an ISP that supplies 10,000 packets for every 1,000 packets it accepts. Since servers, especially Web sites, tend to generate much more traffic than they consume, ISPs with tight networks with many server farms or Web hosting sites often have a hard time peering with anyone. This situation is shown in Figure 1.8.

ISPs without peering arrangements must rely on public exchange and peering points like the NAPs or (formerly) CIX for global connectivity. However, these exchange points are usually congested, which led to the rise of peering in the first place. And routing policies are still in place at the NAPs. A special device called the *route server* applies the routing policies in place between the ISPs that come together at these public peering points.

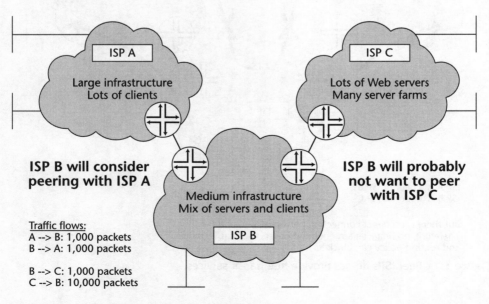

Figure 1.8 Good peer candidates and bad peer candidates.

Public peering arrangements are usually multilateral and applied to all ISPs that connect there, although there are bilateral arrangements in place here as well. The trend today is more toward private peering between pairs of peers. Exchanges are often overwhelmed by traffic, and it is almost impossible to enforce any QoS mechanisms in place on an ISP's network such as differentiated services for voice and video through a public exchange point.

Private peering can be done by simply installing a WAN link between routers at the AS borders of the two ISPs. Alternatively, peering can be done at a *collocation* site where the two peer's routers basically sit side by side. Both types of private peering are common.

The whole point of this chapter is that the Web explosion has created a need for new routing policies between peer ISPs. The Internet today has about 25 percent more routes (about 100,000) than there were *computers* attached to the Internet at the beginning of 1989 (about 80,000). Routing policy is necessary whether the peering is public or private, through a NAP or through a WAN link between routers. Routing information simply cannot be easily distributed everywhere all at once. Even the routing protocols play a role. When the initial NSFNET backbone was installed, only the Routing Information Protocol (RIP) routing protocol was mature enough to run on the backbone. Fully 80 percent of the traffic on the new NSFNET backbone was RIP routing updates, and so the quest for newer routing protocols such as Open Shortest Path First (OSPF) and Intermediate System-Intermediate System (IS-IS) began in earnest. Routing policies help IGPs such as OSPF and IS-IS distribute routing information within an AS more efficiently.

The Internet *must* be segmented into routing domains (the AS), and the flow of routing information between those domains must be controlled by routing policies to enforce the public or private peering arrangements in place between ISPs. Driven mainly by the use of the Web for commercial purposes, the Internet in 1990 was only 3 percent of the size of the Internet in 1996. The goal of this book is to detail the operation of the routing protocols and the creation of routing policies to enforce the aims of internal route distribution and peering between ASs to bring some order into this jungle of connections that is the Internet.

TCP/IP Survivor's Guide

Much of what follows in this book assumes you have at least some familiarity with the Internet Protocol suite, which is now the official name for what everyone still calls TCP/IP (Transmission Control Protocol/Internet Protocol). This chapter serves as a guide for those interested in routing policy, but might not have the level of knowledge regarding TCP/IP that is necessary to fully appreciate the details about protocol operation (especially IP) in the later chapters. Those familiar with TCP/IP might be tempted to skip this chapter, although even if you have used TCP/IP for years, you might want to reconsider, only because TCP/IP is constantly changing and adapting to new networking circumstances.

One change is the name of the protocol stack itself. The name change from TCP/IP to the Internet Protocol suite was made for two reasons. First, TCP/IP was starting to appear on networks other than the Internet, and not only private LANs and corporate networks. All manner of devices that are connected have started at least experimenting with TCP/IP. TCP/IP now runs on cash registers in stores and auto emissions test devices in garages. The name change restores the origin of the protocol stack directly to the Internet. Second, the name change reflects the fact that there is more—much more—to TCP/IP than just TCP and IP. Today, there is a lot of interest in facets of the Internet Protocol suite such as the User Datagram Protocol (UDP) and the Real-time Transfer Protocol (RTP) in addition to TCP, and Multiprotocol Label Switching (MPLS) in addition to IP. This is not to say that IP is not the focus of the first few chapters of the book. It is. This chapter simply explores the current structure of the Internet Protocol suite as it is used on the Internet and by routers today.

In this chapter, we outline all four layers of the Internet Protocol suites and then explore the lower layers in detail, including IP itself. Next, we explain the upper layers of the Internet Protocol suite are explained, starting with TCP. Along the way, we present the detailed structure of the IP packet and header with the intention of providing a firm basis for how routing protocols and routing policies use the information inside the IP packet header to perform their tasks. The chapter closes with a look at some of the operational details of some applications and adjunct protocols that are important in routers and on the Internet.

Internet Protocol Suite: An Overview

The Internet Protocol suite, or TCP/IP, is a *layered* protocol, as is almost every network protocol in use today. It is possible, of course, to create a monolithic network protocol and program that forms a single entity and handles everything from user mouse clicks to the serial sending and receiving of bits out of the connector on the back of the computer, but this is rarely done anymore. There are two main reasons that layers are the rule today when it comes to network protocols. First, the layers simplify the overall implementation (programming) process by isolating features and functions in specific layers. This separation also makes troubleshooting and testing easier and more efficient. Second, as long as the interface between the layers is respected (such as a higher-layer packet placed inside a lower-layer frame), the task of adding features and functions to one layer or another, and so the entire protocol stack is made much simpler.

One consequence of the layering of TCP/IP is that the IP packets can be made to run on any type of network. The IP packet layer is one layer, and the layers below the IP layer are not important in the overall flow of packets from one host (end system) to another across the network. All that matters is that the device at the receiving end of the link understands the type of IP packet *encapsulation* used at the sending end of the link. This is usually taken to mean that IP runs on everything, and that's pretty close to the truth. In fact, in a very real sense the role of the IP router is simply to take an IP packet from one type of network using one form of packet encapsulation and send the packet off to another type of network using another type of packet encapsulation.

If there were only one form of packet encapsulation used everywhere, the IP packets could remain invisible to the router, and the router would be more efficient as a *bridge* (for LANs) or *switch* (for WANs). Oddly, the rise of Ethernet as the dominant form of LAN, coupled with the emergence of Gigabit Ethernet on the WAN, makes the use of bridging/switching schemes such as virtual LANs (VLANs) and Multiprotocol Label Switching (MPLS) popular alternatives to simple IP packet routing. But in this book, the traditional role of the router as IP packet processor is assumed.

TCP/IP is also considered to be a *peer protocol* stack, which means that every implementation of TCP/IP has the same capabilities as every other. So there are no "restricted" or "master" versions of TCP/IP that anyone need be concerned about. Any TCP/IP has all of the capabilities of TCP/IP. All TCP/IP stacks are created equal.

Actually, *almost* all are equal. TCP/IP, like many other protocols, is actually a peer protocol implemented in a distinctly asymmetrical manner known as the *client/server model*. This fact has consequences when it comes to routing policy implementation, so a few words about this are appropriate.

TCP/IP Layers and the Client/Server Model

On the Internet, computers that run TCP/IP are called *hosts*. The hosts fall into one of two major categories: the host could be *client* or the host could be a *server*. However, since most computers are fully multitasking-capable today, it is possible that the same host could be running the client version of a program for one application (for example, a Web browser) and the server version of another program (for example, a file transfer server) at the same time. Dedicated servers are common on the Internet, but most client computers almost act as servers for a variety of applications. The details are not as important as the interplay among layers, applications, and routers. The interplay between the layers of TCP/IP and the implementation of the client/server model is shown in Figure 2.1.

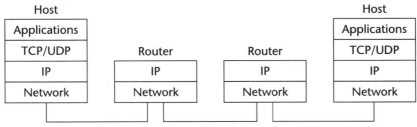

Figure 2.1   The TCP/IP model of operation.

TCP/IP has four layers. Networking is often taught from a seven-layer model for data communications known as the Open Systems Interconnection Reference Model (OSI-RM). The OSI-RM will be discussed in a little more detail in Chapter 11 on the IS-IS routing protocol. IS-IS is based entirely on the OSI-RM, but TCP/IP is not. TCP/IP is a totally independent implementation of layered protocols, and the layers of TCP/IP do not fit very well with OSI-RM, especially at the top of the OSI-RM. But even though TCP/IP has four layers and the OSI-RM has seven, both protocol stacks do exactly the same things for networks and applications: They form the bridge between the bits on the wire and the programs running in local computer memory.

The underlying *network access* layer, often called the *network layer*, with a couple of major exceptions, is not really defined by the RFC specification process at all. What is often defined is just a way to put IP packets inside a given frame structure (the frame is the basic protocol data unit, or PDU, of the network layer) on the sending side of a link and a way to take the IP packets out of the frame on the receiving side of the link. This gives IP almost total independence of the network used to transport the IP packets between hosts, routers, and networked combinations of these device types.

Above the network layer is the IP layer itself. The IP layer not only forms and routes the IP packet (also called a *datagram* in older documentation) but also provides a mechanism for the operation of many routing protocols, the major exception being Border Gateway Protocol (BGP). Technically, all routers that do not run BGP need to do is implement the IP layer above the network layer, since the routing protocols can use IP directly. Only hosts need to add a transport layer to deal with the contents of the packet. Routers are intermediate systems in the sense that they just relay packets from source host to destination host without so much as even looking at the content of transit IP packets. Routers only examine the IP headers.

The transport layer of TCP/IP consists of two major protocols: the Transmission Control Protocol (TCP) and the User Datagram Protocol (UDP). TCP is a "reliable" layer added on top of the "best-effort" IP layer to make sure that even if packets are lost in transit, the hosts will be able to detect and resend missing information. TCP always resends lost data units, called *segments*, even if a segment is spread across many IP packets and only one packet is lost. This means that TCP does not selectively resend lost packets but must back up and resend everything in a corrupt segment. Segments are just used to chop up application content, such as huge, multimegabyte files, into more easily handled pieces. TCP is a *connection-oriented* layer on top of the *connectionless* IP layer, which means that before any TCP segment can be sent to another host, a TCP connection must be established to that host. In contrast, UDP is a connectionless transport layer on top of the connectionless IP layer. UDP segments are simply forwarded to a destination under the assumption that sooner or later a response will come back from the remote host that forms an implied or formal acknowledgement that the UDP segment arrived.

At the top of the TCP/IP stack is the application layer. It is the applications themselves that come in client or server versions, not any other layer of TCP/IP. While a host computer might be able to run a client process and server process at the same time, these processes must be two different applications, since an individual process cannot be a client and a server simultaneously. There is a good reason for this distinct application implementation. A server process when started basically sits and "listens" for clients to "talk" to the server. For example, a Web server is brought up on a host successfully whether there is a browser client pointed at it or not. The Web server just issues what is called a *passive open* to TCP/IP and remains idle until a client requests content. In contrast, the Web browser (client) always issues an *active open* to TCP/IP and attempts to send packets to a Web site right away. Otherwise, why is it running? The Web site can be the default site for the browser, but if the Web site is not reachable, that is an error condition. Clients talk and servers listen. The two cannot be embodied in the same application process at the same time because a program cannot simultaneously issue a passive open and an active open. The application must either talk or listen.

What does this client and server distinction have to do with routing and routing policy? As it turns out, client/service traffic loads are as asymmetric as the software. Many more packets flow from a server to a client than from a client to a server. A simple client mouse click can initiate a deluge of packets lasting an hour or more when a software package is downloaded.

ISPs with lots of home or dial-in users tend to see huge spikes in traffic flows during the day. Once school is out, traffic starts to build, peaking after dinner, and tapering off only late at night. ISPs with mostly server farms tend to see smoother traffic profiles, because although there is always some large pool of users coming in to the server from somewhere in the world, as all of these local time zone peaks spread themselves out over the whole day.

Consider a small ISP with mostly dial-in home users linked to a huge ISP with many server farms, each with Web sites hosting all kinds of services. Few packets will flow onto the large ISP's network from the smaller ISP, but in the return direction the traffic flow will be tremendous. So what? Well, what if the small ISP happens to be between the huge ISP and another large ISP with many dial-in users? Not only will the server-generated traffic for the modest-sized ISP flow into small ISP, but so might all of the many packets bound for the third, large ISP on the other side. Why should the ISP in the middle provide free transit for the high traffic load of packets for the third ISP? This extra traffic could lead to longer delays for the small ISP's paying customers. This is also a good place to apply a routing policy, naturally, but it all starts with an appreciation of client/server differences.

A closer look at the TCP/IP stack is shown in Figure 2.2. The TCP/IP stack basically bridges the gap between interface connector on the network (hardware) and the local memory of the host where the applications run (software). The names of the protocol data units used at each layer are given as well. The

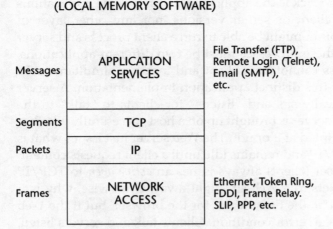

Figure 2.2 The TCP/IP protocol stack in detail.

unit of the network layer is the *frame.* Inside the frame is the data unit of the IP layer, the *packet.* The unit of the transport layer is the *segment* in TCP/IP, and the segment by definition is the content of the information-bearing packet. Finally, applications exchange *messages,* although this term is not a formal definition. Segments taken together form the messages that the applications are sending to each other.

At this point we need to examine a few operational aspects of the TCP/IP protocol stack more closely.

The Network Layer

The network layer of TCP/IP deals with areas such as physical connectors, bit signals, and media access control—in short, everything needed to send and receive a frame. Network layer interfaces have been defined for Frame Relay and X.25 WANs as well as LANs. All IP implementations must be able to support at least one of these interface types.

Interfaces for IP packets have been defined for all of the following:

- Ethernet from DEC, Intel, and Xerox (known as DIX Ethernet)
- IEEE (Institute of Electrical and Electronics Engineers) 802.3 Ethernet-based LANs
- Token Ring LANs (IEEE 802.5)

- Point-to-Point Protocol (PPP from the IP developers themselves, the closest thing TCP/IP has to an official network layer protocol)

- X.25 (an international standard public switched connection-oriented network protocol)

- Frame Relay (another international standard public switched connection-oriented network protocol)

- FDDI (Fiber Distributed Data Interface, a LAN-like network running at 100 Mbps)

- ATM (Asynchronous Transfer Mode, a high-speed public network service using fixed-length cells)

- ISDN (Integrated Services Digital Network, a public switched network in some ways similar to X.25)

- ARCnet (a proprietary LAN protocol from Datapoint)

- IEEE 802.4 LANs (known as Token Bus, from General Motors)

- SLIP (Serial Line Interface Protocol, an older but common way of sending IP packets over a dial-up, asynchronous modem arrangement)

- CDPD (Cellular Digital Packetized Data, a way of sending IP packets over the cellular mobile radio network; CDPD is sometimes loosely called wireless TCP/IP)

- Packet over SONET/SDH (POS, a way to send IP packets directly inside SONET/SDH frames instead of using an intermediate "frame" structure such as Frame Relay or ATM)

More obscure interfaces also exist, such as HYPERchannel or Switched Multimegabit Data Service (SMDS), but these need not be detailed because of their relatively uncommon implementation.

The network layer of TCP/IP basically takes IP packets at the source and puts them inside whichever frame structure is used at the network layer, such as a Frame Relay frame or Ethernet frame. The network layer then sends the frame as a series of 0s and 1s (bits) on the link itself, exactly as expected. At the receiver, the network layer recovers the frame from the arriving sequence of 0s and 1s and extracts the IP packet. The IP packet is then sent to the receiving IP layer for further processing.

The advantage of not tying the IP layer to any specific network at the lower layers is flexibility. A new type of network interface can be added without great effort. Also, it makes the linking of these various network types into an internetwork that much easier.

Note that the router in its role as an intermediate system between source and destination end systems only handles the IP packet for transit traffic. This is not to say that routers are not sometimes clients and/or servers themselves.

It is a common enough practice to Telnet to a router and remotely log in for configuration or network administration purposes, and most routers can also be file transfer clients. But routers are not really used for the *purpose* of sending email or as a Web site, so the convention of showing only the IP layer on a router is accurate enough. And although routers today routinely have a transport and application layer, not so long ago routers did not have enough power to run their routing protocols as well as client/server applications. This is one reason why many routing protocols ride directly inside IP packets instead of relying on TCP or UDP (again, BGP is the major exception).

The IP Layer

The IP layer is a *connectionless* layer. This means that IP packets are routed completely independently through the collection of routers that make up the internetwork and do not follow "paths" or "virtual circuits" or anything else set up by connections in other types of networks. This also means that packets may arrive out of sequence, or even with gaps in the sequence (caused by lost packets), at the destination. IP does not even care which application a packet belongs to: It delivers all packets without a sense of priority or sensitivity to loss. IP itself is not concerned with this aspect of its operation, which is characteristic of all connectionless, best-effort networks. Sequenced traffic, priorities, and guaranteed delivery in the form of acknowledgments, if needed by the application, must be provided by the higher layers of the TCP/IP protocol stack. These "reliable" transport functions are not functions of the IP layer.

This book uses IP addresses in their version 4 format (IPv4) almost exclusively. The Internet today is slowly transitioning to the newer form of IP address, IP version 6 (IPv6). IPv6 is covered in Chapter 3, "IP Addressing and Routing." For this book, all addresses are assumed to be IPv4 addresses unless otherwise stated. IP addresses are usually expressed in a form know as *dotted decimal notation*. IP addresses are 32 bits in length, and each 8-bit byte is expressed as a decimal number between 0 and 255. So examples of valid IP addresses are 10.0.14.200, 172.16.0.0, or 192.168.69.45. More details on the IP address are explored in Chapter 3.

Two other major protocols run at the IP layer besides IP itself. The routers that form the network devices in a TCP/IP network must be able to send the end systems (hosts) error messages in case a router must discard a packet (due to a lack of buffer space because of congestion, for example). This protocol (which must run at this layer because the other layers are technically lacking in routers when performing the packet transfer function) is known as the Internet Control Message Protocol (ICMP). ICMP is not usually considered a complete protocol by itself, because the ICMP messages themselves are sent inside IP packets.

The other major protocol actually has many different functions, depending on the exact network type that IP is running on. These are known as Address Resolution Protocols (ARPs), and their main function is to provide a method for the IP layer protocol itself to determine the proper network layer address to place in the frame header in order for the network beneath the IP layer to deliver the frame containing the IP packet to the proper destination. For instance, if IP is running on a LAN, frames are addressed by media access control (MAC) address, coded into every LAN adapter card. ARP offers a method for the IP layer to send a message onto the LAN saying, in effect, "Who has IP address 192.168.40.69?" The IP software on each system on the LAN examines the ARP message and the system that has the corresponding IP address (192.168.40.69) replies to the sending IP address with the correct MAC layer address in the frame.

The IP layer is also the home of many of the routing protocols in common use on the Internet today. In fact, all of the routing protocols that are Interior Gateway Protocols (IGPs) place their messages directly inside of IP packets. These include RIP, OSPF, IS-IS, and many others. This practice allows routers to run routing protocols without the need to implement a transport and application layer. And even if these upper layers are present, as is common today, the routing protocols can function without the overhead of these upper layers.

The structure of the IP packet is shown in Figure 2.3. The structure illustrated is for IP version 4 (IPv4). The newer IP version 6 (IPv6) header is discussed in Chapter 3. Unless otherwise stated in this book, all references to "IP" refer to IPv4. The minimum (no options; very common) IP header length is 20 bytes (always shown as 4 bytes per line), and the maximum length (rarely seen) is 60 bytes. Some of the fields are fairly self-explanatory, such as the fields for the 4-byte (32-bit) IP source and destination address, but others have specialized purposes.

These fields of the IP packet header are as follows:

Version.   Currently set to 4 for IPv4, the most common form of IP used. The newer version of IP is IPv6.

Header Length.   The length of the IP header in 4-byte (32-bit) units known as *words*.

Type of Service.   Parameters that affect how packet is handled by routers and other equipment.

Total Length of Packet.   Length of the packet in bytes. Maximum is 65,535—a length that is approached by no common TCP/IP implementation. Most IP packets are seldom more than 1,500 bytes or so in length, but a few approach 10,000 bytes. Most hosts will choke if asked to produce or consume an IP packet 10,000 or more bytes long.

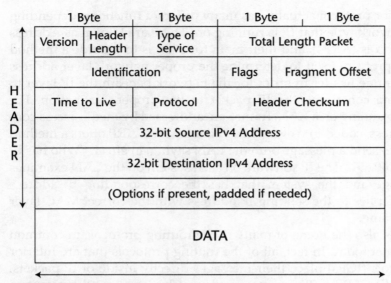

Figure 2.3   The IP packet header.

The next three fields directly figure in the *fragmentation* process. Fragmentation occurs when a larger IP packet (for example, 9,000 bytes) must be broken up to fit inside a smaller frame (for example, the 1,500-byte frame used in most types of Ethernet). The three fields are as follows:

Identification.   A number set for each packet fragment that helps the destination host reassemble these like-identified fragments.

Flags.   Only the first 3 bits are defined. Bit 1 must be 0. Bit 2 is the DF ("don't fragment") bit. It is 0 if fragmentation is allowed (UDP should not allow fragmentation of the packet containing a UDP message), or 1 if fragmentation is *not* allowed (e.g., for UDP). Bit 3 is the MF ("more fragments") bit, and it is set to 0 if the packet is the last fragment, or 1 if there are more fragments to come.

Fragment Offset.   When packets are fragmented, the fragments must fall on an 8-byte boundary. That is, an 800-byte-long packet may be fragmented as two packets of 400 bytes, but not as eight packets of 100 bytes, since 100 is not evenly divisible by 8. This field contains the number of 8-byte units (known as blocks) in the packet fragment.

The rest of the IP header fields are as follows:

Time to Live.   This value is the number of *seconds*, up to 255 maximum, that a packet is supposed to have to reach the destination. Each router is to decrement this field by a preconfigured amount of 1 or more. If the packet has the field set to 0, it is discarded. Unfortunately, there is no easy way for routers to track this time, so most routers interpret this field as a simple *hop count* between routers and decrement this field by 1.

Protocol.   This field contains the number of the transport layer protocol that is to receive and process the data content of the packet. The protocol number for TCP is 6 and UDP is 17. There are 256 possible values, and although many of them are defined, few of them are used in practice.

Header Checksum.   An error check on the IP header fields only, not the data fields. This checksum is primitive compared to newer error-checking methods.

Source and Destination Address.   The IP addresses of the source and destination hosts.

Options.   The options are not often used in user information packets and will not be described further.

Padding.   When options are used, the padding field is used to make certain the packet header ends on a 32-bit boundary. That is, the packet header must be an integer number of 4-byte *words*.

The Transport Layer

The two main protocols that run above the IP layer are TCP and UDP. As time goes on, UDP is assuming more and more importance on the Internet, especially for applications such as voice and streaming audio and video. This is because TCP is not particularly well suited for such real-time applications. TCP's reliability features include sequence numbering with resending to detect and supply missing or out-of-sequence segments, as well as complete flow control to prevent any sender from overwhelming a receiver. Neither of these features, resending nor flow control, is needed or desirable when it comes to real-time audio and video on the Internet.

TCP contains all the functions and mechanisms needed to make up for the best-effort connectionless delivery provided by the IP layer. Packets may arrive at a host with errors, out of sequence, or even with gaps in sequence due to lost or discarded packets. TCP must guarantee that the segment (the TCP protocol data unit) is delivered to the destination application error-free, complete, and in sequence. In keeping with the general philosophy of connection-oriented networks, TCP provides acknowledgments that periodically flow from the destination to the source to assure the sender that all is well with the data sent up to that point in time.

On the sending side, TCP passes segments to the IP layer for placement in packets, which IP will route without connections to the destination. On the receiving side, TCP accepts the incoming segments from the IP layer and delivers the data to the proper application running at the layer above TCP in the exact order in which the data was sent.

The TCP/IP transport layer has another major protocol that runs at the TCP layer besides TCP: the User Datagram Protocol (UDP). UDP is a protocol that is as connectionless as IP. When applications run with UDP instead of TCP, there is no need to establish (or maintain) a connection between a source and destination before sending data. Connection management, of course, adds overhead and delay to the network. UDP offers a way to send data quickly and simply. However, UDP offers none of the services that TCP supplies. Now applications cannot count on TCP to ensure error-free, guaranteed (via acknowledgments), in-sequence delivery of data at the destination.

For some simple applications, purely connectionless data delivery may be sufficient. Single messages between applications may be sent more efficiently with UDP because there is no need to exchange TCP segments to establish a connection in the first place. Most applications will not be satisfied will this mode of operation, however. So all of the primary TCP/IP applications such as file transfer (FTP), remote login (Telnet), Web page transfers, and so on use TCP, and most are expressly forbidden from using UDP. Similarly, several applications in TCP/IP must use UDP only, such as the Domain Name System (DNS), and will not function correctly with TCP.

Generally, TCP is for use with "sustained flows" of information from end-to-end, and UDP is for quick "request/response" message pairs between client and server. Real-time applications use UDP with another header inside called the Real-time Transfer Protocol (RTP). The RTP header takes what is needed from TCP, such as a sequence number to detect (but not resend) missing packets of audio and video and uses these necessary features in UDP.

Figure 2.4 shows the structure of the TCP header. TCP options are seldom used, but if present, the TCP options must form 4-byte units. If the option is less than 4 bytes, the option field is padded to 4 bytes.

The fields of the TCP header are as follows:

Source Port.   The 16-bit application port that loaded the data into the TCP segment.

Destination Port.   The 16-bit application port to which the TCP segment is being sent.

Sequence Number.   A 32-bit field that counts the segments sent from source to destination.

Acknowledgement Number.   A 32-bit field that informs the sender of the next sequence number expected. Together, these fields detect missing and out-of-sequence segments.

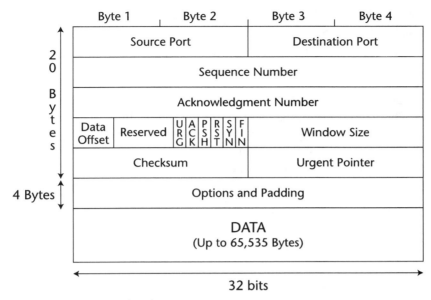

Figure 2.4 The TCP header.

Data Offset.   This field tells the receiver where the data begins. That is, this field contains the number of 4-byte units in the TCP header.

Reserved.   These bits are reserved for future functions. They must be set to 0s.

Control Bits.   Six single-bit fields called *flags* which control the status of the TCP connection across the network. The flags, when set to a one-bit, mean:

- URG: Urgent pointer. There is urgent data present in the segment that should be processed before any other data in the TCP segment. This flag works with the Urgent Pointer field.

- ACK: Acknowledgment. The acknowledgment field is valid and should be checked against the sender's sequence number field.

- PSH: Push. Tells the sender not to buffer the data in the segment, but to "push" it right out in a packet immediately.

- RST: Reset. Essentially resets a connection and begins the TCP three-way handshake all over again. This is also used to not accept a connection request from another host.

- SYN: Synchronize. Used to request a connection and to synchronize sequence numbers.
- FIN: Final. Indicates there is no more data coming from the sender. The connection should be closed.

Window.   Used for flow control so that a sender can never overwhelm a receiver. This 16-bit number is used to tell the sender how many bytes of data the receiver is willing to receive before the sender must stop sending and wait for an acknowledgment. The flow control occurs when the receiver deliberately delays sending the acknowledgment or shrinks the window.

Checksum.   An error-checking mechanism.

Urgent Pointer.   Points to the place in the segment following the urgent data where the "regular" data begins. Only valid when the URG flag is set.

Options.   Used to convey optional fields in the TCP header.

The UDP header is shown in Figure 2.5. In contrast to the TCP header, the UDP header is quite sparse. This is fine for a connectionless protocol used for simple request-response message pair exchanges.

The fields of the UDP header are as follows:

Source Port.   The 16-bit application port that loaded the data into the UDP segment.

Destination Port.   The 16-bit application port to which the UDP segment is being sent.

Message Length.   A 16-bit field used to indicate the size of the UDP header and its data.

Checksum.   An error-checking mechanism (not always used in UDP).

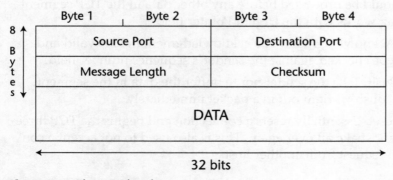

Figure 2.5   The UDP header.

The Application Layer

At the top of the Internet Protocol stack, at the application services layer, are the basic applications and services of the TCP/IP architecture. Application services offers several basic applications themselves. These are typically bundled with the TCP/IP software distributed by various vendors and, fortunately, are generally interoperable.

The standard application services include a file transfer method (File Transfer Protocol, or FTP), a remote terminal access method (Telnet), an electronic mail system (Simple Mail Transfer Protocol, or SMTP), and a Domain Name System (DNS) directory service for domain name to IP address translation (and vice versa). In addition, many TCP/IP implementations include a way of accessing records within files remotely (rather than transferring the whole file) known as Network File System (NFS). There is also the Simple Network Management Protocol (SNMP). For the Web, the application is really a protocol called the Hypertext Transfer Protocol (HTTP). Some of these applications are defined to run on TCP and others are defined to run on UDP.

An important application layer concept in TCP/IP is the *socket*. Sockets in turn relate to the TCP/UDP concept of a *port*. Sockets and ports are important enough in TCP/IP to deserve a little more exploration.

As mentioned, the TCP/IP architecture works by implementing the client/server model of networking by means of a set of peer-to-peer protocols. Peer-to-peer just means that all systems on the TCP/IP network are running the same software, in this case, the TCP/IP software. Each system has the same network capabilities as any other. This is the essence of the peer protocol model. Local systems may not only access data on remote systems but also have remote systems access data on the local system.

At the same time as TCP/IP is peering, TCP/IP implements the client/server model. In TCP/IP, all applications exist as two separate implementations: a client process and a server process. For example, FTP (the File Transfer Protocol application bundled with TCP/IP) comes as both a client version and a server version. To attach to a remote system to transfer files, a user need only run the client process. But to allow remote clients to access the target system, the target system must be running the server version of the FTP process. In fact, on multi-user operating systems, the same physical computer is often running one server FTP process (the passive open to allow remote users to access the local system) and one or more client FTP processes (the active open to allow local users to access remote systems).

The choice of port number on the part of these FTP clients and servers is critical. First, there is usually only one TCP/UDP transport layer, but there are usually many server application processes running to accept mail, file transfer requests, and so on. The transport layer must pass the arriving TCP/UDP segments to the proper application. It makes no sense to pass a file transfer client request to the electronic mail server process. So the receiving server TCP layer must know which port number the FTP server process is using, and the email process, and the port numbers of whatever other processes are running on that computer at that exact time. Second, the client port number is important as well. The server process must know the port number that the client process is using on the client machine. This is the only way that the server process can reply to the proper port number on the client. This is because a remote computer may also have only one transport layer running many FTP client processes at the application services layer.

Fortunately, an easy mechanism exists for sorting out these client and server port numbers. All TCP/IP server processes must "listen" (technically, the server processes issue the passive opens) on a *well-known port*. These well-known port numbers are documented by the Internet Assigned Numbers Authority (IANA) and cannot be used for other purposes. The use of well-known port numbers on the part of servers makes it easy for clients to know the port number on which a server process is listening, if at all.

For example, the well-known port number for the FTP server process (passive open) is 21. Port numbers from 1 to 1023 are reserved for well-known TCP/UDP ports, and almost all of them are assigned. Any TCP segment having a destination port number of 21 is given by the TCP layer to the server FTP process, if this process is running at the application services layer.

But how does the client process (which issues the active open on the remote system) choose a port number? It might seem that the client process should also choose port number 21, since the client process is also running FTP. In fact, this will not work. Well-known port numbers are reserved for use by server processes only and may not be used at all by clients. Otherwise, only one FTP client could be run at a time on the remote system, and this is obviously not a desirable situation when the remote system itself is a multi-user system.

To get around this apparent limitation, TCP/IP client processes must use a client port number that is *not* a well-known port number (that is, greater than 1,023). Since these client processes are the "talkers" and the client port number is included in the TCP segment sent to the remote server process, the remote server process will know what the client process has chosen for a client port number and reply accordingly. There is no confusion between separate clients establishing connections (or *sessions*) with the same client port number because these connections are distinguished by *socket* number (port number plus IP address, and the IP address must be different for different clients running on different hosts). And even if the client connections originate in the same remote system, this system can easily make sure no two client processes choose the same port number. Either the ports are the same and the IP address is different at one end, or the IP addresses are different and the ports are the same: a very elegant yet simple mechanism. This process is illustrated in Figure 2.6. By convention, the socket is indicated by adding the port to the IP

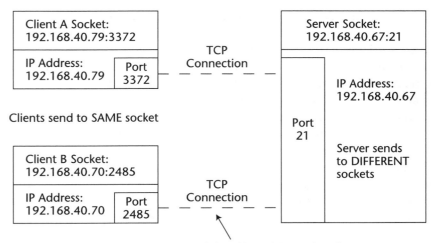

Clients send to SAME socket

TCP Connections are defined by BOTH end sockets

Figure 2.6   Sockets and ports.

address, separated by a colon, such as 192.168.40.67:21. The TCP connections on a client or server are identified by concatenating the socket numbers at each end of the TCP connection. Why invent a numbering scheme just for TCP connections? So sockets have yet another use.

A whole series of well-known ports exists. Since the transport layer has two main protocols, TCP and UDP, each have a set of well-known ports that are not confused by the applications running at the applications services layer (generally, applications run on the same ports with TCP or UDP, but there are some exceptions). The IANA has made efforts to coordinate the port numbers so that applications that may be both connection-oriented (using TCP) and connectionless (using UDP) employ the same port numbers.

So adding the TCP/UDP port number to the IP address to yield the socket is an important way to enumerate connections and sessions in TCP/IP and sort all of the sources and destinations of packets properly. But sockets are important in TCP/IP for another reason entirely. The socket is the real interface between an Internet-ready application program and the TCP/IP protocol stack. There are other ways to write programs according to the client/server model to run over the Internet, but using the sockets interface is by far the most common.

To understand the attraction of the sockets interface in TCP/IP, a brief review of programming concepts is needed. At the very beginning of computer programming, programmers had to know the internals of the computer architecture in order to do something as simple as open a file. Programs written in machine language (0110 1110) or basic assembly language (ADD REG A STO REG B) offered no real alternatives. Once the high-level language COBOL came along, it was possible to teach people how to write programs without teaching them the internals of the computer. In COBOL, it was just OPEN FILE ACCTS and that was it. The COBOL compiler translated the OPEN to whatever was needed to ready the file for processing. Some sneered that the advent of COBOL meant the end of true computer scientists, but most people embraced the ease of programming that the use of COBOL encouraged.

Now consider the situation once the Web came along and the quest was now for programmers who could write applications that ran on the client/server Internet. Without sockets, programmers would have to either duplicate all of TCP/IP (unlikely) or carefully construct segments that could be passed to TCP or UDP with all of the details needed to construct the necessary TCP and UDP and IP headers. With sockets, the network looked and was treated just like a file. And programmers all knew how to read and write to a file—reading from a socket received and writing to a socket sent. Programmers could all create a file, write to a file, read from a file, and close a file. Now programmers could create a socket (attach to TCP/IP), write to a socket (send), read from a socket (receive), and close a socket (detach from TCP/IP). With sockets, programmers could write networked applications without knowing anything about networks.

Putting It All Together

The various pieces of TCP/IP are placed in their respective layers in Figure 2.7.

The TCP/IP protocol stack is very complex. For the sake of simplicity, the preceding presented only enough information for you to understand how TCP/IP supports the rest of the applications and adjunct protocols described in the rest of this chapter.

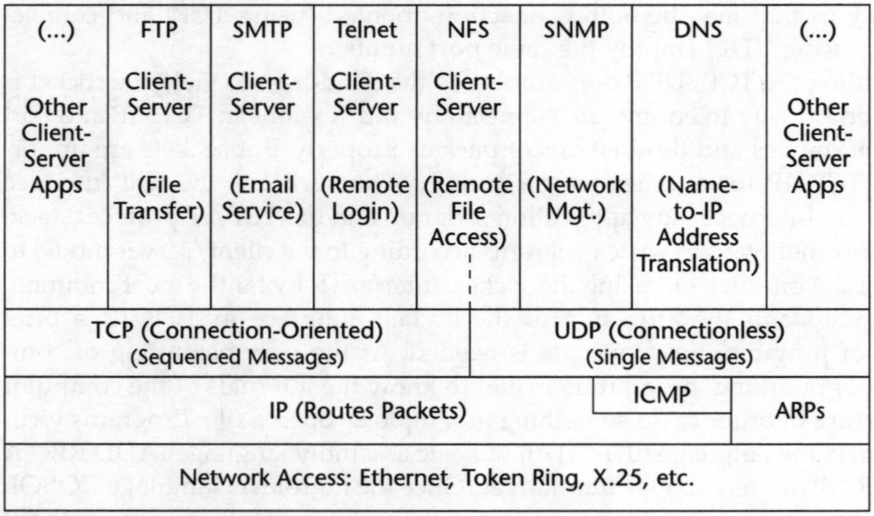

(...)	FTP	SMTP	Telnet	NFS	SNMP	DNS	(...)
Other Client-Server Apps	Client-Server	Client-Server	Client-Server	Client-Server			Other Client-Server Apps
	(File Transfer)	(Email Service)	(Remote Login)	(Remote File Access)	(Network Mgt.)	(Name-to-IP Address Translation)	

TCP (Connection-Oriented) (Sequenced Messages)				UDP (Connectionless) (Single Messages)			

IP (Routes Packets)	ICMP	ARPs

Network Access: Ethernet, Token Ring, X.25, etc.

Figure 2.7 The major pieces of TCP/IP.

Key TCP/IP Applications

So far, the application layer of TCP/IP has been explored only generally. TCP/IP applications originally supplied three main functions: file transfer, electronic mail, and remote login capabilities. These are certainly still very popular applications on TCP/IP networks, but not the only ones by any means. In this section we take a closer look at these three basic applications and several others. However, even this more detailed look comes nowhere near to being an exhaustive list of all the common applications bundled with most TCP/IP software. Some TCP/IP documentation calls these applications services, but this merely reflects the fact that the service is defined, not the actually implementation in program code, which constitutes the application.

This section provides more details and examples for four basic TCP/IP applications: File Transfer Protocol (FTP), the remote login application (Telnet), the Simple Mail Transfer Protocol, and the Domain Name Service (DNS). The first three are self-explanatory; the fourth (DNS) is the application that translates Internet names to IP addresses and IP addresses back to Internet names.

We also explore four additional applications, but these are not as common and are not always bundled with all TCP/IP vendors' products. Sometimes these additional applications must be purchased separately, or they may not even be supported in limited, basic functionality versions of the TCP/IP protocol stack. These four applications are an application for loading a hard-diskless device (such as a small router) from a server (Trivial File Transfer Protocol or TFTP), and the Boot Protocol, or BOOTP, an application for accessing a single record in a file across a TCP/IP network (Network File System, or NFS), an application for managing devices on a TCP/IP network (Simple Network Management Protocol, or SNMP), and a graphical user interface for UNIX-based workstations (X Windows).

These eight applications (which are all applications, despite the presence of *protocol* in some of their names) form a good cross section of the wide selection of network capabilities available to a user on a TCP/IP network or the Internet. An implementer of other network protocol stacks would be hard-pressed to find as rich a collection of applications as are available for TCP/IP. And the presence of well-respected standards for TCP/IP implementations makes the interpretability of these applications almost a certainty. The choice of these applications was made mainly to show the richness and variety of TCP/IP at the application layer.

FTP (File Transfer Protocol)

File transfer capability is part of the basic function of the TCP/IP architecture. FTP enables users on a TCP/IP network to copy an entire file from one system to another (which also must be running FTP). Exactly what FTP can and cannot do must be clearly understood. FTP can make a copy of a file. It cannot *move* a file from one system to another. So, after the FTP transfer terminates, there are now *two* exact copies of the file: one still on the source system and the copy on the destination system. (The FTP user may delete the source file on the source system *after* the transfer, but this procedure requires additional steps and permissions.) FTP can copy an entire file. It cannot copy only a *portion* or a single record from a file from one system to another. FTP is all or nothing. If the file is large and the user only wishes to copy a small portion of the file, FTP is of no use.

FTP deals with only simple file types. The protocol can handle either ASCII text files or files that consist of a sequence of binary (hexadecimal) data. It cannot preserve complex record structures found in some files such as indexed records or linked lists. FTP is bidirectional: Files may be sent as well as received, even in the same FTP session. FTP lets users access files on remote systems for performing simple housekeeping tasks as well, such as deleting or renaming files, or even creating new directories.

File transfer capability may also include optional features that are not generally available with every version of FTP. One of these features is called *third-party transfer* and allows a user on a local system to transfer a file between two remote systems. That is, the local system need be neither the source nor destination of the transferred files. Another optional feature is called *restart recovery* and provides a user with the ability to restart a failed file transfer where it left off. Generally, FTP will require a user to retransfer the entire file, even if the transfer fails on the last bit of the file.

FTP, like almost all TCP/IP applications, requires a client and server process. A standard set of commands is used on the client FTP process to communicate with the server FTP process. These commands allow the user to move up and down the remote filesystem's directory tree (if allowed), obtain file directory information, and transfer the selected files to the user's local system. Often, differences exist among file and directory names on different operating systems—for example, UNIX operating systems are generally more liberal with filenaming conventions than are older operating systems. For instance, you could not transfer a UNIX file named MyFile.Here.anyone.c under that name to an old DOS machine. So, FTP must frequently translate filenames as well.

A remote user must access the FTP server with a login ID and password. Once connected to the remote FTP server, the user may transfer files as ASCII text (the default mode) or as binary files (known as *binary* or *image* mode). Files that are executable code or other nontext formats must be transferred in binary mode. Not doing so is a common mistake that users new to FTP often make.

Two major types of FTP file transfers exist. One type is referred to as *anonymous FTP*, which gives remote users access to public filesystems. The other type has no such special name but is *private FTP* and gives remote users access to a private filesystem. Most FTP server processes allow access to a special public filesystem through an anonymous login ID. The remote user must actually enter the character string "anonymous" when prompted for a user ID by the FTP server system. By convention, the remote user's user ID and fully qualified Internet name is used as the password. If the remote FTP server process does not allow anonymous access, the remote user must have a valid ID and password on the remote system.

Telnet (Remote Login)

Application-to-application connectivity is one of the main offerings of TCP/IP. But frequently applications programs are written to run on exactly one system on a network, usually because that system has access to the files needed to run the application. TCP/IP offers a simple method for allowing remote users to access these applications and run them across the network or Internet. The input keystrokes for the application are transferred from the remote user's keyboard across the network to the remote system and processed. The output messages are sent back across the network and displayed on the remote user's screen.

This is the essence of Telnet. Telnet offers a way for remote users on a system running the Telnet client process to appear as a local user on a system running the Telnet server process. The remote user must supply a valid user ID and password before gaining access to the remote system. On systems that maintain Telnet servers for the purpose of supplying information to the public (for example, bulletin board-type services), a special "guest" or "newuser" login ID may be permitted.

Of course, giving any remote user access to applications and files of information on a given system is sometimes risky, especially in view of the well-publicized activities of hackers. While hackers do not have valid user IDs and passwords on private Telnet server systems, many hackers will happily spend hours entering user IDs and passwords more or less at random in the hopes of gaining access to a remote system. In fact, abuse of Telnet because of intrusions of unauthorized remote users has led some sites to simply shut down Telnet servers or discourage their use.

Many kinds of keyboards and screen displays are in common use. Telnet functions by having the Telnet client and server process implement a very basic set of default terminal functions known as a *network virtual terminal (NVT)*. The NVT is very simple: It functions as an old-fashioned half-duplex keyboard and printer with a scroll of paper as output. (DOS functioned in exactly the same way, which is why a DOS `dir` command's output frequently scrolls off the top of the screen.)

NVT defines special control characters as well as commands typed from a keyboard. These include a special Send Break control character to gain the attention of the Telnet server process, an Abort Output control character for terminating output to the display device, and various other functions. These usually are a combination of the ASCII Control key (written as a ^ in a lot of documentation) and another character. An especially useful control character is the Escape code, which is used to return the user to the Telnet command mode. The exact set of control characters a Telnet server supports and the keyboard sequence to send them is established when the Telnet session is first set up between client and server. A list of these characters and keyboard codes may be obtained by a user during a Telnet session with the `display` command.

DNS (Domain Name Service)

The TCP/IP application that translates Internet domain names to IP addresses and vice versa is known as the Domain Name System, or DNS. Used with both FTP and Telnet, this application also has special records used only by email. So in this section we discuss DNS in an email context.

This DNS application is essentially transparent to TCP/IP users, except when it is absent or fails. Then users are frequently unable to communicate with any other TCP/IP system at all.

Users normally establish FTP and Telnet connections, and send email, not by the IP address of the remote system (although this works as well) but by the remote system's Internet name. For example, `ftp acct.xyz.com` attempts to establish an FTP session with the remote TCP/IP system whose IP address corresponds to acct.xzy.com. This text string is entered by the user directly. Of course, the packets are not really sent to acct.xyz.com, but the IP address of acct.xzy.com. How is the IP address found? It is unreasonable for the TCP/IP protocol to expect the user to supply the IP address as well as the name of the remote system. But it is equally unreasonable to expect the local system's TCP/IP software to know the IP addresses for every other TCP/IP system in the world either.

Fortunately, there is a solution. The TCP/IP standards mandate that the local host have a minimal number of hostnames and associated IP addresses in a configuration file. If the remote destination hostname is not found, the local host (transparently to the user) runs the DNS client process and sends a message to the IP address of a *name server*. This name server runs the DNS server process and is also specified in a configuration file set up when the TCP/IP software is initially installed.

The DNS server process may run on a dedicated system (that is, a system running only DNS and nothing else) or on any regular user system on the TCP/IP network. However, if run on a normal user's system, the DNS service will not be available when the user's system is not powered on and in use.

Some TCP/IP network administrators configure TCP/IP to always try to do a DNS name lookup first and only access the local host table if an entry is not found. Usually at least one DNS dedicated name server is maintained by an organization employing TCP/IP. Some larger organizations maintain several name servers in case one fails.

Not even the largest local TCP/IP name server in a single organization can contain all the possible names and IP addresses for all the TCP/IP hosts in the world. Instead, the Internet maintains huge name servers known as *root servers* that know that IP addresses of every DNS server in a given "zone" (such as the .COM zone or the .EDU zone). These zone DNS servers are in turn capable of *resolving* (that is, translating to an IP address) any hostname supplied to it.

DNS operation sounds complex, but it isn't. All DNS servers cache the results of recent IP address resolution queries and use this cache to respond to subsequent queries. However, since hostnames frequently change, IP addresses obtained in this fashion are called *nonauthoritative*, since the IP address was not supplied by a local DNS server directly.

Figure 2.8 shows how DNS works. At the bottom of the pyramid are the millions of local, but authoritative, DNS servers for all of the LANs and hosts on the Internet. At the organization level (for example, samplecompany.com), there are thousands of DNS servers that know about the entire organization. There are fewer DNS servers for ISPs, and only a handful of root name servers for the Internet. All of them share information and help one another locate IP addresses and names. The only question is how far a DNS server must go to find the information it needs.

Most TCP/IP implementations allow users to access the DNS server directly using a special command called `nslookup`. The output from this command typically is the default server's name and IP address, as configured at installation time.

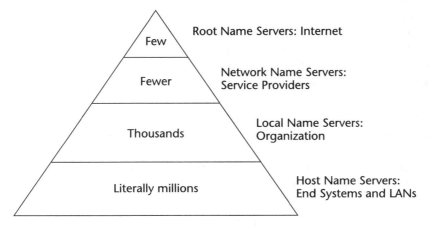

Fewer but larger Domain Name Servers are needed at higher levels

Figure 2.8 The DNS hierarchy.

SMTP (Simple Mail Transfer Protocol) and Post Office Protocol (POP)

The sending and receiving of electronic mail on computer networks is probably the most common application that users access. Even users that use file transfer and other applications awkwardly can usually send a message to other users and read their own email. In fact, some networked systems are used almost exclusively for email and little else.

On host systems running TCP/IP, each system must have a unique IP address. This IP address is associated with a *fully qualified domain name*, which is often just called an *Internet name*. But since many operating systems allow multiple users (for example, UNIX), the TCP/IP email protocol sends email from *account* to *account*. This unique account name is usually the user's login ID (for example, harryd or rsmith), but not always. TCP/IP email addresses are thus in the form harryd@acct.abc.com, where the email account is to the left of the @ ("at") sign and the fully qualified domain name is to the right of the @ sign.

Usually, email involves the use of two protocols. These are the Simple Mail Transfer Protocol and Post Office Protocol (POP). Mentioned earlier in the chapter, SMTP is used to transfer mail between two email servers. POP is used to allow users to collect their email from an SMTP server. SMTP is used to actually transfer the email, but POP makes it possible for hosts that are not attached to the Internet all the time (essentially PCs that are often powered on and off at will) to receive their email when they wish.

SMTP needs more than just itself to form a complete email package. The reason for this is that the complete email process requires more than just a text file to transfer from a source account to a destination account. The text file must originate somewhere, and this usually requires a text editor that allows the email sender to add, delete, copy, and modify the text in the email. The text file must be read or saved to disk or even printed somehow, and this might require a text editor as well. Since the definition and functions of email text editor software is beyond the scope of TCP/IP as a communication protocol, SMTP just defines the actual sending and receiving of email, not the details of its origin or ultimate fate. This means that SMTP is not really useful to end users directly. Instead, implementers have added the necessary editing, saving, and printing capabilities to the SMTP service under a variety of names. Many TCP/IP implementations simply call this application mail, but other email SMTP editors are popular on UNIX-based systems, such as elm and pine.

SMTP differs from FTP and Telnet in another important feature. While both FTP and Telnet establish a real-time connection between a client process and server process, this is not normally done with SMTP email. An email process on each TCP/IP host usually gathers edited and prepared email messages on disk and sends them all out to their respective destinations periodically. At the destination system, the SMTP process distributes the messages to the proper user accounts.

A user's account is therefore actually just some disk space set aside on the local system as the user's mailbox. Arriving messages take up disk space, and unless the user checks the mailbox regularly, the user's allocated space may be consumed and the user's messages lost on arrival or deleted or both. Because of this, most TCP/IP multi-user systems remind users upon login that "you have mail" or "you have new mail" to prompt them to clean up their mailbox areas on the system's hard disk drive. Unfortunately, there is no real way to force users to read, delete, or reply to their email.

Today, most personal computers acting as hosts use both SMTP and POP (the most popular version is POP3). Without POP, not only would hosts have to be up and attached to the Internet all the time, but email could also be received only on the host on which the proper SMTP was running. To overcome these limitations, POP is used to enable users to fetch their email almost from any host anywhere, and whenever the user pleases. Sending email still involves SMTP.

So a user usually does not send email directly to another user but instead to the user's SMTP server. But how do users find one another's SMTP servers on the Internet? The DNS servers have special records, called *MX (mail exchange) records*, which supply the destination user's SMTP server's IP address when the destination user's IP address is resolved by DNS. The interplay between SMTP, POP, and DNS is shown in Figure 2.9.

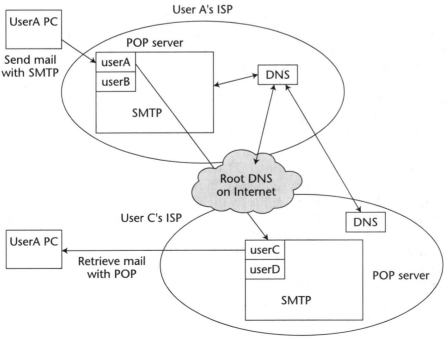

Figure 2.9   SMTP, POP, and DNS.

In Figure 2.9, email is sent from User A to User C. The program used to send email on User A's computer employs SMTP to send the email to the ISP's SMTP email server. A DNS lookup (actually, a series of lookups) is used to find the SMTP server of the recipient. Once the IP address of the SMTP server of the recipient is found, the mail is forwarded using SMTP. User C uses POP to retrieve the email from User A from this SMTP server.

Trivial File Transfer Protocol (TFTP) and Boot Protocol (BOOTP)

We'll deal with the remaining applications discussed in this section more briefly. Many users on TCP/IP networks or the Internet have never used any applications other than FTP, Telnet, and email (these users employ DNS as well, of course, but DNS is seldom used directly or even seen by end users). However, a few more applications are detailed to show the scope of TCP/IP and the wide variety of applications available to users of TCP/IP networks. Also, the Trivial File Transfer Protocol and Boot Protocol are still sometimes supported and used in routers, even those with lots of RAM and hard drives, so a few words about TFTP and BOOTP are in order.

Normally FTP operates with TCP and so is a connection-oriented file transfer mechanism. This is a good thing too, since TCP will not deliver data to an application unless the data is free of errors, in sequence, and complete. However, the vast majority of LANs operate in a connectionless fashion. Many devices attached to LANs today such as hubs and low-end routers have no hard disk drives at all. Yet TCP/IP management standards and applications (see the section *Simple Network Management Protocol* coming up) require a manageable device on a TCP/IP network to have an IP address and run the TCP/IP protocol stack. Since it is important for network managers to be able to manage large internetworks with many of these hubs and routers, and these network devices may have only random access memory (RAM), the question is just how the TCP/IP protocol stack and network management software gets loaded into one of this diskless devices.

FTP is one answer, but it requires TCP and the full FTP application. This is really a case of overkill on a LAN, where the chances of errors are very low. Requiring all of FTP can decrease the availability of already scarce resources such as RAM on a low-end device. And once the router or hub network management or other software is loaded, FTP does not have to be used at all anymore. However, deleting FTP is risky, because if the memory of the device is lost (due to a power failure or other glitch), the software must be downloaded from some router or hub software server all over again.

To address these limitations, many TCP/IP implementations include the Trivial File Transfer Protocol and the Boot Protocol. These are really two applications that work together to load a diskless network device with configuration information and other software that otherwise would have to be loaded by hand from diskette or kept on a hard disk in the device itself (increasing cost and complexity).

Unlike FTP, TFTP uses UDP. UDP is connectionless, as connectionless as the IP layer and the LAN these protocols run on. This is good fit, since the resulting protocol stack of TFTP-UDP-IP-LAN is connectionless from top to bottom. This makes for very compact code implementations and minimal overhead. Since TFTP is not really intended for users to access for file transfer (that is what full FTP with TCP is for), TFTP offers only a subset of FTP functions (for example, there is no "list directory" command). If users do not use TFTP, obviously something else must be using it.

The BOOTP protocol, yet another application service of TCP/IP, uses TFTP. With BOOTP and TFTP, router and hub configuration and other code may be placed on a server on a LAN. This server runs the TFTP and BOOTP server processes. The TFTP and BOOTP client processes are loaded into the diskless hub and router's memory, along with the IP address of the device. The relationship between TFTP and BOOTP is shown in Figure 2.10.

When the hub or router is powered up, the RAM-resident BOOTP client sends a message to the BOOTP server process using TFTP. The BOOTP server replies with a filename. This filename is the file on the server where the network device's current configuration and software is located. The network device then uses TFTP to download the file into its local memory. The hub or router is then ready to go.

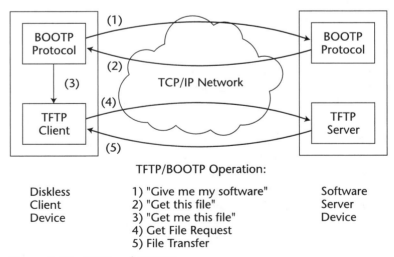

TFTP/BOOTP Operation:

Diskless	1) "Give me my software"	Software
Client	2) "Get this file"	Server
Device	3) "Get me this file"	Device
	4) Get File Request	
	5) File Transfer	

Figure 2.10   FTFP and BOOTP.

Network File System (NFS)

The Network File System is really a family of applications built on top of TCP/IP that mainly address several limitations of FTP. Originally developed by Sun Microsystems, a major UNIX workstation vendor, as part of their Open Network Computing (ONC) product line, Sun released the specifications of many of the components of NFS into the public domain. These components have become important parts of TCP/IP.

NFS allows users to access remote files transparently, as if the files were resident on a local hard drive. Instead of appearing as part of a local UNIX filesystem, these files appear as part of a *network* filesystem, hence the name. FTP limits remote file access to copying a whole file, not just a needed record, across the TCP/IP network. NFS allows a user to open a file on a remote filesystem, read a single record, add or delete records, and close the file, all without copying the entire contents. NFS allows virtual disk drive connections across a TCP/IP network. NFS also allows shared file access among many users.

Because of NFS's origins outside of the TCP/IP definition process, NFS is not tied to a TCP/IP network, but that is its most common implementation. There are three layers to NFS, which establish sessions, file translation mechanisms, and the remote access of the file itself across the network. For the sessions, NFS implements a remote procedure call (RPC) mechanism, which defines the format of messages sent across the TCP/IP network to accomplish NFS tasks. RPC extends the concept of local file management procedure calls (open a file, read a record, and so on) to *remote* file management procedure calls across the TCP/IP network.

To handle differences in file types and formats among operating systems, NFS implements an External Data Representation (XDR) protocol, which provides for a common format in place of native internal representation for data to be sent across the network. NFS itself forms an application layer interface for remote file access and management.

NFS is defined as a *stateless* application. This means that an NFS server process does not keep track of any previous service requests from a specific NFS client process. While this is done mainly for ease of implementation, it makes for some awkward file manipulations in NFS. For example, if a client accesses a remote filesystem (which is what NFS is for) and changes the directory (the UNIX and DOS cd command) to a subdirectory, the user will have difficulty using cd .. (go up one directory level) because the remote NFS server process has no idea what the current directory actually is for that particular user (most Web sites function in exactly the same way). NFS servers process all requests independently, in keeping with stateless operation. NFS servers must enhance basic NFS service to provide state information about a user's interactions in NFS. Oddly, Web sites often store session information on the *client* machine, in the form of cookies.

A *cookie* is a piece of information given by a Web server to a browser. The information has no defined format, since it only needs to be understood by the server software that generated it. Cookies do have some common features, however, and all cookies received by Internet Explorer (for example) are stored in simple, flat text files in a folder called "cookies" in most newer versions of Windows. Cookies store all sorts of useful information about the user. For instance, if a user has established a login and password to a financial Web site and wants his or her Web page to show certain stocks upon login, this information about the user is stored not at the Web site, but on the user's computer by means of a cookie. So millions of user "profiles" add nothing at all to the Web server. Of course, if the user accesses the Web site from another PC, the user's preferences are lost and the default Web page is displayed, because the cookie is on the other PC. Security concerns have led to the reduced role of cookies on the Internet today, but if you set your browser to generate a message or alarm whenever a Web site attempts to give the browser a cookie, as you follow Web links, there will usually be messages or alarms every few minutes. Cookies allow Web sites to be stateless and yet seem to remember details about user sessions.

Nevertheless, stateless operation permits NFS to use UDP instead of TCP. Since UDP is inherently unreliable (UDP's service is often described as "best effort," as is IP's network service), some NFS implementers have begun using TCP instead, especially when NFS is to be used over an internetwork with many WAN links having higher bit error rates than LANs. This use of more reliable TCP connections with NFS, however, has its price. Since a connection takes time to establish with TCP, the net effect is to slow NFS down so much that NFS may not be fast enough for many applications and users. In these cases, an NFS file open may seem to take forever. The NFS protocol stack is shown in Figure 2.11.

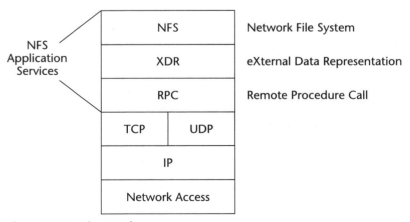

Figure 2.11 The NFS layers.

The use of RPC without NFS allows application developers to write what are known as *distributed applications*. Distributed applications do not require all components of an application (such as DLLs in a Windows environment) to reside on a local disk drive. Since RPC allows remote execution of processes as well as remote file access, these components can be loaded on a central computer and accessed by the main application components over the TCP/IP network. There are several advantages to doing this, of course. It keeps the size of the software loaded on client computers to a minimum and also makes it easy for developers to change the coding of an application component without worrying about how to distribute the update to all users. With RPC all the users access and share the server-based common routines.

Simple Network Management Protocol

Simple Network Management Protocol was introduced in 1989 to manage routers on the Internet. Since then, SNMP has emerged as the industry-standard network management software of choice not just for routers, but for LAN hubs, modems, multiplexers, and even end-user computers. One reason for this is SNMP's purposeful simplicity.

SNMP is extremely elementary. Only five commands and responses are defined in the original version. This original version is now known as SNMPv1. Whenever just *SNMP* is used, it is understood to indicate SNMPv1. The newer version, SNMPv2, was standardized in 1993 but is only slowly being implemented. SNMPv2 is much more complex than SNMPv1, but much better suited to managing complex internetworks of many LANs, routers, hub, modems, and multiplexers. Other enhancements such as better manager authentication and encryption are also part of SNMPv2.

SNMPv1 uses UDP connectionless transfer. Since an unreliable transfer method was of limited utility in managing remote devices (is the device dead or did the message get lost?), SNMPv2 can use TCP to provide reliable TCP/IP network connections. A lot of network management information can be gathered just by knowing a connection can be established to a remote network device (regardless of the problem, at least it is there).

SNMP, naturally, is built on the client/server model. But in SNMP, the client process (the talker) is the central network management software running on a system in a network management operations center. The server process (the listener) runs in each and every SNMP-manageable device on the TCP/IP network. When queried by the network management software, the SNMP server process replies with the current status of some piece of information about the device. There is one exception to this: SNMP defines a *trap* event on a managed device. This special event is sent to the network management client software without being asked. So SNMP is assigned two well-known ports: one for the managed device to listen for SNMP commands (port 161) and the other for the network management software to listen for traps (port 162).

The SNMP manager application is run on a central network management workstation. The device to be managed runs the SNMP process known as the SNMP *agent*. When asked by the network management workstation (the Get parameter), the SNMP agent software accesses the current value of a variable in an SNMP database. This database is technically known in SNMP as a set of *objects*. However, most people refer to this database of information about a managed device as a management information base (MIB). Strictly speaking, a MIB is just a description of this database's structure: The first field is an integer and represents the number of IP datagrams processed, the second field is 20 characters long and represents the vendor of the device, and so on.

Once a MIB is implemented and installed in a managed device and takes on current, valid values (926, XYZcom, etc.), these fields technically become objects accessed by the SNMP agent software. Note that the SNMP agent is only able to access current values in the MIB. Any historical network management information must be kept on the network management workstation. This helps keep the size of the MIB small in the managed device. The components of SNMP are shown in Figure 2.12.

Many vendors define their own private extensions to the MIB defined in SNMP for a specific network device. These are usually low-level hardware extensions with information such as whether the device is on battery backup, has experienced a fan failure, and so on. Most manageable network devices sold today include vendor-installed MIBs that are accessible by most SNMP manager software products.

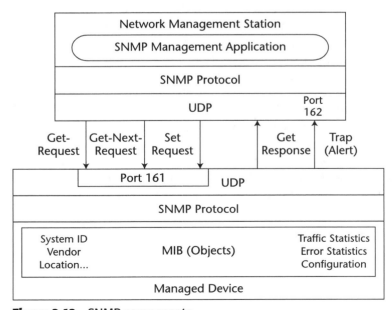

Figure 2.12   SNMP components.

X Windows

The original implementations of TCP/IP were all intended for simple, command-based ASCII display terminals with white (or green) letters on a black background. A user typed in a command at a prompt and pressed the Enter key. TCP/IP did its job and the output was displayed, line by line, on the screen. If the response was long enough, the beginning scrolled off the top of the screen. DOS still functions in exactly this way.

Instead of this dual-color display, computers today offer graphical user interfaces (GUIs) that display many colors and different-looking fonts. GUIs can display the output from several programs running simultaneously in separate windows and will accept information not only from keyboard-entered commands but from pointing and clicking with a mouse. Microsoft Windows is a perfect example of a windows-based GUI.

X Windows was developed at MIT to bring windowing capabilities to a TCP/IP and UNIX environment. X Windows includes specifications and tools so that developers can write their own X Windows interfaces for TCP/IP. With X Windows, a user can run FTP and Telnet, and edit email simultaneously, each in a different window. This multitasking capability accounts for X Windows' popularity.

X Windows is not particularly notable as a TCP/IP application, but it is very common and useful as a TCP/IP interface and is frequently distributed on UNIX-based systems using TCP/IP. In fact, X Windows is rapidly becoming as common on UNIX systems as Microsoft Windows is on PC systems.

X Windows is noteworthy in one other regard. The developers of X Windows actually *reversed* the usual interpretation of the terms clients and servers in TCP/IP. While most documentation about TCP/IP defines a server as a listener issuing a passive open and a client as a talker issuing an active open, to X Windows, the server is the user's workstation and the client is the remote process being accessed, by definition. Because of this unusual terminology, servers and clients on networks using X Windows are often referred to as X *servers* and X *clients*, to distinguish these terms from conventional TCP/IP meanings. Nonetheless, the terminology may still be confusing. This usage of X Windows is shown in Figure 2.13.

A special related device, known as an X terminal, has no native applications of its own, but only accesses remote systems and applications and displays the results on a built-in X Windows GUI. All X implementations use TCP/IP as a network protocol.

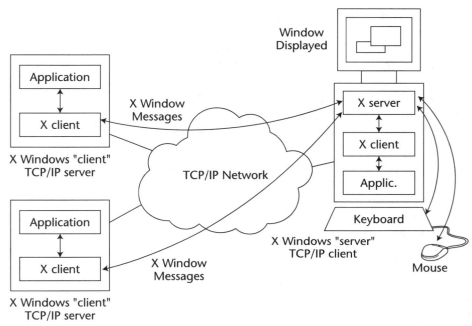

Figure 2.13 Clients and servers in X Windows.

Multimedia and Multicast

One of the main reasons that TCP/IP has thrived over the years and become the network protocol of choice in many situations is the dynamic nature of TCP/IP itself. The standard definition and version of the TCP/IP architecture is constantly being updated to address newer networking technologies and methodologies. These changes take place at all layers of the TCP/IP protocol stack. Application services are continually redefined to reflect new user requirements such as audio and video support. Network access is constantly enhanced to enable TCP/IP to function on transport network technologies undreamed of not too long ago, such as Gigabit Ethernet. Even the TCP and IP protocols are not immune. Each has been through several major revisions in their lifetimes.

This section examines several key aspects of newer TCP/IP capabilities. This survey is by no means exhaustive, but it is representative of the key features that implementations of TCP/IP must address to maintain its place as a leading network technology. The point is that TCP/IP has never been "finished," and given the pace of computer and network technology development over the last 10 years or so, it probably never will be.

There has been much discussion about the suitability of TCP/IP for broadband networks. Rather than formally define just what a broadband network is, suffice it to say that these networks are fundamentally different enough from older networks to maintain a sharp distinction between the two. Most observers would agree that broadband networks must support interactive multimedia. Multimedia support means that the network must have enough bandwidth to allow the transfer of video and audio as well as data. *Interactive* means that the network must have low enough delays (latency) to allow real-time communication between endpoints. Interactive multimedia also implies that the network delays must be consistent. All traffic—voice, video, and data—must arrive with about the same delay during a session to avoid problems with the end-user applications.

If people are someday able to watch sports events and live television over the Internet routinely and without headaches, and exchange all manner of information in email, the two aspects of TCP/IP in this section will play a large role.

MIME (Multipurpose Internet Mail Extensions)

As mentioned earlier, one of the main purposes of the original Internet was sending and receiving email to and from any user on a computer running TCP/IP attached to the Internet. The SMTP application service handled this task on TCP/IP host systems, but it had several limitations that have been addressed through MIME (Multipurpose Internet Mail Extensions). Although MIME explicitly references the Internet, MIME is in no way exclusive to the Internet. Any TCP/IP network, connected or nonconnected (that is, totally private with no links outside the organization to the global, public Internet), may implement MIME support for their TCP/IP email. Indeed, there are compelling reasons for doing so.

Until the MIME specification appeared in 1992, the basic structure of email support in TCP/IP had remained unchanged since 1982, well before the rise of PCs and LANs as the platform and network of choice for most users. The email specification in place from 1982 limited the contents of email messages to short lines of 7-bit ASCII code, which defines 128 characters (basically whatever keys can be typed from a standard PC QWERTY keyboard).

Even then, richer code sets were in use, including 8-bit ASCII code sets that extended the standard 128 characters to 256, adding accents and other special characters to the standard set. IBM used an 8-bit EBCDIC code set that also defined 256 (all different!) characters. But it did not matter: TCP/IP email was limited to 7-bit ASCII. The *short line* limit referred to the fact that most email TCP/IP implementations expected to see a *newline* character every 256 characters or so, regardless of the email format and content.

These limitations were somewhat of a burden throughout the 1980s, but email was sent and received on TCP/IP systems without major problems until the 1990s. Then newer user requirements completely overwhelmed the limited capabilities of TCP/IP email. The new user requirement was, in a word, multimedia.

Multimedia refers to the fact that information is conveyed among users not just by means of text (it is read). Information between users on computers may now consist of text as well as graphics (it is looked at), audio (it is listened to), and video (it is watched and takes the form of graphics that move and may even make sounds). In the early 1980s, multimedia was not a major limitation on email systems for a very good reason: There was little support or need for multimedia on the end users' systems.

The situation quickly changed in the 1990s. Users began creating compound documents that not only consisted of text (and little of it pure 7-bit ASCII) but included graphics like company logos, voice annotations, and even rudimentary animation and video. Advanced graphics began to be called "images" and achieved photographic-quality detail. Applications appeared for sales and training at first, but then for even general use, that required stereo speakers and full-motion capabilities on the computer in order for these multimedia applications to be used properly. All PCs sold today are multimedia-ready and PC manufacturers expect users to want and need multimedia capabilities.

A problem occurred when users wished to share these multimedia documents and application contents across an internetwork using TCP/IP. The 1982 TCP/IP mail specification simply never considered multimedia email. The transfer of email containing not only text but images and audio was never mentioned.

That changed with the MIME specification. The major extension to TCP/IP email applications was the specification of seven distinct *content types* of information that could be included in the body of an email document. Even basic "text" was extended to include not only 7-bit ASCII but several other character sets for Asian languages and other specialized fonts. A special multipart content type allowed the mixing of these various types in the same email message. The application type transfers messages as an unstructured stream of bits, allowing file transfer via email. The message type allows the sending of an email message within another email message, a process known as *encapsulation* in MIME. The image type refers to still images (or pictures, or graphics;

in short, anything that is not read like text). The audio type is for both voice and audio (for example, high-fidelity stereo sound). Finally, the video type is for both full-motion video and moving images (animation), with the possibility of adding an audio sound track. The major MIME types are as follows:

Text.   Many different character sets.

Multipart.   Mixing of various types in a single email message.

Application.   Binary images or executables.

Message.   Encapsulating another email message.

Image.   Still graphics in many formats.

Audio.   Sound encoded in many formats.

Video.   Moving graphics in many formats.

The seven MIME content types were further divided into subtypes. Subtypes exist because the inventors of MIME acknowledged that there was not just one way of representing any of the content types on a computer or within an application. For instance, images are frequently generated and stored and displayed in a number of popular formats. An image may conform to the GIF (graphical interface format, popularized by CompuServe Information Services) or JPEG (Joint Photographic Experts Group, popularized by scanner vendors and others) standard format. MIME allows the inclusion of both in TCP/IP email as subtypes of the content type "image." The MIME subtypes are as follows:

Text.   Plain, richtext.

Multipart.   Mixed, alternative, parallel, digest.

Application.   Octet-stream, PostScript.

Message.   rfc822, partial, external-body.

Image.   JPEG, GIF.

Audio.   Basic, display.

Video.   mpeg.

Even within the structure of these seven major types and their associated subtypes, the MIME specification was meant to be itself extensible. That is, a mechanism is defined for adding both new subtypes and new content types to the standard MIME specification. This registration process is intended to make MIME a good fit with all data types and applications for the foreseeable future. MIME support is included in almost all TCP/IP protocol implementations.

Multicast and the Multicast Backbone

Technically, the Multicast Backbone (MBone) is not part of the TCP/IP protocol at all. However, since the MBone does add considerable functionality to TCP/IP networks connected to the Internet, and there is nothing to prevent the concepts and operations of the MBone to be applied to private, nonconnected TCP/IP networks, we will discuss the MBone as part of TCP/IP networks in general.

The idea behind the creation of the MBone was to extend the multimedia capabilities added to TCP/IP email by MIME to real-time, interactive applications. Such applications are still characterized by a need to send not only text but also audio and video between users. However, the time limitations of email multimedia support provided by MIME (email is typically sent only periodically on most TCP/IP networks) are bypassed with the MBone, which delivers multimedia to users in an as-it-happens manner. The MBone grew out of an attempt on the part of the IETF to create a network to multicast video of its own conferences. As such, the MBone was and is quite successful.

Essentially an experimental network built as part of the Internet, the MBone addresses more than just Internet bandwidth and delay limitations that prevent the use of "live" multimedia on the Internet. The "multicast" capability of the MBone refers to the fact than a source of a video or audio information, or any multimedia information in general, must transmit the packets containing the multimedia information individually to each separate endpoint. In other words, a video data stream sent from a source to 14 destinations would ordinarily be required to send out 14 separate copies of the same packet, each with the unique IP address of each separate destination. This is hardly efficient use of the already scarce bandwidth available, and long delays are inevitable for the attempted employment of real-time multimedia.

The MBone is a *virtual network* layered on top of the normal TCP/IP routers and links of the Internet. Multicast TCP/IP routers known on the MBone as *mrouters* are used to multicast IP packets from a single input port to many output ports. Since the rest of the Internet does not support multicast, the MBone uses a system of *tunnels* to allow multicast packets to be packaged inside "plain" IP packets. This way, the multicast packets will pass through any non-multicast routers transparently. The *unicast* IP routers will pass the multicast IP packets through unknowingly to a multicast IP router (the mrouter), where these multicast IP packets can be processed correctly.

If all this seems great, the natural question is this: Why not just convert the whole Internet to a multicasting MBone and run voice and video and data right to every desktop connected to the Internet in the world? There are three reasons why this is not done. First, not all hosts need to handle the constantly arriving multimedia IP packets. Second, not all organizations have the bandwidth needed to receive MBone traffic. Third, the entire aggregate bandwidth

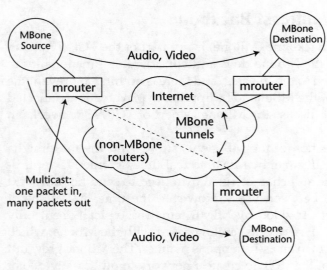

Figure 2.14 The MBone.

in the MBone itself is limited. This means that even though the MBone is fine for rudimentary video, it is hardly a cable TV replacement.

The MBone consists of a series of *virtual circuits* connecting the mrouters together. Since the Internet, and TCP/IP networks in general, are connectionless at the IP layer, some way around the limitations on delay-variation-sensitive applications like voice and video had to be found. The problem with connectionless, independently routed packets with timing-sensitive contents is that the resequencing and missing packet overhead, coupled with the delay "jitter" of each individual packet through the router network, make it next to impossible to employ voice and video on a TCP/IP network, multicast or otherwise. The solution with the MBone was simply to connect the mrouters with more connection-oriented *paths* instead of purely connectionless *routes* from source to destination. These virtual circuits used on the MBone are the tunnels between mrouters. The tunnels connect these mrouters, and all sources may effectively broadcast onto the MBone on an equal-access basis. The overall structure of the MBone is shown in Figure 2.14.

ARP and ICMP

Two other pieces of TCP/IP need to be investigated in more detail before we proceed to IP addressing in Chapter 3: ARP and ICMP. The ARP protocol family is used to map the IP addresses used in packets to and from the network layer addresses used in frames, especially on LANs. ICMP is the part of TCP/IP that conveys IP error information from a router or destination host back to the source of the packet.

ARP Protocols

IP is not the only protocol that runs at the IP layer. A whole class of protocols known as Address Resolution Protocols exist at the IP layer as well. In addition to ARP itself, there is Reverse ARP, Proxy ARP, and even Inverse ARP (InARP). Other ARPs for other network technologies have been proposed as well, such as Asynchronous Transfer Mode ARP (ATMARP). We'll only define the ARP protocol itself in detail in this section and mention briefly the purpose of the other members of the ARP family.

The IP packet must contain the source and destination IP addresses of the systems wishing to communicate. But the real work of getting data around in a network is done by the *frame*, the network layer data unit in the TCP/IP architecture. The frames have their own source and destination addresses: MAC layer addresses of "physical" addresses for LANs, connection identifiers for some public data networks like Frame Relay, and Data Link addresses for other types of WANs. The ARP documentation refers to this frame address as the *hardware address*.

The question is this: How does a source host on a TCP/IP network, which has used the Domain Name Service to find out the destination system's IP address, tell the network access layer which *frame* address to use as the destination address in the frame? Of course, the source system knows its own network layer address: All TCP/IP software installations either configure this by hand (the old way) or by querying the driver software (the current way). This is the key to the whole ARP process; every TCP/IP system known its own IP address and network layer frame address.

The only problem is to find a mechanism for a source system to ask, in effect, who has IP address 192.168.40.67 (for example) and what is the hardware (network layer) address associated with it? This is the mechanism that ARP provides. On LANs, ARP messages are broadcast to all stations on the LAN. The proper destination IP layer realizes that the destination IP address in the packet matches its own and replies directly to the sender by reversing the source and destination IP address in the packet and using its own network layer address as the *source* address in the frame.

The original source system can now cache the network layer address of the destination and proceed with sending live IP packets, supplying the proper frame address to the network layer software. On most WANs, ARP is still used, but as a limited multicast rather than a broadcast.

Two problems occur with ARP. One is when there are duplicate IP addresses on a network (which happens all the time, despite TCP/IP network administrators' efforts to prevent it). Naturally, the source system receives two ARP replies and has no idea which one is correct. The second problem occurs when LAN bridge links fail and then are restored. Recall that bridges make LANs all one big network, so ARP messages must pass through a bridge. When the WAN link between bridges fails, the destinations on that portion of the network are unreachable. The source systems' caches of network layer addresses will purge and empty out. This happens because of a timer that discards any destination system entries not communicated within a given amount of time. But when the LAN bridge link is restored, hosts may begin to generate 30 or 40 ARP requests per second. Each is a broadcast and must be processed by each receiving host. The result is that hosts are swamped with ARP requests and may slow down considerably or even fail.

Figure 2.15 shows a simplified ARP message header and information fields. The figure also illustrates the ARP process. (Ethernet types will be discussed in Chapter 3, "IP Addressing and Routing.")

RARP (Reverse ARP) is used in cases where a device on a TCP/IP network knows the network access layer (hardware address to ARP) but must determine the IP address associated with it. RARP is frequently used for diskless network devices on TCP/IP networks such as low-end or older routers and hubs.

Proxy ARP is an older technique used in early TCP/IP routers and still supported in some routers today. Since routers required different IP address network numbers on each router port, small networks connected by routers wasted IP address space. Proxy ARP was a method of assigning a single IP address to both sides of router without using subnet masking. Proxy ARP has been largely replaced by subnetting (described in Chapter 4, "Subnets and Supernets") in modern TCP/IP networks.

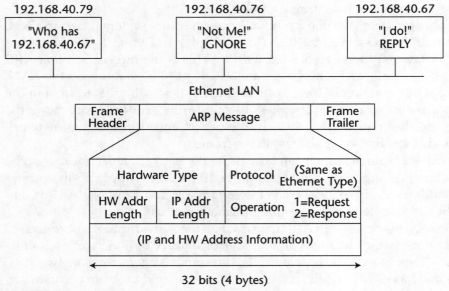

Figure 2.15   The ARP process.

InARP was developed especially for use on Frame Relay networks. Instead of using ARP to find out MAC-layer LAN addresses, TCP/IP networks linked by Frame Relay networks use InARP to determine the Frame Relay DLCI (Data Link Connection Identifier) number to use in the frame when sending IP datagrams. Extensions to ARP will also apply to newer network technologies as TCP/IP network come to be linked by these newer techniques (such as optical networking) in the coming years.

Internet Control Message Protocol (ICMP)

One of the distinct advantages of linking of LANs with routers running TCP/IP instead of relying on LAN bridges is the presence in the TCP/IP architecture of a special protocol at the IP layer for error messages. Bridges have no separate software layer above the frame level and so have no way of sending such error messages to the originator of a message. In the TCP/IP architecture, this protocol, called the Internet Control Message Protocol (ICMP) is particularly important for best-effort connectionless packet networks using IP.

If a packet is sent and no reply is received, the packet may have been lost by the router network, or there may be an error condition that forced a router (or destination) to discard the packet. In these cases, an ICMP message arriving back at the source can help the source system correct the problem (for example, an invalid IP address) or take other recovery steps (such as resending the packet to another router). For TCP/IP network management purposes, ICMP provides very useful diagnostic information about network problems.

TCP/IP implementations vary widely in ICMP interpretation capabilities. TCP/IP documentation states that ICMP must be supported in all cases, but in very limited TCP/IP implementations (such as TCP/IP shareware and freeware), this support may mean no more than that the system will accept ICMP messages. In many cases, these limited implementations will not even generate an error message to the user or affect the operation of the TCP/IP software at the source, defeating the whole purpose of ICMP support. The only way to be sure is to ask the vendor or source, and then ask for documentation or references.

ICMP messages are carried inside IP packets. Therefore, for all intents and purposes, the ICMP messages look just like regular IP packets to routers (except for the source router, if the ICMP message was originated at a router). ICMP error messages may be generated by a router or destination host system and are sent back to the originating address of the packet. The originated system will usually be a host, but not always.

Figure 2.16 shows the basic structure of the ICMP message and the different ICMP message types possible. The ICMP Type field defines codes for router-to-host and host-to-host error messages. The ICMP Code field has different

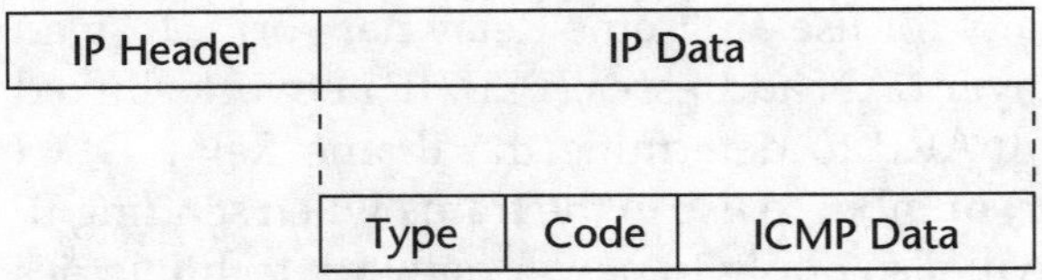

IP Header	IP Data	

Type	Code	ICMP Data

Type Field: Message Type:

0	Echo Reply
3	Destination Unreachable
4	Source Quench
5	Redirect
8	Echo Request
11	Time Exceeded
12	Parameter Problem
13	Timestamp Request
14	Timestamp Reply
15	Information Request
16	Information Reply
17	Address Mask Request
18	Address Mask Reply

Figure 2.16   Basic ICMP message structure and types.

meanings depending on the Type field value. These codes provide more specific information about the type problem indicated. The ICMP Data field varies widely in form and content depending on the Type field. In some cases, the IP header and first 8 bytes of the original packet triggering the ICMP message are sent back to the source host.

Unfortunately, many end users are unaware of ICMP messages at all. Many TCP/IP implementations, in an effort to make life as simple for end users as possible, never actually display the text that goes along with an ICMP error message on an end user's system at all. Instead, a software "statistics counter" is kept that increments with each Type or Type/Code ICMP message received by the host system. This makes information on the general pattern of errors available to the TCP/IP network manager, but since the details of the ICMP source are not kept, this information is usually of limited value.

Although many users of TCP/IP networks are unfamiliar with ICMP in general, one ICMP message is well known to just about all users of TCP/IP. This is the ICMP Echo message known as *ping*, sent from the ICMP layer on a source system to the ICMP layer on a destination system. Usually, the ping message just wants the destination to echo back some random text of variable length. Ping is used as a simple test to see whether or not the device is "alive" and reachable. A series of pings is frequently sent to a hub or router to see if the device is functional. Because ICMP messages are sent as regular packets, a good rule of thumb is that if about 75 percent of all pings are successfully echoed, the remote device is alive and well.

This chapter cannot begin to describe all of TCP/IP. What have been presented, however, are all the essentials necessary to understand what routers do and how they do it. This background now leads us into a fuller discussion of the key role in routing played by the IP address itself, addressed in the next chapter.

IP Addressing and Routing

One of the most confusing aspects of routing protocols and routing policy is that these deal with the IP address. This sounds almost paradoxical. The IP address is so fundamentally a part of the IP layer in general and router behavior in particular that it seems like almost everyone must be familiar with all of the details of IP version 4 (IPv4) addressing. Yet this is not the case, and IP addressing can cause considerable confusion when it comes to detailing the operation of routing protocols and routing policies, especially with regard to the newer version of IP addresses, IPv6 (IP version 6). So in this chapter we'll explore all aspects of IP addressing with regard to routing, with the exception of subnetting and supernetting, which are important enough to warrant a chapter of their own (Chapter 4). IP packet fragmentation is also examined, because packet fragmentation explains how the IPv6 packet header is put together and why compatibility between IPv4 and IPv6 routers and hosts is not necessarily a given.

The IP Address

The first point is that the IP address has nothing at all to do with the TCP/IP network layer address (also called the Layer 2 address), or hardware address, dealt with by ARPs. LANs and WAN serial link network addresses are mapped to IP addresses, but with the important exception of multicast addresses, there is no relationship between LAN media access control (MAC) or WAN serial link addresses in the frame header and IP addresses in the packet header. This chapter presents a simple networking example to point this frame-packet independence out and more precisely distinguish between bridging and routing.

Two types of IP addressing schemes can be used with IP networks. Both types of IP address are 32 bits long, but they differ in how hosts and routers interpret the addresses. The two types are as follows:

Classful.   This was the original IP addressing scheme established in RFC 791. Based on the value of the initial bits in the IP address, the IP address fell into one of several classes. Each *class* differed in the number of IP address bits assigned to the *network* and the *host* portion of the IP address. This chapter deals mainly with classful IP addresses.

Classless.   This newer way of interpreting the 32-bit IP address space assumes no classes exist at all. The boundary between the network and host portion of the IP address is not determined by the initial IP address bits, but by the IP network *mask*. Classless IP addressing is considered in detail in Chapter 4, "Subnets and Supernets."

Primarily, routers, rather than hosts, deal with the differences between classful and classless IP addresses. A good understanding of both classful and classless IP addressing is essential to understanding how routing and routing policy works.

Originally, the IP address was established in RFC 760 as an 8-bit *prefix* that identified the network to which a host was attached. All the early Internet gateways did was look at the prefix and route the packet to one of the 200 or so network sites that could exist. RFC 791 changed this to a classful 32-bit structure, and RFC 1518 (classless interdomain routing, or CIDR) introduced the idea of the *classless prefix* all over again. Routers today do not deal with classful concepts such as "the network portion of a Class A IP address" but rather with classless concepts such as "the IP prefix."

Hosts on the same network (for example, a LAN) must have the same network portion or prefix of their IP addresses. This is the only way that routers can route among networks that form the Internet. So part of the IP address specifies the network, and the whole IP address specifies the host on the network. Whether classful or classless, the boundary between network and host IP address bits is movable. An IP address can be expressed in dotted decimal, binary, octal, or hexadecimal. All are proper and identical.

The basic concepts of the IP address are shown in Figure 3.1. The Internet name assigned to this IP address is given, along with the IP address dotted decimal, binary, and hexadecimal notation.

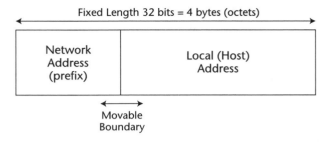

Internet Name: pc1.acct.mycompany.com

IP Address: 192.168.78.26

Binary String: 11000000 10101000 01001110 00011010

Hexadecimal Digits: C0.A8.4E.1A

Figure 3.1   The IP address.

Note that the Internet name is only partially dependent on the IP address. When a user or organization wishes to obtain a public IP address, they actually receive two things that are guaranteed to be globally unique on the Internet. First is the network portion (or prefix) of the IP address, such as 192.168.78.0 (this is actually a private IP address, as are all IP addresses used in this book for security reasons). The ending of 0 indicates an IP network rather than a host. Second is the *top-level domain name*; in this example, the domain name is mycompany.com (again, this is not a valid domain name). These two elements are assigned globally, and the rest of the information needed for domain name and IP address is assigned locally by the network administrator. The PC in the example is configured as pc1.acct.mycompany.com. (This might indicate PC 1 in the accounting department, but the meaning is totally up to the local network administrator.) The IP address assigned and configured locally to go with this fully qualified domain name (Internet name) is 192.168.78.26. Both of these pieces of information are reflected in the local (authoritative) DNS server.

This example uses *static* IP address assignment. In this case, the organization either obtains an IP network address on its own or uses a range of IP addresses assigned the organization's ISP. It is also possible to assign devices *dynamic* IP addresses, using the Dynamic Host Configuration Protocol (DHCP). This is often done for an ISP's dial-in users, although organizations still use DHCP on LANs either for security reasons or to assign a unique IP address only when a device actually needs to access the Internet. There are many more details involving the use of dynamic IP addresses and the Internet, but these have little to do with routing on the Internet and so they are not investigated here further.

IP addresses always take the form <netid, hostid>. When the host portion of the IP address is written with all 0s, then the network itself is meant. To completely identify a particular host on a particular network, the whole address is needed. When all 32 bits of the IP address are specified, this is often called a *host address*. But there is no separation between network and host portion of the IP address. In dotted decimal, the possible IP addresses can run from 0.0.0.0 to 255.255.255.255. When a hypothetical IP address is viewed—for example, 172.17.202.4—determining where the boundary between network and host number happens to be is difficult. How are people, and routers as well, expected to find this movable boundary?

RFC 791 had an interesting solution to this boundary location problem. It divided the entire IP address range into five classes called Class A, Class B, Class C, Class D, and Class E. The different classes were distinguished by the value of the initial bits of the first byte of the IP address. Class D was (and is) used for multicast addresses, and Class E was for experimental use. Classes A, B, and C were used for normal, unicast traffic among clients, servers, and routers.

For network and host identification purposes, Class D is not used, nor is Class E. Class A addresses used the first byte as network address, and the remaining 24 bits in the last 3 bytes as host address. Class B addresses used the first 2 bytes as network address and the remaining 16 bits in the last 2 bytes as host address. Class C addresses used the first three bytes as network address, and the remaining 8 bits in the last byte as host address. The classful IP address scheme is shown in Figure 3.2.

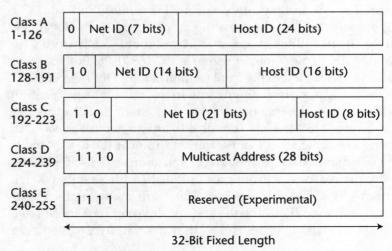

Figure 3.2 Classful IP addresses.

All Class A IP addresses start with a zero-bit and are of the form network. host.host.host in dotted decimal. This automatically limits the decimal number in the first byte to the range 0 to 127 (since the 128 value position in the byte must be 0). Network addresses 0 and 127 are reserved for special use. IP address 127 dot anything is used as a special loopback address. Packets sent to this IP address never leave the host but simply loop back through the TCP/IP software. The 24-bit host field cannot be all 0s or all 1s, since these have special meanings as well. This leaves $2^{24} - 2$, or $16,277,216 - 2 = 16,277,214$ hosts on each of the possible Class A networks allowed on the Internet. But fully 50 percent of the entire IP address space is used by Class A addresses (2^{31} is half of 2^{32})!

Who would build such a huge, yet unified, IP network? And why should half of all IP addresses reside on Class A networks? Recall that LANs using the same IP network address must all be on the same LAN segment. A single LAN with Class A IP address 10.0.0.0 (as an example) could have more the 16 million hosts, but not one single router on the network. All LAN interconnection would have to be done with bridges. Of course, when RFC 791 was new, that is exactly how LANs were connected: with bridges. Bridges were marketed against the newer routers (then often called firewalls or gateways) as simpler devices that were, unlike routers, protocol-independent. This meant that bridges only cared about LAN frames, not the types of packets that the LAN frames carried. In the days when there were many more network layer packet protocols in use besides IP, bridges made a lot more sense than they do today.

In the original vision for the Internet, Class A addresses were mainly for large, national packet-switched networks. A country might get a single Class A address for all of the hosts within its borders. This plan made sense during the dawn of the Internet Age, but it makes little sense today. And many Class A addresses went, not to countries, but to computer companies that helped shape the early Internet. IBM, for example, asked for and got Class A IP address 9.0.0.0.

All Class B addresses start with 1 0 and are of the form network.network .host.host in dotted decimal. This automatically limits the Class B first byte range to 128 to 191. As with Class A, the 16-bit host field cannot be all 0s or all 1s. So there can be 16,384 Class B networks, each with 65,534 hosts. The Class B address space represents 25 percent of the full IP address space. Class B networks were supposed to be for large organizations and multidivisional corporations—smaller than a country but larger than a single company. By and large, most Class B addresses were assigned in exactly this fashion, although many companies with Class A addresses also received Class B addresses.

All Class C addresses start with 1 1 0 and are of the form network .network.network.host in dotted decimal. The automatically limits the Class C first byte range to 192 to 223. As with Class A and Class B, the 8-bit host field cannot be all 0s or all 1s. So there can be 2,097,152 Class C networks, each with 254 hosts. The Class C address space represents 12.5 percent of the full IP address space. This is because although there can be a couple of million Class C networks, there can only be a handful of hosts on each one compared to Class A and Class B networks. Class C networks were supposed to be for single companies, and in those days before the PC, 250 computers was a lot for any company of almost any size to have. Today, a single Class C address is barely enough for most departmental LANs on a single floor of a large company.

Class D multicast addresses start with 1 1 1 0 and are in the range 224 to 239, and Class E addresses start with 1 1 1 1 and are in the range 240 to 255.

The classful IP address structure was intended for a world of a few truly huge, national networks (Class A), many, many small LANs (Class C), and a number of networks in between (Class B). The problem is that today there are many networks with many hosts, and few, if any, fall neatly into one class or another. So today most routers and hosts use classless IP addressing, where the boundary between IP address *prefix* and host identifier is determined by other than the initial address bits. A full discussion of classless IP addressing is presented in Chapter 4.

Private and Martian IP Addresses

RFC 1918 established private Class A, B, and C address spaces to be used on private IP networks and in books such as this when it is not desirable to use public IP addresses for examples. The private IP address ranges are as follows:

Class A.   10.0.0.0 through 10.255.255.255

Class B.   172.16.0.0 through 172.31.255.255

Class C.   192.168.0.0 through 192.168.255.255

These addresses can never appear in a routing table on a router on the public Internet. In addition, there are several "martian addresses" that should not appear on the public Internet either. The story is that packets sent to these destinations might as well be on Mars as far as the Internet was concerned. The currently defined martians are as follows:

- 0.0.0.0 through 0.255.255.255
- 127.0.0.0 through 127.255.255.255
- 128.0.0.0 through 128.0.255.255
- 191.255.0.0 through 191.255.255.255
- 192.0.0.0 through 192.0.0.255
- 223.255.255.0 through 223.255.255.255
- 240.0.0.0 through 255.255.255.255

Martians will be revisited in Chapter 4, since there is actually a subnet mask associated with each of these addresses and subnet masks are discussed in that chapter. Some router vendors lump RFC 1918 private addresses and martian addresses together, usually all as martians. While it is true that private IP addresses and martian IP addresses should not appear in the routing table of an Internet router, they are not necessarily the same thing. In this chapter and the ones that follow, private IP addresses and martian IP addresses are treated as distinct concepts.

Reading IP Addresses

IP addresses are read in a certain way and have special meanings depending on how they are written. For example, 192.168.70.66 is read as "host 66 on IP network 192.168.70.0." All IP network addresses must have zero-bits in the host address field, and this address cannot be assigned to any host (actually, nothing usually prevents this address assignment; it just won't work correctly). The following are some examples of how IP addresses are read and where they are commonly used:

0.0.0.0	As source address, means unknown host.
255.255.255.255	As destination address, means any host (a form of "anycast").
172.16.255.255	As destination address, means any host on 172.16.0.0 ("directed broadcast").
0.0.0.33	As source address, means host 33 on the local network.
192.168.14.0	As source address, means some host on network 192.168.14.0.

Other forms of IP addresses exist, but those listed previously are the most important. When these forms are used outside of their defined roles (that is, something like 172.16.255.255 as a source address instead of a destination address), the result is usually an error condition.

Direct and Indirect Routing

IP addresses are used in routing. Some books and references make extensive use of the concepts of *direct routing* and *indirect routing* of packets. This terminology can be misleading, since direct "routing" of packets can actually occur without a router at all. In this book, the terms *direct delivery* and *indirect delivery* of packets are used instead. A host can use direct delivery to send packets directly to another host, or use indirect delivery if the destination host is reachable only through a router.

But how does the source host know whether the destination host is reachable through direct (local) delivery or indirect (remote) delivery through a router? This is a very interesting question, and answering it will involve understanding exactly how bridges and routers differ in operation, and how routers use the IP address to determine how to handle packets. So let's now examine direct and indirect packet delivery.

Direct Delivery or No Routing Required

The host knows that no router is needed to handle a packet sent from the source host to the destination host because the IP addresses of the source and destination hosts have the *same IP network portion* (prefix) in both source and destination IP addresses—a simple yet effective way to let hosts know whether or not they are on the same LAN.

Although the focus of this chapter is on the IP address, there will also be references to the TCP/IP network layer addresses (usually the MAC address on a LAN) and the TCP/UDP port and socket numbers. This is still very much the client/server world of TCP/IP. The relationship between all of these concepts is shown in Figure 3.3, which is also used to illustrated direct delivery (or direct routing) of IP packets when no routing is required.

Figure 3.3 follows a packet from client to server when both are on the same LAN segment (meaning there is no router in between client and server). This figure outlines direct delivery of the packets. All direct delivery means is that the packet and frame does not pass through a router on the way from source to destination.

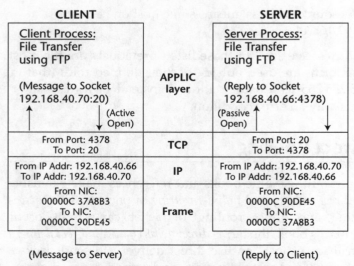

Figure 3.3 The client/server model, the IP address, and direct delivery.

The server must initially issue a passive open on the socket, in this case the well-known port for FTP control messages, port 21. The socket is the combination of dotted decimal IP address and TCP port (FTP uses TCP), in this case 192.168.40.70:20. Once the server is listening, the client FTP process can issue an active open on a not-well-known port to connect to the FTP server. The sockets used at the application layer are "from" socket 192.168.40.66:4378 and "to" socket 192.168.40.70:20.

The TCP/IP protocol stack on the client uses this information to build the TCP header and IP header. The ports go into the TCP segment header, and the IP addresses go into the IP packet. If the IP address of the server is not in the client DNS cache, DNS is used to find the IP address for the FTP server, which might only be known to the user as ftp.mycompany.com.

In the example shown in Figure 3.3, the IP packet is placed inside an Ethernet MAC frame. The MAC source and destination addresses are shown in the figure as well. The client knows its own MAC address, and if the server's MAC address is not cached, then ARP is used to determine the MAC address of the FTP server. In the example, the source MAC address is 00000C 37A8B3 and the destination MAC address is 00000C 90DE45. Note that it is common to specify IP addresses and ports in decimal (dotted decimal), but MAC addresses are always in hexadecimal. The server's reply to the client is also shown in the figure.

LAN MAC addresses are 48 bits (6 bytes) long. The first 24 bits (3 bytes) are assigned by the Institute of Electrical and Electronics Engineers (IEEE) to the manufacturer of the NIC. The last 24 bits (3 bytes) are the NIC manufacturer's serial number for that NIC. The MAC address is used in the LAN frame header.

MAC frames usually have one of two Ethernet frame formats today. There are other MAC frame formats, such as Token Ring and Fiber Distributed Data Interface (FDDI), but by far the most common LAN type today is Ethernet. Ethernet frames more often use the original frame structure used by DEC, Intel, and Xerox in the original Ethernet, known as DIX Ethernet. Alternatively, Ethernet frames can use the official IEEE 802.3 CSMA/CD (Carrier Sense Multiple Access with Collision Detection) frame structure that is supposed to be used on all forms of 10Base-T "Ethernet" LANs. 10Base-T LANs use unshielded twisted-pair (UTP) wiring instead of coaxial cable, and hubs instead of the awkward media attachment units (MAUs) employed in DIX Ethernet LANs. However, the DIX Ethernet frame structure is simpler and allows for more information (the IP packet) inside the frame, so many 10Base-T LANs still use DIX Ethernet frames. The structure of both frame types is shown in Figure 3.4.

DIX Ethernet Frame Structure:

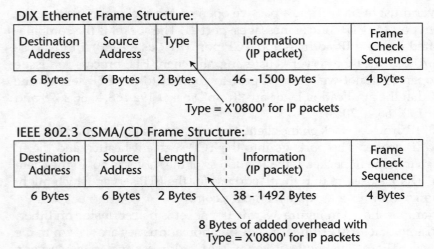

Destination Address	Source Address	Type	Information (IP packet)	Frame Check Sequence
6 Bytes	6 Bytes	2 Bytes	46 - 1500 Bytes	4 Bytes

Type = X'0800' for IP packets

IEEE 802.3 CSMA/CD Frame Structure:

Destination Address	Source Address	Length	Information (IP packet)	Frame Check Sequence
6 Bytes	6 Bytes	2 Bytes	38 - 1492 Bytes	4 Bytes

8 Bytes of added overhead with
Type = X'0800' for IP packets

Figure 3.4   DIX Ethernet and IEEE 802.3 CSMA/CD frames.

Both frame types use the same form of source and destination MAC address, and use a 32-bit (4-byte) frame check sequence (FCS) for frame-level error checking. The FCS in both cases is a standard 32-bit cyclical redundancy check known as CRC-32. The difference is that the DIX Ethernet frame indicates information type (frame content) with a 2-byte Type field (x0800 means "an IP packet inside") and the IEEE 802.3 CSMA/CD frame places this "Ethertype" field at the end of an additional 8 bytes of overhead called the SNAP (Sub-Network Access Protocol) header.

These 8 bytes must be subtracted from the information field (IP packet) length so that the overall frame length is still the same as in DIX Ethernet, since this maximum length is universal in all forms of Ethernet. In DIX Ethernet, frame length is inferred from the frame delimiter indicators on the LAN, while in IEEE 802.3 CSMA/CD an explicit 2-byte Length field replaces the Type field in DIX Ethernet.

One or more LAN bridges might exist between the source and destination host. No matter, this is still direct delivery. ARPs will pass right through bridges, and MAC frames are forwarded through bridges without regard for MAC frame content. Bridges create one big LAN, and all hosts on this LAN must have the same IP network address. Routers operate differently than bridges, as will be shown in the next section, *The IP Router and Indirect Delivery*.

The source host knew to ARP for the MAC address of the destination host because the destination host is on the same LAN as the source. How did the source host know this? Because the network portion of 192.168.40.66 is the same as the network portion of 192.168.40.70: 192.168.40.0. Hosts on the same

LAN segment *must* have the same IP network addresses. And destination hosts on the same LAN are simply "ARP'd" to determine their MAC addresses. The destination MAC address in the frame is thus the MAC address that corresponds to the destination IP address in the IP packet inside the MAC frame.

What is different when the FTP client and server are on different LANs and must communicate through a router? The example in the following section shows what differs.

The IP Router and Indirect Delivery

What precise role does the router play in the world of TCP/IP and the Internet? It is fine to say that the router is the network node of the Internet, and that no one can attach to the Internet today without a router, but what does this mean? What exactly does a router do? This section explains how routers route IP packets to perform what is called *indirect delivery* of packets from source to destination. In contrast to direct delivery, which occurs when packets can be sent between devices on the same LAN segment, indirect delivery uses one or more routers between source and destination. The source and destination could still be quite close in terms of distance, for instance, on separate floors of the same building. All that matters is whether or not there is a router between source and destination.

Consider a simple network consisting of two LANs connected by routers, as shown in Figure 3.5. The Internet consists of thousands of LANs and routers, of course, but all of the essentials of routing can be illustrated with the simple diagram. The routers are just R1 and R2, and the hosts are just named H1.L1.com, H2.L2.com, and so on, but this naming convention is fine for this simple network.

For the purposes of this discussion, all of the LAN segments are assumed to be Ethernets. Although drawn as distributed cables, most Ethernet LANs are built as IEEE 802.3 10Base-T LANs with hubs and UTP wiring. Only the frames on the Ethernet LANs are really Ethernet. Each host has a network interface card (NIC) installed. The interface actually carries the IP address, not the host, but in this scenario each host has only one interface. Note that *routers* are the ones that have more than one TCP/IP interface, and so routers have more than one IP address. As it turns out, this is how routers connect LANs together over the Internet. A router can have 2, 8, 16, or even more interfaces. Each interface usually needs an IP address and typically represents a separate "network" as the term applies to IP.

Each NIC in the host or router has a 48-bit (6-byte) MAC address. These details are unimportant for this discussion, so here the MAC layer addresses are just labeled as M1, M2, and so on. Each host and router interface has an IP address as well, and these are given in Figure 3.5. The hosts also have host-names as well, but the routers are just Router1 and Router2 and the routers are

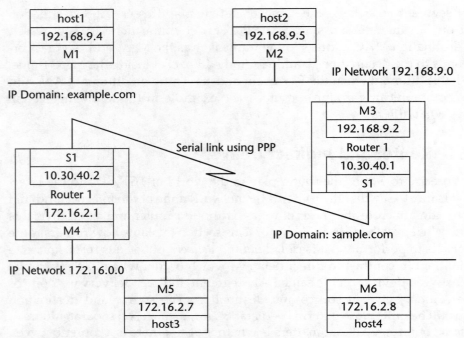

Figure 3.5 Routers, LANs, and indirect delivery.

only shown with network layers and IP layers (although most routers do have application layers and usually hostnames). Since the routers in this example are in different locations, they are connected by a serial link. The serial link is running PPP, and so the packets are placed inside PPP frames on this link between the routers. There is no need for global uniqueness on serial ports, since they are point-to-point links in this illustration, so each one is just labeled S1, for Serial 1, at the TCP/IP network layer.

All IP addresses have two essential parts: the network (some say the sub-network) and host portions of the IP address. Public and private IP addresses also exist. Private IP addresses can be used on any network, as long as these addresses are shielded from the rest of the Internet—usually with some form of network address translation (NAT) running in the router. This example of a simple network uses private addresses as if they were public IP addresses.

Public IP addresses must be obtained from a central authority, such as the Internet Registry, and are globally unique throughout the Internet. Mapping between a hostname like host1.example.com and an IP address such as 192.168.9.4 is done by the local DNS server, which is always authoritative to the local network. DNS information is spread throughout the Internet, but since the locally assigned hostnames and IP addresses can change, only the local DNS can ever be authoritative for a given network.

The hosts on the upper LAN are host1.example.com and host2.example.com. The IP network address is 192.168.9.0 (a private Class C address). The hosts on the lower LAN are host3.sample.com and host4.sample.com. One of the hosts on the lower LAN could have been host1.sample.com, since only the fully qualified domain name need be unique, but the hostnames in this example were chosen for simplicity and clarity. The IP network address on the lower LAN is 172.16.0.0 (a private Class B address). The serial ports on the routers are given IP network addresses from the 10.0.0.0 private Class A address space, although in many cases point-to-point serial links can be "unnumbered" interfaces and not be assigned IP addresses at all. The reason that this is possible will be apparent later on in this example.

Now all of the pieces are in place to follow a packet between client and server on the "internetwork," this time using routers and indirect delivery of packets.

Suppose a client process running on host1.example.com wants to send a packet to a server process running on host4.sample.com. The application is unimportant for this example; it could be FTP, Telnet, or something else. What is important is that the source host knows that the destination host (server) is not on the same LAN. How does it know? For one thing, the domain names are different: example.com for the source and sample.com for the destination. This distinction is easy for people to make but not computers running TCP/IP. But maybe the globally assigned domain is just com and the locally assigned domain is host1.example and host4.sample. More information is needed to decide if the domains are truly different. Fortunately, DNS can be used to resolve the IP address associated with the destination. Now it should be obvious to the source that the destination IP network address (172.16.0.0) is on a different network than the source IP network address (192.168.9.0). (This is a classful example; classless host and router operation is discussed in Chapter 4.)

Now the source knows that the packet to 172.16.2.8 must be sent through at least one router, and perhaps several routers, using indirect delivery. Why is it called indirect delivery? *Because the packet destination address is the destination IP address of the host, but the initial frame destination address is the MAC address of the router.* So the packet is sent "indirectly" to the destination host inside a frame sent to the router. Therefore, the frame constructed and sent on the LAN by host1 is:

Dest.MAC: **M3** Src.MAC: M1 Dest.IP: **172.16.2.8** SourceIP: 192.168.9.4   INFO

Note that the frame is sent to the router (M3), but the packet is sent to 172.16.2.8 (the server). This is how routing works. (Bridges or direct delivery in routing always have frames where the destination MAC is the same as the IP address it represents.)

How did the source host get so smart? That is, how did the source host know the MAC address of the correct router? After all, there could be several routers on a LAN. All that host1 has done so far is to use DNS to determine the

IP address of the destination. However, every TCP/IP configuration on a host must include a *default gateway* that is to be used when packets must leave the local LAN. The default gateway can be set statically or dynamically using DHCP or even other, related protocols. In this example, it is assumed that the default gateway (router) IP address has been entered statically when the host was configured for TCP/IP.

Since the default gateway is by definition on the same LAN as the source host, the source host can simply ARP to obtain the MAC address of the interface on the router attached to the LAN. Note that the IP address of the router is used just to get the MAC address of the router, not so that the source host can send packets directly to the router.

So the router pays attention to the frame when it arrives on the LAN, but host2 ignores the LAN frame (the frame is not for M2). By looking at the packet inside the frame, Router1 knows that the destination host is not directly connected to Router1. The *next hop* is another router. How did Router1 get so smart? In much the same way as host1: Router1 knows the IP addresses assigned to its local interfaces. These are 10.30.40.1 and 192.168.9.2. (Not that a router should or would ever forward a packet out on the same interface the router received the packet from!) The router avoids this situation with a solution called *split horizon*, making sure packets "make progress" toward a destination and avoid heading right back where they came from. Obviously, the destination IP address of 172.16.2.8 does not belong to either of these two networks.

A router might have many interfaces, not just two as in this simple example. So which output port should the router use to forward the packet? The network portion of the IP address is looked up in a *forwarding table* (sometimes called a *routing table*) according to certain rules in order to find out the IP address of the next-hop router and the output interface on which this router is to be found. The rules used for these lookups will be discussed in more detail in the Chapter 4. For now, assume that Router1 finds out that the next hop for the packet to host4 is Router2, and that Router2 is reached on serial port S1.

Router1 now places the packet from host1 to host4 inside a PPP frame for transport on the serial link. Another key feature that distinguishes routers from bridges is the router's ability to *fragment* a packet for transport on an output link (at least in IPv4). Fragmentation involves each router knowing the maximum transmission unit (MTU) size for the link types on all of the router's interfaces. Ethernet LANs, for example, all have an MTU size of 1,500 bytes (1,518 bytes if you include the LAN frame header). Serial links usually have MTU sizes larger than that, so this example assumes that Router1 does not have to fragment the packet it received from the LAN. Fragmentation is important to understanding the differences between IPv4 and IPv6, and it plays a role in routing protocols, so the basics of fragmentation will be covered in a later section of this chapter.

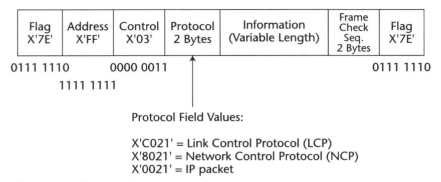

Figure 3.6 The PPP frame.

Figure 3.6 shows the structure of a PPP frame. When the PPP frame carries an IP packet, the Protocol field is set to x0021, as shown in the figure. Note that none of the other fields in the PPP header have a source address for the frame. Point-to-point links only care about the destination, which is always xFF in PPP, and this essentially means "any device at the other end of this link that sees this frame." (This is one reason why serial interfaces on routers do not really need IP addresses.)

So the packet from host1 to host4 arrives at Router2 on the serial link. Router2 knows that the next hop for this packet is not another router, but that Router2 can deliver the packet directly to host4 using direct delivery. How? Simply because the network portion of the IP address in the packet destination, 172.16.2.8, is on the same network as the router itself on interface 172.16.2.1.

So the frame containing the packet is placed on the LAN with the following structure:

Dest.MAC: M4 Src.MAC: **M6** Dest.IP: 172.16.2.8 SourceIP: **192.168.9.4 INFO**

Note that in this case the MAC address of the *source* is the router, and the MAC address of the destination is the MAC address of host4.sample.com. Again, Router2 can always ARP with IP address 172.16.2.8 if the MAC address of the destination host is not in the local ARP cache on the router. The source and destination IP addresses on the packet never change, of course. Host4 must be able to reply to host1.

Again, it is assumed that there is no problem with MTU sizes in this example. But MTU sizes are often important, especially when the operational differences between IPv4 and IPv6 are considered. So before discussing IPv6 addresses and IPv6 router operation, we'll take a brief tour of IP packet fragmentation. Fragmentation and MTU size also play a role in routing protocols. So at least a basic understanding of fragmentation and MTU size is necessary to appreciate some of the details of the routing protocols discussed later in this book. Most importantly, an MTU size mismatch can cause an OSPF link to get stuck and not come up although everything else is fine. And fragments play an important role in IS-IS when finding routing information in the IS-IS database.

Maximum Transmission Unit (MTU)

Every network interface, LAN or WAN, on a TCP/IP network must be configured with a TCP/IP parameter known as the maximum transmission unit (MTU) size. This is the upper limit in size, in 8-bit bytes (octets), of the maximum length of the transmission frame that can be sent on a particular network using the network layer protocol. Most networks have a well-defined MTU size, but a surprising number do not (for instance, Token Ring LAN's MTUs are "tunable," IBM's SDLC WAN protocol for SNA has an "undefined" limit, and so on). It is common in these environments to choose a default or commonly used MTU size for consistency (for example, 4464 bytes for Token Ring and 2048 for SDLC). Typical MTU sizes used in TCP/IP are listed in Figure 3.7. Note that the WAN MTU sizes are very flexible: Smaller sizes are favored to avoid such WAN complications as *serialization delay*. Serialization delay occurs when smaller delay-sensitive packets, such as those containing voice, are delayed while a much longer packet containing lower-priority traffic, such as bulk data transfers with FTP, is being sent bit by bit on the interface.

The TCP/IP network administrator needs to be aware of the MTU size allowed on every link on a path through a TCP/IP from every source to destination. This knowledge is necessary because of the way the IP protocol performs (and the TCP/IP network handles) IP packet fragmentation. If the IP software on a source (host or router) has a packet to send and the packet is larger than the network interface's MTU size, the IP software must perform this process of fragmentation. Simple in principle, all fragmentation means is that the IP packet is split up into two or more frames. These packet fragments are then sent across the TCP/IP network, routed independently to the destination, and then reassembled into the original IP packet at the destination network host system (other routers will *never* reassemble a fragmented packet).

This fragmentation process has two important aspects. First, the fragmentation may be repeated even within the TCP/IP network by many routers. If a frame containing a fragmented IP packet encounters another type of network interface between two routers with an even smaller MTU size, the router has no choice but to "fragment the fragment" for further transport across the TCP/IP network. Second, the reassembly process is *always* done at the destination host running TCP/IP. This avoids the extra effort of reassembling packets in routers just to refragment them later on in the network when a smaller MTU in encountered. This, of course, adds extra processing delay to the destination system, but the TCP/IP network runs faster.

Network Protocol	Typical MTU Size	Maximum IP Packet
Ethernet	1518	1500
IEEE 802.3	1518	1492
IEEE 802.4	8191	8166
IEEE 802.5*	4508	4464
FDDI	4500	4352
SMDS	9196	9180
Frame Relay*	4096	4091
SDLC*	2048	2046

* These protocols have "tunable" frames sizes

Figure 3.7   Typical MTU sizes.

The point for TCP/IP network administrators is simple: *Fragmentation of IP packets is to be avoided if at all possible.* The reason for this far-reaching statement is simple also: Fragmentation on the TCP/IP network means that fragments may be lost (in which case a time-out delay is added to the whole process) or arrive out of sequence. Considerable recovery effort to resequence and reassemble IP packet fragments is needed on the destination host and will be perceived by the user as a TCP/IP network transport delay. In other words, the TCP/IP network appears slow even when all data has arrived at the destination but is still being resequenced and reassembled.

Obviously, the most important MTU size is not at the end user's network that attaches to the router (these are probably Ethernet LANs anyway), but the *smallest MTU size in the entire internetwork*, wherever that may be. Any MTU size from a source to a destination must be factored in, and in a large TCP/IP network with several alternate paths between the routers, this may not be a trivial task. Because of the independent routing characteristics of TCP/IP networks, the path MTU may even change between two end users from minute to minute and even be asymmetrical (the path outbound is not the path inbound for data sent between two users)!

TCP/IP defines a process of *path MTU discovery* for finding out the path MTU at any time. Unfortunately, a path MTU discovered at the beginning of a file transfer may not last for the entire duration of the file transfer session. If the path MTU grows larger, then more packets are sent than necessary; if the path MTU grows smaller, then fragmentation is inevitable.

Since the MTU for most LAN protocols is fixed, the only latitude most organizations have is with the WAN link protocols carrying the IP protocols between routers on the TCP/IP internetwork. These WAN links are usually known as *serial lines* in TCP/IP documentation. It appears that the best solution is to align the serial line MTU size with a LAN protocol, and that would be the optimal situation. In other words, a TCP/IP internetwork linking only Ethernet LANs would set serial-line MTU sizes to 1,500, based on the MTU size of an Ethernet frame.

In fact, the process is more complicated. Serial lines (WAN links) run much slower than LANs (WAN links have less bandwidth and longer signal propagation delays than LANs). TCP/IP network administrators would like to be able to give IP packets with interactive application data (such as Telnet) precedence over IP packets with "bulk data" from other applications (such as FTP). Many implementations allow and support this, since the application port number is included in the TCP or UDP header.

But this is not a perfect solution. Users transferring bulk data prefer larger IP packets to minimize overhead added from layer headers and the raw number of packets sent. Users running many interactive applications prefer smaller packets to minimize buffering delays and transport delays. The selected MTU size must strike a balance between the needs of these two user communities. Of course, a member of the bulk data community doing file transfers in the morning may become a member of the inactive community in the afternoon, so the situation is not clear-cut.

The MTU situation is also complicated with the increasingly frequent use of data compression techniques both in modern modem standards and in some network protocols, such as Compressed Serial Line Interface Protocol (CSLIP) in TCP/IP. There are also newer TCP/IP standards for header compression that complicate the issue even further. The point is that the MTU size configured and used by IP is in no way aware of these compression techniques functions or of their possible existence on a TCP/IP network.

The entire subject of MTU sizes, especially in regard to the MTU size effect on TCP/IP network performance, is frequently a neglected topic. This section has attempted to give TCP/IP network administrators a perspective on the issue.

Fragmentation and Reassembly

Fragmentation in IP routers and hosts is sometimes called *segmentation*. However, because the IP header contains a bit called the *Don't Fragment bit*, we will use *fragmentation* in this section. IP packet fragmentation is important in understanding one of the main differences between IPv4 and IPv6 operation.

The structure of the IPv4 packet is repeated in Figure 3.8. The minimum (no options present; this is very common) IP header length is 20 bytes (always shown as 4 bytes per line), and the maximum length (rarely seen) is 60 bytes. Some of the fields are fairly self-explanatory, such as the fields for the 4-byte (32-bit) IPv4 source and destination address, but others have specialized purposes.

The three fields used in the fragmentation process are as follows:

Identification.   A number set for each packet fragment that helps the destination host reassemble these like-numbered fragments.

Flag.   Only the first 3 bits are defined: Bit 1 must be 0, Bit 2 is 0 if fragmentation is allowed (recall UDP is not supposed to allow fragmentation of the packet containing a UDP message) or 1 if fragmentation is not allowed (for example, for UDP), and Bit 3 is 0 if the packet is the last fragment or 1 if there are more fragments to come.

Fragment Offset.   When packets are fragmented, the fragments must fall on an 8-byte boundary. That is, an 800-byte-long packet may be fragmented as two packets of 400 bytes, but not as eight packets of 100 bytes, since 100 is not evenly divisible by 8. This field contains the number of 8-byte units, known as *blocks*, in the fragmented packet.

The rest of this section concentrates on the fragmentation process and the implications for TCP/IP network administrators. The point has already been made that fragmentation is a processor-intensive operation and should be avoided at all costs, if possible. Of course, if all source hosts were aware of the *minimum* path MTU size before sending an IP packet, the problem would be solved. The trick is to figure it out.

A method to determine this path MTU is commonly used, but it is not perfect, and it is slow. The method works as follows: Before sending live packets to a destination system where the path MTU is not known, the source system sends out an echo packet of a given size, usually using the MTU size of the source system's own TCP/IP network—1,500 for Ethernet, 4,500 for Token Ring, and so on. This packet has the Don't Fragment bit set in the Flags field. If the packet comes back, as echoes should, then the MTU size is fine and is used for live data.

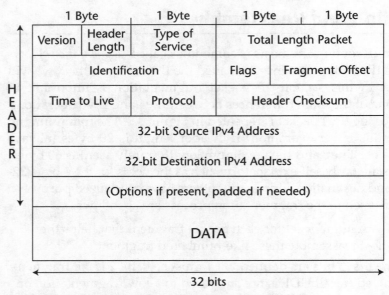

1 Byte	1 Byte	1 Byte	1 Byte

Version	Header Length	Type of Service	Total Length Packet	
Identification		Flags	Fragment Offset	
Time to Live		Protocol	Header Checksum	
32-bit Source IPv4 Address				
32-bit Destination IPv4 Address				
(Options if present, padded if needed)				
DATA				

← 32 bits →

Figure 3.8   The IPv4 header and fragmentation fields.

However, if there is a smaller MTU size on a network that the packet must traverse as it makes its way through the router network, the router attached to this smaller MTU size network *must* discard the packet, since the Don't Fragment (DF) bit is set. But the router will send an ICMP message back to the source indicating an error condition: namely, that the packet has to be discarded because the DF bit was set. The source can then adjust the packet size downward and try again. This process may be repeated several times.

The method works, but it is awkward and slow. The live data basically waits until the path MTU size is determined. And since each packet is independently routed, if there are multiple paths through the router network (and there usually are, since this is the whole point of routers), the MTU size may change with every possible path an IP packet may use from the source to the destination. However, this method is better than a "send and pray" process.

Figure 3.9 shows a portion of a simple TCP/IP network. The arriving IP packet is coming from a WAN with a preconfigured MTU size of 4,500 bytes. The destination host is attached to the router by means of an Ethernet LAN having an MTU size of 1,500 bytes. The figure shows the portions of the IP packet and the values of the fragmentation fields for each fragment. The figure also shows how the destination host interprets the fragmentation fields to reassemble the entire packet at the destination.

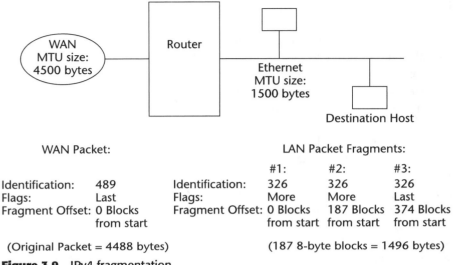

WAN Packet: LAN Packet Fragments:

                                         #1:   #2:   #3:
Identification: 489   Identification: 326   326   326
Flags: Last   Flags: More   More   Last
Fragment Offset: 0 Blocks   Fragment Offset: 0 Blocks 187 Blocks 374 Blocks
                    from start   from start from start from start

(Original Packet = 4488 bytes)   (187 8-byte blocks = 1496 bytes)

Figure 3.9   IPv4 fragmentation.

Fragmentation is to be avoided for two main reasons: the need for time-outs on undelivered fragments and the lack of knowledge on the part of a destination of the reassembled packet size. These reasons are the performance penalty that fragmentation involves. To explore them further, we need to take a quick look at the destination host reassembly process.

A fragmented packet is always reassembled at the destination host. However, since all packets are independently routed, the pieces can arrive out of sequence. When the first piece arrives, some local memory is allocated for the reassembly process. The *fragment offset* of the arriving packets indicates where in the sequence the newly arrived packet should be placed.

Many different packets from several sources may arrive fragmented. All of these pieces may be undergoing the reassembly process at the same time. The destination host IP layer software associates packets having matching Identification, Source Address, Destination Address, and Port fields as belonging to the same packet. However, the Total Length field in a packet fragment's IP header only indicates the length of that particular packet fragment, not the entire packet before fragmentation. Only when the destination system receives the last fragment can the total length of the original packet be recovered.

If a packet is partially reassembled, and the final piece to complete the set has not arrived, the IP software includes a tunable time-out parameter. If the reassembly timer expires, the remaining packet fragments are discarded. If the final piece of the packet finally arrives after the time-out, this long-awaited packet fragment must be discarded as well.

This description of the reassembly process illustrates the two problems of reassembly time-out and memory allocation due to packet size uncertainties. The reassembly time-out value must have a value low enough so as not to unreasonably delay the recovery process of the TCP layer. The TCP layer contains session (connection) information that will detect a missing packet in a sequence of TCP segments (the contents of the packets) and request the missing information be re-sent. Too large a value of the reassembly timer makes this retransmission process very inefficient. Too small a value leads to needlessly discarded packets. In most TCP/IP implementations, the reassembly timer is set by the software vendor and cannot be changed. This is yet another reason to avoid fragmentation.

The second problem is because arriving IP packets have no way of informing the destination system that, say, "I am the first of 10 fragments." If this were the case, the destination system could allocate memory for reassembly that was the best fit of the contiguous available buffer space. But all packet fragments can indicate is "I am the first of many," "I am the second of many," until one finally says "I am the last of many." This uncertainty of reassembled size leads many TCP/IP software implementers to allocate as large a block of memory as available for reassembly. Obviously, a fragmented packet may have been quite large to begin with, since it was fragmented in the first place. But the net result is the local memory becomes quite fragmented. And if smaller blocks of memory are allocated, the resulting noncontiguous pieces must be moved to an adequate-sized memory buffer before the TCP layer can process the reassembled packet.

There used to be a common third problem as well: reassembly deadlock. When memory was a scarce commodity in many hosts and routers, all available local memory could end up holding partially assembled packet fragments. In this case an arriving fragment could not be accepted even if it completed a set and the system ground to a halt. But in these days of inexpensive and plentiful memory, this rarely happens.

All in all, these factors combine to make fragmentation of IP packets an expensive luxury.

Limitations of IPv4

What has all this talk of fragmentation to do with the IP address? Simply that fragmentation behavior changes from IPv4 to IPv6. Fragmentation by routers has been seen as a major limitation of IPv4 that is addressed by IPv6. The need for time-consuming fragmentation is not the only limitation of IPv4, of course. Some of the major limitations of IPv4 are as follows:

- The classful IP addresses of Classes A, B, and C are intended for a world of few large networks and many small networks.

- The Internet today consists of just many large networks ill-suited for classful address assignments.

- Not enough 32-bit IP addresses exist, even without classes, for a world where even toasters and cars might have IP addresses.

- Identification of certain packets with IPv4 is difficult—those that should be sent over the same path to form a *flow* of packets on the Internet, such as packet flows for voice and video.

- Fragmentation is a needless complexity for Internet routers.

The limitations of the original structure of the IP address space has been one of the considerations that has led to a major revision in the TCP/IP protocol, the first one in years. The current structure of IP Class A, B, and C addresses envisioned a world of a few large networks and many small networks running TCP/IP. In fact, the world today consists of just many large networks. The IP Class structure address space is in danger of being exhausted at the current rate of growth. IPv6 was developed for other reasons as well, but the IP address space structure limitations and the threat of IPv4 address exhaustion were uppermost. Once the IP address space issue was addressed, the IPv6 implementers went ahead and fixed a lot of the other limitations of IPv4 as well.

NOTE The current version of IP is version 4 (written IPv4, or just IP). The new version of IP is IP version 6 (IPv6). During development, IPv6 was identified as IPng (which stood for IP: The Next Generation, because the developers were big fans of the TV show *Star Trek: The Next Generation*), but the ng designation was dropped in favor of v6 for continuity purposes. IPv5 exists and is defined in RFC 1819 as the Streams 2 (ST2) Protocol.

Although most of the discussion surrounding IPv6 has focused on the IP address space (in 1990, the exhaustion of Class B IP addresses was predicted for 1994), many aspects of the entire IPv6 standard affect virtually every user of TCP/IP. The one possible exception is the operation of totally private IP networks, with no outside connections to the Internet or even other IP networks. Such private networks will not have to worry about IPv6 for years to come. Most other IP network operators will have to worry about the impact of and transitioning to IPv6 probably within the next few years, and certainly within the next 5 years. Others in the industry, such as some router vendors, have adopted a wait-and-see attitude.

Features of IPv6

This section will emphasize two of the most important aspects of IPv6: the IPv6 header and address and how IPv6 will affect router operation. (A complete examination of IPv6 would need to be exhaustive and is left for other books to cover.)

IPv6 has been around since about 1995, but the pressure to make the transition from IPv4 to IPv6 has only recently become evident. IPv4 address exhaustion, once greatly feared, has been overcome mainly through the use of NAT and Dynamic Host Configuration Protocol (DHCP). But increased address space is still a major reason to make the transition to IPv6.

Pressure to transition from IPv4 to IPv6 comes mainly from network service providers and operators, such as cellular telephone network operators, who are concerned with the exhaustion of the IPv4 address space. The major features of IPv6 are as follows:

- An increase in the size of the IP address from 4 bytes (32 bits) to 16 bytes (128 bits)
- An increase in the size of the IP header from 24 bytes (192 bits) to 40 bytes (320 bits)
- Enhanced security capabilities using IPSec
- Provision of special mobile and autoconfiguration features
- Provision for support of *flows* between routers and hosts for interactive multimedia
- Inclusion of header compression and extension techniques

IPv6 increases the size of the IP address from 4 bytes (32 bits) to 16 bytes (128 bits). For backward compatibility, all currently assigned public IP addresses would be supported as a subset of the new IPv6 address space. The increased IP address would increase the IP packet header size (and thus the total TCP/IP overhead) from the current 24 bytes (192 bits) to 40 bytes (320 bits). Ironically, the new header is longer but actually much simpler than the old IPv4 header.

Enhanced security was a major goal of the IPv6 developers. Many routers today, especially low-end routers, have few additional firewall capabilities or features. Some of these inexpensive network devices are not even capable of having these security features added. These routers are just not powerful enough to both route and perform security checking such as screening source and destination IP addresses and accepting traffic only from trusted routers on the TCP/IP network. These *pass-through routers* without security features have been a real problem in suddenly security-conscious organizations once a virus or intruder has made their way into the target network. But replacing all pass-through routers with firewall-capable devices or special firewall systems has been such a complex and expensive task that many needed security features go unimplemented.

IPv6 essentially makes the decision for both TCP/IP network implementers and router vendors. All devices compliant with the IPv6 standard *must* support authentication between routers. That is, the routers must identify themselves before any routing table updates are accepted by the other devices. There will still be pass-through routers, of course, but these devices must minimally now run the authentication software if they are IPv6-compliant.

IPv6 features autoconfigured address and special support for mobile users. Wireless networks support laptop devices running TCP/IP over special wireless modems today, but the high bit error rates and low bandwidths available with wireless modems make the unreliable delivery of TCP/IP packets today particularly ill-suited for wireless operation. These new mobile features include *chained headers* that allow for the faster forwarding of IP packets through routers and the fact that intermediate fragmentation of IPv6 packets in routers is forbidden. The path MTU must be respected in IPv6 routers.

IPv6 includes support for *flows* to support multimedia traffic. The Flow field in the new IP header structure is to be used by IPv6 routers to ensure that IPv6 packets with voice and video information get priority treatment and follow *virtual circuits* (that is, connections) through the IPv6 router network. For historical reasons, the IPv6 developers are loath to call these virtual circuits *connections* and these flow-enabled routers *switches*, but that is essentially what these terms mean.

IPv6 is perfect for a dynamic environment, unlike IPv4, which expects IP addresses to essentially remain where they are for all time. There are many discovery options bundled with IPv6, including not only support for autoconfiguration, but also for finding the maximum path MTU size (to avoid the need for fragmentation, which IPv6 routers will not do anyway), finding other hosts without using ARP, and finding routers as well.

The last major feature included in the IPv6 specification (exactly which features are major or minor is open to debate, depending on a user's most pressing IPv4 limitation) is a standard for header compression and extension. At first, these two aspects may seem contradictory, but they are actually complementary. The header compression addresses situations in which the new 40-byte IPv6 header consists mostly of "empty" or repeated fields (such as all-zero bit fields). In this case, there is a standard way of compressing the 40 bytes of the header down to 20 or so. However, since the IPv6 header fields are already a simplified structure compared to the current IPv4 header fields, a mechanism exists for extending these fields (for new features) in the future. The idea is that header extensions will be more palatable for implementers and vendors if the hope of efficient header compression is also there.

The effect of the new IPv6 protocol on the layers of the TCP/IP architecture above IP is worthy of consideration as well. The network access layer of

TCP/IP, being the vehicle for IP packet transport inside data link layer frames, is unaffected by any changes to IP itself. However, the TCP layer and the application services are a different matter. TCP heavily depends on IP to deliver TCP segments (or UDP also, for that matter) inside IP packets. There have been serious discussions about necessary changes to TCP in reaction to the changes included in IPv6. For now, however, TCP is not included in the changes due to IPv6 implementation.

The same cannot be said for the application services themselves, such as Telnet or FTP. In many cases, needed changes are merely cosmetic. Most documentation on TCP/IP standard applications claims that IP addresses are 32 bits long. Obviously, this must change. Some applications, such as FTP, carry IP addresses inside what are normally considered data fields in most other applications. Over 58 protocols changed with IPv6, including the socket interface, ICMP (ICMPv6 for IPv6), and routing protocols.

So for IPv6 consistency, any application that is implemented using an IP address must allow for the expanded 128-bit IPv6 address structure as well as the traditional 32-bit IPv4 addresses. This is a minor enough change, but it still must be done for the application to work properly with IPv6. The situation is trickier for applications that carry IP addresses as data. Some mechanism may be needed to figure out whether an IPv4 address or an IPv6 address is being used during an FTP session.

The transition of both the Internet and private TCP/IP networks from IPv4 to IPv6 has been explored by developers as well. This is critical for IPv6 deployment and acceptance. The suggestion to users before they even consider making this transition is simple: Get more memory. All TCP/IP network devices from hosts to routers need to store a number of IP addresses in memory. Hosts need fewer than routers, but there are exceptions. The four-times-larger IPv6 address means that *at least* four times the memory will be required in a network device to hold the same amount of table entries for IP addresses as before.

TCP/IP network hosts on networks with Internet connectivity will get a dual stack of software: one for handling IPv4 and one for handling IPv6. Both are needed because the host will never know if the arriving data is from a remote IPv4 network or a remote IPv6 network. These hosts will have IPv4-compatible IPv6 addresses, as mentioned previously. Private TCP/IP networks may convert to IPv6 whenever they want.

Routers will identify themselves to TCP/IP networks as IPv6 routers. If the host is also IPv6, there is no problem, and a source need not worry about the destination IP version (that is totally up to the destination network). However, the IPv6 router must convert the traffic from an IPv6 host to IPv4 before delivering this traffic to the destination IPv4 network. In other words, for the foreseeable future, there will be no IPv6-*only* routers. All routers must handle both IPv4 and IPv6 for now.

Ironically, most of the added features of IPv6 are currently only used by a few TCP/IP users. Therefore, most users will merely sit and wait for the dust to clear for now before making the transition to IPv6. Of course, the users eagerly awaiting these features will convert to IPv6 right away. But for the vast majority of TCP/IP network users, the best strategy for the time being seems to be to stay with IPv4 until these networks must convert to IPv6.

The IPv6 Header Structure

The structure of the IPv6 header is shown in Figure 3.10. There are only five fields in the entire IPv6 header besides the new expanded 16-byte IP source and destination addresses. This simplified header structure makes for faster processing in the routers.

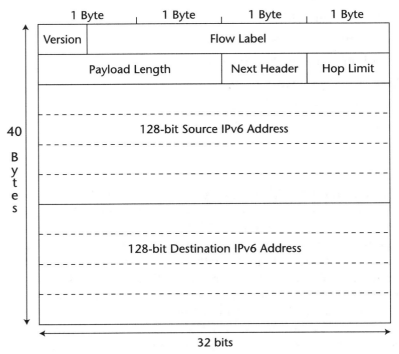

Figure 3.10   The IPv6 header.

The functions of the five fields of the IPv6 header are as follows:

Version.   A 4-bit field for the IP version number (x06).

Flow Label.   A 28-bit field used to label packets request special handling by router (for example, priorities for voice and video packets).

Payload Length.   A 16-bit field indicating the length of the packet in bytes, excluding the IPv6 header.

Next Header.   An 8-bit field indicating the type of header immediately following the IPv6 header (that is, the same function as the Protocol field in IPv4).

Hop Limit.   An 8-bit field set by the source and decremented by 1 at each router. Packet is discarded if Hop Limit is decremented to 0.

IPv6 Header Changes

Following are some of the most important changes in the IPv6 header:

- Longer addresses (32 bits to 128 bits)
- No Fragmentation fields
- No Header Checksum field
- No Header Length field (fixed-length header)
- Payload length in bytes, not blocks (32-bit units)
- Time-to-Live (TTL) field becomes Hop Limit
- Protocol field becomes Next Header (packet content format)
- 64-bit alignment of the packet, not 32-bit alignment
- A Flow Label field has been added
- No Type of Service bits

Notice that many of the IPv4 fields have vanished entirely, especially the fields used for packet fragmentation. IPv6 addresses the fragmentation performance issues and problems by forbidding it altogether in routers once the packet has been sent. Source hosts may still fragment, however, if the source host wishes to send packets larger than the path MTU to a destination. In IPv6, fragmentation may be avoided entirely by making all packets 576 bytes long (the same length worked in IPv4, but resulted in many "extra" packets).

The IPv4 header Checksum field is gone as well, since end system error checking is the preferred method in today's more reliable network technologies, and almost all transmission frames provide better error checking at the network layer. There is no need for a Header Length field either, since all IPv6 headers are the same length. The Payload Length field excludes the IPv6 header fields and is measured in bytes, rather than the awkward 4-byte units of IPv4.

The Time-to-Live field, which was never interpreted as a timer anyway, is gone. In its place is the Hop Limit field, a straightforward indication of the number of routers and network nodes a packet may pass through before it should reach its destination. The Protocol field of IPv4 has become the Next Header field in IPv6. This was more a matter of semantics than technology, but the term *next header* is more accurate, since the information inside the IPv6 packet is not necessarily a higher-layer protocol (for example, TCP segment) in IPv6. There are many other possibilities.

Instead of making the entire packet an integer number of 32-bit (4-byte) units, as in IPv4, the new IPv6 header must be an integer number of 64-bit (8-byte) units. The 32-bit unit was chosen for IPv4 when many high-performance computers were 32-bit machines, meaning memory access and internal bus operations moved 32-bit units (called *words*) around inside the computer. In today's world, which IPv6 was designed for, high-performance computers often support 64-bit words. It only made sense to align the new IPv6 header for ease and speed of processing on the newer-architecture computers.

Finally, in place of the Type of Service field in IPv4, the new IPv6 header defines a Flow Label field used by routers to speed IPv6 packets containing time-sensitive application data such as voice, video, and multimedia on its way. The Type of Service field was usually ignored by router software in IPv4 anyway, and other uses were not standardized.

One other topic involving IPv6 should be mentioned in this necessarily brief overview. The IPv6 specification includes a concept known as Extension Headers. In a sense, Extension Headers take the place of the Options in the IPv4 packet header. IPv6 Extension Headers are only present when needed and are designed to be extensible. In this context, *extensible* means that the use and purpose of Extension Headers are designed to be flexible and new functions may be defined in the future, but "extensible Extension Headers" is not an illuminating phrase.

The currently defined Extension Headers include a Hop-by-Hop Option Header, which is to be examined by every router handling the IPv6 packet, a Routing Header that specifies the IP addresses of the routers on the "path" from source to destination (similar to Source Routing in Token Ring LANs), and an Authentication Header for enhanced security on TCP/IP networks (these can be used in IPv4 as part of IPSec). There is even a Fragmentation Header for the use of the source host when there is no way to prevent the source from sending packet larger than the path MTU size (IPv6 routers cannot fragment, but hosts can). There are several others as well, but these few mentioned give a feel for the kinds of capabilities included in the IPv6 Extension Headers.

IPv6 Addresses

IPv6 addresses can be one of three types. There are broadcast addresses at all in IPv6, even directed broadcasts. In IPv6, multicast serves the same purpose as broadcast in IPv4. The three types are as follows:

Unicast.   This type of IPv6 address is used to identify a single interface.

Anycast.   This type of IPv6 address, new in IPv6, is used to identify a *set* of interfaces, usually on different devices. Anycast addresses can be used to deliver packets to the nearest interface.

Multicast.   This type of IPv6 address is used to identify a *group* of interfaces for multicast purposes. IPv6 relies of multicast addresses for a lot of the discovery features of IPv6.

The differences between anycast and multicast are that packets sent to an anycast IPv6 address are delivered to *one* of several interfaces, while packets sent to a multicast IPv6 address are delivered to *all* of many interfaces.

There is no such thing as dotted decimal in IPv6. All IPv6 addresses are expressed in hexadecimal. They could be expressed in binary as well, but 128 0s and 1s are a lot to write down. IPv6 addresses are written in eight groups of 16 bits each, or eight groups of four hexadecimal numbers, separated by colons. Some examples of IPv6 addresses (which appear over and over in books and articles) are as follows:

FEDC:BA98:7654:3210:FEDC:BA98:7654:3210

1080:0000:0000:0000:0008:0800:200C:417A

Obviously, this form of address still involves a lot of writing and typing. So several ways have been devised to abbreviate IPv6 addresses. For example, any group can leave out leading 0s, and all-0 groups can be expressed as just a single 0. Also, a long string of leading 0s can simply be replaced by a double colon (::). In fact, groups of 0s anywhere in the IPv6 address can be expressed as :: as long as there is no chance of ambiguity. That is, the double colon can only be used once in any IPv6 address.

Even with these conventions, the first IPv6 address given previously cannot be compressed at all. But the second can be expressed as:

1080::8:800:200C:417A

This is lot better than writing out all 128 bits, even as hexadecimal. Do not forget that only one set of double colons can ever be used inside an IPv6 address. So:

1080:0000:0000:9865:0000:0000:0000:4321

could be written as:

1080:0:0:9865::4321 or 1080::9865:0:0:0:4321

but *never* as:

1080::9865::4321

A special case in IPv6 has been made for using IPv4 addresses as IPv6 addresses. For instance, supposed the IPv4 address 10.0.0.1 is transitioned to a network using IPv6 instead of IPv4. The IPv4 address should already be globally unique (this example of 10.0.0.1 is a private IPv4 address, so it is not unique, of course), so another globally unique IPv6 address is not strictly necessary.

The IPv4 address could be written in IPv6 as:

0:0:0:0:0:0:A00:1

or even:

::A00:1

But IPv4 addresses in IPv6 can still be written in dotted decimal as:

::10.0.0.1

In this case, the double colon at the start is the tip-off that this is really an IPv6 address even though it looks just like an IPv4 address.

The IPv6 Address Prefix

Although the idea of classful addressing does not apply to IPv6 addressing, the first few bits of an IPv6 address do reveal something about the IPv6 address. IPv6 addresses have an *address type*, and this is determined by the *format prefix* of the IPv6 address. There are reserved addresses in IPv6 as well, for things like loopback (0:0:0:0:0:0:0:1), multicast (starting with FF), and so on. There is also an *unspecified address* consisting of all 0s (0:0:0:0:0:0:0:0, compressed as just ::) that can be used as a source address by an IPv6 device that has not yet been assigned an IPv6 address. IPv6 address space is also reserved for NSAP (Network Service Attachment Point) addresses used in Open Systems Interconnection (OSI) networks, IPX addresses used with Novell NetWare, and geographical addresses.

The IPv6 format prefixes are shown in Table 3.1. The table lists the allocated use of the format prefix, the format prefix value in binary, and the fraction of the total IPv6 address space used by that format prefix.

Table 3.1 IPv6 Address Prefixes

ALLOCATED USE	PREFIX IN BINARY	FRACTION OF TOTAL SPACE
Reserved	0000 0000	1/256
Unassigned	0000 0001	1/256
Reserved for NSAP allocation	0000 001	1/128
Reserved for IPX allocation	0000 010	1/128
Unassigned	0000 011	1/128
Unassigned	0000 1	1/32
Unassigned	0001	1/16
Aggregatable global unicast addresses	001	1/8
Unassigned	010	1/8
Unassigned	011	1/8
Reserved for geographic-based unicast addresses	100	1/8
Unassigned	101	1/8
Unassigned	110	1/8
Unassigned	1110	1/16
Unassigned	1111 0	1/32
Unassigned	1111 10	1/64
Unassigned	1111 110	1/128
Unassigned	1111 1110 0	1/512
SPECIAL USE ADDRESSES		
Link local use addresses	1111 1110 10	1/1024
Site local use addresses	1111 1110 11	1/1024
Multicast addresses	1111 1111	1/256

These format prefixes are *binary*, not hexadecimal. So, for example, an IPv6 multicast address begins with FF, not 1111:1111.

Provider-based IPv6 addresses are important. Like IPv4 addresses, most IPv6 addresses will be handed out to customers by ISPs. So the most common IPv6 address used will be provider-based, unicast IPv6 addresses beginning with 001. There will also be variable-length fields following in the address for the registry identifier (the authority that assigned this IPv6 address space to the ISP), the provider identifier (the ISP), the subscriber identifier (the customer), the subnet identifier (a group of physical links), and the interface identifier (such as the MAC address).

Two types of local IPv6 addresses exist: *link local* and *site local*. Local IPv6 addresses are just those addresses that do not have global significance and so can be used over and over again as long as they do not cause confusion to hosts or routers. Both types start with the same 8 bits: 1111 1110 or FE in hexadecimal. The FE format prefix acts as a flag to routers on the Internet that they are not to route packets with these destination addresses: they are for local use only. Site local addresses can be used on an entire site (for example, on a LAN). Link local addresses can be used between two devices directly connected by a point-to-point link. Usually, both site local and link local IPv6 addresses end with a 64-bit representation (called EUI-64) of the 48-bit MAC address of the LAN interface (even LANs can be used in a crossover, point-to-point fashion). When this is done, there is no need for hosts or routers to ARP, since the MAC address is now embedded in the IPv6 address.

IPv4 Packet Processing

What is the difference between a router handling an IPv6 packet and a router handling an IPv4 packet? Because for some time to come, routers will have to handle both types of headers, this is a good place to explore this issue in a little more detail.

A router must follow three main steps in IPv4 to process a packet. Processing a packet just means checking an incoming packet for errors and other parameters, determining the proper output port for the packet, and then sending the packet out on that port. Each of these major steps is broken down into a series of smaller steps:

1. Check incoming IPv4 packet.

    - Compute Checksum and compare to received value. If wrong, discard packet.

    - Check Type of Service parameters and provide requested handling.

    - Check Time-to-Live field. If zero, discard packet.

2. Determine output port.

    - Is a Source Route used in Option field? If so, send to specified router.

    - Does the packet allow fragmentation? Is fragmentation needed on the output port?

- Is the Type of Service required available?
- Based on the preceding, a table entry is analyzed and chosen for output. Else the packet is discarded.

3. Send the IPv4 packet:
- Fragment if needed.
- Rebuild packet header: decrement Time-to-Live, set Fragment Offset if needed, and recompute Checksum (since some IPv4 header fields have changed).
- Output packet.

In all cases where a router discards a packet, an ICMP message must be generated and sent back to the source host. Also, recall the performance penalty when fragmentation is needed.

IPv6 Packet Processing

The following outline lists the steps a router follows in an IPv6 TCP/IP network. These steps assume that no Extension Headers that must be examined by the router are used (in this case, the router just checks the Next Header field value). The overall steps are the same as in IPv4 processing but much more efficient.

1. Check incoming IPv6 packet.
- Check Payload Length against received packet. If incomplete, discard.
- Check Hop-Limit field. If zero, discard packet.

2. Determine output port.
- Check Next Header field for Extension Headers.
- Check Flow Label for priority handling.
- Based on the preceding criteria, a table entry is analyzed and chosen for output.

3. Send the IPv6 packet:
- Output packet, with only hop limit changed.

The IPv4/IPv6 Transition: Terminology

What about routers in the transition period between IPv4 and IPv6? How will the two environments coexist? How will IPv4 and IPv6 routers and hosts interoperate? Because this is an important issue, we will explore it in more detail.

Fortunately, a transition plan has been put in place by the IPv6 developers. This plan contains some terminology that is new, so a few words of explanation are in order. The transition plan defines the following terms:

IPv4-only node.   A host or router that implements only IPv4.

IPv6/IPv4 (dual) node.   A host or router that implements both IPv4 and IPv6.

IPv6-only node.   A host or router that implements only IPv6.

IPv6 node.   A host or router that implements IPv6. Both IPv4/IPv6 dual nodes and IPv6-only nodes are included in this category.

IPv4 node.   A host or router that implements IPv4. Both IPv4/IPv6 dual nodes and IPv4-only nodes are included in this category.

IPv4-compatible IPv6 address.   An address assigned to an IPv6 node that can be used in both IPv6 and IPv4 packets. A special format is used for this type of IP address.

IPv4-mapped IPv6 address.   An address assigned to an IPv4-only node represented as an IPv6 address. These addresses always identify IPv4-only nodes, never IPv4/IPv6 or IPv6-only nodes.

IPv6-only address.   An address assigned to any IPv4/IPv6 or IPv6-only node. These addresses always identify IPv6/IPv4 nodes, never IPv4-only nodes.

These terms can be somewhat confusing, but all these terms mean is that hosts and routers can be classified as IPv4 devices, IPv6 devices, or both IPv4 and IPv6 devices. The IPv4/IPv6 devices are capable of understanding and using both IPv4 and IPv6. However, the IPv6-only address can be used in an IPv6/IPv4 device. Otherwise, no older IPv4 devices on a TCP/IP network would be able to communicate with them.

IPv4/IPv6 Device Compatibility

Table 3.2 shows the communication capabilities of IPv4 and IPv6 devices.

Table 3.2 is an attempt to clear away some of the confusion over the interoperability capabilities of the many forms of these various devices. In the table, the entries mean the following:

Direct.   There is direct interoperability capability between the two types of devices.

Translate.   There is indirect interoperability capability between the two types of devices only through the assistance of a special "translating" router. A translating router is one capable of translating IPv4 address to IPv6 addresses and vice versa.

Table 3.2 IPv4 and IPv6 Devices

NODE TYPE:	IPV4-ONLY NODE	IPV6/IPV4 NODE W/ IPV6 COMP. ADDR.	IPV6/IPV4 NODE W/ IPV6-ONLY ADDR	IPV6-ONLY NODE W/ IPV6-COMP. ADDR	IPV6-ONLY NODE W/ IPV6-ONLY ADDR.
IPv4-only node	Direct	Direct	None	Translate	None
IPv4/IPv6 node w/ IPv4-compatible-address	Direct	Direct	Direct	Direct	Direct
IPv6/IPv4 node w/ IPv6-only address	None	Direct	Direct	Direct	Direct
IPv6-only node w/ IPv4-compatible address	Translate	Direct	Direct	Direct	Direct
IPv6-only node w/ IPv6-only address	None	Direct	Direct	Direct	Direct

None. There are no interoperability capabilities between the two types of devices at all. That is, they will not be able to communicate.

Fortunately, the Directs are many and the Nones are few. A couple of Translates are needed in some cases, but not many. IPv4-compatible IPv6 addresses are expected to be used extensively in the early stages of IPv6 deployment. In this case, many organizations can use their existing IPv4 address to compose IPv6 addresses simply and directly by essentially embedding these older IPv4 addresses in IPv6 addresses.

Deploying IPv6

By now it should be apparent that IPv6 deployment is a long, ongoing process. During this transition, some devices, hosts, or routers might even be able to run dual IPv4 and IPv6 layers. These devices can send and receive both IPv4 and IPv6 packets. These devices need both IPv4 and IPv6 addresses, and they may or may not be related. But this way, IPv4-only clients can access services on an IPv6-only server.

IPv6 packets can also be sent inside an IPv4 tunnel. In other words, a complete IPv6 packet can be encapsulated inside an IPv4 packet and sent over a series of IPv4-only routers. Packets can be sent by either a *configured tunnel* or an *automatic tunnel*. Tunneling devices have an IPv4-compatible IPv6 address consisting of 96 zeros followed by the 32 bits of the IPv4 address. With configured tunneling the IPv4 tunnel endpoint is determined by the router performing the encapsulation. With automatic tunneling the IPv4 tunnel endpoint is determined by the IPv4 address inside the IPv6 packet header. No dual-protocol stacks are needed to support tunneling.

Tunneling can be one of four types:

Host to router. Hosts with dual IP stacks can tunnel IPv6 packets to a dual-stack IP router that is only reachable over an IPv4 network.

Router to router. Routers running dual IP stacks connected by an IPv4 only series of other routers can tunnel IPv6 between themselves.

Router to host. Routers with dual IP stacks can tunnel IPv6 packets to a dual-stack IP host that is only reachable over an IPv4 network.

Host to host. Dual IP stack hosts can tunnel IPv6 packets between themselves using direct delivery.

The last two types deliver packets to final destination. In these cases, the tunnel endpoint is the IPv6 destination address of the device. These are examples of automatic tunneling and simply use the IPv4-compatible address in the IPv6 packet to build the IPv4 packet header.

We will discuss further details of routing protocols with regard to IPv6 in later chapters. The next chapter introduces the ideas of subnetting, supernetting, and variable-length subnet masking (VLSM), mostly from an IPv4 perspective. The concept of VLSM is also applied to IPv6 in Chapter 4.

Subnets and Supernets

One major concept deserves a chapter of its own, especially when IPv6 is considered: the *subnet mask*. This feature determines the position of the boundary between network and host portions of the IP address. It does so whether the version of IP being considered is IPv4 or IPv6 or whether classful or classless IP addresses are involved. A subnet mask is always used. Mistaken impressions to the contrary, even with classful IP addresses there is a subnet mask— a *default* subnet mask—that is applied to an IP address, whether or not an explicit mask has been configured.

In this chapter we look at all aspects of finding and perhaps moving the boundary between network and host bits in the IP address. The movable boundary is an important one, because routers performing indirect delivery generally only need to look at the *prefix* (network portion) of the device address to determine what the IP address of the next hop is and what output interface to send the packet to on its way to the destination. Of course, direct delivery does require both prefix and host addressing knowledge, and this is the point of the whole chapter. How do network devices such as routers, switches, and hosts always know *exactly* where the boundary between prefix and host address is within the IP address? Only when this prefix/host boundary is determined will the device know whether a router is the next hop or not. And that, as has been established in the last chapter, makes all the difference.

First, we examine IPv4 addressing, including classful IPv4 addressing. The original need for subnetting is introduced, and then the reverse concept in routing, supernetting, is covered, all in terms of classful IP addresses to this point. Supernetting is the goal of an IPv4 feature called *classless interdomain routing* (CIDR), which became the basis for a more generalized and advanced method of applying masks to classless IP addresses. So the emphasis here is on classless IP addressing using *variable-length subnet masks* (VLSM), the newer way of combining the concepts of subnetting and supernetting into one package.

We close the chapter closes by looking at how routers apply masks to IPv6 addresses. Not only are IPv6 addresses much larger than IPv4 addresses, the variations in notation make the application of normal subnet masking notation to IPv6 challenging. There are also the related issues of how best to organize the IPv6 address space for quick router lookups. The key here is that IPv6 addresses complicate the organization of IP address information and subnet masks in several ways. All of these IPv6 issues are explored in full.

IP Addressing and the Internet

The view of the Internet presented in Figure 1.1 was a little misleading in one respect: The figure was just too neat and organized. The figure presented ISPs in a hierarchical fashion, from small to large, and in order not to make the figure too confusing, the links between the ISPs were not nearly as haphazard and almost random as the links between ISPs in the real Internet are. In the real world of the Internet, links between ISPs can span distances that are local, national, or international. Customers link to more than one ISP. ISPs link to each other, and NAPs, as well as they can.

The decommissioning of the NSFNET backbone has forced ISPs to migrate from a core and backbone structure to a much more distributed architecture increasingly dominated by large commercial Internet service providers. Since many of the "new" Internet service providers are "old " telephone companies, it has become common to call any location inside the ISP cloud with a numbers of routers, servers, and links to customers a *point of presence* (POP). The links between ISPs really link one ISP's POP with another ISP's POP. Even small ISPs can have a POP; the POP term applies to one router and server and a couple of links as well as to a large national ISPs with hundreds of routers, servers, and links. The general form of the Internet today, with the emphasis on POPs and links, is shown in Figure 4.1.

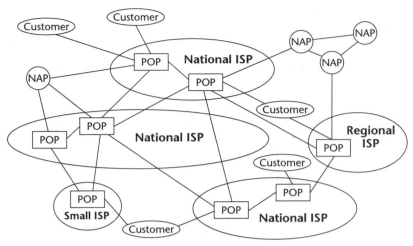

Figure 4.1 The Internet as POPs and Links.

As mentioned in Chapter 1, ISPs that have POPs all across the United States are called *national providers* or *national ISPs,* although there is nothing to prevent any ISP at all from calling itself national. ISPs that cover more focused areas are called *regional providers* or *regional ISPs* and connect to other providers at one or more points. Customers connect their providers with *access links,* although many ISPs customers are also service providers in their own right, as pointed out in Chapter 1. ISPs can avoid *full mesh* requirements by peering at a public peering point (such as a NAP) or peering directly. The term *full mesh* just means that if any number of ISPs want to communicate most efficiently, they should have a complete set of direct connections—a full mesh— among them. Since this is impossible for all of the ISPs on the Internet today, ISPs can still reach each other by connecting (peering) to a public NAP. Many pairs of ISPs peer directly.

Sometimes the phrase *network service provider* (NSP) is still seen and used with regard to the Internet. At one time ISPs were those service providers that furnished Internet connectivity in a given area, mainly to end users. *NSP* was reserved for those service providers that ran and maintained a backbone network that more or less paralleled the NSFNET backbone. Today, the term NSP has little to recommend its continued use, since all ISPs are scrambling for customers and few ISPs can afford the luxury of specialization.

Network access points (NAPs) were established by the NSFNET to form a series of public peering points where different service providers could interconnect. There were two reasons for the NAP structure. First, at the time, the NSF's Acceptable Use Policy (AUP) restricted the use of the Internet to research and education. Companies that wanted to use the Internet to distribute sales and marketing information, commercial software and upgrades, and so on, were technically forbidden from using the NSFNET backbone for this purpose. Second, without NAPs, ISPs would need to be directly connected to each other for commercial purposes unless every ISP was willing to be a free transit ISP to almost anyone else, a situation few ISPs really wanted to think about. So commercial- and general-use traffic on the Internet was supposed to use the NAPs.

Initially, there were four NAPs, and the NSFNET was linked to the NAPs by March 1995. However, it was not very long before Web traffic overwhelmed the NAPs, which were usually built on a combination of 100-Mbps FDDI and 45-Mbps ATM. The routers at the NAPs frequently suffered from routing instabilities and high packet loss, leaving ISPs unable to reach each other, not only in the United States but also in many European countries. Why? Because in many cases it was more cost-effective for European countries to link to the U.S. NAPs than to link directly to each other, given the state at the time of the inter-European link rate structures. So a lot of Internet traffic between France and Germany, for example, traveled first to a parking garage in Reston, Virginia, where the east coast NAP was located.

Each NAP employed a *route server*—part of the overall Routing Arbiter (RA) project—to coordinate the routing information supplied by the routing protocols of all the ISPs that linked to the NAP. Without the assistance of the route server, all ISPs would have to exchange full routing information with every other ISP linking to the NAP. The route server keeps a common database of all of this routing information for each ISP. So ISPs just send and get routing information to and from the route server. The route server also applies any of the routing policies established at the NAPs by the ISPs. The routing polices at the NAPs are kept in the Routing Arbiter Database (RADB). Collectively, the RADB and other routing information databases are known as the Internet Routing Registry (IRR). The routing policies written for the NAP route servers use a language called the *Routing Policy Specification Language* (RPSL).

Few people, even network administrators, need concern themselves with configuring routing policies for use with the route servers at NAPs, so RPSL will not be covered in detail. Instead, the emphasis will be on configuring routing policies on routers directly connected either within an ISP's autonomous system (AS) or between ISPs that are connected as peers. And even when ISPs have a presence at a NAP or other form of public peering point, there is no requirement that the ISPs use a central database or the route server. Direct interconnections are always allowed.

As mentioned, the alternative to the NAP structure was the direct interconnection and peering of pairs of ISPs. There were attractions to direct interconnection, such as reduced reliance on third-party administrators and managers to resolve link and router problems, to configure increased capacity, and the like. Peering also reflects actual traffic flows and necessary Internet topologies much more closely than do NAPs. Links between peers can be easier to provision, upgrade, tune for performance, and fix when broken. Early peering was driven by just such a desire for "NAP avoidance." This benefited the NAPs as well, because the reduced traffic loads freed up bandwidth and alleviated a lot of the congestion that NAPs were noted for. Peering primarily appealed to larger ISPs, mainly because the larger ISPs increasingly desired to keep traffic exchanges more or less equal in both directions. Also, smaller ISPs did not always have the resources to establish and maintain the WAN link infrastructure needed to implement large-scale peering both in regard to monthly links costs as well as the cost of all those "extra" router WAN ports. Despite the emergence of large-scale peering, the large ISPs do maintain a presence at the NAPs; otherwise, it would be even harder for a smaller ISP to reach the world.

What has all this talk about NAPs to do with IP addressing? Everything. After all, routes and routing information are all about *prefixes*, and prefixes are the network portions of classful or classless IP addresses. ISPs exist to link Internet-attached hosts that are *clients* to Internet-attached hosts that are *servers*. The servers are in the vast majority of cases located on LANs that share a common IP network address space (for example, 172.17.0.0).

How do clients find servers (actually, the networks that the servers are on)? It's one thing to say that DNS translates a client request like going to Web server www.example.com to an IP address such as 172.17.48.200 so that the Web browser can try and link to the Web site. But it is quite another to figure out how all of the routers in all of the ISPs that make up the Internet know where network 172.17.0.0 is in the first place.

Clients find servers because the routes to all reachable networks on the Internet are *advertised* by routers. That is, the ISP that links directly to 172.17.0.0 shares this information with other ISPs, with or without NAPs, until the whole Internet knows where the server is located. The links between ISPs can be fast or slow, and therefore some links may be more attractive than others. Figure 4.2 shows what routing protocols and policies do on the Internet.

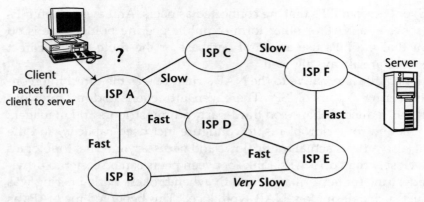

Figure 4.2   Routing protocols and policy on the Internet.

The client attached to ISP A has sent a packet bound for the server attached to ISP F into the Internet. The routers in ISP A must first of all know from the IP address of the destination that the server is not a host attached to ISP A. The routers must also know whether the best way for the packet to reach the next ISP in the chain to the server is through ISP C, ISP D, or ISP B. Perhaps the ISP A routers will consider speed of links above all else to determine the best path. From a pure bandwidth point of view, ISP C might look very attractive, because the links to ISP F through ISP D are all high-speed links. But wait! ISP D will not act as a free transit point to ISP E. How does ISP A know this? Perhaps ISP B should be used to reach ISP F, and ISP B will allow transit of ISP A's traffic. How does ISP B tell ISP A about its transit status to ISP F? However, the link between ISP B and ISP E is very slow, much slower than even the link between ISP A and ISP C. How can ISP B inform ISP A that ISP B is a bad choice to reach ISP F quickly? Perhaps ISP A has decided that the best way to reach ISP F is just through the smallest number of ISPs. In this case, the link to ISP C looks very attractive, but slow. How is this information shared by all other ISPs?

The answer to all of the questions and issues raised in the previous paragraph is that each ISP will configure, apply, and maybe adjust a *routing policy* to influence the way that IP addresses are distributed by the routing protocols. And the routing policies all deal with IP addresses. Clients and servers deal with full, network/host classful or classless IP addresses. Routers, on the other hand, deal with subnetting and supernetting IP addresses, as well as VLSM and the IP route prefixes that VLSM produces. Before we look at VLSM, which applies to classless IP addresses, we'll start with the concept of IP address subnetting, which applies to classful IP addresses.

IP Subnetting

As introduced in Chapter 3, "IP Addressing and Routing," the IP address space was originally classful and contained a number of special-purpose and private addresses. These are summarized in Table 4.1.

Because the first bits of the IP address determine the IP address class, the IP addresses belonging to that class fall into certain numeric ranges, which are shown in the Table 4.1. The examples are all drawn from private address spaces, as established by RFC 1918.

However, there are potentially more than 2 million Class C networks. In contrast, there are only 100 or so Class A networks and about 16,000 Class B networks possible. The problem is that once the Web hit town and everyone needed an IP network address for their PCs and Web sites, it became obvious that Class A and Class B addresses would quickly become exhausted, leaving only Class C addresses for most networks. But routers must have a separate routing table entry for each and every IP network. If most IP networks are Class C networks, then all Internet routers would potentially have to hold in memory (and maintain!) a list of more than 2 million entries. Even in the current era of inexpensive and abundant memory, this size routing table poses challenges.

Table 4.1   The Classful IP Address Space

FIRST BYTE	CLASS	EXAMPLE
0-127	A	10/8
128-191	B	172.18/16
192-223	C	192.168.14/24
224-239	D	224.1.1.1 (multicast)
240-255	E	Reserved (experimental)
PREFIX	**RANGE**	**PURPOSE**
0/0	0.0.0.0	Default (unknown dest.)
10/8	10.0.0.0-10.255.255.255	Private addresses
127/8	127.0.0.0-127.255.255.255	Loopback
172.16/24	172.16.0.0-172.31.255.255	Private addresses
192.168/24	192.168.0.0-192.168.255.255	Private addresses
255.255.255.255	255.255.255.255	Local broadcast

Where IP Addresses Come From

Most people get the IP addresses for their networks, clients, and servers from their ISP. But where do ISPs get their IP addresses? And large organizations can still apply for their own IP addresses independent from any ISP. But apply to whom?

Initially, IP addresses (and the Internet domain names that were associated with them) were handed out by the Internet Assigned Number Authority (IANA). Today the Internet Corporation for Assigned Names and Numbers (ICANN), an international nonprofit organization, oversees the process of assigning IP addresses.

The actual IP addresses are handed out by the following Internet registries:

ARIN (American Registry for Internet Numbers).   Since 1997, ARIN has handed out IP addresses for North and South America, the Caribbean, and Africa below the Sahara.

RIPE NCC (Reseaux IP Europeens Network Coordination Center). RIPE assigns IP addresses in Europe and the surrounding areas.

APNIC (Asian Pacific Network Information Center).   APNIC assigns IP addresses in 62 countries and regions in Central Asia, Southeast Asia, Indochina, and Oceania.

AfriNIC (African Network Information Center).   AfriNIC is to take over assignment of African IP addresses from ARIN.

The collection of these Internet registries databases that determine who has what IP address space are known as the Internet Routing Registry (IRR). Internet domain names are a related activity, but as with IP addresses, names must be globally unique, and unlike IP addresses, they can be almost anything. Internet domain name assignment is also overseen by ICANN and currently administered by security corporation VeriSign.

The IP address space assignments that form the IRR fall into distinct geographical distributions and start with IP Class A address 61.0.0.0. This distribution is shown in Table 4.2.

Note that the figure lists a number of Class A and Class B addresses. Anyone can still ask for a Class A or a Class B address, but most likely people will get a Class C address, or even a group of Class C addresses, since all Class C addresses can only be used for networks with less than 254 hosts.

To make use of the classful IP address space flexible, a single Class A or Class B address would need to be divided into a number of smaller IP networks. The way to do this is known as *subnetting*. At the same time, flexibility would be improved if many small Class C addresses could be combined into one larger IP network. They can—by *supernetting*, which is discussed in the *Classless Interdomain Routing (CIDR)* section of the chapter.

Table 4.2 IP Addresses and Geography

ADDRESSES	ALLOCATION	ADDRESSES	ALLOCATION
61.0.0.0- 61.255.255.255	APNIC-Pac rim	196.0.0.0- 198.255.255.255	Various
62.0.0.0- 62.255.255.255	RIPE NCC-Europe	199.0.0.0- 201.255.255.255	ARIN-North/ South Am.
63.0.0.0- 64.255.255.255	ARIN	202.0.0.0- 203.255.255.255	APNIC-Pac rim
128.0.0.0- 191.255.255.255	Various	204.0.0.0- 209.255.255.255	ARIN
192.0.0.0- 192.255.255.255	Multiple regions	210.0.0.0- 211.255.255.255	APNIC-Pac rim
193.0.0.0- 195.255.255.255	RIPE NCC-Europe	212.0.0.0- 213.255.255.255	ARIN

The Basics of Subnetting

Subnetting is not restricted to IP Class A and Class B addresses. In fact, the original application of subnetting to IP networks was to allow a single Class C IP address to be used on small LANs connected by routers instead of bridges and having fewer than 254 hosts. Bridges would simply shuttle frames between all of the interfaces on the bridge, but routers, because they are packet layer devices, determine the proper output port for a packet based on the network portion of the IP address. If there is only one Class C address assigned to the entire site, but there are two LANs on the site connected through a router, then the Class C address must be subnetted (and the IP host addresses assigned on each LAN segment correctly) so that the router functions properly. These LAN segments now become *subnets* of the main IP address space.

Subnetting is accomplished through the use of an IP address *mask*. The mask is just a string of bits as long as the IP address: 32 bits in the case of IPv4. If the mask bit is a one-bit, it just means that the corresponding bit in the IP address the mask references is part of the network portion of the IP address. If the address bit is part of the host (local) portion, the corresponding mask bit is set to a zero-bit. That's all there is to it. So a mask of 255.255.0.0 means that the first 16 bits of the IP address having this mask are part of the network address, and the last 16 bits are the part of the host portion of the address.

All subnet masks must end in 128, 192, 224, 240, 248, 252, 254, or 255. Those are the values of each bit position as they are "turned on" left to right in any octet. Oddly, subnet masks were once allowed to turn on bits that were *noncontiguous*, or not starting at the left of the address without gaps. So 255.255.19.0 was once a valid subnet mask. But this is no longer true, and the effect is to restrict masks to the ending values listed. Note that 255.224.0.0 is a valid subnet mask, as is 255.255.248.0 and 255.255.255.252. Once the one-bits stop, the rest of the subnet mask must be set to all zero-bits.

Classful IP addresses (Class A, Class B, and Class C) have default subnet masks that correspond to the class of the IP address in question. Default subnet masks do not have to be configured on hosts and routers in many cases, leading some to believe—mistakenly—that classful IP addresses do not need a subnet mask at all. This is simply not true. All hosts and routers need a subnet mask to determine the boundary between the network and host portions of the IP address. If the default mask works, fine. But this does not mean that the mask is not present or used.

Subnet masks can be written in as many forms as there are for IP addresses: dotted decimal notation, bit string, octal, or hexadecimal. It is most common to see subnet masks in either dotted decimal or hexadecimal notation. In *VLSM and the Longest-Match Rule* later in this chapter, the *prefix* or slash notation is introduced. Sometimes the default mask for an IP address class is called the *natural mask* for that type of address. In all cases it is possible to change the default mask to something else in order to move the boundary between the network and host portions of the IP address to wherever the device needs to look for it. Of course, all devices, hosts or routers, that need to route the packets within the subnetted network need to have identical masks. Many routing protocols today exchange subnet mask information right along with the routes.

The default masks for the original classful IP address space are shown in Table 4.3.

Reverse masking is useful on hosts and routers. Instead of indicating the bits to use as the network address, reverse masking indicates which bits are to be used for the host portion of the IP address. The default reverse masks for Class A, B, and C are 0.255.255.255, 0.0.255.255, and 0.0.0.255, respectively.

Table 4.3   Default Classful IP Address Masks

CLASS	DEFAULT MASK	NETWORK/ HOST BITS	EXAMPLE ADDRESS INTERPRETATION
A	255.0.0.0	8/24	10.24.215.86 is host 0.24.215.86 on network 10.0.0.0
B	255.255.0.0	16/16	172.17.44.200 is host 0.0.44.200 on network 172.17.0.0
C	255.255.255.0	24/8	192.168.27.3 is host 0.0.0.3 on network 192.168.27.0

Basically, subnetting moves the boundary between network and host for a particular classful IP address to the *right* of the position where the boundary is normally found. (As will be shown later, supernetting, as well as CIDR and VLSM, move the boundary between network and host for a particular classful IP address to the *left* of this position.)

Suppose a network administrator is faced with the situation in which a single Class C address space, in this case 192.168.77.0, needs to be shared between two LANs linked by a single router to the Internet. Naturally, the total number of devices at the site having IP addresses all at once cannot exceed 254. It cannot because IP addresses 192.168.77.0 (the network itself) and 192.168.77.255 (the directed broadcast) cannot be assigned to hosts. It is assumed that this limitation is not a problem. How can subnetting be used to allow devices on the two LANs to use the router properly between them and yet at the same time appear as one single Class C network to the Internet? Simply by adjusting the default Class C address mask on all of the hosts and the two router ports so that the Class C address space is split into two distinct networks. Recall that routers will not route between LAN ports unless there are two different IP network addresses assigned to the ports.

How can 192.168.77.0 appear to be two networks (subnets)? Just by setting the IP subnet mask on all hosts and the router LAN ports to look at 25 bits for the network portion of the IP address instead of 24 bits. This leaves 7 bits for the host address instead of 8, so each LAN segment can only have 128 addresses (usually with only 126 devices) instead of the full 256 addresses and 254 devices.

The subnet mask used in this example could be written:

255.255.255.128

11111111 11111111 11111111 10000000

FF FF FF 80

All are identical and mean exactly the same thing: On this interface, for this address, use 25 bits for the network address instead of 24. It makes no difference if the address belongs to Class A, B, or C; subnetting can be done to all classful IP addresses.

How does subnetting by the network administrator in the 192.168.77.0 network example work? If the twenty-fifth bit of the IP address is a zero-bit, then the router can send those packets out on interface EN0 (Ethernet 0) to LAN 1. This automatically limits the host address assignments (in most cases) on that LAN to the range 192.168.77.1 to 192.168.77.127 because only those host addresses have a zero-bit in the twenty-fifth position. And if the twenty-fifth bit of the IP address is a one-bit, then the router can send those packets out on interface EN1 (Ethernet 1) to LAN 2. This automatically limits the host address assignments (in most cases) on that LAN to the range 192.168.77.129 to

192.168.77.254 because only those host addresses have a one-bit in the twenty-fifth position. Note that IP address 192.168.77.128 is now technically the "this network" address "ending in zero" for that subnet. Older routers often allow this subnet to be used as a valid address, but the best practice is to use the highest and lowest IP address as intended: to indicate the network and as a directed broadcast. The effect of the subnet is shown in Figure 4.3.

The network administrator in charge of handing out the host IP addresses for the two LANs must be careful. An IP address such as 192.168.77.200 cannot be assigned to LAN 1, and an IP address such as 192.168.77.21 cannot be assigned to LAN 2, because in both cases the bits in the twenty-fifth position do not match the subnet mask.

The hosts on each LAN must have the correct and identical subnet mask configured as well. Why? Because unless the originating host knows that the next hop to the destination is a router, the host will try to ARP for the MAC address of the destination on the same LAN segment. If the ARP fails, the originating host just assumes that the destination is powered off or otherwise unreachable and eventually gives up trying to deliver the packet. Consider a packet sent from a host on LAN 1, say, 192.168.77.26, to a host on LAN 2, perhaps 192.168.77.144. If the default subnet mask is configured on the hosts, then these two addresses appear to be on the same LAN and ARPs are used to try to map the IP address of the destination to the MAC address of the LAN port with that IP address. Only when all hosts have 255.255.255.128 as a mask will they know that destinations on the other LAN segments are reachable only through the router. An ARP might still be used, but only to find the MAC address of the router interface, not the destination. The packet still goes to 192.168.77.144. But the frame goes to the router.

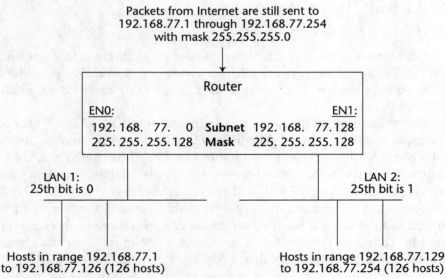

Figure 4.3   A simple subnet example using Class C.

Note that the router interface on the Internet side is unconcerned about the subnet masking used on the other router interfaces. This is because as far as the Internet is concerned, the 192.168.77.0 network is reachable through this router, and that's that. So the 192.168.77.0 route is advertised with its default or natural mask of 255.255.255.0 and all is well.

More Advanced Subnetting

Today, subnetting is often used with Class A and Class B addresses and less commonly with Class C. There's not much to be gained by subnetting a Class C address into 16 subnets (for example), each having 14 hosts on a LAN segment (there are not 16 devices allowed, because the high and low subnet address should not be assigned to hosts). But consider an ISP that has been assigned a Class A address such as 10.0.0.0. There is no possible way that the ISP wants a single "network" without one single router that would cover 16,777,216 hosts. The ISP would most likely want to subnet the address space many times over and assign pieces of this subnetted Class A address to its many customers. Because this is a *logical* division of the address space, not a physical division, all other ISPs need to know is, say, "here's a packet for 10.234.75.0—send it over to that ISP with the Class A space." Only the ISP's internal routers would need to know what to do with the packets from other ISPs in more detail—all based on the subnet masks used.

An important concept in Classful IP addressing is the *major network*. When anything but the natural Class A, B, or C subnet mask is applied to the major network, the result is a number of subnets. For example, the major network for a network of 172.16.55.0 with a mask or 255.255.255.0 is 172.16.0.0. No subnet mask need be specified for a classful major network, because the natural mask is always assumed unless otherwise given. The major network 172.16.0.0 address space has been *subnetted* to 172.16.55.0 with mask 255.255.255.0.

Subnets are not overly complicated, but conceptualizing what they are can be tricky at first. This is especially true when subnetting Class A or Class B addresses. For example, suppose the subnet mask for a Class B network is 255.255.224.0. How many subnets does this subnet mask yield and how many hosts can be allocated on each subnet? In the third byte, the first 3 bits are turned on for the mask (224 = 192 + 64 + 32). Three masked bits give eight subnets, although the first and last subnet is not useful for host addresses. This is because the all zero-bits and all one-bits 255 special addresses rules apply to subnet bits also! So there are technically six subnets available for host addresses, subnet 000 and 111 being unavailable for assignment.

How many hosts on the subnets? There are now not 16 bits for the host address, as in a normal Class B address, but only 13 bits available, since 3 bits were used by the subnet mask. Thirteen bits gives 8,192 possible hosts for each subnet. However, the first and last addresses in each subnet are not available for assignment to a host (the 0 and 255 rule yet again), so there are 8,190 hosts supported on each Class B subnet.

Only six networks with 8,190 hosts might be useful for some ISPs with a Class B address, but that's still only a handful of customers and a lot of hosts per customer. Maybe a tighter subnet mask would help. Consider subnet mask 255.255.240.0 for the same Class B address. Now the subnets are 14 ($2^4 - 2 = 14$) and the hosts on each are 4094 ($2^{12} - 2 = 4094$). A subnet mask of 255.255.248.0 gives 30 subnets and 2,046 hosts on each, a subnet mask of 255.255.252 gives 62 subnets and 1,022 hosts on each, a subnet mask of 255.255.254.0 gives 126 subnets with 510 hosts on each, and so on. The ISP will have to strike a balance between number of subnets and number of hosts if the subnet mask is to be the same all over the network.

A related subnet issue is determining exactly what the subnet address (all zero-bits after the mask) and broadcast address (all one-bits after the mask) are for a given IP address and subnet mask. This can be tricky because subnet masks do not always fall on neat byte boundaries as classful addresses do. An IP address like 172.30.0.128 might not look like network-itself address that cannot be assigned to a host, but it might be.

Consider a Class B address such as 172.17.0.126 with a subnet mask of 255.255.255.192. Is this IP address available for host assignment on this subnet, and just what is the subnet and broadcast address for this subnet? What range of host addresses can be assigned to this subnet? These types of questions come up at ISPs all the time.

There are people who can do this type of calculation in their heads. For the rest of us, the first thing to do is to mask out the network portion of the IP address with the subnet mask by writing down the bits. Then the subnet portion of the address can be simply marked off. Next, forming the subnet and broadcast address for the subnet can be easily done by setting the rest of the bits in the address (the host bits) first to all zero-bits and then to all one-bits. The resulting address range forms the limits of the subnet.

To illustrate, Figure 4.4 shows how to derive these answers for Class B IP address 172.17.0.126 and subnet mask 255.255.255.192.

Exercises like these are important because when subnetting the IP address space, host addresses must be carefully assigned to the proper subnets (router interface). This concern is especially acute with regard to classful IP addresses. Having a *discontinuous* major network that has been subnetted so that part of the space is reached through one interface of the router (10.4.0.0 over here . . .) and the other part of the subnetted major network is reached through another interface (10.5.0.0 over there . . .) can be a problem. Care must be taken in how the router deals with the subnets and the masks that establish them. This aspect of subnets is discussed again in the section *VLSM and the Longest-Match Rule*, coming up in the chapter. Figure 4.5 shows subnetting applied to a Class A address. Now there are 254 subnets (two less than expected at first) each with 65,534 hosts (again two less) in network 10.0.0.0 when the subnet mask is 255.255.0.0.

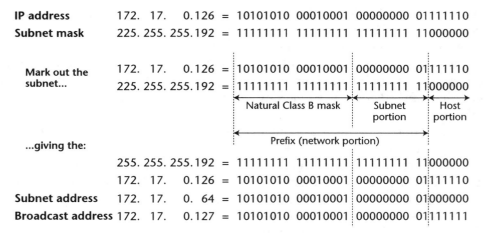

**Valid host address range on subnet 172.17.0.64 =
172.17.0.65 through 172.17.0.126 (62 hosts)**

Figure 4.4 Finding a subnet address, broadcast address, and host range.

The figure introduces a new notation for subnet masking. This is the / (forward slash). Why is it necessary to write out the subnet mask in dotted decimal as if the mask were somehow separate from the IP address to which the mask applies? Subnet masks have no meaning on their own. So the slash notation, introduced with CIDR, ties the subnet mask concisely right to the IP address the mask applies to. So IP address 10.0.0.1 with a subnet mask of 255.255.0.0 is the same as writing 10.0.0.1/16. (Presumably, reverse masking to indicate the *host* bits could be indicated with a backslash as 10.0.0.1\16.)

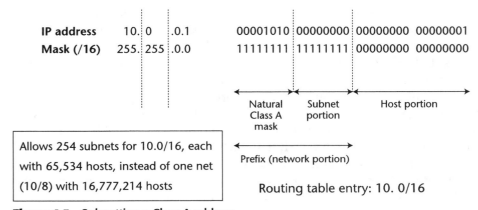

Figure 4.5 Subnetting a Class A address.

An IP address like 192.168.5.14/32 is a host address. Every IP address has a *slash notation*, whether or not the subnet mask slash is explicit. By convention, the absence of a subnet mask means a host address (/32). Classful IP addresses have default slash notations of 10.0.0.0/8, 172.16.0.0/16, and 192.168.0.0/24. But because this notation is primarily used for classless IP addresses, this section on classful IP address subnetting has not used the slash notation at all until now.

Slash notation sometimes is abbreviated even further. Why write 10.0.0.0/8 when you can write 10/8 with a lot less effort? If the rest of the bits are zero-bits, just ignore them. Although fairly common, this abbreviated notation will not be used consistently in this book. So 192.168.14.0 with a subnet mask of 255.255.255.0 is just as likely to appear as 192.168.14.0/24 as it is to appear as 192.168.14/24. Both mean the same thing.

Subnetting was originally introduced to allow the more flexible use of routers in LAN environments, but subnetting also allows an ISP to make more flexible use of former Class A and Class B address spaces. However, classful IP address spaces are officially a thing of the past. Classful addresses have given way to CIDR and VLSM. CIDR came first, so we'll next look at the opposite of subnetting: *supernetting* with CIDR.

Classless Interdomain Routing (CIDR)

Classless interdomain routing was an immediate answer to a couple of problems: first, the impending exhaustion of IP Class A and Class B address space, and second, the rapid and large increase required in routing tables to handle the many Class C addresses required to satisfy Web-hungry users.

Classful addresses are fine in theory, but in practice they leave a lot to be desired. One of the biggest concerns is the limited number of large networks that can exist with classful IP addresses. Only about 16,000 total LANs (networks) can be linked to the Internet in the whole world with Class A and Class B addresses. These networks can have a lot of hosts, but that's not the way that routers work to connect clients and servers. By 1992 the inevitable exhaustion of the classful IP address space was on everyone's mind. Already, the Internet had about 8,500 routes, and projections put the number of routes by 1995 at 80,000 routes. That increase in the number of networks did not happen; growth leveled out because of to the combined effects of CIDR and related IP addressing schemes such as the Dynamic Host Configuration Protocol (DHCP) and Network Address Translation (NAT). But at the time, people were worried.

Class C addresses continued to be the only classful addresses routinely handed out to ISPs and others. But Class C IP addresses could only have 254 hosts per network, which boiled down to a LAN segment on a site router's interface. Now, the "real" IP address space consists only of contiguous bits. This just means that the 32 bits of the IP address have no real built-in concept of classes or anything else. It was the default class mask that determined the whole class structure. Move the mask setting the network/host boundary to the left in a major Class A, B, or C IP address, and the result was subnetting. CIDR invented a way to move the network/host boundary to the *right*, and the result was *supernetting*.

With CIDR, a block of *contiguous* (assigned in a group, with no networks within the range assigned to anyone else) IP Class C addresses could be given to a service provider or large customer and allow them to configure IP networks with anywhere from a few hosts up to 16,384 hosts. The number of contiguous Class C addresses needed was determined by a simple count of the number of host addresses required. This CIDR plan is shown in Table 4.4.

CIDR changed the terminology that applied to the IP address space. Routes to IP networks were now represented by *prefixes*. A prefix consisted of the IP network address ending in zeros, followed by a slash (/), and ending with an indication of how many of the leftmost contiguous bits in the address are part of the network mask that should be applied to the address for routing purposes. For example, before CIDR, the Class C address 192.168.64.0 would ordinarily have a mask of 255.255.255.0 applied to it. Subnetting could add bits to this major network mask, but only in the fixed patterns and values outlined in the previous section. CIDR supernetting enabled a "CIDR-ized" network address to be represented as 192.168.64.0/18, and that was all the information needed. Sometimes this was abbreviated even further to just 192.168.64/18, but the two forms are equivalent. The notation just means that a subnet mask 18 bits long should be applied to 192.168.64.0. This notation is the same as writing "192.168.64.0 with mask 255.255.192.0" but in much more compact form.

Table 4.4   Grouping Contiguous Class C Addresses under CIDR

IF YOU NEED...	REGISTRY WILL GIVE YOU...
Fewer than 256 addresses	1 Class C network
Fewer than 512 but more than 256 addresses	2 contiguous Class C networks
Fewer than 1,024 but more than 512 addresses	4 contiguous Class C networks
Fewer than 2,048 but more than 1,024 addresses	8 contiguous Class C networks
Fewer than 4,096 but more than 2,048 addresses	16 contiguous Class C networks
Fewer than 8,192 but more than 4,096 addresses	32 contiguous Class C networks
Fewer than 16,384 but more than 8,192 addresses	64 contiguous Class C networks

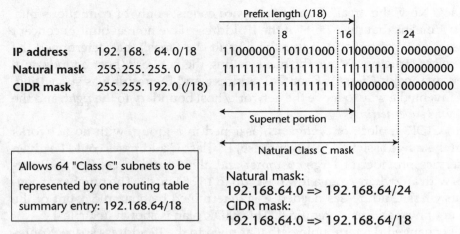

Prefix length (/18)

		8	16	24
IP address	192.168. 64.0/18	11000000	10101000	01000000	00000000
Natural mask	255.255.255. 0	11111111	11111111	11111111	00000000
CIDR mask	255.255.192.0 (/18)	11111111	11111111	11000000	00000000

Supernet portion

Natural Class C mask

Allows 64 "Class C" subnets to be represented by one routing table summary entry: 192.168.64/18

Natural mask:
192.168.64.0 => 192.168.64/24
CIDR mask:
192.168.64.0 => 192.168.64/18

Figure 4.6   CIDR supernet addressing.

Even when CIDR was used, all bits after the IP network address had to be zero, of course. That aspect of IP addressing did not change. So 192.168.64.0/18 was a valid IP network address, but 192.168.64.0/17 was not. This aspect of CIDR is shown in Figure 4.6. The IP network 192.168.64.0/18 is a CIDR super-net because the mask contained fewer bits than the natural mask that would be applied to the address under classful IP addressing.

CIDR allowed for the creation of a network such as 192.168.64.0/18 with 16,384 hosts (14 bits remain for the host portion of the 192.168.64.0 network) instead of requiring 64 separate IP network addresses to be assigned and con-figured. But CIDR did more than allow the grouping of contiguous Class C addresses into bigger networks than formerly possible. Once the principle of supernetting was established, CIDR allowed for the *aggregation* of all of the pos-sible IP addresses under the specified prefix into this one compact notation.

Aggregation just means that instead of having 64 routing table entries to rep-resent the Class C addresses that comprised network 192.168.64.0/18, this entire group of 64,000 or so hosts could be reached with a single routing table entry. Of course, this required that all of the host addresses under this 192.168.64.0/18 *aggregate* be handed out and used correctly, but this was not an unreasonable expectation because the CIDR block was assigned to a single entity such as an ISP. Sometimes the term *route summarization* is used in the same sense as aggregation, and in fact, most people use the terms *aggregation* and *summarization* interchangeably. To add to the confusion, there are the terms *CIDR block* and *supernet* to consider. Technically, CIDR blocks introduced the <prefix/length> notation, supernets have prefixes shorter than the natural mask, and aggregates are used to represent a summary of an IP address space. In this book, all of these terms basically mean exactly the same thing: prefix notation with a slash.

Keep in mind that even though the route to 192.168.64.0/18 can be advertised to another router as a single entity and routing table entry, this does not necessarily mean that all 64,000 hosts that make up network 192.168.64.0/18 are really on a LAN attached to a single router. More specific routes to other networks can still be spread around many routers and many interfaces. As long as the routing protocols know what to advertise where (the major role of routing policy), there should be no confusion (resulting in routing loops or black holes) among the routers.

So a router in another AS can reach all of the 64,000 or so hosts on network 192.168.64.0/18 over a single interface. But once closer to the destination, the routers in the AS that have assigned the 192.168.64.0/18 address space can easily distribute the arriving traffic based on more specific routing information. The more general aggregate routing table entries can coexist with the more specific routing table entries and all will be well. This aggregate/specific concept is shown in Figure 4.7. An informal representation of the routing table information is shown in the figure for some of the routers.

But wait a minute. How does Router C know that an IP packet addressed to, for example, a Web site at IP address 192.168.113.245 should go to Router F and not somewhere else? What makes the routing table in Router B smart enough to know that the path to 192.168.96.0/19 is to be ignored for this particular packet? How does a packet arriving at Router B for host 192.168.97.45 make its way to Router E?

More than CIDR was required to make routers properly route when multiple routing table entries seem to be attractive as a next hop for individual packets to a host. What was needed was VLSM and the *longest-match rule*.

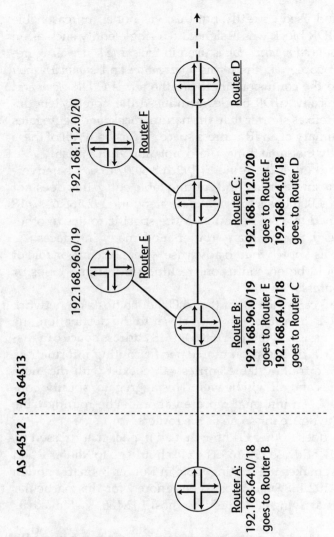

Figure 4.7 Aggregate and more specific IP addresses.

VLSM and the Longest-Match Rule

The term *variable-length subnet masking* just means that one classless network (such as 192.168.64.0/18) can be configured with different-length subnet masks. This can be done on different routers or even on the same router. It just depends on what the router is required to do with the address space. Without VLSM, only one subnet mask could ever be applied to an entire network, and 192.168.64.0/18 could only have its 64,000 hosts reachable through a single router interface. If there were more subnets, there would be fewer hosts on each. This trade-off between routes (networks) and hosts might be okay, but usually more flexibility of assigned IP address space is required by ISPs. VLSM permits this flexibility or IP address space configuration.

Consider a simple example of VLSM in action on a single router. The network administrator of the router has been assigned a traditional Class C IP network address of 192.168.11.0 to divide into three subnets. But the three subnets (LANs) on the three router interfaces are of different sizes. One subnet needs 100 hosts, another requires 50 hosts, and so does the third subnet. In theory, regular subnetting should work, since there are only 200 hosts needed and a Class C address provides 254 host addresses (192.168.11.1 through 192.168.11.254). However, VLSM is needed to do this properly.

It is necessary because the natural mask for a Class C network is 255.255.255.0. Any Class C subnet mask must have contiguous bits set to 1 beyond this 24-bit mask. (Originally, subnet masks were not required to use contiguous bits, which made life very interesting for routers. Now all subnet masks must use contiguous bits from left to right.) Table 4.5 shows the only possible subnets possible for a Class C address. A 32-bit mask is the same as a host address, and 31-bit masks are not generally useful, since the space leaves no room for multiple devices of a "network." (There are, however, special cases where /31 masks are used.)

Nowadays the 255.255.255.252 or /30 mask is commonly used on point-to-point links between routers. This leaves only two IP addresses for each end of the link, and "masking down tight" leaves plenty of other network addresses for other router interfaces on the network. Why assign a subnet with 62 or 126 hosts to a link that can only have two ends?

A lot of routers still use unnumbered interfaces for point-to-point links. Why assign an IP address to such a link at all when the packets and frames on the link do not rely on link IP addressing for delivery across the link in any way? The packets between routers have the client or server (host) source/ destination addresses and the frames on point-to-point links, unlike LANs, have addresses totally independent of IP addressing. There is nowhere for the packet to go to or come from but the other end of the link. Only LANs and *multipoint* types of router interfaces really need IP addresses. However, placing IP addresses on all router interfaces do make using tasks like diagnostic pings and traceroutes easier, and routing protocols today more or less expect IP addresses on all interfaces.

Before VLSM came along, the same mask had to be applied to an IP address across the entire network. So this address could form two subnets with 126 hosts each (192.168.11.0/25), or four subnets with 62 hosts each (192.168.11.0/26), but not the three subnets with the number of hosts needed. With VLSM, subnets do not have to be of equal size everywhere. Since subnets are only locally meaningful, their meaning can change from one interface and LAN segment to another.

VLSM handles the need for variable-sized subnets easily, as is shown in Figure 4.8. The mask 255.255.255.128 (192.168.11.0/25) is configured on the first interface, EN0. This allows the assignment of host addresses 192.168.11.1 through 192.168.11.126 (126 hosts) on this LAN segment. The mask 192.168.11.192 (192.168.11.0/26) is configured on interface EN1, allowing host addresses 192.168.11.129 through 192.168.11.190 (62 hosts) on this LAN segment. Finally, the same mask is applied to the third interface, allowing host addresses 192.168.11.193 through 192.168.11.254 (62 hosts) on the LAN.

Table 4.5 Possible Class C Subnets

LAST OCTET OF MASK	BINARY	NUMBER OF SUBNETS	HOSTS PER SUBNET (EXCLUDES SPECIAL ADDRESSES)
128 (/25)	1000 0000	2	126
192 (/26)	1100 0000	4	62
224 (/27)	1110 0000	8	30
240 (/28)	1111 0000	16	14
248 (/29)	1111 1000	32	6
252 (/30)	1111 1100	64	2

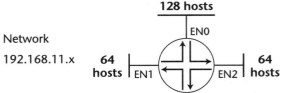

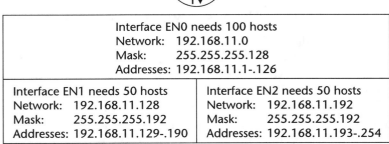

Figure 4.8 Using VLSM.

Masking with VLSM takes some getting used to. At least classful masks 255.255.255.128 and 255.255.255.192 look different enough to make people notice. VLSM creates networks like 192.168.11.0/24 and 192.168.11.0/25 that look almost the same but are distinct networks and IP address spaces. Now, every host on more specific network 192.168.11.0/25 is also covered under the more general aggregate prefix 192.168.11.0/24, but no host on network 192.168.11.128/25 is included in address space 192.168.11.0/25. Part of the confusion comes from the fact that including 25 bits in an IP prefix makes the address in the last byte 128, not 1. Including 26 bits makes the last byte 192, not 3, and so on.

The Longest-Match Rule

VLSM provides an important clue for understanding how routers can mix and match prefixes and differing lengths in a routing table and still route packets to the correct next hop. Suppose a router has two entries in a routing table, based on the simple network introduced in Figure 4.7. Look at a simplified view of the routing table on Router B, along with the first 24 bits of the bit configuration of the two prefixes:

PREFIX	PREFIX IN BITS	NEXT- HOP ROUTER
192.168.64.0/18	Router C	11000000 10101000 01/ 000000
192.168.96.0/19	Router E	11000000 10101000 011/ 00000

A slash and a space marks the division between the prefix and the host portion of the address, based on the subnet mask bits given. What happens when a packet with a destination address of 192.168.97.45 arrives from Router A? The 32-bit destination address in bits is as follows:

DESTINATION ADDRESS	ADDRESS IN BITS
192.168.97.45	**11000000 10101000 0110**001 00101101

No subnet mask is associated with a host address. The bits that are important for this discussion are marked in **bold**. Looking at the simplified routing table, it would seem that either entry is a potential match for the destination address. In fact, the first 18 bits are exactly the same. But the nineteenth bit is a one-bit in the routing table entry for 192.168.96.0/19 and so is the nineteenth bit in the destination address 192.168.97.45. This makes the /19 entry the *longest match* for the destination address, and the packet is forwarded to Router E. The rest of the bits represent the host of the 192.168.96.0/19 network and are used for local delivery of the packet on Router E.

The longest-match rule is also often called the *best match* or the *more specific route* for a given destination IP address. But whatever it is called, the point is the same: The longest-match next hop is always used in favor of a potential, but shorter-match, next hop. This is how VLSM works. What about a packet to a host at 192.168.90.166 arriving at Router B? Now the destination address in bits is as follows:

DESTINATION ADDRESS	ADDRESS IN BITS
192.168.90.166	**11000000 10101000 010**11010 10100110

This time the nineteenth bit is a zero-bit, so the 192.168.96.0/19 next hop is *not* the longest match for the destination. But the first 18 bits *do* match the entry for 192.168.64.0/18, and the packet is sent on to Router C. The same longest-match rules apply at each router, and VLSM requires longest-match rules to allow the flexible use of subnet masks required on the Internet today.

Radix Tree Representation

The use of VLSM complicates the IP address space considerably. It is not always obvious what the longest match will be for a given host address when there are several possibilities closely sharing the IP prefix space. A common way to visualize the IP address space for the purpose of longest matches is to use the *radix tree* representation of the IP address space. Also known as a *binary tree*, the radix tree is a way to compactly visualize the relationships between prefix with similar bases addresses but different subnet mask lengths.

Think of the entire 32-bit IP address space as an underground parking garage with 32 levels. (IP addresses 32 bits long are host addresses, and /31 masks are not generally useful for networking, but they still count.) The ground-level entry point to the Radix Parking Garage is level 0 and is written as /0. The first parking level is /1, the next /2, all the way down to the very bottom at /32. Not only are the levels labeled with slashes, but the Radix Garage has very different numbers of parking spaces at each parking level. The entrance level (/0) has really no place to park at all, the first parking level (/1) has two spaces, the second level (/2) has four, and so on. So all together, there are a *lot* of spaces in the garage. Every one of them is a potential IP network address and prefix.

The root of the radix tree is 0/0 or 0.0.0.0/0. This is the *default* IP network address, in the sense that *anything* is a longer match than 0/0 for a destination IP address. The 0/0 address is not really a place to "park" packets in a real next hop, and it is often called the *route of last resort*. The router that forms the next hop for the default routing table entry is often called the *gateway of last resort*. This just means that if 0/0 happens to be the longest match for a packet's destination address, this router is the next hop. But since this really means "if you don't know what else to do with this packet, send it here," the term *last resort* is a very good one. Routing protocols usually *never* advertise their default routes to other routers unless they are very closely related, because it is easy to form routing loops and black holes ("Send it to the default here!" "No! Send it back!"). Default routes have local significance only, like calling one person in the world "Mom." Siblings call the same person "Mom," but most people in the world have their own "Mom." "Send this packet to Mom" means something different to most people, but it is a real person nonetheless.

At the 0/0 root, all 32 bits of the IP address are zero-bits, and *none* of them are network address bits. That's what 0/0 means. At the first level (/1), only the first bit of the IP address is part of the prefix. This bit can obviously be only either a zero-bit or a one-bit, so the two possible IP network address prefixes at level /1 are 0.0.0.0/1 and 128.0.0.0/1 (the first bit position in the first byte has a value of 128 decimal). These two "parking spaces" can also be written as 0/1 and 128/1.

Note than IP address prefixes 0.0.0.0/0 and 0.0.0.0/1 are two different networks and prefixes. If both are present in a routing table with two different next hops, the longest match will always be 0.0.0.0/1 and not 0.0.0.0/0, as long as the first bit of the packet destination address is a 0 bit and there are no longer matches in the routing table (not likely, but this is only an example).

At the next level (/2), the second bit of the 32-bit IP address is included in the mask. Since each of the network prefixes at level /1 can have either a zero-bit or a one-bit in the second position, there are now *four* entries at the /2 level of the tree. The four entries are 0.0.0.0/2 (00 in the first two bits of the IP address), 64.0.0.0/2 (01 in the first two bits of the IP address), 128.0.0.0/2 (10 in the first two bits of the IP address), and 192.0.0.0/2 (11 in the first two bits of the IP address). The same logic applies to every level of the Radix Parking Garage.

All prefixes at the first three levels of the IP radix tree are shown in Figure 4.9. A selected portion of the tree, much farther down, is also shown applied to the IP address space introduced in Figure 4.7.

The radix tree makes it obvious now that prefix 192.168.64.0/18 is not the same as prefix 192.168.64.0/19. The radix tree also makes it easier to see just what specific IP addresses fall under a particular aggregate. To be part of the aggregate space, the prefix must fall under the radix tree whose root is the point that represents the aggregate. So prefix 192.168.112.0/20 is a more specific route of the aggregate 192.168.96.0/19, but not a more specific route of the aggregate 192.168.64.0/19. The prefix 192.168.112.0/20 is, however, a more specific prefix under 192.168.64.0/18. It all depends on position in the tree.

Aggregates are useful to cut down on the size of the routing tables in routers and the number of routing updates that need to be distributed among routers on the Internet. This use of aggregates is shown in Figure 4.10. Of course, what addresses should be aggregated (summarized) and advertised is an important aspect of routing policy.

This concept of aggregation is very important when the specific routes under a particular aggregate are *suppressed* and not sent as part of a routing protocol's advertisements to other routers. When aggregates are not properly configured and controlled with routing policies, packets can wander around the Internet and never reach their proper destination.

Aggregation

Be aware that concepts like CIDR, VLSM, and aggregation do not work in isolation to solve problems with regard to classful IP addresses. All of these ideas work together in the router and on the network so that packets are always making progress one router at a time toward the one router in the world that has that particular network directly configured on an interface. (Actually, there can be more than one router physically attached to a particular network, but only one will be the *designated router* as far as the Internet is concerned.)

Routing protocols that could deal with only classful IP addresses struggled with aggregation. For example, the original RIP (RIPv1) did not exchange address masks along with routing information, so either the natural masks for

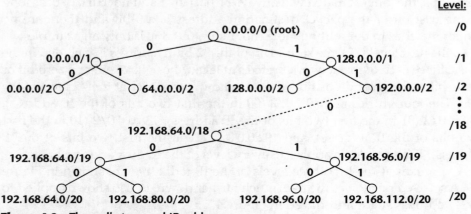

Figure 4.9 The radix tree and IP addresses.

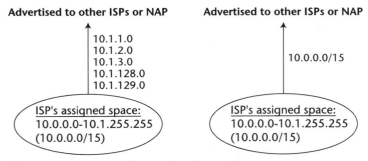

Figure 4.10 Aggregation and routing policy.

each route had to be applied or subnets had to be defined locally on each and every router that needed to know about the subnet. This classful operation severely limited the location and methods that ISPs could use to distribute their IP address spaces for LANs and links.

ISPs and corporations found classful addressing extremely confining because classful routing protocols always perform route aggregation or summarization on major network class boundaries. So a packet to 10.100.17.66 will always be forwarded to the next hop for network 10.0.0.0, because the natural mask for a Class A network is always 255.0.0.0. All 16 million or so potential hosts on the 10.0.0.0 network better be reachable through that same router interface. It made no sense to assign a 10.0.0.0 address to a point-to-point link between routers, because the other 16 million addresses were now totally useless.

If different pieces of a major Class A, B, or C network were separated by another major network, this resulted in a situation called *discontiguous major subnets*. With classful addressing, aggregation was a real problem when discontiguous major subnets were configured. The reason for this problem is shown in Figure 4.11.

The three routers in the figure, Router A, Router B, and Router C, are all attached to the same LAN. The network administrator of Router A has configured network 172.20.29.0/24 (a subnetted Class B address) on another interface, and the network administrator of Router C has configured network 172.20.78.0/24 (another subnetted Class B address) on another interface.

The problem is that classful routing protocols will only aggregate subnetted classful addresses into major network addresses. So both Router A and Router C have no choice but to advertise a route to 172.20.0.0 to Router B. Poor router B learns about 172.20.0.0 from two different interfaces, both with the exact same information: The network is directly connected to a router one hop away. Router B will innocently assume that either Router A or Router C can be used to forward packets to network 172.20.0.0 and usually simply pick one router or the other as the active next hop.

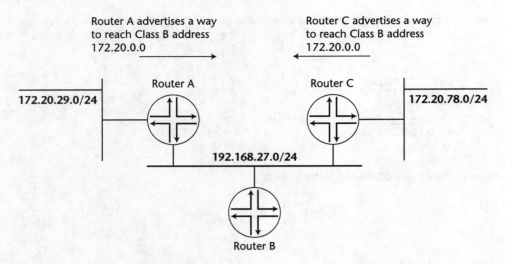

Figure 4.11 Classful routing and discontiguous major networks.

The solution to the discontiguous subnet situation is to use a routing proto-col that understands classless routing, or to make sure subnets are contiguous. Because continuous subnets are so limiting, network administrators faced with this problem will use newer routing protocols that distribute the subnet masks right along with the route information. The way that classless routing protocols handle aggregate prefix distribution is shown in Figure 4.12.

Now the mask is part of the routing information and all is well. It should be noted that it is possible to have different subnet masks lengths on each of the subnets. For example, Router A could be using 172.20.29.0/24 and Router C could be using 172.20.78.0/20. The longest-match rule takes care of any pack-ets addressed to either address space.

Aggregates on the Internet

Just because classless routing protocols with VLSM are in use does not mean that aggregation is now a simple or painless activity. On the Internet, aggre-gation is used still used to cut down the size of routing tables and minimize the amount of routing information distributed, but this requires careful allo-cation of the ISP's address space. Figure 4.13 shows how the edge routers of an ISP usually employed aggregate addresses to advertise into the ISP core of backbone routers.

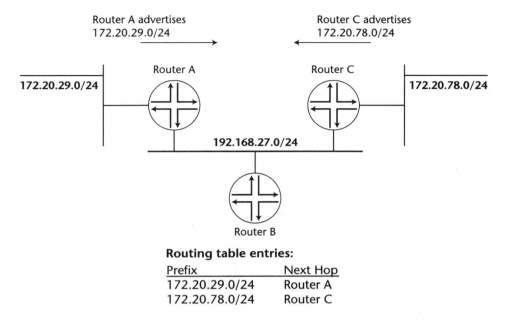

Routing table entries:

Prefix	Next Hop
172.20.29.0/24	Router A
172.20.78.0/24	Router C

Figure 4.12   Classless routing and aggregate prefix distribution.

The choice of IP addresses used in a real ISP network should be anything but haphazard. You should plan carefully if you want to make sure that none of the specifics for the 172.18.0.0/16 prefix end up linked to Router I, for example. But even if it were necessary to assign more-specific IP addresses covered under an aggregate to a router other than one directly attached to the backbone router, the longest-match rule would take care of the exception. Routine assignment of specifics without regard to aggregation on the backbone will not lead to ambiguous routing in and of itself, but such a practice will increase the size of the routing table and the amount of routing information that needs to be maintained by the routing protocols.

Consider the position of network 172.18.4.0/24 in Figure 4.13. This network is attached to Router A, but the aggregate IP address 172.18.0.0/16 is advertised into the core by Router D. A portion of what Router C's routing table would look like is shown in Table 4.6.

The term *self* in the table just means that this network is directly connected to Router C, while the other networks are more than one hop away through the next-hop router in the table. The longest-match rule means that a packet to 172.18.4.5 goes to Router A (as it should) instead of Router D. Even if a routing policy suppresses advertisements of specifics under 172.21.0.0/16, this suppression will not apply to route 172.18.4.0/24, because 172.18.4.0/24 is not under the binary tree rooted at 172.21.0.0/16.

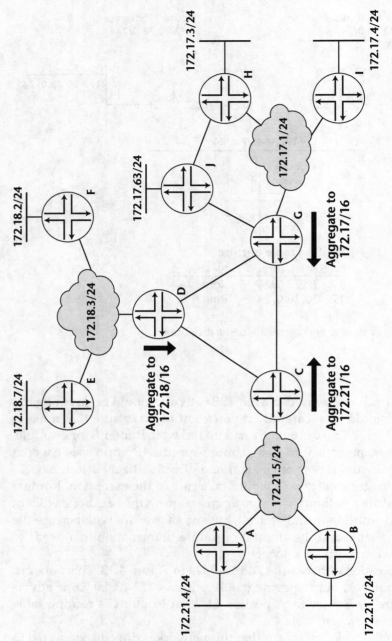

Figure 4.13   Aggregation to the backbone.

Table 4.6   Router C's Routing Table (Portion)

PREFIX	NEXT-HOP ROUTER
172.17.0.0/16	Router G
172.18.0.0/16	Router D
172.18.4.0/24	Router A
172.19.7.0/24	Router D
172.21.5.0/24	Self
172.21.6.0/24	Router B

Aggregation on the Internet occurs repeatedly as routers seek to minimize their routing table size and update information volume. The prefixes that represent the address spaces assigned to ISPs can therefore become shorter and shorter as the information about the address space flows toward the Internet core of exchange points. This effect is shown in Figure 4.14. The left-hand side of the figure shows route distribution without aggregation, and the right-hand side of the figure shows the effects of repeated aggregation as routing information flows toward the heart of the Internet.

In each case, the lowest level represents the address spaces assigned to the ISP's customers. Each ISP's potential address space is shown, with the aggregate that will be used to represent the space when it is advertised outside of the AS.

Care is needed when advertising aggregate routes between ISPs, especially when an ISP uses a default route (0/0) for destinations that are no longer reachable through a longer match because of a failed link or router (unreachable destinations are not represented by entries in the routing table). If the longest match is now the default, the result could be a routing loop (traffic shuttled back and forth endlessly) or a black hole (packets to unreachable destinations are discarded). Both of these situations are shown in Figure 4.15.

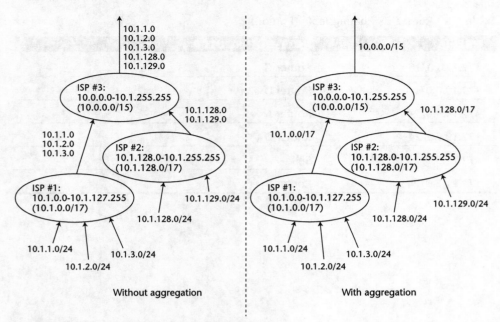

Figure 4.14   Repeated aggregation.

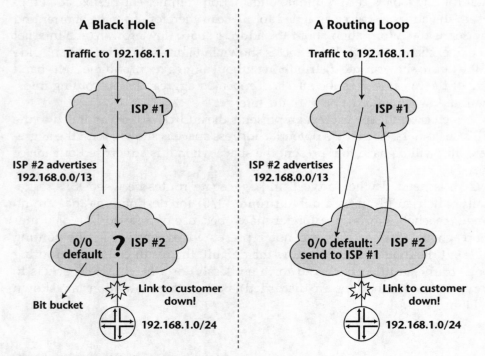

Figure 4.15   Black holes and routing loops.

On the left-hand side of the figure, ISP 2 has defined a 0/0 default route when there is no longer a match for a route in a router's routing table. The next hop for packets to such a route is to simply discard the packet, since there can be no real destination for packets sent to 0.0.0.0 addresses. Network 192.168.1.0/24 is a customer network of ISP 2, and this fact is advertised to ISP 1 as the aggregate 192.168.0.0/13. The black hole occurs when the link from ISP 2 to the customer is down. The route to the more specific 192.168.1.0/24 network now disappears from the routing table. When packets to a host at 192.168.1.1 (for example) arrive from ISP 1, the default route, which is now the longest match, simply discards the packets (in some cases, an ICMP message is returned to the sender, but this does not make the destination any more reachable than it would be without the ICMP message).

A routing loop is shown on the right-hand side of the figure. Again, the only link to the customer 192.168.1.0/24 network has failed. In this case, the 0/0 default points to a real next hop, but this time the next hop is a router in ISP 1's network. ISP 1's router will just loop the packet back to ISP 2, and so on, until the TTL on the packet expires and an ICMP message is sent back to the source. In real routing loops, the loop is not always closed so quickly; packets tend to wander around an ISP network until they either find their way back to the ISP that forwarded them or the TTL expires. In either case, the result is bad. (There can be other causes of routing loops besides default routes; this is just one example.)

Aggregation is often desirable for a router, but it is not magic. There are limits to aggregation just as there are limits that apply to almost anything in networking. For instance, one of the consequences of the longest-match rule is that destinations, whether routing domains such as ASs or customers, connected to multiple other routing domains must always be explicitly announced and advertised in their most specific (nonaggregated) form and should *never* be aggregated along with other addresses.

Figure 4.16 shows why. Here, a host (192.168.1.10) is reachable through both Routing Domain 1 and Routing Domain 2 (the routing domains can be an AS or a complete ISP cloud; the point is the same). However, the host is a customer of the ISP running Routing Domain 1, so all traffic to 192.168.1.10 should flow through Routing Domain 1 unless there is a problem. Routing Domain 2 can always be used, but only as a last resort to reach the host. The aggregate advertisements that these routing domains make to Routing Domain 3, which is directly connected to them both, are shown in the figure.

Note that Routing Domain 1, the preferred path for traffic to the host at 192.168.1.10, advertises 192.168.1.0/24, which is the natural mask for formerly classful addresses in the 192.168.0.0 address space. In contrast, Routing Domain 2 has aggregated the host network into a single advertisement for 192.168.0.0/16. The result is that traffic to 192.168.1.10 follows the longest-match path to Routing Domain 1.

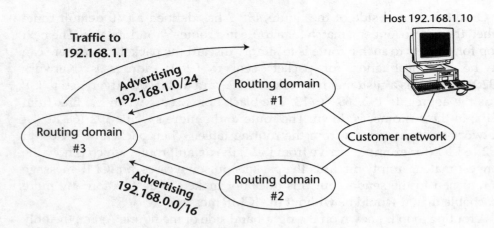

Figure 4.16 Aggregates and longest matches.

Be aware that there are circumstances where *both* routing domains might advertise the /24 route and the /16 aggregate to Routing Domain 3. For example, the owner of the host network might well be a customer of the two ISPs running Routing Domains 1 and 2, or the two routing domains could belong to the same ISP. In either case, the routers in Routing Domain 3 would follow rules other than the longest-match rules to determine the next hop to the host. Some form of *load balancing* or *traffic sharing* could even be used in Routing Domain 3 to try to distribute packets to the host fairly and avoid overwhelming either of the two routing domains.

Aggregates and Routing Policy

There are many reasons that the use of aggregates on the Internet requires careful consideration and the use of a routing policy. The decision to aggregate, what to aggregate, and whether to also advertise the specifics under the aggregated range is a crucial one that every ISP (and even customers with multiple routers) must face. The increased use of NAT and DHCP just complicates the issue, since the IP address space on a customer network might have little to do with the routes *to* the customer network actually advertised across the Internet. The issue used to be even more complicated before RFC 2008 encouraged customers changing ISPs to always renumber their IP addresses (under the *address lending* policy). No customers relished that idea, so before RFC 2008 it was not unusual for a new ISP to advertise more specific routes for a piece of the old ISP's address space. The longest-match rule made sure that traffic found its way to the new ISP.

Other routing polices might be needed when a customer connects to two different ISPs. Since the customer can be reached through both ISPs but presumably has only one IP address space, how should the customer's network best be reached over the Internet? There are some companies that have actually started to advertise their routes to *both* ISPs and let routes point where they will. Few ISPs like this idea, and there is always a routing policy to help the ISPs control their routes.

Generally, it is never a good idea for an ISP to aggregate another ISP's addresses. Otherwise, the situation shown in Figure 4.17 might result.

In the figure, a NAP receives aggregate routes from two national (Tier 1) ISPs. The two national ISPs in turn have several smaller ISPs as customers, and often these customers are linked to both national ISPs. The figure shows the IP addresses used and advertised by each ISP, both as an aggregate and as the real address space assigned to the ISP's customers.

Note that at the NAP, traffic to Small ISP 3 network 10.24.17.0 is sent to National ISP 2 instead of the expected National ISP 1 (all traffic to Small ISP 3 has to flow through National ISP 1 anyway). The problem is that National ISP 2 has chosen to advertise all its reachable addresses as the two aggregates 10.32.0.0/13 and 10.24.0.0/18. National ISP 1 is fine: Every other ISP reachable through National ISP 1 is represented by more specific addresses under 10.24.0.0/13. But National ISP 2 is inadvertently including Small ISP 3's 10.24.16.0/21 aggregate under National ISP 2's 10.24.0.0/18 umbrella. Since the /18 prefix is a longer match than National ISP 1's /13 prefix, all traffic to

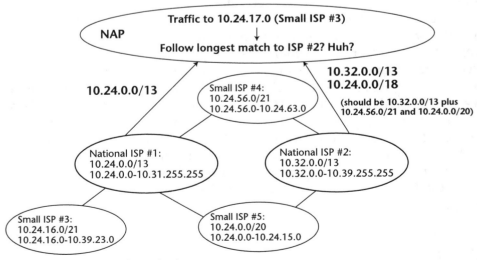

Figure 4.17 Aggregating other's routes.

Small ISP 3 goes through National ISP 2. From there, the transit traffic has no choice but to flow through either Small ISP 4 or Small ISP 5 to get to National ISP 1 if a routing loop is to be avoided (that is, National ISP 2 should *never* send the traffic back to the NAP). This is hardly a good situation for any of the ISPs, least of all Small ISP 4 and 5.

All would be well if National ISP 2 advertised as aggregates 10.32.0.0/13 (this is fine) and 10.24.56.0/21 (for Small ISP 4) and 10.24.0.0/24 (for Small ISP 5). In this case, National ISP 2 should not be aggregating other ISP's routes.

There are two possible exceptions to the "do not aggregate other ISP's routes" rule. The first is when one address space is a complete subnet of the proposed aggregate. The second is when two ISPs are peers and mutually agree just how to represent the aggregates exchanged with other ISPs.

IPv6 Prefixes

This chapter has focused on the use of IPv4 subnets and supernets and applied CIDR and VLSM to IPv4 addressing schemes. This is only expected: IPv4 is still the most common form of IP and will be for some time to come. However, at least a few words about the use of prefixes and masks in IPv6 are in order here, if for no other reason than the vast majority of the rest of this book deals with IPv4 exclusively.

As mentioned in the previous chapter, IPv6 deals with prefixes only. There are no classes on IPv6 addresses, although the uses of the IPv6 address space is often determined by the value of the first few bits of an IPv6 address. IPv6 routing is quite similar to IPv4 with CIDR and VLSM, but there are a few points to be made to clarify this general statement.

For example, IPv6 addresses can be *provider-based* or for *local use*. All provider-based IPv6 addresses for aggregatable global unicast packets begin with either 0010 (2) or 0011 (3) in the first four bit positions of the entire 128-bit IPv6 address. Other bits in the provider-based IPv6 format represent fields for the *top-level aggregator* (TLA: 13 bits), *reserved functions* (8 bits), and the *next-level aggregator* (NLA: 24 bits). The fields form the first 48 bits of the IPv6 address and make up the *public topology* portion of this type of IPv6 address. The next 16 bits form the *site topology* portion of this type of IPv6 address, so the first 64 bits essentially make up the network portion of the IPv6 address. TLAs are usually Internet registries and NLAs are usually large ISPs.

Typical IPv6 address prefixes would look as follows:

2001:0400::/23

2001:05FF::/29

2001:0408::/35

and so on. The 64 bits that make up the low-order bits of the IPv6 address must be in a format known as the EUI-64 (64-bit Extended Unique Identifier) format. Normally, the 48-bit MAC address consists of 3 bytes (24 bits) for the manufacturers identifier and 3 bytes (24 bits) for the node ID, or serial number of the MAC board itself. So a typical MAC address would look like 0000:900F:C27E. The next-to-last bit in the first byte of this address is the *universal/local* bit and is usually set to a 0 bit (local). In EUI-64 format, this bit must be set to a one-bit (universal), making the first byte 02 instead of 00. So 0000:900F:C27E becomes 0200:900F:C27E.

To convert a MAC address to an EUI-64 address that can be used on an interface for the host portion of an IPv6 address, you must also insert the string FFFE between the manufacturer and serial number fields of the MAC address (between the first and last 3 bytes). So the MAC address becomes 0200:90FF:FE0F:C27E. This is more easily shown as follows:

MAC address:	0200:900F:C27E	
Split in half:	0200:90	0F:C27E
Insert FFFE:		FF FE
Form EUI-64:	0200:90FF:FE0F:C27E	

This format is for the provider-based IPv6 addresses. Local-use IPv6 addresses can be subnet local (link local) or subscriber local (site local). Both begin with 1111 1110 (FE in hexadecimal), but link local IPv6 addresses continue with a 10 (making the first two bytes FE80 if all of the trailing 6 bits in the second byte are zero-bits) and site local IPv6 addresses continue with a 11 (making the first two bytes FEC0 if all of the trailing 6 bits in the second byte are zero-bits). Both forms usually end with the 48-bit IEEE MAC address, but again with the added FFFE bits to form a the EUI-64 identifier. The site local form (FEC0) has a 16-bit field for the subnet. These address forms are used as the *private addresses* in IPv6 (just as 10.0.0.0 and the others in IPv4).

For instance, two routers connected by a small LAN can use the link local IPv6 address of FE80::<EUI-64 format MAC address> on their interfaces. This type of address is never advertised by an IPv6 router attached to the Internet, and it cannot be used to span subnets. On point-to-point links, some other distinguishing identifier of the interface card other than the MAC address can be used at the end of the link local address.

Site local addresses include a 16-bit subnet field, so these forms of private IPv6 addresses *can* be used to span subnets (and through routers), but only if there is no connection to the Internet (these addresses are also never advertised onto the Internet). Using link local and site local IPv6 addresses, an organization can build an entire global network, but only if none of the traffic tries to travel across the Internet. Then IPv6 provider-based addresses are needed. This is similar to building a complete corporate network in IPv4 using the 10.0.0.0 private address space, but using NAT for traffic that must travel across the Internet. But with IPv6, the lower-order bits (80 bits) of the site local address (subnet and interface) are just pasted on to the higher fields (48 bits) of the provider-based forms of IPv6 address. This is a lot easier than implementing NAT.

What about private masks and routing in IPv6? As shown in the preceding text, prefix masks in IPv6 have the same general form as prefix masks in IPv4; they just look a little strange at first. For example, the following is a sample IPv6 site local host address (this time in lowercase hex notation) and one possible network prefix for it:

fe80::90:69ff:fea0:8000/128

fe80:: /64

As in keeping with all of the addresses used in this book, this IPv6 address is a private address. The /64 mask tells the router that the first 64 bits of the address are to be used for longest-match routing purposes.

As far as aggregation is concerned, an IPv6 routing table at a customer site would have entries starting with fe80 and fec0 for local links and subnets, and entries starting with 2001:0408:001A::/48 (for example) for links to the Internet. The small ISP to which the customer attached could aggregate the entries for many customers as 2001:0408:0010::/40. The large ISP to which the smaller ISP is linked would aggregate many smaller ISPs address spaces as 2001:0408::/35, and on the Internet backbone this address space could even end up as 2001:0400::/23.

Summary: The Five Roles for Routing Policy

Before moving on the second part of this book and considering the role of routing policy in IGP routing protocols, we should summarize the role of routing policies in the overall routing process as presented in the first chapters. The following are five roles for routing policy in a routing environment:

- To help determine content of the routing table
- To help determine which routes form the forwarding table
- To help determine which routes are advertised to other routers
- To determine if routing protocols should share information
- To modify the routing information associated with a route

In this list, the *routing table*—sometimes called the *routing information base* (RIB)—is assumed to contain everything about routes learned from all of the IGP and EGP routing protocols. Based on this information, the router builds the *forwarding table* containing the next-hop router IP address and physical interface through which the next router is reached. When the routing protocols, IGP or EGP, talk to other routers, routing information is announced (advertised) to the other routers. Not only that, but a router running multiple routing protocols can want one routing protocol to share route information learned from another routing protocol (or source of routing information). Finally, the information associated with the route (for example, the next hop or metric) in either the routing table or the forwarding table can be modified as it arrives or as it leaves the router.

These roles are shown in Figure 4.18.

Although the emphasis in the previous few chapters has been on the underlying mechanisms of TCP/IP and IP addressing, these topics were introduced for better understanding of the routing protocols and routing polices discussed in the rest of this book. The main point is that changes to the Internet, IP addressing, and the way that routers handle these IP addresses in their routing tables has made it necessary to produce more and more elaborate routing polices so that the routing protocols function correctly in all circumstances.

Whether the concern is subnetting or supernetting, IPv4 or IPv6, large national ISPs or small local ISPs, NAPs or private peering, there is always a routing policy that addresses them all. Routing protocols today are only a start toward making a collection of routers perform as needed. The routing policies complete the task.

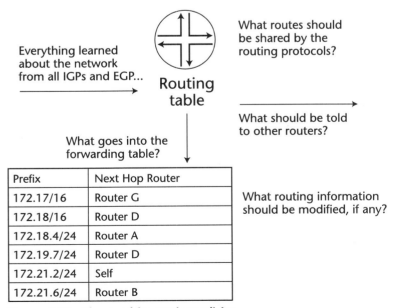

Figure 4.18   The need for routing policies.

Cisco Router Configuration

Before we discuss the specifics of Cisco routers and configuration in this chapter, as we do for Juniper Networks routers in the next chapter, we'll examine the role of routers in general on the Internet today. The basics of routers and routing have already been examined; additional concepts should be covered before the Cisco router product line is discussed in detail.

Routers are the network nodes of the Internet. Packets are relayed using dynamic routing from hop to hop across the Internet from source to destination host. This manner of relay distinguishes Internet routing from other types of network delivery techniques. *Relaying* means that the packets are forwarded to the next hop blindly: The sender assumes that the packets will get there and does not keep a copy of the packet in case retransmission is needed; nor does the sender rely on any packet-layer acknowledgment from the downstream node to know if the packet ever made it there or not. Relaying is a best-effort service. Routing is dynamic in the sense there is no fixed path through the network set up for a packet, and so packets can take widely diverse and sometimes rapidly changing paths from source to destination. The nice thing about dynamic routing is that losing a link or node on the network does not terminate any path-based connections on the network, but dynamic routing also means that it is hard to guarantee certain quality of service (QoS) levels of performance in terms of bandwidth or delay on these changeable paths (so IP is often called an "unreliable" service despite IP's extremely reliable dynamic routing capability). Routing from hop to hop means that the forwarding router has no idea where the packet will go once the packet is beyond the router at the other end of the link. The "horizon" of an Internet router is very close indeed, and one of the challenges of routing protocols is to make sure that the limited vision of routers is still enough to avoid routing loops and black holes that prevent packet delivery to the destination host.

Although routers are indispensable for packet delivery across the Internet, the importance of the router is often overshadowed by the role of the clients and servers that are the sources and destinations of the packets. It is tempting to say just that "routers route" and leave it at that. Packets go in and out of the routers, and the client Web browser fetches information from a Web site anywhere in the world. Much more has been written about the structure of the Web browser and the components of a Web site and Web page than the structure and components of a router. This only reflects the relative importance of these Internet components (client, server, and router) to the end users.

The importance of routers in this book, of course, is that the router runs the routing protocols and that the router is the focus of the routing policies that determine the paths that packets take across the Internet. The details of the router's internals are not as important as the behavior of the routing protocol and policy and how these routing protocols and policies are configured on the router. In fact, the internal organization of the router is almost irrelevant. What does matter is how the routers interact with one another and how the collection of routers that form an ISP's AS or ASs perform and route as a group.

First we take a brief overview of some important router products from Cisco. This list of Cisco products is not exhaustive, just representative. The main point is not to deem one router architecture better than the other but to give you an understanding of how the configuration files that determine the performance of the routing protocols and routing policies are implemented.

After the survey of Cisco router architecture and products, the notation used for configuration and routing policies is introduced. Distinct text styles are used for prompts, user command input, and router console output. These notations are used consistently for all examples in the remainder of this book.

The simplest form of router access is assumed: direct, local access to the router through the terminal console serial port on the router. There are other ways to access a router, naturally. Most routers can be accessed and configured over a modem attached to an auxiliary (AUX) serial port, through the network itself using Telnet or a router Web page, over a special local network management port and LAN, or even through a terminal server. These other router access methods are mentioned and described, but all of the examples are based on direct console connection to the router. Keep in mind that what is actually seen, and the keystrokes actually required to configure the router, might be somewhat different when the router is accessed through something other than the direct-console port. For the most part, however, things should be similar enough to be understood, even when router access is other than local and direct.

Last, we look at the configuration files and commands used to manipulate these files on Cisco routers. The number and location of these configuration files, as well as their "look and feel," is outlined. The commands used to change these files are distinct as well. In some cases, the configuration can be accomplished through a point-and-click Web page interface. But this book will always use the *command-line interface* (CLI) method of typing in a command and then examine the result on the router's configuration file. Even Web-enabled routers still allow this direct CLI configuration. Lately, Web-enabled routers have been seen as a security risk. Web pages on routers are just as vulnerable to hacking as the Web pages on servers. So, many network administrators have disabled the simple Web page configuration capabilities on their routers.

This chapter is limited to the Cisco routers. This limitation is not meant to slight other vendors of routers but only is intended to limit the scope of the chapter, which would otherwise be many times larger than it is. The next chapter introduces the Juniper Networks router architecture and configuration procedures. These are also the two router lines that we investigate in the later chapters on routing protocol and routing policy configuration.

Cisco Router Architecture

It is conventionally believed that Cisco invented the router. This is not strictly true, because there were "routers" before Cisco came along. But Cisco took the humble Internet gateway and LAN-connecting firewall and transformed these into a device that was better than bridges for connecting LANs, added security to customer sites, and popularized Internet connectivity. Today, Cisco is a sprawling networking giant that makes much more than routers. Cisco makes hubs, switches, and a variety of voice and optical networking products.

Even with regard to routers, Cisco is a diverse company. It makes tiny routers that link one or two PCs to a Digital Subscriber Line (DSL) link. Also produced are medium-sized routers that link one or two office LANs to the Internet. And the company makes large, high-end, backbone routers using very fast processors to route up to 60 million packets per second. Despite these differences, all Cisco routers have some hardware and software features in common. We discuss these similarities in the paragraphs that follow.

Cisco Hardware

When it comes to architecture, many Cisco routers seem very much like a PC. This was one of the reasons for the initial success of Cisco: The Cisco routers could be fabricated out of simple, off-the-shelf parts and did not require extensive or customized chipsets or hardware. So Cisco routers have a CPU, memory, interfaces, peripheral ports—in short, everything but a hard drive. Cisco routers do not even have floppy drives or other form of external storage. This makes sense: Routers don't need to store much of anything. A routing table needs to be in memory at all times, because it's much too slow to try and fetch a piece of a routing table off a hard drive when needed. A lot of routers boot themselves from special servers and have nonvolatile random access memory (NVRAM) that keeps whatever information they need to remember whenever their power is cut or turned off. Volatile memory like normal RAM is always erased when power is lost, but NVRAM acts like a disk and keeps its content even when the main power to the router is cut off. Routers do not have to worry about adding cards for video or graphics or other tasks either. The slots in the chassis simply handle various types of networking interfaces such as Ethernet, ATM, SONET/SDH (Synchronous Optical Network/Synchronous Digital Hierarchy), or other types of point-to-point WAN links. Most interface modules have multiple ports, depending on the type of interface they support. In a lot of high-end router models, the interface cards are complex devices all by themselves and are often called *blades*. Interfaces usually can be added as needed for the networking environment: one or more LAN cards for the routers that handle customers and one or more WAN cards for connection to other routers. Backbone routers often have only WAN cards and no customers at all.

Another difference between a Cisco router and a common PC is that PCs almost always have only a single CPU. It doesn't matter what kind of user device it is: Windows/Intel (Wintel) PCs have an architecture based on the x86 architecture, Apples favor the Motorola 68000 series and variations, and Sun Workstations use the SPARC processor, and so on. Because of the central role of these chips in running all of the hardware and software on the computer, single-CPU architectures require very powerful CPU chips.

Cisco routers use a variety of CPU chips, and because the tasks are shared among the processors, these CPU chips do not have to be tremendously powerful. Each CPU set is chosen to fit the mission of the router. For example, small routers such as the Cisco 700 series, use the 25-MHz 80386 Intel CPU, last used in user PCs years ago. That's enough horsepower for the home and small office Cisco 700, and these chips are stable, plentiful, and inexpensive. The Cisco 2500 router line uses the 20-MHz Motorola 68EC030 processor. Farther up the product line, Cisco uses increasingly more powerful, general-purpose processors form Motorola, Silicon Graphics, and other chip makers.

Cisco Memory

Cisco routers use different types of memory. Figure 5.1 shows the general layout of the motherboard of a Cisco 4500 router, one of the most common routers used in the world today. All Cisco router motherboards have four types of memory intended for specific purposes. Each type of memory and its location on the motherboard is shown in the figure.

Every Cisco router ships with at least the factory default minimum of dynamic random access memory (DRAM) and flash memory, but more can be added in the factory or in the field. Generally, the DRAM can be doubled or increased four-fold, depending on the model, and flash memory can be doubled.

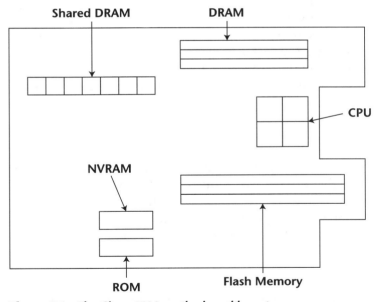

Figure 5.1 The Cisco 4500 motherboard layout.

RAM/DRAM

The RAM/DRAM is sometimes called *working storage* because in the days before hard drives and other types of external storage, memory was all that computers had for storing information outside of the immediate CPU. In a Cisco router, the RAM/DRAM perform the same functions for the router's CPU as the memory in a PC does for its CPU. So when the router is up and running, the RAM/DRAM contains an image of the Cisco Internetwork Operating System (IOS) software, the *running configuration* (running-config) file, the routing table and associated tables built after startup, and the packet buffer. If this seems like a lot of work for one type of memory, this just shows the flexibility of function in a general-purpose architecture router.

The RAM acronym often used by Cisco is somewhat misleading. Almost all RAM in a Cisco router today is DRAM, since static memory—regular RAM—became obsolete some time ago. But people are used to the old RAM acronym, and it's included in a lot of literature just for familiarity.

Small Cisco routers ship with 1.5 MB (megabytes) of DRAM expandable to 2.5 MB. The largest Cisco routers (actually switches) ship with 32 MB minimum DRAM and are expandable to 256 MB. These are just representative figures, because an agile company like Cisco is upgrading equipment all the time.

In addition to the DRAM near the CPU, Cisco routers include shared DRAM or *shared memory*. Also known as *packet memory*, the shared DRAM handles the packet buffers in the router. Splitting the packet buffers from the other DRAM improves I/O performance, because the shared DRAM is physically closer to the interfaces that handle the packets.

NVRAM

As mentioned, nonvolatile RAM is memory that retains information even when power is cut off to the router. Cisco routers use NVRAM to store a copy of the router configuration file. Without NVRAM, the Cisco router would never be able to remember its proper configuration when it was restarted. NVRAM is where the Cisco *startup configuration* (startup-config) is stored.

Flash Memory

Flash memory is another form of nonvolatile memory. Although flash memory is different than NVRAM, it can also be erased and reprogrammed as needed. In Cisco routers, and many other routers, flash memory is used to hold one or more copies of the router's operating system—in this case, IOS. This is important because flash memory allows a network administrator to place newer versions of the router's operating system on routers throughout a network and then "flash the router" to upgrade them all at once to the new operating system. Many Cisco routers, such as the Cisco 2500 product line, can run from flash and do not need the IOS image in RAM.

ROM

ROM is read-only memory and is therefore nonvolatile, but as you might expect, ROM cannot be changed. Cisco routers use ROM to hold what is called the *bootstrap program*. Normally, flash memory and NVRAM hold all of the information that the router needs to come up again properly with current configuration after a shutdown or other power loss. But if there is a catastrophe, the bootstrap program in ROM can be used to boot the router into a minimum configuration. ROM used for this purpose is also called ROMMON (ROM monitor) and has a distinctive rommon>> prompt taken from early UNIX systems. ROMMON at least gets the router to the point where simple commands can be typed in through a system console terminal (monitor). In smaller Cisco routers, ROM holds only a minimal subset of the Cisco IOS software. In larger Cisco routers, the ROM often holds a full copy of the Cisco IOS software.

Cisco Router Access

Users don't generally communicate with routers, but users communicate *through* routers. The situation is different for network administrators and managers. These personnel must communicate directly with the individual routers in order to install, configure, and manage the routers.

Routers are key devices on the Internet and almost any type of network. Many backbone routers handle packets for hundreds or thousands of users, and some handle packets for even more. So when a router goes down, or even slows down because of congestion or a problem, the users get angry and the network managers react immediately. For this reason, network managers need multiple and foolproof ways to access the routers they are responsible for in order to manage them.

Cisco routers do not come with a keyboard, mouse, and monitor. A network administrator can communicate with a Cisco router in any of three ways:

The console port.   This port is for a serial terminal that is at the same location as the router and attached by a short cable from the serial port on the terminal to the console port on the router. The terminal is usually a PC or UNIX workstation running a terminal emulation program. Several physical connector types are used for this port on Cisco routers. Network administrators often have to carry around several different connector types to ensure they have the proper connector for the router they need to manage.

The auxiliary (AUX) port.   This port is for a serial terminal at a remote location. Connection is made through a pair of modems, one connected to the router and the other connected to the terminal. There is little difference if any between the AUX and console ports in terms of characteristics. They are separate because routers might require simultaneous local and remote access that would be impossible if there were only one serial port on the router.

The network.   The router can always be managed over the same network on which it is routing packets. This is often called *in-band management*, in contrast to the console and AUX ports, which are *out-of-band*. This just means that the network access method shares the link to the router in the same bandwidth as user packets transiting the router. There are three ways to access a Cisco router over the network: through Telnet (called *VTY lines*), using a Web browser (HTTP is the protocol), or with Simple Network Management Protocol (SNMP), a protocol invented expressly for remote router management.

The three ways to access a Cisco router for configuration and management purposes are shown in Figure 5.2.

Small Cisco routers only have a console port. With the proper cables, these console ports can be hooked up to a modem for remote access, but obviously they cannot be used simultaneously for local access. On some Cisco routers, the console ports are labeled Admin or Management. Trying to access a console or AUX ports using the normal graphical interface provided by Windows,

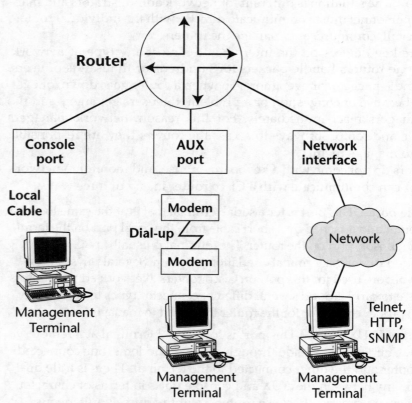

Figure 5.2 Accessing Cisco routers.

Mac OS, or UNIX X Windows is tempting. But the console and AUX ports only understand a simple, character-based serial protocol. On Windows PCs, for example, only HyperTerminal (or another serial terminal emulation program) can communicate with a Cisco router through the console or AUX ports.

Cisco's Router Operating System

Cisco routers have two files that are particularly significant: the *configuration file* and the *Cisco IOS software*. The configuration file can be changed in order to tell the router what to do. The IOS software cannot be changed, only upgraded. Cisco routers also have a lot of dynamic files that are not stored and are built when the router is booted and hold only information, not instructions.

The IOS software is contained in a single file on the router. Depending on the version, IOS files are anywhere from 3 MB to 10 MB in size. IOS files are called *system images* by Cisco. IOS is kept small by separating functions into a series of *feature sets*, each of which must be ordered (and paid for) separately. These feature sets are often also called *software images* or *feature packs*. Feature packs support certain network types (there are feature sets for LANs and WANs) and other router environment characteristics (there are feature sets for routing protocols, security, multicast, and so on).

IOS feature sets can be confusing. All feature sets will not run on all Cisco routers. And even if the feature set as a whole does run, on smaller routers some of the features might not run at all. In addition, feature sets come with three further variants: Basic, Plus (just what is added depends on the hardware platform), and Encryption (two types that can be added to either the Basic or Plus packages to add encryption).

To simplify matters a little, Cisco has established "feature set families" called IP Routing (basic routing support), Desktop (all types of LAN network operating systems such as Novell, IP, AppleTalk, etc. are supported here), Enterprise (adds a lot of WAN and management features), and Enterprise/APPN (adds a lot of IBM specifics to Enterprise, such as support for IBM's Advanced Peer-to-Peer Networking, or APPN). Feature set families help establish firm pricing policies and upgrade paths.

When ordering a Cisco router, customers get the generic IOS and add the proper feature set family for their hardware platform. Then they choose a release level for the IOS package and order the specific ISO part number indicated. So Cisco customers have to say, for example, "I need IOS Feature Set Enterprise Plus 56 for a Cisco 7500 running Release 12.2" in order to get the proper product.

Even Cisco release numbers, which track IOS and the feature sets in time, can be confusing. IOS has major versions and releases within a version, and many people use the terms *version* and *release* interchangeably. The designation of the IOS software consists of four parts, as shown in Figure 5.3.

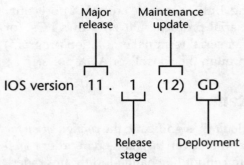

Figure 5.3   The four major parts of an IOS release number.

The first part is the major release—11 in the figure—and this marks a stable version of the software suitable for use by customers for production networks. In addition, IOS release numbers add information on the following:

Release stage.   Each version of IOS usually has several major revisions during its lifetime. This number identifies the stage of the version along its lifeline.

Maintenance update.   Written in parentheses, this number denotes support added to the release. Support is usually added for additional platforms and features that were not available in the first customer shipment (FCS) of the release.

Deployment.   An IOS release can be used without constraint by all customers that want to use it. This is called *general deployment* (GD). Releases for can also be in *early deployment* (ED) or *limited deployment* (LD) for a more restricted group of customers.

Most people just refer to IOS software as, say, release 11.2 or release 11.3 and leave off the rest of the information unless it is important in the context.

Cisco Router Products

One reason Cisco router software is so complex is that the Cisco router product line is so diverse. Cisco routers come is all shapes and sizes, and Cisco makes more than just routers. As mentioned, the company makes switches and hubs, and a variety of specialized devices for network security and the like. This section presents just an overview of the present Cisco router product line. Keep in mind that Cisco introduces new products regularly.

SOHO Routers

SOHO routers are intended for small office/home office networks with perhaps only three or four PCs to link to the Internet. Why have router at all? Without a router, users with multiple PCs would have to link each to the Internet using a separate dial-up line or use one PC as the gateway to an Internet link and a hub to build a LAN for the other PCs. The users would also have to provide their own security for the site. Using a SOHO to ISP router connection saves money, gives better performance, and is more reliable (no worry about getting a free port to dial in to). Many Cisco SOHO routers are furnished (but still sold) by service providers to customers that are using high-speed DSL access to the Internet.

The WAN side of the SOHO router can also be Integrated Services Digital Subscriber Line (ISDN) or normal serial links using dial-up. The products are organized into *series*, meaning the same basic chassis is manufactured into several products with differing features. Different SOHO router series can also support features such as voice over IP (VoIP) and virtual private networks (VPNs). Five series of Cisco SOHO routers are shown in Figure 5.4.

Product Series	Description
Cisco 77	DSL access router for multiple users. Configurable IOS.
Cisco 600 Series	DSL access router for single users. No user-configurable IOS.
Cisco 700 Series	ISDN access router for up to 30 users. No user-configurable IOS.
Cisco 800 Series	ISDN, DSL, or serial line access router for up to 20 users. Configurable IOS and VPN encryption.
Cisco uBR900 Series	Integrated VoIP, VPN, and router for small offices. Configurable IOS.

Figure 5.4   Cisco SOHO routers.

Midrange Routers

Cisco midrange routers can handle small- to medium-sized networking needs. Lots of these networks exist, so Cisco has dozens of products in many series to address this market. All service different types of LANs and WAN links. These products are often called *access routers* or *edge routers* because they usually allow one or more customer LANs to access each other and the Internet and so sit on the edge of the Internet cloud.

These routers are either *modular* or *nonmodular*. Modular routers can be upgraded in the field by inserting one or more added modules to handle other networking situations. Nonmodular routers are fixed in configuration. Seven series of Cisco midrange routers are shown in Figure 5.5.

Backbone Routers

Whenever Cisco wants to emphasize the position of their products with respect to the Internet, the backbone routers are the products they are referring to. The Cisco 4000 series is probably the most successful router line of all time. The 7000 and 12000 series have a large chassis into which blades are inserted.

Product Series	Description
Cisco 1000 Series	Ethernet access router for ISDN or serial WAN link.
Cisco 1400 Series	Ethernet access router for either an ATM or DSL link.
Cisco 1600 Series	Ethernet access router for ISDN or serial WAN link. VPN encryption.
Cisco 1700 Series	Ethernet access router for serial, ISDN, or DSL link. VPN encryption, VoIP, or Voice over Frame Relay (VoFR).
Cisco 2500 Series	Ethernet/Token Ring or dial-access servers connect 1 or 2 LANs to ISDN or serial link.
Cisco 2600 Series	Modular access router, voice/data gateway, or dial-access server. Connects 1 or 2 LANs to ISDN, T1, Ethernet, modems, or ATM. Supports fax and frame relay as well.
Cisco 3600 Series	Similar to 2600, but higher density router for dial-access or router-to-router traffic.

Figure 5.5 Cisco midrange routers.

Backbone routers usually do not have end users attached, so they can take on as many users as there are packets flowing through them. All of these routers are modular and have multiple slots into which various modules with interfaces can be inserted. The interfaces can handle Ethernet and Token Ring LANs, as well as Gigabit Ethernet (GBE), Fiber Distributed Data Interface (FDDI), and High-Speed Serial Interface (HSSI). The WAN interfaces include, but are not limited to, support for SONET OC-12 (Optical Carrier level 12) and OC-48 links that run at 622 Mbps and 2.4 Gbps, channelized T1 (24 channels running at 64 Kbps each), packet over DS3 (45 Mbps) and ATM at a variety of speeds. These routers also include support for Multiprotocol Label Switching (MPLS), VPNs, and IPSec (Secure IP).

Seven series of the Cisco backbone router family are shown in Figure 5.6.

A more complete survey of Cisco networking products would include switches such as the Catalyst ATM switch line and hubs such as the MicroHub. The products mentioned in this section are all routers.

Product Series	Description
Cisco 4000 Series	Three slots for Ethernet, Token Ring (TR), FDDI, HSSI, ISDN, channelized T1, and ATM.
Cisco 6400 Series	DSL router for ISPs and corporations. Supports Ethernet (GBE too), DSL, and ATM.
Cisco 7000 Series	Four to thirteen slots. Ethernet, TR, FDDI, HSSI, ISDN, channelized T1, packets over DS3, and ATM.
Cisco 10000 Series	Ten slot GBE switch-router. Special card for OC-12 links. Supports IPSec, MPLS VPNs and quality of service (QoS) capabilities.
Cisco 12000 Series	Eight to twelve slots. GBE switch-router for IP. Special cards for OC-12 and OC-48 links.
Cisco uBR7200 Series	Two to four slot carrier-class routers. For cable TV operators and ISPs. Residential users to high-speed data and IP telephony.
Cisco uBR10012 Series	Similar to uBR7200. Carrier-class routers. For cable TV operators and ISPs. Residential users to high-speed data and IP telephony.

Figure 5.6 Cisco backbone routers.

Cisco's Hierarchical Vision

One reason that Cisco makes routers large and small is that Cisco sees routers naturally deployed in a hierarchy. Cisco routers are typically deployed in what Cisco calls a hierarchical network design. No matter whether the routers form the network for a large private organization or the router network for an ISP, the structure is pretty much the same. Smaller routers are used on the edge of the network, and larger routers are used on the backbone. There is no requirement for users to deploy their routers according to this plan, but most organizations accept that some form of hierarchy gives the overall network some measure of flexibility, scalability, and reliability, and at the same time reduces congestion, just as Cisco claims.

Cisco calls the three layers of the hierarchy the *access layer*, the *distribution layer*, and the *core layer*. More layers can be added, but these three layers can be used to keep local traffic flows local, and only the core layer is used for traffic between major sections of the network.

The three layers and the types of connectivity usually used at each level are shown in Figure 5.7. Access routers are usually meshed to all distribution routers but only linked directly if traffic flows call for this. Distribution routers are not usually meshed to the core, but they can be. Note that the hierarchy does not call for (or encourage) direct access layer links for the core. Generally, since WAN links are usually paid for by the mile, shorter links between access and distribution routers can be meshed for reliability, but the longer links between core routers are not typically meshed in a large organization or ISP.

The roles for these layer routers, as Cisco loosely defines them, are as follows:

The access layer.   This layer is where end-user devices and LANs connect to the network. Access routers are typically used in an office building or in a campus environment to allow traffic not meant for local client/server delivery to leave the local networks and traffic from the global public Internet to enter the site, so that public Web servers and FTP servers and the like are accessible. These routers typically are configured to run LAN network operating systems such as AppleTalk or NetWare's IPX protocol. Security is also a concern here, but the emphasis in this book is on connectivity to an ISP's larger network rather than on the side of the router that faces the user. Routing tables can be kept to a minimum at the access layer, with a single default route often used to tell the router "if you don't know where else to send this packet, send it here."

The distribution layer.   This layer is intended to form a first level of connectivity for the access routers. These routers usually run routing protocols such as OSPF and IS-IS, and often BGP as well. Routing policies are used to control the redistribution of routing information from one routing protocol to another, as well as what routes are aggregated or summarized for BGP. Routing tables tend to be large and routing policies more complex. In ISP networks, these routers are often called *POP routers* with direct links to the access routers and also to the core.

The core layer.   This layer provides connectivity for all the distribution layer routers and also provides links to other ISPs or routing domains. These are large routers that form the backbone of the entire network, and the routing tables and routing policies can be very complex. ISPs often distinguish between two types of core routers: the core routers themselves and *border routers* (also called *boundary routers*) that handle the links and routing policies to other peer ISPs or the NAPs. Core routers typically implement BGP *route reflection* or *confederations* (also called *sub-confederations*) to better handle and distribute routing information within the routing domain. Core routers usually run IBGP (internal BGP, discussed in Chapter 13) and have links only within the routing domain to POP routers and border routers. Border routers usually run EBGP (external BGP) and really define the role of the ISP with regard to the Internet as a whole. For example, the border routers determine whether the routing domain is a stub (one link only to the Internet at large), multihomed (links to more than one other AS or ISP), or transit network (allowing traffic to/from other routing domain to traverse its backbone).

For purposes of the discussion in this book, the normal Cisco hierarchy terminology is modified somewhat. For example, an "access router" from the service provider perspective is usually a service provider's router that links to the customer's "site routers." In some Cisco documentation, access routers are called *central-site access routers* and site routers are called *remote-site routers*.

In some of the examples in this book, the access routers will have many serial interfaces connecting customers and one Ethernet interface to connect to the service providers' distribution routers. This is the exact opposite of most examples of access routers in other books, where Ethernet links to customers' LANs and serial links connect to service provider distribution routers.

So many of the configuration examples in this book apply mainly to access, POP, core, or border routers, always from the service provider perspective. However, smaller networks might combine functions, especially core/border functions, in the same router. In either case, the configurations will be appropriate, just applied to different routers, or not, depending on the role of the router.

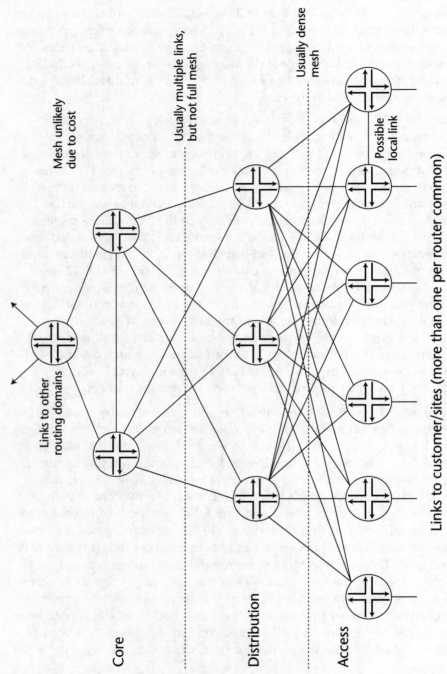

Figure 5.7 Cisco's router hierarchy.

Configuring Cisco Routers

A router is controlled through its configuration file, often just called the *config file* or even just *config*. Besides the IOS software, the only other permanent file on a Cisco router is the configuration file. The IOS software is fixed in nature and cannot be altered by customers. Customers tell the IOS software what to do by editing and adjusting the configuration file. The IOS software consults the configuration file hundreds of times per second so that the router can perform its job correctly.

Two main Cisco configuration files exist: the *startup-config*, stored in NVRAM that is usually used when the router boots, and the *running-config* in RAM, which is the actual configuration used by the router while forwarding packets. Changes made to the running-config take effect immediately, but only changes to the startup-config will "stick" and be used when the router is restarted.

Configuration files are edited differently than files found on an end-user computer. Network administrators cannot just click and place a cursor where they want and typed away just as with a word processing document. Configuration files are not compiled and debugged like a program source file either. Network administrators change configuration files via special IOS commands and then view the result to make sure it is what was intended.

Most router problems are caused not by failing hardware but by simple configuration errors. And the errors are not often obvious. Routers exist to interact with one another, and although the configuration files on each and every router are perfectly correct in isolation, when the routers communicate using their routing protocols, something is wrong. Configuration files must not only be correct on all routers concerned but consistent as well. Changing the configuration file on one router can cause ripple effects throughout the network. Network administrators take configuration changes seriously, and they spend most of their time reviewing configurations and making changes in a coordinated fashion.

Configuration files usually determine which dynamic files come into existence once the router is turned on. The exact contents of these files can be determined by configuration as well. Dynamic router files are usually tables, such as the routing table, the switching (or forwarding) table, ARP tables, and others. These tables change rapidly as the router is running, and so network administrators cannot put anything directly into these tables. Administrators maintain control over the contents of these tables indirectly, by setting parameters in the configuration file.

Getting Started

How does a network administrator gain access to the configuration file on a Cisco router? Cisco configuration can be as complex as Cisco hardware, so it is best to start with a few concepts that apply to Cisco configuration.

Assume that a network administrator is sitting at a Windows PC directly connected by the serial port on the PC to the console port of a Cisco router. All the network administrator has to do is run a terminal emulator program such as HyperTerminal as a VT100 (an old DEC terminal type that still works just fine and has a lot of nice features such as support for the arrow keys). The link itself is usually set for 9600 bps, 8 bits per character, and no parity, and 1 stop bit to delimit the characters. This is typically abbreviated as 9600 8-N-1 and is often the default for a lot of terminal emulator programs.

The cursor is now normally a black lozenge in the upper left corner of the screen. Where's the router? It's there, but routers don't spend a lot of time looking to see if someone has connected to the console port. They have more important things to do. To announce his or her presence, the network administrator just needs to press the Enter key once or twice. This wakes the router up and begins the dialogue with the router.

Operating Modes

The first time a Cisco router is powered up, the user (presumably the network administrator) is in *Setup mode*. Setup mode prompts the user through a dialogue for initial router configuration. The router can also place the user in RXBoot mode (to boot some helper software) and ROM Monitor mode (when things are terribly wrong). In fact, there are *seven* modes that a user can be in when accessing a Cisco router. All modes have distinctive prompts, and paying attention to the prompts lets people know what mode they are in. (Setup mode consists of a dialogue with questions and answers and so does not really have a prompt.) All seven modes have different purposes and management capabilities. Suppose the router has been named RouterA during setup. The seven modes, their purposes and capabilities, and their prompts are shown in Figure 5.8.

Generally, three operating modes are in constant use for Cisco routers. These are Boot, User, and Configuration mode. The Boot modes are not of concern here, since the Setup mode is only used to create a basic configuration file at initial startup, and the other two are for boot failures. User mode (technically, the *User EXEC mode*) is where the user is placed when normal console access is made to a working router. In User mode, the user can only issues a few IOS commands to examine a few general status indicators on the router.

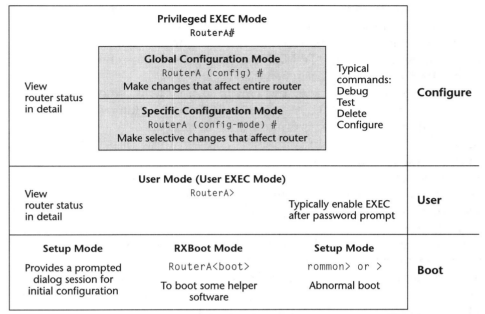

Figure 5.8 The seven operating modes for Cisco routers.

To really see what is going on, and to configure the router, the user must be in *Privileged EXEC mode*. A user enters privileged EXEC mode by typing the IOS command `enable` and supplying the proper password (if one has been set, which is usually the case). Because most network administrators spend little time in User mode except to go to the privileged EXEC mode, they are usually just called *User mode* and *EXEC mode*.

Once in EXEC mode, the user can issue IOS commands that are potentially very dangerous, such as debug, test, delete, and, of course, commands to edit the configuration file. There are two configuration modes, and both are shown inside the EXEC mode because they can only be accessed this way. In *Global Configuration mode*, the changes made affect the entire router, while in *Specific Configuration mode* the changes made are applied selectively to various parts of the configuration file. The prompt now reflects the section to which the configuration changes are applied. For example, at the prompt `RouterA(config-if)#` indicates all changes made apply to the interfaces of the router.

Configuration Files

Two types of configuration files are on every Cisco router: the running-config file and the startup-config file. The running-config file's image is in RAM, so any changes made to the running-config file go into effect immediately but will be lost when the router is restarted unless the changes are stored somewhere else. The router usually boots its configuration from NVRAM. The startup-config is stored in NVRAM, and IOS goes there to find the router's configuration in the first place when it starts up.

Cisco configuration files have seven major sections (called modes) under the global configuration level. These are listed in Table 5.1, along with the part of the router that the section targets and the prompt seen.

Cisco router configuration commands come in three classes: global commands, major commands, and subcommands. *Global commands* are used to set parameters that apply to the router as whole. *Major commands* are used to configure a particular interface or routing process. *Subcommands* are used after a major command to supply configuration details that apply to the interface or routing process.

Global commands are used at the `(config)#` prompt to set parameters such as the router hostname (the name of the router). One very useful global command is `no ip domain-lookup`. This speeds things up when there is a typo in the configuration command. The default Cisco behavior when a command is entered that is not understood (such as typing `wrote` instead of `write`) is to assume that the command is a request to establish a Telnet session with a host called `wrote`. This results in an attempt by the router to resolve this string into an IP address by finding a Domain Name System (DNS) server on the network. A lot of routers might not have a DNS server configured yet, or even if there is one, the strange hostname is not valid anyway. The result is a delay during which no further commands can be entered. Turning the domain lookup off just makes life easier.

Table 5.1   Cisco Configuration Modes and Prompts

CONFIGURATION MODE	PROMPT	CHANGES APPLY TO...
Global	`RouterA(config)#`	Entire configuration file
Interface	`RouterA(config-if)#`	Physical interfaces
Subinterface	`RouterA(config-subif)#`	Logical (virtual) interfaces
Controller	`RouterA(config-controller)#`	Physical router controller
Line	`RouterA(config-line)#`	Terminal lines (console, AUX, VTY)
Router	`RouterA(config-router)#`	IP routing protocols
IPX-Router	`RouterA(config-ipx-router)#`	Novell IPX routing protocol
Route-Map	`RouterA(config-route-map)#`	Routing tables (policies)

Major commands are used in the other modes. Global commands are always self-contained and on one line. Major commands are followed by at least one, and often more, subcommands that relate to the major command. Subcommands are always indented in the configuration.

The Cisco configuration process has some quirks that take some getting used to. First of all, the initial assignment of IP addresses and masks to interfaces, setting some initial routing protocols, and other related parameters is done through the `setup` configuration process. This dialogue can be initiated all over again through the `setup` command, and even interfaces that are `shutdown` (the Cisco term for inactive interfaces that are present but not fully configured) can be configured and activated (through the `no shutdown` command) without using the setup dialogue.

Next, Cisco commands include an *auto-completion* feature that allows the router to interpret abbreviated commands as if the user had typed in the entire string, as long as the string entered is unambiguous. For example, typing `conf t` is the same as typing `configure terminal`, although only `conf t` will actually show up on the screen. Command completion is a great time-saver, and ambiguous commands are flagged with a % prompt. An online help system allows the user to enter a ? almost anywhere to find out what the allowed commands are at that point. The Up arrows or CTRL-P can be used to scroll through a history of commands as well.

A related feature is called *tab-to-complete*. The user can display a partial command like `sh` for `show` by entering `sh` and pressing the Tab key. However, this completion appears on a separate line and can be very disruptive to the flow of the command, so few experienced Cisco users bother with this feature.

Also, Cisco configuration prompts are generic, such as `(config-if)#`. This does not tell the user which interface, for example, is being configured by, say, inserting the name of the interface into the prompt. Care is needed to ensure that changes are being made to the correct portion of the configuration. In practice the interface configuration commands are seldom elaborate or extensive, so this is not that much of a limitation unless the interface configuration process is interrupted.

Finally, there is no easy way to view the changes to the configuration from within Configuration mode. The `show history` command can be used to view the commands entered by the user, but other means are needed to view the changes applied to the configuration file itself, after the <CTRL-Z> (Cisco displays this as Ctrl/Z) ends the process.

Four IOS major commands handle most of the configuration of a Cisco router:

Show. Used to display the status of the router.

Configure. Makes changes to the configuration file.

No. Negates a setting in the configuration file.

Copy or Write. Puts the configuration file changes into effect.

Some related IOS commands are also used to enter Configuration mode and to move around the configuration command lines:

Enable. Takes the user from User EXEC mode to Privileged EXEC mode.

Disable. Takes the user from Privileged EXEC mode to User EXEC mode.

Exit. Exits Configuration mode or ends a login session.

CTRL-A. Moves cursor to the start of a command line.

CTRL-B. Moves cursor back one character in the command line.

CTRL-F. Moves cursor forward one character in the command line.

CTRL-C. Quits a process (such as a multipage display).

ESC-B. Moves cursor to the beginning of the prior word (good for typo corrections).

ESC-F. Moves cursor to the beginning of the next word.

Usually, if the terminal session is set up as a VT100, the arrow keys will do what is expected. But if they do not, these edit commands will always work.

The main initial configuration tasks on the Cisco router are handled by the Setup Mode dialogue and not in Configuration mode at all. That is, the detected physical interfaces are configured and enabled, IP addresses and masks assigned, the router given a name (Hostname), passwords and login IDs assigned, all through an interactive dialogue. Setup mode can be invoked from the EXEC mode. Now, once set up, these criteria can be changed through Configuration modes, but the initial configuration is through the Setup Mode dialogue.

A Cisco router can be configured three main ways. The router can be configured from memory (commands stored in NVRAM), from a network (commands stored on a TFTP server), or through user configuration commands entered from a terminal. The method used in this book is `configure terminal` (`config term` or `conf t`) and is used through the console port or through a Telnet session. Configuration changes made this way are not really applied to the configuration at all. The configuration commands and subcommands are stored and applied only at the end of the terminal configuration session. The key sequence to end a configuration session is `<CTRL-Z>` and this basically creates what Cisco calls a *configuration command script* that is merged into the running-config in RAM. These changes need to be applied to the startup-config file if the changes are to be made permanent by copying this new file into NVRAM memory. This can be done with the `write memory` or `copy running-config startup-config` commands. When used to copy the configuration file in NVRAM to RAM the `copy startup-config running-config` is used, but this will merge the contents of NVRAM with the current RAM configuration file.

Naturally, keeping all configuration information on a router in memory, nonvolatile or not, can be risky. So there are Cisco configuration commands to copy either configuration files to and from a TFTP server. TFTP is trivial FTP, a very minimal version of FTP for use on a single LAN. The TFTP server stores the router configuration information on its hard drive. Either the running (RAM) or the startup (NVRAM) configurations can be copied to or from the TFTP server. For example, to load a configuration file from the TFTP server into NVRAM to become the startup-config, the command `copy tftp startup-config` is used. When a configuration from a TFTP server is loaded into RAM to become the running-config, the operation is a merge and the existing running-config is added to, not overwritten. Finally, a completely blank configuration can be placed into NVRAM with the `erase startup-config` command. The relationship among all these commands is shown in Figure 5.9. Note that operations that add to the running-config in RAM are merged. This makes sense because the contents of RAM determines the packet-forwarding operations of the router directly.

The following example shows how a user first runs Setup mode and then uses Configuration mode to add some things to the router configuration.

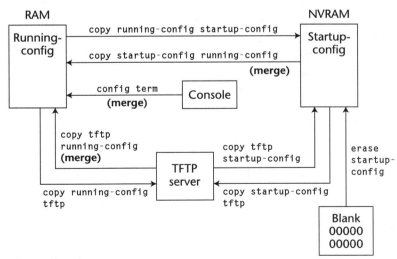

Figure 5.9 Cisco configuration file commands.

Cisco Configuration Example

The following paragraphs show how Cisco routers are initially configured. Then the configuration is modified. This is a working example in the sense that the router configuration established in this section is useful toward building up a complete series of networks later on in this book.

In this example, a setup configuration is performed on an access router with one Ethernet interface, and a serial interface is used to link to other routers. Later on, only Ethernet interfaces are used for router connectivity. Ethernet is only used for simplicity, not to suggest that access routers routinely link to other routers over Ethernet links. Plenty of other sources provide information on configuring other types of interfaces on Cisco routers

After the initial configuration, this section creates an address for the *loopback* interface on the router, adds some static routes to the configuration, and configures an aggregate to cover the range of the static routes. Loopback interfaces are used on routers not so much for loopback purposes (in fact, a 127 loopback IP address is often the worst thing that can be configured on the loopback interface) as for *stability* purposes. The loopback interface is intended to be a stable interface that can be used to identify the router in routing protocols, form a convenient single address for Telnet or traceroute purposes, and can still be used for diagnostic purposes as well. If a router did not have a stable loopback interface, and the interface that the router was known by is down, the router would be unreachable over the network by Telnet and routing protocol sessions, even those on other interfaces, might fail. The loopback should always be reachable as long as one interface is up and running.

Also, Cisco routers allow for a serial interface to be *unnumbered* and without an IP address at all. Unnumbered interfaces "borrow" the IP address of another interface as specified and make the serial link more or less transparent between the routers. This is often done to preserve IP addresses, especially in a classful IP environment. In this book, all serial interfaces receive IP addresses. A router having all unnumbered serial interfaces and without a loopback IP address would be all but isolated from the network as a whole.

Static routes are the opposite of dynamic routes. Dynamic routes can come and go in the routing table as the routing protocols detect new networks or failed links. Static routes are always there in the routing table. Even if the link to the static addresses' next hop is down, the entry never goes away. The network is just unreachable. Complete networks can be built up entirely out of static routes, and sometimes they are. But today static routes have a special role in the access router: Static routes are used to map the links to the customer sites. After all, most customer sites have only a single serial link to an off-site router. If the link to the site from the access router is down, then the customer is effectively isolated and unreachable. Customer links tend to be very stable as well and do not move much among interfaces on the router, get new IP addresses often, and so on. So customer LANs with end-user clients and servers are always represented by static routes on the access routers in this book.

A special type of static route is the *default route*, which is closely related to the concept of the "gateway of last resort," as Cisco calls it. The default route is used when there is no more explicit match for an IP address in the routing table. This default address is typically 0.0.0.0/0 and essentially passes as a longest match for anything not in the routing table. The configuration example sets this default address as well.

Cisco also has commands to set a `default-gateway` and `default-network` for the router. The default gateway should only be used and set when there is no IP routing taking place on the router and therefore the Cisco router is acting as a host. For example, a low-end Cisco router in Boot mode uses the default gateway to load its software. Setting the default network is a way to identify routes that the router will consider for the gateway of last resort when no route to 0.0.0.0/0 exists. There can be several "candidate" default networks, and the advantage is that there is no need for a static default to be defined: The router chooses its own gateway of last resort from among the default networks based on reachability and routing metric. This simple example does not set the `default-gateway` but uses the `default-network` in conjunction with aggregates.

Finally, the example configures an aggregate route to cover the range of the static routes used in the example. A simple procedure is given to figure out the most appropriate aggregate to use, and several cautionary notes are also included to prevent the later use of the aggregate-causing routing loops or black holes.

Initial Setup

Initial setup of a Cisco router is performed either when the router is powered up for the first time, or the `setup` command is explicitly invoked. Either way, automatic or command-driven, running setup results in the user being stepped through an interactive System Configuration dialogue. The `setup` command facility in the router allows the user to configure some global parameters right away. Setup also detects which interfaces have been installed and prompts the user for basic configuration information for each installed interface, one by one. Finally, setup prompts the user to store the result in NVRAM.

The System Configuration dialogue has changed a little from IOS 11 to IOS 12. This example uses IOS 12.2. When assigning IP addresses to interfaces, IOS still considers the subnet mask to be an *extension* of the number of bits in the major (classful) network. So the subnet mask of /24 assigned to a major network 10.0.0.0 (formerly Class A) in this example is entered as 16 and *not* as 24, because the natural Class A mask is already 8 bits long.

Since this is an access router, a lot of LAN operating system protocols are turned on in this example, just in case any user LAN segments are directly attached to the router. One notable protocol that is *not* configured here is IGRP, Cisco's proprietary upgrade to RIP. The reason for this apparent omission will be explained in Chapter 7, "Routing Information Protocol (RIP)." SNMP is absent also, but this is common unless secure SNMP methods are used. Also, no unnumbered serial interfaces are used in these examples. Although still popular as a way to conserve classful IP addresses, all serial interfaces on the network examples in this book have IP addresses.

The following simple example only configures one Ethernet link (Ethernet0) and one serial link (Serial0), just to show the process rather than offer a full tutorial on Cisco router setup procedures. In many cases, the default action in square brackets (such as [yes]) is taken by just pressing the Enter key. The actual replies typed by the user are shown in **bold**. Initially, Cisco routers have a default name of Router and there is no password on the enable command to enter privileged EXEC mode.

```
        --- System Configuration Dialog ---

At any point you may enter a question mark '?' for help.
Use ctrl-c to abort configuration dialog at any prompt.
Default settings are in square brackets '[]'.

Continue with configuration dialog? [yes]:

First, would you like to see the current interface summary? [yes]:
Any Interface listed with OK? value "NO" does not have a valid
configuration

Interface          IP-Address      OK?  Method    Status   Protocol
Ethernet0          unassigned      NO   not set   up       down
Serial0            unassigned      NO   not set   down     down

Configuring global parameters:

  Enter host name [Router]: Cisco_access

The enable secret is a one-way cryptographic secret used
instead of the enable password when it exists.

  Enter enable secret [<Use current secret>]: lab
The enable password is used when there is no enable secret
and when using older software and some boot images.
  Enter enable password [ww]: lab
  Enter virtual terminal password [ww]: lab
  Configure SNMP Network Management? [yes]: no
  Configure DECnet? [no]:
```

```
  Configure AppleTalk? [yes]:
    Multizone networks? [no]:

  Configure IPX? [yes]:
  Configure IP? [yes]:
    Configure IGRP routing? [yes]: no
  Configure Async lines? [yes]: no

Configuring interface parameters:

Configuring interface Ethernet0:
  Is this interface in use? [yes]:
  Configure IP on this interface? [yes]:
    IP address for this interface: 10.0.32.1
    Number of bits in subnet field [8]: 16
    Class A network is 10.0.0.0, 16 subnet bits; mask is /24
  Configure AppleTalk on this interface? [yes]: no
  Configure IPX on this interface? [yes]:
    IPX network number [1]:

Configuring interface Serial0:
  Is this interface in use? [no]: yes

  Configure IP on this interface? [no]: yes

  Configure IP unnumbered on this interface? [no]: no
      IP address for this interface: 10.0.33.1
      Number of bits in subnet field [8]: 16
      Class A network is 10.0.0.0, 16 subnet bits; mask is /24

    Extended AppleTalk network? [yes]: no
  Configure IPX on this interface? [no]: no

The following configuration command script was created:

hostname Cisco_access
!
enable secret 5 $1$ryTe$ekYqoFhp9fjSTQ4pDy9fy/
enable password lab
line vty 0 4
password lab
snmp-server community public
!
no decnet routing
appletalk routing
ipx routing
ip routing
!
interface Ethernet0
no ipx network
```

```
interface Serial0
no ipx network
interface Serial1
no ipx network
!
interface Ethernet0
ip address 10.0.32.1 255.255.255.0
ipx network 1
no mop enabled
!
interface Serial0
no shutdown
ip address 10.0.33.1 255.255.255.0
no mop enabled
!
network 10.0.0.0
!
end

Use this configuration? [yes/no]: yes


Building configuration...

Use the enabled mode 'configure' command to modify this configuration.


Cisco_access#
```

Further configuration can now be done using the `configure terminal` (or `conf t`) command. It is common enough to configure some additional password protection on Cisco routers and to set the router for at least some logging. Because later configurations in this will not display all details of all configurations, this section covers some of the most common additional tasks performed in an initial Cisco router setup.

This book uses direct console access for configuration. In many cases, however, routers are commonly accessed over the network using what Cisco calls *vty lines*. These are virtual terminal lines used for remote Telnet access and should always be password-protected. More than one user can Telnet to the router at the same time, if the number of vty lines is set higher than 0 (0 is the first vty session identifier used). This example sets up vty lines 0 through 4 for five remote users and then assigns the password lab to them:

```
Cisco_access#conf t
Cisco_access(config)#line vty 0 4
Cisco_access(config-line)#password lab
Cisco_access(config-line)#<ctrl-Z>
```

The line section of the configuration now displays the following:

```
!
line vty 0 4
 password lab
 login
!
```

Another handy feature to configure on any router is to establish a date- and time-stamped log file for messages such as interface transitions, errors, and so on. The internal buffer is circular, so that newer messages replace older ones. The commands usually used are logging buffered and service timestamp log datetime. Without datetime, the router only records dates and times in terms of router uptime, which is not usually very helpful in pinpointing the message timeframe. Using datetime does require that the router's clock has already been set with the clock set command in Global Configuration mode:

```
Cisco_access#conf t
Cisco_access(config)#clock set 10:25 2 January 2002
Cisco_access(config)#logging buffered
Cisco_access(config-line)#service timestamp log datetime
Cisco_access(config-line)#<ctrl-Z>
```

This information shows up right at the front of the configuration file:

```
Current configuration:
!
service timestamp log datetime
...
!
```

The contents of the log can be displayed using the show log command. Routine administration configuration can be as simple or complex as required and include message-of-the-day (motd) banners and so on.

Cisco routers are inherently classful IP devices. That is, Cisco routers historically always viewed an IP address as Class A, B, or C and attempted to summarize and advertise addresses along classful lines and make routing decisions accordingly. To make sure that the Cisco router treats IP addresses in a totally classless manner, you can use the global configuration command ip classless:

```
Cisco_access(config)#ip classless
```

What the ip classless command really does is to allow the Cisco router to perform longest-match lookups on routes and allow arbitrary and multiple boundaries between network and host portions of IP addresses on the same router. The `ip classless` command was introduced in IOS 10.0. Since IOS 11.3, this command has been the default behavior and is turned off with the `no ip classless` global configuration command.

Much more could be said in general about Cisco router configuration. It is more important, however, that the router be configured with some IP addresses for the routing protocols and polices to work on.

Loopback, Static Routes, and an Aggregate Route

If the router was not already in privileged EXEC mode, this mode could be entered by using the `enable` command. The user must provide the correct password (`lab` in this example). Configuration mode is then entered, with input taken from the terminal attached to the console port:

```
Cisco_access#conf t

Enter configuration commands, one per line. End with Ctrl/Z.
Cisco_access(config)#
```

Note that if the abbreviated command `conf t` is used, the Cisco auto-completion feature allows the router to understand the command (as long as the command is unambiguous), but the terminal screen will still display `conf t`. Few people bother with the tab-to-complete feature, so logs of Cisco configuration sessions tend to be filled with many terse and somewhat puzzling clusters of two or three letters. In this book, except for the most common and routine commands, configuration commands are spelled out in full.

Setting the Loopback IP Address

Cisco routers can have more than one loopback interface, designated Loopback0, Loopback1 (and abbreviated Lo0, Lo1), and so on. In addition, each loopback interface can have more than one IP address. This example only assigns one loopback IP address to interface Loopback0 and then exits from interface configuration:

```
Cisco_access(config)# interface loopback 0
Cisco_access(config-if)# ip address 10.100.32.1 255.255.255.255
Cisco_access(config-if)# exit
Cisco_access(config)#
```

That is all there is to it. Note that Cisco uses the traditional 255 mask notation, which sets the loopback address to a host route. Loopback addresses play an important role in many routing protocols, so the loopback address must be a reachable destination on the network. Some degree of care is needed in selecting loopback addresses.

Adding Static Route Addresses

Just as router loopback addresses do, static routes play an important role in router networks. In smaller networks consisting of three or four routers connected by a minimal number of links, static routing might be used for the whole network, since dynamic routing will never be able to find an alternate route once a link or router is down. Even in larger networks, static routes make sense for links that have no alternate paths and do not change much, if at all.

A good example of single, stable links in a router network are the links to customers' site routers from a service provider's access routers. These links can be serial links if the access router is some distance from the customer, or just Ethernet ports on the router if the access router is located close to a cluster of customer LANs. If the link is down, the customer cannot be reached in any other way. If the customer link is restored, the customer still has the same address and appears on the same router interface. So static routes work fine here.

The destination of a static route configured on a Cisco router can be one of three general types:

1. The IP address of the next-hop interface along the path to the destination.

2. The IP address of another route in the routing table, which is used to find the correct output interface.

3. The designation of a directly connected interface.

Generally, all you need to configure static routes is an IP network address and a next-hop IP address. Naturally, if the next hop is to be reachable, then the IP address used as the static route next hop should be reachable through the router, or else the packet will be discarded and an ICMP message sent back to the source. So if the next-hop destination for the static route is entered as `Serial1`, and the Serial1 physical interface happens to be down, the next hop is unreachable. If a router IP address or IP network address is used as a next hop, then dynamic routing protocols might be able to use an alternate path to the next hop. If the next hop is a network address (such as 10.0.32.0/24) and not a host route (10.0.32.1 or the equivalent 10.0.32.1/32), then the router can perform some load sharing if there are multiple interfaces that can be used to reach the next-hop IP address. But both interfaces and IP addresses can be used in static routes. If a next hop is reachable only over a single serial link and that link is down, why bother using IP addresses for next hops?

Sometimes it makes sense to have a static route next hop that explicitly discards packets. This could be helpful, for example, when a new customer site is being prepared for linking to an access router. The address assignment is known, and testing needs to be done to make sure that the routing information is distributed properly among the other routers. One way to perform this testing is to simply configure the new customer route with a next hop of "discard" until the customer site is ready to go.

All you need to define a static route on a Cisco router is the `ip route` configuration command, the static route's IP address, the subnet mask, and the next-hop IP address. The following adds some static routes to the example Cisco access router:

```
Cisco_access(config)# ip route 10.200.1.0 255.255.255.0 10.0.32.1
Cisco_access(config)# ip route 10.200.2.0 255.255.255.0 null0
Cisco_access(config)# ip route 10.200.3.0 255.255.255.0 serial0
```

The first line adds the static route 10.200.1/24 to the Cisco access router and sets the next hop to the Ethernet0 interface defined in the startup configuration routine. An optional value for the Cisco *administrative distance* of a static route is not used in this example, because this value is only used by Cisco routers.

The second line adds the static route 10.200.2/24 but sets the next hop to `null0`. On a Cisco router, any packet routed to the null0 interface is simply discarded as if it had never existed. So packets that arrive at this router for network 10.200.2.0 are sent to null0 and discarded.

The third line adds the static route 10.200.3/24 and sets the next hop to the `serial0` interface. This works as well as specifying the IP address and will always forward packets to this IP address out the specified interface, regardless of the IP address assigned to the interface. Now, packet forwarding always resolves two facts about the output interface: IP address and physical port. So it does not really matter so much which one is given as the next hop: The router always finds out both. But in one case, the IP address is used to determine the interface, no matter where the interface is, and in the other case, the interface is used to find out the IP address, no matter what the IP address is.

A special case of a static route is the *default route*. The default route, if it exists, is used to forward packets that do not match a more specific entry in the routing table. Typically, the default route is in the form 0.0.0.0/0, which will match any IP address that has no longer match in the routing table.

The following configuration command sends all packets without longer matches in the routing table out onto the `ethernet0` interface on the `Cisco_access` router:

```
Cisco_access(config)# ip route 0.0.0.0 0.0.0.0 ethernet0
```

Why is this entry important? Consider the situation shown in Figure 5.10, which is common enough in access router configurations. There are three serial interfaces to customer sites and one Ethernet interface to link access routers to other service provider routers.

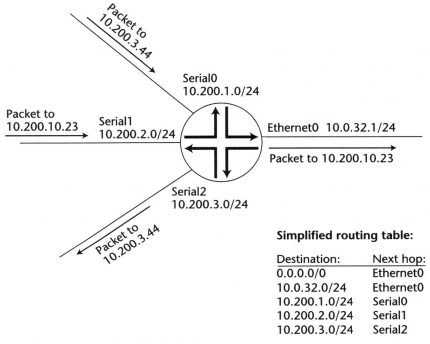

Figure 5.10 The role of the default route.

Packets arriving on any interface for destinations on network 10.200.3.0/24 are sent to Serial2 based on the longest match. Packets for *any* other destination not on these three serial interfaces are sent to the default next hop and out of interface Ethernet0, which is exactly what is needed.

Cisco routers also have a concept of the *gateway of last resort*. This is similar to the idea of a default route. To set the gateway of last resort, you use the following configuration command:

```
Cisco_access(config)# ip default-network 10.0.32.0
```

As long as there is an entry in the routing table for 10.0.32.0, then this next-hop interface will be used to forward packets without longer matches in the routing table.

Since both default routes and gateways of last resort have only local significance, these routes are not usually advertised to other routers by the routing protocols. However, there are exceptions to this general rule.

Setting the Aggregate

Aggregate, or summary, routes are used to keep routing information advertisements between routers to a minimum, as well as to keep the size of routing tables. Aggregation is often done on access routers as long as the customer addresses are assigned in a way that is consistent with the aggregation policy of the service provider. This means that access routers should use contiguous IP address spaces, at least to the extent feasible based on the service provider's address space allocation. Haphazard assignment of IP addresses can easily lead to "holes" in the address space that make aggregation inefficient at best and just wrong at worst.

The trick when establishing aggregates is to make sure the aggregate route is general enough to cover all of the more specific routes beneath the aggregate and still be specific enough so that routing loops or black holes do not happen.

Following is a relatively simple procedure to follow for determining aggregate mask length:

1. Put the candidate routes for aggregation in numerical order.
2. Write out the addresses as bit strings.
3. Account for any holes in the aggregate address space.
4. Use a mask that covers all of the bits in the aggregate space that are the same.

This procedure is easier to show as an example rather than explain in the abstract. Suppose an access router has been configured with the following IP addresses on the serial links to customers:

```
10.200.1.0/24
10.200.2.0/24
10.200.5.0/24
10.200.6.0/24
```

What aggregate can be used to summarize this address space? The addresses are already in numerical order, so the second step is to write them down as bit strings (a space is used to indicate the mask length):

```
10.200.1.0/24    00001010 11001000 00000001    00000000
10.200.2.0/24    00001010 11001000 00000010    00000000
10.200.5.0/24    00001010 11001000 00000101    00000000
10.200.6.0/24    00001010 11001000 00000110    00000000
```

There are several holes in this range. Subnet 0 (10.200.0.0/24) should not be assigned to a customer anyway, and 10.200.7.0/24 turns out to be the directed broadcast address, so those absences are understandable. But where are 10.200.3.0/24 and 10.200.4.0/24? If these addresses are assigned to other access routers, then aggregation should not take place. After all, if the network administrator on the other router decided to aggregate those two addresses with the same aggregate route used on the Cisco_access router, there will be two routes floating around on the network each claiming to be the best way to deliver packets to that address space. In this case, assume that these two addresses are reserved for customers and serial interfaces on this access router, but these addresses have not yet been assigned.

The final step is to establish the point where the addresses differ. This is shown in **bold** in the following:

```
10.200.1.0/24    00001010 11001000 00000001    00000000
10.200.2.0/24    00001010 11001000 00000010    00000000
10.200.5.0/24    00001010 11001000 00000101    00000000
10.200.6.0/24    00001010 11001000 00000110    00000000
```

So the address space in the example can be safely aggregated as 10.200.0.0/21. This is represented in 255 notation as a mask of 255.255.248.0.

Because Cisco routers are inherently classful IP devices, aggregation can be complicated on a Cisco router. For example, to a basic Cisco router, the summary network for the range 10.200.1.0/24 through 10.200.6.0/24 is 10.0.0.0/8, period. The "natural" aggregate for this range is not 10.200.0.0/21 but 10.0.0.0/8! A Class A is a Class A, and that is that. Of course, a service provider with a Class A address having some 16 million possible hosts will not be happy to be forced to use this address space for a handful of hosts on a single access router.

Fortunately, Cisco routers can act in a classless manner through the use of the `ip classless` command, and this is the default in newer IOS versions. When this is configured on a collection of Cisco routers, the routers and routing protocols will not complain that 10.200.1.0/24 appears on one router while 10.200.14.0/24 appears on another router four hops away. So, many Cisco routers routinely use `ip classless` today.

However, just making a Cisco router classless is not the same as having an easy way to set aggregates of arbitrary length on the router. For instance, there is no global `aggregate` configuration command at all in Cisco. Instead, Cisco routers can use a variation on the `ip  route` command and `default-network` command to establish arbitrary classless aggregates (there are other ways to represent aggregates on Cisco routers).

When a static route is used as an aggregate (or summary route), the address used is in a fashion "halfway" between a route that provides a longest match for a specific network such as 10.200.1.0/24 and the global default route (0.0.0.0/0) that matches anything without a more specific route in the routing table. So a `default-network` of 10.200.0.0/21 could be used to produce the longest match for destinations such as 10.200.1.0/24 through 10.200.6.0/24 without needing specific entries for those networks on the router. Naturally, the specifics about networks 10.200.1.0/24 through 10.200.6.0/24 still must *exist* on the router with the interfaces leading to those networks, but only the aggregate address of 10.200.0.0/21 need be advertised to other routers.

To create a routing table entry for the aggregate 10.200.0.0/21, you need another static route. The static route for the aggregate must have the proper subnet mask and a valid next hop. The `ip route` command is used for this. However, there is no real next hop associated with this aggregate, because only the specifics under the aggregate have reachable interfaces on the router. So it is also necessary to use a network for the next hop of the aggregate on the router that will be reachable in the routing table. This is called the *summary route* version of the static `ip route` command.

For example, the following command sets a static aggregate route for 10.200.0.0/21 and gives it a next-hop network address of 10.0.32.0 (no mask needed). The mask is entered in 255 format. This next hop is, of course, the network address of the Ethernet interface and so will be found in the routing table. This next hop is also the next hop for the aggregate that will be advertised when the static aggregate is advertised to other routers with a routing protocol:

```
Cisco_access(config)#ip route 10.200.0.0 255.255.248.0 10.0.32.0
```

Cisco routers can also explicitly set aggregate addresses in certain routing protocols. Unlike using static routes as aggregates, this method is not used at the global level of the configuration, but at the routing protocol level for the routing protocols that recognize and commonly use aggregation, particularly BGP.

To set an aggregate for a routing protocol to use on the Cisco access router, you use the `aggregate-address` configuration command (technically, this is a subcommand). Note that this is done under the config-router section (*not* the global config section) of the Cisco configuration, because Cisco routers usually tie aggregation (or summarization) to a specific routing protocol and *not* to the router in general. There is nothing in any way wrong with Cisco routers tying aggregation to a routing protocol: Routers do not exist in isolation and routers are expected to be running at least one routing protocol, and most routers run several.

More details of the Cisco use of the aggregate will be discussed in Chapter 13, "Border Gateway Protocol (BGP)," and Chapter 17, "Basic BGP Routing Policies." The following is provided just to show how aggregation *would* be configured under a routing protocol such as BGP:

```
Cisco_access(config-router)# aggregate-address 10.200.0.0 255.255.248.0
```

Even when an aggregate address is established for some routing protocols, the Cisco router continues to advertise the more specific routes such as 10.200.1.0/24 and so on. To suppress the specifics and advertise only the summary route, you can use the `summary-only` option:

```
Cisco_access(config-router)# aggregate-address 10.200.0.0 255.255.248.0
summary-only
```

To make these configuration statements permanent, you must exit Configuration mode with Ctrl/Z and then simply do a `write  memory` or `copy running-config startup-config` to apply the changes to the router.

Viewing the Results

What will the Cisco configuration look like when the loopback and static routes have been added to the configuration? What will the routing table look like? The following commands and listings show this, now using an older IOS, IOS 11.2:

```
Cisco_access#show configuration
Building configuration...
Current configuration:
!
version 11.2
service password-encryption
!
enable secret 5 $1$ryTe$ekYqoFhp9fjSTQ4pDy9fy/
enable password lab
line vty 0 4
password lab
snmp-server community public
!
no decnet routing
appletalk routing
ipx routing
ip routing
!
interface Ethernet0
 no ipx network
interface Serial0
 no ipx network
interface Serial1
 no ipx network
!
Interface Loopback 0
 ip address 10.100.32.1 255.255.255.255
!
interface Ethernet0
 ip address 10.0.32.1 255.255.255.0
 ipx network 1
 no mop enabled
!
 interface Serial0
 no shutdown
 ip address 10.0.33.1 255.255.255.0
 no mop enabled
!
network 10.0.0.0
```

```
!
ip route 0.0.0.0 0.0.0.0 Ethernet0
ip route 10.200.1.0 255.255.255.0 10.0.32.1
ip route 10.200.2.0 255.255.255.0 Null0
ip route 10.200.3.0 255.255.255.0 Serial0
!
end
```

The `aggregate-address` command, tied as it is in Cisco to a routing protocol, is not shown. Aggregates will be configured and used in Chapter 17 on BGP.

Even this simple configuration has a number of IP addresses, but not much shows up yet in the Cisco routing table. To see the contents of the IP routing table, you use the Cisco operational command `show ip route`:

```
Cisco_access#show ip route
Codes: I - IGRP derived, R - RIP derived, O - OSPF derived
       C - connected, S - static, E - EGP derived, B - BGP derived
       i - IS-IS derived, D - EIGRP derived
       * - candidate default route, IA - OSPF inter area route
       E1 - OSPF external type 1 route, E2 - OSPF external type 2 route
       L1 - IS-IS level-1 route, L2 - IS-IS level-2 route
       EX - EIGRP external route

Gateway of last resort is not set

     10.0.0.0 is subnetted (mask is 255.255.255.0), 1 subnets
S       10.200.2.0 is directly connected, Null0
Cisco_access#
```

The codes used essentially show the source of the routing information. For example, a C, or connected, network is one that is directly configured on a physical interface on the router, and static routes are marked as S.

Where are the IP addresses for the Ethernet and serial interfaces, the loopback, and the default? Furthermore, only one static is listed, the one with the next hop to Null0. What happened?

All is well. Cisco routers exist to *route* through connections to other routers and networks. This router is still totally isolated from the rest of the world and does not even have any physical link connectors plugged in yet. Since no interfaces are up except the internal Null0 "bit bucket," there are no active routes to display even though the configuration shows them. Once a true network is built with active links, routing protocols, and routing policies, the contents of the Cisco routing table changes dramatically.

More Cisco Configuration Tools

Cisco also has two tools available to simplify configuration chores: Config-Maker and Fast Step. Neither of these will be mentioned further in this book, because the material in this book assumes direct console configuration and these tools run on external system platforms.

In the next chapter, we compare and contrast the Juniper Networks architecture and configuration procedures with Cisco.

Juniper Networks Router Configuration

Juniper Networks routers share many of the same features as Cisco routers. Yet they also differ from Cisco routers in many important respects. We handle our discussion of Juniper Networks in this chapter in much the same manner as in the previous chapter on Cisco routers. The parallel structure between the two chapters allows you to easily compare and contrast the Cisco way and the Juniper Networks way of doing things with routers. In fact, Chapters 5 and 6 can be thought of as companion chapters. The method used with respect to configuration is intended to be as neutral as possible and permit readers to form their own opinions about what is easy and intuitive and what is difficult and complicated with regard to basic configuration tasks.

First, we look at the basic Juniper Networks router architecture and products. Not all router variations currently available from Juniper Networks are surveyed, only the main products. Nevertheless, the whole Juniper Networks approach to routing is explored. As is evident, Juniper Networks is a more specific, hardware-based routing architecture than is Cisco. Next, a basic startup and static route configuration example is given—the same one as in Chapter 5. The same notation used in this book for configuration and routing policies is used in the example, with distinct text styles for prompts, user command input, and router console output.

Router access in this coverage is assumed to be the simplest type: direct, local access to the router through the terminal console serial port on the router.

Other router access methods are mentioned and described, but all of the examples are based on direct console connection to the router. Keep in mind that what you actually see, and the keystrokes actually required to configure the router, might be somewhat different if you were to access the router through something other than the direct console port. For the most part, however, elements should be similar enough among the different means of router access for the method to be understood even when router access is other than local and direct.

Finally, we look at the configuration files and commands used to manipulate these files on Juniper Networks routers. The number and location of these Juniper Networks configuration files, as well as their look and feel, are quite different than on the Cisco router platforms. The commands used to change these files are distinct as well. This chapter always uses the *command-line interface* (CLI) method of typing in a command and then examining the result on the router's configuration file.

The discussion in this chapter concerns Juniper Networks routers only. Other vendors of routers exist; no slight is intended toward them. But for the sake of brevity, this subject matter is limited in scope. Cisco and Juniper Networks are also the two router lines that are investigated in Chapters 17 through 19, on routing protocol and routing policy configuration.

Router Architecture: Juniper Networks

Some say that the architecture of a Juniper Networks router could not be more different than that of a Cisco router. Where Cisco's basic router architecture is CPU-based and general, Juniper Networks router architecture is hardware-based and specific. This contrast, as detailed later, could extend to other aspects of the routers as well, from the fractured IOS of Cisco to the unified JUNOS software of Juniper Networks, from the sprawling product line of Cisco to the focused one of Juniper Networks, and so on. For now, all you need to know is that Juniper Networks routers are very different in many ways than Cisco routers. You can decide the degree for yourself.

Cisco might have invented the router, but Juniper Networks invented a distinct type of router based not on a PC or workstation architecture but on "hardware" that allowed the router to perform packet forwarding at *wire speeds* (this term, once common, is now not used), as fast as the link could deliver packets. The hardware was really a collection of application-specific integrated circuits (ASICs) that were programmed with *microcode* (very low level and fast instructions) and could perform only the specific tasks that were burned onto the ASICs when they were made. Now, just like Cisco, Juniper Networks did not really invent hardware-based architectures, or ASICs, or microcode. But Juniper Networks applied these techniques to IP routing and extended them with their own breakthroughs to produce a router that did essentially not need to buffer packets while they were being routed. And this high-speed capability enabled Juniper Networks to produce routers that could still route at link bit rates far above their competitors, up to 10 Gbps. In fact, a lot of early performance numbers of Juniper Networks routers, even when produced by independent lab testing, were met with skepticism.

In contrast to Cisco, Juniper Networks is a tightly focused company. They make very fast routers—period. Some of these routers are smaller than others, but no Juniper Networks router is intended for small offices or SOHO applications. There are no feature sets or options: Any Juniper Networks router can perform multicasting or form a VPN or be anywhere along a Multiprotocol Label Switching (MPLS) path, as long as the proper interface hardware is present. In describing Cisco routers, the task is to find enough hardware and software similarities to talk about. With Juniper Networks routers, the task is often to find enough differences between the products to make the discussion interesting.

Juniper Networks Hardware: An Overview

No one would accuse a Juniper Networks router of looking or acting like a PC. This was one of the reasons for the initial success of Juniper Networks: Routers based on a central CPU had just about run out of gas once links speeds moved into the multigigabit ranges with OC-48 (2.4 Gbps) and OC-192 (10 Gbps). And with 10-Gigabit Ethernet and OC-768 (40 Gbps) emerging, the time was right for a change to the basic architecture of the router.

Juniper Networks routers, oddly enough, *do* have hard drives, and some of them have floppy drives (although very large ones) as well. In fact, every Juniper Networks router has a complete PC built right in (some even have two PCs), and the JUNOS operating system runs on a modified version of UNIX called FreeBSD UNIX. But isn't the PC architecture much too slow for heavy-duty, high-speed routing? And isn't a hard drive useless when it comes to routing because the routing table has to be in memory? Right on both counts. The PC in the Juniper Networks router, called the Routing Engine (RE), does not forward packets at all. Packets are routed and forwarded by the Packet Forwarding Engine (PFE) where all the specialized ASICs are located. The RE controls the router, handles the routing protocols and performs all of the other tasks that can be handled more leisurely than high-speed packet transit traffic.

The fundamental principle in Juniper Networks router design is the idea that the functions of a router can be split into two distinct parts: one portion for handling routing and control operations and another for forwarding packets. By separating these two operations, the router hardware can be designed and optimized to perform each function well.

This division of labor makes perfect sense. It has already been pointed out several times that no one really sends traffic *to* a router. The vast majority of packets just pass *through* the router. So transit packets never leave the hardware-based PFE, and control packets, such as those for the routing protocols, which only come along even few seconds or so, can be handled as required by the RE.

Just like other routers, Juniper Networks routers can handle a variety of types of networking interfaces. But Juniper Networks routers are intended mainly for an ISP backbone, although many corporations are attracted to smaller, edge-oriented Juniper Networks routers as well. So Juniper Networks routers do not include support for a lot of older, or more obscure, interface types and protocols. There is no configuring of IPX or AppleTalk on a Juniper Networks router, or Token Ring either. Juniper Networks routers tend to support only the fast and the current with regard to links and protocols.

The overall concept of the division between routing protocol control and management and line-rate routing transit traffic is shown in Figure 6.1. The components are discussed in detail in the sections that follow.

Before we examine each piece of the Juniper Networks router in detail, here is a short explanation of what each piece in the figure does in the router.

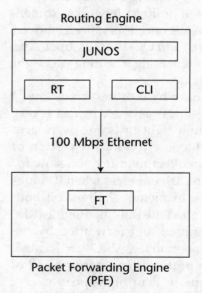

Figure 6.1   The Juniper Networks router architecture.

As mentioned, the section of the Juniper Networks router that is designed to handle the general routing operations is the *Routing Engine,* or RE. The RE is designed to handle all the routing protocols, user interaction, system management, and OAM&P (operations, administration, maintenance, and provisioning), and so on. The second section of the Juniper Networks router is referred to as the *Packet Forwarding Engine* (PFE) and is specifically designed to handle the forwarding of packets across the router from input to output interface. Transit packets never enter the Routing Engine at all.

The communications channel between the Routing Engine and the PFE is a standard 100-Mbps Fast Ethernet. This might seem somewhat surprising at first, because the interfaces on a Juniper Networks router can be many gigabits per second. But only control information needs to enter the Routing Engine. The vast majority of packets only transit the PFE at link speeds. There are many advantages to using a standard interface, even internally. A standard interface is easier to implement than creating a new proprietary interface, standard chipsets are readily available, inexpensive, and so on.

The RE contains the JUNOS operating system itself, the CLI for configuration and control, and the *routing table* (RT). The routing table in a Juniper Networks router contains all of the routing information gathered from all routing protocols running on the router, as well as miscellaneous information such as interface addresses, static routes, and so forth. Cisco routers also have a routing table, of course. But the routing table in a Cisco router more closely resembles what is called the *forwarding table* in a Juniper Networks router. This will become apparent later in this chapter.

The RE does not have to be very powerful or have a large hard drive, but it usually does only because it is hard to find older chipsets that will gracefully handle newer and more powerful features, and it is really hard to even buy a hard drive under 20 GB today.

The PFE is where the *forwarding table* (FT) resides. The FT contains all the active route information that is actually used to determine the packet's next hop without needing to send the packet to the RE. In many ways, what is displayed by the Cisco `show ip route` command used in the previous chapter, more closely resembles what ends up in the Juniper Networks forwarding table.

There is no counterpart in Juniper Networks to the memory types used in the Cisco router product line. Juniper Networks routers employ ASICs instead of memory for router functions. These next sections explore in more depth the overall architecture of the Juniper Networks router introduced above.

The Routing Engine (RE)

The RE is designed to be a robust, quick, PC-like host responsible for the operation of routing protocols, troubleshooting and provisioning operations, and general management of the router. The RE hardware consists of the following:

- An Intel Pentium-based compact Peripheral Component Interconnect (PCI) platform
- A nonrotating compact flash drive (often called a RAM disk)
- A standard rotating hard drive, the same as on any PC
- A removable PC Card (formerly PCMCIA) media drive

The JUNOS operating system software resides on the compact flash drive, and an alternate copy is on the system hard drive. This is one of many reasons that Juniper Networks routers include a hard drive as part of the RE. The hard-drive copy of the JUNOS software serves as a backup copy of the operating system for disaster-recovery situations.

The RE is primarily responsible for the protocol intelligence of the router. It is therefore responsible for creating the *routing table*, which consists of all routes learned by all protocols running on the router. The RE goes through the routing table periodically to generate a subset of routes that will be used for all forwarding purposes. These *active routes* are placed in the *forwarding table*. A copy of the forwarding table is in turn given to the PFE so that proper decisions can be made for packet handling. As route updates come into the RE by means of the routing protocols, the PFE's forwarding table is incrementally updated.

The incremental update of route changes is important. Rather than flushing the entire forwarding table and then replacing it with the new one, the RE sends a simple add, delete, or modify message to update the forwarding table. When you are routing on the Internet, it is common to see routing tables that consist of 100,000 routes or more. If a single route were to disappear, it is obviously simpler to remove the single route.

Packet Forwarding Engine (PFE)

The second major component of a Juniper Networks router is the PFE, the portion of the router that is specifically designed to forward transit packets. General-purpose processors are not necessary or desired in the PFE because of the specific job functions that are required of the PFE (such as packet encapsulation and route lookup). By designing microchips, or ASICs, specifically for these forwarding functions, the entire packet forwarding process can be implemented in hardware. This design technique allows for a more robust, consistent, and efficient packet forwarding implementation. The PFE is therefore highly efficient hardware that is responsible for forwarding packets as quickly as possible. It can also deliver wire-rate packet filtering, rate limiting, and accounting services with minimal impact on packet forwarding.

The PFE consists of four separate hardware components: *Physical Interface Cards* (PICs), *Flexible PIC Concentrators* (FPCs), the *midplane*, and a *control board*. Each component has its own ASIC (or sometimes several ASICs) that account for a single piece of the forwarding puzzle. Only when all four components are brought together can a packet be received on one port and forwarded out another.

Let's take a more detailed look at each component.

Physical Interface Card (PIC)

The PIC port is the interface connecting the router to physical transmission facilities. In other words, the PIC is where the network cable is plugged in. Located on each PIC is an ASIC that is designed to handle media-specific functions, such as encapsulation, checksums, and media-specific signaling. Separate ASICs have been designed for each media type supported by Juniper Networks. For example, an ASIC has been designed for Synchronous Optical Network (SONET) functions, for ATM functionality, and to handle Fast Ethernet operations.

On some router models, PICs are equipped with an ejector lever. These PICs are *hot-swappable*, which means that insertion and removal is accomplished without significantly affecting the operation of the rest of the router.

PICs for some earlier router models do not have ejector levers and require that the FPC be removed prior to PIC removal. While removal of this PIC will disrupt the operation of any ports on that particular FPC, the rest of the router's ports will continue to operate without significant disruption.

Flexible PIC Concentrator (FPC)

Simply put, the FPC is a chassis card that houses multiple PICs. Each FPC can hold between one and four PICs of any type (with the exception of certain OC-192c and OC-48 PIC/FPC combinations that exist for certain router models). For most models, the FPC also houses 128 MB of buffer memory that is utilized for storing data as it traverses the router, as well as a specially designed ASIC. The relationship between PIC and FPC is shown in Figure 6.2.

There is a PowerPC 603e processor on every FPC. While this general-purpose processor has nothing to do with forwarding packets, the 603e is used for supervisory processes such as monitoring communication between the PFE ASICs and bringing up and taking down PFE components. It also monitors items such as the temperature sensors located on the FPC. This information is then relayed to the JUNOS software for proper processing.

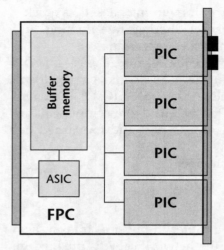

Figure 6.2 An FPC with PICs.

FPCs are designed to be fully hot-swappable. To properly remove or insert an FPC from the system, you must first prepare the router. Online and offline buttons are associated with each FPC. When you want to remove an FPC from an operational router, you simply press the button for 3 seconds until the associated status light goes off. Once the status light goes off, you can safely remove the FPC from the router.

To activate a currently installed FPC, you must again press the proper button for 3 seconds until the status light begins to flash green, indicating that the FPC is coming online. This procedure is necessary only in the case of an FPC that has been brought offline in the manner described in the preceding paragraph. FPCs installed at boot time will come online automatically, as will newly installed FPCs. Again, the insertion or removal of any particular FPC will not significantly interrupt the operation of the router as a whole.

The Router Midplane

Whenever an FPC is inserted into the router chassis, the electrical connectors on the FPC make contact with mating connectors on the midplane. The midplane is nothing more than a passive connection between the FPC and the control board that allows mechanical interconnection of the various components.

The Control Board

The control board (which oddly enough has different names on different router models) contains the central decision maker for the PFE, the *Internet*

Processor II ASIC (IP2). It is the control board that allows the IP2 to reference the information kept in the forwarding table in the PFE in order to properly route packets. The IP2, as well as some other important ASICs, is resident on the control board.

The IP2 is also where *firewall filtering* operations are implemented. Firewall filters establish security rules for routers. The IP2 contains a powerful, line-rate filtering mechanism that allows you to control IP traffic based on many characteristics. Since it is centrally located, a firewall filter can be implemented on any interface, flow, or traffic stream with the same level of performance.

In addition to the IP2 processor, the control board in a Juniper Networks router also contains a PowerPC 603e processor for supervisory functions. Again, this processor does not play any role in forwarding packets across the router. It is used for monitoring the environmental systems, maintaining communication between the RE and PFE, as well as managing the FPCs and all PFE ASICs. This processor is also responsible for loading and maintaining the forwarding table and handling so-called *exception packets*, which are packets that must be sent to the Routing Engine for further processing (such as routing protocol packets).

Packet Flow

The role of the ASICs in the PFE can best be understood by following the flow of a packet through the router—first into a PIC, then through the switching fabric, and finally out another PIC for transmission on a network link. The overall role of the ASICs is shown in Figure 6.3.

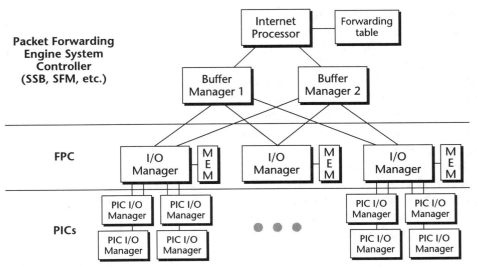

Figure 6.3 The role of the ASICs.

When a packet arrives on an input interface, a media-specific ASIC on the PIC performs all the media-specific details such as framing and checksum verification. Each PIC has an I/O manager ASIC for this purpose. For instance, ATM PICs have an ASIC for cell assembly and reassembly, T3 serial line PICs have an ASIC for all T3 framing, and so on.

The PIC then passes the serial stream of bits inside the frame to the FPC, which has an ASIC that parses and appropriately decapsulates (unwraps) the packet. Packets routinely carry extra headers in front of the IP packet itself, especially when ATM is used. The FPC also breaks the packet into fixed-length 64-byte memory blocks (in Juniper Networks documentation, these Juniper Networks-specific, fixed-length "cells" are sometimes called *j-cells*) and passes each memory block to the Distributed Buffer Manager ASIC on the system control board. The Distributed Buffer Manager ASIC then writes the memory blocks into packet buffer memory, which is distributed evenly across all the FPCs installed in the router. This is a nice feature, because memory on an FPC that has very active ports can always use buffer space on a less active FPC. This avoids buffer starvation on the router.

In parallel with this buffering, the Distributed Buffer Manager ASIC extracts the information from the packet header needed for route lookup and passes that information to the Internet Processor ASIC. The IP ASIC, usually the IP2, performs a lookup in its full forwarding table and finds the outgoing interface and the specific next hop. The forwarding table can forward all unicast packets that do not have options and multicast packets that have been previously cached. Unicast packets with options and noncached multicast packets (and other exception packets) are sent to the Routing Engine for resolution.

After the Internet Processor ASIC has determined the next hop, it passes the results of the lookup to a second Distributed Buffer Manager ASIC, which in turn passes it to the outgoing interface. (Note that there could be multiple outgoing interfaces in the case of multicast.)

At this stage a pointer to the packet is queued, *not* the packet itself. Even though routing is proceeding at line rates, output ports can only handle one packet at a time. If two input ports point to the same next-hop output interface, one packet goes while the other must wait in a queue.

Each output port has four queues, each of which can have a configured share of the link bandwidth. Several factors can account for queuing order, including the value of the precedence bits, utilization of the input interface, destination address, and even more sophisticated algorithms. If the outgoing interface decides to queue the packet for transmission, when the packet reaches the front of the queue and is ready for transmission, the memory blocks are read from packet buffer memory. Then the packet is reassembled and passed to the media-specific PIC for transmission on the line.

Juniper Networks Router Access

Like most routers, Juniper Networks routers do not come with a monitor and keyboard. Router management is accomplished in four ways, although the Juniper Networks router only comes with one of these methods enabled by default. Juniper Networks routers' access for management purposes is always to the Routing Engine. The PFE has enough to do forwarding traffic, and there is no ASIC that would pay attention to a user login request anyway. The four ways that a network administrator can communicate with a Juniper Networks router are as follows:

The console port.   This port is for a serial terminal that is at the same location as the router and attached by a short cable from the serial port on the terminal to the console port on the router. The terminal is usually a PC or UNIX workstation running a terminal emulation program. In contrast to Cisco, there is only one physical connector type used for this port: a DB9 connector. Network administrators never have to carry around several different connector types so they can be sure to have the proper connector for the router they need to manage. On Juniper Networks routers, this is the only management port enabled by default.

The auxiliary (AUX) port.   This port is for a serial terminal that is at a remote location. Connection is made through a pair of modems, one connected to the router and the other connected to the terminal. There is little difference if any between the AUX and console ports in terms of characteristics. They are separate because routers might require simultaneous local and remote access that would be impossible if only one serial port was on the router. On Juniper Networks routers, this management port is disabled by default and must be configured before use.

The network.   The Juniper Networks router can always be managed over the same network that it is routing packets on. This is often called *in-band management* in contrast to the console and AUX ports, which are *out-of-band*. This just means that the network access method shares the link to the router in the same bandwidth as user packets transiting the router. There are three ways to access a Juniper Networks router over the network: through Telnet, through secure shell (ssh), or with Simple Network Management Protocol (SNMP), a protocol invented expressly for remote router management. Telnet, ssh, and SNMP must be configured on the router before they can be used. Remote access through Telnet or ssh is usually made to the *lo0* interface over the *fxp1* interface from PFE to RE. The RE end of the fxp1 interface is called *loopback0* (lo0).

Management Ethernet.   Juniper Networks routers also include an out-of-band Ethernet 10/100Base-T LAN port that can be configured to allow many routers to be managed over a special Ethernet LAN that handles only management sessions and is invisible to user transit packets. This LAN essentially networks the Routing Engines together and does not affect the PFEs at all. This port is the *fxp0* port. Access is through Telnet, ssh, or SNMP.

The four ways to access a Juniper Networks router for configuration and management purposes are shown in Figure 6.4.

Some Juniper Networks routers can be configured with two Routing Engines for redundancy purposes. In that case, there are two of each type of access port on each router. Only the console ports are enabled by default. The two AUX and management Ethernet ports must be configured on each RE, and in-band network access must be to one RE or the other. Just as with Cisco, the console and AUX ports only understand a simple, character-based serial protocol. On a PC or workstation, only a terminal emulation program like HyperTerminal can communicate with a Juniper Networks router through the console or AUX ports. The management Ethernet allows Telnet or SNMP access.

Juniper Networks Router Operating System

In stark contrast to Cisco routers, the routing engine on a Juniper Networks router is a completely functional UNIX platform that runs the JUNOS operating system, also called the JUNOS Internet software. It is even possible to "shell out" of the router interface on the RE and enter the UNIX realm, but this is usually only done at the instruction of a Juniper Networks technician during troubleshooting or diagnostic procedures.

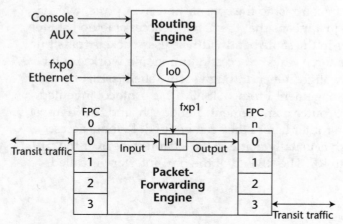

Figure 6.4   Accessing Juniper Networks routers.

The JUNOS Internet software provides IP routing protocol software—as well as software for interface, network, and chassis management—specifically designed for the large production networks typically supported by Internet service providers. The complete JUNOS Internet software runs on all Juniper Networks routers, so there are no feature sets to worry about.

The JUNOS Internet software runs on the router's RE. It consists of software processes that support Internet routing protocols, control the router's interfaces and the router chassis itself, and allow router system management. All these processes run on top of a *kernel* that enables communication among all the processes and has a direct link to the PFE software. The JUNOS software is used to configure the routing protocols that should run on the router and to configure properties of the router's interfaces. Afterward, the JUNOS software is used to monitor the router and to troubleshoot protocol and network connectivity problems.

The JUNOS Internet software is preinstalled on the router. Once the router is powered on, it is ready to be configured. The primary copy of the software is installed on a nonrotating flash disk (UNIX device *ad0*). Two backup copies are included, one on the router's rotating hard disk (ad1 or ad2, depending on the model) and a second on the removable media (either a 120-MB LS-120 floppy disk or a PCMCIA card, which can be afd0 or ad4) that is shipped with the router.

When the router boots, it first attempts to start the software image from the removable media if one is installed in the router. If this fails, the router next tries the flash disk, then finally the hard disk. Normally, the router boots from the flash disk. If the router is booted from an *alternative media*, users are informed of this.

Each JUNOS software release consists of the following components:

- Base package, which contains additions to the operating system
- Kernel and network tools package, which contains the operating system
- Routing package, which contains the software that runs on the Routing Engine
- Packet Forwarding Engine software package
- Crypto package, which contains security software (domestic version)
- Documentation package, which contains the documentation for the software

A *package* is a collection of files that make up a software component. These software packages are provided as a single unit, called a *bundle*, which you can use to upgrade all the packages at once. Packages can also be upgraded individually, but this is usually done as part of a troubleshooting procedure. When you upgrade to a new major release, the bundle must be used; individual packages should not be used. Between 4.X and 5.Y releases, a special package called *jinstall* is needed.

Generally, the software is downloaded by authorized customers over the Internet. The price that is paid by bundling all of the JUNOS software features in one bundle is that the JUNOS software is much larger than most Cisco packages. Presumably, bandwidth is not a problem for Internet core backbone service providers.

Two sets of JUNOS software packages are provided, one for customers in the United States and Canada and another for other customers. The worldwide version does not include any capabilities that provide encryption of data leaving the router. Otherwise, the two packages are identical.

An example of a JUNOS software release number is shown in Figure 6.5. A JUNOS software release has a name in the following format:

```
JUNOS-m.nZnumber
```

In this notation, `m.n` are two integers that represent the software release number, and `m` denotes the major release number. `Z` is a capital letter that indicates the type of software release. In most cases, it is an `R`, to indicate that this is released software. If you are involved in testing prereleased software, this letter might be an `A` (for alpha-level software), `B` (for beta-level software), or `I` (for internal, test, or experimental versions of software). `Number` represents the version of the major software release (sometimes called the "build").

The following is an example of a software release name:

```
JUNOS-5.0R2.4
```

For distribution and upgrade purposes, a JUNOS software package has a name in the following format:

```
Package-name-release.tgz
```

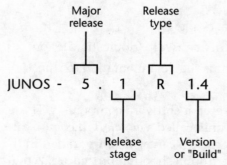

Figure 6.5 The major parts of a JUNOS software release number.

(This is a file in the usual UNIX "tar and gzip" format.) `Package-name` is the name of the package. Examples are `jroute` (the routing protocol package) and `jkernel` (the JUNOS operating system kernel package). `Release` is the JUNOS software release number; for example, 5.0R1 or 4.4R1.5.

Although not technically part of the JUNOS software version designation, the packages usually have a final extension before the "tgz" ending indicating whether the package is for *domestic* (encryption) or *export* (no encryption) purposes. The following are examples of JUNOS software package names:

```
jroute-5.1R1.4-domestic.tgz
jkernel-5.1R1.4-export.tgz
jpfe-5.1R1.4-domestic.tgz
jbundle-5.1R1.4-domestic.tgz (jbundle contains all needed packages:
used within 4.X or 5.Y)
jinstall-5.1R1.4-domestic.tgz  (jinstall must be used to
upgrade/downgrade between 4.X and 5.Y)
```

There is much more to the JUNOS software than this brief overview supplies. Other books are available that give more details of the structure of the JUNOS operating system. Most of the details we explored were just to contrast the Juniper Networks approach with Cisco's IOS philosophy.

Juniper Networks Router Products

Unlike Cisco, which makes just about every type of networking device, the product line of Juniper Networks is much more focused. Juniper Networks makes very fast routers, mostly intended for the core network of an ISP. This is not to say that there are not differences among the routers. Some can be used as cable TV headends for cable modem services, others can be used for wireless and mobile IP environments, and so on. But this section emphasizes the similarities among the product line.

Every Juniper Networks router is built on the same basic foundation of RE/PFE. While the idea of using a dedicated PFE along with a physically separate RE for handling routing protocols remains consistent, each product is slightly different from its predecessors. In this section we examine the features of each router that comprised the Juniper Networks product line at the end of 2001.

In August 1998, the M40 router debuted. Impressive as the M40 was as a high-speed router, the product that really put Juniper Networks on the map was the introduction of the M20 router in December of 1999. No one had ever seen a router that could cram so much speed and functionality into a form factor so small. The number of high-speed interfaces that an M20 router could jam into a small amount of telecommunications rack space was the talk of the industry. In contrast to the M40, it was even possible to consider using M20s closer to the edges of the network, although most M20s were firmly placed on the service provider backbone. Juniper Networks returned to the core with a vengeance in March 2000 with the M160 router. If the M20 opened eyes with regard to size, the M160 opened eyes with regard to speed and capacity. The M160 could handle and route packets at a full 10 Gbps on each interface, an impressive accomplishment. Finally, the company turned more toward the edge with the introduction of the M5/M10 routers in September 2000. These two routers shared a common chassis and could be used in the core or at the edge of the network.

Table 6.1 shows the general features of the Juniper Networks product line, this time in order of size and capacity. In the table, the FPCs are called "slots" since the M5 and M10 do not use FPCs. Four PICs per slot are typically supported, but the number of physical interfaces per PIC can vary depending on the speed of the interface (a major exception is the OC-192c or STM-16 PIC on the M160; only one 10 Gbps interface is supported on the entire FPC). Racks are assumed to be standard 7-foot (2-meter+) telecommunications racks.

Now let's take a closer look at each of these major platforms, this time in chronological order.

M40

During initial product development, the largest potential customers of Juniper Networks wanted a router to provide line-rate performance on a stable platform, and they wanted it immediately. The large carriers who wanted to deploy the M40 insisted that if they desired redundancy, they would deploy the routers in pairs. So the M40 had no redundancy when it comes to hardware, with the exception of redundant power supplies. Otherwise desirable optional features such as redundancy and firewall capabilities were pushed aside to deliver the product to market in minimal time. The result was the half-rack-sized M40.

Table 6.1 The Juniper Networks Product Line

ROUTER	SLOT BANDWIDTH	SLOTS	MAXIMUM PICS	POWER	SIZE
M5	3.2 Gbps	1	4	AC/DC	15 per rack
M10	3.2 Gbps	2	8	AC/DC	15 per rack
M20	3.2 Gbps	4	16	AC/DC	5 per rack
M40	3.2 Gbps	8	32	AC/DC	2 per rack
M160	12.8 Gbps	8	32	DC only	2 per rack

The power supplies in an M40 can be either alternating current (AC) or direct current (DC), but not both simultaneously, and are fully redundant. While a single power supply can provide sufficient power for the entire router, if two are operating correctly, they will share the load. The DC power supplies have a maximum output of 1,500 watts (W) and an input current rating of 35 amps at minus 48 volts (35 A @ -48 V). The input voltage can be in the range of -40 through -75 V DC. The AC power supplies also run a maximum of 1,500 W and have an input current rating of 8 A @ 208 V. The acceptable input voltage range is from 180 to 264 V AC.

The M40 has a single RE and a single board for PFE control, and it can contain up to eight FPCs. The control board for the PFE is referred to as the *System Control Board (SCB)* and is located in the middle of the PFE. One significant difference between the M40 and the remaining product line is that the Distributed Buffer Manager ASICs are located on the backplane of the M40 rather than on the control board as in the other router models.

M20

The M20 platform was designed for greater port density and holds up to four FPCs in a chassis that is only 14 inches high. This model also addresses customer concerns about redundancy.

The power supplies in an M20 can also be either AC or DC and are fully redundant. The DC power supplies have a maximum output of 750 W and an input current rating of 24 A @ -48 V. The input voltage can be in the range of -40 through -72 V DC. The AC power supplies also run a maximum of 750 W and have an input current rating of 13 A @ 90 V. The acceptable input voltage range is from 90 to 264 V AC.

In the M20 platform the Distributed Buffer Manager ASICs are moved from the backplane to the control board. For this reason, the control board was renamed the *System Switching Board (SSB)* to reflect the change. The M20 also implements full redundancy with dual REs and dual SSBs. Both the REs and the SSBs are redundant in that during normal operation, one is operational while the second is in standby mode. In the event of a failure, the second unit assumes control of the router, although not instantaneously.

M160

Like the M20, the M160 implements dual REs that provide failure redundancy. The PFE, however, is handled in a completely different manner. The basic architecture used in the M40 and M20 that moved packet information around inside the chassis could not handle 10-Gbps line rates. The basic speed was about 3.2 Gbps. So to quadruple the throughput of the basic architecture, the M160 moved to a system that allows the forwarded traffic to be load balanced over several control boards. Think of the M160 architecture as four M40s running in parallel.

The M160 implements four control boards that work together to handle the traffic transiting the router. The change in operation for the control board causes yet another name change, this time to *Switching and Forwarding Module (SFM)*. In essence, each of the four SFMs does the job of a single SCB in an M40. Since the M160 FPCs have four times the throughput of the M40 platform, each SFM is effectively handling one-quarter of the traffic on each FPC. Should one of the SFMs become inoperable, one-quarter of the router's throughput would be lost, but it can still continue to forward packets at the reduced rate until the failed SFM is replaced.

The M160 has another feature due to this parallel architecture. When the serial stream of bits leaves the FPC, it must be directed to one of the four M160 SFMs. To accomplish this, two *Packet Director (PD)* ASICs are utilized. The PD ASICs determine to which SFM to send the packet and direct the serial stream of bits to one of four I/O manager ASICs that have been installed on each FPC. Each I/O manager is assigned to a particular SFM and therefore directs packet chunks toward a designated control board.

The M160 also improves on modularity in hardware, in part to make the replacement of failed parts easier, but mostly because of centralizing operation of common components found on the control board of other Juniper Networks routers. Because the M160 has four SFMs that work together, it is necessary to centralize operations such as internal clocking and system management.

So on the M160, the *Miscellaneous Control System (MCS)* works in conjunction with the RE to monitor communications among the internal router components and to provide clocking for SONET interfaces. The MCS monitors system components and sensors to gather information to send to the RE for processing. It also handles the power-up cycle for components when the system is first started, as well as the power-down sequence when the user requests that the unit be taken offline. The master MCS is hot-pluggable, and the backup MCS is hot-swappable. In other words, the router does not need to be powered down when inserting/removing the master MCS, but the routing will be interrupted. The backup MCS can be inserted/removed without affecting the router operations.

The *PFE Clock Generator (PCG)* generates a clocking signal to synchronize the internal components. The PCG supplies a 125-MHz clock to modules of the PFE including the ASICs. The PCGs are also hot-pluggable.

Another key difference in the M160 architecture is the separation of the out-of-band management ports. The Ethernet and RS-232 connectors are located on a separate card on the left side of the FPCs called the *Connector Interface Panel (CIP)*. The CIP is used for management connectivity to the M160's two REs. The upper set of connectors is labeled Host0 and connects directly to RE0. The second set of connectors is labeled Host1 and connects directly to RE1.

The final key differentiator for the M160 is the DC-only power supplies. Mostly because AC power rectification produces a large amount of heat, the M160 does not offer AC power modules. The DC power supplies are fully redundant, but in the case of the M160, two options exist for DC power. The original DC power supply provides a maximum output of 2,600 W with an input current rating of 65 A @ -48 V. The nominal DC input voltage should be in the range of -48 to -60 V DC. The enhanced DC power supply provides slightly more power at 3,200 W max with a slightly higher input current rating of 80 A @ -48 V. The "enhanced" power supply is needed only in rare occasions when the M160 is loaded with numerous cards drawing very high power.

M5/M10

It makes sense to talk about the M5 and M10 as one. They share a common chassis, but the M10 offers double the interface capacity as the M5. The M5 and M10 routers are reduced in size to increase port density. The loss of physical space inside and outside the router causes these smaller routers to move, combine, and even drop certain components that exist in the other platforms.

For example, the FPC in the M5/M10 has been combined with the control board to form a single *Forwarding Engine Board (FEB)*. This allows for consolidation of the main PFE functions and saves valuable space.

The PICs used for an M5/10 router have their own ejector handle and can therefore be installed or removed without powering down the router. This is necessary since the PIC inserts directly into the router chassis. PIC offline/online buttons are located on the front of the router. Since the M5/10 have a single RE, only a single set of the Ethernet and RS-232 connectors are required for out-of-band management.

The only aspect that externally differentiates the M5 from the M10 is the number of PICs that it can hold. The M5 router is capable of holding up to four PICs (one FPC), while the M10 can consist of up to eight PICS (two FPCs). Considering that both routers are only 5.25 inches high, this provides for outstanding port density.

Finally, the power supplies in the edge access routers are again available in both AC and DC and are fully redundant. The DC power supplies can provide up to 434-W maximum output with an input current rating of 13.5 A @ -48 V DC. The acceptable input voltage range is from -42.5 through -72 V DC. The AC power supplies also provide a maximum of 434-W output with an input current rating of either 8 A @ 100 volts AC, or 4 A @ 240 V AC.

All product lines evolve and change, and Juniper Networks is no exception. Look for newer router and related products to appear at almost any time as the T640 did in mid-2002.

Configuring Juniper Networks Routers

A Juniper Networks router's transit traffic might be controlled through a UNIX-based routing engine, but the Juniper Networks Routing Engine is as controlled through its configuration file as much as any other router is. Just as in Cisco's IOS, the JUNOS software is fixed in nature and cannot be altered by customers. Customers tell the JUNOS software what to do by editing and adjusting the configuration file.

Also as in Cisco, JUNOS software configuration files are edited differently than files found on an end-user computer, despite the similarities of the Routing Engine to a UNIX computer. Network administrators cannot just click and place a cursor where they want in the JUNOS software configuration file and type away just as with a word processing document. JUNOS software configuration files are changed using special JUNOS command-line interface (CLI) commands and then viewing the result to make sure it is what was intended.

And just as in Cisco, most Juniper Networks router problems are caused not by failing hardware, but by simple configuration errors. Configuration files must not only be correct on all routers concerned, but consistent as well. Changing the configuration file on one router can cause ripple effects throughout the network. Network administrators take configuration changes seriously, and they spend most of their time reviewing configurations and making changes in a coordinated fashion.

Getting Started

Juniper Networks routers lack the Cisco `setup` command dialogue sequence for initial router configuration. This is not to say that no initial configuration needs to be done on a Juniper Networks router, far from it. Juniper Networks recommends that a complete initial router configuration include setting at least the following:

- Name of the machine (hostname)
- The router's domain name
- IP address and prefix length information for the router's management Ethernet interface (fxp0)
- IP address of a default router to be used when the router cannot route properly on its own
- IP address of a DNS server for domain name lookups
- Password for the user "root" in good UNIX fashion

The following assumes that a network administrator is sitting at Windows PC directly connected by the serial port on the PC to the console port of a Juniper Networks router. All the network administrator has to do is run a terminal emulator program such as HyperTerminal as a VT100 (an old DEC terminal type that still works just fine and has a lot of nice features such as support for the arrow keys). The link itself is usually set for 9,600 bps, 8 bits per character, and no parity, and 1 stop bit to delimit the characters. This is typically abbreviated as 9,600 8-N-1 and is often the default for a lot of terminal emulator programs.

Initially, Juniper Networks routers have no users other than "root" defined. On initial startup, the console port is the only one active on the router. The router will not even boot into the CLI on initial startup. If a terminal is connected to the router, startup messages scroll across the screen, and then the user (network administrator) logs in as root with no password. The design engineers could have created a default password, but since this is for initial router configuration and only local console access is enabled, having no password is simpler. Since there is no hostname yet assigned, the router does not even know its name. The sequence to begin initial configuration is as follows:

```
no-name (ttyd0)

login: root

--- JUNOS 5.1R2.4 built 2001-12-11 02:11:09 UTC

Terminal type? [vt100] <Enter>
```

Once logged in as root, the user can run the JUNOS software CLI to begin configuration. The prompt for root login is %, but this is not really part of the router software. Again, the lack of a hostname explains the root@ prompt:

```
root@% cli
root> configure
Entering configuration mode

[edit]
root#
```

Note that the prompt is > in *Operational mode* and then # in *Configuration mode*. Since there is not yet a hostname for the router, the user is just "root at no_name."

"Operating" Modes

In contrast to the Cisco routers, there are only *two* modes for CLI commands on a Juniper Networks router. Both modes have distinct prompts: > for Operational mode and "#" for Configuration mode. As the names imply, Operational mode is for commands used to check on the overall functioning and status of the router, while Configuration mode is used to configure the router. Users can be limited to several levels of operational and configuration commands, but this feature is beyond the scope of this chapter. In the text that follows we'll assume that users are defined to have all privileges to run both operational and configuration commands alike (a UNIX *superuser*).

To enter Configuration mode, a user in Operational mode types either `configure` or `edit`, although `configure` is the recommended command. Note the change in prompt:

```
root> configure
Entering configuration mode

[edit]
root@#
```

Unlike Cisco routers, Juniper Networks configuration files have a structure and language all their own. A Juniper Networks configuration file looks almost like a C-language program and is sprinkled with "curly braces," or { and }, semicolons at the end of lines, and many levels of indentation.

The Juniper Networks configuration file has a strict hierarchical structure with major sections relating to the major function of the router. For example, physical interfaces are configured in the interfaces section of the configuration hierarchy, users are added at the system level, and so on. Initially, users are always placed at the highest level of the CLI configuration hierarchy. The level is always shown to the user in square brackets before the prompt, as shown in the preceding code. The highest level is just [edit]. To move about the hierarchy, the CLI `edit` command is used to move down, and there are several ways to move back up. Direct "side-to-side" movement in the configuration hierarchy is forbidden.

For example, to move to the `system` section of the configuration hierarchy, you simply type:

```
[edit]
root@#edit system
[edit system]
root@#
```

To move up one level in the hierarchy, you can use the `up` command. Many configuration sections are very deep in terms of levels, so `up` N can be used to move the user up N levels in the hierarchy until the top level is reached. For example, `up 2` moves the user up two levels in the configuration hierarchy. The command `top` always places the user at the top of the hierarchy. The `exit` command leaves Configuration mode if the user is at the top of the hierarchy. When used below the top level, the `exit` command often gives the same results as up (there are important exceptions, but this is not intended to be an exhaustive CLI tutorial).

There are currently 13 high-level sections in the configuration statement hierarchy. These are shown in alphabetical order in Table 6.2, along with a brief description of their general purpose.

Just as in Cisco, Juniper Networks router commands include an *auto-completion* feature that allows the router to interpret abbreviated commands as if the user had typed in the entire string, as long as the string entered is unambiguous. For example, typing conf is the same as typing configure. However, there is a key difference between how Cisco and Juniper Networks auto-completion works. Cisco just keeps the terse form of the command string on the screen: conf t, for example. Juniper Networks auto-completion is initiated whenever the <spacebar> is pressed and will always display the entire command string on the terminal. So conf<spacebar> results in the text string configure on the terminal.

Table 6.2   The Juniper Networks Configuration Command Hierarchy

HIERARCHY LEVEL	GENERAL PURPOSE
[edit accounting-options]	Sets overall accounting parameters for the router.
[edit chassis]	Sets environmental parameters such as alarms.
[edit class-of-service]	Sets parameters for preferred packet treatment on the router.
[edit firewall]	Sets up security-related firewall filters for the router.
[edit forwarding-options]	Sets sampling and other traffic-related parameters for the router.
[edit groups]	Sets up groups of statements repeated in the configuration.
[edit interfaces]	Sets addresses and related parameters for physical/logical interfaces.
[edit policy-options]	Sets up routing policies for the router.
[edit protocols]	Sets up the routing protocols used on the router.
[edit routing-instances]	Sets multiple, independent routing processes on the router.
[edit routing-options]	Sets overall global parameters, such as static routes, for the router.
[edit snmp]	Sets overall network management parameters for the router.
[edit system]	Sets up user and logging parameters for the router.

As with Cisco, there is an online help system that allows the user to enter a ? almost anywhere to find out what the allowed commands are at that point. The Up arrows or CTRL-P can be used to scroll through a history of commands as well.

Configuration Files

Juniper Networks configuration files are just text files. Since the Routing Engine is essentially a complete UNIX computer, editing capabilities for the configuration files are very robust.

When a user enters Configuration mode on a Juniper Networks router with `configure` or `edit`, the user is given a copy of the currently running *active configuration* called the *candidate configuration*. It is this candidate configuration file that is edited. When all changes are made to the candidate configuration, the candidate configuration is made the active configuration with the `commit` configuration command. The router performs a syntax check of the file, converts the file to machine-readable code, installs it as the active configuration, and returns to the command prompt:

```
[edit]
lab@MyRouter#commit
commit complete
[edit]
lab@MyRouter#
```

There are several options to the `commit` command for syntax checking (`commit check`) and to make the changes only tentative (`commit confirmed`). When `commit confirmed` is used, the *interim configuration* will automatically `rollback` to the previous configuration after 10 minutes, but this interval can easily be changed when the command is issued. To make a "confirmed" configuration permanent, you must issue the `commit` command again within the rollback interval.

The two main ways to make changes to the candidate configuration are with the `set` command to add information and the `delete` command to delete information. At any point in the configuration process, the `show` command can be used to see the level of the hierarchy being edited and all sections below. At the `[edit]` level, the entire configuration is displayed with the `show` command. Portions of the candidate configuration can displayed at whatever level of the hierarchy the user is parked.

Because the Routing Engine has a hard drive available, Juniper Networks routers can keep a number of copies of former configurations right on the router. There are actually 10 copies of committed configuration information. The text of the running configuration is called juniper.conf. The older copies are named juniper.conf.1 through juniper.conf.9. When a user does a `commit`,the oldest copy is deleted and all of the other copies are renumbered accordingly.

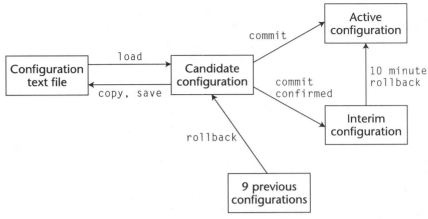

Figure 6.6   Juniper Networks router configuration files and commands.

To retrieve a copy of a previously committed configuration, the user uses the `rollback N` command, where N is the number of the configuration to be made the candidate configuration for editing. A `rollback` by itself is the same as `rollback 0` and always restores the current configuration as the candidate configuration (a nice feature for correcting global `delete` mistakes).

You can save configurations, and even portions of configurations, to flash memory or the hard drive on the Routing Engine. The `save` or `copy` commands can be used to save all or part of a candidate configuration with a user-specified filename (for example, my-config.txt). To make the saved configuration all or part of the candidate configuration, the command `load` is used (for example, `load override my-config.txt` makes the previously saved configuration file my-config.txt the new candidate configuration.

The relationship between the various configuration files on a Juniper Networks router and the commands that link them are shown in Figure 6.6.

Much more could be said about Juniper Networks router configuration. But to limit the size of this section, it will be enough to close with an example of a user entering Configuration mode and then using configuration commands to add a few things to the router configuration.

Juniper Networks Configuration Example

This section offers an example of how Juniper Networks routers are initially configured. Then we modify the configuration. This is a working example in the sense that the router configuration established here will be used in building up a complete network later on in this book.

Unlike Cisco routers, there is no special setup configuration on a Juniper Networks router. So this section shows the steps to perform a simple configuration on an access router with one Ethernet interface and a serial interface used to link to POP routers. Later on, only Ethernet interfaces will be used for router connectivity. Ethernet is only used for simplicity, not to suggest that access routers routinely link to POP routers over Ethernet links.

After the simple initial configuration, we create an address for the *loopback* interface on the router, add some static routes to the configuration, and configure an aggregate to cover the range of the static routes. Loopback interfaces are used on routers not so much for loopback purposes (in fact, a 127 loopback IP address is often the worst thing that can be configured on the loopback interface) as for *stability* purposes. The loopback interface is intended to be a stable interface that can be used to identify the router in routing protocols or to form a convenient single address for Telnet or traceroute purposes, and it can still be used for diagnostic purposes as well. If a router did not have a stable loopback interface, and the interface that the router was known by is down, the router would be unreachable over the network by Telnet, and routing protocol sessions, even those on other interfaces, might fail. The loopback should always be reachable as long as one interface is up and running. As in the previous chapter, all serial interfaces will have IP addresses and so are not unnumbered interfaces.

Static routes are the opposite of dynamic routes. Dynamic routes can come and go in the routing table as the routing protocols detect new networks or failed links. Static routes are always there in the routing table. Even if the link to the static addresses' next hop is down, the entry never goes away. The network is just unreachable. Complete networks can be built up entirely out of static routes, and sometimes they are. But today static routes have a special role in the access router: static routes are used to map the links to the customer sites. After all, most customer sites have only a single serial link to an off-site router. If the link to the site from the access router is down, then the customer is effectively isolated and unreachable. Customer links tend to be very stable as well and do not move much among interfaces on the router, get new IP addresses often, and so on. So customer LANs with end-user clients and servers are always represented by static routes on the access routers in this book.

A special type of static route is the *default route*. Juniper Networks routers have no concept of Cisco's "gateway of last resort," but there is a default route. The default route is used when there is no more explicit match for an IP address in the routing table. This default address is typically 0.0.0.0/0 and essentially passes as a longest match for anything not in the routing table. The configuration example sets this default address as well.

In contrast to Cisco, Juniper Networks routers have commands to set a `backup-router`. The backup router is used while the router is booting and cannot otherwise route packets. This simple example does not use the `backup-router` command.

Finally, the example configures an aggregate route to cover the range of the static routes used in the example. A simple procedure is given to figure out the most appropriate aggregate to use, and several cautionary notes are also included to prevent the later use of the aggregate causing routing loops or black holes.

Initial Setup

Initial setup of a Juniper Networks router is very different than the Cisco Interactive System Configuration Dialog. By taking advantage of the underlying UNIX environment of the Routing Engine, the initial Juniper Networks router setup for users is similar to a UNIX computer. That is, there is only root access to the router (with no password), and any users and their passwords must be added. Users are given a user identification (uid), a class that defines the user's capabilities (such as "superuser," "operator," and so forth), and an authentication method (simple password, RADIUS, or TACACS+). This example establishes a user called "lab" with the same as an encrypted password, a uid of 2000, and class superuser. The root user is given a password as well with the `root-authentication` command.

There is a default factory configuration on the Juniper Networks router, but this only turns on some system logging and establishes a file called "messages" for logged information. This is all according to traditional UNIX system practices. The `syslog` section of the configuration is included here, but no configuration of this section is required.

Although the console port is enabled by default on the Juniper Networks router, this initial configuration configures the console port as well as the aux port. This is because the configuration can set the terminal type to VT100 so the user will not be repeatedly prompted for the terminal type. The aux port must be enabled specifically, and the speed on both ports is explicitly set to 9,600 bps in this example.

Unlike many other routers, Juniper Networks routers have no TCP/IP ports enabled by default. None. Zero. There are simply no backdoors of any kind of the router. In fact, when it comes to TCP/IP application services, there are only four things that a Juniper Networks router can be made to do: Telnet, finger, ssh (secure shell), and FTP (oddly, until recently, this was a totally undocumented service). This example will turn on the FTP, ssh, and Telnet services.

Finally, the hostname of the router is set to Juniper_access. The following reproduces the initial `root` login for the sake of completeness. The commands to accomplish the preceding are as follows:

```
no-name (ttyd0)

login: root

--- JUNOS 5.1R2.4 built 2001-12-11 02:11:09 UTC
```

```
Terminal type? [vt100] <Enter>

root@% cli
root> configure
Entering configuration mode

[edit]
root#
```

The show command reveals the factory default configuration with it's system logging:

```
[edit]
root#show
system {
    syslog {
        user * {
            any emergency;
        }
        file messages {
            any notice;
            authorization info;
        }
    }
}
```

Now we add users and passwords, configure the console and aux ports, set the hostname, and turn on the services. Even though the command used is plain-text-password, the password entered is not displayed on the screen and the password is stored as encrypted-password. The plain-text-password just means that the password will be entered in plain text, not in an encrypted form (although entering pre-encrypted passwords is also allowed). These steps are accomplished by parking at several levels of the configuration hierarchy just to show a variety of methods and demonstrate the flexibility of the CLI:

```
[edit]
root#edit system
[edit system]
root#set login user lab uid 2000 class superuser authentication plain-
text-password
New password:(not displayed)
Retype new password:(not displayed)

[edit system]
root#up
[edit]
root#set system ports console speed 9600 type vt100
```

```
[edit]
root#set system ports auxiliary speed 9600 type vt100
[edit]
root#set system host-name Juniper_access
[edit]
root#set system services ftp
[edit]
root#edit system services
[edit system services]
root#set telnet
[edit system services]
root#set ssh
[edit system services]
root#top
[edit]
root#
```

Now we commit and log back in as user lab. The command commit and-quit commits the configuration and returns us to Operational mode (the > prompt). Note that the hostname changes immediately. Passwords do not display on the screen:

```
[edit]
root#commit and-quit
commit complete
root@Juniper_access>exit

Juniper_access (ttyd0)

login: lab
Password:

--- JUNOS 5.1R2.4 built 2001-12-11 02:11:09 UTC

lab@Juniper_access>
```

So far so good. But how do the IP addresses get assigned to the interfaces of the router? Come to think of it, where *are* the interfaces anyway? Cisco auto-detects the interfaces and presents them during the initial setup dialogue. Juniper Networks routers auto-detect installed interfaces as well, but not as part of a special dialogue. The easiest way to see what interfaces are on the Juniper Networks router is with the show interfaces terse operational command:

```
lab@Juniper_access> show interfaces terse
Interface       Admin Link Proto Local              Remote
fe-0/0/0        up    down
fe-0/0/1        up    down
```

```
fe-0/0/2        up      down
fe-0/0/3        up      down
t1-0/0/0        up      down
t1-0/0/1        up      down
t1-0/0/2        up      down
t1-0/0/3        up      down

(more lines not shown...)
```

The Juniper Networks routers `interface` naming will be explained shortly. A number of other lines about internal interfaces and other interfaces such as fxp0 and lo0 will be displayed as well, but this output only shows the transit packet interfaces on the PFE. The Admin field value of up shows that the interface has been detected by the JUNOS software, but the Link field value of down shows that the link has not yet been connected to anything.

Before we configure an Ethernet and serial port on the Juniper Networks access router, a few words about the interface naming convention used in Juniper Networks routers are in order. All physical interfaces on the PFE are identified by a two-letter abbreviation followed by three numbers separated by slashes, such as `fe-0/0/0`.

The abbreviation stands for the type of PIC. The current abbreviations for the most common physical links are as follows:

at- (ATM).   Supports ATM at speeds of 155 Mbps and 622 Mbps.

e1- (E1).   Standard 2.048-Mbps E1 serial links. Can be used for Frame Relay.

e3- (E3).   Standard Mbps E3 serial links. Can be used for Frame Relay.

fe- (Fast Ethernet).   Standard 100-Mbps Ethernet. This PIC can also support 10 Mbps Ethernet.

ge- (Gigabit Ethernet).   Standard 1,000-Mbps Ethernet.

so- (SONET/SDH).   Standard SONET/SDH speeds up to 10 Gbps.

t1- (T1).   Standard 1.544-Mbps T1 serial links. Can be used for Frame Relay.

t3- (T3).   Standard 45-Mbps T3 serial links. Can be used for Frame Relay.

Each of the link types has a variety of encapsulations that can be used for the link as a whole, such as PPP or Packet over SONET (POS). The three numbers that follow the letter abbreviation represent the following:

1. The Flexible PIC Concentrator (FPC) slot for the interface. This can be 0 to 7 on the M40 and M160, 0 to 3 on the M20, 0 or 1 on the M10, and only 0 on the M5.

2. The position of the PIC on the FPC. This number is usually 0 to 3 on all models.

3. The position of the port on the PIC. This number is usually 0 to 3 as well.

So, for example, interface so-2/1/2 means a SONET/SDH interface in FPC slot 2, PIC position 1, and port 2 on that PIC. Interface fe-1/1/0 means a fast Ethernet interface in FPC slot 1, PIC position 1, and port 0 on that PIC.

In this example, the Ethernet interface fe-0/0/0 and serial T1 interface t1-0/0/0 are configured with IP addresses 10.0.64.1/24 and 10.0.65.1/24, respectively.

There are other quirks of interface configuration on a Juniper Networks router, mainly because the ASIC on the PIC is intelligent enough to allow for many parameters of operation to be set. These operational parameters can be for the physical link itself or for the *logical units* on the interface. Some interfaces, such as Frame Relay or ATM, can have many logical units, each with its own parameters such as connection identifiers. Most other interface can have only one logical unit defined, and this must be unit 0. In this example, only logical unit 0 is used.

An interface on a Juniper Network router can have one of several *families* of packet structures defined on the logical interface. One family is simply inet for IP packets. But the content of frames arriving on an interface could also be ISO packets (necessary for the IS-IS routing protocol), MPLS, and so on. This example uses only IP packets.

Finally, interfaces have one or more IP addresses under family inet. Address and mask are supplied in prefix/mask notation.

Here is how to configure the interfaces on a Juniper Networks router, starting right where the example left off:

```
lab@Juniper_access>configure
[edit]
lab@Juniper_access#edit interfaces
[edit interfaces]
lab@Juniper_access#set fe-0/0/0 unit 0 family inet address 10.0.64.1/24
[edit interfaces]
lab@Juniper_access#set t1-0/0/0 unit 0 family inet address 10.0.65.1/24
```

A nice feature of the Juniper Networks CLI is the ability to display all or part of the candidate configuration as it is being built. To view the interface information added in the preceding code, the show command is used at the interfaces level of the configuration hierarchy:

```
[edit interfaces]
lab@Juniper_access#show
interfaces {
```

```
        fe-0/0/0 {
            unit 0 {
                family inet {
                    address 10.0.64.1/24;
                }
            }
        }
        t1-0/0/0 {
            unit 0 {
                family inet {
                    address 10.0.65.1/24;
                }
            }
        }
    }
[edit interfaces]
lab@Juniper_access#
```

Note that no changes are made to the active configuration until a `commit` command is executed. Before we proceed with a `commit`, we first need to add the loopback, static routes, and aggregate route.

Loopback, Static Routes, and Aggregate Routes

If the router was not already in Configuration mode, this mode could be entered by using the `configure` command. The user must have configuration privileges, but this is assumed.

Setting the Loopback IP address

Juniper Networks routers have only one loopback interface, designated Loopback0 (lo0), but the loopback interface can have more than one IP address. This example only assigns one IP address to interface lo0:

```
[edit]lab@Juniper_access# set interface lo0 unit 0 family inet address
10.100.64.1
```

That is all there is to it. Note that Juniper Networks routers do not require the use of a mask if the mask is a 32-bit host mask. In fact, only a 32-bit address can be used on the loopback interface. Loopback addresses play an important role in many routing protocols, so the loopback address must be a reachable destination on the network. Some degree of care is needed in selecting loopback addresses.

Adding Static Route Addresses

Just as router loopback addresses, static routes play an important role in router networks. In smaller networks consisting of three or four routers connected by a minimal number of links, static routing might be used for the whole network, since dynamic routing will never be able to find an alternate route once a link or router is down. Even in larger networks, static routes make sense for links that have no alternate paths and do not change much if at all.

A good example of single, stable links in a router network are the links to customers' site routers from a service provider's access routers. These links can be serial links if the access router is some distance from the customer, or just Ethernet ports on the router if the access router is located close to a cluster of customer LANs. If the link is down, the customer cannot be reached in any other way. If the customer link is restored, the customer will still have the same address and appear on the same router interface. So static routes work fine here.

Generally, all you need to configure static routes is an IP network address and a next-hop IP address. Naturally, if the next hop is to be reachable, then the IP address used as the static route next hop should be reachable through the router, or else the packet will be discarded and an ICMP message sent back to the source. Sometimes it makes sense to have a static route next hop that explicitly discards packets. This could be helpful, for example, when a new customer site is being prepared for linking to an access router. The address assignment is known, and testing needs to be done to make sure that the routing information is distributed properly among the other routers. One way to perform this testing is to simply configure the new customer route with a next hop of "discard" until the customer site is ready to go.

Static routes on a Juniper Networks router are configured under the routing-options section of the configuration hierarchy. All that is needed to define a static route on a Juniper Networks router is the static route's IP address, the subnet mask, and the next-hop IP address, although there are other parameters, of course. The following adds some static routes to the example Juniper Networks access router, picking up where the previous code section ended:

```
[edit]
lab@Juniper_access# edit routing-options
[edit routing-options]
lab@Juniper_access# set static route 10.200.9.0/24 next-hop 10.0.64.2
lab@Juniper_access# set static route 10.200.10.0/24 discard
lab@Juniper_access# set static route 10.200.11.0/24 reject
```

The first line adds the static route 10.200.9/24 to the Juniper Networks access router and sets the next hop to the fe-0/0/0 interface defined earlier.

The second line adds the static route 10.200.10/24 but sets the next hop to `discard`. On a Juniper Networks router, any packet arriving for this address space is simply discarded as if it had never existed. So packets that arrive at this router for network 10.200.10.0 are discarded.

The third line adds the static route 10.200.11/24 and sets the next hop to `reject`. This is almost the same as `discard`, except that an ICMP message is sent back to the source.

A special case of a static route is the *default route*. The default route, if it exists, is used to forward packets that do not match a more specific entry in the routing table. Typically, the default route is in the form 0.0.0.0/0, which will match any IP address that has no longer match in the routing table.

The following configuration command sends all packets without longer matches in the routing table out onto the `fe-0/0/0` interface on the `Juniper_access` router:

```
[edit routing-options]
lab@Juniper_access# set static route default next-hop 10.0.64.2
```

The command `set static route 0.0.0.0/0 next-hop 10.0.64.2` would have the same result. Since both default routes and gateways of last resort have only local significance, these routes are not usually advertised to other routers by the routing protocols. However, there are exceptions to this general rule.

Setting the Aggregate

Aggregate, or summary, routes are used to keep routing information advertisements between routers to a minimum and keep the size of routing tables to a minimum as well. Aggregation is often done on access routers as long as the customer addresses are assigned in a way that is consistent with the aggregation policy of the service provider. This means that access routers should use contiguous IP address spaces, at least to the extent feasible based on the service provider's address space allocation. Haphazard assignment of IP addresses can easily lead to holes in the address space that make aggregation inefficient at best and just wrong at worst.

The trick when establishing aggregates is to make sure that the aggregate route is general enough to cover all of the more specific routes beneath the aggregate and still be specific enough so that routing loops or black holes do not happen.

Following is a relatively simple procedure to follow for determining aggregate mask length:

- Put the candidate routes for aggregation in numerical order.
- Write out the addresses as bit strings.

- Account for any holes in the aggregate address space.
- Use a mask that covers all of the bits in the aggregate space that are the same.

This procedure is easier to show as an example rather than explain in the abstract. Suppose an access router has been configured with the following IP addresses on the serial links to customers:

```
10.200.9.0/24
10.200.10.0/24
10.200.12.0/24
10.200.14.0/24
```

What aggregate can be used to summarize this address space? The addresses are already in numerical order, so the second step is to write them down as bit strings (a space is used to indicate the mask length):

```
10.200.9.0/24    00001010 11001000 00001001    00000000
10.200.10.0/24   00001010 11001000 00001010    00000000
10.200.12.0/24   00001010 11001000 00001100    00000000
10.200.14.0/24   00001010 11001000 00001110    00000000
```

There is a hole in this range. Where are 10.200.11.0/24 and 10.200.13.0/24? If these addresses are assigned to another access routers, then aggregation should not take place. After all, if the network administrator decided to aggregate those two addresses with the same aggregate route, there will be two routes floating around on the network each claiming to be the best way to deliver packets to that address space. In this case, assume that these two addresses are reserved for customers and serial interfaces on this access router, but they have not yet been assigned.

The final step is to establish the point where the addresses differ. This is shown in **bold** in the following:

```
10.200.9.0/24    00001010 11001000 00001001    00000000
10.200.10.0/24   00001010 11001000 00001010    00000000
10.200.12.0/24   00001010 11001000 00001100    00000000
10.200.14.0/24   00001010 11001000 00001110    00000000
```

So the address space in the example can be safely aggregated as 10.200.8.0/21. (Note that in proper subnet fashion, the addresses 10.200.8.0/24, which is the subnet 0 address, and 10.200.15.0/24, the directed broadcasts address for the subnet, have not been assigned to customers, although Juniper Networks routers will not mind if these addresses were assigned or not.)

To set an aggregate for a routing protocol to use on the Juniper Networks access router, you use syntax very similar to that used to configure the static routes. However, unlike static routers, aggregate routes on a Juniper Networks router *cannot* have a "real" next hop. This is understandable since an aggregate route is not really a place to send packet: The aggregate just summarizes a collection of places as on-route advertisement. Now, if the aggregate is advertised to another router using a routing protocol and routing policy, then the next hop of the advertised aggregate will by default be the router that advertised the aggregate. This is like saying to the other router, "If you get any packets bound for 10.200.8.0/21 or below it on the IP address radix tree, send it to me." But naturally the router advertising the aggregate route must have more detailed information about the destinations of these more specific addresses in the form of reachable next hops.

So the default next-hop value for an aggregate is `reject`. This will always send an ICMP message back to the source. This is always a good idea for innocently misdirected traffic, but in many cases, hackers rely on ICMP information about unreachable destinations to map out networks and router connectivity. If this is a concern, you can always configure aggregates with a next hop of `discard` that will silently discard packets arriving in response to the aggregate advertisement that do not have more specific places to go once the packets reach the router advertising the aggregate.

It is always important to keep in mind the differences between *configuring* an aggregate and *advertising* an aggregate on a Juniper Networks router. Aggregates are configured with `reject` or `discard`. Aggregates are advertised with "real" next hops if and only if they are *active routes*. Active routes are actually used for forwarding packets and only active routes are eligible to be advertised to other routers through a routing protocol (why advertise a route that is not is use?). Static routes are *always* active because of their static configuration. So the aggregate in this example becomes instantly active because of the presence of the static routes beneath it.

Aggregate routes become active if and only if they have more specific routes active beneath them. In other words, the aggregate 10.200.8.0/21 only becomes active and therefore eligible for advertisement if there is also an active route on the aggregating router to, for example, 10.200.9.0/24. These more specific routes are called *contributing routes* to the aggregate. Any route can only contribute to one aggregate, although a contributing route can be an aggregate itself. So, for instance, 10.200.9.0/24 becoming active in turn activates the aggregate 10.200.8.0/21, which in turn activates the aggregate 10.200.0.0/16 (if it exists on the router).

The concept of a contributing route is not always an easy one to grasp or visualize. The binary tree representation of the IP address space can help, as shown in Figure 6.7. In the figure, the aggregate route is in **bold**, and the static routes are <u>underlined</u>.

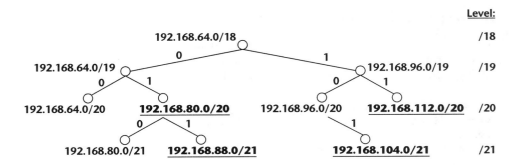

Contributing routes to aggregate 192.168.64.0/19?

192.168.80.0/20 *is* a contributing route (it is under the aggregate)
192.168.88.0/21 *is* a contributing route (it is under the aggregate)

192.168.112.0/20 is *not* a contributing route
192.168.104.0/21 is *not* a contributing route

Figure 6.7 Aggregates and the idea of contributing routes.

The aggregate route in question is 192.168.64.0/19. Suppose there are four static routes more specific than this aggregate configured on the router: 192.168.80.0/20, 192.168.88.0/21, 192.168.104.0/21, and 192.168.112.0/20. Will the aggregate be active or not? The figure shows that only two of these static routes (which are always active) contribute to the 192.168.80.0/19 aggregate. However, only one active contributing route is needed to make the aggregate an active route. So the aggregate will indeed be active.

Aggregates take some getting used to, but they are used over and over again in some of the chapters to come, so you will become quite comfortable with them. For now, it is enough to simply set the aggregate using the default next hop of `reject`:

```
[edit routing-options]
lab@Juniper_access# set aggregate route 10.200.8.0/21
```

Even when an aggregate address is established for the routing protocols, the Juniper Networks router continues to advertise the more specific routes such as 10.200.9.0/24 and so on. To suppress the specifics and advertise only the summary route, you need a routing policy. This is discussed in a later chapter, Chapter 16.

Viewing the Results

What will the Juniper Networks configuration look like when the loopback and static routes have been added to the configuration? What will the routing table look like? The following commands and listings show this:

```
lab@Juniper_access>show configuration
version 5.1R2.4;
system {
    host-name Juniper_access;
    ports {
        console {
            speed 9600;
            type vt100;
        }
        auxiliary {
            speed 9600;
            type vt100;
        }
    }
    login {
        user lab {
            uid 2000;
            class superuser;
            authentication {
                encrypted-password "$1$dQDrM$stzjHa1Vk5AQgE49grCtb1"; #
SECRET-DATA
            }
        }
    }
    services {
        ftp;
        ssh;
        telnet;
    }
    syslog {
        user * {
            any emergency;
        }
        file messages {
            any notice;
            authorization info;
        }
    }
}
interfaces {
    fe-0/0/0 {
        unit 0 {
            family inet {
                address 10.0.64.1/24;
```

```
                    }
                }
            }
            lo0 {
                unit 0 {
                    family inet {
                        address 10.100.64.1/32;
                    }
                }
            }
            t1-0/0/0 {
                unit 0 {
                    family inet {
                        address 10.0.65.1/24;
                    }
                }
            }
        }
        routing-options {
            static {
                route 10.200.9.0/24 next-hop 10.0.64.2;
                route 10.200.10.0/24 discard;
                route 10.200.11.0/24 reject;
                route 0.0.0.0/0 next-hop 10.0.64.2;
            }
            aggregate {
                route 10.200.8.0/21;
            }
        }
```

Entries at the same level of the configuration hierarchy are usually listed in alphabetical order, but there are exceptions, such as the statics and aggregates. Note that the default route is just another static.

Even this simple configuration has a number of IP addresses, and more show up than in the Cisco routing table, which more closely resembles the Juniper networks forwarding table. To see the contents of the IP routing table, you use the Juniper Networks operational command show route:

```
lab@Juniper_access>show route

inet.0: 6 destinations, 6 routes (6 active, 0 holddown, 0 hidden)
+ = Active Route, - = Last Active, * = Both

10.0.64.1/32        *[Local/0] 00:04:38
                       Reject
10.0.65.1/32        *[Local/0] 00:04:38
                       Reject
10.100.64.1/32      *[Direct/0] 00:04:38
                     > via lo0.0
```

```
10.200.8.0/21        *[Aggregate/130] 00:03:12
                        Reject
10.200.10.0/24       *[Static/5] 00:04:38, metric 0
                        Discard
10.200.11.0/24       *[Static/5] 00:04:38, metric 0
                        Reject


lab@Juniper_access>
```

The output of this command looks very different than the Cisco show ip route. The table shown with the show route command is inet.0, the main unicast IP routing table (the show forwarding-table command shows the contents of the forwarding table in the PFE). The six destinations in the table are reachable through six routes; when multiple protocols are running, destinations can be reached through many routes. All six are active (installed in the forwarding table and used for routing packets), none are in hold-down (retained even if not present in routing updates), and none are hidden (not eligible to become active). The routes listed (*) are both the currently active routes (+) and the last active route (-) to their destinations.

The information in brackets is the source, or protocol, of the routing information. Both Local and Direct sources are connected directly to the router, but locals are always host addresses with 32-bit masks, whereas directs are usually network entries and normally appear with masks less than 32 bits in length. An exception is the loopback address, 10.100.64.1/32 in the above example, which is always a direct even though it is a 32-bit address (the reason has to do with routing policy implementation). This example uses a router with no active links, so the routing table information is minimal. The number in the brackets is the internal Juniper Networks *preference* of the protocol, or source of routing information. If two routes could be the active route to a destination, the first tiebreaker is to choose the route with the *lower* preference. Preferences can be changed in several ways. This table shows the default values for local, direct, static, and aggregate. The maximum preference value is 255. The use and meaning of the route metric is covered in the next chapter.

Note the absence of some IP addresses. The *host* addresses for the Ethernet and T1 interfaces appear, but not the network entries. As with the Cisco router, this is because the Juniper Networks router is still totally isolated from the rest of the world and does not even have any physical link connectors plugged in yet. However, the aggregate is active because at least one of the contributing static routes is active.

Since no interfaces are up except the internal loopback interface, any routes with next hops that represent the IP address at the other end of the link do not appear. Normally, if the link on the 10.0.64.1 interface was up and running with another router, the entries for 10.0.64.0 would look as follows:

```
10.0.64.0/24        *[Direct/0] 00:00:04
                    > via fe-0/0/0.0
10.0.64.1/32        *[Local/0] 00:00:04
                      Local via fe-0/0/0.0
```

Both entries are created from the same 10.0.64.1/24 configuration information. The `Local` address is always the host address, and the `Direct` address is always the network based on the configured mask. So packets addressed to 10.0.64.2 or 10.0.64.100 or whatever will always find their way out onto `fe-0/0/0`.

Once a true network is built with active links, routing protocols, and routing policies, the contents of the Juniper Networks routing table will change.

More Juniper Networks Configuration Tools

Juniper Networks also has two tools available to simplify configuration chores. The first is actually a way to edit the router configurations anywhere with any UNIX, Windows, or other operating system text editor. When using a terminal emulator program as the console, you can load these simple text files onto the router by copying the configuration text, running the `load override terminal` command, and then pasting the configuration into the terminal screen. Entering CTRL-D twice (or Enter followed by CTRL-D) ends the terminal input mode. Placement of braces and semicolons can be crucial in creating a good configuration, so it is a good idea to run a quick `commit check` to make sure the syntax is correct.

There is also an entire JUNOScript language for remote configuration tasks. Neither of these will be mentioned further in this book, because this book assumes direct console configuration and these tools run on or require external system platforms.

PART

Two

Interior Routing Protocols

The six chapters that make up the second part of this book investigate the operation of all major *interior* routing protocols. Interior routing protocols, called *interior gateway protocols* (IGPs) in the older Internet terminology, run between the routers *inside* a single AS, or routing domain. An ISP or large organization might have a single AS, but many global networks often divide their networks into one or more ASs. For instance, a multinational ISP might have one AS for North America, another AS for Europe, and a third AS for the Pacific Rim and the rest of the world in general. In all cases, IGPs run within these routing domains and do not share information learned across AS boundaries except occasionally when physical interface addresses might be shared.

IGPs are used to make sure that every network and interface within the AS is reachable from every other place within the AS. IGPs essentially bootstrap themselves into existence and send information about their IP addresses and interfaces to other routers directly attached to the source router. These other routers are called *neighbor* or *adjacent* routers depending on the routing protocols. This information may be distributed various ways, and all are discussed in this part of the book.

Three main IGPs are given full treatment in this part of the book: RIP, OSPF, and IS-IS. The Routing Information Protocol (RIP), often declared hopelessly obsolete and to be avoided in all circumstances, is still used and actually remains a popular routing protocol for small subnets. Usually the "updated" version of RIP, known as RIPv2, is used, and that will be the version of RIP emphasized in this book. RIP is a relatively simple protocol; nonetheless, two chapters are devoted to the subject, to cover the subjects of routing protocol (Chapter 7, "Routing Information Protocol,") and configuration (Chapter 8, "Configuring RIP"). The two chapters deal with RIP configuration on both Cisco and Juniper Network routers.

Open Shortest Path First (OSPF) and Intermediate System–Intermediate System (IS-IS) routing protocols also receive two chapters each in this part of the book. The first chapter on each protocol (Chapter 9, "Open Shortest Path First (OSPF)" and Chapter 11, "Intermediate System–Intermediate System (IS-IS)," respectively) presents the details of the protocol, router topologies, and design considerations. The second chapter on each protocol (Chapter 10, "Configuring OSPF," and Chapter 12, "Configuring IS-IS," respectively) gives a sample configuration for the protocol using Cisco and Juniper Networks routers. Special consideration for multivendor environments for mixed networks is given as well.

RIP is a *distance-vector* routing protocol, while OSPF and IS-IS are *link-state* routing protocols. Distance-vector routing protocols are simple and base routing decisions on one thing only: How many routers (hops) are there between here and the destination? It does not matter how fast the links are or how congested the network might be near another router: The best route has the fewest number of hops (routers).

Link-state protocols attempt to find out more about the network than just how many routers are along the path to the destination. So link-state protocols tend to be much more complex than distance-vector routing protocols, although link-state protocols are much more suited for networks with links of many different speeds (as is almost always the case today). However, link-state protocols require a fairly complicated and elaborate database of information about the network, not only about the local router addressing and interface environment but about each and every router in the immediate area and sometimes in the entire AS. All of these details are fully discussed.

These chapters do not deal much with routing policies. Routing policies for IGPs are discussed in full in Chapter 16, "IGP Routing Policies."

Routing Information Protocol (RIP)

Despite its age, the Routing Information Protocol (RIP) is still one of the most popular routing protocols in use on the Internet and on all types of TCP/IP networks. The basics of RIP were spelled out in RFC 1058 from 1988, but this is a little misleading. The truth is that RIP was in use long before 1988, but no one had really bothered to document RIP in detail. RIP was bundled with almost all implementations of TCP/IP, so networks often ran RIP and RIP alone. Why pay for something more advanced when RIP was there and available for free?

RIP version 1 (RIPv1 or just RIP) as specified in RFC 1058 has a number of annoying limitations, all of which are investigated in this chapter. Yet RIP was so popular that simply doing away with RIP was never a realistic consideration. Instead, RFC 1388 introduced RIP version2 (RIPv2 or sometimes RIP-2) in 1993. RIPv2 did what it could to improve RIP operation, and the improvements helped a lot but could not turn a simple distance-vector protocol like RIP into a more sophisticated routing protocol along the lines of link-state routing protocols such as OSPF and IS-IS. RIPv2 was intended to be backward-compatible with RIPv1, and most RIP implementations today run RIPv2 by default and allow RIPv1 to be configured as needed. In this chapter, the term RIP signifies a version of RIP that runs RIPv2 by default but can also be configured as RIPv1 as required. When only RIPv1 or RIPv2 is meant in this chapter, those more specific terms are used instead.

Cisco was among those who were deeply dissatisfied with RIPv1 limitations. Almost immediately, Cisco set about creating its own vendor-specific (proprietary) version of a distance-vector routing protocol, which Cisco called the Interior Gateway Routing Protocol (IGRP). IGRP improved upon RIPv1 in several ways, but, naturally, pure IGRP could only run between Cisco routers. As good as IGRP was, IGRP was still basically a distance-vector protocol that selected the best route based on minimizing the number of routers between the router handling the packet and the destination. As networks grew more and more complex in terms of link speeds and router capacities, using more than just simplistic topology information to route packets became desirable. It was always possible to switch to a link-state protocol such as OSPF or IS-IS, but many network administrators at the time felt that these new protocols were not stable or mature enough for working, production networks. So Cisco invented Enhanced IGRP (EIGRP) as a sort of hybrid routing protocol that combined features of both distance-vector and link-state routing protocols all in one package.

Because of the proprietary nature of IGRP and EIGRP, only the basics of these routing protocols are covered in this chapter. No equivalent of either IGRP or EIGRP exists on Juniper Networks routers, so IGRP and EIGRP has no real place in a book emphasizing the multivendor aspects of routers. There will be no details on configuring IGRP or EIGRP, since this is impossible on Juniper Networks routers.

For the purposes of completeness, however, we will discuss at least some of the issues related to the use of IGRP and EIGRP at the end of this chapter.

Distance-Vector Routing

RIP, both RIPv1 and RIPv2, is a very simple distance-vector routing protocol. Other distance-vector routing protocols besides RIP are in use, and these types are classified as *Bellman-Ford routing protocols*. They are so called because they all choose the best path to a destination based on the shortest-path computation algorithm first described by R. E. Bellman in 1957; later, in 1962, they were applied to a distributed network of independent, dynamic routers by L. R. Ford Jr. and D. R. Fulkerson.

Distance-vector routing was used on the early ARPANET and in other packet networks. Xerox, the birthplace of many networking and computing developments from the PC to Ethernet, also developed the Xerox Network System Routing Information Protocol, or XNS-RIP, for running inside a routing domain or AS. Xerox also has a Gateway Information Protocol (GIP) for an EGP between routing domains or routers in different ASs. The XNS version of RIP became the basis for Novell's IPX RIP and AppleTalk's Routing Table Maintenance Protocol (RTMP). The RIP used on the Internet today was first ported from Xerox to TCP/IP as a part of Berkeley Software Distribution UNIX (BSD UNIX) in 1982 and bundled with their TCP/IP implementation.

Just about every version of UNIX today also bundles RIP with TCP/IP, usually as the *routed* ("route management daemon" and pronounced "route-dee") process, but sometimes as the *gated* ("gate-dee") process.

All routing protocols make use of a *metric* that represents the relative "cost" of sending a packet from the current router to the destination out one router interface or another. As expected when costs are involved, the lowest cost is the best way to send a packet. Distance-vector routing protocols have only one possible metric: distance. The distance is expressed in terms of the number of routers between the router handling the packet at present and the router directly attached to the destination network. The distance metric is carried between routers running the same distance-vector routing protocol as a *vector*, which is just a field in a routing protocol update. Technically, a vector in engineering has both *magnitude* and *direction*, so this definition also fits: The magnitude is the cost, and the direction is implied from the interface that the routing update is received on. In practice, the use of the distance vector just means that the distance metric associated with a route in one router is told to another router in a field of the routing protocol update message.

The real revolution behind routing protocols like RIP is that they required minimal configuration of static routes. RIP was a dynamic routing protocol that allowed adjacent (directly connected) routers to exchange routing table information periodically and so in a sense "bootstrap themselves into existence" and try to build up a sense of the topology of the router network as a whole by passing information received by adjacent neighbors on the other routers.

Initially, a router knows nothing but its own local configuration. After some period of running a routing protocol among a collection of routers, all routers will have a consistent collection of routing tables with correct information. The time to construct these consistent tables is called the time for *convergence* of the routing protocol. When changes in the network due to failed links or routers cause the routing tables to be outdated, the routing tables on the router collection are inconsistent. At these times routing loops and black holes can occur. The faster a routing protocol converges, the better the routing protocol is for large-scale deployment.

To try to prevent routing loops, routing protocols should also seek to route packets closer to the ultimate destination rather than away from the destination. This is known as *making progress* toward a destination. One consequence of the making-progress concept is that packets should never be sent out on the same physical interface that they are received on. This is the *split horizon* concept, based on the idea that a router should "see" a split between where a packet came from and where the packet is going to (the horizon).

Ultimately, all routing protocols succeed because networking is basically very simple. Networking is not quantum physics. No advanced degrees in math or science are needed to understand how routing protocols work. This is a good thing since computers have to perform networking and routing, and computers are about the dumbest machines around and will only do exactly what they are told. In fact, even lawn mowers are more suited to a specific task than computers are at networking. And while small children entering a store with a parent intuitively understand instructions like "stay right here and follow me," given the same instructions, computers are hopelessly confused.

Complexity is generally a very bad thing when it comes to networks. The simple seems to always push the more complex aside. Ethernet's simplicity doomed Token Ring. Pure and simple IP routing has almost made vast and complex ATM obsolete. And so RIP still has a place in the world of networking. The place for RIP might be larger to some and smaller to others, but few today would condemn RIP to the junk pile.

Simple Hop-Count Routing

To illustrate many of the principles that all routing protocols simple and complex must deal with, let's look at a simple example of how distance-vector, or hop count, routing works. All routing protocols must pass along network information received from adjacent routers to all other routers in a routing domain, a concept known as *flooding*. Flooding is the easiest way to ensure consistency of routing tables, but convergence time might be high as routers at one end of a chain of routers wait for information from routers at the far end of the chain to make its way through the routers in between. Flooding also tends to maximize the bandwidth consumed by the routing protocol itself, but there are ways to cut down on this.

The example network only uses addresses employed as *router IDs* for distribution around the network. In most cases, the router ID is the same as the address on the router's loopback interface (lo0), but not always. Routers need IDs so that network administrators and many routing protocols have stable and consistent addresses to use for things like Telnet sessions, diagnostic messages, and for routing protocol message exchanges.

Consider the router network shown in Figure 7.1, which has five routers and six links. In reality, each router would most likely have many more IP addresses than just the loopback addresses. But this network shows how distance-vector protocols function by using only these five IP addresses so that all of the routers can at least reach each other. The links are given simple Ethernet (E1, E2, E3) or serial (S1, S2, S3) identifiers rather than IP addresses, but that is all that is needed for this example. Later in this chapter, we'll use more realistic networks and link addresses with RIP.

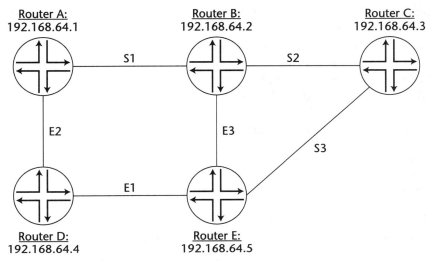

Figure 7.1 The distance-vector network.

When these routers are initially powered on, all the routers initially know about are their own interfaces and interface addresses (ignored here) and router IDs. This *local knowledge* must be shared to create the global topology knowledge needed to perform routing across the whole network. Initially, none of these routers even knows how many other routers there are or even what addresses are used at the ends of the links.

The initial routing tables are very simple, to say the least. Each router has an entry similar to Router A's:

```
From Router A to:       Next-Hop Interface:   Cost:
    192.168.64.1            local               0
```

This just means that to go from Router A to 192.168.64.1, use the local interface on which this 32-bit mask host route is defined (lo0 in this case), and that the cost of reaching this network from Router A is 0 (it's right here).

The distance vector that represents this information on each router is just as simple:

```
Router A: 192.168.64.1 = 0
Router B: 192.168.64.2 = 0
Router C: 192.168.64.3 = 0
Router D: 192.168.64.4 = 0
Router E: 192.168.64.5 = 0
```

Now each router has to share the information about this network with all other routers. Nothing is known about the details of the network, but Router A, for example, does know that there are two interfaces configured. So the easiest thing to do is just send a routing protocol update out on both interfaces, LAN or not, as a broadcast (i.e., "everybody pay attention to this") frame.

Router B and Router D receives this routing protocol update from Router A. The Next-Hop interface can be inferred simply as the interface over which the update is received. At this point, Router B's table looks as follows:

```
From Router B to:    Next-Hop Interface:   Cost:
192.168.64.1         S1                    1
192.168.64.2         local                 0
```

Router B receives the distance vector for 192.168.64.1, which is 0, and increments this cost for the route to 1 ("there is one other router between here and the destination network"). The 192.168.64.1 network is reached by sending the packet out on the S1 interface. Router D has the same kind of information, but with a different outbound interface:

```
From Router D to:    Next-Hop Interface:   Cost:
192.168.64.1         E2                    1
192.168.64.4         local                 0
```

Router B now has a routing update with two distance vectors: 192.168.64.1=1 and 192.168.64.2=0. How is this information passed along to the other routers? One simple way is to wait for number of seconds (perhaps 30 seconds) just to make sure that all routing updates from adjacent routers have been received and then perform another cycle of routing update messages.

So Router B can now flood, or pass along, this information to the other routers it is directly connected to: Router C and Router E. Note that Router B also sends this information out on S1; it's just simpler to send everything everywhere. How does Router A avoid confusion? Router A takes the distance vectors received from Router B on interface S1 and increment the cost. So now 192.168.64.1=2 and 192.168.64.2=1. When Router A looks in its routing table, Router A sees that the cost (2) to 192.168.64.1 (itself) is greater than the cost of 0 (local), so Router A ignores the update about 192.168.64.1 from Router B.

Note that Router E receives *three* routing updates concerning Router A: one advertised by Router B, one advertised by Router D, and one advertised by Router C. These are interpreted to show that 192.168.64.1 is two hops away over interfaces E1 and E3, but three hops away over interface S3.

This three-hop metric over S3 is because Router C first hears about Router A from Router B's update containing the vectors 192.168.64.1=1 and 192.168.64.2=0. Router C increments these and create table entries as:

```
From Router C to:      Next-Hop Interface:    Cost:
     192.168.64.1             S2                 2
     192.168.64.2             S2                 1
     192.168.64.3             local              0
```

During the next routing update cycle, Router C advertises this information to Router E over S3 as 192.168.64.1=2, 192.168.64.2=1, and 192.168.64.3=0. Incrementing the cost to Router A gives 192.168.64.1=3 over S3 on Router E.

Of these three choices (E1, E3, or S3), which one should Router E use to forward traffic to Router A? It has already been pointed out that a routing update that has a *higher* metric than an entry already in the routing table should never be used to forward traffic. This takes care of S3. But what about choosing between E1 and E3? Usually, distance-vector implementations simply use whichever update arrived first. If Router B told Router E first, the "send it over E3" entry is used on Router E for forwarding packets to 192.168.64.1. If the update from Router D arrived first, the "send it over E1" entry is used on Router E for forwarding packets to 192.168.64.1.

Note that routing information about Router A takes at least 30 seconds to reach Router C, if that is the routing update interval used. The information that arrives at Router B from Router A takes at least one update cycle to make its way to Router C, and the same is true in the other direction. Long chains of routers can take quite a long time to converge when a network address is added or when a link fails. A newer method called *triggered updates* that flood whenever changes occur can cut down on this convergence time dramatically.

When this network converges, each routing table is consistent and each router is reachable from every other router over one of the interfaces. The network topology has been "discovered" by the routing protocol. These tables are shown in Figure 7.2.

Note that several of the routers have alternatives other than those shown in the table. For example, the cost to reach 192.168.64.1 (Router A) from Router E is the same (2) over E3 as it is over E1. The E3 interface is most likely in the table just because the update from Router B indicating that it should be sent there arrived before the update from Router D, which indicated the same thing. When costs are equal, routing tables tend to stick with what they know.

Broken Links

The distance-vector information has now been exchanged and the routers all have a way to reach each other. Usually, the routing protocol updates an internal database in the router just for that routing protocol, and one or more entries based on the database are made in the routing table, which might contain

From Router A to:	Next Hop Interface:	Cost:
192.168.64.1	local	0
192.168.64.2	S1	1
192.168.64.3	S1	2
192.168.64.4	E2	1
192.168.64.5	S1	2

From Router B to:	Next Hop Interface:	Cost:
192.168.64.1	S1	1
192.168.64.2	local	0
192.168.64.3	S2	1
192.168.64.4	E3	2
192.168.64.5	E3	1

From Router C to:	Next Hop Interface:	Cost:
192.168.64.1	S2	2
192.168.64.2	S2	1
192.168.64.3	local	0
192.168.64.4	S3	2
192.168.64.5	S3	1

From Router D to:	Next Hop Interface:	Cost:
192.168.64.1	E2	1
192.168.64.2	E2	2
192.168.64.3	E1	2
192.168.64.4	local	0
192.168.64.5	E1	1

From Router E to:	Next Hop Interface:	Cost:
192.168.64.1	E1	2
192.168.64.2	E3	1
192.168.64.3	S3	1
192.168.64.4	E1	1
192.168.64.5	local	0

Figure 7.2 Routing tables after convergence.

information from other routing protocols as well. The routing table information is then used to compute the best routes to be used in the forwarding table (sometimes called the switching table) of the router. This example essentially merges and blurs the distinctions between routing protocol information database, routing table, and forwarding table for the sake of simplicity and clarity. This is okay as long as the detailed process is kept in mind to some degree.

What happens to the network if link S1 breaks and can no longer be used to forward traffic? This situation is shown in Figure 7.3. In a static routing world, this would be disastrous. But when using a dynamic routing protocol, even one as simple as a distance-vector routing protocol, the network should be able to converge around the new topology. How it works is as follows.

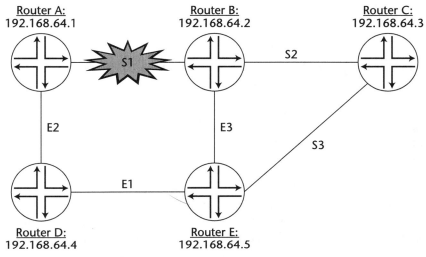

Figure 7.3 Link break.

Router A and Router B, since they are locally connected to the interface (direct), notices the link outage first because routers constantly monitor the state of their interfaces at the physical level. Distance-vector protocols note this absent link by indicating that link S1 now has an "infinite" cost. All routers formerly reachable through link S1 are now located an infinite distance away.

The routing tables on Router A and Router B almost instantly reflect this change:

```
From Router A to:        Next-Hop Interface:      Cost:
   192.168.64.1             local                 0
   192.168.64.2             S1                    INF
   192.168.64.3             S1                    INF
   192.168.64.4             E2                    1
   192.168.64.5             S1                    INF


From Router B to:        Next-Hop Interface:      Cost:
   192.168.64.1             S1                    INF
   192.168.64.2             local                 0
   192.168.64.3             S2                    1
   192.168.64.4             E3                    2
   192.168.64.5             E3                    1
```

For the next routing update cycle, Router A advertises distance vectors on link E2 to Router D (Router B is no longer reachable):

```
192.168.64.1=0
192.168.64.2=INF
```

```
192.168.64.3=INF
192.168.64.4=1
192.168.64.5=INF
```

For the next routing update cycle, Router B advertises distance vectors on link S2 to Router C and link E3 to Router E:

```
192.168.64.1=INF
192.168.64.2=0
192.168.64.3=1
192.168.64.4=2
192.168.64.5=1
```

The routing update from Router A is received and processed by Router D. Since an infinite value cannot be incremented, the distance vectors as seen from Router D in relation to link E2 back to Router A are as follows:

```
192.168.64.1=1
192.168.64.2=INF
192.168.64.3=INF
192.168.64.4=2
192.168.64.5=INF
```

These values are now compared to Router D's current routing table. This is what that looked like before the link failure:

From Router D to:	Next-Hop Interface:	Cost:
192.168.64.1	E2	1
192.168.64.2	E2	2
192.168.64.3	E1	2
192.168.64.4	local	0
192.168.64.5	E1	1

Note that every value of the new distance vector received on E2 is the same as or higher than the current values in the table. And only the way to reach Router A (192.168.64.1) over E2 is the same. The cost to reach Router B (192.168.64.2) over E2 is now an infinite value. Since that is the current way to reach Router B, Router D must reflect that change. Router D's table now looks like the following:

From Router D to:	Next-Hop Interface:	Cost:
192.168.64.1	E2	1
192.168.64.2	E2	INF
192.168.64.3	E1	2
192.168.64.4	local	0
192.168.64.5	E1	1

Meanwhile, in the same update cycle, Router C and Router E will get similar distance-vector information from Router B on links S2 and E3 respectively. So Router C and Router E updates their tables to:

```
From Router C to:        Next-Hop Interface:        Cost:
   192.168.64.1              S2                       INF
   192.168.64.2              S2                       1
   192.168.64.3              local                    0
   192.168.64.4              S3                       2
   192.168.64.5              S3                       1


From Router E to:        Next-Hop Interface:        Cost:
   192.168.64.1              E3                       INF
   192.168.64.2              E3                       1
   192.168.64.3              S3                       1
   192.168.64.4              E1                       1
   192.168.64.5              local                    0
```

Naturally, when the next update cycle comes around, Router D, Router C, and Router E advertises their new distance vectors to their neighbors. Router D now sends out on links E1 and E2:

```
192.168.64.1=1
192.168.64.2=INF
192.168.64.3=2
192.168.64.4=0
192.168.64.5=1
```

Router C will now send out on links S2 and S3:

```
192.168.64.1=INF
192.168.64.2=1
192.168.64.3=0
192.168.64.4=2
192.168.64.5=1
```

Router E will now send out on links E1 and E3, and S3:

```
192.168.64.1=INF
192.168.64.2=1
192.168.64.3=1
192.168.64.4=1
192.168.64.5=0
```

These messages trigger routing table updates on Router A, Router B, Router D, and Router E (nothing will change on Router C). Router A is the main beneficiary of this update cycle, because the update message received from Router D on E2 now provides a less-than-infinite way to reach Router C and Router D over interface E2. So Router A uses the new information:

```
From Router A to:          Next-Hop Interface:        Cost:
  192.168.64.1               local                    0
  192.168.64.2               S1                       INF
  192.168.64.3               E2                       3
  192.168.64.4               E2                       1
  192.168.64.5               E2                       2
```

One more cycle is needed to remove the infinites on Router A and Router B and replace link S1 with link E2 on Router A and with link E3 on Router B. This is because of the one-hop-at-a-time convergence pattern of strictly periodic updates. The routing update information about the new way to reach Router B from Router A must pass through Router E and Router D on its way to Router A, and the same is true in reverse.

But ultimately the routing tables converge on the new topology, as shown in Figure 7.4.

Distance vectors work well when the network consists of links that are of the same speed and routers that all handle routing protocol update messages at about the same speed as well. But in many cases distance-vector routing protocols are prone to a number of effects that limit convergence time and so do not route packets correctly for some time after many types of changes in network topology.

Distance-Vector Consequences

In some cases distance-vector updates are generated so closely in time by different routers that a link failure can occur. This can cause a routing loop to occur and packets to easily bounce back and forth between two adjacent routers until the packet TTL expires, even though the destination is reachable over another link. The bouncing effect will last until the network converges on the new topology.

This convergence can take some time, however, since routers not located at the end of a failed link have to gradually increase their costs to infinity one hop at a time. This is called *counting to infinity* and can drag out convergence time considerably if the value of infinity is set high enough. On the other hand, a low value of infinity limits the maximum number of routers that can form the longest path through the network from source to destination.

To minimize the effects of bouncing and counting to infinity, most implementations of distance-vector routing protocols such as RIP also implement *split horizon* and *triggered updates*.

From Router A to:	Next Hop Interface:	Cost:
192.168.64.1	local	0
192.168.64.2	E2	3
192.168.64.3	E2	3
192.168.64.4	E2	1
192.168.64.5	E2	2

From Router B to:	Next Hop Interface:	Cost:
192.168.64.1	E3	3
192.168.64.2	local	0
192.168.64.3	S2	1
192.168.64.4	E3	2
192.168.64.5	E3	1

From Router C to:	Next Hop Interface:	Cost:
192.168.64.1	S3	3
192.168.64.2	S2	1
192.168.64.3	local	0
192.168.64.4	S3	2
192.168.64.5	S3	1

From Router D to:	Next Hop Interface:	Cost:
192.168.64.1	E2	1
192.168.64.2	E1	2
192.168.64.3	E1	2
192.168.64.4	local	0
192.168.64.5	E1	1

From Router E to:	Next Hop Interface:	Cost:
192.168.64.1	E1	2
192.168.64.2	E3	1
192.168.64.3	S3	1
192.168.64.4	E1	1
192.168.64.5	local	0

Figure 7.4 The converged routing tables after the link failure.

Split Horizon

Split horizon is easy enough to understand: If Router A is sending packets to Router B to reach Router E, then it makes no sense at all for Router B to try to reach Router E through Router A. All Router A will do is turn around and send the packet right back to Router B.

So Router A should never advertise a way to reach Router E to Router B. The change that this would require to the example in this section is minimal; instead of using the same distance vector on each interface, each router would delete any distance vectors that are using the interface that the update is being sent on. In other words, suppose Router A has the following routing table:

```
From Router A to:          Next-Hop Interface:        Cost:
  192.168.64.1               local                     0
  192.168.64.2               S1                        1
  192.168.64.3               S1                        2
  192.168.64.4               E2                        1
  192.168.64.5               S1                        2
```

Without split horizon, the same distance-vector information would be sent out on both links E2 and S1. But why would Router A ever want Router B to send packets for Router C (192.168.64.3) over link S1 to Router A? The same logic applies to packets to Router E (192.168.64.1).

Using simple split horizon, Router A simply omits the references to these routers from its advertisements to Router B. So only Router A and Router D reachability over link S1 would be advertised to Router B. Initial advertisements flooded at startup will age out of the database. A more sophisticated form of split horizon is known as *split horizon with poison reverse*. In this form, the advertisement from Router A to Router B would advertise the distances to routers reached over S1 (Router B, Router C, and Router E) as infinite. Split horizon with poison reverse eliminates a lot of counting-to-infinity problems caused by single link failures. However, many multiple link failures will still cause routing loops and counting-to-infinity problems even when split horizon with poison reverse is in use.

Triggered Updates

Networks should be stable enough so that routing updates do not have to be sent many times per second on all links. This cuts down on the amount of bandwidth consumed by routing protocols. However, if a simple timer is used to schedule cyclical routing updates, this raises the convergence time as information makes its way hop by hop though the chain of routers.

Several distance-vector protocols, including the original version of RIP, use a fixed interval to schedule routing updates. The original RIP used a 30-second interval timer to schedule the sending of distance-vector information. This value seemed low enough to detect failures rapidly, yet was high enough so that a lot of unchanged information about the routing tables did not congest the network.

In addition, a timer is associated with each routing table entry. If the information about the route is not refreshed in a certain interval (usually set as a simple multiple of the update timer), then the router that advertised the information is assumed down and the routing table entry is set to infinity. The RIP RFC suggests that this timer be set at six times the update interval, or 180 seconds (3 minutes). So even if the network is so congested that only one out of every six RIP update packets makes it to an adjacent router, routes will not start to disappear.

With triggered updates, a router running a distance-vector protocol such as RIP can remain silent if there are no changes to the information in the routing table. If a link failure is detected, triggered updates will send the new information.

Triggered updates, like split horizon, will not eliminate all cases of routing loops and counting to infinity. However, triggered updates always help the counting process to reach infinity much faster.

RIPv1

The basic RIP (RIPv1) packet structure is used to share routing information between routers running RIP. In this section, all references to RIP mean RIPv1. The basic RIP packet structure appears in Figure 7.5. RIP packets use UDP port 520 both as destination and source port.

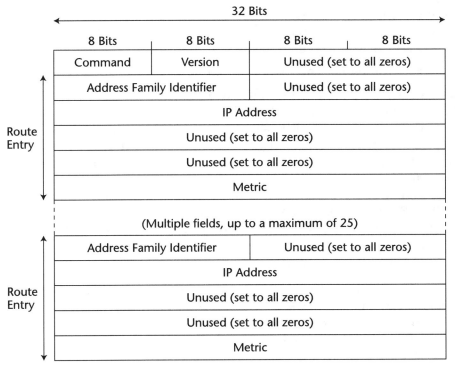

Figure 7.5 The RIPv1 packet format.

The fields in the packet are as follows:

A 1-byte command field. There are actually five values defined for this field, but in practice only two of them are used on the Internet in almost all cases. The values are shown in Table 7.1.

A 1-byte version number field. RIPv1 uses a value of 1 in this field, and RIPv2 uses a value of 2.

A 2-byte field that must be set to all zero-bits. But if the field is unused, why specify that it must be all zeros? Simply because software implementations are fond of taking unused bits in many protocol packet formats and using them to extend and enhance their own vendor-specific, proprietary features when the same vendor's routers are used. But this makes interoperability more difficult and often impossible. Forcing the unused fields to all zeros, or some other specific bit pattern, discourages this practice and makes multivendor interoperability much more likely. In spite of this, many router vendors make "check zero" a RIP configuration option. Network administrators usually have a choice whether or not to discard RIP packets that have nonzero values in these fields.

A 2-byte Address Family Identifier (AFI) field. The AFI field was included to make sure that RIP was compatible with the other versions of RIP used to carry non-IP addresses (such as when RIP is used for AppleTalk). The field is set to a value of 2 when IP packet and routing information is exchanged. Naturally, this book assumes that IP addresses are all that the RIP packet will carry.

Another 2-byte field. This must be set to all zero-bits.

A 4-byte (32-bit) IPv4 address. This field and the three that follow can be repeated up to 25 times in the RIP Response packet. The 25-route limit makes sure that the RIP packet does not need to be fragmented for any link. However, large routing tables require many packets to exchange information. Every 1,000 routes in a RIP routing table needs 40 RIP packets. This is one reason that RIP was deemed totally unsuitable for Internet backbone routers, which can have up to 100,000 routes and thus require 4,000 RIP packets to be exchanged between every router every 30 seconds. A RIP Request packet has the IP address of the originator in this field.

Another pair of 4 byte all-zero fields. These fields are a way to extend RIP and add future functionality to RIP.

A 4-byte metric field. These 32 bits are used to carry the distance vector associated with the route. Each router increments this field when the packet is processed. Routers are actually allowed to add more than 1 to this metric field (perhaps for particularly slow links), but in practice this is rarely, if ever, done. After all, it's bad enough that the maximum RIP hop count is 15; why make it easier to reach this limit with even fewer routers? The valid ranges for this field are 1 through 15 (so local networks are advertised with a hop count of 1). The metric can actually be 16, which is infinity in RIP, but this value is not a valid hop-count value. (This section is correct; a 32-bit field is used to carry the 4 bits that actually mean something in RIP.)

The address used in the RIPv1 address field can be one of four types:

- A host address with all 32 bits in use
- A classful network address such as 10.0.0.0 or 172.17.0.0
- A subnet of the classful major network (in which case all routers running RIP must use the same subnet mask for that network, since the subnet mask is not included in the RIPv1 update)
- A default route (IP address 0.0.0.0)

If a RIP router sees bits set beyond the normal classful major network boundary, the router knows that this is either a subnetted network or a host route. The router usually checks to see if there is subnet mask that fits the address configured on one of its local interfaces. If there is, then that mask is used on the RIP route. If not, the classful major network mask is assumed. So if the route received is 172.17.45.0, the router's local interfaces are checked. Suppose there is a network address and mask configured on one interface: 172.17.45.0/24. Then this is a subnetted IP address. (If bits are set beyond even this boundary, the route is interpreted as a host route.) If there is no local address and mask that fits, the route is interpreted as the natural Class B network 172.17.0.0/16.

Table 7.1 Values and Purpose of RIP Command Field

RIP COMMAND VALUES	PURPOSE
1	Identifies a request for routing table information.
2	Identifies a response containing routing table information.
3	Turn trace on (obsolete).
4	Turn trace off (obsolete).
5	For Sun Microsystems' internal use.

However, this method requires that the router have a local interface address and mask that fits the address in the update. What about routes that are advertised through a chain of routers and contain information about network addresses far removed from the local router? All that can be advertised is the single routing table entry that summarizes the classful major network to which the IP address belongs. This is not necessarily a bad thing, because it keeps the size of the routing tables to a minimum as well as the update messages.

Therefore, RIP routers can be *boundary routers* that perform automatic summarization (also called *subnet hiding*) of classful IP addresses, regardless of the subnet masks in use on the routers on either side of the boundary router. The operation of a RIP boundary router is shown in Figure 7.6.

In the figure, the router located at the boundary between classful networks 10.0.0.0 and 172.16.0.0 will only advertise these major networks between the two networks. The summarization used with RIP is automatic. So all routers in the 172.16.0.0 address space will have a single routing table entry pointing to

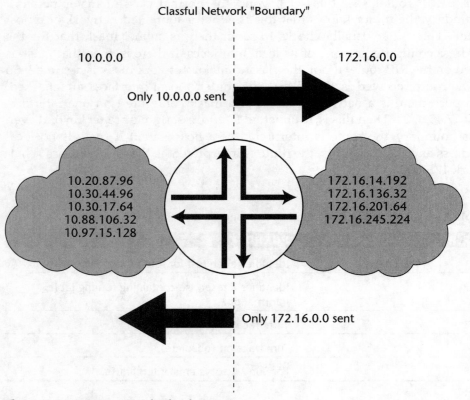

Figure 7.6 Route summarization in RIP.

the 10.0.0.0 boundary router. The boundary router *will* have a local interface having the proper subnet mask for the 10.0.0.0 address space (10.0.0.0/24 in this example), and so can figure out the proper route advertisements within the 10.0.0.0 address space.

At startup, RIP routers send a Request message out on each interface running RIP. The router then listens for a Response. If the router receives a Request on a RIP interface, the router responds with a Response message. Updates about routes not in the routing table are added. Entries for a particular route are replaced only if the new route has a lower hop count. There is one exception: If a higher hop count for a route is advertised by the router listed as the Next-Hop router for more than a configurable period of time (typically 90 seconds), then the higher hop count is accepted.

A RIP Request for a full routing table update has the AFI field set to 0, all zeros in the address field (0.0.0.0), and a metric of 16. RIP routers can also Request information about specific routes.

A RIP packet must be 512 bytes or smaller, including the header. RIP packets have no implied sequence, and each update packet is processed independently by the router that received the update. The RIP routing table (database) must contain the following fields:

- The destination IP address, which is usually in major network summary form such as 192.168.64.0.

- The metric (distance vector). The lower the total cost (hop count) to the destination, the more attractive the route is.

- The Next-Hop IP address, derived from the source interface on the router that received the update packet.

- The *route change flag* field, which is used to indicate that the next hop has recently changed.

- The timers associated with the route. The two timers defined in RIP are *route timeout* and *route-flush*, but routers usually add an *update timer* or even other timers for internal use to these two timers.

A router is only required to keep *one* entry associated with each route. But in practice, routers might keep up to four or more routes (next hops) to the same destination so that convergence time is lowered. However, a routing table that is required to have only a single route to a summary network that might contain thousands of hosts (10.0.0.0, for example) must be updated as often as possible.

So the original RIP required routers running RIP to *broadcast* the entire contents of their routing tables at fixed intervals. On LANs, this meant that the RIP packets were sent inside broadcast MAC frames, of course. But broadcast MAC frames tell not only every router on the LAN but every *host* on the LAN "pay attention to the contents of this frame." Inside the frame, the host would find a RIP update packet and probably ignore the contents. But every 30 seconds, every host on the LAN had to interrupt its own application processing and start throwing away RIP packets.

Each host could keep the information inside the RIP update packet. Some hosts on LANs with RIP routers had as elaborate a routing table as the routers themselves. And hackers loved RIP: With a few simple coding changes, any host could impersonate a RIP router and start blasting out fake routing information, as many college and university network administrators found out in the late 1980s.

Table updates in RIP are initiated on each router at approximate 30-second intervals. Strict synchronization is to be avoided, since RIP traffic spikes can easily lead to discarded packets. This is bad enough for user application traffic flowing between RIP routers, but it is even worse when RIP packet themselves are the casualties. The *update timer* usually adds or subtracts a small amount of time to the 30-second interval to avoid RIP router synchronization.

However, this fixed update interval means that a missing RIP update packet for a series of routes (as many as 25) does not necessarily means the route is invalid. The route is usually still used for 180 seconds. This *route timeout* timer is re-initialized every time an update for the route is received. If 3 minutes elapse with no update on a route, the route is assumed to be unreachable over the current interface and the route is flagged as invalid. This results in the metric for the route being set to infinity (16) and the route change flag bit being set. The route metric of infinity is then advertised to the RIP router's neighbors during the next update cycle.

So a route can *expire* on a router and be advertised as unreachable to other RIP routers. Either way, the route is now invalid as far as RIP is concerned. But invalid routes are not immediately purged from the RIP routing table. The invalid entry stays in the routing table for a short time, although the router will not be able to send packets to the destination by using RIP. The time interval beyond the route timeout is determined by the *route-flush timer*. The value of the route-flush timer is typically set at 90 seconds. So after a total of 270 seconds (4.5 minutes), the invalid route entry is finally removed from the RIP routing table.

RIP supports split horizon with poisoned reverse and triggered updates. To further minimize the risk of slow counting to infinity to invalidate and purge routes that are totally useless, RIP adds a *hold-down timer*. As soon as a triggered update has been used to advertise the infinite metric on a useless route, the hold-down timer is set (usually at 90 seconds) and starts counting down to zero. During this time interval, the router will not accept any updates from any neighbors about that route. This further lowers the risk of creating routing loops in RIP.

Network devices running RIP can be either *active* or *passive* (silent) mode. Active RIP devices listen for RIP update packets and also generate their own RIP update packets. Passive RIP devices only listen for RIP updates and never generate their own update packets. Many hosts, for example, which must process the broadcast RIP updates sent on a LAN, are purely passive RIP devices.

RIPv1 Limitations

The original RIP (RIPv1) had a number of limitations that made RIP difficult to use in large networks. The term *large* can be hard to define, but most network administrators will feel quite comfortable using RIP in routing domains with perhaps 9 or 10 routers. Certainly, there is little reason not to use RIP when there are only a handful or routers in a routing domain or AS. However, there are good reasons not to use RIP in networks that might have 20 or more routers connected by links of widely varying speeds and using classless subnetting/ supernetting. The larger the routing domain, the more severe and annoying the limitations of RIP become.

Everything in the RIP packet seems "super-sized." All of the fields are larger than they need to be, sometimes many times larger. Even one route/metric pair with 36 bits that mean something (the 32-bit IP address and the 4-bit metric) requires 192 bits to send (six *words* of 32 bits each). Of these 192 bits, 96 of them are required to be set to zero-bits and not used for anything else. So there are almost three times as many zero-bits as routing information bits in a RIP packet.

This "unused" format goes a long way in explaining why RIP has earned a reputation as a bandwidth hog. In fact, the early Internet was plagued by lost packets that seemed to peak at 30-second intervals. This surge in traffic and the corresponding buffer overruns and tail drops that the rise in traffic caused was easily traced to RIP updates flooding the network. A short-term fix was to add some variation to the strict fixed interval for RIP message exchanges. The long-term fix was to migrate from RIP to something else more suited to a network with many routers, large routing tables, and links with widely varying speeds and delays.

The major limitations of RIP are as follows:

- As a network grows, the distance vector might require a metric greater than 15, which is, of course, unreachable (infinite). Using distance vectors greater than 1 for slow links only makes this problem worse.

- The simple hop-count metric will always result in packets being sent, for example, over two hops using low-speed 64-Kbps links rather than three hops using SONET/SDH links. The more different speed links that are used with RIP, the worse this problem becomes.

- RIP devices will accept RIP updates from any other device. Hackers love RIP for this very reason, but even an innocently misconfigured router can disrupt an entire network using RIP.

- RIP requires all routers to use the same subnet mask, because RIP updates do not carry any subnet mask information. Discontiguous subnets drive RIP crazy, and so the use of RIP severely limits the useful range of IP addresses available.

- Convergence can be painfully slow with RIP: up to five minutes or more when links result in long chains of routers instead of neat meshes. And circles of RIP routers maximize the risk of counting to infinity.

- Split horizon with poison reverse only prevents bouncing routing loops between adjacent routes. The nonzero hold-down required to counter the most common causes of these larger routing loops increases convergence time.

- RIP wastes a lot of bandwidth because routing updates are sent at fixed intervals even when the network is totally stable and there are no changes to the routing tables at all (unless triggered updates are used).

Nevertheless, the use of RIP for small, homogeneous networks is nearly universal. The closer a router is to the end user, the more likely it is that the router is running RIP on at least some interfaces. RIP runs on many of the interfaces of most access and site routers.

RIPv2

RIPv2 first emerged as an update to RIPv1 in RFC 1388 issued in January 1993. This initial RFC was superseded by RFC 1723 in November 1994. The only real difference between RFC 1388 and RFC 1723 is that RFC 1723 deleted a 2-byte Domain field from the RIPv2 packet format, designating this space as unused. No one was really sure how to best use the Domain field anyway.

RIPv2 was not intended as a replacement for RIPv1, but RIPv2 was designed to extend the functions of RIPv1 to make RIP more suitable for variable-length subnet masking (VLSM). The RIP message format was changed as well to allow for authentication and multicasting. This was done to make RIP attractive despite emerging competition from OSPF and IS-IS as routing protocols.

This section emphasizes the differences between RIPv1 and RIPv2. Despite the changes, RIPv2 is still RIP and suffers from many of the same limitations as RIPv1. Most router vendors support RIPv2 by default but allow interfaces or whole routers to be configured for backward compatibility with RIPv1.

RIPv2 is still an IGP, but it distributes subnet masking information along with routes. The major RIPv2 improvements are that RIPv2 allows the following to happen:

- Authentication between RIP routers
- Subnet masks to be sent along with routes
- Next-hop IP addresses to be sent along with routes
- Multicasting of RIPv2 messages

The RIPv2 packet format is shown in Figure 7.7.
The fields in the RIPv2 packet are as follows:

A 1-byte command field. This is the same as in RIPv1; a value of 1 is for a request and a value of 2 is for a response.

A 1-byte version number field. RIPv1 uses a value of 1 in this field, and RIPv2 uses a value of 2.

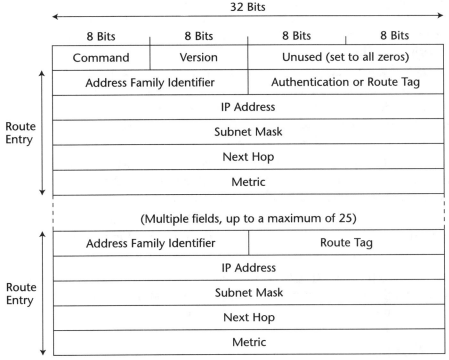

Figure 7.7 The RIPv2 packet format.

A 2-byte field that must be set to all zero-bits. This was the Domain field in RFC 1388. Now officially unused in RFC 1723, this field is ignored by routers running RIPv2 (but this field must be set to all zero-bits for RIPv1 routers).

A 2-byte Address Family Identifier (AFI) field. This field is set to a value of 2 when IP packet and routing information is exchanged. RIPv2 also defines a value of 1 to ask the receiver to send a copy of its entire routing table. When set to all one-bits (0xFFFF), the AFI field is used to indicate that the 16 bits following the AFI field, ordinarily set to zero-bits, now carry information about the type of authentication being used by RIPv2 routers.

A 2-byte Authentication or Route Tag field. When the AFI field is not 0xFFFF, this is the Route Tag field. The Route Tag field identifies *internal* and *external* routes in RIPv2. Internal routes are those learned by RIP itself, either locally or through other RIP routers. External routes are routes learned from another routing protocol such as OSPF or BGP.

A 4-byte (32-bit) IPv4 address. This field and the three that follow can be repeated up to 25 times in the RIPv2 Response packet. This field is almost the same as in RIPv1. This address can be a host route, a network address, or a default route. A RIPv2 Request packet has the IP address of the originator in this field.

A 4-byte Subnet Mask field. Reflecting the biggest change made in RIPv2, this field contains the subnet mask that goes with the IP address in the previous field. If the network address does not use a subnet mask different than the natural classful major network mask, then this field can be set to all zeros, just as this field is in RIPv1.

A 4-byte Next-Hop Field. This field contains the Next-Hop IP address that traffic to this IP address space should use. This was a vast improvement over the implied next hop used in RIPv1.

A 4-byte metric field. Unfortunately, the RIPv2 metric field is unchanged. The range is still 1 to 15, and a metric value of 16 is considered unreachable.

RIPv2 is still RIP. But RIPv2's additions for authentication, subnet masks, next hops, and the ability to multicast routing information increase the sophistication of RIP and have extended RIP's usefulness.

Authentication

Authentication was added in RIPv2 for the Response messages. It is the Response messages that contain the routing update information, and authenticating the responder to a Request message is a good way to minimize the risk of a routing table becoming corrupted either by accident or through hacker activities.

However, there were really only 16 bits available for authentication, hardly adequate for modern authentication techniques. So the authentication actually takes the place of one routing table entry and authenticates the entire update message. This gives 16 bytes (128 bits) for authentication, which is not state-of-the-art but is better than nothing.

The trick then was to come up with a simple way to let the receiver know if authentication was being used, and therefore there was one less a routing entry than expected in the update message. The group working on RIPv2 decided to limit the authentication to the first, and only the first, group of four fields (16 bytes) in the update message. When the AFI field was set to 0xFFFF (all one-bits), the 16 bits that followed identified the authentication method used. This implied that there could be several different authentication schemes in RIPv2, but only one method was actually defined in RFC 1388: a simple plaintext password. This was specified with a value of 2 in the Authentication Type field following the AFI of 0xFFFF.

When authentication is used with RIPv2, each routing update message has the format shown in Figure 7.8.

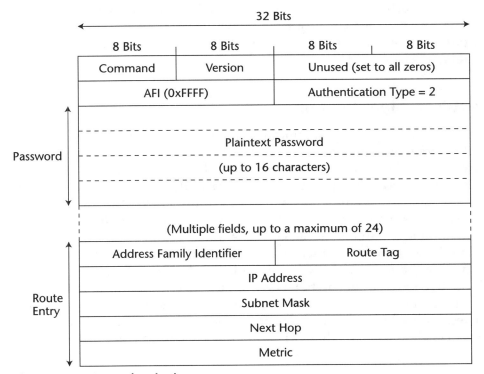

Figure 7.8 RIPv2 authentication.

RIPv2 devices must make sure that the password is correct before accepting the routing information that follows the authentication fields. Obviously, the use of a plaintext password offered only minimal authentication in RIPv2. Ordinarily, encrypted passwords 16 bytes long would be a modest challenge to hackers. But plaintext is there in the packet for all to see. And there is nothing to force network administrators to use 16-character-long passwords at all, and few network administrators bother with passwords that long.

The really nice feature of RIPv2 authentication is that router vendors can add their own Authentication Type values and schemes to the basics of RIPv2, and many do. For example, Cisco and Juniper Networks routers can be configured to use MD5 (Message Digest 5) authentication encryption to RIPv2 messages. So most routers can have three forms of authentication on RIP interfaces: none, simple password, or MD5. Naturally, the MD5 authentication keys used must match up on the routers.

Subnet Masks

The biggest improvement from RIPv1 to RIPv2 was the ability to carry the subnet mask along with the route itself. This allowed RIP to be used in classless IP environments with VLSM.

RIPv2 is much more capable than RIPv1 in deciding whether a route entry in an update message is a host route, network, or subnet. RIPv2 can handle discontiguous subnets and is still completely compatible with older, classful addressing schemes.

Next-Hop Identification

Identifying the next hop specifically in RIPv2 is especially helpful when multiple routing protocols are in use. This is fairly common in today's router networks, so a few words about this aspect of RIPv2 are in order.

Consider a network where there are several routers with only one or a couple of small LANs. In the terminology used in this book, these would be site routers. One or more of these small routers with only a few routes are attached to larger routers with Internet access, either directly or through a core of other routers. These are access routers in the terminology used in this book.

The small routers run RIPv2 between themselves and the access router. It makes little sense to run anything else. On the other hand, the access routers, which may or may not be part of a service provider's network, run OSPF between themselves. As is common, the two access routers have different speed links to the Internet as a whole. The situation is shown in Figure 7.9.

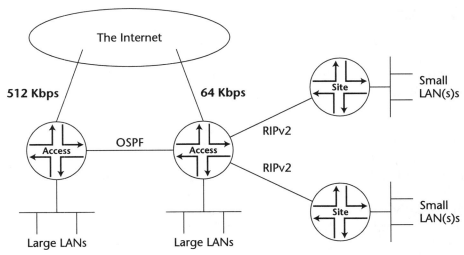

Figure 7.9   Use of next hop in RIPv2.

Obviously, the traffic from the two small routers on the right of the figure would be better off using the router with the 512-Kbps link and not the router with the 64-Kbps link. Now, there might be reasons for those particular site routers *not* to be allowed to use the higher-speed link, but this example assumes that the lower-speed link is only there for redundancy and backup purposes.

The router on the left of the figure would be a much better next hop for the small routers on the right of the figure than the access router running RIPv2. But how can this information be given to the small routers? Turning on RIPv2 between the routers running OSPF will not work: The higher-speed link is still one hop farther than any route reachable through the router with the low-speed link. And running more than one routing protocol on the same interface is not good practice anyway.

The Next-Hop field in RIPv2 is used in this case to override the ordinary metric method of deciding active routes in RIP. RIPv2 routers check the Next-Hop field in the routing update message. If the Next-Hop field is set for a particular route, the RIP router uses this as the next hop for the route, regardless of distance-vector considerations.

This RIPv2 Next-Hop mechanism is sometimes called *source routing* in some documents. But true source routing information is always set by a *host*, not a router. This is just RIPv2 *Next-Hop identification*.

Multicasting

Multicasting is a kind of halfway distribution method between unicast (one source to one destination) and broadcast (one source to all possible destinations). Multicasting can still optimize routing update traffic by not requiring routers on the same LAN to unicast an exact copy of each routing update message to every other router on the LAN, but still not just blast every device with broadcast information that only routers really need. Multicasting is a way to simultaneously deliver packets to multiple devices belonging to the same *multicast group,* but not every device.

RIPv2 multicasting also offers a way to filter out RIPv2 messages from a RIPv1-only router. This can be important, since RIPv2 messages look very much like RIPv1 messages. But RIPv2 messages are all invalid by RIPv1 standards. For example, RIPv1 devices would either discard RIPv2 messages because the mandatory all-zero fields are not all zeros, or they would accept the routes and ignore the additional RIPv2 information such as the subnet mask. RIPv2 multicasting makes sure that only RIPv2 devices see the RIPv2 information. So RIPv1 and RIPv2 routers can easily coexist on the same LAN, for instance.

The multicast group used for RIPv2 routers is 224.0.0.9. A full discussion of multicasting is beyond the scope of this book. It is enough to note that RIPv2 routers will send and receive routing updates to this multicast group.

RIPv2 is still limited in several ways. The 15 maximum hop count is still there, as well as counting to infinity to resolve routing loops. And RIPv2 does nothing to improve on the fixed distance-vector values that are a feature of all versions of RIP.

RIPng for IPv6

The continued popularity and widespread use of RIP has led to the creation of a special version of RIP just for use with IPv6. This version is called *RIPng*, where "ng" stands for "next generation" (IPv6 itself was often called IPng in the mid-1990s). So there is no need to fear migration to IPv6 because a routing protocol other than RIP must be used on low-end routers and networks.

RIPng uses exactly the same hop-count metric as RIP as well as the same logic and timers. So RIPng is still good old distance-vector RIP, with two important differences:

- The RIP packet formats have been extended to carry the longer IPv6 addresses.
- IPv6 security mechanisms are used instead of RIPv2 authentication.

The overall format of the RIP packet is the same as the format of the RIPv2 packet. There is a 32-bit header followed by a set of 20-byte route entries. The header fields must be the same as those used in RIPv2; there is a 1-byte Command code field, followed by a 1-byte Version field (now 6), and then 2 unused bytes of bits that must still be set to all zero-bits. However, the 20-byte router entry fields in RIPng are totally different that those in RIPv2.

IPv6 addresses are 16 bytes long, leaving only 4 bytes for any other information that must be associated with the IPv6 route. First, there is a 2-byte Route Tag field with the same use as in RIPv2: The Route Tag field identifies *internal* and *external* routes. Internal routes are those learned by RIP itself, either locally or through other RIP routers. External routes are routes learned from another routing protocol such as OSPF or BGP. Then there is a one byte Prefix Length field that tells the receiver where the boundary between network and host is in the IPv6 address. Finally, there is a 1-byte Metric field (this field was a full 32 bits in RIPv1 and RIPv2). Since infinity is still 16 in RIPng, this is not a problem.

The fields of the RIPng packet are shown in Figure 7.10.

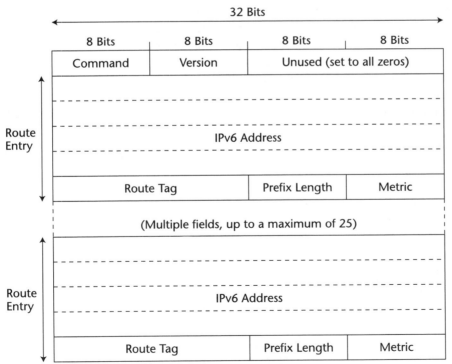

Figure 7.10   The fields of the RIPng packet used with IPv6.

The combination of IPv6 address and Prefix Length do away with a need for the Subnet Mask field in RIPv2 packets. The Address Format Identifier (AFI) field from RIPv2 is not needed in RIPng, since only IPv6 routing information can be carried in RIPng.

However, IPv6 still needs a Next-Hop field. This RIPv2 field contained the Next-Hop IP address that traffic to this IP address space should use, and it was a vast improvement over the implied next hop used in RIPv1. Now, IPv6 does not always need this Next-Hop information, but in many cases the next hop should be included in an IPv6 routing information update. An IPv6 next hop needs another 128 bits (16 bytes). The creators of RIPng decided to essentially reproduce the same route entry structure for the IPv6 next hop, but use a special value of the last field (the Metric) to indicate that the first 16 bytes in the route entry was an IPv6 Next Hop, not the route itself. The value chosen for the metric was 255 (0xFF), because this was far beyond the legal hop-count limit of 15 for RIP.

When the route entry used as an IPv6 Next Hop, the 3 bytes preceding the 0xFF Metric must be set to all zero-bits. This is shown in Figure 7.11.

At first it might seem that the amount of the IPv6 routing information sent with RIPng must instantly double in size, since now each 20-byte IPv6 route requires a 20-byte IPv6 Next-Hop field. This certainly would make IPv6 very unattractive to current RIP users. But it was not necessary to include a Next-Hop entry for each and every IPv6 route, because the creators of RIPng used a clever mechanism to optimize the use of the Next-Hop entry.

A Next-Hop entry always qualifies any IPv6 routes that follow it in the string of route entries until another Next-Hop entry is reached or the packet stream ends. This keeps the number of "extra" Next-Hop entries needed in

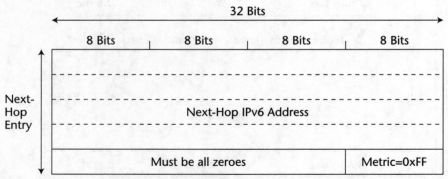

Figure 7.11 The Next-Hop IPv6 address is RIPng.

RIPng to an absolute minimum. And because the Next-Hop field in RIPv2 has only specialized use, a lot of IPv6 routes need no Next-Hop entry at all.

Figure 7.12 shows a RIPng packet that contains information about six IPv6 routes. The first three require no special Next-Hop entry, the next one needs a special Next Hop, and the last two IPv6 routes also need a different Next Hop. The first three route entries use the advertising router as the next hop, as usual. Note the position of the two Next-Hop entries in the packet that supply the Next-Hop information for the routes that require it.

The whole packet occupies only 160 bytes for the routes and next hops instead of 240 bytes. And this example is probably an extreme when it comes to the use of Next-Hop information.

The decision to replace RIPv2 authentication with IPv6 security mechanisms was based on the superior security used in IPv6. Recall that the use of MD5 authentication was not specified in the RIPv2 RFC. The IPv6 Authentication Header protects both the data inside the packet and the IP addresses of the packet, but this is not the case with RIPv2 authentication no matter which method is used. And IPv6 encryption can be used to add further protection.

The RIPng protocol is simpler as a result. No mechanism is needed to distinguish between authentication and route entries in RIPng. The existence of RIPng all but ensures the continued survival of RIP in the IPv6 world.

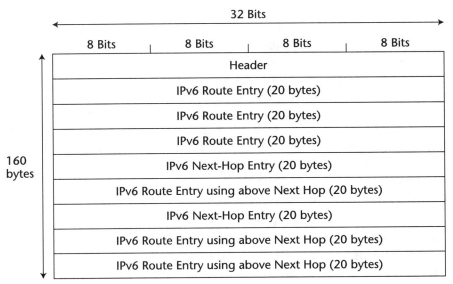

Figure 7.12 Next-Hop entries and Route Entries in RIPng.

Interior Gateway Routing Protocol (IGRP) and Enhanced IGRP (EIGRP)

Cisco routers often use a proprietary IGP known as the Interior Gateway Routing Protocol (IGRP) instead of RIP. Later, features were added to IGRP in the form of Enhanced IGRP (EIGRP). In this section, we only briefly outline IGRP and EIGRP, since IGRP/EIGRP interoperability with Juniper Networks routers is currently impossible.

IGRP and EIGRP might appear to be open standards, but this is only because of the wide-ranging deployment of Cisco routers. No router vendor other than Cisco supports IGRP or EIGRP. Cisco has never published the details of IGRP internals (EIGRP is based on these) and is not likely to. So multivendor interoperability, even if desired by other router vendors, is not really possible. In multivendor environments, the solution to routing protocol compatibility is simple: Use OSPF or IS-IS between Cisco and Juniper Networks routers.

IGRP improves on RIP in several areas, but IGRP is still essentially a distance-vector routing protocol. EIGRP, on the other hand, is advertised by Cisco as a "hybrid" routing protocol that includes aspects of link-state routing protocols such as OSPF and IS-IS among the features of EIGRP.

IGRP

IGRP does not have a single metric (hop count) as does RIP, but rather a whole series of metrics with a wide range of values that can be hashed against a mathematical value that Cisco calls a *weight*. The result of the routing computation on each weighted metric produces a single value that forms a *composite metric* for the route. Network administrators can adjust the metrics and weights to favor some characteristics of a route over others. For example, the composite metric can heavily favor high-bandwidth interfaces or more reliable interfaces when computing active routes to a particular destination.

IGRP also supports *multipath routing*. RIP and other protocols like RIP only use a single route (the best route) to a destination. IGRP can remember up to four ways to reach a particular IP address space and load-balance among these diverse paths. A failed link is not fatal to a route with multipath routing.

Six metrics are used in IGRP:

Hop count.   The default maximum is 100 hops (routers). The configurable maximum is 255. However, IGRP uses hop counts only to prevent routing loops, not to compute active routes. The real power of IGRP is the ability to use the other five metrics for actual route computation, especially the last four.

Packet (MTU) size.   The maximum transmission unit (MTU) determines the largest-sized packet an IGRP router will accept. Large packets with routing information have to be buffered or fragmented, which slows the whole routing process down. Small packets chew up bandwidth. Tuning the MTU size for routing information updates across a network can strike a balance between the two extremes.

Bandwidth. The outbound link bandwidth can be set between 1,200 bps to 10 Gbps, and the default is 1.544 Mbps (T1 speed). IGRP favors higher bandwidth links, but it is possible to understate the actual bandwidth on a link to force IGRP to avoid the link. If only the default value is used on each link, then IGRP cannot use this metric to help route computation at all; all the links appear to be the same.

Delay. This IGRP metric measures the latency on the outbound link. That is, this is the time it takes to send a packet of a given MTU size over the link, assuming the link is free to be used without buffering delays. This metric can have a value from 1 to 16,777,215. The *aggregate delay* of the route is the sum of the delays on each outbound router interface on the path. The aggregate delay sum is divided by 10 for route computation purposes. The default delay is 21,000, which is appropriate for the default T1 1.544-Mbps link speed. If links are given other bandwidth metrics, the delay is adjusted automatically based on the speed relative to this default delay value. In other words, a 10-Mbps Ethernet will be assigned 10 times the delay of a 100-Mbps Ethernet interface. This value can always be explicitly overridden.

Load. The delay metric assumes that there is no congestion on the outbound interface. The load metric adds information about the load on the outbound link to the route computation process. In theory, this should be very helpful. In practice, outbound link loads vary so widely and quickly that basing routing on link-load factors is a risky proposition, because a simple FTP session over a single link might cause traffic rerouting! So the default load metric effectively disregards load in route computations. The allowed range is from 1 to 255, but extreme care is needed whenever load and the associated weight is turned on in IGRP.

Reliability. The last IGRP metric is a measure of how stable the link is. This metric automatically tracks the error rate (based on packet loss) on the link. The default value is 1, but this value often grows over time as errors occur on the link. The allowed range is from 1 to 255.

IGRP does not just compare the various metrics assigned to a route. IGRP uses the metrics (and their associated weights) to derive a single composite metric that represents the cost of the route. The lower the cost, the better. If all IGRP default values are used without modification, the result is essentially the same as the hop-count metric used in RIP. The details of the IGRP formula are not discussed here, but this information is available from many other sources.

EIGRP

EIGRP is, of course, based on IGRP. The enhancements include support for classless IP addressing using CIDR or VLSM. Other improvements in EIGRP were better routing loop detection and faster alternate path discovery.

EIGRP was designed to be backward-compatible with IGRP and remains as firmly Cisco-proprietary as IGRP. The same set of six metrics is used in EIGRP as in IGRP. The only real difference is that while IGRP composite metric is 20 bits long, EIGRP metric is 32 bits long. This is many times larger when the numbers are expressed as powers of two. EIGRP automatically translates its larger metrics when sent to IGRP routers.

Cisco calls EIGRP an *advanced distance-vector* routing protocol or *hybrid* routing protocol. This is because despite the similarities between IGRP and EIGRP, EIGRP reacts differently than IGRP to changes in topology due to link or router failures, advertises routes differently, and even updates routing table entries differently than IGRP. These aspects of EIGRP behavior are very different than RIP or IGRP, but very similar to link-state routing protocols such as OSPF or IS-IS. Whether these differences and similarities justify creating a new category of routing protocol just for EIGRP is open to debate.

The main improvements of EIGRP over IGRP are as follows:

Low-bandwidth use on stable networks.   When there are no changes to routing tables, all that EIGRP routers exchange periodically are simple Hello messages.

Convergence through partial, bounded updates.   EIGRP routers will only send routing table changes to neighbors, and then only to neighbors that need to know about the changes.

Alternate route retention.   EIGRP stores every path it has learned to a destination. So convergence is rapid after a failure if this alternate route is not affected by the routing change.

Independence from IP.   EIRGP works with any protocol that can be routed, not just with IP.

Support for CIDR and VLSM.   The IP addresses used in EIGRP can have completely arbitrary network/host boundaries both for network addresses and subnet masks.

A more complete section on EIGRP would investigate features of EIGRP such as neighbor discovery and recovery, the use of the Reliable Transport Protocol (RTP) in EIGRP, and so on. But this information is readily available from other sources and is beyond the scope of this book.

Configuring RIP

In keeping with the utter simplicity of RIP, the configuration of RIP on most routers and interfaces is also very simple. There are only a handful of options to consider, so RIP is a good place to start an investigation into routing protocols.

Neither RIPv1 nor RIPv2 support unnumbered serial links (the RIP RFC calls them *addressless links*). This is not a problem in the examples provided in this book, since all links are given an explicit IP address, but you should keep this apparent limitation in mind.

Mixing different versions of RIP on the same router is never a great idea. Doing so can cause problems, which is understandable given the differences between RIPv1 and RIPv2 message formats and functions. Sometimes, however, using RIPv1 and RIPv2 on the same router is unavoidable, since extremely low-end devices might only understand RIPv1. For the sake of simplicity, the examples that follow use only RIPv1 for some router configurations and only RIPv2 for others. The commands needed to configure RIPv1 on some interfaces and RIPv2 on others are given but not used in the example network. The examples are always explicit about when RIPv1 or RIPv2 is used.

Previous chapters detailed the general configuration steps for both Cisco and Juniper network access routers. Ethernet (actually 100-Mbps Fast Ethernet) and serial interfaces were configured with IP addresses used, loopback addresses assigned, and several statics and aggregates configured. The example networks in this chapter start with a similar basic configuration, except for the aggregates, which are used later. The examples build on the basic interface, loopback, and static addresses, using RIPv1 and RIPv2 as the routing protocol between the access routers (central-access) and smaller site (remote site) routers. The smaller routers are presumed only able to run RIPv1 or RIPv2.

Access routers frequently use static routes to send packets over the single link to a site router. These static routes are still present in the examples in this chapter. On many occasions, however, running a routing protocol between access and site routers might be preferable. So RIP is added to the static routes. RIP is configured on both a Fast Ethernet and serial interface, using the proper interface notation, depending on whether the router is a Cisco or Juniper Networks router.

The example networks used in the configuration examples are shown in Figure 8.1. The site routers are assumed to be close enough to the access routers for the site routers to attach using Fast Ethernet, while those that are more remote require a short serial WAN link. Any number of scenarios might involve site routers and access routers linked by LANs and WANs; the details are unimportant. Even if every router in the figure were called an access router, the configurations would not change. In the networks in the examples, there is only one Ethernet-attached router and one serial-link-attached router, but the points and configuration steps are basically the same no matter how many links and routers there are.

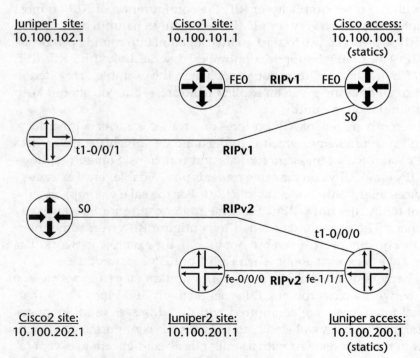

Figure 8.1   The example networks for RIP configuration.

The loopback addresses assigned to the routers are also shown in the figure. In the example networks, there are both Cisco and Juniper Networks access routers. These two access routers will eventually communicate with each other and form one larger network, but they will not be running RIP to communicate with each other, so they are shown separate in this example.

The rest of the example network use a number of multivendor combinations and RIP version variations. Not all possible combinations of router vendors, RIP, and links are represented here, but we explore the major multivendor scenarios (Cisco/Juniper RIPv1 and Cisco/Juniper RIPv2). Both RIPv1 and RIPv2 are used over both serial and LAN interfaces. The interfaces link routers from the same vendor as well as routers from the other vendor. The goal here is to provide as many interoperability variations as possible and not to suggest this arrangement is recommended or even realistic.

The example networks in this book all include "Ethernet" for interface configuration examples. But Ethernet comes in regular-size 10-Mbps Ethernet, large-size 100-Mbps Fast Ethernet, and super-size 1,000-Mbps Gigabit Ethernet. These example networks all use 100-Mbps Fast Ethernet for the Ethernet interfaces, which is common enough today.

Fast Ethernet for Multivendor Connectivity

Caution is required in the example networks with regard to situations where a Cisco router is required to interoperate over Ethernet with a Juniper Networks router. The PICs used in some Juniper Networks routers will not auto-sense the speed difference between regular 10-Mbps Ethernet and 100-Mbps Fast Ethernet. Explicit configuration for 10-Mbps operation is required for these PICs. Many Cisco routers include support for Fast Ethernet, but not all. In this example, support for 100-Mbps Fast Ethernet on all of the Cisco routers is assumed. The Cisco ports in the figure are labeled FE to reflect this requirement. Cisco routers also support several types of multiport Fast Ethernet cards, such as the Fast Ethernet Interface Processor (FEIP) used on the Cisco 7000 series of routers. The Cisco configuration commands here assume that some form of Fast Ethernet is used. But the configuration commands are generic in the sense that no specific model of Fast Ethernet card is assumed. For simplicity, the various forms of Fast Ethernet used on the Cisco routers in these examples have been edited to a basic Fast Ethernet0, Fast Ethernet1, and so on.

RIP and Static Routes

The RIP configurations will include the advertisement of the static routes by RIP so that universal reachability is achieved. If a large corporation ran all of the routers in the example RIP networks, this would be required. If the example network in this scenario were a service provider's access routers linking to a variety of customers' site routers, this global connectivity might not be required or even desired at this level. But this is just a simple networking example, and global connectivity is always assumed to be the goal.

So at the end of the configuration, the local LANs attached to the site routers, all three of the router loopback addresses, and the static routes on the access routers will all be reachable by all routers. Any ping or traceroute to those addresses from any of the three routers will succeed. Limiting this access is just as easy as enabling it, but in this case the need for such reachability is assumed.

The *redistribution* of static routing information by the RIP routing protocol provides the first example of a routing policy used in a router configuration. Sometimes a protocol advertises information from another protocol or source of routing information—a process known as *injecting* static routes into RIP. All of the details of routing policies are discussed later in this book. For now, only the routing policy or optional commands needed to redistribute static routes by RIP are examined.

These examples only give full configuration details on the access routers. This is done only to limit the size and complexity of the configuration examples given. Configuration of the site routers will closely mirror the configurations of the access routers. Nonetheless, the routing tables on all three of the routers in each configuration are shown.

Cisco RIP Configuration

By default, Cisco routers can receive and understand both RIPv1 and RIPv2 messages. But also by default, Cisco routers only send RIPv1 messages. This is not much of an issue, and it is simple enough to turn on or off whatever version of RIP is needed. In fact, each interface on the Cisco router can be configured to send and receive RIPv1 and RIPv2 messages—or even both at the same time.

Cisco Fast Ethernet

As already noted, Cisco routers support several types of multiport Fast Ethernet cards. The Cisco 7000 series, for example, supports the Fast Ethernet Interface Processor (FEIP) used on the Cisco 7000 series of routers. The FEIP uses a three-part port identifier similar to the Juniper Networks PIC port identification system. These represent the slot/interface/interface port of the Fast Ethernet connection. An FEIP port would be referred to as:

```
Router(config)# interface fastethernet 0/0/0
```

Other models of Cisco routers, such as the Cisco 2600 series, and other Fast Ethernet interfaces use a two-part port identifier (slot/unit):

```
Router(config)# interface fastethernet 0/0
```

The Cisco configuration commands used in this chapter assume that some form of Fast Ethernet is used. But the configuration commands uses only one digit (specifically, 0/0) to identify the Fast Ethernet port. In some cases, a third digit must be entered. The Fast Ethernet port itself is identified as either FE0 or FE1 in this chapter and configuration commands simply use FastEthernet0 and FastEthernet1. This is all in line with standard naming conventions.

Cisco Access Router RIPv1 Configuration

Just to cut down on the number of interfaces that have to be configured and accounted for, this example uses some of the static routes, a concept that was introduced for the Cisco_access router in Chapter 5, "Cisco Router Configuration." But since there are no real customer networks on real interfaces to point these static addresses toward, the next hop for each static route is Null0. Packets sent to this next-hop interface are discarded. The key point here is that static routes, no matter if their next hop is a real interface or Null0, are not automatically advertised by RIP. A simple routing policy is needed to redistribute the static routes by RIPv1.

To configure RIPv1 on a Cisco router, you simply enter privileged EXEC mode and configure RIP under that section of the configuration. No version is needed: The router sends RIPv1 by default but understands both RIPv1 and RIPv2 when either is received. The interfaces that RIPv1 will run on are determined by the addresses assigned to the interfaces on the router. The network subcommand enables RIP on a specific interface based on this IP address.

The default for the whole router is to receive either RIPv1 or RIPv2 and to send RIPv1. But including the version subcommand is recommended, for the sake of specificity. This inclusion is especially important when multivendor interoperability with Juniper Networks routers is required, because Juniper Networks routers default to RIPv2 operation on the interfaces on which RIP has been configured.

Setting RIPv1 or RIPv2 on the whole router works in this configuration example. But it will not always work in a real-world situation. For example, suppose one interface needs to run RIPv1 and the other needs to run RIPv2. To set the version of RIP individually on separate interfaces, the ip rip send version and ip rip receive version would have to be used for each interface on which RIP is running. This is done here. In addition, even though the initial RIPv1 configuration will use classful IP addresses, keep in mind that ip classless is usually the default behavior on the Cisco router.

The following shows the static routes, this time each with a Null0 next hop. This example adds another static route from a completely different address space as well, but with the same-length mask (/24):

```
Cisco_access#conf t
Enter configuration commands, one per line. End with Ctrl/Z.
Cisco_access(config)# ip route 10.200.1.0 255.255.255.0 null0
Cisco_access(config)# ip route 10.200.2.0 255.255.255.0 null0
Cisco_access(config)# ip route 10.200.6.0 255.255.255.0 null0
Cisco_access(config)# ip route 172.17.9.0 255.255.255.0 null0
```

The loopback (lo0) address on the router is 10.100.100.1/32. The loopback address is set on the Cisco_access router as follows:

```
Cisco_access(config)# interface loopback0
Cisco_access(config-if)# ip address 10.100.100.1 255.255.255.255
```

The interface addresses are just as simple to configure:

```
Cisco_access(config)# interface fastethernet0
Cisco_access(config-if)# ip address 10.0.32.1 255.255.255.0
Cisco_access(config)# interface serial0
Cisco_access(config-if)# ip address 10.0.33.1 255.255.255.0
```

There is no default route set on the Cisco_access router, although the site routers might have a default route set. But this makes no difference to the Cisco_access router itself, since the default will not be advertised to the access routers.

The addresses used by RIPv1 in the rest of this section are shown in Figure 8.2.

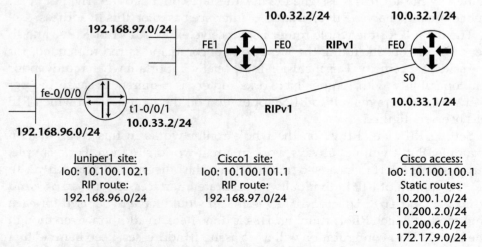

Figure 8.2 The addresses in the Cisco access router example.

This figure adds several details to the overall figure shown previously. All interfaces are given IP addresses for each end of their links. The site routers, in keeping with their networking role, only have a single LAN interface that supports all of the hosts at the site. These networks need to be advertised using RIPv1. The IP addresses for the LANs are shown in the figure, along with the site router's loopback addresses. Note that there are patterns to the assignment of the IP addresses for all of these devices, as there should be.

In this case, the Juniper1_site routers and Cisco1_site routers are assumed to have been configured properly with the associated LAN's IP address and interfaces to the Cisco_access router, that RIP is running on the correct interfaces, and anything else that is needed. The basic RIPv1 configuration for the Cisco_access router is as follows:

```
Cisco_access(config)# router rip
Cisco_access(config-router)# version 1
Cisco_access(config-router)# network 10.0.0.0
```

That's all that is needed. Now, the version 1 could have been omitted, since that is the default, but it is included here for completeness. RIPv1 is always classful and performs automatic summarization, so only the major network designation is required. RIPv1 does not pay attention to anything but network 10 as far as routing is concerned. But because all of the rest of the examples in this book are classless, keep in mind that RIPv1 is the exception in this regard.

Possibly, another interface on the Cisco router might have to run RIPv2. Although this is not done in this example, the following shows how another interface on the same router would be made to send and receive RIPv2:

```
Cisco_access(config)# interface fastethernet1
Cisco_access(config-if)# ip rip receive version 2
Cisco_access(config-if)# ip rip send version 2
```

So the version 1 applies to all interfaces that have network 10 configured, except for those specific interfaces that receive and send version 2. The same method would apply to RIPv2 on the whole router and RIPv1 on an interface, so this format is not repeated later. However, the default behavior of RIPv2 on a Cisco router is still to summarize major networks in a classful manner. Therefore, usually when RIPv2 is configured on a Cisco router, the command no auto-summary is also used so that subnets are advertised properly wherever they are configured in a collection of Cisco routers.

The following is the completed configuration for the Cisco_access router. Only the sections of the configuration necessary for this example are shown:

```
Cisco_access#sh run
Building configuration...
```

```
Current configuration:
!
version 12.1
!
hostname Cisco_access
!
interface Loopback0
 ip address 10.100.100.1 255.255.255.255
!
interface FastEthernet0
 ip address 10.0.32.1 255.255.255.0
!
interface Serial0
 ip address 10.0.33.1 255.255.255.0
!
router rip
 version 1
 network 10.0.0.0
!
ip route 10.200.1.0 255.255.255.0 Null0
ip route 10.200.2.0 255.255.255.0 Null0
ip route 10.200.6.0 255.255.255.0 Null0
ip route 172.17.9.0 255.255.255.0 Null0
!
end
```

This is simple but complete enough to form a functioning network with three routers when all three are configured correctly.

Viewing the Results for RIPv1

The routing table on the Cisco_access router is now more interesting than it was without any active interfaces:

```
Cisco_access#sh ip route
Codes: C - connected, S - static, I - IGRP, R - RIP, M - mobile,
B - BGP
       D - EIGRP, EX - EIGRP external, O - OSPF, IA - OSPF inter area
       N1 - OSPF NSSA external type 1, N2 - OSPF NSSA external
type 2
       E1 - OSPF external type 1, E2 - OSPF external type 2, E - EGP
       i - IS-IS, L1 - IS-IS level-1, L2 - IS-IS level-2, * - candidate
default
       U - per-user static route, o - ODR

Gateway of last resort is not set

R    192.168.97.0/24 [120/1] via 10.0.32.2, 00:00:23, FastEthernet0
```

```
R      192.168.96.0/24 [120/1] via 10.0.33.2, 00:00:27, Serial0
       10.0.0.0 is variably subnetted, 8 subnets, 2 masks
C        10.100.100.1/32 is directly connected, Loopback0
R        10.100.101.1/32 [120/1] via 10.0.32.2, 00:00:23, FastEthernet0
R        10.100.102.1/32 [120/1] via 10.0.33.2, 00:00:27, Serial0
C        10.0.32.0/24 is directly connected, FastEthernet0
C        10.0.33.0/24 is directly connected, Serial0
S        10.200.1.0/24 is directly connected, Null0
S        10.200.2.0/24 is directly connected, Null0
S        10.200.6.0/24 is directly connected, Null0
       172.17.0.0/24 is subnetted, 1 subnets
S        172.17.9.0 is directly connected, Null0
```

Note that RIPv1 is doing its job. The first two R routes—192.168.97.0/24 on the Cisco1_site router and 192.168.96.0/24 on the Juniper1_site router—have been learned by RIPv1. As an aside, this only happens if and when RIP has been configured to run on the 192.168 interfaces on the site routers and these two LANs are up and running. Routers will not advertise routes to configured but down interfaces. Since both routes show up in the access router's routing table, all is well on the site routers with regard to these two LANs. Note that the next-hop interface is listed, as is the *remote* IP address on that interface.

The [120/1] notation in the RIP routes is interesting. The 120 gives the *administrative distance* of the routing protocol, which is Cisco's internal value assigned to the routing protocol. The lower the administrative distance of the routing protocol, on a scale of 0 to 255, the more attractive the route is to use for forwarding. The 1 is the metric for this route according to RIP, meaning there is one other router between this router and the LAN represented by the 192.168 addresses. This other router is the site router, of course.

The other two RIP routes are for the loopback addresses of the site routers. These addresses are advertised by RIP in this case only because the loopback addresses are drawn from the same major network space, 10.0.0.0, as the interface addresses. Otherwise, separate network commands would have been needed to cover the loopback addresses on the site routers.

The access router now realizes that the 10.0.0.0 major network has been *variably subnetted*, meaning that more than one subnet mask has been used to subnet this address space on the router. There are two masks in use with the eight subnets, and the routing table lists the masks for each route: the /32 (255.255.255.255) for the loopback and /24 (255.255.255.0) for everything else.

Now, the goal of this exercise is to make everything reachable. Juniper Networks router configurations and routing tables are shown shortly, so this section looks at the Cisco site router to make sure that this router is receiving all the routes that it should from the access routers. The following is the routing table on the Cisco1_site router:

```
Cisco1_site#sh ip route
Codes: C - connected, S - static, I - IGRP, R - RIP, M - mobile,
       B - BGP
       D - EIGRP, EX - EIGRP external, O - OSPF, IA - OSPF
       inter area
       N1 - OSPF NSSA external type 1, N2 - OSPF NSSA external
       type 2
       E1 - OSPF external type 1, E2 - OSPF external type 2, E - EGP
       i - IS-IS, L1 - IS-IS level-1, L2 - IS-IS level-2,
       * - candidate default
       U - per-user static route, o - ODR

Gateway of last resort is not set

C    192.168.97.0/24 is directly connected, FastEthernet1
     10.0.0.0 is variably subnetted, 6 subnets, 2 masks
C       10.0.32.0/24 is directly connected, FastEthernet0
C       10.100.101.1/32 is directly connected, Loopback0
R       10.100.100.0/24 [120/1] via 10.0.32.1, 00:00:18, FastEthernet0
R       10.200.2.0/24 [120/1] via 10.0.32.1, 00:00:18, FastEthernet0
R       10.200.1.0/24 [120/1] via 10.0.32.1, 00:00:18, FastEthernet0
R       10.200.6.0/24 [120/1] via 10.0.32.1, 00:00:18, FastEthernet0
```

There are two masks for the variably subnetted 10.0.0.0 network, even though RIPv1 does not care at all about the masks. That is why the access router's loopback address, 10.100.100.0, appears with a /24 mask instead of its given /32 mask. The site router must derive a mask for the 10.0.0.0 routes based on its own mask for the 10.0.0.0 network, which is /24.

But wait! Where is the 172.17.9.0 static route from the Cisco_access router? The 10.0.0.0 subnet static routes are there for a very good reason: RIP is configured to run on network 10.0.0.0 and these static routes were included in that classful address space. Now, pings to the 172.17.9.0 address space could still work if a default address to the Cisco_access router is set on the site router. But this relies on a configuration step to be taken on another router. It is better to make sure that the 172.17.9.0 static route is advertised to the site routers using RIPv1.

A Routing Policy to Redistribute Static Routes

The routing policy to redistribute static routes with RIPv1 is not much of a routing policy at all. It's just a configuration command. Normally, in the rest of this book, any and all routing policies required to make the routing protocols function properly are included in the initial configuration. But since this is the first application of a routing policy to change the default behavior of the routing protocol, contents of the routing tables, and advertisements of the routes, this simple routing policy application is shown as a separate step.

The redistribute statics subcommand is applied to the Cisco_access router configuration as follows:

```
Cisco_access#conf t
Enter configuration commands, one per line. End with Ctrl/Z.
Cisco_access(config)# router rip
Cisco_access(config-router)# redistribute static
```

The RIP section of the configuration now appears as follows:

```
!
.router rip
 redistribute static
 version 1
 network 10.0.0.0
!
```

A quick look at the routing table on the Cisco1_site router now shows that the 172.17.9.0 route is present due to RIPv1:

```
Cisco1_site#sh ip route
Codes: C - connected, S - static, I - IGRP, R - RIP, M - mobile,
B - BGP
       D - EIGRP, EX - EIGRP external, O - OSPF, IA - OSPF
inter area
       N1 - OSPF NSSA external type 1, N2 - OSPF NSSA external
type 2
       E1 - OSPF external type 1, E2 - OSPF external type 2, E - EGP
       i - IS-IS, L1 - IS-IS level-1, L2 - IS-IS level-2,
* - candidate default
       U - per-user static route, o - ODR

Gateway of last resort is not set

C    192.168.97.0/24 is directly connected, FastEthernet1
     10.0.0.0 is variably subnetted, 6 subnets, 2 masks
C       10.0.32.0/24 is directly connected, FastEthernet0
C       10.100.101.1/32 is directly connected, Loopback0
R       10.100.100.0/24 [120/1] via 10.0.32.1, 00:00:18, FastEthernet0
R       10.200.2.0/24 [120/1] via 10.0.32.1, 00:00:18, FastEthernet0
R       10.200.1.0/24 [120/1] via 10.0.32.1, 00:00:18, FastEthernet0
R       10.200.6.0/24 [120/1] via 10.0.32.1, 00:00:18, FastEthernet0
R    172.17.0.0/16 [120/1] via 10.0.32.1, 00:00:10, FastEthernet0
```

Note that the default classful Class B mask has been applied to the 172.17.9.0 route.

Juniper Networks RIP Configuration

The Juniper_access router links to the Cisco router in a RIPv2 environment. There also is another set of static routes to represent other networks linked to the router. As with Cisco, setting RIPv1 or RIPv2 can be done on the whole router or on an individual interface. So one interface can run RIPv1 while another runs RIPv2. Juniper Networks routers are inherently classless, so there is no need on a Juniper Networks router to worry about IP classless operation. The Ethernet interface to the Cisco site router is assumed to run at 100 Mbps, so no explicit configuration is required to set the speed on the Juniper Networks router interface.

Juniper Access Router RIPv2 Configuration

The following shows the static routes, this time each with a `reject` next hop that generates an ICMP message back for any packets sent to one of these static routes. This example adds another static route from a completely different address space as well, but with the same-length mask (/24).

```
[edit routing-options]
lab@Juniper_access# set static route 10.200.9.0/24 reject
lab@Juniper_access# set static route 10.200.10.0/24 reject
lab@Juniper_access# set static route 10.200.12.0/24 reject
lab@Juniper_access# set static route 172.17.10.0/24 reject
```

The loopback address on the Juniper_access router is 10.100.200.1/32. This is set as follows:

```
[edit]

lab@Juniper_access# set interface lo0 unit 0 family inet address
10.100.64.1
```

The interface addresses are just as simple to configure:

```
[edit]
lab@Juniper_access#edit interfaces
[edit interfaces]
lab@Juniper_access#set fe-0/0/1 unit 0 family inet address 10.0.35.1/24
[edit interfaces]
lab@Juniper_access#set t1-0/0/0 unit 0 family inet address 10.0.34.1/24
```

It is also assumed that there is no default route set on the Juniper_access router. The addresses used by RIP in the rest of this section are shown in Figure 8.3.

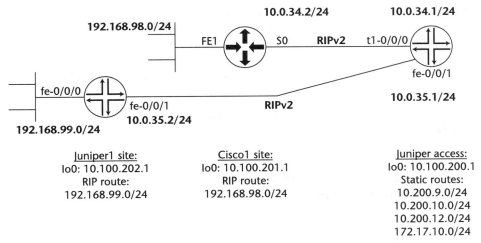

Figure 8.3 The addresses in the Juniper Networks access router example.

This figure adds several details to the overall figure shown previously. All interfaces are given IP addresses for each end of their links. The site routers, in keeping with their networking role, only have a single LAN interface that supports all of the hosts at the site. These are the networks that need to be advertised using RIP, of course. The IP addresses for the LANs are shown in the figure, along with the site router's loopback addresses. Note that there are patterns to the assignment of the IP addresses for all of these devices, as there should be.

The Juniper2_site routers and Cisco2_site routers are assumed to have been configured properly with the associated LANs IP addresses and interfaces to the Juniper_access router, that RIP is running on the interfaces, and anything else that is needed. Juniper Networks routers require that a *group* be established for RIP configurations, which makes it a lot easier to mix RIPv1 and RIPv2 interfaces. The Juniper Networks "group" terminology identifies an "instance" of the routing protocol running on the router. The following is the basic RIPv2 configuration for the Juniper_access router:

```
[edit protocols]
lab@Juniper_access# set rip group rip2-site
lab@Juniper_access# set rip group rip2-site neighbor t1-0/0/0
lab@Juniper_access# set rip group rip2-site neighbor fe-0/0/1
```

Note that there is no mention of IP addresses in the RIPv2 configuration. There is also no need to specify the version because by default the Juniper Networks router will understand both RIPv1 and RIPv2 routing protocol packets on all interfaces.

If you needed to specify a particular version of RIP for a particular interface, all you would need to do would be to add the proper send and receive configuration statements:

```
lab@Juniper_access# set rip group cisco2-site neighbor t1-0/0/0 send
version-1

lab@Juniper_access# set rip group cisco2-site neighbor t1-0/0/0 receive
version-1
```

These configuration statements are used as an example only and are not used in the example network, which runs RIPv2. The relevant portions of the configuration on the Juniper_access router are as follows:

```
interfaces {
    fe-0/0/1 {
        unit 0 {
            family inet {
                address 10.0.35.1/24;
            }
        }
    }
    t1-0/0/0 {
        unit 0 {
            family inet {
                address 10.0.34.1/24;
            }
        }
    }
    lo0 {
        unit 0 {
            family inet {
                address 10.100.200.1/32;
            }
        }
    }
}
routing-options {
    static {
        route 10.200.9.0/24 reject;
        route 10.200.10.0/24 reject;
        route 10.200.12.0/24 reject;
        route 172.17.10.0/24 reject;
    }
}
protocols {
    rip {
        group rip2-site {
            neighbor t1-0/0/0.0;
```

```
        neighbor fe-0/0/1.0;
    }
}
```

Viewing the RIPv2 Results

A useful operational command to verify the proper operation of RIPv2 on the Juniper_access router is as follows:

```
lab@Juniper_access> show rip neighbor
                        Source       Destination  Send    Receive   In
Neighbor        State   Address      Address      Mode    Mode      Met
--------        -----   -------      -----------  ----    -------   ---
fe-0/0/1.0      Up      10.0.35.1    224.0.0.9    mcast   both      1
t1-0/0/0.0      Up      10.0.34.1    224.0.0.9    mcast   both      1
```

The destination address of the RIPv2 routing protocols is the multicast group address assigned to RIPv2, 224.0.0.9. The router can receive both multicast RIPv2 packets and broadcast RIPv1 packets. The metric added to routes received before they are placed in the routing table is 1. The show rip statistics operational command can be used to give statistics for both RIPv1 and RIPv2 updates sent and received.

The routes placed in the Juniper_access router's routing table by RIPv2 are revealed as follows:

```
lab@Juniper_access> show route

inet.0: 14 destinations, 14 routes (14 active, 0 holddown, 0 hidden)
+ = Active Route, - = Last Active, * = Both

10.0.34.0/24        *[Direct/0] 00:18:39
                     > via t1-0/0/0.0
10.0.34.1/32        *[Local/0] 00:36:50
                      Local via t1-0/0/0.0
10.0.35.0/24        *[Direct/0] 00:36:15
                     > via fe-0/0/1.0
10.0.35.1/32        *[Local/0] 00:36:50
                      Local via fe-0/0/1.0
10.100.200.1/32     *[Direct/0] 00:36:50
                     > via lo0.0
10.100.201.1/32     *[RIP/100] 00:18:39, metric 2
                     > to 10.0.34.2 via t1-0/0/0.0
10.100.202.1/32     *[RIP/100] 00:32:35, metric 2
                     > to 10.0.35.2 via fe-0/0/1.0
10.200.9.0/24       *[Static/5] 00:36:50, metric 0
                      Reject
```

```
10.200.10.0/24      *[Static/5] 00:36:50, metric 0
                       Reject
10.200.12.0/24      *[Static/5] 00:36:50, metric 0
                       Reject
172.17.10.0/24      *[Static/5] 00:36:50, metric 0
                       Reject
192.168.98.0/24     *[RIP/100] 00:18:39, metric 2
                       > to 10.0.34.2 via t1-0/0/0.0
192.168.99.0/24     *[RIP/100] 00:18:39, metric 2
                       > to 10.0.34.2 via fe-0/0/1.0
224.0.0.9/32        *[RIP/100] 00:14:46, metric 1
```

The routing protocol *preference*, Juniper Network's form of administrative distance, assigned to RIP (both versions) is 100. The site router's loopback addresses are in the table, as are the LAN addresses on the site routers. Note that in contrast to Cisco, the metric for the routes on the site routers is 2, not 1, because Juniper Networks routers always include the local router as a hop. Now, inet.0 is the Juniper Networks *unicast* routing table. So what is the RIPv2 multicast address 224.0.0.9/32 doing in the unicast table? Its inclusion was simply a design decision. Establishing a completely separate table for the few multicast routes used by routing protocols (OSPF uses two) makes little sense. The multicast addresses are well known and easily distinguished. So they are listed in the unicast routing table.

Examination of the following routing table on the Juniper1_site router reveals something interesting (as it would in Cisco site router table, were we to study that):

```
lab@Juniper1_site> show route

inet.0: 6 destinations, 6 routes (6 active, 0 holddown, 0 hidden)
+ = Active Route, - = Last Active, * = Both

10.0.35.0/24        *[Direct/0] 00:46:45
                       > via fe-0/0/1.0
10.0.35.2/32        *[Local/0] 00:46:45
                        Local via fe-0/0/1.0
10.100.202.1/32     *[Direct/0] 00:46:45
                       > via lo0.0
192.168.98.0/24     *[RIP/100] 00:11:08, metric 3
192.168.99.0/24     *[Direct/0] 00:46:45
                       > via fe-0/0/0.0
192.168.99.1/32     *[Local/0] 00:46:45
                        Local via fe-0/0/0.0
224.0.0.9/32        *[RIP/100] 00:11:08, metric 1
```

Where are the interface, loopback, and static route addresses from the Juniper_access router? RIP is up and running, and the access router is receiving RIPv2 information from the site routers. What is going on?

Earlier in this section, it was assumed that the site routers were configured correctly, and that assumption still holds. This proper operation is confirmed by the site routing information showing up correctly on the access router. So the problem must be on the access router.

The problem is only the default RIP behavior of Juniper Networks routers. By default, Juniper Networks routers "listen" to RIP updates, but they do not "speak" RIP unless explicitly told what routes to advertise. Not even the remote interface address shows up on the site routers with the default RIP operation.

Just as the problem of the Cisco routers in the RIPv1 example was solved by using a simple routing policy, a simple routing policy on the Juniper_access router will solve the RIPv2 routing problem on the site routers. And also as before, if a default route is used on the site routers, sending all traffic without explicit routes to the access router, this might not be a problem at all. But this example does rely on explicit routes to the static route destinations on the access router, however.

The Send-Statics Routing Policy

Instead of a configuration statement like `redistribute statics` used in Cisco, Juniper Networks routers consider redistributing information from one routing to another to be a complete routing policy. It's a rudimentary routing policy to be sure, but a routing policy nonetheless. As a routing policy, even an action a simple as having RIP readvertise the static routes configured on the router must be done using a routing policy configured in the policy-options section of the Juniper Networks configuration hierarchy.

All aspects of Juniper Networks routing policies are explored later on in this book. For now, it is enough to give the configuration of a routing policy to take `from` a "protocol" (information origin) called `static` routes and `then` `accept` these routes for advertisement by the routing protocol. The `policy-statement` is given a name of `send-statics` and then applied to RIP as an `export` (advertising) policy. The following shows how the routing policy is configured:

```
[edit]
lab@Juniper_access# edit policy-options policy-statement send-statics
[edit policy-options policy-statement send-statics]
lab@Juniper_access# set term 1 from protocol static
[edit policy-options policy-statement send-statics]
lab@Juniper_access# set term 1 then accept
[edit policy-options policy-statement send-statics]
lab@Juniper_access# show
term 1 {
    from protocol static;
    then accept;
}
```

The show command only displays the rules of the routing policy send-statics because the command was entered at the [edit policy-options policy-statement send-statics] level of the configuration command hierarchy.

The routing policy as written only advertises the static routes defined on the access router to the site routers. If the interface address and loopback address are also to be advertisedto the Juniper1_site router, another term needs to be added to select these sources of information. The loopback address is added as follows:

```
[edit policy-options policy-statement send-statics]
lab@Juniper_access# set term 2 from interface lo.0
[edit policy-options policy-statement send-statics]
lab@Juniper_access# set term 2 then accept
[edit policy-options policy-statement send-statics]
lab@Juniper_access# show
term 1 {
    from protocol static;
    then accept;
}
term 2 {
    from interface lo0.0;
    then accept;
}
```

Once a routing policy has been defined on a Juniper Networks router, the policy does absolutely nothing until it is applied as either an import (receiving) or export (sending) policy within a routing protocol. The following is how the send-statics policy is applied so that RIPv2 will advertise the static routes and the loopback address to the other routers:

```
[edit]
lab@Juniper_access# set protocols rip group rip2-site export send-statics
```

The RIPv2 configuration now looks like this:

```
[edit]
lab@Juniper_access# show protocols
protocols {
    rip {
        group rip2-site {
            export send-statics
            neighbor t1-0/0/0.0;
            neighbor fe-0/0/1.0;
        }
    }
}
```

The simplest way to verify proper operation of the routing policy is just to check the routing table on the Juniper1_site router. The Cisco site router shows almost exactly the same information:

```
lab@Juniper1_site> show route

inet.0: 11 destinations, 11 routes (11 active, 0 holddown, 0 hidden)
+ = Active Route, - = Last Active, * = Both

10.0.35.0/24        *[Direct/0] 00:41:40
                     > via fe-0/0/1.0
10.0.35.2/32        *[Local/0] 00:41:40
                     Local via fe-0/0/1.0
10.100.200.1/32     *[RIP/100] 00:15:08, metric 2
                     > to 10.0.35.1 via fe-0/0/1.0
10.100.202.1/32     *[Direct/0] 00:41:40
                     > via lo0.0
10.200.9.0/24       *[RIP/100] 00:15:08, metric 2
                     > to 10.0.35.1 via fe-0/0/1.0
10.200.10.0/24      *[RIP/100] 00:15:08, metric 2
                     > to 10.0.35.1 via fe-0/0/1.0
10.200.12.0/24      *[RIP/100] 00:15:08, metric 2
                     > to 10.0.35.1 via fe-0/0/1.0
172.17.10.0/24      *[RIP/100] 00:15:08, metric 2
                     > to 10.0.35.1 via fe-0/0/1.0
192.168.98.0/24     *[RIP/100] 00:11:08, metric 3
192.168.99.0/24     *[Direct/0] 00:41:40
                     > via fe-0/0/0.0
192.168.99.1/32     *[Local/0] 00:41:40
                     Local via fe-0/0/0.0
224.0.0.9/32        *[RIP/100] 00:09:33, metric 1
```

All is now well, and explicit routing table entries exist for the loopback address and the static routes from the access router.

A Note on RIPv1 Juniper Network Router Operation

The previous examples used RIPv1 on the Cisco access router and RIPv2 on the Juniper Networks access router. The situation could have been reversed—RIPv2 run on the Cisco access router and RIPv1 run on the Juniper Networks access router. But then there would have been an interesting side effect with regard to the 172.17.10.0/24 static route defined on the access router.

RIPv1 is totally classful, but the normally Class B 172.17.0.0 network is now subnetted to 172.17.10.0/24 on the Juniper Networks access router. The issue is that the site routers do not have a clue as to how the 172.17.0.0 should be subnetted once they receive this route with RIPv1, since there is no 172.17.0.0 network defined on the site routers at all. RIPv1 sends no mask information, so how the site routers choose to represent the 172.17.10.0/24 network in their routing tables is completely implementation-dependent.

But note that however the 172.17.10.0/24 route is represented in the site routers' routing tables is totally compliant with the RIPv1 specification. The RIPv1 specification only describes how routing information is exchanged by routers, not what should be done with that information once it arrives at the receiving router. As it turns out, Cisco and Juniper Networks routers handle the same information in different ways.

As seen in the previous section, *Cisco Access Router RIPv1 Configuration*, the Cisco1_site router stores the 172.17.10.0 route (there is no mask supplied in RIPv1) as 172.17.0.0/16. This only makes sense: The normal classful mask applied to 172.17.*anything* would be /16.

But Juniper Networks routers behave differently than Cisco routers when confronted with the 172.17.10.0 route. As an inherently classless router, the Juniper Networks router relies on the mask information (/24) sent with RIPv2 to figure out how the 172.17.10.0 route should be handled. This is mask information now absent in RIPv1. So the Juniper Networks router, seeing bits set beyond the normal classful Class B 172.17.0.0 boundary, simply stores the 172.17.10.0 route as a host route:

```
172.17.10.0/32      *[RIP/100] 00:22:52, metric 2
                    > to 10.0.35.1 via fe-0/0/1.0
```

This behavior more or less renders the 172.17.10.0 route useless on the Juniper1_site router. A host route assigned to a real device cannot end in 0. Any packets sent to "host" 172.17.10.0 produces a longest match on the host route in the routing table on the Juniper Networks site router, but no other packets in this address space are forwarded to the access router unless there is a default route configured on the Juniper Networks site router to handle this situation. This does not require a lot of effort, and it might have been done already. But keep this in mind if no packets to 172.17.10.0/24 show up at the access router even though the route is advertised with RIPv1.

So when it comes to RIP, whenever possible, use RIPv2. But it is probably even better to use OSPF or IS-IS as the IGP for a collection of routers, even when only small site routers are included.

CHAPTER 9

Open Shortest Path First (OSPF)

In contrast to the simplicity of RIP, this chapter explores one of the most powerful and complex of all IGPs: Open Shortest Path First (OSPF). OSPF is not a distance-vector protocol like RIP, but a *link-state* protocol with an ambitious set of metrics that can be used to reflect much more about a network than just the number of routers encountered between the source and destination. In OSPF, a router attempts to route based on the state of the links between source and destination, which is where the name link state comes from.

There's a reason the word "attempts" appears in the preceding paragraph. As originally envisioned, OSPF can be equipped with metrics for computing the shortest path through a collection of routers; they are based on link and router characteristics such as highest throughput, lowest delay, lowest cost (in terms of money), and link reliability. For now, OSPF is used very cautiously, with default metrics based entirely on link bandwidth.

Even with the most conservative use of OSPF, link states are a vast improvement over simplistic hop counts based on the number of routers. Why? Because distance-vector routing protocols like RIP were fine for networks constructed out of equal-speed links but struggled when networks started to be built out of WAN links with a wide variety of available speeds. For instance, when RIP first appeared as an IGP, almost all WANs were composed of low-speed analog links running at 9,600 bps. Even digital links running at 56 or 64 Kbps were mainly valued for their ability to carry five 9,600-bps channels on the same physical link. Commercial T1s at 1.544 Mbps were not widely available until 1984, and then only in major metropolitan areas. Digital equipment to terminate these circuits was very expensive, and as recently as 1991, a 9,600-bps analog modem listed for $799.

Today, there are many choices available for WAN links, and the costs are a fraction of what they once were. Routers can be connected by T1s (1.5 Mbps) or T3s (45 Mbps), E1s (2 Mbps) or E3s (34.368 Mbps), and SONET/SDH from 155 Mbps to 10 Gbps (and many speeds in between). Even LANs can run at 10 Mbps or 100 Mbps or 1 Gbps, and 10-Gbps Ethernet changes the landscape even more. The quickest way to send packets from one router to another in such a mixed link environment is not always through the smallest number of routers.

As a simple example, consider the three routers in Figure 9.1. This is not a contemporary example (although it might be), but it reflects the situation that led to the creation of link-state protocols in the first place. There are two T1 links running at 1.544 Mbps and one link running at 64 Kbps.

Distance-vector routing protocols like RIP have always sent packets from Router A to Router C over the 64-Kbps link, since that is only one hop. But obviously it would be very attractive to send packets over the higher-speed links through Router B. But two hops is longer than one hop—unless the routing protocol can somehow to be made to recognize that it should use the shortest path based on metrics other than simple hop count.

RIP was also slow to converge on a new network topology. Even with triggered updates that set routes to infinity immediately and sent that information to neighbors, RIP's counting-to-infinity behavior had forced every router to increment the distance to the unreachable network through every value between the current value and infinity (16 hops). During the convergence time, routing loops were common, and even split horizon and poison reverse did not avoid all routing loops. Adding a *hold-down* to prevent routing loops helped a lot, but it could also increase convergence time. OSPF was designed to correct all of these limitations of RIP.

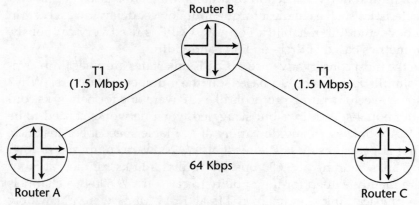

Figure 9.1 The case for link-state routing.

The *open* in OSPF refers to the fact that the Shortest Path First (SPF) algorithm to compute and converge on routes based on distributed information was not owned by anyone and could be used by all implementations of OSPF. The SPF algorithm is often called the *Dijkstra algorithm* after the computer and network pioneer E. W. Dijkstra, who first worked it out mathematically from graph theory. Dijkstra himself modestly called his new method SPF, first described in 1959, because compared to a distance-vector protocol's counting to infinity to produce convergence on a new shortest path to a destination, his algorithm found the *shortest path first*.

The initial appearance of OSPF was a shock to routing protocol specialists everywhere. The RIP specification that needed less than 20 pages of simple text to describe was suddenly augmented by an OSPF specification that required more than 100 pages of complex diagrams and explanations in PostScript (a very sophisticated page description language) to detail. Many early Internet coders, who could write and debug a program to implement RIP in a day, were now faced with a document that they had trouble finding a printer on which to print the RFC, let alone being able to read and understand it.

The complexity of OSPF meant that early implementations were unstable, incomplete, and anything but interoperable among different router vendor versions. In fact, OSPF version 1 (OSPFv1), described in RFC 1131, never really matured beyond the experimental stage. But the current version of OSPF, OSPFv2, which first appeared as RFC 1247 in 1991 and is now defined by RFC 2328 issued in 1998, changed all of that. OSPF today is the recommended replacement for RIP, although a strong argument for a RIP replacement routing protocol could be made in favor of IS-IS, another link-state routing protocol that is discussed in Chapter 11, "Intermediate System-Intermediate System (IS-IS)," and Chapter 12, "Configuring IS-IS."

Link States and Shortest Paths

Link-state protocols are all based on the idea of a *distributed map* of the network. All of the routers that run a link-state protocol have the same copy of this network map, which is built up from scratch by the routing protocol itself and not imposed on the network from an outside source at all. The network map and all of the information about the routers and links (and the routes that the routers know about) are kept in a *link-state database* on each router. The database does not contain a "map" in the usual sense of the word; instead, records exist that represent the topology of the network as a series of links from one router to another. The database must be identical on all of the routers in an *area* (defined in the *OSPF Areas and Router Types* section later in the chapter) for OSPF to work properly.

Initially, each router only knows about a piece of the entire network. The local router knows only about itself and the local interfaces. However, the local router must be considered the definitive source of information about itself. So *link-state advertisements* (LSAs), the OSPF information sent to all other routers from the local router, always identify the local router as the source of the information.

The OSPF routing protocol floods this information to all of the other routers so that a complete picture of the network is generated and stored in the link-state database. *Flooding* just means that one router takes the information it has learned as input on one interface and immediately passes it along as output on all other interfaces. OSPF uses *reliable flooding*, which means that OSPF routers have ways to find out if the information passed to another router was received or not. Naturally, networks change as links fail or are added, and the same might be true of the network routers. When any router detects a change in the network topology, this information must be shared with all of the other OSPF routers. This flooding is needed because any alteration of the network topology might change the shortest path, sometimes drastically.

For example, if the T1 link between Router B and Router C in Figure 9.1 fails, then Router A must quickly realize that the shortest path to Router C is now the 64-Kbps link. Counting to infinity is too slow, but OSPF flooding is potentially a faster way to converge the network on the new topology. This fast convergence through the recomputation of every route in the network link-state database has not always been possible. Many routers in the past struggled just to route packets fast enough without worrying about the added burden of processor-intensive flooding and database maintenance. The actual periodic rerunning of algorithms like SPF were not as much of a problem; routers were just computers and as such excelled at performing the quick computations that route calculation required. It was the activities relating to the link-state database that were more of a problem in early OSPF implementations. The more routers and links that OSPF had to deal with, the larger the link-state database that had to be maintained above and beyond the routing and forwarding tables that were required to move packets on their way through the router.

OSPF almost sank beneath the weight of its own link-state database. The breakthrough with OSPFv2 was to introduce the idea of *stub areas* into an OSPF routing domain. A stub area could function with a greatly reduced link-state database, although the stub areas still relied on a very special *backbone area* to have a more complete map of the entire network. The various types of areas defined and used in OSPF are discussed in the *OSPF Areas and Router Types* section coming up in the chapter. The intent is just to show how OSPF needed certain optimizations, including the isolation of small routers in stub areas and the deployment of powerful backbone routers, to get off the ground in the first place. In today's world of resource-rich, high-speed routers, we can easily forget that what are now considered trivial tasks—flooding and database maintenance—were once crushing burdens for low-end routers to perform efficiently.

What OSPF Can Do

The design goals of OSPF were ambitious. Even in 1987, when work on OSPF began, the Internet was struggling with routing protocols. The NSFNET backbone and many autonomous systems (ASs) ran RIP as an Interior Gateway Protocol (IGP), but a lot of routes on the Internet were just static routes. There was also a lot of default routing; if a router did not know how to deliver the packet locally, a static default route sent it somewhere else. RIP was just too slow to converge and consumed a lot of bandwidth. Routers ran the Exterior Gateway Protocol (EGP) between ASs, but EGP was awkward and required a tree topology among routing domains.

By 1992, OSPF had matured enough to be the recommended IGP for the Internet. OSPF largely delivered on most of the following design goals:

Better routing metrics for links.   OSPF employs a configurable link metric with a range of valid values between 1 and 65,535. The total cost of a path between routers from source to destination is unlimited, as long as all the routers are in the same AS. Network administrators, for example, could assign a metric of 10,000 to a low-bandwidth link and 10 to a very high bandwidth SONET/SDH link. Supposedly, since all of the routers were within a single AS or formed a single ISP network, these values could be manually assigned through a central authority. In practice, no one wanted to assign values to links this way. So most implementations of OSPF divide a *reference bandwidth* by the actual bandwidth on the link, known through the router's interface configuration. The default reference bandwidth is usually 100 Mbps (Fast Ethernet). Since the metric cannot be less than 1, all links at 100 Mbps or faster use a 1 as a link metric and thus revert to a simple hop count when longest cost paths are computed. If needed, the reference bandwidth can be altered (usually raised), but this again requires a central authority to impose.

Equal-cost multipaths.   In many collections of routers, numerous ways exist to reach the same destination network, some of which might be computed by the routing protocol as having the same cost. When equal-cost paths exist, whether three hops or a link-state metric of 40, OSPF routers can find and use them. This means that multiple next hops can be installed in a forwarding table with OSPF. OSPF does not specify how to use these multipaths; routers can use simple round-robin (one next hop after another, then repeat) per packet, round-robin per flow, hashing, or other mechanisms.

Router hierarchies.   OSPF made very large routing domains possible by introducing a two-level hierarchy of areas. This hierarchy enabled networks to be built with literally hundreds of routers. With OSPF, the concepts of an edge and backbone router became common and well understood.

Internal and external routes.   Once the AS structure emerged, distinguishing between routing information that originated within the AS (internal routing information) and routing information that came from another AS (external routing information) became necessary. RIP trusted everything equally, but OSPF could tell if the routing information was generated locally or remotely. Internal routing information is generally more trustworthy than external routing information that might have passed from AS to AS or ISP to ISP across the Internet.

Classless addressing.   OSPF was first designed in a classful Internet environment with Class A, Class B, and Class C addresses. However, OSPF is comfortable with the arbitrary network/host boundaries used by classless interdomain routing (CIDR) and variable-length subnet masking (VLSM). So OSPF routing information has always associated the network mask with the route explicitly.

Security.   RIPv1 routers have accepted updates from anyone, and even RIPv2 routers only officially have used simple plaintext passwords that could be sniffed out by anyone with access to the link. Hackers loved spoofing routers and disrupting RIP routing tables. OSPF allows not only for simple password authentication but also for strong MD5 key mechanisms on routing updates.

TOS routing.   The original OSPF was intended to support the bit patterns established for the Type of Service (TOS) field in the IP packet header. Routers at the time had no way to enforce TOS routing, but OSPF anticipated the use of the Internet for all types of traffic such as voice and video and went ahead and built into OSPF ways to distribute multiple metrics for links. So OSPF routing updates can include TOS routing information for five IP TOS service classes, defined in RFC 1349. The service categories and OSPF TOS values are normal service (TOS=0), minimize monetary cost (2), maximize reliability (4), maximize throughput (8), and minimize delay (16). Since all current implementations of OSPF support only a TOS value of 0, little will be said about the other TOS metrics in this chapter.

What is the relationship between the OSPF use of a reference bandwidth and TOS routing? Use of the OSPF link reference bandwidth is different than and independent of TOS support, which relies on the specific settings in the packet headers. OSPF routers were supposed to keep separate link-state databases for each type of service, since the least-cost path in terms of bandwidth could be totally different than the least-cost path computed based on delay or reliability. This was not feasible in early OSPF implementations, which struggled to maintain the single, normal TOS=0 database. And it turned out the Internet users did not want lots of bandwidth *or* low delay *or* high reliability when they sent packets. Internet users wanted lots of bandwidth *and* low delay *and* high reliability. So the reference bandwidth method is about all the link state that OSPF can handle, but that is still better than nothing.

The Theory of OSPF

You don't need an advanced knowledge of mathematics or graph theory to understand how OSPF uses the link-state database to compute the entries that should be in the routing table. Even though the SPF algorithm isn't easy to understand or even describe, the operation of OSPF with regard to route computation can be explained very simply.

The OSPF database consists of a table of entries that represent a collection of routers and their local interfaces and routes as a *directed graph*. A directed graph consists of *leafs* that represent the routers and *links* between that leafs that represent the physical links between the routers. The graph is "directed" in the sense that each link is assigned a metric (cost) in one direction only. So each link advertisement is generated by two routers: the routers at each end of the link. Links are not even required to have the same metric or cost in both directions, although they usually do. The link doesn't really have to be point-to-point to typically have the same metric or cost in both directions; Frame Relay and ATM usually work this way too. For the purpose of route calculation, OSPF always sees routers as directly connected by unidirectional links. Both routers must advertise a link before the link can be used for route calculations, although information about the links is kept in each router's link-state database for an hour (3,600 seconds).

In addition to the IP addresses that represent the router itself (the Router ID) and the interfaces on the router, the IP routes that each router knows about are associated with each leaf (router) in the graph. These routes can be static routes or other types of routes learned from "outside" OSPF itself. Technically, any IP route learned from a source other than OSPF itself is an external route from the OSPF link-state database perspective.

To see how OSPF works in the real world, consider a simple collection of six routers, as shown in Figure 9.2. Each router is shown with its loopback address, and this address is assumed to be the Router ID for OSPF purposes. There are only two types of links used in this simple network: 10-Mbps Ethernet and 100-Mbps Ethernet. Also for simplicity, even though both link types are LANs, the links between the routers are shown as point-to-point links using some form of Ethernet crossover cabling. Finally, there are no link IP addresses at all; the next hop associated with each link is assumed to be the Router ID (loopback address) of the router in the figure.

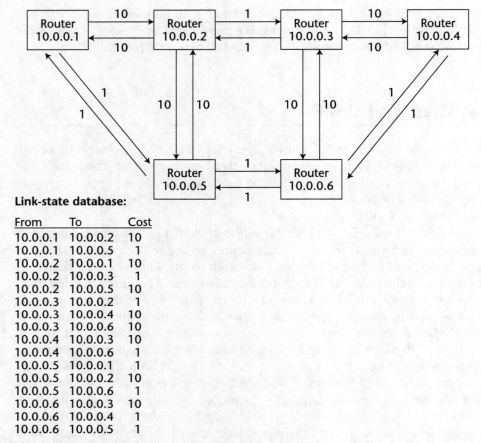

Link-state database:

From	To	Cost
10.0.0.1	10.0.0.2	10
10.0.0.1	10.0.0.5	1
10.0.0.2	10.0.0.1	10
10.0.0.2	10.0.0.3	1
10.0.0.2	10.0.0.5	10
10.0.0.3	10.0.0.2	1
10.0.0.3	10.0.0.4	10
10.0.0.3	10.0.0.6	10
10.0.0.4	10.0.0.3	10
10.0.0.4	10.0.0.6	1
10.0.0.5	10.0.0.1	1
10.0.0.5	10.0.0.2	10
10.0.0.5	10.0.0.6	1
10.0.0.6	10.0.0.3	10
10.0.0.6	10.0.0.4	1
10.0.0.6	10.0.0.5	1

Figure 9.2 An example network for SPF route calculation.

The reference bandwidth is 100 Mbps, as usual. So each link in the figure has either a metric of 1 (100 Mbps/100 Mbps) or 10 (100 Mbps/10 Mbps). Note the directed graph nature of the metrics, although both are the same in each direction. This simple network will show how the SPF algorithm builds its routing table, including next hops and costs, from the link-state database.

The link-state database is shown in the figure as well. Each router is assumed to have reliably flooded its local information to all the other routers. All that is left for the routers to do is perform their route calculations.

The link-state databases must be identical within an OSPF area, and this is one of the main jobs of reliable·flooding. However, each router has its own perspective on the database. So even though the database is the same, the resulting routing tables will be totally different, depending on which router is actually running the link-state algorithm. This example will use the perspective of Router 10.0.0.5.

Any OSPF routing update with new information triggers the OSPF route calculation process. This almost always means running the Dijkstra algorithm against the database to produce the least-cost active route to every IP address destination in the area.

The algorithm starts by making the router itself the root of a tree. The link-state database reveals the routers that are directly connected to the calculating router, and these *neighbors* are added to what becomes the *candidate list*. The costs of the links to these routers (leafs) are associated with the candidate list, as is the next-hop address and interface.

The next step is to consider only the router in the candidate list with the least cost. If there are multiple routers with the same cost, as often happens, each is added to the tree. The router, or routers, with the least cost is added at the proper "branch" to the tree rooted on the calculating router. If there are any higher-cost paths to the same route still in the candidate table, these can be deleted since the goal is the find the least-cost path. Then the neighbors of *this* router (or these routers) are added to the candidate list. Only routers not currently on the tree are considered as new candidates. The cost to reach these new routers is taken from the sum of the link metrics needed to get there from the calculating router, again based on the entries in the link-state database. The selection process then repeats itself, with the least-cost router being added to the tree. Each step is called an *iteration* of the algorithm. At each step, the cost and next hop associated with the router is added to the tree as well. This process continues until the candidate list is empty and all routers in the area have been added to the tree leading away from the calculating router.

The step-by-step approach that Router 10.0.0.5 takes to generate its shortest-path tree is shown in Figure 9.3. The candidate list shows the next-hop interface (router) and cost to that destination in parentheses.

The tree-building method avoids routing loops, and the incremental addition of routers to the tree ensures that each link in the network is examined only once. There is no concern that once on the tree, a router might be reachable through a path with a lower cost, since only the lowest-cost path to a router is ever added to the tree in the first place. So the cost to reach any router already on the tree is guaranteed to be minimal whenever a packet has to start out from the router at the root of the tree.

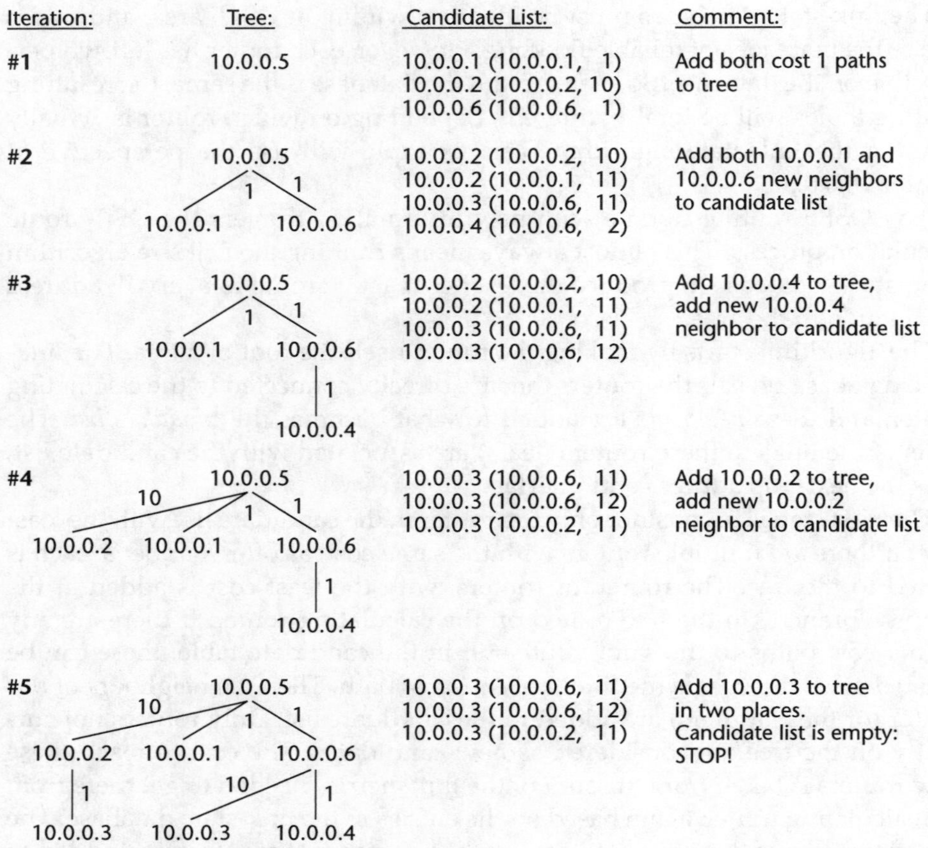

Iteration:	Tree:	Candidate List:	Comment:
#1	10.0.0.5	10.0.0.1 (10.0.0.1, 1) 10.0.0.2 (10.0.0.2, 10) 10.0.0.6 (10.0.0.6, 1)	Add both cost 1 paths to tree
#2	10.0.0.5 1 ⟋ ⟍ 1 10.0.0.1 10.0.0.6	10.0.0.2 (10.0.0.2, 10) 10.0.0.2 (10.0.0.1, 11) 10.0.0.3 (10.0.0.6, 11) 10.0.0.4 (10.0.0.6, 2)	Add both 10.0.0.1 and 10.0.0.6 new neighbors to candidate list
#3	10.0.0.5 1 ⟋ ⟍ 1 10.0.0.1 10.0.0.6 │ 1 10.0.0.4	10.0.0.2 (10.0.0.2, 10) 10.0.0.2 (10.0.0.1, 11) 10.0.0.3 (10.0.0.6, 11) 10.0.0.3 (10.0.0.6, 12)	Add 10.0.0.4 to tree, add new 10.0.0.4 neighbor to candidate list
#4	10.0.0.5 10 ⟋ 1 ⟍ 1 10.0.0.2 10.0.0.1 10.0.0.6 │ 1 10.0.0.4	10.0.0.3 (10.0.0.6, 11) 10.0.0.3 (10.0.0.6, 12) 10.0.0.3 (10.0.0.2, 11)	Add 10.0.0.2 to tree, add new 10.0.0.2 neighbor to candidate list
#5	10.0.0.5 10 ⟋ 1 ⟍ 1 10.0.0.2 10.0.0.1 10.0.0.6 │ 1 10 ⟋ │ 1 10.0.0.3 10.0.0.3 10.0.0.4	10.0.0.3 (10.0.0.6, 11) 10.0.0.3 (10.0.0.6, 12) 10.0.0.3 (10.0.0.2, 11)	Add 10.0.0.3 to tree in two places. Candidate list is empty: STOP!

Figure 9.3 Running the SPF algorithm.

The final directed graph of the network, shown in Figure 9.4, illustrates how the SPF algorithm views router connectivity. The figure also shows the routing table that Router 10.0.0.5 will use to reach every other router, the next-hop interface (router in this example), and the cost to each router. Note the presence of two equal-cost paths to Router 10.0.0.3. Router 10.0.0.5 could simply pick one to install in the forwarding table—or make both routes active, if the router is capable of load balancing.

Once the tree construction is complete, meaning that the candidate list is empty, the routes in the link-state database associated with each router can be pasted on to the completed tree. The next hop and cost associated with each route can then be used to generate the active route for each destination.

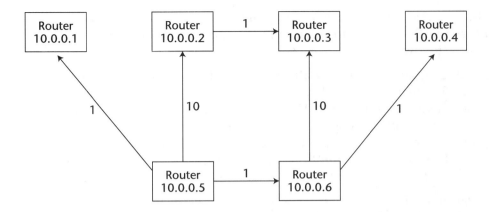

Figure 9.4   The network and routing table as seen by Router 10.0.0.5.

OSPF Network Types

The key to making OSPF work properly is the structure of the link-state database. At each step along the way when running the SPF algorithm, the calculating router moves out one link more to consider the neighbor routers on the network. Doing this was simple enough when routers were almost always connected by point-to-point WAN links. But now the types of physical links used to connect routers can be more complex, ranging from LANs to Frame Relay to ATM. So OSPF has actually defined five types of networks that might be used to link routers together. Even though these are called network types, each one really describes the type of link that can be used between OSPF routers. OSPF sends its messages back and forth slightly differently on each type of network. It also has separate rules for how the information about the routers connected by this type of link is represented in the link-state database.

The five OSPF network types are point-to-point, broadcast, nonbroadcast multi-access (NBMA), point-to-multipoint, and virtual links. Descriptions of each type follow:

Point-to-point.   These are traditional WAN links such as TI/E1 or SONET/SDH. Two OSPF routers connected by a point-to-point link will always become what OSPF calls *fully adjacent* and exchange the full set of OSPF messages. IP addresses do not matter much in terms of frame addressing on point-to-point links, so IP packets carrying OSPF messages use a multicast address of 224.0.0.5 on these packets. This is the *AllSPFRouters* multicast address.

Broadcast.   These are traditional LAN networks such as Ethernet. Each and every station is physically adjacent to another, and one frame sent by one is heard by all, even though the MAC frame is addressed to only one station. OSPF routers on LANs will always elect a *designated router* (DR) and *backup designated router* (BDR). This ensures that every router on the LAN does not end up sending multiple copies of the same LSA information to every other router. On a LAN, OSPF routers use the multicast AllSPFRouters 224.0.0.5 for *Hello packets* (for a definition and discussion, see the section *The Hello Packet* later in the chapter) and the DR and BDR use this multicast destination address on all OSPF packets. All other routers will send the other types of OSPF messages with the AllDRouters multicast destination address of 224.0.0.6. The AllDRouters on a LAN are those routers that are the DR and BDR. Only these two routers use the 224.0.0.6 multicast group. All other routers on the LAN are DRRouters (because they could potentially become a DR or BDR some day) and use the multicast group for AllSPFRouters, 224.0.0.5.

NBMA networks.   These are networks like Frame Relay and ATM. They are multi-access because they can reach more than one router on the same physical interface but do not broadcast. NBMA networks elect a DR and BDR but cannot use multicast addresses. Unicast IP addresses are used instead.

Point-to-multipoint.   These are special types of NBMA network configurations with a hub-and-spoke structure. Because of this, these networks are treated as a set of point-to-point links. But a DR and BDR are elected, and OSPF packets use the 224.0.0.5 and 224.0.0.6 multicast addresses.

Virtual links.   These are used in special situations to connect OSPF routers over a kind of transparent IP point-to-point connection. OSPF packets are unicast over a virtual link.

Somewhat confusingly, these network link types can further be classified as either *transit networks* or *stub networks*, but this designation has nothing to do with link type and everything to do with where the link types are used in a collection of OSPF routers. This added classification has caused considerable confusion with *stub areas*, discussed previously, which are totally different.

Officially, transit networks have two or more attached routers. Packets on a transit network do not have to originate on or be delivered to a transit network; the packets are just passing through. Stub networks have only a single router and are usually LANs. Packets on a stub network always either originate on or are delivered to the stub network. OSPF advertises stub networks as host routes (routes with a /32 mask) and router loopback interfaces are always stub networks.

OSPF Areas and Router Types

OSPF routers might have to maintain multiple databases, flood a lot of information, and repeatedly run complex algorithms. Flooding only incremental changed information is one thing, but as the number of routes and routes grows, the burden on each router can grow very quickly. OSPFv2 introduced areas as a way to cut down on the size of the link-state database, the amount of information flooded, and the time it takes to run the SPF algorithm, at least on areas other than the special backbone area.

An OSPF area is a logical grouping of routers sharing the same 32-bit Area ID. The Area ID can be expressed in dotted decimal notation similar to an IP address, such as 192.168.17.33. The Area ID can also be expressed as a decimal equivalent, so Area 260 is the same as Area 0.0.1.4. When the Area ID is less than 256, usually only a single number is used, but Area 250 is still really Area 0.0.0.250.

OSPF areas handle three types of traffic. *Intra-area* traffic flows between routers entirely within a single area. *Inter-area* traffic flows between routers in different areas. *External* traffic flows between the OSPF routing domain and another AS.

OSPF Area Types

OSPF contains five area types. The position of a router with respect to OSPF areas is important as well. Since OSPF areas are so important to OSPF use and router configuration, we'll look at them more closely in this section. The basic OSPF area types, router types, and their relationships are shown in Figure 9.5. A variety of formats for area IDs are shown in the figure, but in most cases only one format is used for all areas.

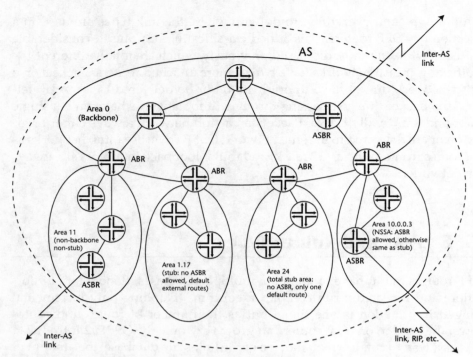

Figure 9.5 OSPF areas and routers.

The OSPF Area 0 (0.0.0.0) is very special. This is the backbone area of an OSPF routing domain. An OSPF routing domain (AS) can consist of a single area, but in that case the single area must be Area 0. Only the backbone area can generate the summary routing topology information that is used by the other areas. This is why all inter-area traffic must pass through the backbone area (some *backdoor links* can be configured on some routers to bypass the backbone area, but these violate the OSPF specification). In a sense, the backbone area knows everything. Not so long ago, only powerful high-end routers could be used on an OSPF backbone.

All areas other than the backbone area connect to the backbone area through an area border router (ABR). An ABR by definition has links in two or more areas. In OSPF, routers always form the boundaries between areas. A router with links outside the OSPF routing domain is called an *autonomous system boundary router* (ASBR). Routing information about destination IP addresses not learned from OSPF always are advertised by an ASBR. Even when static routes, or RIP routes, are redistributed by OSPF, that router technically becomes an ASBR. ASBRs are the source of *external routes* that are outside of the OSPF routing domain, and external routes are often very numerous in an

OSPF routing domain attached to the global Internet. If a router is not an ABR or ASBR, it is either an *internal router* and has all of its interfaces within the same area, or a *backbone router* with at least one link to the backbone. However, these terms are not as critical to OSPF configurations as ABRs or ASBRs, and they are often too fuzzy to be of much use. For example, not all backbone routers are ABRs or ASBRs, and backbone routers can also be internal routers.

The four OSPF area types besides the backbone are as follows:

Nonbackbone, nonstub areas.   These types of areas are really just smaller versions of the backbone area. There can be links to other routing domains (ASBRs) and the only real restriction on a nonbackbone, nonstub area is that it cannot be Area 0.

Stub area.   Stub areas (not to be confused with stub *networks*) cannot have any links outside the AS. So there can be no ASBRs in a stub area. This minimizes the amount of external routing information that needs to be distributed into the link-state databases of the stub area routers. Because an AS might be an ISP on the Internet, the number of external routes required in an OSPF routing domain is usually many times larger than the internal routes of the AS itself. Stub area routers only obtain information on routes external to the AS from the ABR.

Total stub area.   Also called a *totally stubby area*. Stub areas cannot have ASBRs within them by definition. But stub areas only reach all the ASBRs, which have the links leading to and from other ASs, through an ABR. So including detailed external route information in the stub area router's link-state database would be foolish. All that is really needed is the proper default route as advertised by the ABR. Total stub areas only know how to reach their ABR when confronted with a route that is not within their area.

Not-so-stubby-area (NSSA).   The banning of ASBRs from stub areas proved very restrictive. As mentioned in the preceding text, even the simple advertisement of static routes into OSPF made a router an ASBR. So did the presence of a single LAN running RIP with routes that needed to be advertised by OSPF. Not only that, as ISPs merged and grew through acquiring smaller ISPs, "pasting" the new OSPF area with its own ASBRs onto the backbone area of the other ISP became difficult. The easiest thing to do was to make the new former AS a stub area, but the presence of an ASBR prevented that solution. The answer was to introduce the concept of a not-so-stubby-area (NSSA) in RFC 1587. An NSSA can have ASBRs, but the external routing information introduced by this ASBR into the NSSA is either kept within the NSSA or translated by the ABR into a form useful on the backbone Area 0 and to other areas.

OSPF area discussions must sooner or later address the issue of how many routers should be in an OSPF area. There is no hard-and-fast rule, since the number of links and routes is just as important, and perhaps even more important, than the number of routers. The use of aggregate routes complicates the issue even more. Some OSPF areas have just 4 routers and others may have up to 40 routers. This apparent nonanswer is not meant to be evasive, just realistic.

Designated Router (DR) and Backup Designated Router (BDR)

OSPF ABRs and ASBRs are special types of OSPF routers. But an OSPF router can also be a designated router (DR) and backup designated router (BDR). These have nothing to do with ABRs and ASBRs, and concern only the relationship between OSPF routers on links that deliver packets to more than one destination at the same time.

OSPF DRs and BDRs mostly exist on LANs, although pure NBMA networks also elect a DR and BDR to represent a collection of routers. There are two major problems with LANs and NBMA networks. First, the link-state database represents links and routers as a directed graph. A simple LAN with five OSPF routers would need $N(N-1)/2$, or $5(4)/2 = 20$ link-state advertisements just to represent the links between the routers, even though all five routers are mutually adjacent on the LAN and any frame sent by one is received by the other four. Second, and just as bad, is the need for flooding. Flooding over a LAN with many OSPF routers is chaotic, as link-state advertisements are flooded and "reflooded" on the LAN.

To address these issues, multi-access networks such as LANs always elect a DR for OSPF. The DR solves the two problems by (1) representing the multi-access network as a single "virtual router" or "pseudonode" to the rest of the network and (2) managing the process of flooding link-state advertisements on the multi-access network. So each router on a LAN, for example, forms an OSPF adjacency only with the DR (and also the BDR, as mentioned in the following paragraphs). All link-state advertisements go only to the DR (and BDR), and the DR forwards them on to the rest of the network and internetwork routers.

DR failure is a big problem. So each network that elects a DR also elects a BDR that will take over the functions of the DR if and when the DR fails. The DR and BDR form OSPF adjacencies with all of the other routers on the multi-access network, and the DR and BDR also form an adjacency with each other.

How does a LAN, for example, elect a DR and BDR in the first place? Each OSPF router is assigned a router priority with valid values in the range of 0 to 255. A router priority of 0 means that the router is not eligible to become the DR or BDR. There are not separate procedures to elect a DR and BDR, as might be expected. Instead, there is only one procedure, and it elects the BDR. Once the election takes place, if there is no current DR making itself known on the LAN, the BDR promotes itself to DR and the BDR election process repeats itself. This time there *is* a DR, so the process halts. If the BDR even detects that the DR has "disappeared" from the LAN, the BDR takes over as the new DR with minimal disruption.

The BDR election process is very simple. The router with the highest router priority wins. Few network administrators bother to change the default router priority value, which is 1 for Cisco and 128 for Juniper Networks routers. So this method rarely works well. The next tiebreaker, which always works, uses the highest OSPF Router ID as the choice for DR/BDR. Since the OSPF Router ID must be an IP address, and it is usually the loopback interface address, there is always a unique high value on the LAN. Once a DR and BDR are selected for the network, they remain in their roles even if a new router with a higher priority or Router ID appears on the multi-access network.

Care is needed when assigning a router priority of 0 (in other words, it cannot become DR or BDR). If only one router is eligible to become DR/BDR, there will only be a DR on the network and no BDR at all. If there are *no* routers eligible, then no OSPF adjacencies can form at all.

OSPF Packets

As might be expected, OSPF routers communicate with IP packets. But instead of using UDP or TCP, OSPF messages ride directly inside of IP packets as IP protocol number 89. Because OSPF does not use UDP or TCP, in contrast to RIP, the OSPF protocol is fairly elaborate and must reproduce many of the features of a transport protocol to move OSPF messages between routers.

There can be one of five OSPF packet types inside the IP packet, all of which share a common OSPF header. The structure of the common OSPF header is shown in Figure 9.6.

The Version field is 2, for OSPFv2, and the Type has one of the five values detailed below. The Packet Length is the length of the OSPF packet in bytes. The Router ID is the IP address selected as OSPF Router ID (usually the loopback interface address), and the area ID is the OSPF area of the router that originates the message. The Checksum is the same as the one used on IP packets and is computed on the whole OSPF packet.

The AuType is the authentication type, either none (0), simple password authentication (1), or cryptographic authentication (2). The simple password is an eight-character plaintext password, but the use of AuType = 2 authentication gives the authentication field the structure shown in the figure. In this case, the Key ID identifies the secret key and authentication algorithm (MD5)

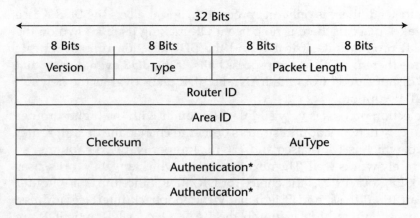

Figure 9.6   The common OSPF packet header.

used to create the message digest, the Authentication Data Length specifies the length of the message digest appended to the packet (which does not count as part of the packet length), and the Cryptographic Sequence Number always increases and prevents hacker "replay" attacks.

The Hello Packet

The Hello packets form a complete protocol all by themselves. These packets establish the initial OSPF adjacency between routers but are also used to maintain the adjacency and so detect link and router failures as quickly as possible. The Hello packets carry parameters on which neighbor OSPF routers must agree in order to establish an adjacency. The Hello packet is shown in Figure 9.7. Note that this is OSPF packet Type = 1.

The fields of the Hello packet are as follows:

Network Mask.   This is the mask of the interface originating the packet. If this mask does not match the receiving interface mask, then the routers will not become OSPF neighbors.

Hello Interval.   This is the time in seconds between Hellos on the interface. These values must match in both directions on the link.

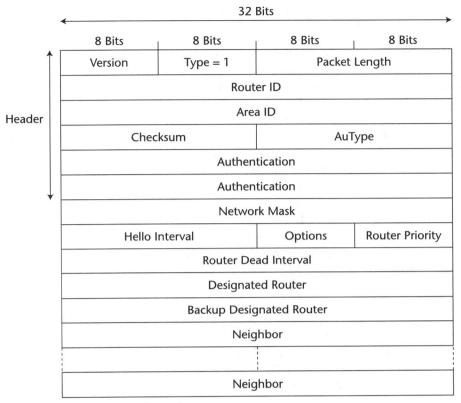

Figure 9.7 The OSPF Hello packet.

Options. There are six defined OSPF options in the 8-bit Options field that must be compatible. The Options field is discussed in detail in the *The Link-State Acknowledgment Packet* section of this chapter.

Router Priority. This field is used for DR and BDR election.

Router Dead Interval. The length of time in seconds that the originating router will wait for a hello before declaring the other router dead. Neighbors must agree on the value of this parameter.

Designated Router and **Backup Designated Router.** These are the IP addresses, not the Router IDs, of the interface of the "proposed" DR and BDR on the network. They are used during the DR/BDR election process, and until there is a DR or if the link does not require a DR, these fields are set to 0.0.0.0.

Neighbor. This field is a recurring field in the Hello packet that lists all of the OSPF neighbors from which the router originating the hello has received valid hellos in the past router dead interval seconds.

The Database Description Packet

Once OSPF routers have established an adjacency with Hello packets, the Database Description (DD) packets are used so that the routers can determine if their link-state databases match or not. The originator describes its link-state advertisements (LSAs) as a sequence of headers, which the receiver checks against its own LSAs in its database.

Many DD packets may be exchanged when a new router is connected to a stable OSPF router, mostly in one direction; but in other cases, the exchange of DD packets can be more symmetrical. To manage this flurry of DD packets, flags are used within a master/slave relationship between the routers. (The term is unfortunate, but it's used in the specification.) The DD packet is shown in Figure 9.8. Note that this is OSPF packet type = 2.

The Interface MTU field is the size in bytes of the largest IP packet that can be sent on the originating interface without fragmentation. These fields *must* match, and a common OSPF problem called "stuck in ExStart" occurs when one side of a link changes the MTU size but the other does not. The link is still up and running, but OSPF fails.

The Options field is that same as in the Hello packet.

Only the last 3 bits of the next byte are defined. The first 5 bits are set to 00000. The I (initial) bit set to 1 identifies the first of a series of DD packets. The rest of the DD packets in a sequence have I = 0. The M (more) bit is set to 1 to indicate that the DD packet is not the last of a sequence. The last DD packet has M = 0. The MS (master/slave) bit is set to 1 when the originator is the master

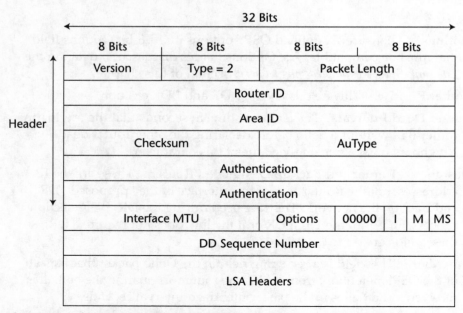

Figure 9.8 The OSPF Database Description packet.

and MS = 0 when the originator is the slave. The only role of the master/slave relationship is to ensure the use the DD sequence numbering (next field) of the master for the DD exchange.

The DD Sequence Number field is set by the master to some unique value in the first DD packet, and then incremented in subsequent DD packets. This makes sure that the full sequence of DD packets is received.

Finally, the LSA Headers field lists some or all of the LSA headers in the originator's link-state database. The LSA header structure is detailed in the *OSPF LSA Types* section, but LSA headers contain enough information so that the receiver can uniquely identify the LSA and its "age."

The Link-State Request Packet

As the DD packets are exchanged, each router records in a link-state request list the LSA headers of any LSA that is not in its link-state database or is more recent. Once the DD exchange is complete, each router can send one or more link-state request packets to its neighbor asking for the full copy of the LSA. The other router always replies with the most recent LSA. The link-state request packet is shown in Figure 9.9. Note that this is OSPF packet Type = 3. There are multiple instances of three repeating fields:

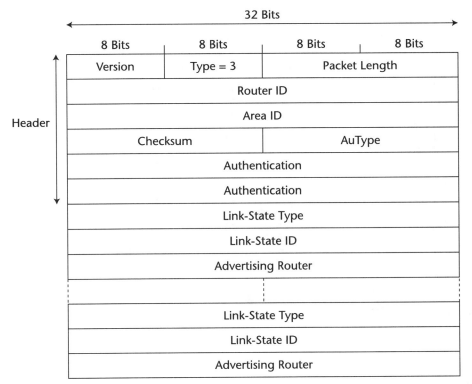

Figure 9.9 The OSPF Link-State Request packet.

Link-State Type.   This field identifies the LSA type, as described in the *OSPF LSA Types* section.

Link-State ID.   This varies by LSA type. Link-state IDs are also detailed in the *OSPF LSA Types* section.

Advertising Router.   The OSPF Router ID of the router that originated the LSA. (This is not necessarily the router originating the link-state request).

The Link-State Update Packet

The Link-State Update packets are the real workhorses of OSPF. All of the other packet types do not include LSAs or just list LSA headers. The Link-State Updates send the full contents of the LSAs to neighbors in response to Link-State Requests and when things change in the link-state database. It is the Link-State Update packets that get passed along router by router during reliable flooding. The Link-State Update packet is shown in Figure 9.10. Note that this is OSPF packet Type = 4. There are just two fields:

Numbers of LSAs.   This field just gives the number of LSAs in the packet.

LSAs.   This field contains the full LSAs themselves. These are detailed in the *OSPF LSA Types* section.

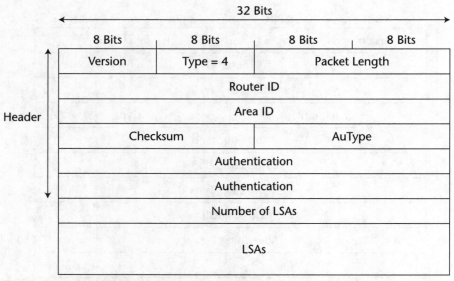

Figure 9.10   The OSPF Link-State Update packet.

The Link-State Acknowledgment Packet

Link-State Acknowledgment packets are used to make flooding reliable. Each LSA must be explicitly acknowledged by the receiver by using Link-State Acknowledgment packets. The LSAs are acknowledged through their LSA headers, and multiple LSAs can be acknowledged by a single packet. The contents are just a list of LSA headers, as shown in Figure 9.11. Note that this is OSPF packet Type = 5.

The 8-bit Options field is of special interest in OSPF packets. This Options field is also confusingly present in the LSA header, as well as in the Hello and DD packets. This field begins with 2 unused bits, which are usually set to 0. The last 6 bits are used to represent the following:

DC: Demand circuit support.   When set, this bit indicates that the originator supports demand circuits.

EA: External attributes support.   When set, this bit indicates that the originator supports external attributes, which are not discussed further in this book.

N/P: NSSA support.   When set, this bit indicates that the originator supports NSSA External LSAs (discussed shortly). If N = 1, then the E bit described in the following must be set to 0. If N = 0, then the router will not support NSSA External LSAs. Routers without matching N bits will not become adjacent. This bit becomes the P bit at the ABR of an NSSA and appears *only* in NSSA LSA headers (which is why this bit can be used in the same position as the N bit; an N bit cannot appear in a packet that the N bit is used to prohibit). The P bit controls whether the NSSA ABR should translate NSSA external routes into LSA types used in the rest of the AS or not.

MC: Multicast support.   When set, this bit indicates that the originator supports MOSPF.

E: External support.   When set, this bit indicates that the originator accepts AS External LSAs, described in the *OSPF LSA Types* section. This bit is set to 0 in all LSAs that originate in a stub area. The backbone and nonstub areas set this bit to 1. In the Hello packet, this bit identifies stub routers. Neighboring routers must match E bit values to become adjacent.

T: TOS support.   When set, this bit indicates that the originator supports IP packet TOS metrics. No routers do this today.

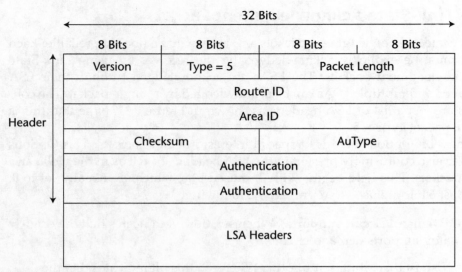

Figure 9.11   The OSPF Acknowledgment packet.

Database Synchronization and Neighbor States

OSPF routers always attempt to establish an OSPF adjacency if the parameters of the hellos match. With the matched setting of the Interface MTU size in the DD packet, the OSPF routers will become neighbors. For LANs and NBMAs, the DR and BDR are adjacent to all their neighbors, but no adjacencies will exist between the DRothers.

Figure 9.12 shows the general process where two OSPF routers synchronize their link-state database and the OSPF states that each router transitions through until the routers are fully adjacent. The routers are assumed to be connected by a point-to-point link, and no DR or BDR is needed.

Both routers are initially in the down state, and one router will always send a Hello packet before the other router because the routers are not synchronized in any way. In this example, Router1 sends the first hello and Router2 receives it. At this point, the DR field in the hello is set to 0.0.0.0, and there are no Neighbors seen yet on the interface. If the Options field in the received hello is compatible with the Options set on Router2, then Router2 replies with its own hello, with the DR field also set to 0.0.0.0 but with the Neighbors Seen field set to Router1's Router ID taken from the received Hello packet. Router2 now transitions to the Init (Initial) state.

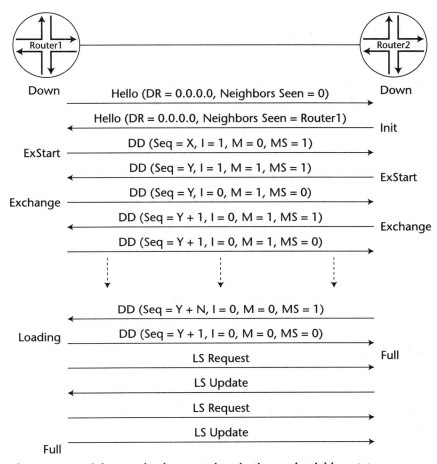

Figure 9.12 Link-state database synchronization and neighbor states.

Receiving the Hello, Router1 puts itself in ExStart (Exchange Start) and begins a DD exchange phase to synchronize the link-state databases. The receipt of the DD from Router1 puts Router2 into the ExStart state, and the first two DDs exchange empty DD packets with the master/slave bit set to 1 so that each essentially wants to be the master. The status of the I and M bits are also shown. The I bit is set to 1 when the DD packet is the first in the sequence. The M bit set to 0 to indicate that there are more DD packets to come, while the M bit set to 1 indicates the last DD in the sequence.

The router with the higher Router ID in the packet header becomes the master. All this really means is that the master's sequence numbering will be used for the DD exchange. In this case the master is Router1, and Router1's sequence numbering is used during the DD Exchange state, which begins once the master has been determined.

In the exchange state, link-state database synchronization begins in earnest. The neighbors describe every entry in their link-state databases by exchange LSA headers inside DD packets. If either router sees an LSA that is not in its link-state database, or if either sees an LSA header that is more recent, the router places the LSA header on a Link-State Request list. At the end of the DD exchange, Router2 is in the full state (indicating a full adjacency), because its Link-State Request list is empty. Router1, on the other hand, enters the loading state while its Link-State Request list is conveyed to Router2 in Link-State Request packets. Router2 replies with Link-State Updates containing the full LSAs (not just the LSA headers) requested.

All of the LSAs sent in Link-State Update packets must be individually acknowledged, since the updates contain the information of interest in building a full link-state database. LSAs are acknowledged either *implicitly*, meaning that an Update packet containing the same "instance" of the LSA is received by the router that sent it, or *explicitly* using LinkState Acknowledgment packets.

OSPF LSA Types

The section details the OSPF link-state advertisement types, which are distinct from the OSPF packet types just described. All OSPF packet types use LSA headers, except the Link-State Update packets, which always contain all of the details of the LSA.

The 11 LSA types defined for OSPF are shown in Table 9.1.

Table 9.1 LSA Types

TYPE CODE	DESCRIPTION
1	Router LSA: describes local router environment, including link cost.
2	Network LSA: From DRs, describes all routers on multi-access network.
3	Network Summary LSA: From ABRs, advertises routes outside area.
4	ASBR Summary LSA: From ABRs, advertises ASBR host route.
5	AS External LSA: From ASBRs, advertise routes external to AS.

Table 9.1 *(Continued)*

TYPE CODE	DESCRIPTION
6	Group Membership LSA: Used in Multicast OSPF (MOSPF).
7	NSSA External LSA: From ASBRs in NSSAs, advertises routes external to AS.
8	External Attributes LSA: Potential replacement for IBGP.
9	Opaque LSA (link-local scope): Used in MPLS.
10	Opaque LSA (area-local scope): Used in MPLS.
11	Opaque LSA (AS scope): Used in MPLS .

Of these 11 types of LSA, we will discuss only six of them in detail. The use of LSA types 6, 8, 9, 10, and 11 is specialized and far beyond the scope of this chapter. However, LSA types 1, 2, 3, 4, 5, and 7 appear with regularity in OSPF configuration and so will be investigated in some detail.

All LSAs share a common header. The DD and acknowledgment packets carry only these LSA headers to identify the LSA and determine how long it has been since the information has been refreshed. The three fields in the LSA header used to uniquely identify an LSA are the Type, the Link-State ID, and the Advertising Router. The three fields used to identify the most recent instance of an LSA are the Age, Sequence Number, and Checksum. The Checksum field excludes the Age field, since this changes as LSAs sit in a link-state database. But because LSAs sit for long periods in link-state databases, the checksum is useful to detect possible memory parity errors. The *age* of an LSA is the time, in seconds, since the LSA originated. LSAs age as they sit in a link-state database and must be refreshed by the originating router periodically in order to be used in route calculations. The LSA header also has two other fields. The Options field is the same in the Hello and DD packets and has already been described. The Length field gives the length of the LSA in bytes, including the LSA header.

The Router LSA

In a very real sense, the Router LSA is the most important LSA of all. Initially, a collection of OSPF routers knows nothing about the other routers even in their own area. But they do know their own environment in terms of Router ID, local links, and the outbound metrics assigned to these links. So every OSPF router details this information and shares it with its neighbors in the area in a Router LSA (Type 1). The format of the Router LSA is shown in Figure 9.13.

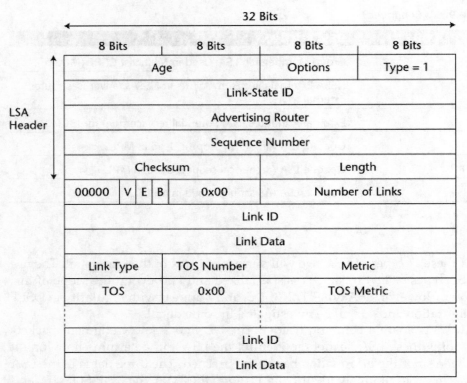

Figure 9.13 The Router LSA (Type = 1).

The contents of the header fields have already been described. The Router LSA itself begins with 3 flag bits embedded in a string of zero-bits. These flags are the V (virtual endpoint) bit, which is set when the router is the endpoint of a virtual link, the E (external) bit, which is set when the originating router is an ASBR, and the B (border) bit, which is set when the originating router is an ABR (a router can easily be both ASBR and ABR).

The Number of Links field gives the number of links that the router is describing in the LSA.

The fields labeled Link ID through TOS Metric appear one or more times in the Router LSA. As mentioned, OSPF can support four TOS metrics in addition to TOS = 0 (Normal Service). But since the only currently supported TOS value is 0 (as of RFC 2328), only the Link ID, Link Data, and Link Type fields are vital and therefore described here.

Although it appears last in this group, the value of the Link Type field actually determines the content of the Link ID and Link Data fields. Four link types are defined in Table 9.2.

Table 9.2 Link Type Values

LINK TYPE	CONNECTION TYPE	COMMENT
1	Point-to-point	A connection to another router.
2	Transit network	Carries transit traffic.
3	Stub network	Must carry packets with local source and/or destination.
4	Virtual link	Used to "paste" areas onto the backbone.

The Link ID field identifies the object to which the link is connected. When this is another router, this field will be the same as the Link-State ID field in the header of the *neighboring* router's LSA, so that the neighboring router can find the LSA in its own link-state database. The Link ID values depend on the Link Type and are listed in Table 9.3.

The Link Data field content also depends on the Link Type field. These are listed in Table 9.4.

Table 9.3 Link ID Values

LINK TYPE	VALUE PLACED IN LINK ID FIELD
1	Neighbor router's Router ID (typically loopback interface host route)
2	IP address of the DR's interface
3	IP network address
4	Neighbor router's Router ID (typically loopback interface host route)

Table 9.4 Link Data Values

LINK TYPE	VALUE PLACED IN LINK DATA FIELD
1	Host IP address of the originating router's interface
2	Host IP address of the originating router's interface
3	Stub network's IP address or subnet mask
4	Virtual link's MIB-II ifIndex value (virtual links are not "real")

Router LSAs are flooded within their originating area. The information that they contain, most importantly the IP routes that the local router knows about authoritatively, are shared using other LSA type so that every OSPF router in the entire AS knows exactly what to do with an IP packet for a particular destination address.

The Network LSA

Designated routers originate Network LSAs. Since a lot of OSPF information flows through the DRs on multi-access networks such as LANs, all of the routers in an area must know just where the DRs are located. These LSAs are flooded only within an area. The structure of the Network LSA is shown in Figure 9.14.

The structure of the Network LSA is much simpler than the Router LSA. The Link-State ID field in the header is the IP address of the DR's network interface. The Network Mask field in the LSA itself is the mask used on the network, and the Attached Router field lists the Router IDs of all routers on the network fully adjacent to the DR. The number of entries is derived from the Length field in the header.

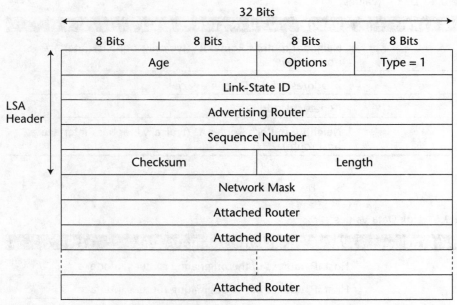

Figure 9.14 The Network LSA (Type = 2).

The Network Summary and ASBR Summary LSAs

The format of the Network Summary (Type = 3) and ASBR Summary LSAs (Type = 4) is identical. The only difference (besides the Type field) is in the use of the Link-State ID field in the LSA header. These LSAs are produced by an ABR and flooded into a single area (*other* LSAs of these types are flooded into other areas, naturally). The Network Summary LSAs (Type = 3) advertise routes *external to an area* so that routers in an area can find out about networks not in their local area. ASBR summaries LSAs (Type = 4) advertise the ASBRs themselves that are located outside the local area. The structure of both of these Summary LSAs is shown in Figure 9.15.

Network Summary LSAs carry the IP address of the external network in the Link-State ID field. This can be an aggregate representing a large block of IP addresses, because of the presence of the Network Mask field. If the external route advertised is the default route, then the Link-State ID and Network Mask fields are both 0.0.0.0.

ASBR Summary LSAs carry the OSPF Router ID (usually the IP address of the loopback interface) on the Link-State ID field. The Network Mask field is therefore meaningless and set to 0.0.0.0.

The Metric and TOS fields have been covered earlier and need not be detailed again. Only TOS = 0 is currently supported.

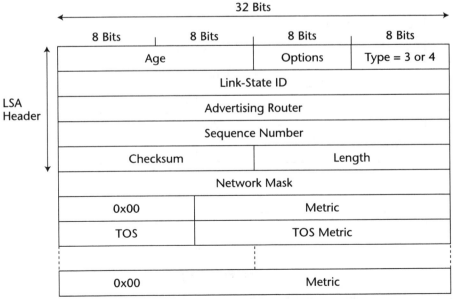

Figure 9.15 The Network Summary and ASBR Summary LSAs (Type = 3 or 4).

The AS External LSA

The AS External LSAs (Type = 5) come from the ASBRs. These LSAs advertise routes external to the AS and are flooded into all nonstub areas. The structure of the AS External LSA is shown in Figure 9.16.

The Link-State ID is the route being advertised, and the Network Mask applies to this destination. Default routes are advertised with 0.0.0.0 in these fields. The E bit is the *external metric* of the route. If the E bit is set to 1, the metric type is E2. If the E bit is set to 0, the metric type is E1. Type 1 external paths (E1) are routes that include the external cost to the destination, as well as the

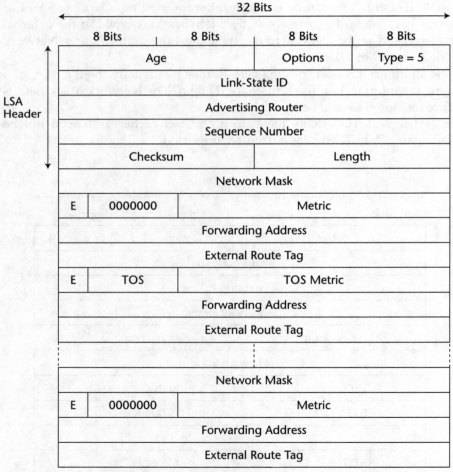

Figure 9.16   The AS External LSA (Type = 5).

cost (metric) to reach the ASBR that originates the routing information. Type 2 external paths (E2) are routes that also include the external cost to the destination, but they ignore the cost (metric) to reach the ASBR that originates the routing information. E2 is the default. ASBRs must explicitly set the E bit to 1 if the cost to reach the ASBR is to be factored into the total cost of the route.

The cost of the route is in the Metric field, and the Forwarding Address is the place to send packets to this destination. If this field is 0.0.0.0, the packets are forwarded to the originating ASBR.

The External Route Tag field is not used by OSPF itself. This is just a way to carry additional, external information about the route. These are used in routing policy and will be discussed more fully in a later chapter on OSPF routing policies.

TOS fields can be included in the External LSA. Each nonzero TOS has its own metric, E bit, forwarding address, and external route tag. Only TOS = 0 is currently supported.

The NSSA External LSA

The NSSA External LSAs (Type = 7) also come from ASBRs but from those located in not-so-stubby areas (NSSAs). All of the fields of the NSSA External LSA are used in the same way as the AS External LSA fields with the exception of the Forwarding Address field. The structure of the NSSA External LSA is shown in Figure 9.17.

The Forwarding Address field is the next-hop address on the network if the network between the NSSA ASBR and the other AS is advertised as an internal route, meaning the destination appears to be within the local AS itself. The Forwarding Address field is the NSSA ASBR's Router ID if the network between the NSSA ASBR and the other AS is *not* advertised as an internal route, meaning the destination appears to be outside of the local AS itself. Sometimes the NSSA ASBR is just readvertising RIP routes (internal), and sometimes the NSSA ASBR is advertising truly external routes from an NSSA pasted on to OSPF Area 0.

OSPF for IPv6

The changes made to OSPF for IPv6 are minimal, oddly enough. This makes it easy to transition from OSPF for IPv4 to OSPF for IPv6, and configuration will be familiar. There is new version number, OSPF version 3 (OSPFv3), and some necessary format changes, but fewer than might be expected. The basics are described in RFC 2740, "OSPF for IPv6," from December 1999.

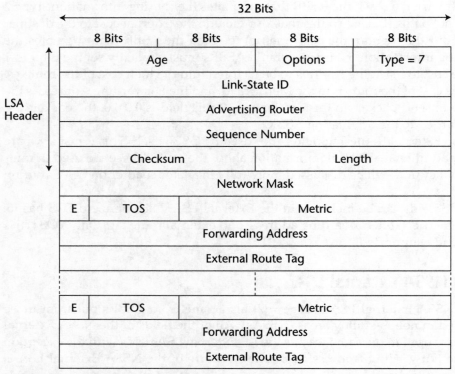

Figure 9.17 The NSSA External LSA (Type = 7).

OSPF for IPv6 (OSPFv6) uses link local IPv6 addresses and IPv6 multicast addresses. The IPv6 link-state database is totally independent of the IPv4 link-state database, and both can operate on the same router.

Oddly, there is no change in the OSPFv6 Router ID field; it is still 32 bits long. But this Router ID no longer represents an IPv4 address on a loopback or other interface. It is just a 32-bit-long string that is a unique identifier for the OSPFv6 router. Also, OSPFv6 has no AuType field, because the authentication now relies on IPv6 authentication. This field now becomes the instance ID and is used in IPv6 when an IPv6 link is shared by independent OSPF networks.

Naturally, OSPFv6 must make some concessions to the larger IPv6 addresses and next hops. But the common LSA header has a few changes as well. The Link-State Identifier field is still there, but it is now a pure identifier and not an IPv4 address. There is no longer an Options field, since this field also appears in the packets that need it, and the LSA Header Type field is enlarged to 16 bits. Naturally, when LSAs carry the details of IPv6 addresses, those fields are now large enough to handle the 128-bit IPv6 addresses.

A full discussion of OSPFv6 operation is not necessary and is beyond the scope of this book.

OSPF in the Real World

OSPF areas, ABRs, and ASBRs seem to produce a bewildering array of LSA types. But in the real world, an OSPF router seldom produces more than a few types of LSAs. All routers produce Type 1 LSAs, and Type 2 LSAs if the network interfaces elect a designated router (DR), as on a LAN. ABRs produce Type 3 and Type 4 LSAs as well, and ASBRs can produce Type 5 or Type 7 LSAs.

Figure 9.18 shows the types of LSAs produced by each type of OSPF router. The actual content of the LSAs depends on the kind of area on the interface. All of these LSAs have *area scope* (they are not flooded outside of their area) with the exception of Type 5 (AS External) LSAs. The Type 5 (AS external) LSAs are flooded throughout the entire AS.

Although frowned upon by OSPF purists, in reality both *virtual links* and *backdoor links* are used with regularity. A full discussion of OSPF would include more details on the use of virtual links and backdoor links, but this chapter will only mention what these types of links are used for.

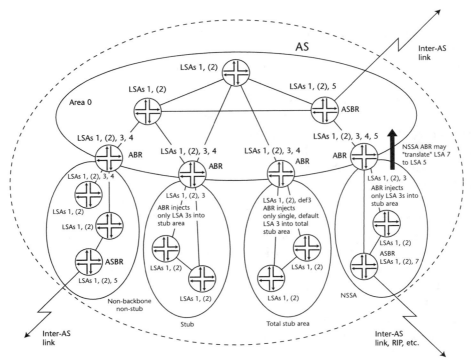

Figure 9.18 LSA types produced by OSPF routers.

Virtual links are a kind of "duct tape" used to paste areas onto a distant backbone area. It is common enough for an ISP to acquire a smaller ISP. Both might be running OSPF, and the intention is to merge to formerly separate ASs into one large AS with a single backbone area. Collapsing a smaller AS into one nonbackbone area is not hard, and the smaller AS might only have a single area to begin with. But suppose the smaller ISP has service only within Arizona (this is only an example) and the nearest ABR of the acquiring ISP is in Kansas City, Missouri. Now, a long WAN link can be bought to attach the nearest Arizona router to Kansas City. But suppose the acquiring ISP already has a router in Phoenix, linked to the Kansas City router. The Phoenix router is not an ABR, but it is nearby. Making the Phoenix router into an ABR is possible. However, doing so might still require new WAN links to the rest of the backbone area, and the Phoenix router might not scale up to backbone size and speed, so this is not a good solution. It would be easier to make the Phoenix router appear to be the Kansas City ABR as far as the routers in Arizona are concerned. This is exactly what an OSPF virtual link does. Once a virtual link from the Phoenix router to the Kansas City router has been defined, all of the other Arizona routers can just link to Phoenix and appear to be at the ABR.

A similar situation would be a good place to use a backdoor link. However, while virtual links are supported by OSPF, backdoor links are supposedly forbidden in OSPF, but used anyway. Backdoor links are used to allow areas to exchange traffic without using the backbone Area 0.

Consider a larger ISP acquiring a smaller ISP again. The smaller ISP has routers in Orlando, Florida, Charlotte, South Carolina, and other locations up and down the east coast of the United States. The larger ISP has an ABR in Atlanta, Georgia, and a nonbackbone router in Tampa, Florida. Because of the way the smaller ISP's area has been fit into the larger ISP's OSPF structure, the smaller ISP now has the router in Orlando linked to its "new" ABR in Charlotte, close to the larger ISP's backbone area. OSPF rules would make the Orlando router send packets destined for Tampa to Charlotte, then to Atlanta, and finally to Tampa, assuming that the Charlotte and Atlanta ABRs have a direct link (they probably would).

But some router vendors would allow for the configuration and provisioning of an OSPF backdoor link directly between Orlando and Tampa, less than 100 miles apart, even though neither is an ABR on the backbone area. Such inter-area routing without using the OSPF backbone area is not allowed in OSPF, but in the real world it is done all the time. Why burden the OSPF backbone with a lot of traffic sent in such a roundabout fashion?

OSPF purists would look at this situation and recommend a realignment of the nonbackbone areas, perhaps moving the Tampa router over to the Charlotte ABR. But this move might affect other traffic flows, and service providers are not often happy to change things that are perceived to be just fine the way they are, especially if a backdoor link can be configured.

The examples in the next chapter use neither virtual links nor backdoor links. But in the real world of the Internet, these are used quite frequently when possible.

Configuring OSPF

OSPF configurations can quickly grow in complexity until the whole point of an exercise is lost in the midst of huge link-state databases and large routing tables. This chapter attempts to configure a worthwhile example of OSPF in action and yet at the same time limit the size and complexity of both the link-state database and routing tables. What works for one route should work for several. Exploring the varieties of OSPF areas and their interactions is more important than trying to load up an autonomous system (AS) with a realistic number of routes.

This chapter is much more ambitious than the earlier chapter on RIP configuration. With RIP, there were only two real variations to explore: RIPv1 and RIPv2. OSPF has five area types alone, plus five link types, a couple of network types, and so on. When two router vendors are thrown in for good measure, the number of interoperability scenarios that could potentially be investigated is large. So we'll limit our exploration to the basics. It is more important to consider essential interoperability features than to try to enumerate all of the details of every possible configuration.

From this point onward, no configuration details for interfaces and addresses are necessary. These have been presented in Chapter 5, "Cisco Router Configuration," and Chapter 6, "Juniper Networks Router Configuration," and then are repeated in Chapter 8, "Configuring RIP." Information about interfaces and addresses is limited to statements such as "Serial1 (or t1-0/0/0) has been configured with IP address 10.0.32.1/24 and the loopback address is

172.16.0.10," without showing all the steps needed to do this. Details in this chapter are reserved for OSPF specifics. Configurations shown are limited in scope to the sections that affect OSPF operation. Also, for simplicity, all of the links in the example in this chapter are point-to-point Ethernet links using crossover cables.

We limit the information in this chapter to only two OSPF area types and their link-state advertisements (LSAs) at first; only at the end of the chapter are all of the scenarios merged together. First, a backbone area is established, and then one of four types of OSPF area are added individually. For example, a backbone OSPF Area 0 is configured with an autonomous system boundary router (ASBR) running BGP to another AS and an area border router (ABR) to a nonbackbone, nonstub area (Area 1). This area also has an ASBR, but this time a simple router running RIP on one interface. Then a configuration of three Juniper Networks routers is presented, for the Area 0 ASBR, the ABR between Area 0 and Area 1, and then the ASBR in Area 1. After explaining the LSA types seen in each router's link-state database, along with the routing table appearances, we replace the Juniper Networks routers one by one by Cisco routers and present the equivalent configuration and link-state database information.

This basic procedure is then repeated as a stub area (Area 2), a total stub (totally stubby) area (Area 3), and finally a not-so-stubby-area (NSSA, Area 4) are added to the backbone Area 0. By the end of this chapter, both Juniper Networks and Cisco routers are configured as an ASBR, an ABR, and just a plain, ordinary router running OSPF. Interoperability is explored as a Juniper Networks router is replaced in one OSPF role or another with a Cisco router.

At the end of the chapter, a complete AS routing domain with 12 routers is presented. Nine of these routers will run OSPF, and the remaining three will just be sources of non-OSPF (external) routing information. Just to illustrate where all of this configuration activity is heading, Figure 10.1 shows the final state of the network when all area types have been explored.

The information needed for all of the configurations is shown in the figure. The figure is quite complex, however, so a few words of explanation are needed even before we start out. The AS numbers used are from the private AS numbering range (64512 through 65535). All of the routers shown in AS 64512 are initially Juniper Networks routers, with one exception. The external router in the upper right of the figure in AS 64555 is a Cisco router, and this router runs BGP to the ASBR router in Area 0. Because we have not yet discussed BGP, no configuration details are given for this ASBR interface. Sufficient notation would be that the routing information from AS 64555 will be redistributed into AS 64512 by OSPF—and that the OSPF routing information from AS 64512 will also reach AS 64555. (This is not to suggest that it would be realistic to use an IGP like OSPF to redistribute external BGP routes from another AS. But the emphasis in this chapter is on OSPF. More realistic BGP/IGP scenarios will be discussed in Chapter 13, "BGP.")

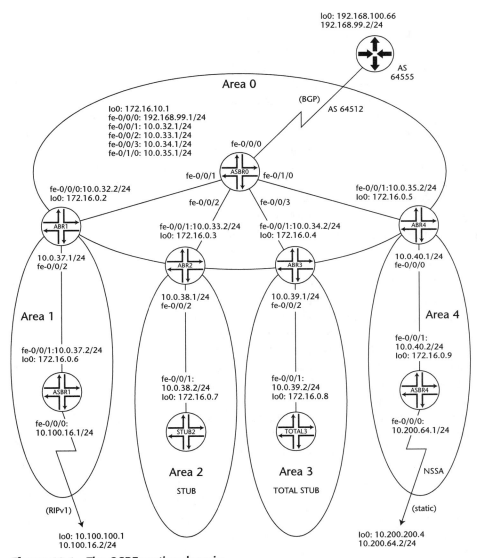

Figure 10.1 The OSPF routing domain.

In keeping with the smaller-is-better theme in this chapter, the router in AS 64555 will not contribute much to the OSPF routing domain. In fact, only the router's loopback address (192.168.100.66) and interface address (192.168.99.2/24) will ever appear on any of the routers in the AS 64512 domain. Now, in the real world, the routes contributed by AS 64555 might number in the thousands, even when aggregated. But again, the idea here is to explore OSPF in a small, controlled network environment.

The ASBR router in Area 0 (ASBR0) has a more complex configuration, but really only with regard to interfaces. ASBR0's loopback address is given (172.16.0.1) and so are the addresses on all four of the interfaces to the ABRs, all drawn from the 10.0.3X.0/24 address space. Each ABR also has its loopback and interface addresses given, and as ABRs these routers have one interface in the backbone Area 0 and the other interface in the nonbackbone area.

Area 1 is a nonbackbone, nonstub area. The ABR with interfaces on both the backbone Area 0 and in Area 1 is ABR1. An ASBR in Area 1, named ASBR1, runs RIPv1 on the 10.100.16.1/24 interface. The pool of private addresses is limited, but it is hoped that the use of the 10.100 prefix makes this network distinct enough from the 10.0 prefix interfaces used in the OSPF AS to easily distinguish the source of these routes. As before, the details of the router at the other end of ASBR1's non-OSPF interface are unimportant and are not discussed in this chapter. However, the loopback and interface addresses on the RIP router are given, and as before, the RIP information will be distributed into OSPF by the ASBR.

Area 2 is a stub area. The ABR here is ABR2. The non-ABR router is just STUB2 with the single interface and loopback address shown.

Area 3 is a total stub (or totally stubby) area. The ABR is ABR3. The non-ABR router is TOTAL3 with the single interface and loopback address shown.

Area 4 is a not-so-stubby-area (NSSA). The ABR is ABR4. This NSSA has a router named ASBR4 and is most likely the reason for making this an NSSA in the first place. At the end of this chapter, this ASBR will have a static route mapped to a link outside the NSSA.

The previous RIP examples used a mixture of WAN and LAN links. This chapter uses only LAN links, mainly to make the OSPF metrics uniform (they will basically be hop counts) and reflect the actual lab environment where this network was built. All LAN links are 100-Mbps Ethernet having an OSPF metric of 1. The links are used as point-to-point links by employing simple crossover cables between the interfaces. WAN links such as T1 or E1 will have higher metrics and just complicate the routing tables in the examples. There are no virtual links or backdoor links used in this chapter.

In a real service provider network, the ABR routers would most likely be *POP (point-of-presence) routers* and the non-ABR routers outside of the backbone area would be the *access routers* that have been configured as part of the RIP configuration chapter. In the real world, this structure makes perfect sense, as ASBR1 and ASBR4 would usually be running RIP to remote site routers or injecting static routes to the site routers into OSPF. The STUB2 and TOTAL3 routers would typically have their own links to site routers, but this time running OSPF, so these routers are not ASBRs from the OSPF perspective. The ASBR0 would be a *border router* that links the OSPF routing domain (AS 64512) to its peers on the Internet, a role played by the router in AS 64555 in this example.

Basic OSPF Backbone Configuration

In this section we simply configure OSPF on the ASBR0 and ABR1 routers. Both are initially Juniper Network routers. Configuration of OSPF on ASBR0 is straightforward:

```
[edit protocols]
lab@ASBR0# set ospf area 0 interface fe-0/0/1
lab@ASBR0# set ospf area 0 interface fe-0/0/0
```

All that is really needed is an area number (0 for the backbone) and the interfaces to run OSPF on. There is usually no need to specifically run OSPF on the lo0 (loopback) interface, because the JUNOS software automatically configures lo0 as a stub network (not stub *area*) if the OSPF router ID is found on lo0, as it usually is. Since the loopback is always the router ID in this book, OSPF packets will go to and come from the lo0 stub in the routing engine without any problem.

An important point is that if an explicit OSPF Router ID is configured on a Juniper Networks router (in the routing-options portion of the JUNOS software configuration file), then OSPF will not run automatically on the loopback interface. In other words, the only reason that OSPF runs automatically on the lo.0 is that the OSPF Router ID is there. So even though the LSAs will have something like 172.16.10.1 as an OSPF Router ID as originator, there will be no route to 172.16.10.1 in the routing table!

Best practice is to include in the OSPF configuration lo.0 as a *passive* interface in some area. Passive interfaces advertise their addresses but do not attempt to form adjacencies. This is good, because the loopback really has nothing to form an adjacency with anyway. In these examples, no Router ID is set on the Juniper Networks routers, the loopback interface is the Router ID, and so no explicit configuration for lo.0 passive is used.

The OSPF section on ASBR0 looks like the following:

```
[edit protocols]
lab@ASBR0# show
ospf {
    area 0.0.0.0 {
        interface fe-0/0/1.0;
    }
}
```

The only difference on router ABR1 for the backbone is the interface name and address:

```
[edit protocols]
lab@ABR1# set ospf area 0 interface fe-0/0/0
```

However, the ABR also has an interface to Area 1. This will be added later. For now, the ASBR0 and ABR1 routers are linked in Area 0 by a single link. The successful operation of OSPF is revealed on ABR1 by the following:

```
lab@ABR1> show ospf neighbor
Address       Interface       State     ID            Pri  Dead
10.0.32.1     fe-0/0/0.0      Full      172.16.10.1   128  34
```

The ABR1 router has a full OSPF adjacency on the interface and the remote link IP address to Area 0's ASBR0 is given. The other router's OSPF Router ID is listed, as is the priority for this router to become DR on a broadcast network (default = 128) and the current number of seconds (default in the JUNOS software is equal to four times the Hello interval) until this neighbor is declared dead. This value should never really drop below 30 when Hello packets are sent with the default 10-second interval.

One of the most common things that can go wrong with OSPF neighbor establishment is an *area mismatch* when one router is configured as, for instance, Area 1 and the other is configured as Area 0. But this is easy to verify. A more tricky condition, discussed in Chapter 9, "OSPF," is the stuck-in-ExStart condition encountered when the MTU sizes in DD packets do not match. Because the links in this network are all Fast Ethernet, and the MTU sizes are not changed, these OSPF links come right up.

Viewing the Routing Table

Something interesting happens when the routing table on ASBR0 is compared to the routing table on ABR1. (The details of the BGP routing information are discussed in Chapter 14, "Configuring BGP.") The comparison would look as follows:

```
lab@ASBR0> show route
inet.0: 8 destinations, 8 routes (8 active, 0 holddown, 0 hidden)
+ = Active Route, - = Last Active, * = Both

10.0.32.0/24       *[Direct/0] 01:05:27
                    > via fe-0/0/1.0
10.0.32.1/32       *[Local/0] 01:05:32
                      Local via fe-0/0/1.0
172.16.0.2/32      *[OSPF/10] 00:05:17, metric 1
                    > to 10.0.32.2 via fe-0/0/1.0
172.16.10.1/32     *[Direct/0] 01:05:32
                    > via lo0.0
192.168.99.0/24    *[Direct/0] 01:05:32
                    > via t1-0/0/0.0
```

```
                              [BGP/170] 01:02:26, MED 0, localpref 100
                                  AS path: 64555 ?
                              > to 192.168.99.2 via fe-0/0/0.0
      192.168.99.1/32         *[Local/0] 01:05:32
                               Local via fe-0/0/0.0
      192.168.100.0/24        *[BGP/170] 01:02:26, MED 0, localpref 100
                                  AS path: 64555 ?
                              > to 192.168.99.2 via fe-0/0/0.0
      224.0.0.5/32            *[OSPF/10] 01:05:33, metric 1

lab@ABR1> show route
inet.0: 5 destinations, 5 routes (5 active, 0 holddown, 0 hidden)
+ = Active Route, - = Last Active, * = Both

      10.0.32.0/24           *[Direct/0] 01:03:44
                              > via fe-0/0/0.0
      10.0.32.2/32           *[Local/0] 01:03:46
                               Local via fe-0/0/0.0
      172.16.0.2/32          *[Direct/0] 01:03:46
                              > via lo0.0
      172.16.10.1/32         *[OSPF/10] 00:00:08, metric 1
                              > to 10.0.32.1 via fe-0/0/0.0
      224.0.0.5/32           *[OSPF/10] 01:03:47, metric 1
```

The OSPF metric for the routes in this single-link network is 1. This is derived by dividing the reference bandwidth (100 Mbps) by the actual bandwidth on the interface (100 Mbps). All destinations so far are one hop away over the single link. When a 1.544-Mbps T1 link is used, the OSPF metric for the link is 64.

But where is the BGP route on ABR1 for the loopback0 interface relating to AS 64555? The absence of the information of the 192.168.99.0/24 link is understandable, since this link is external to the AS. But why is the network for the lo0 address 192.168.100.66 not showing up on ABR1?

As with RIP, an explicit but simple routing policy is needed to redistribute the information learned from BGP on ASBR0 into OSPF. (The same is true from OSPF to BGP, but this type of redistribution is discussed in Chapter 13, on BGP.) External BGP information is not usually redistributed by OSPF today at all due to the number of BGP routes. But this OSPF chapter will redistribute this single BGP route for the purposes of illustration. The routing policy required on ASBR0 to redistribute BGP routes with OSPF is as follows:

```
policy-statement from_bgp {
        term 1 {
            from protocol bgp;
            then accept;
        }
    }
```

This `from_bgp` routing policy is applied as an export (output) policy to OSPF on ASBR0:

```
ospf {
    export from_bgp;
    area 0.0.0.0 {
        interface fe-0/0/1.0;
    }
}
```

Now the routing table on ABR1 looks like this:

```
lab@ABR1> show route
inet.0: 6 destinations, 6 routes (6 active, 0 holddown, 0 hidden)
+ = Active Route, - = Last Active, * = Both

10.0.32.0/24        *[Direct/0] 01:33:56
                     > via fe-0/0/0.0
10.0.32.2/32        *[Local/0] 01:33:46
                      Local via fe-0/0/0.0
172.16.0.2/32       *[Direct/0] 01:33:46
                     > via lo0.0
172.16.10.1/32      *[OSPF/10] 00:30:08, metric 1
                     > to 10.0.32.1 via fe-0/0/0.0
192.168.100.0/24    *[OSPF/150] 00:12:52, metric 0, tag 0
                     > to 10.0.32.1 via fe-0/0/0.0
224.0.0.5/32        *[OSPF/10] 01:33:47, metric 1
```

The default routing protocol preference for *internal* OSPF routes (those located within the AS) is 10. The routing preference for routes outside the AS advertised by OSPF is 150. Note that the metric and tag on the 192.168.100.0/24 route is 0. This is an OSPF E2 external route, the default, which does not consider the internal cost of reaching the ASBR, only the external cost of reaching the route. Since this is a BGP route, no OSPF metric has been assigned to 192.168.100.0/24 by ASBR1. A routing policy could easily assign a metric and tag value, however.

ASBR0 Cisco Configuration

It is already possible to give the configuration for a Cisco router instead of a Juniper Networks router as ASBR0. In fact, it is probably better to do this now than later, since there are only two interfaces to worry about instead of the five in the full ASBR0 configuration.

Although this router also runs BGP, only the OSPF configuration for `Cisco_ASBR0` is shown here:

```
Cisco_ASBR0#conf t
Enter configuration commands, one per line.  End with CNTL/Z.
Cisco_ASBR0(config)#router ospf 10
Cisco_ASBR0(config-router)#redistribute bgp 64512
Cisco_ASBR0(config-router)#network 10.0.32.1 0.0.0.0 area 0
Cisco_ASBR0(config-router)#network 172.16.10.1 0.0.0.0 area 0
```

The `router ospf 10` configuration command ends with the *process identifier,* also called the *process number.* Process numbers for OSPF in Cisco reflects the ability to run more than one *routing instance* of OSPF on the same router. (Juniper Networks routers can do this too.) Different routing instances have different OSPF tables, databases, and so on. But in these examples, only one instance of OSPF will run on every router. The process number is locally significant and can vary from router to router, since the process number is only used internally.

The `redistribute bgp 64512` is the Cisco equivalent of the simple routing policy that takes BGP routes from AS 64555 and advertises them into AS 64512.

Specifying the network or interface that OSPF will run on can be done several ways. The `network` configuration command uses a *reverse mask* to separate the host portion from the entire IP prefix. It is possible to use network 10.0.32.0 0.0.0.1 Area 0, or if OSPF was to run on all 10.0.32.0/24 interfaces, network 10.0.32.0 0.0.0.255 Area 0. This example uses the most specific form: the complete interface address with a 0.0.0.0 reverse mask.

The second `network` statement makes OSPF advertise the loopback address, 172.16.10.1, into Area 0. Without this statement, since the loopback address is from a different network address space than the interface, OSPF will include the loopback address in the link-state database for Area 0 (it is also the OSPF Router ID). However, the routing tables on neighbor OSPF routers will not have an entry for 172.16.0.1! By default, loopback addresses are not advertised by Cisco routers, but OSPF automatically runs as a stub network on the Juniper Networks router's loopback address.

The following are the relevant portions of the configuration:

```
hostname Cisco_ASBR0
!
autonomous-system 64512
!
router ospf 10
  redistribute bgp 64512 metric 0 metric-type internal level-2
  network 10.0.32.1 0.0.0.0 area 0
  network 172.16.10.1 0.0.0.0 area 0
!
```

Several defaults for the BGP redistribution have been added automatically in the configuration. The Cisco_ASBR0 routing table looks like the following:

```
Cisco_ASBR0#sh ip route
Codes:C - connected,S - static,I - IGRP,R - RIP,M - mobile,B - BGP
      D - EIGRP,EX - EIGRP external,O - OSPF,IA - OSPF inter area
      E1 - OSPF external type 1,E2 - OSPF external type 2,E - EGP
      i - IS-IS,L1 - IS-IS level-1,L2 - IS-IS level-2,* - candidate
default

Gateway of last resort is not set

     10.0.0.0 255.255.255.0 is subnetted, 1 subnets
C       10.0.32.0 is directly connected, FastEthernet1
C    192.168.99.0 is directly connected, FastEthernet0
B    192.168.100.0 [20/0] via 192.168.99.2, 00:38:46
     172.16.0.0 255.255.255.255 is subnetted, 2 subnets
C       172.16.10.1 is directly connected, Loopback0
O       172.16.0.2 [110/1] via 10.0.32.2, 00:01:16, FastEthernet1
```

There are now routes learned from OSPF (O) and BGP (B). The administrative distance is 20 for the BGP route (actually, the *external* BGP route because it is outside the AS) and 110 for OSPF on Cisco routers. The BGP route has a metric of 0. The metric for the OSPF route, derived with the same reference bandwidth as on a Juniper Networks router, is 1 (100-Mbps Ethernet). All of the routing information is the same as when ASBR0 was a Juniper Networks router, but it is more compact (there are no Direct and Local entries for each interface).

The routing table on the Juniper Networks ABR1 router is almost identical to what it was before, even though Cisco_ASBR0 is now a Cisco router. One interesting difference (another is discussed in the next section) is shown in the route advertised by the Cisco_ASBR0, as follows:

```
192.168.100.0/24   *[OSPF/150] 00:12:08, metric 1, tag 64555
                   > to 10.0.32.1 via fe-0/0/0.0
```

The BGP route, which had a metric of 0 and a tag of 0 when ASBR0 was a Juniper Networks router, is now 1 and 64555, respectively. By default, Cisco advertises the OSPF external route with a metric of 1 (which will not change, since the default is a Type E2 external route) and a tag value reflecting the source AS of the BGP route. These differences can potentially affect routing in a mixed Cisco and Juniper Networks router environment. The default behaviors can be changed with routing policy, of course, and that's exactly what routing policies are for.

As with the Juniper Networks OSPF configurations, the rest of this chapter does not go into the configuration details of OSPF further. The steps are simple and straightforward. Only the results of the configuration steps are shown.

Nonbackbone, Nonstub Area Configuration

Before the Juniper Networks ABR router is swapped for a Cisco router, in this section we complete the configuration of the ABR1 router, which still needs its Area 1 interface. This interface is added to the Area 0 interface configuration, as shown in the following:

```
[edit protocols]
lab@ABR1# set ospf area 1 interface fe-0/0/2
lab@ABR1# show
ospf {
    area 0.0.0.0 {
        interface fe-0/0/0.0;
    }
    area 0.0.0.1 {
        interface fe-0/0/2.0;
    }
}
```

Naturally, this Area 1 configuration must match up with the configuration on ASBR1 in Area 1:

```
[edit protocols]
lab@ASBR1# set ospf area 1 interface fe-0/0/1
lab@ASBR1# show
ospf {
    area 0.0.0.1 {
        interface fe-0/0/1;
    }
}
```

The OSPF interface for ASBR1 also requires a routing policy to redistribute the RIP routing information (such as it is) into OSPF. The routing policy is as follows:

```
policy-statement from_ripv1 {
        term 1 {
            from protocol rip;
            then accept;
        }
    }
```

This `from_ripv1` routing policy is applied as an export (output) policy to OSPF on ASBR1:

```
ospf {
    export from_ripv1;
    area 0.0.0.1 {
        interface fe-0/0/1.0;
    }
}
```

The rest of this chapter does not go into the configuration details of OSPF further, unless something new is added. The steps are simple and straightforward, and very repetitious. Only the results of the configuration steps are shown.

The Juniper Network default for nonbackbone areas is for the area *not* to be a stub and therefore allow ASBRs in the nonbackbone areas. This still helps to keep the link-state database in Area 1 smaller than it would be on routers other than the ABR, although this will not be very apparent until Area 0 becomes more populated.

At this point, the network looks as shown in Figure 10.2.

Viewing the Routing Table and Link-State Database

The routing tables and link-state databases for routers ASBR0, ABR1, and ASBR1 can now be examined in some detail. ASBR1 in Area 1 would appear as follows:

```
lab@ASBR1> show route
inet.0: 12 destinations, 12 routes (12 active, 0 holddown, 0 hidden)
+ = Active Route, - = Last Active, * = Both

10.0.32.0/24        *[OSPF/10] 00:03:32, metric 2
                     > to 10.0.37.1 via fe-0/0/1.0
10.0.37.0/24        *[Direct/0] 02:04:08
                     > via fe-0/0/1.0
10.0.37.2/32        *[Local/0] 02:04:08
                      Local via fe-0/0/1.0
10.100.16.0/24      *[Direct/0] 02:04:08
                     > via fe-0/0/0.0
10.100.16.1/32      *[Local/0] 02:04:08
                      Local via fe-0/0/0.0
10.100.100.0/24     *[RIP/100] 01:50:43, metric 2
                     > to 10.100.16.2 via fe-0/0/0.0
172.16.0.2/32       *[OSPF/10] 00:03:32, metric 1
                     > to 10.0.37.1 via fe-0/0/1.0
172.16.0.6/32       *[Direct/0] 02:04:08
                     > via lo0.0
```

```
172.16.10.1/32      *[OSPF/10] 00:03:32, metric 2
                    > to 10.0.37.1 via fe-0/0/1.0
192.168.100.0/24    *[OSPF/150] 00:03:32, metric 0, tag 0
                    > to 10.0.37.1 via fe-0/0/1.0
224.0.0.5/32        *[OSPF/10] 02:04:11, metric 1
224.0.0.9/32        *[RIP/100] 02:04:11, metric 1
```

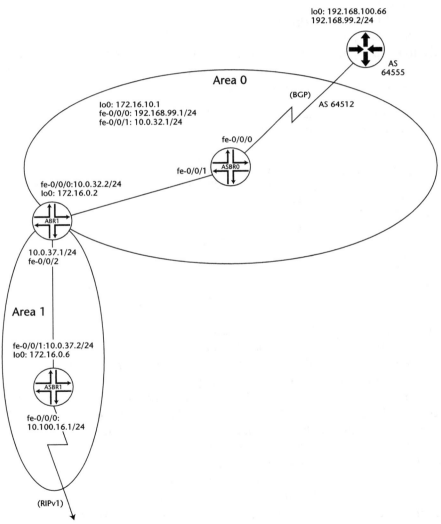

Figure 10.2 OSPF Area 0 and Area 1.

This table holds few surprises. The 10.0.32.0/24 link in Area 0 is there, now with a metric of 2 because two links with a metric of 1 are used to get there (note that the link itself counts). In fact, all destinations in Area 0 will have an OSPF metric of 2 on ASBR1, such as the lo0 route on ASBR0, 172.16.10.1. Area 1 routes not on ASBR1 itself will have a metric of 1. The external BGP route from ASBR0, 192.168.100.0/24 still has a metric of 0, as expected. The RIP route, 10.100.100.0/24, has a metric of 2 in RIP itself. This reflects the two routers (ASBR1 itself and the other router) between this location and the destination.

The link-state databases are identical within an OSPF area because of the effects of flooding. So looking at the link-state database for Area 1 on ABR1 is the same as looking at the link-state database for Area 1 on ASBR1. The asterisks only mark the contributions to the link-state database by the local router and are not really indications of differences in the link-state database itself. Here is the link-state database on ASBR1:

```
lab@ASBR1> show ospf database
    OSPF link state database, area 0.0.0.1

Type      ID          Adv Rtr         Seq          Age   Opt   Cksum   Len
Router    172.16.0.2  172.16.0.2      0x80000016   1264  0x2   0x246b  48
Router    *172.16.0.6 172.16.0.6      0x8000000a     99  0x2   0x6528  48
Network   *10.0.37.2  172.16.0.6      0x80000002    399  0x2   0x578c  32
Summary   10.0.32.0   172.16.0.2      0x8000000b    437  0x2   0xde8a  28
Summary   172.16.10.1 172.16.0.2      0x8000000a    137  0x2   0xc606  28
ASBRSum   172.16.10.1 172.16.0.2      0x80000004   1268  0x2   0xc40d  28
    OSPF external link state database
Type      ID          Adv Rtr         Seq          Age   Opt   Cksum   Len
Extern    *10.100.100.0 172.16.0.6    0x80000005    699  0x2   0xb086  36
Extern    192.168.100.0 172.16.10.1   0x80000005    741  0x2   0xf93f  36
```

The fields in the output list LSA type, the Link State ID, and the originating router. The Sequence number on the LSA helps to identify newer versions of the LSA from the same router, and the Age field increments in seconds until the LSA is refreshed by the originator. The Age should never exceed 3,600 seconds (1 hour). The OSPF Options field values are shown, as well as the LSA checksum and length of the LSA. The LSA Checksums are used to see if link-state databases are identical: If the checksum of the checksums match on two routers, it is assumed that their link-state databases are identical.

Area 1 has five types of LSAs present. Instead of LSA number, Juniper Networks routers use a text version of the LSA type. The originating router is always the source of the LSA information in the area. The relationships among these entries in the Juniper Networks representation of the link-state database are shown in Table 10.1.

Table 10.1   LSAs and Originators

LSA TYPE	JUNIPER NETWORKS NAME	ORIGINATOR (ADV RTR)
1	Router	Local router
2	Network	Local DR
3	Summary	ABR
4	ASBRSum	ABR
5	External	ASBR in backbone or nonstub
7	NSSA	ASBR (and ABR for default route) in NSSA

The purpose of each LSA type should be apparent as well. Router LSAs (Type 1) describe the local router's environment: links, metrics, addresses, and so on. The details carried in the Router LSAs can be displayed with other CLI commands. Network LSAs (Type 2) let other routers in the area know where the DRs are located. There is one LAN link in Area 1 running OSPF, so there is one Network LSA.

Summary LSAs (Type 3) let routers in other areas know about IP address spaces. Note, for example, that the Summary LSAs in Area 1 on ASBR1 represent the link between ABR1 and ASBR0 (10.0.32.0) and ASBR0's OSPF Router ID (172.16.0.1). Both of these addresses are completely within Area 0, but the Type 3 Summary LSAs make them known to routers in Area 1. Naturally, what is summarized into Area 0 will be the 10.0.27.0 and 172.16.0.6 addresses from Area 1.

ABRs are the best place to see what is going on in OSPF. Here is the routing table and link-state database for ABR1 (which is now back to being a Juniper Networks router):

```
lab@ABR1> show route
inet.0: 10 destinations, 10 routes (10 active, 0 holddown, 0 hidden)
+ = Active Route, - = Last Active, * = Both

10.0.32.0/24       *[Direct/0] 02:45:46
                    > via fe-0/0/0.0
10.0.32.2/32       *[Local/0] 02:45:48
                     Local via fe-0/0/0.0
10.0.37.0/24       *[Direct/0] 00:29:41
                    > via fe-0/0/2.0
10.0.37.1/32       *[Local/0] 00:29:41
                     Local via fe-0/0/2.0
```

```
10.100.100.0/24     *[OSPF/150] 00:29:31, metric 2, tag 0
                     > to 10.0.37.2 via fe-0/0/2.0
172.16.0.2/32       *[Direct/0] 02:45:48
                     > via lo0.0
172.16.0.6/32       *[OSPF/10] 00:29:31, metric 1
                     > to 10.0.37.2 via fe-0/0/2.0
172.16.10.1/32      *[OSPF/10] 00:29:41, metric 1
                     > to 10.0.32.1 via fe-0/0/0.0
192.168.100.0/24    *[OSPF/150] 00:29:41, metric 0, tag 0
                     > to 10.0.32.1 via fe-0/0/0.0
224.0.0.5/32        *[OSPF/10] 02:45:49, metric 1

lab@ABR1> show ospf database
    OSPF link state database, area 0.0.0.0

Type      ID           Adv Rtr        Seq          Age  Opt  Cksum   Len
Router   *172.16.0.2   172.16.0.2     0x8000000c   1277 0x2  0xcdd5  48
Router    172.16.10.1  172.16.10.1    0x8000000f   682  0x2  0xd4b0  48
Network   10.0.32.1    172.16.10.1    0x8000000c   82   0x2  0x8451  32
Summary  *10.0.37.0    172.16.0.2     0x80000001   1804 0x2  0xbbb2  28
Summary  *172.16.0.6   172.16.0.2     0x80000001   1799 0x2  0x15c5  28
ASBRSum  *172.16.0.6   172.16.0.2     0x80000001   1799 0x2  0x7d2   28

    OSPF link state database, area 0.0.0.1
Type      ID           Adv Rtr        Seq          Age  Opt  Cksum   Len
Router   *172.16.0.2   172.16.0.2     0x80000017   77   0x2  0x226c  48
Router    172.16.0.6   172.16.0.6     0x8000000a   642  0x2  0x6528  48
Network   10.0.37.2    172.16.0.6     0x80000003   42   0x2  0x558d  32
Summary  *10.0.32.0    172.16.0.2     0x8000000b   977  0x2  0xde8a  28
Summary  *172.16.10.1  172.16.0.2     0x8000000a   677  0x2  0xc606  28
ASBRSum  *172.16.10.1  172.16.0.2     0x80000005   377  0x2  0xc20e  28
    OSPF external link state database
Type      ID           Adv Rtr        Seq          Age  Opt  Cksum   Len
Extern 10.100.100.0    172.16.0.6     0x80000006   342  0x2  0xae87  36
Extern 192.168.100.0   172.16.10.1    0x80000006   382  0x2  0xf740  36
```

In this example, there is only one other router besides the ABR—ASBR0—in Area 0. So this router gets an ASBRSum (Type 4) LSA as well. Normally, there would be non-ASBR routers on the backbone, so there would usually be more Summary LSAs than Network LSAs.

The External (Type 5) LSAs are not associated with any OSPF area; they are *external* to OSPF. There are only two external routes in the AS so far: 192.168.100.0 (/24, although the mask is not shown) from ASBR 172.16.0.1 (ASBR0) and 10.100.100.0 from ASBR 10.100.100.1 (ASBR1). These routes simply represent the loopback addresses of the external BGP and RIP routers. There is no change in the OSPF/150 E2 metrics for these routes from router to router.

Finally, here is the routing table and link-state database for ASBR0 in Area 0:

```
lab@ASBR0> show route
inet.0: 11 destinations, 11 routes (11 active, 0 holddown, 0 hidden)
+ = Active Route, - = Last Active, * = Both

10.0.32.0/24        *[Direct/0] 03:02:59
                    > via fe-0/0/1.0
10.0.32.1/32        *[Local/0] 03:03:04
                    Local via fe-0/0/1.0
10.0.37.0/24        *[OSPF/10] 00:46:47, metric 2
                    > to 10.0.32.2 via fe-0/0/1.0
10.100.100.0/24     *[OSPF/150] 00:46:42, metric 2, tag 0
                    > to 10.0.32.2 via fe-0/0/1.0
172.16.0.2/32       *[OSPF/10] 01:41:55, metric 1
                    > to 10.0.32.2 via fe-0/0/1.0
172.16.0.6/32       *[OSPF/10] 00:46:42, metric 2
                    > to 10.0.32.2 via fe-0/0/1.0
172.16.10.1/32      *[Direct/0] 03:03:04
                    > via lo0.0
192.168.99.0/24     *[Direct/0] 03:03:04
                    > via fe-0/0/0.0
                    [BGP/170] 02:59:58, MED 0, localpref 100
                       AS path: 64555 ?
                    > to 192.168.99.2 via fe-0/0/0.0
192.168.99.1/32     *[Local/0] 03:03:04
                    Local via fe-0/0/0.0
192.168.100.0/24    *[BGP/170] 02:59:58, MED 0, localpref 100
                       AS path: 64555 ?
                    > to 192.168.99.2 via fe-0/0/0.0
224.0.0.5/32        *[OSPF/10] 03:03:05, metric 1

lab@ASBR0> show ospf database
     OSPF link state database, area 0.0.0.0

Type         ID          Adv Rtr       Seq         Age  Opt  Cksum   Len
Router    172.16.0.2    172.16.0.2    0x8000000c  2291  0x2  0xcdd5  48
Router   *172.16.10.1   172.16.10.1   0x80000010   793  0x2  0xd2b1  48
Network  *10.0.32.1     172.16.10.1   0x8000000d   193  0x2  0x8252  32
Summary   10.0.37.0     172.16.0.2    0x80000002   791  0x2  0xb9b3  28
Summary   172.16.0.6    172.16.0.2    0x80000002   491  0x2  0x13c6  28
ASBRSum   172.16.0.6    172.16.0.2    0x80000002   191  0x2  0x5d3   28
     OSPF external link state database
Type         ID          Adv Rtr       Seq         Age  Opt  Cksum   Len
Extern    10.100.100.0  172.16.0.6    0x80000007   455  0x2  0xac88  36
Extern*192.168.100.0    172.16.10.1   0x80000007   493  0x2  0xf541  36
```

The appearance of the routing table can be contrasted with its content shown earlier in this chapter. The link-state database is identical to that for Area 0 on ABR1.

ABR1 Cisco Configuration

In this section we make ABR1 into a Cisco router and configure the Cisco_ABR1 router to communicate with ASBR0 in Area 0 and ASBR1 in Area 1. IP classless operation is assumed. The basic configuration is very simple. Note the use of the process number, which will be kept uniform across the AS in this example:

```
Cisco_ABR1#conf t
Enter configuration commands, one per line.  End with CNTL/Z.
Cisco_ABR1(config)#router ospf 10
Cisco_ABR1(config-router)#network 10.0.32.2 0.0.0.0 area 0
Cisco_ABR1(config-router)#network 10.0.37.1 0.0.0.0 area 1
```

Here is the relevant portion of the configuration:

```
hostname Cisco_ABR1
!
router ospf 10
 network 10.0.32.2 0.0.0.0 area 0
 network 10.0.37.1 0.0.0.0 area 1
!
```

Now the routing table on Cisco_ABR1 looks like this:

```
Cisco_ABR1#show ip route

Codes:C - connected,S - static,I - IGRP,R - RIP,M - mobile,B - BGP
      D - EIGRP,EX - EIGRP external,O - OSPF,IA - OSPF inter area
      E1 - OSPF external type 1,E2 - OSPF external type 2,E - EGP
      i - IS-IS,L1 - IS-IS level-1,L2 - IS-IS level-2,* - candidate
default


Gateway of last resort is not set

     10.0.0.0 255.255.255.0 is subnetted, 3 subnets
O E2    10.100.100.0 [110/2] via 10.0.37.2, 00:01:21, FastEthernet1
C       10.0.32.0 is directly connected, FastEthernet0
C       10.0.37.0 is directly connected, FastEthernet1
O E2 192.168.100.0 [110/0] via 10.0.32.1, 00:01:21, FastEthernet0
     172.16.0.0 255.255.255.255 is subnetted, 3 subnets
O       172.16.10.1 [110/1] via 10.0.32.1, 00:01:41, FastEthernet0
O       172.16.0.6 [110/1] via 10.0.37.2, 00:01:21, FastEthernet1
C       172.16.0.2 is directly connected, Loopback0
```

The external routes learned from RIP and BGP are tagged as E2 (the default). So the cost is what the router gets from outside the AS: a metric of 2 for the RIP route from the Juniper Networks ASBR1 router, and a metric of 0 for the BGP route. (This means that ASBR0 is back to being a Juniper Networks router.)

One *very* important point to remember with regard to OSPF and loopback0 interfaces when Cisco routers are mixed with Juniper Networks routers: On Juniper Networks routers, by default, OSPF is run on the loopback interface as a stub network (unless the loopback is not the Router ID). Advertisement of the lo0 address is automatic in this case, as has been shown already. But on Cisco routers, also by default, OSPF does *not* advertise the loopback0 address unless it is included in the interface reverse mask (which it is not in these examples). If the loopback0 address on Cisco_ABR1 were in the same address space as an interface (loopback0 = 10.0.37.10, for example), then this loopback address *would* be advertised by OSPF.

The following is what the routing table on ASBR0 (a Juniper Networks router) in Area 0 looks like with regard to the loopback addresses now that Cisco_ABR1 is in place:

```
lab@ASBR0> show route 172.16/16
inet.0: 10 destinations, 10 routes (10 active, 0 holddown, 0 hidden)
+ = Active Route, - = Last Active, * = Both

172.16.0.6/32      *[OSPF/10] 00:16:55, metric 2
                    > to 10.0.32.2 via fe-0/0/1.0
172.16.10.1/32     *[Direct/0] 03:14:50
                    > via lo0.0
```

There is no entry for Cisco_ABR1's loopback (172.16.0.2). It cannot be pinged, used for Telnet, or anything else. This might be okay. But loopback addresses are often used not only as OSPF Router IDs but also as stable interfaces to Telnet for configuration, ping for diagnostics, and so on. So it is usually a good idea to make the loopback address reachable by neighboring routers. To do this, we just need to add the loopback address to the OSPF configuration on Cisco_ABR1:

```
Cisco_ABR1#conf t
Enter configuration commands, one per line.  End with CNTL/Z.
Cisco_ABR1(config)#router ospf 10
Cisco_ABR1(config-router)#network 10.0.32.2 0.0.0.0 area 0
```

It makes sense to assign the loopbacks on ABRs to the backbone area. Now the ASBR0 routing table looks like the following:

```
lab@ASBR0> show route 172.16/16
inet.0: 11 destinations, 11 routes (11 active, 0 holddown, 0 hidden)
+ = Active Route, - = Last Active, * = Both

172.16.0.2/32      *[OSPF/10] 00:11:06, metric 2
```

```
                        > to 10.0.32.2 via fe-0/0/1.0
172.16.0.6/32          *[OSPF/10] 00:16:55, metric 2
                        > to 10.0.32.2 via fe-0/0/1.0
172.16.10.1/32         *[Direct/0] 03:14:50
                        > via lo0.0
```

But how can both 172.16.0.2 (Cisco_ABR1) and 172.16.0.6 (ASBR1, another Juniper Network router) *both* claim to have the same metric? Because when the loopback address is advertised in this way by a Cisco router, the metric associated with the loopback route is already 1. The Juniper Networks router increments this and sees the metric as the sum of the two. (If the interface to Cisco_ABR1 was a 10-Mbps Ethernet, the metric for 172.16.0.2 on ASBR1 would be 11.)

Even though the Cisco_ABR1 loopback has been assigned to OSPF Area 0, the route to 172.16.0.2 shows up the same way on Juniper Networks router ASBR1 in Area 1:

```
lab@ASBR1> show route 172.16/16
inet.0: 12 destinations, 12 routes (12 active, 0 holddown, 0 hidden)
+ = Active Route, - = Last Active, * = Both

172.16.0.2/32          *[OSPF/10] 00:10:30, metric 2
                        > to 10.0.37.1 via fe-0/0/1.0
172.16.0.6/32          *[Direct/0] 03:09:38
                        > via lo0.0
172.16.10.1/32         *[OSPF/10] 00:16:26, metric 2
                        > to 10.0.37.1 via fe-0/0/1.0
```

Note the identical metric for routes really located "one hop" (172.16.0.2) and "two hops" (172.16.10.1) away. This default behavior can always be changed with a routing policy, of course.

The following is the OSPF link-state database:

```
Cisco_ABR1#show ip ospf data
        OSPF Router with ID (172.16.0.2) (Process ID 10)

                Router Link States (Area 0)
Link ID         ADV Router      Age     Seq#        Checksum Link count
172.16.0.2      172.16.0.2      23      0x8000000F 0xBCA9    1
172.16.10.1     172.16.10.1     386     0x8000001F 0xB4C0    2

                Net Link States (Area 0)
Link ID         ADV Router      Age     Seq#        Checksum
10.0.32.1       172.16.10.1     395     0x80000003 0x9648

                Summary Net Link States (Area 0)
Link ID         ADV Router      Age     Seq#        Checksum
```

```
10.0.37.0          172.16.0.2      183    0x80000007 0xA55
172.16.0.6         172.16.0.2      367    0x80000001 0x6F62

              Summary ASB Link States (Area 0)
   Link ID         ADV Router      Age    Seq#       Checksum
172.16.0.6         172.16.0.2      367    0x80000001 0x616F

              Router Link States (Area 1)
   Link ID         ADV Router      Age    Seq#       Checksum Link count
172.16.0.2         172.16.0.2      4      0x80000041 0xC267   1
172.16.0.6         172.16.0.6      368    0x80000015 0x4F33   2

              Net Link States (Area 1)
   Link ID         ADV Router      Age    Seq#       Checksum
10.0.37.2          172.16.0.6      377    0x80000003 0x558D

              Summary Net Link States (Area 1)
   Link ID         ADV Router      Age    Seq#       Checksum
10.0.32.0          172.16.0.2      208    0x80000009 0x3D25
172.16.10.1        172.16.0.2      390    0x80000001 0x3399

              Summary ASB Link States (Area 1)
   Link ID         ADV Router      Age    Seq#       Checksum
172.16.10.1        172.16.0.2      390    0x80000001 0x25A6

              AS External Link States

   Link ID         ADV Router      Age    Seq#       Checksum Tag
10.100.100.0       172.16.0.6      384    0x80000006 0xAE87   0
192.168.100.0      172.16.10.1     407    0x80000009 0xF143   0
```

With the exception of formatting, the contents of the link-state database are identical to when ABR1 was a Juniper Networks router.

Stub Area Configuration

In a real AS running OSPF, the external routes could easily overwhelm the rest of the contents of the area link-state databases. ASBR1, perhaps a small access router with a single LAN interface running RIP to a handful of PCs, has to keep track of potentially thousands of routes that are all reached through the same router: ABR1. There are exceptions to this, however. External routes generated by the ASBR in Area 1 are *not* reached though ABR1. Since there is no easy way to distinguish these routers, banishing External LSAs (Type 5s) from Area 1 means banishing the ASBR as well.

An OSPF area without External LSAs or ASBRs is a stub area (there are a few more restrictions). This section configures a new ABR to link to ASBR0 in

Area 0. The new ABR, ABR2, links to Area 2, which is defined as a stub area. Another router, STUB2 is added to the stub Area 2. The Juniper Network JUNOS software configuration steps for ABR2 and STUB2 are given, but not for ASBR0. Then the routing tables and link-state databases for ABR2 and STUB2 are investigated. The portion of the network configured in this section is shown in Figure 10.3.

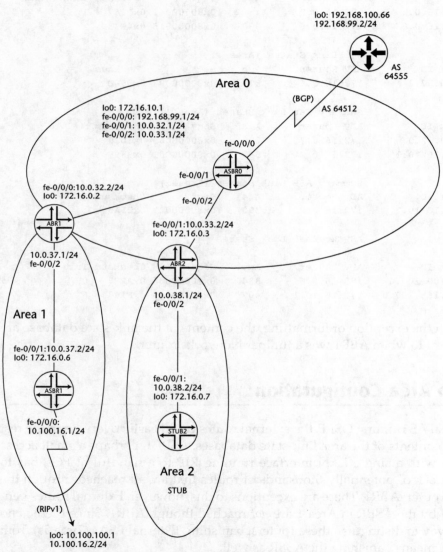

Figure 10.3 Adding the stub Area 2 configuration.

The stub OSPF area configuration for STUB2 is as follows:

```
[edit protocols]
lab@STUB2# set ospf area 2 stub
[edit protocols]
lab@STUB2# set ospf area 2 interface fe-0/0/1
[edit protocols]
lab@STUB2# show
ospf {
    area 0.0.0.2 {
        stub;
        interface fe-0/0/1.0;
    }
}
```

Only the use of the stub statement distinguishes an OSPF stub configuration from a nonstub area in the JUNOS software. The stub statement must be matched on the ABR2 interface, or OSPF will not form an adjacency on the link (there will be an OSPF Options mismatch).

```
[edit protocols]
lab@ABR2# set ospf area 2 stub
[edit protocols]
lab@ABR2# set ospf area 2 interface fe-0/0/2
[edit protocols]
lab@ABR2# set ospf area 0
[edit protocols]
lab@ABR2# set ospf area 0 interface fe-0/0/1
[edit protocols]
lab@STUB2# show
ospf {
    area 0.0.0.0 {
        interface fe-0/0/1.0;
    }
    area 0.0.0.2 {
        stub;
        interface fe-0/0/2.0;
    }
}
```

Viewing the Routing Table and Link-State Database

Focusing on the ABRs is always a good idea in OSPF. The following is the routing table and link-state database for ABR2. The link-state database, but not the routing table, will be identical on ASBR0 and all other Area 0 routers.

```
lab@ABR2> show route
inet.0: 14 destinations, 14 routes (14 active, 0 holddown, 0 hidden)
+ = Active Route, - = Last Active, * = Both


10.0.32.0/24        *[OSPF/10] 00:02:19, metric 2
                      > to 10.0.33.1 via fe-0/0/1.0
10.0.33.0/24        *[Direct/0] 00:51:34
                      > via fe-0/0/1.0
10.0.33.2/32        *[Local/0] 06:07:16
                       Local via fe-0/0/1.0
10.0.37.0/24        *[OSPF/10] 00:02:19, metric 3
                      > to 10.0.33.1 via fe-0/0/1.0
10.0.38.0/24        *[Direct/0] 00:56:56
                      > via fe-0/0/2.0
10.0.38.1/32        *[Local/0] 00:56:56
                       Local via fe-0/0/2.0
10.100.100.0/24     *[OSPF/150] 00:02:19, metric 2, tag 0
                      > to 10.0.33.1 via fe-0/0/1.0
172.16.0.2/32       *[OSPF/10] 00:02:19, metric 2
                      > to 10.0.33.1 via fe-0/0/1.0
172.16.0.3/32       *[Direct/0] 06:07:16
                      > via lo0.0
172.16.0.6/32       *[OSPF/10] 00:02:19, metric 3
                      > to 10.0.33.1 via fe-0/0/1.0
172.16.0.7/32       *[OSPF/10] 00:01:10, metric 1
                      > to 10.0.38.2 via fe-0/0/2.0
172.16.10.1/32      *[OSPF/10] 00:02:19, metric 1
                      > to 10.0.33.1 via fe-0/0/1.0
192.168.100.0/24    *[OSPF/150] 00:02:19, metric 0, tag 0
                      > to 10.0.33.1 via fe-0/0/1.0
224.0.0.5/32        *[OSPF/10] 06:07:17, metric 1
```

This table is already growing large, and there are only a handful of real
routes to consider. Only a few routes are new, however. STUB2 is now present
(172.16.0.7), along with the link to the STUB2 router (10.0.38.0/24 and
10.0.38.2/32) and the link to ASBR0 (10.0.33.0/24 and 10.0.33.2/32). The OSPF
internal (OSPF/10) metrics are the simple sums of the metrics on the links (all
100-Mbps Ethernet with a metric of 1). The OSPF external (OSPF/150) metrics
(Type E2) are distributed unchanged:

```
lab@ABR2> show ospf database
    OSPF link state database, area 0.0.0.0


Type       ID         Adv Rtr        Seq         Age  Opt  Cksum   Len
Router     172.16.0.2 172.16.0.2     0x80000011  178  0x2  0xc3da  48
Router    *172.16.0.3 172.16.0.3     0x80000005  468  0x2  0x9a02  48
Router     172.16.10.1 172.16.10.1   0x8000001d  127  0x2  0x8580  60
```

Network	10.0.32.1	172.16.10.1	0x80000017	427	0x2	0x6e5c	32
Network	10.0.33.1	172.16.10.1	0x80000002	1281	0x2	0x9b42	32
Summary	10.0.37.0	172.16.0.2	0x80000006	724	0x2	0xb1b7	28
Summary	*10.0.38.0	172.16.0.3	0x80000003	768	0x2	0xa6c3	28
Summary	172.16.0.6	172.16.0.2	0x80000006	480	0x2	0xbca	28
Summary	*172.16.0.7	172.16.0.3	0x80000002	470	0x2	0x3d4	28
ASBRSum	172.16.0.6	172.16.0.2	0x80000006	424	0x2	0xfcd7	28

```
          OSPF link state database, area 0.0.0.2
```

Type	ID	Adv Rtr	Seq	Age	Opt	Cksum	Len
Router	*172.16.0.3	172.16.0.3	0x80000003	789	0x0	0x841b	48
Router	172.16.0.7	172.16.0.7	0x80000005	1641	0x0	0xa3ed	48
Network	10.0.38.2	172.16.0.7	0x80000001	1646	0x0	0x7e64	32
Summary	*10.0.32.0	172.16.0.3	0x80000002	168	0x0	0x6dfb	28
Summary	*10.0.33.0	172.16.0.3	0x80000002	1279	0x0	0x5811	28
Summary	*10.0.37.0	172.16.0.3	0x80000001	1279	0x0	0x4222	28
Summary	*172.16.0.2	172.16.0.3	0x80000001	1279	0x0	0xb91c	28
Summary	*172.16.0.6	172.16.0.3	0x80000001	1279	0x0	0x9b35	28
Summary	*172.16.10.1	172.16.0.3	0x80000001	1279	0x0	0x4b82	28

```
          OSPF external link state database
```

Type	ID	Adv Rtr	Seq	Age	Opt	Cksum	Len
Extern	10.100.100.0	172.16.0.6	0x80000011	689	0x2	0x9892	36
Extern	192.168.100.0	172.16.10.1	0x80000011	727	0x2	0xe14b	36

The link-state database on ABR2 is growing as well. There is a third router (ABR2, 172.16.0.3) on the backbone, and a new Summary LSA for STUB2 (172.16.0.7). Note that the link-state database for Area 2 has only two routers, but already contains six Summary LSAs.

Now look at the routing table and link-state database on STUB2:

```
lab@STUB2> show route
inet.0: 11 destinations, 11 routes (11 active, 0 holddown, 0 hidden)
+ = Active Route, - = Last Active, * = Both

10.0.32.0/24       *[OSPF/10] 00:00:04, metric 3
                    > to 10.0.38.1 via fe-0/0/1.0
10.0.33.0/24       *[OSPF/10] 00:00:04, metric 2
                    > to 10.0.38.1 via fe-0/0/1.0
10.0.37.0/24       *[OSPF/10] 00:00:04, metric 4
                    > to 10.0.38.1 via fe-0/0/1.0
10.0.38.0/24       *[Direct/0] 01:40:16
                    > via fe-0/0/1.0
10.0.38.2/32       *[Local/0] 01:40:19
                    Local via fe-0/0/1.0
172.16.0.2/32      *[OSPF/10] 00:00:04, metric 3
                    > to 10.0.38.1 via fe-0/0/1.0
172.16.0.3/32      *[OSPF/10] 00:00:04, metric 1
                    > to 10.0.38.1 via fe-0/0/1.0
```

```
172.16.0.6/32        *[OSPF/10] 00:00:04, metric 4
                      > to 10.0.38.1 via fe-0/0/1.0
172.16.0.7/32        *[Direct/0] 01:40:19
                      > via lo0.0
172.16.10.1/32       *[OSPF/10] 00:00:04, metric 2
                      > to 10.0.38.1 via fe-0/0/1.0
224.0.0.5/32         *[OSPF/10] 06:36:29, metric 1
```

At first glance, this is not very different from the routing table on ASBR1 in the nonstub area. There are no RIP routes, of course, but this gain is offset by the need to represent the new routers in Area 2 and their links. There is a real change in the appearance of the link-state database on STUB2, however:

```
lab@STUB2> show ospf database
    OSPF link state database, area 0.0.0.2

Type       ID          Adv Rtr        Seq        Age  Opt  Cksum  Len
Router    172.16.0.3  172.16.0.3   0x80000007   23   0x0  0x7c1f  48
Router   *172.16.0.7  172.16.0.7   0x80000007   22   0x0  0x9fef  48
Network  *10.0.38.2   172.16.0.7   0x80000004   22   0x0  0x7867  32
Summary   10.0.32.0   172.16.0.3   0x80000003  137   0x0  0x1160  28
Summary   10.0.33.0   172.16.0.3   0x80000002  1639  0x0  0xfd74  28
Summary   10.0.37.0   172.16.0.3   0x80000002  1637  0x0  0xe586  28
Summary   172.16.0.2  172.16.0.3   0x80000002  1337  0x0  0x5d80  28
Summary   172.16.0.6  172.16.0.3   0x80000002  1067  0x0  0x3f99  28
Summary   172.16.10.1 172.16.0.3   0x80000002  1037  0x0  0xeee6  28
```

The change is not in Area 2, which is identical in content to the Area 2 link-state database on ABR2. The change is in the absence of the external (Type = 5) LSAs for routes outside the AS: 10.100.100.1 and 192.168.100.66. No Type 5 LSAs (external) are flooded into stub areas by the ABR attached to the stub. Without the externals, no Type 4 ASBRSum LSAs are needed in Area 2 either.

This is the real savings of the size of the link-state database and routing table in an OSPF stub area. On the Internet the number of routes advertised as external (outside of the AS) can be huge. None of these details are sent into the OSPF stub areas, greatly reducing the size and complexity of the stub routing tables and OSPF link-state databases.

But now the two external routes in this example, 10.100.100.1 and 192.168.100.66, are no longer even pingable from STUB2. There are no entries for those prefixes in the STUB2 routing table. How can the STUB2 router ever reach destination outside the AS? One way is to configure a default static route with the link to ABR2 as the next hop on STUB2. This route is added to the routing table on STUB2 as the very first entry:

```
lab@STUB2> show route

inet.0: 12 destinations, 12 routes (12 active, 0 holddown, 0 hidden)
```

```
+ = Active Route, - = Last Active, * = Both

0.0.0.0/0               *[Static/5] 00:03:56
                        > to 10.0.38.1 via fe-0/0/1.0
```

Now all pings and traceroutes sent with the STUB2 loopback address (172.16.0.7) as the source address will succeed. Alternatively, ABR2 could advertise a default route to STUB2 for external routes. This will be done in the next section when a total stub area is configured.

However, the Summary LSAs (Type = 3) are still numerous. And as the AS grows in terms of links and routers, the number of Summary LSAs in the stub areas just gets bigger and bigger, even though the number of routers and links in the stub area itself is small. This just chews up space in the routing table and link-state database. A look at the STUB2 routing table shows that out of 12 destinations (including the default), 10 of them use the link to ABR2 as the next hop. Only the loopback address and OSPF multicast address do not use this next hop. Why not just summarize all destinations outside of the stub area with one default Summary LSA?

This is, of course, the idea behind a total stub area in OSPF. But before creating a total stub area to add to the overall AS configuration, in the next section we make ABR2 into a Cisco router.

ABR2 Stub Cisco Configuration

In this section we make ABR2 into a Cisco router and configure the Cisco_ABR2 router to communicate with ASBR0 in Area 0 and STUB2 in stub Area 2. These other routers remain Juniper Networks routers, and the default static route (0.0.0.0/0) remains on STUB2. IP classless operation is assumed. The basic configuration is not very complicated:

```
Cisco_ABR2#conf t
Enter configuration commands, one per line.  End with CNTL/Z.
Cisco_ABR2(config)#router ospf 10
Cisco_ABR2(config-router)#network 10.0.33.2 0.0.0.0 area 0
Cisco_ABR2(config-router)#network 172.16.0.3 0.0.0.0 area 0
Cisco_ABR2(config-router)#network 10.0.38.1 0.0.0.0 area 2
Cisco_ABR2(config-router)#area 2 stub
```

Here is the relevant portion of the configuration:

```
hostname Cisco_ABR2
!
router ospf 10
 network 10.0.33.2 0.0.0.0 area 0
 network 172.16.0.3 0.0.0.0 area 0
 network 10.0.38.1 0.0.0.0 area 2
 area 2 stub
```

The following is the Cisco_ABR2 routing table, which has exactly the same information as in the Juniper Networks router ABR2 routing table:

```
Cisco_ABR2#sh ip route

Codes:C - connected,S - static,I - IGRP,R - RIP,M - mobile,B - BGP
      D - EIGRP,EX - EIGRP external,O - OSPF,IA - OSPF inter area
      E1 - OSPF external type 1,E2 - OSPF external type 2,E - EGP
      i - IS-IS,L1 - IS-IS level-1,L2 - IS-IS level-2,* - candidate
default


Gateway of last resort is not set

      10.0.0.0 255.255.255.0 is subnetted, 5 subnets
O E2    10.100.100.0 [110/2] via 10.0.33.1, 00:06:03, FastEthernet0
O       10.0.32.0 [110/2] via 10.0.33.1, 00:06:23, FastEthernet0
C       10.0.33.0 is directly connected, FastEthernet0
C       10.0.38.0 is directly connected, FastEthernet1
O IA    10.0.37.0 [110/3] via 10.0.33.1, 00:06:04, FastEthernet0
O E2 192.168.100.0 [110/0] via 10.0.33.1, 00:06:04, FastEthernet0
      172.16.0.0 255.255.255.255 is subnetted, 5 subnets
O       172.16.10.1 [110/1] via 10.0.33.1, 00:06:24, FastEthernet0
O IA    172.16.0.6 [110/3] via 10.0.33.1, 00:06:04, FastEthernet0
O       172.16.0.7 [110/1] via 10.0.38.2, 00:06:04, FastEthernet1
O       172.16.0.2 [110/2] via 10.0.33.1, 00:06:24, FastEthernet0
C       172.16.0.3 is directly connected, Loopback0
```

For the first time, a route marked as an inter-area (IA) destination shows up. These are routes within the AS but not in the local area or on the backbone (the loopbacks on the Cisco ABRs are assigned to the backbone). The metrics are the same as they were on the Juniper Networks ABR2 but display the same skewing on the other routers as discussed in the previous section.

For example, on ASBR0, the loopbacks appear as follows (note equidistant Cisco_ABR2 and STUB2):

```
lab@ASBR0> show route 172.16/16
inet.0: 16 destinations, 16 routes (16 active, 0 holddown, 0 hidden)
+ = Active Route, - = Last Active, * = Both

172.16.0.2/32      *[OSPF/10] 00:39:38, metric 1
                    > to 10.0.32.2 via fe-0/0/1.0
172.16.0.3/32      *[OSPF/10] 00:17:56, metric 2
                    > to 10.0.33.2 via fe-0/0/2.0
172.16.0.6/32      *[OSPF/10] 00:39:38, metric 2
                    > to 10.0.32.2 via fe-0/0/1.0
172.16.0.7/32      *[OSPF/10] 00:16:19, metric 2
                    > to 10.0.33.2 via fe-0/0/2.0
172.16.10.1/32     *[Direct/0] 04:32:46
                    > via lo0.0
```

Here is the link-state database for Cisco_ABR2:

```
Cisco_ABR2#sh ip ospf da
        OSPF Router with ID (172.16.0.3) (Process ID 10)
                Router Link States (Area 0)

Link ID            ADV Router        Age     Seq#        Checksum Link count
172.16.0.2         172.16.0.2        941     0x80000014 0xBDDD    2
172.16.0.3         172.16.0.3        1259    0x80000007 0x4851    2
172.16.10.1        172.16.10.1       420     0x80000027 0x718A    3

                Net Link States (Area 0)
Link ID            ADV Router        Age     Seq#        Checksum
10.0.32.1          172.16.10.1       720     0x80000004 0x9449
10.0.33.1          172.16.10.1       120     0x80000002 0x9B42

                Summary Net Link States (Area 0)
Link ID            ADV Router        Age     Seq#        Checksum
10.0.37.0          172.16.0.2        289     0x80000004 0xB5B5
10.0.38.0          172.16.0.3        1226    0x80000003 0x160
172.16.0.6         172.16.0.2        43      0x80000003 0x11C7
172.16.0.7         172.16.0.3        1231    0x80000001 0x5F70

                Summary ASB Link States (Area 0)
Link ID            ADV Router        Age     Seq#        Checksum
172.16.0.6         172.16.0.2        1245    0x80000002 0x5D3

                Router Link States (Area 2)

Link ID            ADV Router        Age     Seq#        Checksum Link count
172.16.0.3         172.16.0.3        1242    0x8000001C 0x311C    1
172.16.0.7         172.16.0.7        1243    0x8000000C 0x95F4    2

                Net Link States (Area 2)
Link ID            ADV Router        Age     Seq#        Checksum
10.0.38.2          172.16.0.7        1248    0x80000001 0x7E64

                Summary Net Link States (Area 2)
Link ID            ADV Router        Age     Seq#        Checksum
0.0.0.0            172.16.0.3        1254    0x80000001 0xEEAF
10.0.32.0          172.16.0.3        1254    0x80000002 0x6DFB
10.0.33.0          172.16.0.3        1254    0x80000002 0x5811
10.0.37.0          172.16.0.3        1255    0x80000002 0x4023
172.16.0.2         172.16.0.3        1255    0x80000002 0xB71D
172.16.0.3         172.16.0.3        1255    0x80000002 0x4994
172.16.0.6         172.16.0.3        1255    0x80000002 0x9936
172.16.10.1        172.16.0.3        1255    0x80000002 0x4983

                AS External Link States
Link ID            ADV Router        Age     Seq#        Checksum Tag
10.100.100.0       172.16.0.6        446     0x8000000D 0xA08E    0
192.168.100.0      172.16.10.1       1025    0x8000000B 0xED45    0
```

The only addition is the Summary LSA (Type = 3) for the default route in Area 2 that was added to STUB2 at the end of the previous section.

Total Stub Area Configuration

In a real AS running OSPF, the summary routes in a stub area could easily overwhelm the rest the routing table and link-state database space in a small router. STUB2, probably a small access router with a few links to customer sites, has to handle a lot of routes that are all reached through ABR2. Why flood a lot of summaries into the stub area that are all saying essentially the same thing?

An OSPF area without Type 5 External LSAs (or ASBRs), and using only a default route to reach the ABR, is a *total stub* (or totally stubby) area. In this section we configure a new ABR to link to ASBR0 in Area 0. The new ABR, ABR3, links to Area 3, which is defined as a total stub area without summaries flooded by the ABR from Area 0. Another router, TOTAL3, is added to the total stub Area 3. The Juniper Network JUNOS software configuration steps for ABR3 and TOTAL3 are given, but not for ASBR0. Then the routing tables and link-state databases for ABR3 and TOTAL3 are investigated. The portion of the network configured in this section is shown in Figure 10.4.

The following is the total stub OSPF area configuration for TOTAL3:

```
[edit protocols]
lab@TOTAL3# set ospf area 3 stub

[edit protocols]
lab@TOTAL3# set ospf area 3 interface fe-0/0/1

[edit protocols]
lab@TOTAL3# show
ospf {
    area 0.0.0.3 {
        stub;
        interface fe-0/0/1.0;
    }
}
```

Note that the configuration for TOTAL3 in total stub Area 3 is exactly the same as STUB2 in stub Area 2. This is because the difference between an OSPF stub and total stub area only has to do with the configuration of the ABR. It is the ABR that needs to suppress Summary LSAs and inject the default route that characterizes the total stub area.

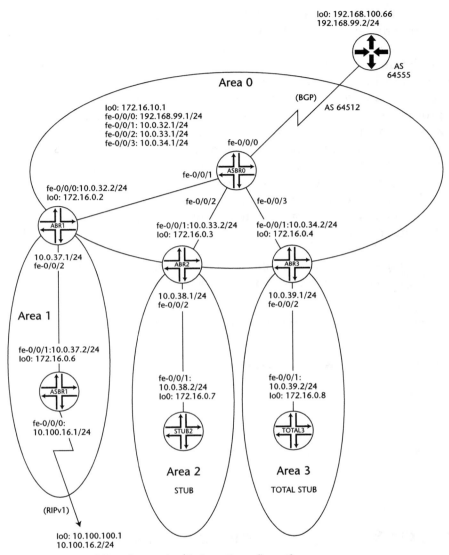

Figure 10.4 Adding the total stub Area 3 configuration.

The configuration for ABR3 is quite different. ABR3 needs an interface to ASBR0 (not shown here), plus a configuration for Area 3, also with the `stub` and `no-summaries` statements. However, this eliminates all Type 3 Summary LSAs from Area 3. The Type 3 Summary LSAs represent routes within the AS, but not in the total stub Area 3. Without this information, the TOTAL3 router (and any other routers in Area 3 besides ABR3) will not know how to reach the ABR. This is similar to the situation in the simple stub Area 2 configuration, when the elimination of Type 5 External LSAs left STUB2 with no way to reach destinations outside of the AS. Now, without even Summary LSAs as a guide, TOTAL2 will be unable to reach destinations outside of Area 3.

The problem was solved in Area 2 by configuring a default route on STUB2. But it was also mentioned that the ABR could inject a default route into the stub area. This is helpful when there is more than one ABR or when the non-ABR routers in the stub areas are under the control of another network administrator (as would be the case if the non-ABR routers are customer site routers). In the JUNOS software, the default route advertised into the stub area is given a metric independent of link considerations. This can help when there are multiple ABRs but you want to use one of them as a first choice and use the other in case of link or ABR failure.

The following shows how to configure the total stub Area 3 with a default route having a metric of 10 on the ABR:

```
[edit protocols]
lab@ABR3# set ospf area 3 stub default-metric 10 no-summaries

[edit protocols]
lab@ABR3# set ospf area 3 interface fe-0/0/2

[edit protocols]
lab@ABR3# show
ospf {
    area 0.0.0.3 {
        stub default-metric 10 no-summaries;
        interface fe-0/0/2.0;
    }
}
```

Viewing the Rzouting Table and Link-State Database

The following is the routing table and link-state database for ABR3. The link-state database, but not the routing table, will now be identical on ASBR0 and all other Area 0 routers.

```
lab@ABR3> show route
inet.0: 18 destinations, 18 routes (18 active, 0 holddown, 0 hidden)
+ = Active Route, - = Last Active, * = Both

10.0.32.0/24        *[OSPF/10] 00:32:37, metric 2
                    > to 10.0.34.1 via fe-0/0/1.0
```

```
10.0.33.0/24        *[OSPF/10] 00:32:37, metric 2
                    > to 10.0.34.1 via fe-0/0/1.0
10.0.34.0/24        *[Direct/0] 00:43:52
                    > via fe-0/0/1.0
10.0.34.2/32        *[Local/0] 00:43:52
                    Local via fe-0/0/1.0
10.0.37.0/24        *[OSPF/10] 00:32:37, metric 3
                    > to 10.0.34.1 via fe-0/0/1.0
10.0.38.0/24        *[OSPF/10] 00:32:37, metric 3
                    > to 10.0.34.1 via fe-0/0/1.0
10.0.39.0/24        *[Direct/0] 00:43:50
                    > via fe-0/0/2.0
10.0.39.1/32        *[Local/0] 00:43:52
                    Local via fe-0/0/2.0
10.100.100.0/24     *[OSPF/150] 00:32:37, metric 2, tag 0
                    > to 10.0.34.1 via fe-0/0/1.0
172.16.0.2/32       *[OSPF/10] 00:32:37, metric 2
                    > to 10.0.34.1 via fe-0/0/1.0
172.16.0.3/32       *[OSPF/10] 00:32:37, metric 2
                    > to 10.0.34.1 via fe-0/0/1.0
172.16.0.4/32       *[Direct/0] 00:43:52
                    > via lo0.0
172.16.0.6/32       *[OSPF/10] 00:32:37, metric 3
                    > to 10.0.34.1 via fe-0/0/1.0
172.16.0.7/32       *[OSPF/10] 00:32:37, metric 3
                    > to 10.0.34.1 via fe-0/0/1.0
172.16.0.8/32       *[OSPF/10] 00:05:37, metric 1
                    > to 10.0.39.2 via fe-0/0/2.0
172.16.10.1/32      *[OSPF/10] 00:32:37, metric 1
                    > to 10.0.34.1 via fe-0/0/1.0
192.168.100.0/24    *[OSPF/150] 00:32:37, metric 0, tag 0
                    > to 10.0.34.1 via fe-0/0/1.0
224.0.0.5/32        *[OSPF/10] 00:49:13, metric 1
```

By now the additions and metrics should be familiar. Note that the default route configured for Area 3 is not in the ABR3 routing table. This default route is not for ABR3; it is for TOTAL3. This route shows up in the ABR3 link-state database for Area 3:

```
lab@ABR3> show ospf database
     OSPF link state database, area 0.0.0.0

Type     ID          Adv Rtr       Seq         Age   Opt  Cksum   Len
Router   172.16.0.2  172.16.0.2    0x8000001c  1567  0x2  0xade5  48
Router   172.16.0.3  172.16.0.3    0x8000000f    94  0x2  0xe3b7  48
Router  *172.16.0.4  172.16.0.4    0x80000006  1370  0x2  0x1c82  48
Router   172.16.10.1 172.16.10.1   0x8000002d   343  0x2  0xc4ce  72
Network  10.0.32.1   172.16.10.1   0x80000024   643  0x2  0x5469  32
```

```
Network   10.0.33.1    172.16.10.1   0x8000000c   943   0x2   0x874c   32
Network  *10.0.34.2    172.16.0.4    0x80000003   170   0x2   0xe2fd   32
Summary   10.0.37.0    172.16.0.2    0x80000010  2048   0x2   0x9dc1   28
Summary   10.0.38.0    172.16.0.3    0x8000000c  1686   0x2   0x94cc   28
Summary  *10.0.39.0    172.16.0.4    0x80000005   554   0x2   0x91d4   28
Summary   172.16.0.6   172.16.0.2    0x80000005  1867   0x2   0xdc9    28
Summary   172.16.0.7   172.16.0.3    0x80000005  1594   0x2   0xfcd7   28
Summary  *172.16.0.8   172.16.0.4    0x80000001   554   0x2   0xf4e1   28
ASBRSum   172.16.0.6   172.16.0.2    0x80000005  1747   0x2   0xfed6   28

     OSPF link state database, area 0.0.0.3
Type      ID          Adv Rtr        Seq        Age  Opt  Cksum  Len
Router  *172.16.0.4   172.16.0.4    0x80000009   559  0x0  0x94ff  48
Router   172.16.0.8   172.16.0.8    0x80000008   556  0x0  0xb9cf  48
Network  10.0.39.2    172.16.0.8    0x80000004   558  0x0  0x7f5c  32
Summary *0.0.0.0      172.16.0.4    0x80000002   770  0x0  0x4152  28
     OSPF external link state database
 Type      ID          Adv Rtr        Seq        Age  Opt  Cksum  Len
Extern  10.100.100.0 172.16.0.6    0x8000001c   315  0x2  0x829d  36
Extern  192.168.100.0 172.16.10.1   0x8000001a    43  0x2  0xcf54  36
```

The default route advertised by ABR3 into Area 3 shows up as the last entry in the Area 0.0.0.3 link-state database. The effects of this default route can be seen on TOTAL3:

```
lab@TOTAL3> show route
inet.0: 6 destinations, 6 routes (6 active, 0 holddown, 0 hidden)
+ = Active Route, - = Last Active, * = Both

0.0.0.0/0          *[OSPF/10] 00:12:24, metric 11
                    > to 10.0.39.1 via fe-0/0/1.0
10.0.39.0/24       *[Direct/0] 00:50:42
                    > via fe-0/0/1.0
10.0.39.2/32       *[Local/0] 00:55:03
                      Local via fe-0/0/1.0
172.16.0.4/32      *[OSPF/10] 00:12:24, metric 1
                    > to 10.0.39.1 via fe-0/0/1.0
172.16.0.8/32      *[Direct/0] 00:55:03
                    > via lo0.0
224.0.0.5/32       *[OSPF/10] 08:03:59, metric 1
```

Only routes within Area 3 appear separate from the default route. All other destinations are reached through ABR3 by way of the default route (with metric 11, as expected). All AS destinations, and even the external routes (10.100.100.1 and 192.168.100.66), are pingable thanks to this default route. Total stubs feature minimal link-state databases, as well as minimal routing tables:

```
lab@TOTAL3> show ospf database

     OSPF link state database, area 0.0.0.3
```

```
Type        ID          Adv Rtr          Seq      Age  Opt  Cksum  Len
Router   172.16.0.4   172.16.0.4     0x80000009   983  0x0  0x94ff  48
Router  *172.16.0.8   172.16.0.8     0x80000008   978  0x0  0xb9cf  48
Network *10.0.39.2    172.16.0.8     0x80000004   980  0x0  0x7f5c  32
Summary  0.0.0.0      172.16.0.4     0x80000002  1194  0x0  0x4152  28
```

This shows how the default route made its way into TOTAL3's routing table. Total stub areas allow OSPF to be used on even the smallest of routers in terms of memory and speed.

ABR3 Total Stub Cisco Configuration

In this section we make ABR3 into a Cisco router and configure the Cisco_ABR3 router to communicate with ASBR0 in Area 0 and TOTAL3 in total stub Area 3. These other routers will remain Juniper Networks routers. IP classless operation is assumed. The basic configuration adds one word to the stub configuration:

```
Cisco_ABR3#conf t
Enter configuration commands, one per line.  End with CNTL/Z.
Cisco_ABR2(config)#router ospf 10
Cisco_ABR2(config-router)#network 10.0.34.2 0.0.0.0 area 0
Cisco_ABR2(config-router)#network 172.16.0.4 0.0.0.0 area 0
Cisco_ABR2(config-router)#network 10.0.39.1 0.0.0.0 area 3
Cisco_ABR2(config-router)#area 3 stub no-summary
```

The command `area 3 default-cost 10` could have been used to set the 0/0 metric to 10, as before. The default value is 1.

The following is the relevant portion of the configuration:

```
hostname Cisco_ABR3
!
router ospf 10
 network 10.0.34.2 0.0.0.0 area 0
 network 172.16.0.4 0.0.0.0 area 0
 network 10.0.39.1 0.0.0.0 area 3
 area 3 stub no-summary
```

The Cisco_ABR3 routing table follows; it has exactly the same information as in the Juniper Networks router ABR3 routing table:

```
Cisco_ABR3#sh ip route

Codes:C - connected,S - static,I - IGRP,R - RIP,M - mobile,B - BGP
      D - EIGRP,EX - EIGRP external,O - OSPF,IA - OSPF inter area
      E1 - OSPF external type 1,E2 - OSPF external type 2,E - EGP
      i - IS-IS,L1 - IS-IS level-1,L2 - IS-IS level-2,* - candidate
default

Gateway of last resort is not set
```

```
        10.0.0.0 255.255.255.0 is subnetted, 7 subnets
O E2    10.100.100.0 [110/2] via 10.0.34.1, 00:01:00, FastEthernet0
C       10.0.34.0 is directly connected, Ethernet0
O       10.0.32.0 [110/2] via 10.0.34.1, 00:01:01, FastEthernet0
O       10.0.33.0 [110/2] via 10.0.34.1, 00:01:01, FastEthernet0
O IA    10.0.38.0 [110/3] via 10.0.34.1, 00:01:01, FastEthernet0
C       10.0.39.0 is directly connected, Ethernet1
O IA    10.0.37.0 [110/3] via 10.0.34.1, 00:01:01, FastEthernet0
O E2 192.168.100.0 [110/0] via 10.0.34.1, 00:01:01, FastEthernet0
        172.16.0.0 255.255.255.255 is subnetted, 7 subnets
O       172.16.0.8 [110/1] via 10.0.39.2, 00:01:11, FastEthernet1
O       172.16.10.1 [110/1] via 10.0.34.1, 00:01:01, FastEthernet0
C       172.16.0.4 is directly connected, Loopback0
O IA    172.16.0.6 [110/3] via 10.0.34.1, 00:01:01, FastEthernet0
O IA    172.16.0.7 [110/3] via 10.0.34.1, 00:01:01, FastEthernet0
O       172.16.0.2 [110/2] via 10.0.34.1, 00:01:01, FastEthernet0
O       172.16.0.3 [110/2] via 10.0.34.1, 00:01:03, FastEthernet0
```

Then, again, the real advantage of a total stub is on the TOTAL3 router, which has not changed and still shows the default route to the ABR. The following is the link-state database on Cisco_ABR3:

```
Cisco_ABR3#sh ip ospf da
        OSPF Router with ID (172.16.0.4) (Process ID 10)


                Router Link States (Area 0)

Link ID         ADV Router      Age     Seq#        Checksum Link count
172.16.0.2      172.16.0.2      1013    0x80000015 0xBBDE    2
172.16.0.3      172.16.0.3      444     0x8000000E 0xE5B6    2
172.16.0.4      172.16.0.4      422     0x80000006 0x7223    2
172.16.10.1     172.16.10.1     428     0x80000036 0x90FA    4

                Net Link States (Area 0)
Link ID         ADV Router      Age     Seq#        Checksum
10.0.32.1       172.16.10.1     732     0x80000006 0x904B
10.0.33.1       172.16.10.1     433     0x80000005 0x9545
10.0.34.1       172.16.10.1     429     0x80000001 0xA03C

                Summary Net Link States (Area 0)
Link ID         ADV Router      Age     Seq#        Checksum
10.0.37.0       172.16.0.2      301     0x80000005 0xB3B6
10.0.38.0       172.16.0.3      745     0x80000006 0xA0C6
10.0.39.0       172.16.0.4      420     0x80000015 0xCB81
172.16.0.6      172.16.0.2      122     0x80000004 0xFC8
172.16.0.7      172.16.0.3      538     0x80000002 0x3D4
172.16.0.8      172.16.0.4      420     0x80000011 0x2F8E

                Summary ASB Link States (Area 0)
Link ID         ADV Router      Age     Seq#        Checksum
```

172.16.0.6	172.16.0.2	2	0x80000004 0x1D5

Router Link States (Area 3)

Link ID	ADV Router	Age	Seq#	Checksum	Link count
172.16.0.4	172.16.0.4	435	0x8000001B	0x3911	1
172.16.0.8	172.16.0.8	441	0x8000000C	0xB1D3	2

Net Link States (Area 3)

Link ID	ADV Router	Age	Seq#	Checksum
10.0.39.2	172.16.0.8	442	0x80000001	0x8559

Summary Net Link States (Area 3)

Link ID	ADV Router	Age	Seq#	Checksum
0.0.0.0	172.16.0.4	441	0x80000011	0xC8C4

AS External Link States

Link ID	ADV Router	Age	Seq#	Checksum	Tag
10.100.100.0	172.16.0.6	457	0x8000000F	0x9C90	0
192.168.100.0	172.16.10.1	135	0x8000000E	0xE748	0

NSSA Configuration

The last OSPF area type to be investigated is the not-so-stubby-area (NSSA). Stubs are fine in that they keep the size of the link-state databases and routing tables to a minimum, but at the cost of not allowing an ASBR in the stub area at all. This does not seem too restrictive, but there are three cases when an otherwise good candidate for an OSPF stub area needs an ASBR:

- An ISP has acquired a very small ISP with small routers but one or more ASBRs. The formerly independent ISP is usually running BGP on these links. This situation is similar to ASBR0 in the example OSPF network.

- A router in the candidate stub area has one or more links running RIP. This situation is similar to ASBR1 in the example OSPF network.

- A router in the candidate stub area has one or more links that are represented by static routes. This occurs when customers are reached by single, stable links and it is not even necessary to run a routing protocol on the link. (So the ISP is less dependent on customer configuration skills.)

Since we have already explored the first two ASBR situations in this chapter already, for the NSSA example, we will use the last scenario. Here, the static route redistributed by OSPF makes the router into an OSPF ASBR, since this routing information did not come from OSPF but from an "external" source (the static route).

In this section we configure a new ABR to link to ASBR0 in Area 0. The new ABR, ABR4, links to Area 4, which is defined as an NSSA. Another router, ASBR4, is added to the NSSA Area 4. The Juniper Networks JUNOS software configuration steps for ABR4 and ASBR4 are given, but not for ASBR0. Then we investigate the routing tables and link-state databases for ABR4 and ASBR4. The portion of the network configured in this section is shown in Figure 10.5.

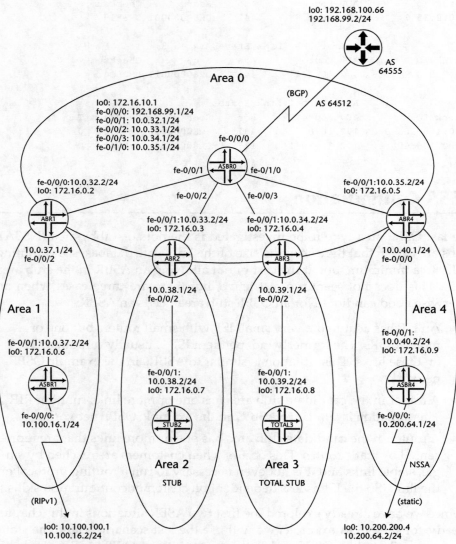

Figure 10.5 Adding the NSSA Area 4 configuration.

This section assumes that ASBR4 has a static route defined for customer network 10.200.64.0/24 on interface fe-0/0/2 with IP address 10.200.64.1/24. The configuration of static routes has been covered several times earlier in this book and is not detailed again. The 10.200.64.0/24 static route is redistributed into OSPF on ASBR4 using a simple `send-statics` routing policy applied as an OSPF `export` policy on the interface to ABR4. This procedure also has been covered before and is not detailed.

Like other stubs, the ABR for an NSSA will not send Type 5 External LSAs into the stub area. But an NSSA is not necessarily a total stub, and in fact the RFC 1587 for NSSAs explicitly states that Summary LSAs should be sent into the NSSA to guarantee optimal routing to the ABRs. However, it is common to make a "total stub not-so-stubby-area" by sending only a default Summary LSA into the NSSA. Unless `no-summaries` is specified in the ABR configuration, all of the details about destinations in other areas, but within the AS, will be flooded into the NSSA. Again, most of these routes will be reached through ABR4, so it makes sense to turn off summaries and advertise a single default route into the NSSA from ABR4.

The following is the NSSA area configuration for ASBR4, including the policy to have OSPF redistribute the static route:

```
[edit protocols]
lab@ASBR4# set ospf area 4 nssa
[edit protocols]
lab@ASBR4# set ospf area 4 interface fe-0/0/1
[edit protocols]
lab@ASBR4# set ospf export send-static
[edit protocols]
lab@ASBR4# show
ospf {
    export send-static;
    area 0.0.0.4 {
        nssa;
        interface fe-0/0/1.0;
    }
}
```

Following is the NSSA OSPF Area 0 and Area 4 configuration for ABR4, including the default metric that replaces the Type 3 Summary LSAs:

```
[edit protocols]
lab@ABR4# set ospf area 4 nssa default-metric 20 no-summaries
[edit protocols]
lab@ABR4# set ospf area 4 interface fe-0/0/0
[edit protocols]
lab@ABR4# show
```

```
ospf {
    area 0.0.0.0 {
        interface fe-0/0/1.0
    area 0.0.0.4 {
        nssa {
            default-metric 20;
            no-summaries;
        }
        interface fe-0/0/0.0;
    }
}
```

The metric on the default route is now set to 20. The configuration looks a little different because an NSSA has more options than other types of stubs.

Viewing the Routing Table and Link-State Database

The routing table and link-state database for ABR4 are shown as follows. The link-state database, but not the routing table, is now identical on ASBR0 and all other Area 0 routers. The routing table on ABR4 now shows just about every route in the entire AS:

```
lab@ABR4> show route
inet.0: 23 destinations, 23 routes (23 active, 0 holddown, 0 hidden)
+ = Active Route, - = Last Active, * = Both

10.0.32.0/24       *[OSPF/10] 00:06:29, metric 2
                    > to 10.0.35.1 via fe-0/0/1.0
10.0.33.0/24       *[OSPF/10] 00:06:29, metric 2
                    > to 10.0.35.1 via fe-0/0/1.0
10.0.34.0/24       *[OSPF/10] 00:06:29, metric 2
                    > to 10.0.35.1 via fe-0/0/1.0
10.0.35.0/24       *[Direct/0] 00:26:44
                    > via fe-0/0/1.0
10.0.35.2/32       *[Local/0] 00:26:47
                     Local via fe-0/0/1.0
10.0.37.0/24       *[OSPF/10] 00:06:29, metric 3
                    > to 10.0.35.1 via fe-0/0/1.0
10.0.38.0/24       *[OSPF/10] 00:06:29, metric 3
                    > to 10.0.35.1 via fe-0/0/1.0
10.0.39.0/24       *[OSPF/10] 00:06:29, metric 3
                    > to 10.0.35.1 via fe-0/0/1.0
10.0.40.0/24       *[Direct/0] 00:26:47
                    > via fe-0/0/0.0
10.0.40.1/32       *[Local/0] 00:26:47
                     Local via fe-0/0/0.0
10.100.100.0/24    *[OSPF/150] 00:06:29, metric 2, tag 0
                    > to 10.0.35.1 via fe-0/0/1.0
```

```
10.200.200.0/24     *[OSPF/150] 00:06:19, metric 0, tag 0
                     > to 10.0.40.2 via fe-0/0/0.0
172.16.0.2/32       *[OSPF/10] 00:06:29, metric 2
                     > to 10.0.35.1 via fe-0/0/1.0
172.16.0.3/32       *[OSPF/10] 00:06:29, metric 2
                     > to 10.0.35.1 via fe-0/0/1.0
172.16.0.4/32       *[OSPF/10] 00:06:29, metric 2
                     > to 10.0.35.1 via fe-0/0/1.0
172.16.0.5/32       *[Direct/0] 00:26:47
                     > via lo0.0
172.16.0.6/32       *[OSPF/10] 00:06:29, metric 3
                     > to 10.0.35.1 via fe-0/0/1.0
172.16.0.7/32       *[OSPF/10] 00:06:29, metric 3
                     > to 10.0.35.1 via fe-0/0/1.0
172.16.0.8/32       *[OSPF/10] 00:06:29, metric 3
                     > to 10.0.35.1 via fe-0/0/1.0
172.16.0.9/32       *[OSPF/10] 00:06:19, metric 1
                     > to 10.0.40.2 via fe-0/0/0.0
172.16.10.1/32      *[OSPF/10] 00:06:29, metric 1
                     > to 10.0.35.1 via fe-0/0/1.0
192.168.100.0/24    *[OSPF/150] 00:06:29, metric 0, tag 0
                     > to 10.0.35.1 via fe-0/0/1.0
224.0.0.5/32        *[OSPF/10] 09:13:27, metric 1
```

Note that the third external route, the static route on ASBR4 to 10.200.200.4, is now listed and distributed to all of the other OSPF areas. The ABR4 link-state database follows:

```
lab@ABR4> show ospf database
     OSPF link state database, area 0.0.0.0


Type       ID            Adv Rtr       Seq         Age   Opt  Cksum   Len
Router     172.16.0.2    172.16.0.2    0x8000001e  1545  0x2  0xa9e7  48
Router     172.16.0.3    172.16.0.3    0x80000011  492   0x2  0xdfb9  48
Router     172.16.0.4    172.16.0.4    0x80000009  870   0x2  0x1685  48
Router    *172.16.0.5    172.16.0.5    0x80000007  638   0x2  0x3c5a  48
Router     172.16.10.1   172.16.10.1   0x80000032  142   0x2  0xf32d  84
Network    10.0.32.1     172.16.10.1   0x80000028  442   0x2  0x4c6d  32
Network    10.0.33.1     172.16.10.1   0x80000010  742   0x2  0x7f50  32
Network    10.0.34.2     172.16.0.4    0x80000005  1170  0x2  0xdeff  32
Network   *10.0.35.2     172.16.0.5    0x80000003  151   0x2  0xdb02  32
Summary    10.0.37.0     172.16.0.2    0x80000013  210   0x2  0x97c4  28
Summary    10.0.38.0     172.16.0.3    0x8000000f  33    0x2  0x8ecf  28
Summary    10.0.39.0     172.16.0.4    0x80000007  1770  0x2  0x8dd6  28
Summary   *10.0.40.0     172.16.0.5    0x80000005  623   0x2  0x80e3  28
Summary    172.16.0.6    172.16.0.2    0x80000008  75    0x2  0x7cc   28
Summary    172.16.0.7    172.16.0.3    0x80000007  1992  0x2  0xf8d9  28
Summary    172.16.0.8    172.16.0.4    0x80000003  1471  0x2  0xf0e3  28
```

```
Summary  *172.16.0.9  172.16.0.5   0x80000001  623  0x2  0xe4ef  28
ASBRSum   172.16.0.6  172.16.0.2   0x80000008   45  0x2  0xf8d9  28
ASBRSum  *172.16.0.9  172.16.0.5   0x80000001  623  0x2  0xd6fc  28

     OSPF link state database, area 0.0.0.4
  Type      ID          Adv Rtr       Seq      Age  Opt  Cksum  Len
Router  *172.16.0.5  172.16.0.5   0x80000005  628  0x0  0xbed2  48
Router   172.16.0.9  172.16.0.9   0x80000009  205  0x0  0xd9a7  48
Network  10.0.40.2   172.16.0.9   0x80000004  633  0x0  0x8651  32
NSSA    *0.0.0.0     172.16.0.5   0x80000001  638  0x0  0x7904  36
NSSA     10.200.200.0 172.16.0.9  0x80000003  505  0x8  0xbde3  36
     OSPF external link state database
  Type      ID          Adv Rtr       Seq      Age  Opt  Cksum  Len
Extern  10.100.100.0 172.16.0.6  0x80000021  414  0x2  0x78a2  36
Extern*10.200.200.0  172.16.0.5   0x80000001  623  0x2  0xa5cf  36
Extern  192.168.100.0 172.16.10.1 0x8000001d 1042  0x2  0xc957  36
```

The Area 0 link-state database grows and grows, adding information about every router and link, even in other areas. This is what the OSPF backbone is for. Yet the NSSA link-state database is quite compact. The NSSA default 0.0.0.0 route (LSA Type = 7) is originated by ABR4 (172.16.0.5), and the NSSA External LSA is originated by ASBR4 (172.16.0.9).

Note that the other Type 7 LSA for the static route on ASBR4 (10.200.200.0) is translated into a Type 5 LSA (extern) by ABR4. This is the default behavior for ABRs attached to NSSAs. It is possible to block Type 7 LSAs at the ABR and prevent their circulation around the AS as Type 5 LSAs by IP address range. For example, to block the 10.200.200.0 route information from leaving the NSSA as a Type 5 LSA, the statement `area-range 10.200.200.0/24 restrict` can be added to the NSSA configuration on ABR4.

Here is the routing table and link-state database for ASBR4:

```
lab@ASBR4> show route
inet.0: 9 destinations, 9 routes (9 active, 0 holddown, 0 hidden)
+ = Active Route, - = Last Active, * = Both

0.0.0.0/0            *[OSPF/150] 00:19:13, metric 21, tag 0
                     > to 10.0.40.1 via fe-0/0/1.0
10.0.40.0/24         *[Direct/0] 00:42:14
                     > via fe-0/0/1.0
10.0.40.2/32         *[Local/0] 00:42:16
                       Local via fe-0/0/1.0
10.200.64.0/24       *[Direct/0] 00:42:16
                     > via fe-0/0/0.0
10.200.64.1/32       *[Local/0] 00:42:15
                       Local via fe-0/0/0.0
10.200.200.0/24      *[Static/5] 00:42:16
                     > to 10.200.64.2 via fe-0/0/0.0
```

```
172.16.0.5/32        *[OSPF/10] 00:19:13, metric 1
                     > to 10.0.40.1 via fe-0/0/1.0
172.16.0.9/32        *[Direct/0] 00:42:16
                     > via lo0.0
224.0.0.5/32         *[OSPF/10] 00:47:10, metric 1
```

Note that for an NSSA, the default route is now an *external* route (OSPF/150) and the default is now an NSSA LSA (Type = 7).

```
lab@ASBR4> show ospf database
    OSPF link state database, area 0.0.0.4


Type        ID          Adv Rtr        Seq        Age  Opt  Cksum   Len
Router    172.16.0.5  172.16.0.5   0x80000005  1159  0x0  0xbed2   48
Router   *172.16.0.9  172.16.0.9   0x80000009   734  0x0  0xd9a7   48
Network  *10.0.40.2   172.16.0.9   0x80000005   434  0x0  0x8452   32
NSSA      0.0.0.0     172.16.0.5   0x80000002    82  0x0  0x7705   36
NSSA    *10.200.200.0 172.16.0.9   0x80000004   134  0x8  0xbbe4   36
```

ASBR4 NSSA Cisco Configuration

All previous Cisco configurations have made the Cisco router an ABR or Area 0 backbone router. For the sake of variety, in this final section we'll make the Cisco router Cisco_ASBR4 and keep ABR4 as a Juniper Networks router. The static route remains on Cisco_ASBR4 mapped to the "customer" link, but the configuration for that route is not shown. Of course, OSPF will have to redistribute this static, as did the Juniper Networks ASBR4. The basic OSPF configuration is as follows:

```
Cisco_ASBR4#conf t
Enter configuration commands, one per line.  End with CNTL/Z.
Cisco_ASBR4(config)#router ospf 10
Cisco_ASBR4(config-router)#redistribute static subnets
Cisco_ASBR4(config-router)#network 10.0.40.2 0.0.0.0 area 4
Cisco_ASBR4(config-router)#network 172.16.0.9 0.0.0.0 area 4
Cisco_ASBR4(config-router)#area 4 nssa
```

Although not used in this example, it should be noted that no-summary is an allowable option, as with Juniper Networks routers. The following is the relevant portion of the configuration:

```
hostname Cisco_ASBR4
!
router ospf 10
```

```
        network 10.0.40.2 0.0.0.0 area 4
        network 172.16.0.9 0.0.0.0 area 4
        area 4 nssa
```

The Cisco_ASBR4 routing table, which has exactly the same information as in the Juniper Networks router ASBR4 routing table, follows:

```
Cisco_ASBR4#sh ip route

Codes:C - connected,S - static,I - IGRP,R - RIP,M - mobile,B - BGP
      D - EIGRP,EX - EIGRP external,O - OSPF,IA - OSPF inter area
      N1 - OSPF NSSA external type 1, E2 - OSPF NSSA external type 2
      E1 - OSPF external type 1,E2 - OSPF external type 2,E - EGP
      i - IS-IS,L1 - IS-IS level-1,L2 - IS-IS level-2,* - candidate
default


Gateway of last resort is 10.0.40.1 to network 0.0.0.0

     172.16.0.0/32 is subnetted, 2 subnets
C       172.16.0.9 is directly connected, Loopback0
O       172.16.0.5 [110/1] via 10.0.40.1, 00:02:57, FastEthernet0
     10.0.0.0/24 is subnetted, 4 subnets
S       10.200.200.0 [1/0] via 10.200.64.1, 00:02:57, FastEthernet1
C       10.0.40.0 is directly connected, FastEthernet0
C       10.200.64.0 Is directly connected, FastEthernet1
O*N1 0.0.0.0/0 [110/21] via 10.0.40.1, 00:02:57, FastEthernet0
```

Note that the default route is tagged as an N1 OSPF route. N1 and N2 are special tags used in the same way as E1 and E2 to identify the cost of routes outside the NSSA. N1 means that the external cost (20) advertised by the Juniper Networks ABR4 is added to the internal cost of getting to ABR4 (1). If the route were an N2 route, the cost would be 20 instead of 21.

The following is the link-state database on Cisco_ASBR4:

```
Cisco_ASBR4#sh ip ospf database
OSPF Router with ID (172.16.0.9) (Process ID 10)

                Router Link States (Area 4)

Link ID         ADV Router      Age     Seq#        Checksum Link

172.16.0.5      172.16.0.5      41      0x8000000E 0xA2E6    2
172.16.0.9      172.16.0.9      45      0x80000007 0xCD5D    2


                Net Link States (Area 4)
Link ID         ADV Router      Age     Seq#        Checksum
```

```
10.0.40.2        172.16.0.9       46            0x80000001 0xBE21


                 Type-7 AS External Link States (Area 4)
Link ID          ADV Router       Age           Seq#       Checksum Tag
0.0.0.0          172.16.0.5       136           0x80000003 0x7506   0
10.200.200.0     172.16.0.9       134           0x80000004 0xbbe4   0
```

Although this example did not configure a Cisco router as NSSA ABR4, there is not much difference in the configurations. The default route from a Cisco_ABR4 router would be generated with the area 4 nssa no-summary statement. Translation of the NSSA Type 7 LSA for 10.200.200.0 into a Type 5 LSA for the rest of the AS is automatic, as in Juniper Networks routers. The Type 7 LSA information for 10.200.200.0 can be restricted to the NSSA itself with the summary-address 10.200.200.0 255.255.255.0 not-advertise statement.

CHAPTER 11

Intermediate System–
Intermediate System (IS-IS)

OSPF is not the only link-state routing protocol that ISPs use within an AS. The other common link-state routing protocol is IS-IS, which stands for Intermediate System–Intermediate System. Although most people just use the term IS-IS (properly pronounced as individual letters—*I-S-I-S*), or even ISIS (pronounced *eye-sis*), when IS-IS is used with IP, the proper term to use is *Integrated IS-IS*. The reason for such seemingly odd terminology as "intermediate system" in IS-IS is that this protocol is a product of the International Organization for Standardization (ISO). The acronym ISO comes from their standards series, all of which are ISO ("equal" in Greek), or open with respect to implementation— in theory at least. Despite its successful use on the Internet, IS-IS is not an IP routing protocol at all. It is an ISO protocol that has been adapted (integrated) for IP in order to carry IP routing information inside of non-IP packets.

The non-IP roots of IS-IS should never be forgotten or underestimated. IS-IS packets are not IP packets; they are CLNP (Connectionless Network Protocol) packets. CLNP packets do not have IP source and destination addresses; they have ISO addresses. CLNP packets are not used for the transfer of user traffic from client to server, at least not normally. Instead, they are used for the transfer of link-state routing information between routers alone. In fact, IS-IS does not have routers at all. Routers are called *intermediate systems* to distinguish them from the client and server *end systems* (ESs) that send and receive traffic.

The nondependence of IS-IS on IP has advantages and disadvantages. One advantage is that network problems can often be isolated to IP itself if IS-IS is up and running between two routers. One big disadvantage is that there are now sources and destinations on the network (the ISO addresses) that are not even pingable. And if a link between two routers is misconfigured with incorrect IP addresses (such as 10.0.32.2/24 on one router and 10.0.33.1/24 on the other), IS-IS will still come up and exchange routing information over the link, but IP will not work correctly, leaving network administrators wondering why the routing protocol is fine but the routes are broken. Independence and invisibility go hand in hand with IS-IS.

Naturally, much more can be said about IS-IS than appears in this chapter. We devote much of this chapter to introducing IS-IS terminology such as link-state protocol data unit (LSP) for OSPF's link-state advertisement (LSA) and contrasting IS-IS's behavior with OSPFs.

The Attraction of IS-IS

If IS-IS is used instead of OSPF as an IGP within an AS, there must be strong reasons for doing so. No one ever wants to introduce a new type of packet onto the network just for fun, and even the seemingly simple task of assigning ISO addresses to routers can be a chore. As it turns out, many ISPs see IS-IS as much more flexible and forgiving than OSPF with regard to structuring the AS.

IS-IS routers can form both Level 1 (L1) and Level 2 (L2) adjacencies. L1 links connect routers in the same IS-IS area, and L2 links connect routers in different areas. More details about IS-IS levels and areas are discussed later in this chapter.

IS-IS does not demand that traffic sent between areas traverse a special backbone area (Area 0.0.0.0) as does OSPF. OSPF backdoor links are a workaround but frowned upon in OSPF specifications. IS-IS does not care if inter-area traffic uses a special area or not; the traffic just needs to get there. In the example used in Chapter 9, "Open Shortest Path First (OSPF)," the Tampa-to-Orlando traffic would not have to travel through two other states to get to its destination. A simple link configured correctly using IS-IS between Tampa and Orlando can carry the traffic and not violate the sensibilities of purists.

The same is true when it comes to pasting new areas onto existing areas, as when a larger ISP acquires a smaller one. Again using an example from Chapter 9, a router in Phoenix need not be made into an ABR or use a virtual link or employ some other workaround. Just paste the new area wherever it makes sense and configure IS-IS L1/L2 routers in the right places. IS-IS takes care of everything else.

A backbone area, such as it exists in IS-IS, is simply a contiguous collection of routers in different areas capable of running L2 IS-IS. That the routers must be directly connected (contiguous) to form the backbone is not too much of a limitation, since most non-edge routers considered for a backbone usually have multiple connections. Each and every IS-IS backbone router can be in a different area. If a more traditional AS structure along the lines of a centralized OSPF is desired, IS-IS could accomplish this simply enough. It would just add certain routers (properly connected) as L2-only routers in one selected area (the backbone), connect areas adjacent to this central area with L1/L2 routers, and make the rest of the routers in the outlying areas L1-only routers.

The attraction of IS-IS today is in this type of flexibility compared to OSPF. This certainly makes more sense that the dogmatic protocol wars that raged from the mid-1980s into the 1990s, until the Web hit town.

My Protocol's Better Than Yours

How should computers with different architectures and internal representations talk to one another over networks? The problem is similar but nowhere near as complex as the need for all humans to communicate despite the vastly different languages spoken. About 6,000 languages are in use around the world (half of them in New Guinea, oddly enough). How can any two people who meet anywhere, anytime, communicate?

In actuality, there are only two real ways to establish this universal linguistic interoperability. Either everyone speaks just one language or everyone speaks exactly two languages: their native tongue and one (constructed) language to be used whenever a person is encountered that speaks a different language than the local dialect. The Internet and IP take the first approach. Want to communicate over the Internet? Learn IP. Forget anything else. The second approach was advocated by a networking group in the late 1970s working within ISO and the International Telecommunication Union (ITU). Their solution is called the Open Systems Interconnection Reference Model, or OSI-RM. This "language" is not advocated as a replacement for anything else, as is sometimes claimed. The OSI-RM is simply a way for computers running IBM's SNA, for example, to communicate in an open and standard fashion with computers running, for instance, DEC's DECnet protocol.

The OSI-RM enjoyed a brief period of popularity in the mid-1980s, when the U.S. government, faced with a computer industry known as "IBM and the seven dwarfs," was struggling to build networks out of IBM, DEC, Wang, Xerox, HP, CDC, and a few others computers, when all of them ran only their own proprietary protocols such as DECnet, WangNet, and so on. (No one accused these companies of being overly imaginative.) After all, who knew better how to network IBM computers than IBM? Only Wang knew the internals of their minicomputers well enough to tune its networking protocols, and so on, or so the feelings at the time went.

The U.S. government went so far as to announce that after a certain date, only computers running open and standard implementations of the OSI-RM would be bought. This sent everyone in the industry into a frenzy, not only because the U.S. government was the largest buyer of computers in the world but also because at the time no stable implementations of OSI-RM existed anywhere. It struck the Internet people as odd that the federal government, quietly using IP all over its own network, had seemingly shoved IP aside in favor of a vision of world protocol harmony. But IP at the time was perceived as a research protocol, unfit for everyday use on production networks, and it was looked at with suspicion by other countries as a military protocol. Even so, in the United States only DEC really embraced OSI-RM-compliant, open software for networking, some thought as a way to embarrass IBM over its highly proprietary SNA.

The conflict was brief and the outcome never really in doubt. ISO had nothing to compare with the Internet. The OSI-RM was and is best seen as a *model* of a network, not really as a way to do networking in and of itself. Any lasting interest in the OSI-RM died when the Web became a part of everyone's life. When the Soviet Union fell (one of the few remaining champions of OSI-RM software) the Internet came to Moscow, and the Russian decision makers decided that IP was not a capitalist plot after all. (The other outpost of the OSI-RM was France, where until recently there were fewer Web sites per capita than in any other industrialized country.)

The OSI-RM lives on today mainly as a teaching tool, and a very successful one at that. The seven-layer OSI-RM is often a student's first introduction to networking. Anyone who refers to IP as a Layer 3 protocol is speaking of the OSI-RM, because in the TCP/IP stack, IP remains firmly at the second layer of the TCP/IP architecture. The other lasting legacy of the OSI-RM is IS-IS.

IS-IS and OSPF

ISO's version of a packet network protocol was CLNP. To distribute routing information from router (IS to the OSI-RM) to host (End System in the OSI-RM), ISO also invented ES-IS to get routing information from routers to and from clients and servers, and IS-IS to move this information around between routers. Everyone was painfully aware of the limitations of RIP, and maybe a stable, well-functioning link-state protocol would be just the thing to give OSI-RM-compliant software the push it needed to give IP (and the other vendor-specific offerings) some real competition if IS-IS proved better than OSPF.

IS-IS came out of DEC as part of that company's effort to complete DECnet Phase V. Standardized as ISO 10589 in 1992, for a while it was even thought that IS-IS would be the natural progression from IP and OSPF to a better place where OSI-RM-compliant software ran on networks everywhere. And OSPF was indeed struggling at the time. To ease the forecast transition period from IP to OSI-RM, *Integrated IS-IS* (sometimes called *Dual IS-IS*) was developed to carry routing information for both IP and ISO protocols.

ISO let a huge early lead over OSPF evaporate in an awkward environment of political and parochial maneuvering that saw standards rejected because of spelling, of all things (it's "routeing" not "routing" in some places). The offending IS-IS terms had to be fixed and the approval process repeated from step one. OSPF soon got its act together, somewhat ironically by freely borrowing what had been shown to work in IS-IS. Today OSPF is the recommended IGP to run on the Internet, but IS-IS still has adherents for the reasons of flexibility cited previously. Of course, one person's flexibility is another person's chaos, and OSPF has much to recommend it as well.

Similarities between IS-IS and OSPF

IS-IS and OSPF share a lot of similarities, namely:

- Both IS-IS and OSPF are link-state protocols that maintain a link-state database and run an SPF (shortest path first) algorithm based on the Dijkstra algorithm to compute a shortest-path tree of routes.

- Both use Hello packets to create and maintain adjacencies between neighboring routers.

- Both use areas that can be arranged into a two-level hierarchy of inter-area and intra-area routes.

- Both can summarize addresses advertised between their areas.

- Both are classless protocols and can handle VLSM with ease.

- Both will elect a designated router on broadcast networks, although IS-IS calls it a Designated Intermediate System (DIS).

- Both can be configured with authentication methods.

Differences between IS-IS and OSPF

Many of the differences between IS-IS and OSPF are differences of terminology. For example, IS-IS uses the term *intermediate systems* and *end systems* for routers and hosts, as already mentioned; a Subnetwork Point of Attachment (SNPA) is used instead of an interface, and protocol data units (PDUs) instead of packets. OSPF LSAs are now IS-IS Link-State PDUs (LSPs) and LSPs are packets all on their own and do not use OSPF's LSA-OSPF Header-IP packet encapsulation.

But not all IS-IS and OSPF differences are minor. Many of them are quite profound and worthy of some investigation in detail.

Areas

Perhaps the most fundamental difference between IS-IS and OSPF is the way that they define their areas. In OSPF, ABRs sit on the borders of areas, with one or more interfaces in one area and other interfaces in other areas. In IS-IS, a router (technically, an IS) is either totally in one area or another, and it is the links between the routers that connect the areas. This difference between OSPF and IS-IS is shown in Figure 11.1. One reason that IS-IS routers must sit in one area or another is that unlike IP, which assigns addresses to every interface, IS-IS typically assigns only one ISO address to the whole router.

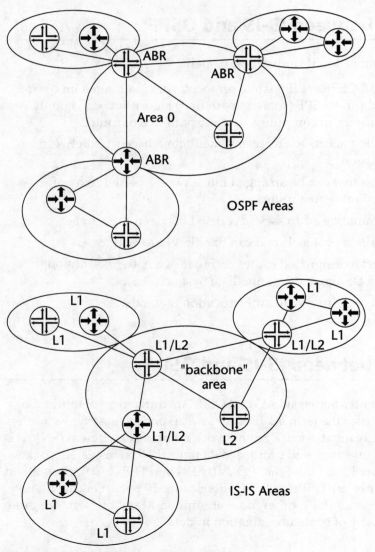

Figure 11.1 OSPF areas and IS-IS areas.

Routers that have all of their links within the same area are called L1 (Level 1) routers and routers that have links to connect other areas are called L2 (Level 2 routers). Some routers have both types of links and so are L1/L2 (sometimes seen as L2/L1) routers. L1 routers are very much like OSPF routers in a total stub area. That is, L1 routers know little more than how to reach an L2 router for routes beyond their immediate area. L2 routers are like OSPF backbone routers, and an IS-IS backbone area is frequently just an area where all of the routers are configured to run L2 only on all their links, although technically L1/L2 routers adjacent to these L2 only routers are part of the IS-IS backbone. L1/L2 routers are much like OSPF ABRs, but IS-IS L1/L2 routers do not send any L2 routes to L1 routers, in keeping with the total stub nature of L1 routers. Instead, a single default route is advertised to L1 routers to reach all other areas in the AS. There are even completely separate metrics for L1 and L2 routes.

L1/L2 routers maintain two link-state databases, one for L1 and the other for L2. All of the L1 routers have identical link-state databases, and all inter-area traffic transits L1/L2 routers. L1 routers lack the specifics of external routes and so must forward packets to an L1/L2 router for destinations outside their local area. An L1 router can find an L1/L2 router because when an L1/L2 router sends its LSPs on an L1 only link, it sets the Attached (ATT) bit in the LSP.

Two routers running IS-IS become neighbors in the following situations:

For Level 1.   The two routers sharing a common network segment must have their interfaces configured to be in the same area if they are to have a Level 1 adjacency.

For Level 2.   The two routers sharing a common network segment must be configured as Level 2 if they are in different areas and want to become neighbors.

Authentication.   The two routers must agree on authentication method (if used) and the password. IS-IS allows configuration of a password for an individual link, area, or for an entire routing domain (AS).

Route Leaking

This L1 routing toward an L1/L2 router by default might seem haphazard at best, since L1 routers have no information about the structure of the AS as a whole. When there are multiple L1/L2 routers available to an L1 router, the L1 router simply picks the closest one in terms of the IS-IS metric without regard for the destination of the packet. An L1/L2 router in an area might have a direct link to the destination, but if another L1/L2 router in the area is closer, the source router has no choice but to use the default to the closer L1/L2 router. L1 routers have a link-state database with information only about their local area, while L1/L2 routers maintain separate L1 and L2 link-state data-bases and topology information and so know a lot more about the network than the L1 routers.

Having a mechanism in IS-IS to allow L2 information to be made available to L1 routers would be helpful. L2 information being redistributed into L1 areas is called *route leaking*, defined in RFC 2966. A bit called the Up/Down bit is used to distinguish routes that are local to the L1 area (Up/Down = 0) from those that have been leaked in the area from an L1/L2 router (Up/Down = 1). This is necessary to prevent potential routing loops. An L1/L2 router will never redistribute an L1 route with the Up/Down bit set to 1 to an L2 router, since that route originated in L2 in the first place. This possibility is shown in Figure 11.2.

Router A's LSP is leaked into an L1 area. But why would this LSP, which knows how to reach Router A, ever be sent back to L2? Using L1 is a very roundabout way to reach Router A at that point. Route leaking is really a way to make IS-IS areas with LI-only routers as smart as OSPF routers in not-so-stubby-areas (NSSAs).

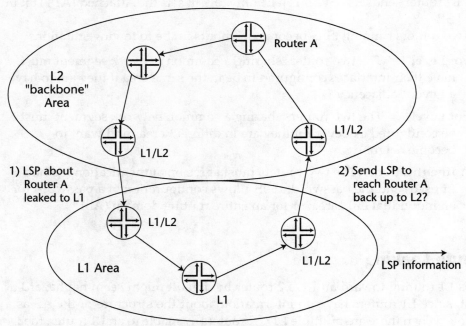

Figure 11.2 Route leaking and the Up/Down bit.

Network Addresses

IS-IS is not an IP protocol, and CLNP does not use IP addresses in its packets. IS-IS packets use a single *ISO area address* (Area ID) for the entire router because the router must be within one area or another. Every IS-IS router can have up to three different area ISO addresses, but this chapter only uses one ISO address per router. The ISO Area ID is combined with an *ISO system address* (System ID) to give the ISO *Network Entity Title*, or NET. Every router running IS-IS must be given an ISO NET as described in ISO 8348.

Because the NET is used on networks other than router networks, such as X.25 or Telex networks, the NET is designed to be very flexible. The length can range from 8 to 20 bytes (octets). The Area ID portion of the NET is used by L2 routers to route packets between IS-IS areas, and the System ID portion is used by L1 routers to route within an area. In both Cisco and Juniper Networks router implementations, the System ID field is always 6 bytes long. There is a 1-byte *Selector* field (SEL) at the end of the NET that is usually set to 0x00 and called an *N-selector* in router networks. Nonzero SEL values function a little like sockets in TCP/IP, but routers only send CLNP packets back and forth between themselves with SEL = 0x00, meaning a packet for the network (routing protocol) layer itself.

The Area ID is itself composed of a variable number of fields. Routers usually just take whatever length NET is configured and subtract the last 7 bytes for System ID and SEL fields. Whatever is left is by definition the Area ID. Routers do not usually parse the Area ID field further: If the Area IDs match, it's an L1 route; otherwise, it's an inter-area L2 route.

When ISO NETs are used with IS-IS on IP routers, the structure of the NET should comply with RFC 1237, which maps NETs for use on IP networks. When used on routers, this means that the NET should begin with a single byte with the value 0x47. This is the *Authority and Format Identifier* (AFI) field, and the number 47 is used on the Internet. However, this requires the acquisition of a public and unique prefix from a recognized authority. So this book will use an AFI of 49 for examples. This value is for the private or local use of NETs and should not be used on networks connected to the Internet or another public network. Usually, a 2-byte area value follows the private AFI value of 49, although other forms are allowed. So in its simplest form, an ISO NET used on an IS-IS router is 10 bytes long and looks like 49.XXXX.YYYY.YYYY.YYYY.00, where XXXX is the Area ID and YYYY.YYYY.YYYY is the System ID.

The Area IDs are just assigned as a network administrator pleases, usually 0000 for the IS-IS backbone, if there is one, and 0001, 0002, and so on for the other IS-IS areas in the AS. The only real question remaining is how to assign the System ID address. Typically, this is the IP address of the loopback interface on the router, and so might be the equivalent of the OSPF Router ID, especially when OSPF and IS-IS are running on the same router (not common, but possible). The alternative, commonly used in Cisco router networks, is to use the 6-byte MAC address of one of the interfaces on the router as the 6-byte System ID field in the NET. Since the router does not rely on this physical interface for IS-IS purposes, even if the interface is down, the IS-IS NET is still reachable and functioning on the other interfaces.

You can map IP addresses to the System ID field of the NET two ways. Neither is perfect, and both are often used. The first way is to simply take an IP address such as 172.16.10.1 and rewrite it with leading zeros as 172.016. 010.001. Then the dots are moved to create the three fields of the ISO System ID: 1720.1601.0001. This is fine, but it is sometimes hard to see the IP address buried in the System ID. A second method just zero-fills and moves the dots differently. So 172.16.10.1 becomes 0172.0016.1001. This method works fine as long as the third and fourth bytes of the IP address are only two digits (common enough on most networks). The advantage of the second method is that it is easier to read the System ID as the IP address of the router. The advantage of the first method is that it places no restrictions at all on the IP address and always works.

All of these possibilities are shown in Figure 11.3.

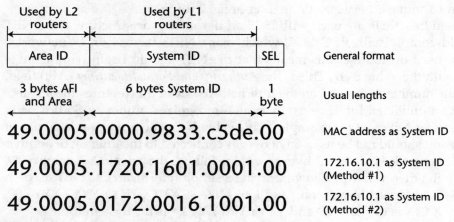

Figure 11.3 NET format and the values of the ISO System ID.

Network Types

OSPF has five different link or network types that OSPF can be configured to run on: point-to-point, broadcast, nonbroadcast multiaccess (NBMA), point-to-multipoint, and virtual links. In contrast, IS-IS defines only two types of links or *subnetworks*: broadcast (LANs) and point-to-point (called *general topology*) links. This really boils down to links that can support multicasting (broadcast) and so should use a Designated Router (IS-IS calls it a Designated Intermediate System, or DIS) and links that do not support multicasting.

IS-IS forms separate adjacencies for L1 and L2 neighbors with separate L1 and L2 Hello PDUs. L1 routers become adjacent to L1 and L1/L2 routers, and L2 routers become adjacent to L2 and L1/L2 routers. Adjacent L1/L2 routers form both L1 and L2 adjacencies (sometimes called L3 adjacencies to keep the single-digit format). Unlike OSPF, the dead interval is not four times the default Hello interval, but three times the Hello interval.

The default Hello interval also varies by IS-IS link type. LANs use a default 3/9 second Hello/dead timer, and nonbroadcast links use a default 9/27 second Hello/dead timer. This is mainly because, unlike OSPF, there is no backup DIS and so DIS failures must be detected quickly and a new DIS elected rapidly.

Designated Intermediate System (DIS)

Although IS-IS technically uses a Designated Intermediate System, it is still common to refer to these devices as a designated router (DR). The point is still the same: The DIS or DR represents the entire multi-access network link (such as a LAN) as a single *pseudonode*. The pseudonode (a *virtual node* in some documentation) does not really exist, but there are LSPs that are issued for the entire multi-access network as if the pseudonode were a real device. LSPs issued on behalf of the pseudonode by the DIS are identified by a non-zero Pseudonode ID (such as 0x02) that is usually appended to the System ID field in the LSP ID field of the router's link-state database. When this final field is 0x00, the link is not a broadcast link using a DIS.

Unlike OSPF, all IS-IS routers on a pseudonode (such as a LAN) are always fully adjacent to the pseudonode. This is because of the lack of a backup DIS, and new DIS elections must take place quickly.

IS-IS DISs also have a priority like OSPF, but the IS-IS priority runs between 0 (not DSI eligible) and 127 (highest priority). There are both L1 and L2 priorities, and both Cisco and Juniper Networks routers make the default value 64.

A router can be an L1 DIS and not the L2 DIS or the other way around, because of the different priorities. Nonbroadcast links have a priority of 0. In case of a priority tie, the numerically highest System ID is elected DIS. (Some texts say highest MAC address, but this is true only if the MAC address is mapped to the System ID of the NET).

In contrast to OSPF, an IS-IS DIS can be preempted if a new router with a higher priority appears on the network. Presumably, if a router is assigned a higher DIS priority, there is a reason and this new router should be the DIS. This is even true if the new router with equal priority only has a higher System ID. So all things being equal, if a new router with a higher loopback address appears on a LAN, the DIS immediately shifts to the new router, and all new LSPs are flooded on behalf of the pseudonode. If DIS stability is desired in IS-IS (for instance, the router on the LAN with the main WAN link is desired to be the DIS), then priorities should reflect this.

LSP Handling

IS-IS routers handle LSPs differently than OSPF routers handle LSAs. While OSPF LSAs age from 0 to a maximum (MaxAge) value of 3,600 seconds (1 hour), IS-IS LSPs age downward from a MaxAge of 1,200 seconds (20 minutes) to 0. The normal refresh interval is 15 minutes. Since IS-IS does not use IP addresses, use of multicast addresses cannot be used in IS-IS for LSP distribution. Instead, a MAC destination address of 0180.c200.0014 (AllL1ISs) is used to carry L1 LSPs to L1 ISs (routers), and a MAC destination address of 0180.c200.0015 (AllL2ISs) is used to carry L2 LSPs to L2 ISs (routers)

A more technical difference between IS-IS and OSPF involves the purging of link-state database entries. Suppose, for example, an IS-IS router receives an LSP with an invalid checksum. This router immediately sets the LSP remaining lifetime value to 0 and refloods the LSP, effectively purging this LSP from the IS-IS routers' databases and causing the originator to reissue a new LSP. In OSPF, only the originator is supposed to purge an LSA, but most router vendors implement a `purge ospf database` command that makes OSPF mimic the IS-IS behavior. However, the IS-IS-anybody-purge behavior can increase LSP traffic. OSPF relies on acknowledgments to detect errored LSAs and so ignores these LSAs. IS-IS can mimic this ignore-bad-LSPs behavior on most routers with some form of `ignore lsp errors configuration` command and rely on only certain types of LSPs for acknowledgments.

OSPF uses a system of LSA headers to synchronize link-state databases and detect newer LSAs. In contrast, IS-IS uses a system of Partial Sequence Number PDUs (PSNPs) and Complete SNPs (CSNPs) to perform the same chore. PSNPs are used as acknowledgments on nonbroadcast links and to request a new version of an LSP on a LAN. CSNPs contain the details of the link-state database and are broadcast every 10 seconds on LANs.

If the LSP that contains the details and metrics of the routes is too large for the IP link it is being sent across, the LSP can be fragmented across several LSPs. Most routers append a nonzero number to the LSP ID in the link-state database to indicate this, since these fragmented LSPs will have the same System ID and Pseudonode ID and so be otherwise indistinguishable. For example, LSP ID 1720.1601.0001.00-00 is an LSP on a nonbroadcast link that has not been fragmented. But LSP IDs 0172.0016.1001.02-01 and 0172.0016.1001.02-00 are a pair of fragmented LSPs that originated on a LAN with Pseudonode ID = 02.

Metrics

Like OSPF, IS-IS can use one of four different metrics to calculate least-cost paths (routes) from the link-state database. For IS-IS, these are default (all routers must understand the default metric system), delay, expense, and error (reliability in OSPF). We discuss only the default metric system here because, as with OSPF, that is the only system that most router vendors support.

The original IS-IS specification used a system of metric values that could only range from 0 to 63 on a link, and paths (the sum of all link costs along the route) could have a maximum cost of 1023. This was seen as very limiting compared to OSPF's 32-bit metric field, especially if the reference bandwidth system is to be applied. The bandwidth ratio between a 10-Gb Ethernet link and a 64-Kbps link is about 1,000 to 1. So a 64-level system of link metrics is not granular enough for many network service providers to base path costs on a reference bandwidth. Instead, Cisco and Juniper Networks routers simply assigned a default value of 10 to every link. Today, IS-IS implementations allow for "wide metrics" to be used with IS-IS. This makes the IS-IS metrics also 32 bits wide.

IS-IS also has a concept of *internal* (within the AS) and *external* (outside the AS) routes, as does OSPF. But where there are both internal and external L2 routes, there are only internal L1 routes in IS-IS. An L1 route to a destination is always preferred over an L2 route, but then the lowest metric wins.

IS-IS PDUs

IS-IS defines nine different types of PDUs. Each PDU has a 5-bit type number and falls into one of three categories. The IS-IS PDU types are shown in Table 11.1.

Table 11.1 IS-IS PDU Types

IS-IS PDU	PDU TYPE NUMBER
Hello PDUs:	
L1 LAN IS-IS Hello PDU	15
L2 LAN IS-IS Hello PDU	16
Point-to-point IS-IS Hello PDU	17
Link-State PDUs:	
L1 LSP	18
L2 LSP	20
Sequence Number PDUs:	
L1 CSNP	24
L2 CSNP	25
L1 PSNP	26
L2 PSNP	27

All IS-IS PDUs share a common 8-byte header. In contrast to OSPF packet types and most other Internet protocols, IS-IS PDUs are usually represented in 1-octet (8-bit) lines instead of the familiar 32-bit lines. The IS-IS header is shown in Figure 11.4. The header is always followed by PDU-specific fields. The PDU ends with a series of variable-length fields that are one of the reasons that IS-IS is in many ways easier and simpler to extend than OSPF. These are the Code/Length/Value (CLV) fields in some documents, or Type/Length/ Value (TLV) fields according to others. This chapter calls them TLVs because that term is more common.

The fields in the IS-IS PDU header are the Intradomain Routeing (sic) Protocol Discriminator (always 0x83 for IS-IS), the Length Indicator (PDU length in octets/bytes), the Version/Protocol ID Extension (always 1), the ID Length (length of the System ID used, set to 0 to indicate a 6-byte System ID), the PDU Type (three zero-bits are reserved, leaving the 5-bit Type field), the Version (also set to 1), the Reserved field (set to all zero), and finally the Maximum Area Address, which is not typically used to indicate the maximum number of areas. Paradoxically, although the Maximum Area Address can be used to indicate the number of areas allowed in the AS (1 to 254 are the allowed values), this field is usually set to 0 and means that the router supports three ISO addresses.

	Length in Octets	Normal Value
Intradomain Routing Protocol Descriminator	1	0x83
Length Indicator	1	Varies
Version/Protocol ID Extension	1	0x01
ID Length	1	0x00
R R R PDU Type	1	0 0 0 Varies
Version	1	0x01
Reserved	1	0x00
Maximum Area Addresses	1	0x00
PDU Specific Fields	N	Highly Variable
Variable-Length Fields (TLVs/CLVs)	N	Highly Variable

Figure 11.4 The IS-IS PDU header and format.

So there are really only two fields in the IS-IS PDU header that vary: the Length Indicator and PDU Type fields. The usual values of the rest of the header fields are also shown in the figure.

Type/Length/Value (TLV)

All routing protocols need to be extended to deal with new networking capabilities. For example, a router network that supports multicast or MPLS must have a way to distribute not only basic local reachability information to other routers but also any local information that all the routers need to know with regard to multicast or MPLS. Sometimes a completely new routing protocol is created, as the Distance Vector Multicast Routing Protocol (DVMRP) was for multicast networks. But all agree today that it is better to simply extend the existing routing protocols for new capabilities, as OSPF was for multicast in the form of Multicast OSPF (MOSPF).

The way that IS-IS makes itself more flexible for new networking methods, and extends and enhances its capabilities, is with a system of Type/Length/ Value (TLV) fields in the IS-IS PDU. The TLV system in IS-IS is quite elegant, and many prefer it to the OSPF method of adding new LSA types.

As mentioned, a lot of ISO and vendor documentation speaks of Code/ Length/Value (CLV) fields, and older documentation uses the final term *vector* instead of *value*, but this book uses the term TLV. The three terms are always used together: the Type is the number identifying what the Value represents, the Length is the length of the Value field, and the Value field contains the value itself. The Type and Length fields are always 1 byte long, but the Value field can be more than 1 byte long, depending on the number in the Length field. Table 11.2 lists these TLVs and notes which ones are specified by IS-IS and which ones are specified for IP use. Only the TLVs used with IP routing implementations are detailed in this chapter.

Table 11.2   TLV Codes Used in IS-IS

CODE	TLV TYPE	IS-IS? (ISO 10589)	IP? (RFC 1195)
1	Area Addresses		Yes
2	IS Neighbors (LSPs)	Yes	
3	ES Neighbors	Yes (not used in IP)	
4	Partition Designated L2 IS-IS	Yes (not detailed)	
5	Prefix Neighbors	Yes (not used in IP)	
6	IS Neighbors (Hellos)	Yes	
8	Padding	Yes	
9	LSP Entries	Yes	
10	Authentication Information	Yes	
128	IP Internal Reachability Information	Yes	
129	Protocols Supported		Yes
130	IP External Reachability Information		Yes
131	Inter-Domain Routing Protocol Information		Yes
132	IP Interface Address		Yes
133	Authentication Information (same as Type 10)		Obsolete

Table 11.2   *(Continued)*

CODE	TLV TYPE	IS-IS? (ISO 10589)	IP? (RFC 1195)
134	Traffic Engineering Router ID		Added in Draft
135	Traffic Engineering IP Reachability		Added in Draft
137	Dynamic Hostname		RFC 2753

Many of the TLV type codes were established for use in the original IS-IS for the OSI-RM in ISO 10589. RFC 1195 uses many of them and added several more for IP use. Internet drafts have adjusted the original RFC 1195 TLVs and added others. If a router does not understand a TLV included in an LSP, the router simply ignores the TLV. Many of these TLVs are used by more than one IS-IS PDU type, but the Authentication TLV is used in all PDUs. Table 11.3 lists the major TLV types and notes which IS-IS PDU types these are used in.

Table 11.3   TLVs Used in IS-IS PDUs

TLV TYPE	IS-IS PDU TYPE								
	15	16	17	18	20	24	25	26	27
Area Addresses	X	X	X	X	X				
IS Neighbors (LSPs)				X	X				
ES Neighbors				X					
Partition Designated L2 IS-IS			X						
Prefix Neighbors					X				
IS Neighbors (Hellos)	X	X							
Padding	X	X	X						
LSP Entries						X	X	X	X

(continues)

Table 11.3   TLVs Used in IS-IS PDUs *(Continued)*

TLV TYPE	IS-IS PDU TYPE								
	15	16	17	18	20	24	25	26	27
Authentication Information	X	X	X	X	X	X	X	X	X
IP Internal Reachability Information	X	X							
Protocols Supported	X	X	X	X	X				
IP External Reachability Information		X							
Inter-Domain Routing Protocol Info		X							
IP Interface Address	X	X	X	X	X				
Traffic Engineering Router ID			X	X					
Traffic Engineering IP Reachability	X	X							
Dynamic Hostname					X	X			

Each of the major IS-IS PDU types and their TLVs deserves a short section of its own. The TLV is detailed only the first time it is mentioned in the rest of this chapter.

IS-IS Hello PDU

IS-IS Hello PDUs allow neighbors to discover each other. Once neighbors have become adjacent, the Hellos have keepalive functions on the link and report any changes in parameters affecting adjacencies. All IS-IS PDUs have a curious behavior with regard to the maximum MTU size for the link.

IS-IS PDUs do not have to worry as much about link MTU size as OSPF does. IS-IS can decide on the upper limit for a PDU by the link buffer size of the originating router or through explicit configuration. IS-IS Hellos are supposed to be padded (extended) to within 1 byte (octet) of this maximum, so that no explicit MTU size needs to be passed between the routers. Also, some links can fail in a way that passes smaller PDUs but drops larger ones. In any case, the advantage of adding a lot of maximum-sized traffic very often to a network link is debatable and is often one of the first points raised against the use of IS-IS, especially on low-speed WAN links. Many router vendors, in spite of the specification, tailor the IS-IS PDU size to the amount of information sent on WAN links once the MTU size has been determined by the Hello PDUs. For example, Cisco allows the configuration to turn off padding on broadcast or point-to-point links (or both) and even allows the configuration to turn off padding on individual interfaces.

IS-IS has two different Hellos for its two link types: LAN Hellos and point-to-point Hellos. There are also L1 and L2 LAN Hellos, making a total of three Hello types. The LAN Hello format is identical for L1 and L2. Both the LAN and point-to-point Hello PDUs are shown in Figure 11.5. The figure shows the common header, the PDU-specific fields, and the position of the TLVs (Variable-Length fields).

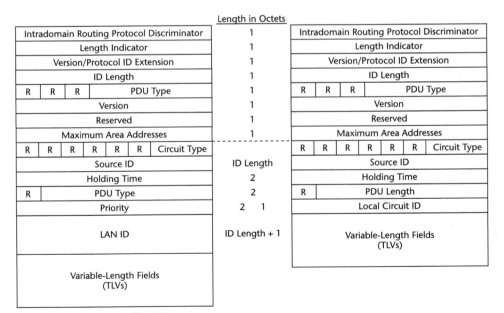

Figure 11.5   IS-IS Hello PDUs.

The LAN Hello PDUs start with a Circuit Type. The first 6 bits are reserved and set to 0, and the last 2 bits are 01 for an L1 router, 10 for L2, or 11 for both L1/L2. If the bits are 00, the PDU is ignored. The Source ID is the System ID of the originating router and is usually 6 bytes (octets) long. The Holding Time is the time in seconds the neighbor should wait for a Hello before declaring the other router dead. The PDU Length is the length of the entire PDU in bytes, the Priority is a 7-bit field used for DIS election (L1 priority may be different than L2 priority), and the LAN ID is the System ID of the DIS with the Pseudonode ID added (1 byte) to distinguish this LAN from another LAN with the same DIS. The IS-IS Hello PDU uses the following TLVs:

Area Address (Type 1).   One per area address is generated. Many routers use only one, and most are limited to three area addresses.

Intermediate System Neighbors (Type 6).   Lists the System IDs of all routers heard from since the last Hello. This TLV is used only on LAN Hellos and lists L1 and L2 routers in their own Hellos. This field is limited to 6 bytes, since many LAN-attached routers use the MAC address as the System ID.

Padding (Type 8).   Used to pad the IS-IS PDU to the MTU size. Since the length can only be 255 bytes, multiple Padding TLVs are often used. The value bits are ignored and are usually set to all zeros.

Authentication Information (Type 10).   Used by Cisco for this purpose in place of Type 133. A value between 0 and 255 is used to indicate the type of authentication. Type 0 is reserved, and Type 255 is used for private authentication methods inside the AS. Cleartext passwords are Type 1. MD5 authentication is also supported by router vendors.

Protocols Supported (Type 129).   Used to indicate whether the originator understands IP only, CLNP only, or both. The values are the ISO-defined Network Layer Protocol ID (NLPID), and IP has the value 0x81. Support for more than IP is rare among router vendors.

IP Interface Address (Type 132).   Carries the IP address (or addresses) assigned to the originating interface. It is rare that an interface has more than two or so IP addresses.

Authentication Information (Type 133).   Specified for authentication by RFC 1195 in place of ISO Type 10. It is illegal to use these today, and they are obsolete.

The point-to-point Hello PDU is also shown in the figure. The only difference is the lack of a Priority field, which is replaced by the Local Circuit ID field. This field is the local "interface index" of this link on the originating router and need not match the value on the other end of the link.

The point-to-point Hello PDUs does not use the Intermediate System Neighbor TLV, but otherwise the TLVs used are the same. The structures of the TLVs used in the Hello PDUs, except for the trivial Padding (Type 8) TLV, are shown in Figure 11.6.

The IS-IS Link-State PDUs (LSPs) do the same thing as the OSPF LSAs: flood information about the originating router and its links within the area. Naturally, there are distinct L1 and L2 LSPs. The L1 routers describe only their immediate environment, while the L2 routers describe not only themselves, but the IP routes that they can reach.

The format of the LSP is the same for L1 and L2, as shown in Figure 11.7. The figure shows the common header, the PDU-specific fields, and the position of the TLVs (Variable-Length fields).

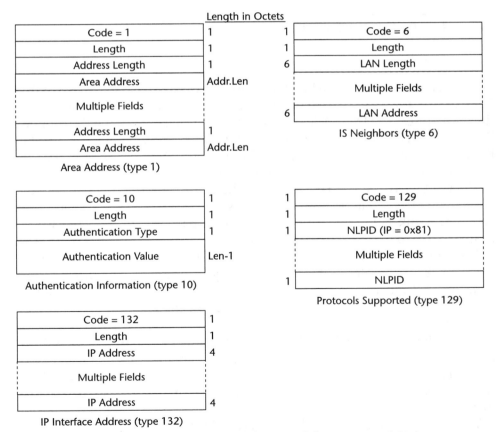

Figure 11.6 The IS-IS Hello PDU TLVs and the IS-IS Link-State PDUs (LSPs).

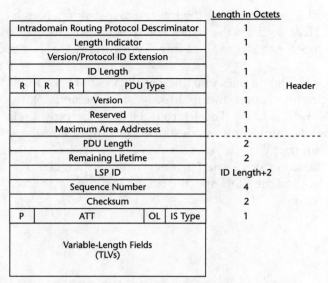

		Length in Octets	
Intradomain Routing Protocol Descriminator		1	
Length Indicator		1	
Version/Protocol ID Extension		1	
ID Length		1	
R R R PDU Type		1	Header
Version		1	
Reserved		1	
Maximum Area Addresses		1	
PDU Length		2	
Remaining Lifetime		2	
LSP ID		ID Length+2	
Sequence Number		4	
Checksum		2	
P ATT OL IS Type		1	
Variable-Length Fields (TLVs)			

Figure 11.7 The IS-IS Link-State PDU (LSP).

The LSP starts with a PDU Length field expressing the length of the entire PDU in bytes (octets). The Remaining Lifetime is the time in seconds until the LSP expires. The LSP ID field is made up of the System ID, the Pseudonode ID, and the LSP number of the LSP. This field was described in more detail in the previous section of this chapter. The Sequence Number field in a 32-bit unsigned integer, and the Checksum is the checksum of the LSP contents.

The last byte of the LSP is interesting. There is a P (Partition Repair) bit that applies only to L2 routers, although it exists in L1 LSPs as well. IS-IS can detect and repair link failures that would otherwise partition an area and isolate routers. Most router vendors do not support this action, so the bit is set to zero.

The ATT (Attachment) field is 4 bits and meaningful only in L1 LSPs originated by L1/L2 routers. The 4 bits identify the metrics supported by the "attachment" and are an Error (bit 7), Expense (bit 6), Delay (bit 5), and Default (bit 4) metric. Most router vendors only support the default metric, so only bit 4 will be 1.

The OL field is the link-state database OverLoad bit. Usually, this bit is 0. But the originating router can set this bit to 1 to tell other routers that its memory is overloaded. Only packets that terminate on the originating router's links should be sent until this bit is cleared, and this router should not be used for transit traffic.

The IS Type is a 2-bit field that indicates if the originating router is an L1 router (01) or an L2 router (11). The values 00 and 10 are unused. Since separate L1 and L2 LSPs are generated, an L1/L2 router will use both IS Types.

The IS-IS L1 LSP PDU can use the following TLVs:

Area Address (Type 1).   Same use as in the Hello PDU.

Intermediate System Neighbors (Type 2).   Not the same as the Type 6. This TLV is very elaborate and has a detailed structure. It lists the originating router's IS-IS neighbors and the link metrics to each of its neighbors. There is a 8-bit Virtual Flag that is 0x01 if the link described is used to repair a partitioned L2 area, but usually it is 0x00, since this feature is rarely supported. R (Reserved) bits are always 0. The I/E bit indicates if the neighbor is internal (0) or external (1) to the AS (it is always 0 because neighbors cannot be outside of the AS). The Default Metric is the default metric to the neighbor, a value between 0 and 63. The S (Supported) bits for the other metric fields are set to 1 (unsupported) for the other metrics (the metric = all 0) in all current implementations. Finally, the Neighbor ID is the System ID (plus nonzero Pseudonode ID for a DIS on a LAN) of the neighbor.

End System Neighbors (Type 3).   Used in L1 routers for attached hosts. Not used for IP.

Authentication Information (Type 10).   Same use as in the Hello PDU.

IP Internal Reachability Information (Type 128).   This TLV lists IP addresses and masks within the AS that are directly connected to the originating router. This TLV appears in both L1 and L2 LSPs (but not LSPs for a Pseudonode). The metric fields are the same as the Intermediate System Neighbors TLV, except there is no I/E bit. This bit position is now the Up/Down bit and is set to 0 to indicate an L1 internal route and set to 1 to indicate route leaking from L2. Backward compatibility is an issue with older IS-IS implementations when the Up/Down bit position was reserved and had to be set to 0.

Protocols Supported (Type 129).   Same use as in the Hello PDU.

IP Interface Address (Type 132).   Same use as in the Hello PDU.

Traffic Engineering Router ID (Type 134).   This TLV is used to carry the Router ID of the router originating the LSP. This is good for OSPF compatibility when both are running in the same AS and also to provide a stable address for traffic engineering.

Traffic Engineering IP Reachability (Type 135).   This TLV adds wide metrics and route leaking to IS-IS. Most routers require TLV Type 135 support to perform both route leaking and the advertisement of IS-IS metrics greater than 63. There are 32 bits for the wide metrics, the same as in OSPF. Then there is an Up/Down bit, followed by a bit set to 1 if traffic engineering *sub-TLVs* are present (sub-TLVs add information to the main TLV and are not discussed further), and a 6-bit Prefix Length field carrying the VLSM information. From 0 to 4 bytes of the IP prefix follows, depending on the value of the Prefix Length field. The TLV ends with 0 to 250 bytes of sub-TLV information.

Dynamic Hostname (Type 137).   This TLV carries the hostname of the router originating the LSP. This is to be the fully qualified domain name (FQDN; for example, Juniper_router@example.com) of the router. Having the hostname available in the IS-IS link-state database helps to map IS-IS packets, which are not IP packets, to the IP router topology.

The IS-IS L2 LSP PDU can use the following TLVs:

Area Address (Type 1).   Same use as in the Hello PDU.

Intermediate System Neighbors (Type 2).   Same use as in the L1 LSP PDU.

Partitioned Designated Level 2 IS (Type 3).   For partitioned area repair. Not used by most router vendors and so not discussed further.

Prefix Neighbors (Type 5).   Not used in IP.

Authentication Information (Type 10).   Same use as in the Hello PDU.

IP Internal Reachability Information (Type 128).   Same use as in the L1 LSP PDU.

IP External Reachability Information (Type 130).   This TLV lists IP addresses and masks *external* to the AS, but reachable over one of the originating router's interfaces. The format is the same as the Internal Reachability TLV, except for the code. This TLV is used by L2 LSPs only. The I/E bit is 0 for internal metrics and 1 for external metrics. There is also an Up-Down bit in this TLV.

Inter-Domain Routing Protocol Information (Type 131).   This TLV lets L2 LSP carry information from external routing protocols through the IS-IS routing domain transparently. This TLV serves much the same purpose as the Tag fields in RIPv2 or OSPF. There is an Inter-Domain Information Type field that is 0x01 if the external information is in a format used by the local routing protocol. Routing policies often set this field explicitly. If this field is 0x02, the External Information is a 16-bit AS number used to tag all of the rest of the External IP Reachability entries through the end of the LSP or until the next Inter-Domain Routing Protocol Information TLV.

Protocols Supported (Type 129).   Same use as in the Hello PDU.

IP Interface Address (Type 132).   Same use as in the Hello PDU.

Traffic Engineering Router ID (Type 134).   Same use as in the L1 LSP PDU.

Traffic Engineering IP Reachability (Type 135).   Same use as in the L1 LSP PDU.

Dynamic Hostname (Type 137).   Same use as in the L1 LSP PDU.

The structures of the TLVs introduced in the LSP PDUs are shown in Figure 11.8.

The IS-IS Sequence Number PDUs (SNPs) are used to keep the IS-IS link-state databases synchronized. They describe some or all of the LSPs in the router's link-state database. There are actually four types of SNPs: Complete and Partial SNPs, and one each for L1 and L2.

A DIS will periodically multicast Complete SNP (CSNP) that describes all of the LSPs in the pseudonode's L1 and L2 link-state databases (if both exist). Naturally, some link-state databases become so large that they cannot be listed inside one CSNP. So the CSNP has a Start LSP field and End LSP field to allow the receiver to determine the range of LSPs described in the CSNP. The range starts with System ID/Pseudonode ID/SNP 0000.0000.0000.00.00 and ends with System ID/Pseudonode ID/SNP ffff.ffff.ffff.ff.ff.

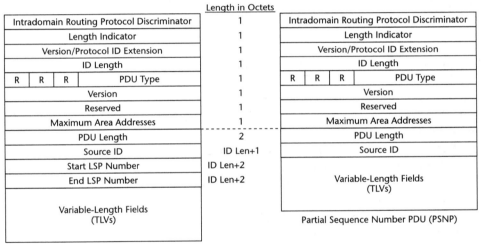

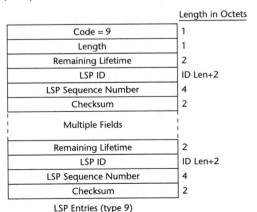

Figure 11.8 The IS-IS LSP PDU TLVs and the IS-IS Sequence Number PDUs (SNPs).

The Partial SNP (PSNP) is similar to the CSNP in form, except that the PSNP lists only part of the L1 or L2 link-state database. So no Start and End fields are needed in the PSNP. An IS-IS router sends a PSNP on a point-to-point link to acknowledge received LSPs. On broadcast links, PSNPs are used to request missing LSPs or LSPs that need to be updated.

SNPs use only two TLVs. These are used whether it is a PSNP or CSNP, and represents the L1 or L2 link-state database.

LSP Entries (Type 9).   This TLV summarizes the LSP by listing the Remaining Lifetime, LSP ID, Sequence Number, and Checksum of the LSP. These fields identify not only the LSP but also a particular instance of an LSP in time.

Authentication Information (Type 10).   Same use as in the Hello PDU.

The IS-IS CSNP and CSNP PDUs, along with the LSP Entries TLV are shown in Figure 11.9.

IS-IS for IPv6

Just as OSPF, IS-IS is busily adapting itself for use with IPv6. One advantage that IS-IS has over OSPF is that IS-IS is not an IP protocol and is not as intimately tied up with IPv4 as OSPF is. So IS-IS has fewer cares about changing for IPv6: IPv4 is already strange enough to IS-IS.

IS-IS for IPv6 will use all of the "normal" IS-IS PDUs and TLVs for Hellos, LSPs, and sequence numbers. The structure of the new TLVs (the drafts call them TLVs) for IPv6 are shown in Figure 11.10.

The basic mechanisms of RFC 1195 are still used, but the two new TLVs defined for IPv6 are as follows:

IPv6 Interface Address (Type 232).   This TLV just modifies the interface address field for the 16-byte IPv6 address space.

IPv6 Reachability (Type 236).   This TLV starts with a 32-bit-wide metric. Then there is an Up/Down bit for route leaking, an I/E bit for external (other routing protocol or AS) information, and a Sub-TLVs Present? bit. The last 5 bits of this byte are reserved and must be set to 0. There is then 1 byte of Prefix Length (VLSM) and from 0 to 16 bytes of the prefix itself, depending on the value of the Prefix Length field. Zero to 248 bytes of sub-TLVs end this TLV.

Both of these have sub-TLVs fields defined, but none have been standardized for IPv6 yet.

Length in Octets

Field	Length in Octets
Code = 2	1
Length	1
Virtual Flag	1
ID Length	1
R | I/E | Default Metric	1
S | I/E | Delay Metric	1
S | I/E | Expense Metric	1
S | I/E | Error Metric	1
Neighbor ID	ID Len+1
Multiple Fields	
R | I/E | Default Metric	1
S | I/E | Delay Metric	1
S | I/E | Expense Metric	1
S | I/E | Error Metric	1
Neighbor ID	ID Len+1

IS Neighbors (type 2)

Length in Octets	Field
1	Code = 128 and 130
1	Length
1	Virtual Flag
1	U/D | I/E | Default Metric
1	S | R | Delay Metric
1	S | R | Expense Metric
1	S | R | Error Metric
4	IP Address
4	Subnet Mask
	Multiple Fields
1	U/D | I/E | Default Metric
1	S | R | Delay Metric
1	S | R | Expense Metric
1	S | R | Error Metric
4	IP Address
4	Subnet Mask

IP Internal Reachability (type 128)
IP External Reachability (type 130)

Field	Length in Octets
Code = 131	1
Length	1
Inter-Domain Information Type	1
External Information	Varies

Inter-Domain Routing Protocol Information (type 131)

Length in Octets	Field
1	Code = 134
1	Length
4	Originating Router ID

TE Router ID (type 134)

Field	Length in Octets
Code = 137	1
Length	1
FQND of router	Varies

Dynamic Hostname (type 137)

Length in Octets	Field
1	Code = 135
1	Length
4	Wide Metric
1	U/D | Sub-TLV | Prefix Length
0-4	Prefix
0-250	Optional Sub-TLVs

TE IP Reachability (type 135)

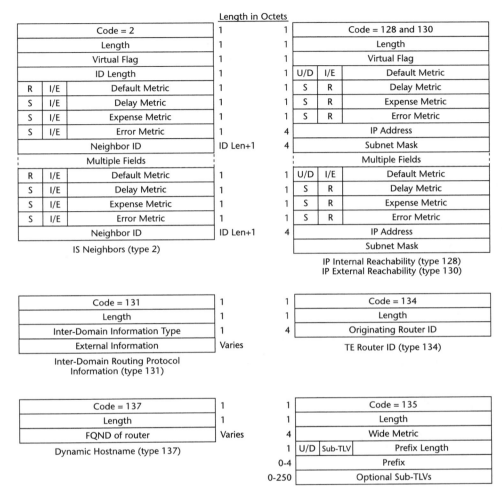

Figure 11.9 The IS-IS CSNP, PSNP, and LSP Entries TLV.

Length in Octets

Field	Length in Octets
Code = 232	1
Length	1
IP Address	16
Multiple Fields (from 0 to 15)	
IP Address	16

IPv6 Interface Address (type 232)

Length in Octets	Field
1	Code = 236
1	Length
4	Wide Metric
1	U/D | I/E | Sub-TLV | Reserved (0s)
1	Prefix Length
0-16	IPv6 Prefix
1	Sub-TLV Length
0-249	Optional Sub-TLVs

IPv6 Reachability (type 236)

Figure 11.10 IS-IS for IPv6.

Configuring IS-IS

IS-IS configurations are not as bewildering as OSPF configurations. There are just not as many areas types, options, or router types to worry about in IS-IS. However, there are the complexities of ISO addresses (the NET), and the L1_only, L2_only, and L1/L2 routers to worry about. In this chapter we attempt to configure a worthwhile example of IS-IS in action and yet at the same time limit the size and complexity of both the link-state database and routing tables. As with the OSPF network example, what works for one route should work for several. It is more important to explore IS-IS than to try to load up an autonomous system (AS) with a realistic number of routes.

This chapter on configuring IS-IS is based on the configuration established in the earlier chapter on OSPF configuration. There should be a certain amount of familiarity with the IP addresses and links used, but this chapter only deals with three IS-IS areas. There are still L1_only, L2_only, and L1/L2 routers, as well as external routes from RIPv1 and BGP. This helps shift attention from IP addresses and links to IS-IS specifics such as the NET and LSPs. There are still interoperability scenarios to consider, but in this chapter we limit the exploration to the basics. It is more important to consider essential interoperability features than try to enumerate all of the details of every possible configuration.

In Chapter 10 on configuring OSPF, one way of limiting the size of the chapter was to drop the configuration details for interfaces and addresses. These were presented in earlier chapters on basic Juniper Networks and Cisco router configuration, and then repeated in the chapter on RIP configuration. This chapter further tries to limit and focus the material by dropping all of the configuration steps, even for the routing protocols. From now on in this book, it will be enough to say something like "the Cisco_L1 router has been configured with this NET address and no padding for point-to-point links" without showing all the steps needed to do this. The completed configuration section for IS-IS is still shown, of course, but not every configuration command needed to get there.

As with OSPF, details in this chapter are reserved for IS-IS specifics. Configurations shown are limited in scope to the sections that affect IS-IS operation. All of the links in the example in this chapter are again point-to-point Ethernet links using crossover cables. This is even less of a compromise than in the OSPF lab, since there are only two types of link, broadcast and point-to-point, in IS-IS. Keep in mind that even though the crossover Ethernet links appear to be point-to-point, they are still broadcast networks and will elect an IS-IS DIS, form a pseudonode, and in short perform in the normal way that LANs do in IS-IS.

Another OSPF strategy to limit the amount of information presented in this chapter is by examining only two ISIS areas initially and their link-state PDUs (LSPs) to start, and then merging the other area together by the end of the chapter. First an IS-IS backbone area is established with L2_only routers, and then another area is added. So a backbone IS-IS area 0001 is configured with an L2_only router running BGP to another AS and two other L2 routers to link to the other IS-IS areas (Area 0002 and 0003). One of these areas also has a router with a link to another network, again running RIP on one interface. The configuration of three Juniper Networks routers are presented for IS-IS Area 0001. After some explanation of the LSP types seen in each router's link-state database, and the routing table appearances, the Juniper Networks routers is replaced by individual Cisco routers and the equivalent configuration and link-state database information presented.

This basic procedure is then repeated as other IS-IS areas are added to this backbone area. By the end of this chapter, both Juniper Networks and Cisco routers are configured as an L1_only router, an L2_only router, and an L1/L2 router. Interoperability is explored as a Juniper Networks router is replaced in one IS-IS role or another with a Cisco router.

As at the end of Chapter 10, a complete AS routing domain, this time with 11 routers, is presented. Nine of these routers will run IS-IS, and the remaining two will just be sources of non-IS-IS ("external") routing information. Figure 12.1 shows the final state of the network when all of basic IS-IS has been explored.

All of the information needed for all of the configurations is shown in the figure. Although this is not as complex as the OSPF topology, a few words of explanation are in order. All of the routers shown in AS 64512 are initially Juniper Networks routers, with one exception. The external router in the upper

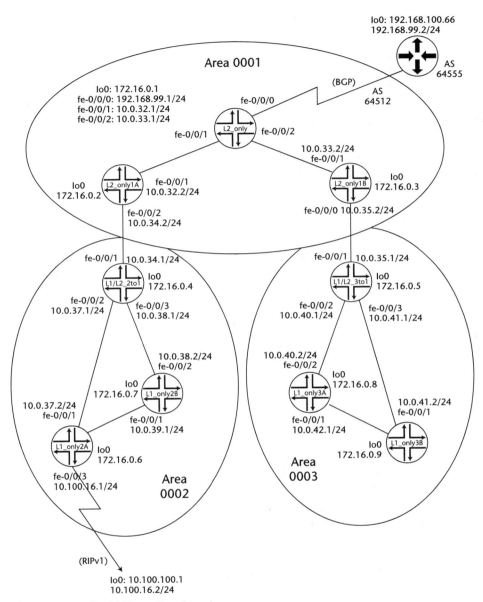

Figure 12.1 The IS-IS routing domain.

right of the figure in AS 64555 is a Cisco router, and this router runs BGP to the L2_only backbone router in Area 0001. Because we haven't discussed BGP yet, no configuration details are given for this interface. It is enough to note that the routing information from AS 64555 will be redistributed into AS 64512 by IS-IS (not realistic in practice, but done here to illustrate IS-IS behavior), and the IS-IS routing information from AS 64512 will also reach AS 64555.

The router in AS 64555 only contributes the router's loopback address (192.168.100.66) and interface address (192.168.99.2/24) to the IS-IS routing domain. As with OSPF, the idea here is to explore IS-IS in a small, controlled network environment.

The L2_only router with BGP in Area 0001 has a more complex configuration, but really only with regard to interfaces. The L2_only BGP router's loopback address is given (172.16.10.1) and so are the addresses on both of the interfaces to the other routers in Area 0001 (they are L1/L2 routers here, but could also be L2_only routers), all drawn from the 10.0.3X.0/24 address space. Each router in Area 0001 also has its loopback and interface addresses given, and these routers have one interface connecting to the Area 0001 L2_only BGP router and the other interface connecting to an L1/L2 router in another area.

Area 0002 has three routers. Two of the routers are L1_only routers. One of them is running RIPv1 on the 10.100.16.1/24 interface. As before, the details of the router at the other end of this router's non-IS-IS interface are unimportant and are not discussed in this chapter. However, the loopback and interface addresses on the RIP router are given, and as before, the RIP information is distributed into IS-IS by this router.

Area 0003 also has three routers. Two of them are L1_only routers. There are no external routes to worry about in Area 0003.

There are only LAN links in this network. All of the LAN links are 100-Mbps Ethernet with an IS-IS metric of 10, the default IS-IS metric for all links. The links are used as point-to-point links by employing simple crossover cables between the interfaces, but keep in mind these links are still broadcast networks as far as IS-IS is concerned and so elect a DIS and generate pseudonode LSPs.

In a real service provider network, the L1/L2 routers would probably be *POP (point-of-presence) routers*, and the L1_only routers outside of the backbone would be the *access routers* that have been configured as part of the RIP configuration chapter. In the real world, this structure makes perfect sense, as access routers would usually be running RIP to remote site routers or injecting static routes to the site routers into IS-IS. The L2_only BGP router would be a *border router* that links the IS-IS routing domain (AS 64512) to its peers on the Internet, a role played by the router in AS 64555 in this example.

To run IS-IS, each router needs an ISO NET to use as an address. The simple private AFI format introduced in the previous chapter is used, as is the simpler conversion method to make the router's loopback address into a System ID. So the L2_only router uses 49.0001 as its Area ID and converts 172.16.10.1 into 0172.0016.1001 for the System ID. The N-Selector is 00 for the router. The routers should have distinct hostnames, so, for example, the L1/L2 routers in the same area can be distinguished. So in Area 0001, the router running BGP will be

Table 12.1   IS-IS Router NETs

HOSTNAME AND AREA	LOOPBACK ADDRESS	NET
L2_Only Area 0001	172.16.10.1	49.0001.0172.0016.1001.00
L2_only1A Area 0001	172.16.0.2	49.0001.0172.0016.0002.00
L2_only1B Area 0001	172.16.0.3	49.0001.0172.0016.0003.00
L1/L2_2to1 Area 0002	172.16.0.4	49.0002.0172.0016.0004.00
L1_only2A Area 0002	172.16.0.6	49.0002.0172.0016.0006.00
L1_only2B Area 0002	172.16.0.7	49.0002.0172.0016.0007.00
L1/L2_3to1 Area 0003	172.16.0.5	49.0003.0172.0016.0005.00
L1_only3A Area 0002	172.16.0.8	49.0003.0172.0016.0008.00
L1_only3B Area 0002	172.16.0.9	49.0003.0172.0016.0009.00

L2_Only and the other routers will be designated L2_only1A (172.16.0.2) and L2_only1B (172.16.0.3.) In Area 0002, one of the L1/L2 routers will be L1/L2_2to1 (connecting Area 0002 to Area 0001) and the other will be L1/L2_3to1 (connecting Area 0003 to Area 0001). The L1_only routers will just be designated 2A or 2B by area. Table 12.1 shows the router hostnames, loopback addresses, and NETs that are used for the entire IS-IS network.

No mention of IS-IS L2 to L1 route leaking is in this chapter. This topic is more properly covered when routing policies for IGPs are covered in more detail later in this book in Chapter 16 "IGP Routing Policies."

Basic IS-IS Area 0001 Configuration

In this section we configure IS-IS on the L2_Only and the other L2 routers in Area 0001. All are initially Juniper Network routers. Configuration of IS-IS on any IP router is not as straightforward as it is for OSPF, because IS-IS is not an IP protocol. Router interfaces assume that any arriving frame has an IP packet inside. However, IS-IS PDUs arrive inside the same types of frames but are not IP packets. Unless the router interface is told that the frame *could* contain an IS-IS PDU, the IS-IS PDU will more than likely cause an error when the interface tries to interpret the IS-IS PDU header as an IP packet.

So the first thing to do on L2_Only is enable ISO packet interpretation capabilities on the router interfaces running IS-IS ("family iso"). The second step is to assign the NET to the entire router. Technically, the NET could be assigned to any interface, but it makes the most sense to assign the NET to the stable loopback interface. This way, if any single interface is down, there is no worry about losing the NET for the router. The configuration steps are not shown, only the result from L2_Only:

```
[edit interfaces]
lab@L2_Only# show
fe-0/0/1 {
    unit 0 {
        family inet {
            address 10.0.32.1/24;
        }
        family iso;
    }
}
fe-0/0/2 {
    unit 0 {
        family inet {
            address 10.0.33.1/24;
        }
        family iso;
    }
}
lo0 {
    unit 0 {
        family inet {
            address 172.16.10.1/32;
        }
        family iso {
            address 49.0001.0172.0016.1001.00;
        }
    }
}
```

Once this has been done, the configuration of the IS-IS protocol on L2_Only can proceed. All that is needed here is to set the interfaces that IS-IS is to run on and to specify that the interfaces are to establish L2 adjacencies only. The Juniper Networks router default is to establish both L1 and L2 adjacencies on all interfaces, but L1 is not need on an IS-IS router within the designated backbone collection of routers.

The IS-IS section on L2_Only looks like this:

```
[edit protocols]
lab@L2_Only# show
isis {
```

```
        export for_bgp;
        level 1 disable;
        interface fe-0/0/1.0;
        interface fe-0/0/2.0;
        interface lo0.0 {
            passive;
        }
    }
```

As with OSPF, the L2_Only router exports the BGP routing information into IS-IS with the routing policy for_bgp. A common error in IS-IS configuration on a Juniper Networks router is to forget that IS-IS *must* be specified to run on the loopback interface (the passive keyword is not required, but recommended). The loopback interface has the NET, and without running IS-IS to the routing engine, no adjacencies will be formed. Note that this is in contrast to the Juniper Networks router OSPF default behavior, which always runs OSPF on loopback0 whether told to or not, as long as the OSPF Router ID is on loopback0, which it is usually is.

The differences on the other L2 routers will be the NET, and the interface names and addresses. Here is what router L2_only1A's IS-IS configuration looks like:

```
[edit protocols]
lab@L2_only1A# show
isis {
    interface fe-0/0/0.0;
    interface lo0.0 {
        passive;
    }
}
```

However, both of the other L2 routers have another interface to another area. These will be added later. For now, the L2_Only and the other L2 routers are linked inside Area 0001 by two links. The successful operation of IS-IS is revealed on L2_only1A with two useful commands:

```
lab@L2_only1A> show isis adjacency
Interface          System      L State Hold (secs) SNPA
fe-0/0/0.0         L2_Only     2 Up          20  0:3:47:8:3e:38

lab@L1/L2_1to2> show isis interface
IS-IS interface database:
Interface    L CirID Level 1 DR      Level 2 DR        L1/L2 Metric
fe-0/0/0.0   2  0x2 Disabled        L2_only1A.02          10/10
lo0.0        0  0x1 Disabled        Passive               0/0

lab@L2_only1A> show isis adjacency
```

```
Interface              System      L State    Hold (secs) SNPA
fe-0/0/0.0             L2_Only     2 Up          20  0:3:47:8:3e:38


lab@L1/L2_1to2> show isis interface
IS-IS interface database:
Interface         L CirID Level 1 DR       Level 2 DR       L1/L2
Metric
fe-0/0/0.0        2  0x2 Disabled          L2_only1A.02       10/10
lo0.0             0  0x1 Disabled          Passive             0/0
```

The first command output shows that there is a Level 2 adjacency up and running on the link to L2_Only. The hold time is the time to wait for the next IIH packet before declaring the link dead. The SNPA is the IS-IS *Subnet Point of Attachment* and is used by IS-IS to represent the IP network in a more ISO-friendly manner.

The next command output shows that the L2_only1A router has a full IS-IS L2 adjacency on the interface fe-0/0/0 and that IS-IS runs passively on the loopback interface (this occurs whether the passive keyword is configured on lo0 or not). IS-IS runs passively here because there is no need to become adjacent to the loopback interface; the loopback interface is internal to the router. Level 1 adjacencies are disabled. Note that the *hostname* of the designated router (technically, DIS) on this LAN link shows up and not the ISO address, followed by the pseudonode identifier (02). The hostname is there because Juniper Networks by default supports the Dynamic Hostname TLV (TLV 137 from RFC 2753). This just makes it easier to see which routers are running IS-IS. The IS-IS System IDs for these routers can be shown with the show isis hostname command. IS-IS also maintains two separate databases, DRs, and sets of metrics for both L1 and L2 routing information, even though the information in this case is identical.

This is what the same commands show on L2_Only:

```
lab@L2_Only> show isis adjacency
Interface         System        L State Hold (secs) SNPA
fe-0/0/1.0        L2_only1A      2 Up       7  0:3:47:8:67:4c
fe-0/0/2.0        L2_only1B      2 Up       8  0:a0:c9:d7:f9:4


lab@L2_Only> show isis interface
IS-IS interface database:
Interface       L CirID Level 1 DR     Level 2 DR        L1/L2 Metric
fe-0/0/1.0      2  0x2 Disabled        L2_only1A.02        10/10
fe-0/0/2.0      2  0x3 Disabled        L2_only1B.02        10/10
lo0.0           0  0x1 Disabled        Passive              0/0
```

One of the most common things that can go wrong with IS-IS neighbor establishment is a *level mismatch* when one router is configured for L1_only and the other is configured for L2_only. But this is easy to verify. Also, Area IDs between L1_only routers must match. Also, if authentication is used, the authentication methods and passwords or keys must match on the link. Because the configurations are correct, and authentication is not used (in the real world, it probably would be), these IS-IS links come right up.

Viewing the Routing Table

Something interesting happens when the routing table on L2_Only is displayed:

```
lab@L2_Only> show route
inet.0: 10 destinations, 10 routes (10 active, 0 holddown, 0 hidden)
+ = Active Route, - = Last Active, * = Both

10.0.32.0/24       *[Direct/0] 03:38:47
                    > via fe-0/0/1.0
10.0.32.1/32       *[Local/0] 03:38:47
                     Local via fe-0/0/1.0
10.0.33.0/24       *[Direct/0] 01:13:21
                    > via fe-0/0/2.0
10.0.33.1/32       *[Local/0] 03:38:47
                     Local via fe-0/0/2.0
172.16.0.2/32      *[IS-IS/18] 00:57:45, metric 10, tag 2
                    > to 10.0.32.2 via fe-0/0/1.0
172.16.0.3/32      *[IS-IS/18] 00:55:21, metric 10, tag 2
                    > to 10.0.33.2 via fe-0/0/2.0
172.16.10.1/32     *[Direct/0] 03:38:47
                    > via lo0.0
192.168.99.0/24    *[Direct/0] 03:38:47
                    > via fe-0/0/0.0
                     [BGP/170] 03:35:41, MED 0, localpref 100
                       AS path: 64555 ?
                    > to 192.168.99.2 via fe-0/0/0.0
192.168.99.1/32    *[Local/0] 03:38:47
                     Local via fe-0/0/0.0
192.168.100.0/24   *[BGP/170] 03:35:41, MED 0, localpref 100
                       AS path: 64555 ?
                    > to 192.168.99.2 via fe-0/0/0.0

iso.0: 1 destinations, 1 routes (1 active, 0 holddown, 0 hidden)
+ = Active Route, - = Last Active, * = Both

49.0001.0172.0016.1001.00/80
                   *[Direct/0] 01:13:08
                    > via lo0.0
```

The JUNOS software default protocol preference for IS-IS internal routes learned through an L2 adjacency is 18 (the OSPF internal preference was 10). The default metric for the IS-IS routes (only the loopbacks to this point) is 10, and the routes are advertised with a tag of 2 (Level 2). The BGP link and route information was discussed in the OSPF configuration chapter and need not be repeated. (IS-IS can use the same reference bandwidth scheme as OSPF on Juniper Networks routers, but this method is not interoperable and is therefore not used in this chapter.)

Notice that enabling the ISO address family creates a separate table, iso.0, just for the ISO routes to the NET destinations. This table will not grow any larger, since IS-IS cannot be used to route ISO traffic, only IP. But the NET on the loopback interface has to be kept *somewhere*.

The following is what the routing table looks like on L2_only1B:

```
lab@L2_only1B> show route
inet.0: 7 destinations, 7 routes (7 active, 0 holddown, 0 hidden)
+ = Active Route, - = Last Active, * = Both

10.0.32.0/24        *[IS-IS/18] 00:00:13, metric 20, tag 2
                     > to 10.0.33.1 via fe-0/0/1.0
10.0.33.0/24        *[Direct/0] 00:02:19
                     > via fe-0/0/1.0
10.0.33.2/32        *[Local/0] 02:16:17
                      Local via fe-0/0/1.0
172.16.0.2/32       *[IS-IS/18] 00:04:47, metric 20, tag 2
                     > to 10.0.33.1 via fe-0/0/1.0
172.16.0.3/32       *[Direct/0] 04:43:11
                     > via lo0.0
172.16.10.1/32      *[IS-IS/18] 00:02:02, metric 10, tag 2
                     > to 10.0.33.1 via fe-0/0/1.0
192.168.100.0/24    *[IS-IS/165] 00:01:50, metric 20, tag 2
                     > to 10.0.33.1 via fe-0/0/1.0

iso.0: 1 destinations, 1 routes (1 active, 0 holddown, 0 hidden)
+ = Active Route, - = Last Active, * = Both

49.0001.0172.0016.0003.00/80
                    *[Direct/0] 02:16:17
                     > via lo0.0
```

Note that the metric to the other link in IS-IS Area 0001, 10.0.32.0, is now 20 (two hops), as is the metric to the 172.16.0.2 loopback on the L2_only1A router. The BGP route outside the AS is distributed with IS-IS has an IS-IS metric of 20 (two hops) and has a preference of 165 (the default for external routes learned through an L2 adjacency). The routing protocol preference for IS-IS internal routes learned though an L2 adjacency is 18, as many of the routes show.

This table should not change at all when a Cisco router becomes the L2_only router. This is done in the next section.

L2_Only Cisco Configuration

It is already possible to give the configuration for a Cisco router instead of a Juniper Networks router as L2_Only. This router also runs BGP, and the BGP configuration for Cisco_L2_only is shown here. No interface details or configuration steps are shown, just the result. The configuration for the Cisco_L2_only router is as follows:

```
hostname Cisco_L2_Only
!
clns routing
!
interface Loopback0
 ip address 172.16.10.1 255.255.255.255
 ip router isis
!
interface FastEthernet0
 ip address 192.168.99.1 255.255.255.0
!
interface FastEthernet1
 ip address 10.0.32.1 255.255.255.0
 ip router isis
!
interface FastEthernet2
 ip address 10.0.33.1 255.255.255.0
 ip router isis
!
autonomous-system 64512
!
router isis
 redistribute bgp 64512 metric 0 metric-type internal level-2
 net 49.0001.0172.0016.1001.00
 is-type level-2-only
!
router bgp 64512
 neighbor 192.168.99.2 remote-as 64555
!
ip classless
```

The `clns routing` statement is not entered during configuration but appears whenever IS-IS is configured to run on the router. Although Cisco routers might not be routing OSI CLNS packets at all, this statement must still be present in the configuration for legacy reasons. Even if the Cisco router does no CLNS routing at all, and only uses IS-IS for IP, many of the Cisco IOS commands are of the form `show clns...` and not `show isis...` as might be expected. The interfaces running IS-IS must have `ip router isis` configured, even the loopback interface (without this statement, the loopback address will not be advertised with IS-IS). It is common among Cisco routers to run IS-IS passively on the loopback interface with the `passive-interface Loopback0` statement under `router isis`, but this is not done here. It does no harm to actually send IS-IS packets to the loopback interface.

In contrast to the JUNOS software, the NET is not placed on the loopback interface, but on the IS-IS routing process with the `net` statement. In contrast to OSPF, IS-IS does not require a list of network addresses. This is taken care of by the `ip router isis` statement on the specific interfaces IS-IS is to run on. The `is-type level-2-only` statement is self-explanatory. The BGP configuration is the same as in the OSPF chapter. Redistributing BGP into IS-IS results in the 192.168.100.0 network from AS 64555 being advertised in AS 64512.

The following is the routing table for the Cisco_L2_only router, which has the same information as when this router was a Juniper Networks router:

```
Cisco_L2_Only#sh ip route
Codes:C - connected,S - static,I - IGRP,R - RIP,M - mobile,B - BGP
      D - EIGRP,EX - EIGRP external,O - OSPF,IA - OSPF inter area
      E1 - OSPF external type 1,E2 - OSPF external type 2,E - EGP
      i - IS-IS,L1 - IS-IS level-1,L2 - IS-IS level-2,* - candidate
default

Gateway of last resort is not set

     10.0.0.0 255.255.255.0 is subnetted, 2 subnets
C       10.0.32.0 is directly connected, FastEthernet1
C       10.0.33.0 is directly connected, FastEthernet2
C    192.168.99.0 is directly connected, FastEthernet0
B    192.168.100.0 [20/0] via 192.168.99.2, 00:02:57
     172.16.0.0 255.255.255.255 is subnetted, 3 subnets
C       172.16.10.1 is directly connected, Loopback0
i L2    172.16.0.3 [115/10] via 10.0.33.2, FastEthernet2
i L2    172.16.0.2 [115/10] via 10.0.32.2, FastEthernet1
```

There are now routes learned from IS-IS (as *i* because the uppercase *I* is used for Cisco's proprietary IGRP protocol) and BGP (B). The loopback addresses of the other routers were distributed with IS-IS. The administrative weight assigned to these IS-IS internal routes learned through L2 is 115 (OSPF was 110). These are Level 2 routes (i L2), and the metric, as before, is 10 per hop (link). All of the routing information is the same as when L2_Only was a Juniper Networks router, but more compact (there are no Direct and Local entries for each interface).

The ISO NET address is not shown with the `show ip route` command. To display the NET assigned to the router, you can use the command `show clns route`.

The routing table on L2_only1B has exactly the same routing information as it had before:

```
lab@L2_only1B> show route
inet.0: 7 destinations, 7 routes (7 active, 0 holddown, 0 hidden)
+ = Active Route, - = Last Active, * = Both

10.0.32.0/24        *[IS-IS/18] 00:08:49, metric 20, tag 2
                    > to 10.0.33.1 via fe-0/0/1.0
10.0.33.0/24        *[Direct/0] 00:11:03
                    > via fe-0/0/1.0
10.0.33.2/32        *[Local/0] 02:07:03
                      Local via fe-0/0/1.0
172.16.0.2/32       *[IS-IS/18] 00:08:49, metric 20, tag 2
                    > to 10.0.33.1 via fe-0/0/1.0
172.16.0.3/32       *[Direct/0] 00:08:49
                    > via lo0.0
172.16.10.1/32      *[IS-IS/18] 00:08:49, metric 20, tag 2
                    > to 10.0.33.1 via fe-0/0/1.0
192.168.100.0/24    *[IS-IS/165] 00:08:49, metric 10, tag 2
                    > to 10.0.33.1 via fe-0/0/1.0

iso.0: 1 destinations, 1 routes (1 active, 0 holddown, 0 hidden)
+ = Active Route, - = Last Active, * = Both

49.0001.0172.0016.0003.00/80
                    *[Direct/0] 02:07:03
                    > via lo0.0
```

The routing table on the Juniper Networks L2_only1B router is not quite identical to what it was before, when L2_Only was a Juniper Networks router. There is the same interesting difference in loopback metric as there was with OSPF: Both L2_Only (172.16.10.1) and L2_only1A (172.16.0.2) now both have a metric of 20. The reason for this, first explained in the OSPF Chapter 10, is that when a loopback address is advertised with OSPF or IS-IS on a Cisco router, the Cisco router adds a hop to the metric. Juniper Networks routers do not add anything to the loopback address metric when advertised by OSPF or IS-IS. This difference can be addressed with a routing policy if the result is bothersome (usually it matters very little).

Also, the BGP route, 192.168.100.0, which had a metric of 20 and a tag of 2 when L2_Only was a Juniper Networks router, is now only 10 (the OSPF tag for this route had the AS number, 64555). By default, Cisco advertises the IS-IS external route with the default IS-IS metric of 10. The Juniper Networks router advertises the external routes injected into IS-IS with a metric of 20 (on L2_Only, both with Juniper Networks and Cisco routers, the BGP metric is 0). These differences can potentially affect routing in a mixed Cisco and Juniper

Networks router environment. The default behaviors can be changed with a routing policy, of course, and that's exactly what routing policies are for.

IS-IS Area 0002 Configuration

Before swapping a Juniper Networks L1/L2 router for a Cisco router, in this section we complete the configuration of IS-IS Area 0002. There is still a lot to be done to configure this area. The L2_only1A router needs a second interface. Then three more routers are added to Area 0002:

L1/L2_2to1. This router links to the L1/L2_1to2 router in Area 0001, as well as the two other routers in Area 0002. Since the L1/L2_2to1 router is running L2 on the interface to L1/L2_1to2 router in Area 0, the router is part of the IS-IS extended backbone even though the router is on Area 0002.

L1_only2A. This router links to L1/L2_2to1 and the L1_only2B router. This is a Level 1-only router and so cannot have any IS-IS links outside of the area. However, this router has a RIPv1 link outside the AS and must redistribute this RIP information to the rest of the routers in the AS. This router resembles an ASBR in the OSPF world.

L1_only2B. This router links to L1/L2_2to1 and to the L1_only2A router. This is also a Level 1-only router and so cannot have any IS-IS links outside of the area.

Again, without all of the configuration step details, here is the configuration showing the second IS-IS interface added L2_only1A:

```
[edit protocols]
lab@L2_only1A# show
isis {
    level 1 disable;
    interface fe-0/0/0.0;
    interface fe-0/0/2.0;
    interface lo0.0 {
        passive;
    }
}
```

The interface fe-0/0/2 must also be configured with the family iso statement and the proper IP address.

L1/L2_2to1 Configuration

This router has three links to configure: one to the L2_only1A router in Area 0001, and two to each of the two other routers in Area 0002. The L1/L2_2to1 router is part of the IS-IS extended backbone even though the router is on Area 0002. This router must be able to run both IS-IS Level 1 and Level 2. The following is the configuration:

```
[edit interfaces]
lab@L1/L2_2to1# show
fe-0/0/1 {
    unit 0 {
        family inet {
            address 10.0.34.1/24;
        }
        family iso;
    }
}
fe-0/0/2 {
    unit 0 {
        family inet {
            address 10.0.37.1/24;
        }
        family iso;
    }
}
fe-0/0/3 {
    unit 0 {
        family inet {
            address 10.0.38.1/24;
        }
        family iso;
    }
}
lo0 {
    unit 0 {
        family inet {
            address 172.16.0.4/32;
        }
        family iso {
            address 49.0002.0172.0016.0004.00;
        }
    }
}
```

There is no need to disable Level 1 or Level 2 on L1/L2_2to1. This router must form both L1 and L2 adjacencies in IS-IS. The IS-IS section on L1/L2_2to1 looks like the following:

```
[edit protocols]
lab@L1/L2_2to1# show
isis {
    interface fe-0/0/1.0;
    interface fe-0/0/2.0;
    interface fe-0/0/3.0;
```

```
        interface lo0.0 {
            passive;
        }
    }
```

L1_only2A Configuration

The L1_only2A router links to L1/L2_2to1 and the L1_only2B router. This is a Level 1-only router and so cannot have any IS-IS links outside of the area. This is the router that has the RIPv1 link outside the AS and must redistribute this RIP information to the rest of the routers in the AS. The following is the configuration:

```
[edit interfaces]
lab@L1_only2A# show
fe-0/0/0 {
    unit 0 {
        family inet {
            address 10.100.16.1/24;
        }
        family iso;
    }
}
fe-0/0/1 {
    unit 0 {
        family inet {
            address 10.0.37.2/24;
        }
        family iso;
    }
}
fe-0/0/2 {
    unit 0 {
        family inet {
            address 10.0.39.2/24;
        }
        family iso;
    }
}
lo0 {
    unit 0 {
        family inet {
            address 172.16.0.6/32;
        }
        family iso {
            address 49.0002.0172.0016.0006.00;
        }
    }
}
```

For the rest of this chapter, we don't need to look at the router interface configurations in detail. Juniper Network routers need family iso on all interfaces running IS-IS, and Cisco routers need ip routing isis. Juniper Network routers need the NET assigned to the loopback interface under family iso and Cisco routers assign the NET to the router as a whole with the net statement. Only the IS-IS protocol sections of the configurations are shown from now on in this chapter.

The IS-IS protocol on the L1_only2A router also requires a routing policy to redistribute the RIP routing information (such as it is) into IS-IS. The routing policy is the same as used for OSPF and is as follows:

```
policy-statement from_ripv1 {
      term 1 {
            from protocol rip;
            then accept;
      }
   }
```

This from_ripv1 routing policy is applied as an export (output) policy to IS-IS on L1_only2A. The following is the complete configuration:

```
isis {
    export from_ripv1;
    level 2 disable
    interface fe-0/0/0.0;
    interface fe-0/0/1.0;
    interface fe-0/0/2.0;
    interface lo0.0 {
        passive;
    }

}
```

L1_only2B Configuration

The L1_only2B router links to L1/L2_2to1 and the L1_only2A router. This is a Level 1-only router and cannot have any IS-IS links outside of the area. The IS-IS protocol configuration looks like this:

```
isis {
    level 2 disable
    interface fe-0/0/1.0;
    interface fe-0/0/2.0;
    interface lo0.0 {
        passive;
    }
}
```

At this point, the network looks as shown in Figure 12.2.

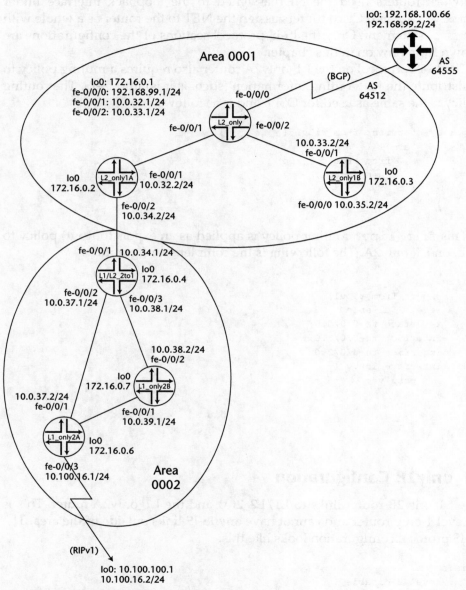

Figure 12.2 IS-IS Area 0001 and Area 0002.

Viewing the Routing Table and Link-State Database

Now all of the routers in Area 0002 have been configured and the link to Area 0001 defined. The routing tables and link-state databases for routers L2_only1A, L1/L2_2to1, L1_only2A, and L1_only2B can now be examined in some detail.

L1_only2A Routing Table and Link-State Database

This section starts with L1_only2A in Area 0002 and works backward toward the backbone Area 0001. This router can only form L1 adjacencies:

```
lab@L1_only2A> show isis interface
IS-IS interface database:
Interface    L CirID Level 1 DR      Level 2 DR       L1/L2 Metric
fe-0/0/1.0   1  0x2  L1_only2A.02    Disabled            10/10
fe-0/0/2.0   1  0x3  L1_only2A.03    Disabled            10/10
lo0.0        0  0x1  Passive         Disabled             0/0
```

The following is the routing table:

```
lab@L1_only2A> show route
inet.0: 14 destinations, 14 routes (14 active, 0 holddown, 0 hidden)
+ = Active Route, - = Last Active, * = Both

0.0.0.0/0          *[IS-IS/15] 00:06:21, metric 10, tag 1
                   > to 10.0.37.1 via fe-0/0/1.0
10.0.34.0/24       *[IS-IS/15] 00:06:33, metric 20, tag 1
                   > to 10.0.37.1 via fe-0/0/1.0
10.0.37.0/24       *[Direct/0] 00:20:04
                   > via fe-0/0/1.0
10.0.37.2/32       *[Local/0] 00:20:04
                     Local via fe-0/0/1.0
10.0.38.0/24       *[IS-IS/15] 00:19:30, metric 20, tag 1
                   > to 10.0.37.1 via fe-0/0/1.0
                     to 10.0.39.1 via fe-0/0/2.0
10.0.39.0/24       *[Direct/0] 00:19:50
                   > via fe-0/0/2.0
10.0.39.2/32       *[Local/0] 00:20:04
                     Local via fe-0/0/2.0
10.100.16.0/24     *[Direct/0] 00:20:04
                   > via fe-0/0/0.0
10.100.16.1/32     *[Local/0] 00:20:04
                     Local via fe-0/0/0.0
10.100.100.0/24    *[RIP/100] 00:01:42, metric 2
                   > to 10.100.16.2 via fe-0/0/0.0
```

```
172.16.0.4/32        *[IS-IS/15] 00:19:30, metric 10, tag 1
                      > to 10.0.37.1 via fe-0/0/1.0
172.16.0.6/32        *[Direct/0] 00:20:04
                      > via lo0.0
172.16.0.7/32        *[IS-IS/15] 00:19:01, metric 10, tag 1
                      > to 10.0.39.1 via fe-0/0/2.0
224.0.0.9/32         *[RIP/100] 00:20:06, metric 1

iso.0: 1 destinations, 1 routes (1 active, 0 holddown, 0 hidden)
+ = Active Route, - = Last Active, * = Both

49.0002.0172.0016.0006.00/80
                     *[Direct/0] 00:20:04
                      > via lo0.0
```

This routing table has few surprises. This is a Level 1-only IS-IS router, similar to an OSPF total stub, so there is a default (0.0.0.0) route toward the nearest L1/L2 router. There is only one L1/L2 router in Area 0002, so this route leads there (fe-0/0/1). The default route is advertised as an internal L1 route by the L1/L2 router, and in Juniper Networks routers an IS-IS route learned through an L2 adjacency has a routing protocol preference of 15. (Internal routes learned by an L2 adjacency have a preference of 18, so internal routes learned by L1 are preferred to internal routes learned through L2; why use the backbone if you don't have to?)

IS-IS also distributes the link information inside of Area 0002, and the IS-IS router loopbacks (Router IDs) as well. The local RIP route information (10.100...) is here as well. IS-IS is a lot more forgiving than OSPF when linking external networks to stub routers. No special area type is needed in IS-IS. An L1 IS-IS router can have external links as easily as an L2 IS-IS router. (The related issue regarding whether these external L1 routes should be sent onto the L2 backbone are considered later on in this chapter.)

But no information about links outside the area is present, all in keeping with the stub nature of the IS-IS areas. The metrics assigned to the routes are not remarkable, but note that the tag is 1 on the internal L1 IS-IS routes.

The link-state databases are identical within an IS-IS area, as in OSPF, because of the effects of flooding. So looking at the link-state database for Area 0002 on L1_only2A is the same as looking at the link-state database for Area 0002 on L1_only2B or L1/L2_2to1 (the Level 1 database). These databases tend to be larger in IS-IS than in OSPF, because there are separate L1 and L2 databases. This section looks at the details of the database on the L1/L2_2to1 router. For now, only the default information on the LSPs is given:

```
ab@L1_only2A> show isis database
IS-IS level 1 link-state database:

LSP ID                      Sequence Checksum Lifetime Attributes
```

```
L1/L2_2to1.00-00        0x21   0x4064    803 L1 L2 Attached
L1_only2A.00-00         0xa    0x842a   1086 L1
L1_only2A.02-00         0x3    0xd611    815 L1
L1_only2A.03-00         0x2    0xa43d    829 L1
L1_only2B.00-00         0x7    0xa012    690 L1
L1_only2B.03-00         0x2    0xf9ea    851 L1


    6 LSPs

IS-IS level 2 link-state database:
    0 LSPs
```

As expected, there is only a Level 1 link-state database on L1_only2A. Note that the Hostname is substituted for the System ID, thanks to TLV 137 Dynamic Hostname support. The Attributes reflect whether the originating router is an L1, L2, or L1/L2 router. The LSP from the L1/L2 router has the Attached bit set and is capable of both L1 and L2 adjacencies. The non-00 LSPs are for LAN pseudonodes, and L1_only2A is the DR on two of the links. All of the LSPs fit in a single packet, so the suffix is -00. The sequence field and checksum come from the LSPs, and the lifetime counts down from 1,200 seconds (20 minutes). There is a further hold-down time if the lifetime goes to 0 without a fresh LSP from the originator.

L2_only2B Routing Table and Link-State Database

Before we turn to the L1/L2 router, here is a quick look at how the Area 0002 routes show up on L1_only2B. The following is the routing table:

```
lab@L1_only2B> show route
inet.0: 11 destinations, 11 routes (11 active, 0 holddown, 0 hidden)
+ = Active Route, - = Last Active, * = Both

0.0.0.0/0          *[IS-IS/15] 00:07:40, metric 10, tag 1
                    > to 10.0.38.1 via fe-0/0/2.0
10.0.34.0/24       *[IS-IS/15] 00:07:52, metric 20, tag 1
                    > to 10.0.38.1 via fe-0/0/2.0
10.0.37.0/24       *[IS-IS/15] 00:20:19, metric 20, tag 1
                      to 10.0.39.2 via fe-0/0/1.0
                    > to 10.0.38.1 via fe-0/0/2.0
10.0.38.0/24       *[Direct/0] 00:20:57
                    > via fe-0/0/2.0
10.0.38.2/32       *[Local/0] 00:20:57
                      Local via fe-0/0/2.0
10.0.39.0/24       *[Direct/0] 00:20:57
                    > via fe-0/0/1.0
10.0.39.1/32       *[Local/0] 00:20:57
                      Local via fe-0/0/1.0
```

```
10.100.100.0/24    *[IS-IS/160] 00:02:59, metric 12, tag 1
                    > to 10.0.39.2 via fe-0/0/1.0
172.16.0.4/32      *[IS-IS/15] 00:20:10, metric 10, tag 1
                    > to 10.0.38.1 via fe-0/0/2.0
172.16.0.6/32      *[IS-IS/15] 00:20:19, metric 10, tag 1
                    > to 10.0.39.2 via fe-0/0/1.0
172.16.0.7/32      *[Direct/0] 00:20:57
                    > via lo0.0

iso.0: 1 destinations, 1 routes (1 active, 0 holddown, 0 hidden)
+ = Active Route, - = Last Active, * = Both

49.0002.0172.0016.0007.00/80
                   *[Direct/0] 00:20:57
                    > via lo0.0
```

The L1_only2B routing table is smaller by the three routes representing RIP and the link to the RIP router on L1_only2A. The RIP is there, of course, with a metric of 12: 10 for the link and 2 for the RIP metric itself. The routing preference for the *external* routes learned through an L1 adjacency is 160. External routes from L2 adjacencies have a preference of 165, so as with internal routes, an L1 route is preferred to an L2 route, although these preferences can be changed. Table 12.2 shows the default Juniper Networks routing protocol preferences for IS-IS routes. The L1 routes are always preferred to routes that must use the IS-IS backbone.

Table 12.2. Juniper Networks' Default IS-IS Routing Preferences

HOW LSP IS LEARNED	PREFERENCE		
	L1	L2	EXAMPLE
L1 Internal	15		Loopback and link addresses inside area (172.16.0.6, etc.)
L2 Internal		18	Loopback and link addresses inside AS (172.16.0.3, etc.)
L1 External	160		Other protocol's routes by L1 (10.100.100.0 RIP)
L2 External		165	Other protocol's routes by L2 (192.168.100.0 BGP)

The link-state database on L1_only2B is indeed the same as the database on L1_only2A:

```
lab@L1_only2B> show isis database
IS-IS level 1 link-state database:
LSP ID                   Sequence Checksum Lifetime Attributes
L1/L2_2to1.00-00           0x21    0x4064       727 L1 L2 Attached
L1_only2A.00-00            0xa     0x842a      1008 L1
L1_only2A.02-00            0x3     0xd611       737 L1
L1_only2A.03-00            0x2     0xa43d       751 L1
L1_only2B.00-00            0x7     0xa012       615 L1
L1_only2B.03-00            0x2     0xf9ea       777 L1
   6 LSPs

IS-IS level 2 link-state database:
   0 LSPs
```

The only other router in Area 2 that we have not looked at is L1/L2_2to1.

L1/L2_2to1 Routing Table and Link-State Database

So far, all of the routers we've examined in detail have been L2_only or L1_only routers. To see what is happening on a routers that can form both L1 and L2 IS-IS adjacencies, in this section we look at router L1/L2_2to1. The adjacencies formed by this router on the interfaces are now a little different than the L2_only or L1_only routers:

```
lab@L1/L2_2to1> show isis adjacency
Interface       System       L State  Hold (secs) SNPA
fe-0/0/1.0      L2_only1A     2 Up           7   0:3:47:8:67:4d
fe-0/0/2.0      L1_only2A     1 Up           8   0:a0:c9:8d:2:b0
fe-0/0/3.0      L1_only2B     1 Up           7   0:50:8b:6d:9a:5c

lab@L1/L2_2to1> show isis interface
IS-IS interface database:
Interface   L CirID Level 1 DR     Level 2 DR     L1/L2 Metric
fe-0/0/1.0  3 0x2 L1/L2_2to1.02    L2_only1A.03   10/10
fe-0/0/2.0  3 0x3 L1_only2A.02     L1/L2_2to1.03  10/10
fe-0/0/3.0  3 0x4 L1_only2B.03     L1/L2_2to1.04  10/10
lo0.0       0 0x1 Passive          Passive        0/0
```

For the first time, interfaces can form either L1 or L2 adjacencies (or both, but that is not the case here because of configuration). The fact the interfaces can form L1/L2 adjacencies is shown in the `show isis interface` command where L is now 3 (for L1, L2, or both). And even though there is no adjacency on one level or the other, the LAN interfaces elect both an L1 and L2 DR.

The following is the routing table on L1/L2_2to1:

```
lab@L1/L2_2to1> show route
inet.0: 17 destinations, 17 routes (17 active, 0 holddown, 0 hidden)
+ = Active Route, - = Last Active, * = Both

10.0.32.0/24       *[IS-IS/18] 00:08:39, metric 20, tag 2
                    > to 10.0.34.2 via fe-0/0/1.0
10.0.33.0/24       *[IS-IS/18] 00:08:39, metric 30, tag 2
                    > to 10.0.34.2 via fe-0/0/1.0
10.0.34.0/24       *[Direct/0] 00:08:56
                    > via fe-0/0/1.0
10.0.34.1/32       *[Local/0] 01:27:33
                     Local via fe-0/0/1.0
10.0.37.0/24       *[Direct/0] 00:22:24
                    > via fe-0/0/2.0
10.0.37.1/32       *[Local/0] 01:27:33
                     Local via fe-0/0/2.0
10.0.38.0/24       *[Direct/0] 00:22:06
                    > via fe-0/0/3.0
10.0.38.1/32       *[Local/0] 01:27:33
                     Local via fe-0/0/3.0
10.0.39.0/24       *[IS-IS/15] 00:21:46, metric 20, tag 1
                    > to 10.0.37.2 via fe-0/0/2.0
                      to 10.0.38.2 via fe-0/0/3.0
10.100.100.0/24    *[IS-IS/160] 00:03:56, metric 12, tag 1
                    > to 10.0.37.2 via fe-0/0/2.0
172.16.0.2/32      *[IS-IS/18] 00:08:39, metric 10, tag 2
                    > to 10.0.34.2 via fe-0/0/1.0
172.16.0.3/32      *[IS-IS/18] 00:08:39, metric 30, tag 2
                    > to 10.0.34.2 via fe-0/0/1.0
172.16.0.4/32      *[Direct/0] 01:27:33
                    > via lo0.0
172.16.0.6/32      *[IS-IS/15] 00:21:46, metric 10, tag 1
                    > to 10.0.37.2 via fe-0/0/2.0
172.16.0.7/32      *[IS-IS/15] 00:21:16, metric 10, tag 1
                    > to 10.0.38.2 via fe-0/0/3.0
172.16.10.1/32     *[IS-IS/18] 00:08:39, metric 20, tag 2
                    > to 10.0.34.2 via fe-0/0/1.0
192.168.100.0/24   *[IS-IS/165] 00:08:39, metric 30, tag 2
                    > to 10.0.34.2 via fe-0/0/1.0

iso.0: 1 destinations, 1 routes (1 active, 0 holddown, 0 hidden)
+ = Active Route, - = Last Active, * = Both

49.0002.0172.0016.0004.00/80
                   *[Direct/0] 01:27:33
                    > via lo0.0
```

This routing table contains more routes than the stub L1_only routers in Area 0002. This router is more like an OSPF ABR but is still firmly an Area 0002 router, as the ISO NET address shows. Note that both the 192.168.100.0/24 BGP route and the 10.100.100.0/24 RIP routes are present on this router.

There is a mixture of internal Area 0002 routes learned through an L1 adjacency (IS-IS/15), internal Area 0001 routes learned through an L2 adjacency (IS-IS/18), external routes learned from L1 (IS-IS/160, the RIP route), and external routes learned from L2 (IS-IS/165, the BGP route). All IS-IS routes have a tag reflecting their origin, L1 or L2 adjacencies.

Because of the ABR nature of the L1/L2 routers is IS-IS, this is the only time in this chapter we look at the link-state database(s) in detail. Here are the detailed L1 and L2 link-state databases from the L1/L2_2to1 router, although they will be the same throughout Area 0001 (all contiguous, L2 routers form the IS-IS backbone area):

```
lab@L1/L2_2to1> show isis database detail
IS-IS level 1 link-state database:

L1/L2_2to1.00-00 Sequence: 0x21,Checksum: 0x4064, Lifetime: 665 secs
    IS neighbor:              L1_only2B.03  Metric:       10
    IS neighbor:              L1_only2A.02  Metric:       10
    IP prefix:          10.0.34.0/24 Metric:       10 Internal
    IP prefix:          10.0.38.0/24 Metric:       10 Internal
    IP prefix:          10.0.37.0/24 Metric:       10 Internal
    IP prefix:          172.16.0.4/32 Metric:        0 Internal
L1_only2A.00-00  Sequence: 0xa,Checksum: 0x842a, Lifetime: 944 secs
    IS neighbor:              L1_only2A.03  Metric:       10
    IS neighbor:              L1_only2A.02  Metric:       10
    IP prefix:        10.100.100.0/24 Metric:        2 External
    IP prefix:          10.0.39.0/24 Metric:       10 Internal
    IP prefix:          172.16.0.6/32 Metric:        0 Internal
    IP prefix:          10.0.37.0/24 Metric:       10 Internal
L1_only2A.02-00  Sequence: 0x3,Checksum: 0xd611, Lifetime: 673 secs
    IS neighbor:              L1/L2_2to1.00 Metric:        0
    IS neighbor:              L1_only2A.00  Metric:        0
L1_only2A.03-00  Sequence: 0x2,Checksum: 0xa43d, Lifetime: 687 secs
    IS neighbor:              L1_only2B.00  Metric:        0
    IS neighbor:              L1_only2A.00  Metric:        0
L1_only2B.00-00  Sequence: 0x7, Checksum: 0xa012, Lifetime: 549 secs
    IS neighbor:              L1_only2B.03  Metric:       10
    IS neighbor:              L1_only2A.03  Metric:       10
    IP prefix:          172.16.0.7/32 Metric:        0 Internal
    IP prefix:          10.0.39.0/24 Metric:       10 Internal
    IP prefix:          10.0.38.0/24 Metric:       10 Internal
L1_only2B.03-00  Sequence: 0x2, Checksum: 0xf9ea, Lifetime: 711 secs
    IS neighbor:              L1/L2_2to1.00 Metric:        0
    IS neighbor:              L1_only2B.00  Metric:        0

IS-IS level 2 link-state database:
```

```
L2_only1A.00-00  Sequence: 0x20,Checksum: 0xde3e, Lifetime: 661 secs
    IS neighbor:                L2_only1A.03  Metric:        10
    IS neighbor:                L2_only1A.02  Metric:        10
    IP prefix:             10.0.34.0/24 Metric:        10 Internal
    IP prefix:             10.0.32.0/24 Metric:        10 Internal
    IP prefix:           172.16.0.2/32 Metric:         0 Internal
L2_only1A.02-00  Sequence: 0xf, Checksum: 0x913a, Lifetime: 654 secs
    IS neighbor:                L2_Only.00    Metric:         0
    IS neighbor:                L2_only1A.00  Metric:         0
L2_only1A.03-00  Sequence: 0xe, Checksum: 0x1bca, Lifetime: 661 secs
    IS neighbor:                L1/L2_2to1.00 Metric:         0
    IS neighbor:                L2_only1A.00  Metric:         0
L2_only1B.00-00  Sequence: 0x17,Checksum: 0x1806, Lifetime: 587 secs
    IS neighbor:                L2_only1B.02  Metric:        10
    IP prefix:             10.0.33.0/24 Metric:        10 Internal
    IP prefix:           172.16.0.3/32 Metric:         0 Internal
L2_only1B.02-00  Sequence: 0x9, Checksum: 0xc509, Lifetime: 590 secs
    IS neighbor:                L2_Only.00    Metric:         0
    IS neighbor:                L2_only1B.00  Metric:         0
L1/L2_2to1.00-00 Sequence:0x53,Checksum: 0xdce5, Lifetime: 1193 secs
    IS neighbor:                L2_only1A.03  Metric:        10
    IP prefix:             10.0.34.0/24 Metric:        10 Internal
    IP prefix:           172.16.0.7/32 Metric:        10 Internal
    IP prefix:           172.16.0.6/32 Metric:        10 Internal
    IP prefix:             10.0.39.0/24 Metric:        20 Internal
    IP prefix:             10.0.38.0/24 Metric:        10 Internal
    IP prefix:             10.0.37.0/24 Metric:        10 Internal
    IP prefix:           172.16.0.4/32 Metric:         0 Internal
L2_Only.00-00  Sequence: 0x13, Checksum: 0x1312, Lifetime: 489 secs
    IS neighbor:                L2_only1B.02  Metric:        10
    IS neighbor:                L2_only1A.02  Metric:        10
    IP prefix:          192.168.100.0/24 Metric:       10 External
    IP prefix:          172.16.10.1/32 Metric:         0 Internal
    IP prefix:             10.0.33.0/24 Metric:        10 Internal
    IP prefix:             10.0.32.0/24 Metric:        10 Internal
```

All of the information in the routing table is derived from these databases. This detailed database is presented here for one very good reason: Notice that the 10.100.100.0/24 RIP route is present in the L1 database (LSP L1_only2A.00-00) but *not* in the Level 2 link-state database on the L1/L2 (LSP L1/L2_2to1.00-00).

A look at the routing table on L2_only1A in Area 0001 confirms the absence of 10.100.100.0/24:

```
lab@L2_only1A> show route
inet.0: 15 destinations, 15 routes (15 active, 0 holddown, 0 hidden)
+ = Active Route, - = Last Active, * = Both

10.0.32.0/24       *[Direct/0] 00:24:58
                    > via fe-0/0/1.0
```

```
10.0.32.2/32        *[Local/0] 00:25:08
                       Local via fe-0/0/1.0
10.0.33.0/24        *[IS-IS/18] 00:24:22, metric 20, tag 2
                       > to 10.0.32.1 via fe-0/0/1.0
10.0.34.0/24        *[Direct/0] 00:10:17
                       > via fe-0/0/2.0
10.0.34.2/32        *[Local/0] 00:25:08
                       Local via fe-0/0/2.0
10.0.37.0/24        *[IS-IS/18] 00:10:00, metric 20, tag 2
                       > to 10.0.34.1 via fe-0/0/2.0
10.0.38.0/24        *[IS-IS/18] 00:10:00, metric 20, tag 2
                       > to 10.0.34.1 via fe-0/0/2.0
10.0.39.0/24        *[IS-IS/18] 00:10:00, metric 30, tag 2
                       > to 10.0.34.1 via fe-0/0/2.0
172.16.0.2/32       *[Direct/0] 00:25:08
                       > via lo0.0
172.16.0.3/32       *[IS-IS/18] 00:23:57, metric 20, tag 2
                       > to 10.0.32.1 via fe-0/0/1.0
172.16.0.4/32       *[IS-IS/18] 00:10:00, metric 10, tag 2
                       > to 10.0.34.1 via fe-0/0/2.0
172.16.0.6/32       *[IS-IS/18] 00:10:00, metric 20, tag 2
                       > to 10.0.34.1 via fe-0/0/2.0
172.16.0.7/32       *[IS-IS/18] 00:10:00, metric 20, tag 2
                       > to 10.0.34.1 via fe-0/0/2.0
172.16.10.1/32      *[IS-IS/18] 00:24:22, metric 10, tag 2
                       > to 10.0.32.1 via fe-0/0/1.0
192.168.100.0/24    *[IS-IS/165] 00:23:14, metric 20, tag 2
                       > to 10.0.32.1 via fe-0/0/1.0

iso.0: 1 destinations, 1 routes (1 active, 0 holddown, 0 hidden)
+ = Active Route, - = Last Active, * = Both

49.0001.0172.0016.0002.00/80
                    *[Direct/0] 00:25:08
                       > via lo0.0
```

By default, a Juniper Networks router will *not* take an external route learned from an L1 adjacency and propagate that route to an L2 router. So RIP route 10.100.100.0/24, learned from an L1 adjacency, will not be sent onto the L2 adjacency link to L2_only1A by default. In this behavior, the Juniper Networks L1/L2_2to1 router resembles an OSPF NSSA ABR that does not convert Type 7 LSAs from an NSSA ASBR to Type 5 LSAs for the OSPF backbone. If it is desirable to allow the 10.100.100.0/24 route to be advertised into Area 0001, this is easily done with a routing policy.

L1/L2_2to1 Cisco Configuration

In Area 0001, the Cisco router became a backbone router running L2 only. In this section we make the L1/L2_2to1 router into a Cisco router and configure the Cisco_L1/L2_2to1 router to communicate with the same Juniper Networks routers around it. IP classless operation is assumed. The basic configuration is very simple. The following is the relevant portion of the configuration:

```
Cisco_L1/L2_2to1#sh run
!
hostname Cisco_Cisco_L1/L2_2to1
clns routing
!
interface Loopback0
 ip address 172.16.0.4 255.255.255.255
 ip router isis
 clns router isis
!
interface FastEthernet0
 ip address 10.0.34.1 255.255.255.0
 Ip router isis
!
interface FastEthernet1
 ip address 10.0.37.1 255.255.255.0
 ip router isis
!
interface FastEthernet2
 ip address 10.0.38.1 255.255.255.0
 ip router isis
!
router isis
 net 49.0002.0172.0016.0004.00
!
ip classless
!
```

It is not necessary to configure L1/L2 operation because this is the default. Each interface has `ip router isis` configured, and the loopback interface has one addition: `clns router isis`. Without this statement on at least one interface, the Cisco router will not advertise the default 0.0.0.0 route to other Level 1 routers. This is because the Attach bit is a CLNS function, and although the Cisco router has `cnls routing` enabled at the general level, it is also necessary to apply CLNS to an interface running IS-IS to send LSPs with the Attach bit set.

The routing table on Cisco_L1/L2_2to1 looks like the following:

```
Cisco_L1/L2_2to1#sh ip route

Codes:C - connected,S - static,I - IGRP,R - RIP,M - mobile,B - BGP
      D - EIGRP,EX - EIGRP external,O - OSPF,IA - OSPF inter area
      E1 - OSPF external type 1 E2 - OSPF external type 2,E - EGP
      i - IS-IS,L1 - IS-IS level-1,L2 - IS-IS level-2,* - candidate
```

```
default

Gateway of last resort is not set

     10.0.0.0 255.255.255.0 is subnetted, 7 subnets
i L1    10.100.100.0 [115/12] via 10.0.37.2, FastEthernet1
C       10.0.34.0 is directly connected, FastEthernet0
i L2    10.0.32.0 [115/20] via 10.0.34.2, FastEthernet0
i L2    10.0.33.0 [115/30] via 10.0.34.2, FastEthernet0
C       10.0.38.0 is directly connected, FastEthernet2
i L1    10.0.39.0 [115/20] via 10.0.37.2, FastEthernet1
                   [115/20] via 10.0.38.2, FastEthernet2
C       10.0.37.0 is directly connected, FastEthernet1
i L2 192.168.100.0 [115/30] via 10.0.34.2, FastEthernet0
     172.16.0.0 255.255.255.255 is subnetted, 6 subnets
i L2    172.16.10.1 [115/20] via 10.0.34.2, FastEthernet0
C       172.16.0.4 is directly connected, Loopback0
i L1    172.16.0.6 [115/10] via 10.0.37.2, FastEthernet1
i L1    172.16.0.7 [115/10] via 10.0.38.2, FastEthernet2
i L2    172.16.0.2 [115/10] via 10.0.34.2, FastEthernet0
i L2    172.16.0.3 [115/30] via 10.0.34.2, FastEthernet0
```

All of the same information is here, but in a more concise form, since Cisco routing tables are more like Juniper Networks routers' forwarding tables. All route metrics are the same. Note that Cisco routers, in contrast to Juniper Networks routers, do not assign four different preferences (administrative weights) to the four different ways to learn IS-IS routing information. All IS-IS routes are 115, although whether the routes are learned from an L1 or L2 adjacency is shown (i L1 or i L2).

There is another important difference between the Cisco L1/L2 router's and the Juniper Networks router's default behavior. A look at the routing on L2_only1A shows that the Area 0002 RIP route, 10.100.100.0/24, is now in the L2_only1A router's routing table:

```
lab@L2_only1A> show route 10.100/16
inet.0: 16 destinations, 16 routes (16 active, 0 holddown, 0 hidden)
+ = Active Route, - = Last Active, * = Both

10.100.100.0/24    *[IS-IS/18] 00:10:20, metric 22, tag 2
                    > to 10.0.34.1 via fe-0/0/2.0
```

This route now appears in the L2_only1A link-state database in the LSP from Cisco_L1/L2_2to1:

```
CiscoL1/L2_2to1.00-00Sequence:0x66,Checksum:0x2146,Lifetime:730 secs
    IS neighbor:              L2_only1A.03  Metric:      10
    IS neighbor:              L1/L2_2to1.04  Metric:      10
    IS neighbor:              L1/L2_2to1.06  Metric:      10
```

```
          IS neighbor:            L1/L2_2to1.08  Metric:      10
          IP prefix:            172.16.0.7/32 Metric:      10 Internal
          IP prefix:            172.16.0.6/32 Metric:      10 Internal
          IP prefix:            172.16.0.4/32 Metric:      10 Internal
          IP prefix:             10.0.37.0/24 Metric:      10 Internal
          IP prefix:             10.0.39.0/24 Metric:      20 Internal
          IP prefix:             10.0.38.0/24 Metric:      10 Internal
          IP prefix:             10.0.34.0/24 Metric:      10 Internal
          IP prefix:           10.100.100.0/24 Metric:      12 Internal
```

Here is adjacency information, showing the L1 and L2 adjacencies on the Cisco router:

```
Cisco_L1/L2_2to1#sh clns ne
System Id    SNPA             Interface  State Holdtime Type Protocol
L1_only2A    00a0.c98d.02b0   Et1        Up    8        L1   IS-IS
L1_only2B    0050.8b6d.9a5c   Et2        Up    8        L1   IS-IS
L2_only1A    0003.4708.674d   Et0        Up    8        L2   IS-IS
```

Finally, a look at the routing table on L1_only2B shows that nothing has changed:

```
lab@L1_only2B> show route
inet.0: 11 destinations, 11 routes (11 active, 0 holddown, 0 hidden)
+ = Active Route, - = Last Active, * = Both

0.0.0.0/0          *[IS-IS/15] 00:02:27, metric 10, tag 1
                    > to 10.0.38.1 via fe-0/0/2.0
10.0.34.0/24       *[IS-IS/15] 00:02:58, metric 20, tag 1
                    > to 10.0.38.1 via fe-0/0/2.0
10.0.37.0/24       *[IS-IS/15] 00:02:58, metric 20, tag 1
                    > to 10.0.39.2 via fe-0/0/1.0
                      to 10.0.38.1 via fe-0/0/2.0
10.0.38.0/24       *[Direct/0] 00:03:24
                    > via fe-0/0/2.0
10.0.38.2/32       *[Local/0] 00:03:24
                      Local via fe-0/0/2.0
10.0.39.0/24       *[Direct/0] 00:03:24
                    > via fe-0/0/1.0
10.0.39.1/32       *[Local/0] 00:03:24
                      Local via fe-0/0/1.0
10.100.100.0/24    *[IS-IS/160] 00:02:58, metric 12, tag 1
                    > to 10.0.39.2 via fe-0/0/1.0
172.16.0.4/32      *[IS-IS/15] 00:02:58, metric 20, tag 1
                    > to 10.0.38.1 via fe-0/0/2.0
172.16.0.6/32      *[IS-IS/15] 00:02:58, metric 10, tag 1
                    > to 10.0.39.2 via fe-0/0/1.0
172.16.0.7/32      *[Direct/0] 00:03:24
                    > via lo0.0
```

```
iso.0: 1 destinations, 1 routes (1 active, 0 holddown, 0 hidden)
+ = Active Route, - = Last Active, * = Both

49.0002.0172.0016.0007.00/80
                    *[Direct/0] 00:03:24
                    > via lo0.0
```

Actually, the active route installed in the forwarding table to reach the 10.0.37.0/24 link between L1_only2A and Cisco_L1/L2_2to1 has shifted from through the Cisco router to through L1_only2A. But this is a "pick one" decision because the routes are identical in all respects in the link-state database.

IS-IS Area 0003 Configuration

In a real AS running IS-IS, it would be unusual to find an area running only IS-IS on every link. This is because in spite of the nice features of IS-IS, there are many more routers running RIP or OSPF. Nevertheless, in this section we configure a totally IS-IS area, Area 0003, and show how the routes appear in a completely IS-IS environment.

The portion of the network configured in this section is shown in Figure 12.3.

Three new routers have to be added to the network: L1/L2_3to1, L1_only3A, and L1_only3B.

L1/L2_3to1 Configuration

This router has three links to configure: one to the L2_only1B router in Area 0001, and two to each of the two other routers in Area 0002. The L1/L2_3to1 router is part of the IS-IS extended backbone even though the router is on Area 0002. This router must be able to run both IS-IS Level 1 and Level 2.

There is no need to disable Level 1 or Level 2 on L1/L2_3to1. This router must form both L1 and L2 adjacencies in IS-IS. The IS-IS section on L1/L2_3to1 looks like this:

```
[edit protocols]
lab@L1/L2_3to1# show
isis {
    interface fe-0/0/1.0;
    interface fe-0/0/2.0;
    interface fe-0/0/3.0;
    interface lo0.0 {
        passive;
    }

}
```

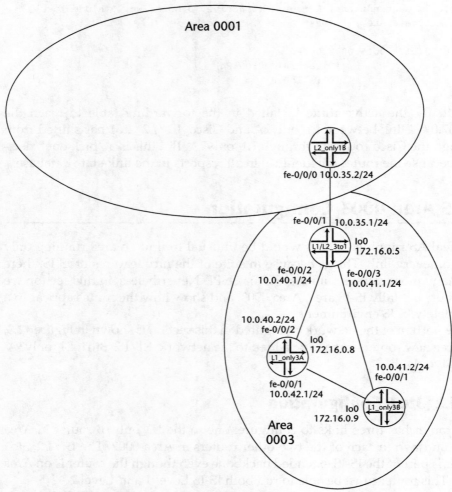

Figure 12.3   Adding the Area 0003 configuration.

L1_only3A and L1_only3B Configuration

The L1_only3A router links to L1/L2_3to1 and the L1_only3B router. The L1_only3B router links to L1/L3_2to1 and the L1_only3A router. These are both Level 1-only routers, and so cannot have any IS-IS links outside of the area. The interface addresses and protocol families and NETs are assumed to be configured correctly.

The following are the IS-IS configurations for both:

```
[edit protocols]
lab@L1_only_3A# show
```

```
isis {
    interface fe-0/0/1.0;
    interface fe-0/0/2.0;
    interface lo0.0 {
        passive;
    }

}

[edit protocols]
lab@L1_only3B# show
isis {
    interface fe-0/0/0.0;
    interface fe-0/0/1.0;
    interface lo0.0 {
        passive;
    }
}
```

The configurations differ only with respect to interfaces.

Viewing the Routing Table and Link-State Database

Now the entire network has been configured. All routers are back to being Juniper Networks routers. The routing tables and link-state databases for routers L2_only1B, L1/L2_3to1, L1_only3A, and L1_only3B can now be examined in some detail. This section starts with L2_only1B in Area 0001:

```
lab@L2_only1B> show route
inet.0: 22 destinations, 22 routes (22 active, 0 holddown, 0 hidden)
+ = Active Route, - = Last Active, * = Both

10.0.32.0/24      *[IS-IS/18] 00:09:56, metric 20, tag 2
                   > to 10.0.33.1 via fe-0/0/1.0
10.0.33.0/24      *[Direct/0] 00:10:46
                   > via fe-0/0/1.0
10.0.33.2/32      *[Local/0] 00:10:46
                    Local via fe-0/0/1.0
10.0.34.0/24      *[IS-IS/18] 00:09:51, metric 30, tag 2
                   > to 10.0.33.1 via fe-0/0/1.0
10.0.35.0/24      *[Direct/0] 00:07:15
                   > via fe-0/0/0.0
10.0.35.2/32      *[Local/0] 00:07:15
                    Local via fe-0/0/0.0
10.0.37.0/24      *[IS-IS/18] 00:09:43, metric 40, tag 2
                   > to 10.0.33.1 via fe-0/0/1.0
10.0.38.0/24      *[IS-IS/18] 00:09:43, metric 40, tag 2
                   > to 10.0.33.1 via fe-0/0/1.0
10.0.39.0/24      *[IS-IS/18] 00:09:43, metric 50, tag 2
```

```
                            > to 10.0.33.1 via fe-0/0/1.0
    10.0.40.0/24        *[IS-IS/18] 00:06:04, metric 20, tag 2
                            > to 10.0.35.1 via fe-0/0/0.0
    10.0.41.0/24        *[IS-IS/18] 00:06:04, metric 20, tag 2
                            > to 10.0.35.1 via fe-0/0/0.0
    10.0.42.0/24        *[IS-IS/18] 00:06:04, metric 30, tag 2
                            > to 10.0.35.1 via fe-0/0/0.0
    172.16.0.2/32       *[IS-IS/18] 00:09:51, metric 20, tag 2
                            > to 10.0.33.1 via fe-0/0/1.0
    172.16.0.3/32       *[Direct/0] 00:10:46
                            > via lo0.0
    172.16.0.4/32       *[IS-IS/18] 00:09:43, metric 30, tag 2
                            > to 10.0.33.1 via fe-0/0/1.0
    172.16.0.5/32       *[IS-IS/18] 00:06:04, metric 10, tag 2
                            > to 10.0.35.1 via fe-0/0/0.0
    172.16.0.6/32       *[IS-IS/18] 00:09:43, metric 40, tag 2
                            > to 10.0.33.1 via fe-0/0/1.0
    172.16.0.7/32       *[IS-IS/18] 00:09:43, metric 40, tag 2
                            > to 10.0.33.1 via fe-0/0/1.0
    172.16.0.8/32       *[IS-IS/18] 00:06:04, metric 20, tag 2
                            > to 10.0.35.1 via fe-0/0/0.0
    172.16.0.9/32       *[IS-IS/18] 00:06:04, metric 20, tag 2
                            > to 10.0.35.1 via fe-0/0/0.0
    172.16.10.1/32      *[IS-IS/18] 00:09:56, metric 10, tag 2
                            > to 10.0.33.1 via fe-0/0/1.0
    192.168.100.0/24    *[IS-IS/165] 00:08:45, metric 20, tag 2
                            > to 10.0.33.1 via fe-0/0/1.0

iso.0: 1 destinations, 1 routes (1 active, 0 holddown, 0 hidden)
+ = Active Route, - = Last Active, * = Both

49.0001.0172.0016.0003.00/80
                    *[Direct/0] 00:10:46
                        > via lo0.0
```

All routes on this L2_only router are learned from L2 adjacencies, of course. Most are internal routes (IS-IS/18), but the external BGP route (192.168.100.0/24) is still IS-IS/165. This router knows about all areas, as expected. The only absent route is the RIP route (1.100.100.0/24) from Area 0001, which is not automatically distributed into L2 by the Juniper Networks L1/L2_2to1 router. Here is the link-state database on L2_only1B:

```
lab@L2_only1B> show isis database
IS-IS level 1 link-state database:
  0 LSPs

IS-IS level 2 link-state database:
LSP ID                          Sequence Checksum Lifetime Attributes
L2_only1A.00-00                 0x9   0x43f0     1004 L1 L2
```

```
L2_only1A.02-00            0x2   0xab2d    1188 L1 L2
L2_only1A.03-00            0x2   0x33be     383 L1 L2
L2_only1B.00-00            0xa   0xe31b    1021 L1 L2
L2_only1B.02-00            0x5   0xcd05     617 L1 L2
L2_only1B.03-00            0x1   0xa34a     620 L1 L2
L1/L2_2to1.00-00           0xe   0x48bf    1013 L1 L2
L1/L2_3to1.00-00           0x9   0xccdc     619 L1 L2
L2_Only.00-00              0xb   0xbc70    1028 L1 L2
   9 LSPs
```

There is only an L2 database, but it contains LSPs from both the L2_only and the L1/L2 routers. Although not detailed here, all of the L2_only routers contain the same 22 routes (L2_Only has two additional routes for the BGP link), and all of the L2 databases on the L2_only and L1/L2 routers contain the same nine LSPs.

L1/L2_3to1 Routing Table and Link-State Database

Here is the final appearance of the routing table and link-state database on the L1/L2 router in Area 0003:

```
lab@L1/L2_3to1> show route
inet.0: 23 destinations, 23 routes (23 active, 0 holddown, 0 hidden)
+ = Active Route, - = Last Active, * = Both

10.0.32.0/24       *[IS-IS/18] 00:14:37, metric 30, tag 2
                    > to 10.0.35.2 via fe-0/0/1.0
10.0.33.0/24       *[IS-IS/18] 00:14:47, metric 20, tag 2
                    > to 10.0.35.2 via fe-0/0/1.0
10.0.34.0/24       *[IS-IS/18] 00:14:37, metric 40, tag 2
                    > to 10.0.35.2 via fe-0/0/1.0
10.0.35.0/24       *[Direct/0] 00:19:31
                    > via fe-0/0/1.0
10.0.35.1/32       *[Local/0] 00:19:33
                    Local via fe-0/0/1.0
10.0.37.0/24       *[IS-IS/18] 00:14:37, metric 50, tag 2
                    > to 10.0.35.2 via fe-0/0/1.0
10.0.38.0/24       *[IS-IS/18] 00:14:37, metric 50, tag 2
                    > to 10.0.35.2 via fe-0/0/1.0
10.0.39.0/24       *[IS-IS/18] 00:14:37, metric 60, tag 2
                    > to 10.0.35.2 via fe-0/0/1.0
10.0.40.0/24       *[Direct/0] 00:19:33
                    > via fe-0/0/2.0
10.0.40.1/32       *[Local/0] 00:19:33
                    Local via fe-0/0/2.0
10.0.41.0/24       *[Direct/0] 00:19:33
                    > via fe-0/0/3.0
10.0.41.1/32       *[Local/0] 00:19:33
                    Local via fe-0/0/3.0
```

```
10.0.42.0/24          *[IS-IS/15] 00:18:58, metric 20, tag 1
                         to 10.0.40.2 via fe-0/0/2.0
                       > to 10.0.41.2 via fe-0/0/3.0
172.16.0.2/32         *[IS-IS/18] 00:14:37, metric 30, tag 2
                       > to 10.0.35.2 via fe-0/0/1.0
172.16.0.3/32         *[IS-IS/18] 00:14:47, metric 10, tag 2
                       > to 10.0.35.2 via fe-0/0/1.0
172.16.0.4/32         *[IS-IS/18] 00:14:37, metric 40, tag 2
                       > to 10.0.35.2 via fe-0/0/1.0
172.16.0.5/32         *[Direct/0] 00:19:33
                       > via lo0.0
172.16.0.6/32         *[IS-IS/18] 00:14:37, metric 50, tag 2
                       > to 10.0.35.2 via fe-0/0/1.0
172.16.0.7/32         *[IS-IS/18] 00:14:37, metric 50, tag 2
                       > to 10.0.35.2 via fe-0/0/1.0
172.16.0.8/32         *[IS-IS/15] 00:18:58, metric 10, tag 1
                       > to 10.0.40.2 via fe-0/0/2.0
172.16.0.9/32         *[IS-IS/15] 00:18:58, metric 10, tag 1
                       > to 10.0.41.2 via fe-0/0/3.0
172.16.10.1/32        *[IS-IS/18] 00:14:37, metric 20, tag 2
                       > to 10.0.35.2 via fe-0/0/1.0
192.168.100.0/24      *[IS-IS/165] 00:14:37, metric 30, tag 2
                       > to 10.0.35.2 via fe-0/0/1.0

iso.0: 1 destinations, 1 routes (1 active, 0 holddown, 0 hidden)
+ = Active Route, - = Last Active, * = Both

49.0003.0172.0016.0005.00/80
                      *[Direct/0] 00:19:33
                       > via lo0.0
```

This is a very full table but has no real surprises. There are both L1 and L2 link-state databases as well:

```
lab@L1/L2_3to1> show isis database
IS-IS level 1 link-state database:
LSP ID                   Sequence Checksum Lifetime Attributes
L1/L2_3to1.00-00           0xb    0x4018     581 L1 L2 Attached
L1_only3A.00-00            0xd    0xa24f     479 L1
L1_only3A.02-00            0x5    0x8253     670 L1
L1_only3A.03-00            0x2    0x6877     683 L1
L1_only3B.00-00            0x12   0xf6f3    1014 L1
L1_only3B.03-00            0x2    0x904c     626 L1
  6 LSPs


IS-IS level 2 link-state database:
LSP ID                   Sequence Checksum Lifetime Attributes
L2_only1A.00-00            0x9    0x43f0     512 L1 L2
L2_only1A.02-00            0x2    0xab2d     697 L1 L2
L2_only1A.03-00            0x3    0x31bf     732 L1 L2
```

```
L2_only1B.00-00                    0xa    0xe31b    530 L1 L2
L2_only1B.02-00                    0x6    0xcb06    746 L1 L2
L2_only1B.03-00                    0x2    0xa14b    959 L1 L2
L1/L2_2to1.00-00                   0xe    0x48bf    521 L1 L2
L1/L2_3to1.00-00                   0xa    0xcadd    725 L1 L2
L2_Only.00-00                      0xb    0xbc70    536 L1 L2
    9 LSPs
```

L1_only3A and L1_only3B Routing Table and Link-State Database

In this section we take a quick look at the two remaining routers. There is not much to complicate these routers' roles in the network.

The following is what the routing tables look like:

```
lab@L1_only3A> show route
inet.0: 10 destinations, 10 routes (10 active, 0 holddown, 0 hidden)
+ = Active Route, - = Last Active, * = Both

0.0.0.0/0          *[IS-IS/15] 00:19:04, metric 10, tag 1
                    > to 10.0.40.1 via fe-0/0/2.0
10.0.35.0/24       *[IS-IS/15] 00:23:18, metric 20, tag 1
                    > to 10.0.40.1 via fe-0/0/2.0
10.0.40.0/24       *[Direct/0] 00:23:54
                    > via fe-0/0/2.0
10.0.40.2/32       *[Local/0] 00:25:17
                     Local via fe-0/0/2.0
10.0.41.0/24       *[IS-IS/15] 00:23:50, metric 20, tag 1
                    > to 10.0.42.2 via fe-0/0/1.0
                      to 10.0.40.1 via fe-0/0/2.0
10.0.42.0/24       *[Direct/0] 00:25:17
                    > via fe-0/0/1.0
10.0.42.1/32       *[Local/0] 00:25:17
                     Local via fe-0/0/1.0
172.16.0.5/32      *[IS-IS/15] 00:23:18, metric 10, tag 1
                    > to 10.0.40.1 via fe-0/0/2.0
172.16.0.8/32      *[Direct/0] 00:25:17
                    > via lo0.0
172.16.0.9/32      *[IS-IS/15] 00:24:42, metric 10, tag 1
                    > to 10.0.42.2 via fe-0/0/1.0

iso.0: 1 destinations, 1 routes (1 active, 0 holddown, 0 hidden)
+ = Active Route, - = Last Active, * = Both

49.0003.0172.0016.0008.00/80
                   *[Direct/0] 00:25:17
                    > via lo0.0


ab@L1_only3B> show route
```

```
inet.0: 10 destinations, 10 routes (10 active, 0 holddown, 0 hidden)
+ = Active Route, - = Last Active, * = Both

0.0.0.0/0          *[IS-IS/15] 00:22:18, metric 10, tag 1
                   > to 10.0.41.1 via fe-0/0/1.0
10.0.35.0/24       *[IS-IS/15] 00:26:31, metric 20, tag 1
                   > to 10.0.41.1 via fe-0/0/1.0
10.0.40.0/24       *[IS-IS/15] 00:27:03, metric 20, tag 1
                   > to 10.0.42.1 via fe-0/0/0.0
                     to 10.0.41.1 via fe-0/0/1.0
10.0.41.0/24       *[Direct/0] 00:27:08
                   > via fe-0/0/1.0
10.0.41.2/32       *[Local/0] 00:30:19
                     Local via fe-0/0/1.0
10.0.42.0/24       *[Direct/0] 00:28:38
                   > via fe-0/0/0.0
10.0.42.2/32       *[Local/0] 00:30:19
                     Local via fe-0/0/0.0
172.16.0.5/32      *[IS-IS/15] 00:26:31, metric 10, tag 1
                   > to 10.0.41.1 via fe-0/0/1.0
172.16.0.8/32      *[IS-IS/15] 00:27:56, metric 10, tag 1
                   > to 10.0.42.1 via fe-0/0/0.0
172.16.0.9/32      *[Direct/0] 00:30:19
                   > via lo0.0

iso.0: 1 destinations, 1 routes (1 active, 0 holddown, 0 hidden)
+ = Active Route, - = Last Active, * = Both

49.0003.0172.0016.0009.00/80
                   *[Direct/0] 00:30:19
                   > via lo0.0
```

In each case, only the Area 0003 details are present. The default route leads to the L1/L2 exit point for Area 0003. Here are the link-state databases:

```
lab@L1_only3A> show isis database
LSP ID                     Sequence Checksum Lifetime Attributes
L1/L2_3to1.00-00             0xb     0x4018     376 L1 L2 Attached
L1_only3A.00-00              0xe     0xa050    1028 L1
L1_only3A.02-00             0x5     0x8253     468 L1
L1_only3A.03-00             0x2     0x6877     481 L1
L1_only3B.00-00             0x12    0xf6f3     810 L1
L1_only3B.03-00             0x2     0x904c     423 L1

IS-IS level 1 link-state database:
LSP ID                     Sequence Checksum Lifetime Attributes
  6 LSPs

IS-IS level 2 link-state database:
```

```
   0 LSPs

lab@L1_only3B> show isis database
IS-IS level 1 link-state database:
L1/L2_3to1.00-00             0xc     0x3e19       1121 L1 L2 Attached
L1_only3A.00-00             0xe     0xa050        920 L1
L1_only3A.02-00             0x6     0x8054       1105 L1
L1_only3A.03-00             0x3     0x6678       1159 L1
L1_only3B.00-00            0x12     0xf6f3        706 L1
L1_only3B.03-00             0x2     0x904c        318 L1

   6 LSPs

IS-IS level 2 link-state database:
   0 LSPs
```

As expected, there is only an L1 database in each case. Note the Attached bit set in the L1/L2_3to1 LSP.

L1_only3B Cisco Configuration

In the previous sections we configured a Cisco router as an L2_only router and an L1/L2 router. Here we explore L1_only operation by making the L1_only3B router into a Cisco router and configuring the Cisco_L1_only3B router to communicate with the same routers. IP classless operation is assumed. Here is the relevant portion of the configuration:

```
Cisco_L1_only3B#sh run
!
hostname Cisco_L1_only3B
!
clns routing
!
interface Loopback0
 ip address 172.16.0.9 255.255.255.255
 ip router isis
!
interface FastEthernet0
 ip address 10.0.42.2 255.255.255.0
 ip router isis
!
interface FastEthernet1
 ip address 10.0.41.2 255.255.255.0
 ip router isis
!
router isis
 net 49.0003.0172.0016.0009.00
```

```
 is-type level-1
!
ip classless
!
```

Now the routing table on Cisco_L1_only3B looks like this:

```
Cisco_L1_only3B#sh ip route

Codes:C - connected,S - static,I - IGRP,R - RIP,M - mobile,B - BGP
      D - EIGRP,EX - EIGRP external,O - OSPF,IA - OSPF inter area
      E1 - OSPF external type 1,E2 - OSPF external type 2,E - EGP
      i - IS-IS,L1 - IS-IS level-1,L2 - IS-IS level-2,* - candidate
default

Gateway of last resort is 10.0.41.1 to network 0.0.0.0

     10.0.0.0 255.255.255.0 is subnetted, 4 subnets
C       10.0.42.0 is directly connected, FastEthernet0
i L1    10.0.40.0 [115/20] via 10.0.41.1, FastEthernet1
                  [115/20] via 10.0.42.1, FastEthernet0
C       10.0.41.0 is directly connected, FastEthernet1
i L1    10.0.35.0 [115/20] via 10.0.41.1, FastEthernet1
     172.16.0.0 255.255.255.255 is subnetted, 3 subnets
i L1    172.16.0.8 [115/10] via 10.0.42.1, FastEthernet0
C       172.16.0.9 is directly connected, Loopback0
i L1    172.16.0.5 [115/10] via 10.0.41.1, FastEthernet1
I*L1 0.0.0.0 0.0.0.0 [115/10] via 10.0.41.1, FastEthernet1
```

Note there is a default route in the Cisco router's routing table because the Attached bit is set on the LSP from the L1/L2 router. Here is the link-state database showing that the Juniper Networks router is indeed setting the Attached bit:

```
Cisco_L1_only3B#sh isis dat
IS-IS Level-1 Link-state Database
LSPID              LSP Seq Num   LSP Checksum  LSP Holdtime  ATT/P/OL
L1/L2_3to1.00-00   0x00000013    0xB99C        1040          1/0/0
L1/L2_3to1.04-00   0x00000002    0x04D9        518           0/0/0
L1_only3A.00-00    0x00000016    0x41A7        975           0/0/0
L1_only3A.02-00    0x0000000B    0x7659        455           0/0/0
L1_only3A.03-00    0x00000009    0x5A7E        1170          0/0/0
L1_only3B.00-00*   0x0000001B    0x6D52        1108          0/0/0
```

The same number of LSPs are present as before, although a new DIS has replaced L1_only3B on the link to the L1/L2 router. Although not shown, the routing tables on the other Juniper Network routers in Area 0003 have not changed.

Linking L1_only2B and L1_only3A

The entire AS routing domain is now up and running. As mentioned in the previous chapter, IS-IS routes traffic from one area to the nearest L1/L2 router and from there across a backbone to the destination. As configured, the AS in this chapter closely mimics the OSPF AS behavior in that traffic from Area 0002 or Area 0003 will cross the Area 0001 backbone of L2_only routers.

In an AS running OSPF, that's as good as it gets. But one of the main attractions of IS-IS for ISPs is that IS-IS is more flexible and forgiving than OSPF with regard to inter-area traffic. OSPF might be better than IS-IS at limiting the sizes of link-state databases, thanks to various kinds of stub areas, but the size of the link-state database is seldom an issue for most ISP routers today. This is good news for IS-IS, which does after all require two separate link-state databases for L1 (intra-area) and L2 (inter-area) routing. OSPF figures on the shortest path with an OSPF area but not *between* OSPF areas.

However, the main concern of ISPs today is not link-state databases but traffic flow. An OSPF backbone can quickly become jammed with traffic that has nowhere else to go to get from one area to another in OSPF. But IS-IS can use shortcuts between areas to keep backbone traffic flows to a minimum.

Consider the AS network in this chapter. How does traffic flow from L1_only3A to L1_only2B at 172.16.0.7? Over six hops through five other routers: L1/L2_3to1, L2_only1B, L2_Only, L2_only1A, and L1/L2_2to1. The following is a traceroute:

```
lab@L1_only3A> traceroute 172.16.0.7
traceroute to 172.16.0.7 (172.16.0.7), 30 hops max, 40 byte packets
 1  10.0.40.1 (10.0.40.1)  0.474 ms  0.267 ms  0.186 ms
 2  10.0.35.2 (10.0.35.2)  0.364 ms  0.386 ms  0.266 ms
 3  10.0.33.1 (10.0.33.1)  0.389 ms  0.336 ms  0.328 ms
 4  10.0.32.2 (10.0.32.2)  0.452 ms  0.421 ms  0.394 ms
 5  10.0.34.1 (10.0.34.1)  0.513 ms  0.470 ms  0.463 ms
 6  172.16.0.7 (172.16.0.7)  0.651 ms  0.548 ms  0.541 ms
```

Now, suppose these routers generated a lot of traffic to each other, were located relatively close together, or both. Isn't there a better way for traffic to flow between them?

If the AS is using OSPF, there is no help. There are backdoor links in some implementations of OSPF, but these are frowned upon by purists and not covered in any standard. IS-IS, on the other hand, can be a real help with inter-area issues and situations like these, which occur all the time as ISPs grow, merge, or evolve their service network.

Figure 12.4 shows the AS network with something new added. There is now a link between L1_only3A and L1_only2B. However, since this link crosses the

area boundaries, these routers can no longer be L1_only routers. In this section, we just refer to them as 3A and 2B.

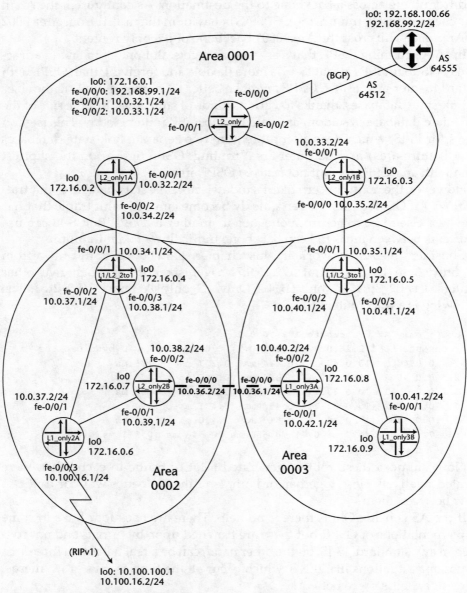

Figure 12.4   A new link between Area 0002 and Area 0003.

All that is needed is to delete `level 2 disabled` from the configuration on these routers and run IS-IS (and `family iso`) on the interfaces between them. Since both routers link directly to an L1/L2 router in their areas, they now form part of the contiguous, but free-flowing, IS-IS backbone.

The configuration details need not be of concern. What is important is what the traceroute now looks like from 3A to 2B:

```
lab@3A> traceroute 172.16.0.7
traceroute to 172.16.0.7 (172.16.0.7), 30 hops max, 40 byte packets
 1  172.16.0.7 (172.16.0.7)  0.479 ms  0.232 ms  0.201 ms
```

There is now a shortcut from Area 0003 to Area 0002. This is easy to do in IS-IS but is not allowed in the OSPF specifications. The new routing table on 3A looks as follows:

```
lab@3A > show route
inet.0: 24 destinations, 24 routes (24 active, 0 holddown, 0 hidden)
+ = Active Route, - = Last Active, * = Both

10.0.32.0/24       *[IS-IS/18] 00:20:33, metric 40, tag 2
                    > to 10.0.40.1 via fe-0/0/2.0
                      to 10.0.36.2 via fe-0/0/0.0
10.0.33.0/24       *[IS-IS/18] 00:20:33, metric 30, tag 2
                    > to 10.0.40.1 via fe-0/0/2.0
10.0.34.0/24       *[IS-IS/18] 00:20:33, metric 30, tag 2
                    > to 10.0.36.2 via fe-0/0/0.0
10.0.35.0/24       *[IS-IS/15] 00:25:35, metric 20, tag 1
                    > to 10.0.40.1 via fe-0/0/2.0
10.0.36.0/24       *[Direct/0] 00:08:34
                    > via fe-0/0/0.0
10.0.36.1/32       *[Local/0] 00:21:11
                      Local via fe-0/0/0.0
10.0.37.0/24       *[IS-IS/18] 00:20:33, metric 30, tag 2
                    > to 10.0.36.2 via fe-0/0/0.0
10.0.38.0/24       *[IS-IS/18] 00:20:33, metric 20, tag 2
                    > to 10.0.36.2 via fe-0/0/0.0
10.0.39.0/24       *[IS-IS/18] 00:20:33, metric 20, tag 2
                    > to 10.0.36.2 via fe-0/0/0.0
10.0.40.0/24       *[Direct/0] 01:46:38
                    > via fe-0/0/2.0
10.0.40.2/32       *[Local/0] 01:48:01
                      Local via fe-0/0/2.0
10.0.41.0/24       *[IS-IS/15] 00:25:35, metric 20, tag 1
                    > to 10.0.42.2 via fe-0/0/1.0
                      to 10.0.40.1 via fe-0/0/2.0
10.0.42.0/24       *[Direct/0] 01:04:11
                    > via fe-0/0/1.0
```

```
10.0.42.1/32          *[Local/0] 01:48:01
                       Local via fe-0/0/1.0
172.16.0.2/32         *[IS-IS/18] 00:20:33, metric 30, tag 2
                      > to 10.0.36.2 via fe-0/0/0.0
172.16.0.3/32         *[IS-IS/18] 00:20:33, metric 20, tag 2
                      > to 10.0.40.1 via fe-0/0/2.0
172.16.0.4/32         *[IS-IS/18] 00:20:33, metric 20, tag 2
                      > to 10.0.36.2 via fe-0/0/0.0
172.16.0.5/32         *[IS-IS/15] 00:25:35, metric 10, tag 1
                      > to 10.0.40.1 via fe-0/0/2.0
172.16.0.6/32         *[IS-IS/18] 00:20:33, metric 20, tag 2
                      > to 10.0.36.2 via fe-0/0/0.0
172.16.0.7/32         *[IS-IS/18] 00:20:33, metric 10, tag 2
                      > to 10.0.36.2 via fe-0/0/0.0
172.16.0.8/32         *[Direct/0] 01:48:01
                      > via lo0.0
172.16.0.9/32         *[IS-IS/15] 00:25:35, metric 20, tag 1
                      > to 10.0.42.2 via fe-0/0/1.0
172.16.10.1/32        *[IS-IS/18] 00:20:33, metric 30, tag 2
                      > to 10.0.40.1 via fe-0/0/2.0
192.168.100.0/24      *[IS-IS/165] 00:20:33, metric 40, tag 2
                      > to 10.0.40.1 via fe-0/0/2.0

iso.0: 1 destinations, 1 routes (1 active, 0 holddown, 0 hidden)
+ = Active Route, - = Last Active, * = Both

49.0003.0172.0016.0008.00/80
                      *[Direct/0] 01:48:01
                      > via lo0.0
```

Note how many of the routes now use the new shortcut to Area 0002 and reflect the shorter metrics. All of the Area 0001 routes can now use this link. The price for this inter-area link is a more complex and fuller link-state database on two routers, but the benefit for traffic flow might be considerable and well worth it.

In summary, both OSPF and IS-IS work well as IGPs for AS networks large and small. The attraction of OSPF for stub-sized link-state databases is offset by the requirement for all traffic to transit the OSPF backbone. The drawback of IS-IS in terms of ISO addressing and non-IP packets is offset by ease of extension for new TLVs and a less rigid area structure.

Again, both will work; which you use is a matter of choice.

PART

Three

Exterior Routing Protocols

In contrast to the six chapters on interior gateway protocols (IGPs) that made up the second part of this book, this section contains only two chapters. The two chapters investigate the Border Gateway Protocol (BGP), which is the exterior gateway protocol (EGP) of choice on the Internet. IGPs such as OSPF or IS-IS run between the routers *inside* a single AS, or routing domain. EGPs such as BGP run between different ASs. An ISP or large organization might have multiple ASs, but many networks run even by large IPS have only a single AS. In all cases, an EGP runs on the *border routers* of these routing domains and shares information about the routes within the AS or learned by the AS from other ASs.

An EGP is used to make sure that every network and interface in any AS located anywhere on the Internet is reachable from every other place in any other AS. Unlike IGPs, which essentially bootstrap themselves into existence and send information about their IP addresses and interfaces to other routers directly attached to the source router, EGPs do not generate any routing information on their own and instead rely on an underlying IGP as the source of the EGP's information.

There are EGPs other than BGP, just as there are IGPs other than RIP, OSPF, and IS-IS. For example, the Inter-Domain Routing Protocol (IDRP) from ISO is the EGP that was to be used with IS-IS as an IGP. IDRP is also sometimes promoted as the successor to BGP, or the best way to carry IPv6 routing information between ISPs and ASs. However, with the Internet as it exists today, the only EGP worth considering for real-world application is BGP.

In a very real sense, EGPs are not really routing protocols at all. As mentioned, EPGs rely on an IGP for routing information. EGPs do not really carry routing information from AS to AS. Rather, EGPs really carry information *about* routes from AS to AS. EGPs are routing protocols without routes or metrics.

In fact, what BGP describes is not even called a "route" but rather Network Layer Reachability Information (NLRI). BGP "routes" do not have metrics, like IGP routes, but *attributes*. Together, the BGP NLRI and associated attributes allow other ASs to make decisions about the best way to reach a route (network) in another AS. Once it arrives at the correct AS through BGP, the packet is delivered locally using the IGP.

So BGP forms a kind of meta-routing in relation to IGP routing. BGP is "routing about routing." The term *meta-* is a Greek prefix meaning *beyond* or *after*. Metaphysics is "beyond-physics" and metamathematics is "beyond mathematics." Metaphysics is "physics about physics" and metamathematics is "mathematics about mathematics." Where physics describes the behavior of objects with mass, metaphysics asks *why* objects have mass. Mathematics defines division, but metamathematics tries to figure out what dividing a number by 0 really means. To use a networking example, ATM meta-signaling uses signaling to set up special ATM channels to be used for "regular" signaling—that is, signaling about signaling. ATM meta-signaling is not the same as the ATM signaling used for setting up voice circuit and data channels. BGP routing to send packets to another AS is not the same as the IGP routing used to deliver packets within an AS.

This difference between BGP and IGPs should always be kept in mind. Some people new to BGP struggle with BGP terminology and concepts because they attempt to interpret BGP features in terms of more familiar IGP features. BGP does not work like an IGP because BGP is *not* an IGP and cannot and should not work like an IGP.

These chapters do not deal much with routing policies for BGP. Routing policies for BGP are discussed in full in a later part of this book.

CHAPTER 13

Border Gateway Protocol (BGP)

The Border Gateway Protocol (BGP) is the glue that holds the Internet together. One ISP cannot usually link to another ISP at all unless both run BGP between them. Despite what is sometimes claimed, it is not necessary for customer networks, even large customer networks with many routers and multiple ASs, to run BGP between their own networks and their ISP. Smaller customers especially are just as well served by a limited number of static routes defined by the ISP, and for larger customers it might be enough to run an IGP passive (no adjacency formed) on the interface to the ISP. It all depends on the complexity of the customer's and ISP's network. But if a routing protocol is deemed appropriate to run between an ISP and a customer network, this will be BGP.

BGP summarizes all that is known about the IP address space inside the local AS and advertises this information to other ASs. The other ASs pass this information along, until all ASs running BGP know exactly what is where on the Internet. Without BGP, a single default route must handle all destinations outside the AS. This is fine for single-homed ASs but hardly adequate for ASs or ISPs that have numerous connections to other ASs and ISPs.

BGP was not the original exterior gateway protocol (EGP) used on the Internet. The first was Exterior Gateway Protocol (also EGP, an unfortunate choice of acronym). EGP is still around, but only in isolated portions of what made up the original Internet, such as used by the U.S. military. However, an appreciation of EGP's limitations helps to understand why BGP looks and acts the way it does.

As the Internet (then called ARPANET) grew to include almost 1,000 computers in the early 1980s, several people noted that distance vector routing protocols such as the original Gateway-to-Gateway Protocol (GGP) would not be able to scale to a large network environment. If every router needed to know everything about every route, then convergence when links failed would be a nightmare. And changes to GGP had to be made globally, universally, and in a coordinated fashion. There was little sense in even pretending that a huge network with many different types of computers and routers run by many different organizations was in any way a single, integrated network.

The solution was to divide the emerging Internet into independent but interconnected autonomous systems (ASs). The AS was identified by a 16-bit number, assigned by the same authorities that assign IP addresses. The AS range 64512 through 65535 is reserved for private AS numbers. Inside the AS, the network could be assumed to be under the control of a single network administrator, at least at the top of the organization. Within an AS, local network matters (addressing, links, new routers, and so on) could be addressed locally by running GGP. But GGP, as an IGP, ran only within the AS. Between ASs, some way had to be found to communicate what networks were reachable within (or through) one AS to the other AS.

The solution was EGP. EGP ran on the routers (gateways) with links to other ASs. If there were two routers in an AS with links to other ASs, then EGP could be run between these two routers so that each had a full and complete set of EGP information. The two routers within the AS did not have to be connected directly, because even then the IGP was used to deliver EGP information.

RIP was also becoming popular at the time as a routing protocol. One AS running GGP could use EGP to communicate routing information to another AS running RIP. Without the concept of an AS or an EGP, the whole world would have to run the same IGP, and the routing databases, routing tables, and forwarding tables on every router would be truly huge instead of just very, very large.

EGP just sent a list of routers (gateways) and the classful major networks that the router could reach. This cut down on the amount of information that needed to be sent between ASs. Today, aggregation is used as often as possible with BGP instead of major networks, but the intent and result are the same.

The point is that there is no need for an EGP to reproduce the features of an IGP. An IGP needs to tell every router in the AS which router has which interfaces and what IP addresses are attached to these interfaces or reachable through that router (such as static routes). But all that other ASs need to know is which IP addresses are reachable in a particular AS and how to get to a border router on, or at least nearer to, that AS.

Consider a driver (packet) needing instructions on how to drive across the United States from San Jose, California, to Minneapolis, Minnesota. It is possible to give this driver a complete set of turn-by-turn directions before ever leaving San Jose. But then the San Jose "router" would have to be able to supply directions for every city, town, and village in Minnesota and every other state of the union. And the turns to take in Minnesota to get to Minneapolis are not even needed until the driver gets to Minnesota.

Perhaps there is a better way. Consider each state as an AS with a "border router" that can give drivers directions as they arrive from other states. San Jose only needs to supply 49 sets of directions to enable drivers to reach every other state in the union (presumably, the directions to Hawaii include special consideration for water routes). The directions only have to be a list of states to pass through on the way to Minnesota, perhaps Nevada, Utah, Wyoming, and South Dakota. There are lots of other ways, of course, but this "path" seems shortest to the San Jose router. The driver does not even need to know anything beyond the Next-Hop state. The San Jose router supplies details on how to get to Nevada, and that's all.

So the driver sets out and arrives in Nevada. The destination is still Minnesota, and the Nevada border router knows how to get to Minnesota. But it turns out that Utah has become congested (post-Olympic related?) or the road to Utah has even "gone down" since California sent the driver on their way, and Nevada now gives the driver directions to Idaho. Sooner or later, the driver arrives at Minnesota and is given detailed directions to Minneapolis.

Now, packets do not drive themselves through an AS. And drivers would not follow "silly" paths that went "California, Nevada, California . . ." or "California, Florida . . ." But the point here is that directions to every state can be handled very concisely by letting each state (AS) know the details (IGP) and share only essentials (EGP).

BGP Is Born

EGP worked, but it suffered from a number of limitations. There was no routing loop detection mechanism, so EPG could take more than 12 hours to count to its "infinity" of 255. The network itself had to be engineered to be loop-free, hard enough in the 1980s and now impossible. There was a tree built around a core network in EGP, and that was how it worked.

Once the NSFNET and ASs arrived, the need to carry routing policy (or *policy-based routing* or *policy routing*) along with basic routing information was impossible with EGP. Traffic for "education and research" could use the NSFNET backbone. Commercial traffic was supposed to use private backbones. But there was no way to tell a router receiving an EGP advertisement that this route, even though much closer through this next hop and not that one, had to use the longer route to comply with the Acceptable Use Policy (AUP) in place at the time.

EGP packets, like RIP packets, could be easily spoofed, making a misbehaving EGP router or hacker source appear like a great way to reach a lot of places. And EGP distances were also often interpreted as RIP hop counts. Naturally, EGP metrics greater than 15 caused all kinds of problems with RIP as the IGP.

Finally, EGP packets that were fragmented had to be reassembled once all the pieces had arrived. Missing pieces meant that whole messages had to be re-sent. EGP had to do all of this housekeeping itself, and this just slowed the already leisurely convergence time of EGP to a crawl.

After some attempts to create a more sophisticated version of EGP, it was decided to create a better EGP (as a class of routing protocol, in contrast to IGPs) than EGP, to be called BGP. BGP came along in 1989 with RFC 1105 (BGP1 or BGP-1 or BGPv1), revised in 1990 as RFC 1163 (BGP2), and revised again in 1991 as RFC 1267 (BGP3). But the version of BGP used today on the Internet, BGP4, emerged in 1994 as RFC 1654 and was extended for classless operation in 1995 as RFC 1771, which remains the baseline BGP specification today. This chapter describes BGP4.

Although BGP4 is the most common EGP in use today, BGP is not necessary to link IGP routing domains. Smaller networks can use static routes, with or without aggregation, and even huge, global ISPs can link OSPF or IS-IS routing domains with yet another well-planned OSPF Area 0 that aggregates all routing information to the rest of the Internet or a series of L2-only IS-IS routers that serve the same purpose. But when an EGP is needed to link AS routing domains, BGP is available.

Although not discussed in this book in any detail, BGP has recently been extended for new roles on the Internet. BGP *extended communities* are used with virtual private networks (VPNs). And BGP routes are often the only ones that can use Multiprotocol Label Switching (MPLS) Label Switched Paths (LSPs). BGP is as easily extensible as IS-IS and OSPF to support new functions and add routing information that needs to be circulated between ASs.

BGP as a Path Vector Protocol

One of the problems with EGP was that the metrics looked very much like RIP hop counts. Simple distance vectors were not helpful at the AS level, because hop counts could not account for the fast backbone links that were beginning to appear in major ISP's networks. Destinations that appeared close over 56- or 64-Kbps links took much longer to reach than through more hops over 45-Mbps links. And distance vectors had no protection against routing loops.

Link-state protocols could have dealt with the problem by implementing some of the alternative TOS metrics described in the OPSF and IS-IS chapters. However, these would rely not only on consistent implementation among all ISPs but on the correct setting of bits in IP packets by the originators. In the brave new world of independent and highly competitive ISPs, this consistency would be next to impossible to achieve.

So neither distance vectors without loop protection nor link states with unrealistic TOS features were deemed proper for BGP. Instead, BGP became a *path vector* protocol.

In BGP, each routing update carries a full list of transit networks (ASs) that must be traversed between the AS receiving the update and the AS that can deliver the packet using its IGP. A loop occurs when an AS path list contains the same AS that is receiving the update. This update is rejected and loops prevented. If the update is accepted, that AS will add its own AS to the list when advertising the routing update to other ASs. This allows ASs to apply routing policies to the updates and avoid using routes that lead through an AS that is not the preferred way to reach a destination.

Path vectors do not imply that all ASs are created equal. Numerous small ASs might get traffic through faster than one huge AS. But more aspects of a route are described in BGP than just the length of the AS path to the destination. The nicest part of this system is that it allows each AS to represent the route with different metrics that mean something to the AS originating the route. All that need matter to another AS is how many other ASs are on the path to the destination.

Associating a potentially lengthy path with each and every route on the Internet was initially seen as posing a considerable issue with scalability. More ASs generate more routes with more path information. RFC 1774 in 1995 estimated that 100,000 routes generated by 3,000 ASs (ISPs) would have paths about 20 ASs long. There was a real concern about router memory and processor requirements to store and maintain all of this information, especially in smaller routers.

Several mechanisms are built into BGP to address this concern. One is support for aggressive route aggregation and classless routing. For a long time, ISPs would not accept a BGP route advertisement with a mask more than 19 bits long (/19). This was called the *universally reachable* address level. The price paid for smaller routing tables and maintenance is a loss of routing accuracy, and many ISPs have relaxed this policy. The other BGP mechanisms to cut down on routing table size and maintenance complexity are route reflectors, confederations (also called subconfederations), and route damping. All of these are discussed in later sections of this chapter.

IBPG and EBGP

BGP is an EPG that runs between individual routing domains, or ASs. When BGP *speakers* (the official term for routers that are configured to peer with BGP neighbors) are in different ASs, the routers use an *exterior* BGP (EBPG) session to exchange information. When BGP peers are within the same AS, the routers use *interior* BGP (IBGP) for the same purpose. These terms often appear in the forms E-BPG/I-BGP or eBGP/iBGP as well.

Now wait a minute. Isn't BGP an *exterior* gateway protocol? And doesn't BGP typically require a fully functioning IGP to reach the destination? Yes, both of these statements are true. Then what is *interior* BGP?

IBGP is not some IGP version of BGP. It is still necessary for BGP routers to exchange BGP routing information inside the same AS. To understand why this is the case, consider the collection of ASs shown in Figure 13.1

As shown in the figure, IBGP sessions are usually only required when an AS is *multihomed* and has multiple links to other ASs. These multiple links can be to the same AS or to different ASs. An AS with only a single link to one other AS need only run EBGP on the border router and can rely on the IGP to distribute routes learned by EBPG to the other routers. Of course, in the case where there is only one exit point for the entire AS, a single static, default route to the border router can be used effectively as well.

EBGP sessions usually peer to the *physical interface* address of the neighboring router. These are typically point-to-point WAN links and are the only way to reach another AS. If the link is down, then the other AS is unreachable over that link anyway, so there is little point in trying to keep a BGP session going to the peer. IBGP sessions usually peer to the stable *loopback interface* address of the peer. An IBGP peer can typically be reached over more than one physical interface within the AS, so even if an IBGP peer's most direct interface is down, the BGP sessions can stay up because BGP packets use the IGP routing table to find their way to the peer.

When two BGP neighbors, EBGP or IBGP, first see each other, they exchange their entire BGP routing tables. After that, only incremental or partial table information is exchanged when routing changes occur. BGP Keepalives are exchanged because in stable networks long periods of time might elapse before something interesting happens. There is no standard Keepalive interval, but most router vendors use 60 seconds as a default Keepalive interval

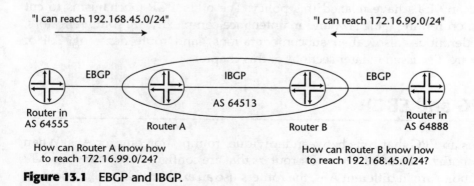

Figure 13.1 EBGP and IBGP.

and 180 seconds as the hold timer, although these can be changed. Unlike IGPs, which must match timer parameters, BGP peers use the lower of two conflicting values on EBGP sessions, since one AS has no real control over the parameters set in another AS.

BGP "Next Hops" and IGP Next Hops

This chapter positions BGP as a "meta-routing" protocol that carries not so much routing information like an IGP does as "routing information about routing information." IGPs have nothing like BGP AS paths to communicate, BGP routes (NLRIs, or Network Layer Reachability Information) are not really routes, and BGP next hops are not really like IGP next hops at all.

BGP NLRIs are the way one AS tells another "I know how to reach IP address space 192.168.14.0/24 and 172.16.24.0/24 and..." The AS does not say that it is the AS that has assigned that IP address space locally—many of the addresses might be from other ASs beyond the AS advertising the routes. That's what the AS path is for: to allow an AS to figure out just how far away a destination is through the AS that has advertised the route, or NLRI.

With an IGP, the next hop associated with a route is usually the IP address of the physical interface on the next-hop router. But the BGP next hop (also sometimes called the protocol next hop) is supposed to be the IP address of the *router* that is advertising the BGP NLRI information. The BGP next hop is the address of the BGP peer, usually the loopback interface address (the *BGP Identifier*) for IBGP and the physical interface address for EBGP. The BGP next hop is the way that one BGP router tells another "If you have a packet for this IP address space, send it here."

For a BGP next hop to be useful, the BGP next hop *must* be reachable through the receiving router's IGP routing table. To resolve a BGP next hop, the route must recursively look up IP addresses in the local routing table until a local physical interface and address is found and the packet forwarded in the general direction of the destination.

This reliance on the underlying IGP is one reason that BGP does not have to bootstrap itself into existence like an IGP. There is no need for BGP to have a mechanism for network topology discovery and information sharing; the IGP has done this already. BGP, like the meta-routing protocol it is, sits on top of the IGP and sends information about IP address spaces to other ASs around the local AS. Of course, it is necessary to give BGP something to advertise in the first place, but that is what routing policy is all about.

Because of the way BGP sets its next hops, there is a well-known unreachable condition in BGP that must be solved with a simple routing policy known as *Next Hop Self*, or just NHS. This is discussed more fully in the next chapter. It is enough here to note that an EBGP route, or NLRI, typically arrives from another AS with the physical address of the remote interface as the BGP next hop. If the EBGP route is readvertised through IBPG, it is likely that the BGP next hop will be completely unknown to the IGP routing tables inside the receiving AS. Why should a router deep within an AS know or care about how to reach a physical interface IP address in another AS? Next Hop Self is just a way to have the router advertising the route through IBGP use *itself* as the next hop for the EBGP route. Not BGP next-hop-is-the-physical-interface-in-another-AS, but BGP next-hop-is-me-in-this-AS or BGP next-hop-self.

IBGP and the IGP

There are two more reasons that IBGP cannot effectively be used as an IGP by itself within an AS. The first reason is that BGP is not a routing protocol built directly on top of IP. BGP relies on TCP connections to reach its peers and so resembles an IP application more than an IGP routing protocol. Without the IGP to provide connectivity, TCP sessions for the BGP messages cannot be established except on links to adjacent routers. The second reason is that BGP does not flood information with IBPG. So what an IBGP router learns from its IBGP peers is never passed along to another IBGP neighbor. To fully distribute BGP information among the routers within an AS, a full mesh of IBGP connections (adjacencies) is necessary. That is, every IBGP router must send complete routing information to every other IBGP router in the AS. In a large AS with many external links to other ASs, this meshing requirement can add a lot of overhead traffic and configuration maintenance to the network. This is where route reflectors and confederations come in later in this chapter.

Why was BGP built this way, with TCP for message transport and no flooding? The main reasons were to keep BGP as simple as possible and to prevent routing loops inside the AS.

Routing protocols like OSPF ride directly inside best-effort IP packets. IP does not resequence packets, resend missing information, or fragment large messages across multiple packets. If these features are needed by the routing protocol (and they are always a good idea), either the routing protocol must provide them or the routing protocol must rely on another layer of the protocol to perform these tasks. OSPF builds support for these features in, but BGP, in the name of simplicity, relies on TCP to provide these features. The result is a less complex protocol, but one that relies on the IGP to provide TCP reachability before the BGP session can be established. No TCP reachability, no BGP.

Also, BGP relies on the AS path for loop prevention. But within an AS, the AS path does not change, by definition. So there is no loop prevention for BGP inside the AS, and flooding of IBGP information could easily lead to a situation where many routers claim to be closer to a destination outside the AS, but none of the routers ever passes the packet to another AS.

The dependency on TCP and the lack of flooding means that IBGP must communicate directly with every other router that needs to know BGP routing information. This does not mean that every router must be adjacent (connected by a direct link), since TCP can be routed through many routers to reach its destination. What it does mean is that routers connected by IBGP inside an AS must create a *full mesh* of IGBP peering sessions.

Nevertheless, it is possible to use IBGP alone, without any IGP running between BGP routers at all. However, this requires all of the routers running IBGP to be directly connected and adjacent. This direct connectivity is not often available in anything but the smallest of ASs.

Without a full IBGP mesh, some routers might not know how to reach some destinations. Because IBGP does not flood, one router receiving IBGP information on one interface will never send that information out on another IBGP interface. It is all too common to find situations with IBGP as shown in Figure 13.2.

In the figure, Router A has network 192.168.122.0/24 to advertise to Router B with IBGP, and Router C has 172.16.12.0/24. Router B passes along both routes to Router D in AS 65001. Router D in turn passes the routing information along to Router E and Router F with IBPG. Ironically, while all of the routers in AS 65001 can reach 172.16.12.0/24 and 192.168.122.0/24, Router A cannot reach 172.16.12.0/24 and Router C cannot reach 192.168.122.0/24 inside their own AS! This is because IBGP will not flood. To allow full connectivity, Router A and Router C need to run IBGP between them, or inject the BGP routes into the IGP.

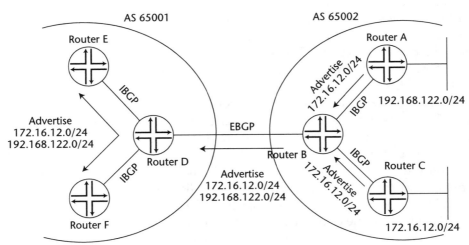

Figure 13.2 The need for a full IBGP mesh.

Perhaps IBGP could just function with a partial mesh instead of a full mesh inside the AS. Maybe the IGP, which usually has to be running inside the AS already, could assist in distributing BGP information. This idea is closely related to another question: Should BGP information from other ASs be redistributed into the IGP? In other words, should a border router take all of the BGP routers received from another AS and just dump them into OSPF or IS-IS or RIP? Is it necessary for all routers in an AS, not just border routers with external links, to know about every single external destination outside the AS?

Consider the situation shown in Figure 13.3. The center ISP has arranged to act as a transit AS for traffic from the ISP on the left to the ISP on the right. Only one route is needed to understand the principle applied to all routes received from ISP 1. The routers inside of ISP 2 do not need to know all the details about the IP address space outside of the AS, just where the border routers are. So IBGP only runs between the two border routers. But when the route for 192.168.77.0/24 is propagated from ISP 1 to ISP 3, ISP 3 begins to send traffic for 192.168.77.0/24 to the ISP 2 border router, naturally. The ISP 2 border router 2 looks this route up in the routing table, and the next hop for the packet is ISP 2 border router 1 facing ISP 1. The *BGP next hop* should be ISP 2 border router 1, but the packet will end up at ISP 2 internal router 3 (there is nowhere else to send it), where the destination address 192.168.77.0/24 is unknown because this internal router is not running BGP. Note that this argument applies only to *transit* traffic through ISP 2.

What should be done to correct this situation and allow packets to transit ISP 2 correctly? There are two ways. The first way is to require the IGP on all routers to know how to reach all external destinations. So every router's IGP table knows how to reach 192.168.77.0/24 through ISP 2 border router 1. This is called *IGP synchronization*. In many BGP implementations, a border router learning a route through IBGP will not advertise the route through EBGP unless the route is reachable through the IGP. To prevent black-hole situations as just described, all EBGP routes learned by ISP 2 border router 1 are redistributed into the IGP. Problem solved.

The second task is to have all of the routers in the AS fully meshed with IBGP. Then IGP synchronization can be turned off, since all routers, even internal routers, will learn about the external routes directly from BGP. Of course, no link-state database calculations can then be applied to figure out how best to reach these routes, but since external and link-state calculations only work within the AS, there is little harm in keeping BGP routes out of the IGP.

Initially, it was assumed that this injection of external BGP information into the IGP would be done routinely. No router would accept an IBGP route unless the route was in the IGP table already, per the rule already described as BGP/IGP synchronization. The problem was that once the Internet grew in leaps and bounds from 1995 on, the last thing anyone wanted to do was to

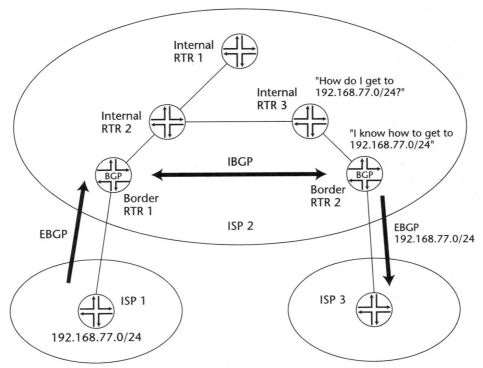

Figure 13.3   BGP synchronization with the IGP.

inject *all* external routes into the IGP. A huge link-state database would choke on the whole Internet routing table, so external routes were typically isolated from IGP routing protocols.

Faced with the choice of overwhelming the IGP with all external routes or running IBGP as a full mesh to all routers inside the AS, most ISPs made the only reasonable choice in the face of link-state database complexities. The ISPs turned off synchronization (if that was the default behavior) and ran IBGP as a full mesh to all routers.

The BGP next hop must also be reachable through the IGP, because of how BGP routing table lookups recurse through the table until an output interface is found. This is, of course, just another application of the Next Hop Self rule.

This seemingly simple rule that BGP destinations must be reachable is the cause of a lot of headaches on networks running BGP. A perfectly good route from another AS is advertised with IBGP to other routers in the AS. But the route is never sent any farther and seems to disappear inside of the receiving AS. A check of the routing table on the outgoing border router shows no route to the destination, yet a check of the routing protocol's operation shows that the route has arrived through an IBGP update. A common reason for this (and there are other reasons that this might happen) is that the BGP destination is unreachable in the routing table. BGP will never install a route in the routing table (and forwarding table) that cannot be used and will also refuse to advertise the route.

There are other rules governing the relationship between IBGP and EBGP with regard to advertising routes. The rules for distributing routing information between IBPG and EBGP are shown in Figure 13.4.

The figure, based on Figure 13.2, shows that Router D will advertise routes learned from EBGP into IBGP in AS 65001. Router B in AS 65002 will advertise anything learned from IBGP (or EBGP) into EBGP to AS 65001. But Router B (or Router D) will never advertise anything learned from IBGP to another IBGP router. Any other routes advertised by BGP must be added through the use of a routing policy.

Other Types of BGP

The major flavors of BGP are EBGP for external peers outside the AS and IBGP for internal peers within the same AS. These are usually the only types of BGP mentioned in most books and articles. But variations of BGP that have somewhat different functions than IBGP or EBGP are used in other situations.

One BGP variation that is becoming very important, especially where VPNs are concerned, is *Multiprotocol BGP*, often seen as MBGP or MP-BGP. Originally defined in RFC 2545, Multiprotocol BGP originally extended BGP to support IP multicast routes and routing information. But the usefulness of MBGP

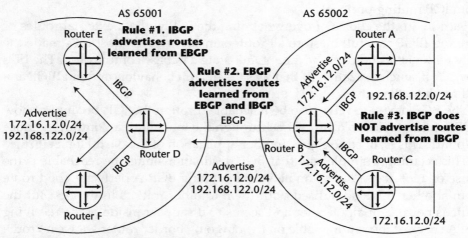

Figure 13.4   IBGP to and from EBGP.

for carrying all types of additional information is already apparent. MBGP is being used to support IP-based VPN information and to carry IPv6 routing information, such as from RIPng and OSPF for IPv6. MBGP work on IPv6 is just beginning, so unlike the IGP chapters, no special consideration of using BGP for IPv6 appears in this chapter other than to note that MBGP will be used for this purpose.

Then there is *Multihop BGP*, sometimes seen as EBGP Multihop. Multihop BGP is only used with EBGP and allows an EBGP peer in another AS to be more than one hop away. Usually, EBGP peers are directly connected by a point-to-point WAN link. But sometimes it is necessary to peer with a router beyond the border router that actually terminates the link, especially if the router at the end of the direct link happens to be very small and under-powered (not often a problem for border routers, but it does happen). Normally, BGP packets have a TTL of 1, so they never travel beyond the adjacent router. Multihop BGP packets have a TTL greater than 1, and the peer is beyond the adjacent router. Multihop BGP is also used in load-balancing scenarios when there is more than one link between two border routers. Multihop BGP is not considered further in this book.

Finally, there is a slight change of behavior in the BGP that runs between confederations. Confederations are discussed more fully later and the differences detailed then. In most cases, the version of BGP that runs between confederations is just called EBGP. However, there are slight differences in the EBGP that runs between ASs and the EBGP that runs between confederations, which are always inside the same AS. Sometimes the variant of BGP that runs between confederations is known as Confederation BGP, or CBGP, although use of this term is still uncommon.

BGP Attributes

The meta-routing information that all forms of BGP carry is associated with a route (NLRI) as a series of *attributes*. This is the major difference between BGP and IGPs. IGP routes carry just the route, next hop, metric, and maybe an optional tag (or two). BGP routes can carry a staggering amount of information, all intended to allow an AS to pick and choose the best way to reach a destination.

Most implementations of BGP understand 10 attributes, and some use and understand even more. Before we list them, you should know that every BGP attribute is characterized by two major parameters. An attribute is either *well-known* or *optional*. Well-known attributes must be understood and processed by every implementation of BGP regardless of vendor. Optional attributes are exactly that; there is no guarantee that a given BGP implementation will understand or process that particular attribute. BGP implementations that do not support an optional attribute simply pass that information on if that is what is called for, or they ignore it.

In addition, a well-known BGP attribute is either *mandatory* or *discretionary*. Mandatory BGP attributes must be present in every BGP update message for EBGP, IBGP, or something else. Discretionary BGP attributes are present not at the vendor's pleasure, as might be assumed by the use of the term *discretionary*. Rather, these attributes appear only in some types of BGP update messages, such as those used by EBGP only.

Finally, optional BGP attributes are *transitive* or *nontransitive*. Transitive BGP optional attributes are passed from peer to peer even if the router does not support the option. Nontransitive BGP optional attributes can be ignored by the receiver BGP process if not supported and not sent along to peers.

The 10 BGP attributes discussed in this chapter are listed with their characteristics in Table 13.1.

The rest of this section briefly describes each of the BGP path attributes in the table.

Table 13.1. BGP Attributes

| | CLASS | | | |
| | WELL-KNOWN | | OPTIONAL | |
ATTRIBUTE (TYPE CODE)	MANDATORY	DISCRETIONARY	TRANSITIVE	NONTRANSITIVE
ORIGIN (1)	X			
AS_PATH (2)	X			
NEXT_HOP (3)	X			
LOCAL_PREF (4)		X		
ATOMIC_AGGREGATE (5)		X		
AGGREGATOR (6)			X	
COMMUNITY (7)			X	
MULTI_EXIT_DISC (MED) (8)				X
ORIGINATOR_ID (9)				X
CLUSTER_LIST (10)				X

The ORIGIN Attribute

The Origin attribute reflects where BGP obtained knowledge of the route in the first place. This attribute can have one of the following values:

IGP (0).   The NLRI was learned from an IGP in the originating AS. This is the *highest* value for Origin in the BGP route selection process.

EGP (1).   The NLRI was learned from EGP.

INCOMPLETE (2).   BGP does not have completion knowledge of the NLRI origin. For example, BGP will not know when redistribution occurs for static routes. This is the *lowest* value for Origin.

The AS_PATH Attribute

This attribute is a sequence of AS numbers that lead to the originating AS for the NLRI. When one AS advertises a BGP route to another with EBGP, it *prepends* its own AS number to this list. So the list is from most recent transit AS to the originating AS. The main use of the AS Path is for loop avoidance among ASs. But it is common to artificially extend the AS Path attribute through a routing policy so that a particular path through a certain router looks very unattractive.

The AS Path attribute can consist of an ordered list of AS numbers (AS_SEQUENCE) or just a collection of AS numbers in no particular order (AS_SET). If an aggregate is formed by merging two or more routes with ordered AS Path, the AS Path attribute for the new aggregate can also merge all of the AS Path members into an AS_SET instead of an AS_SEQUENCE and so try to preserve some information about the more specific routes.

The NEXT_HOP Attribute

This is the BGP Next Hop (or protocol next hop) and quite distinct from an IGP's bootstrap next hop. Outside of an AS, the BGP Next Hop is most likely the border router, not the actual router inside the other AS that has this network on a local interface. The BGP Next Hop is used to determine the *IGP Next Hop* to be used for the packet inside the AS that originates the route.

Usually, if the advertising router and the receiving router are in different ASs, the BGP Next Hop is the IP address of the physical interface of the advertising router. If the advertising router and the receiving router are in the same AS, and the NLRI is also in the same AS, the BGP Next Hop is the IP address of the advertising router. Finally, if the advertising router and the receiving router are in the same AS, and the NLRI is *outside* the AS, the BGP Next Hop is the IP address of the external peer. In this last case, Next Hop Self is the typical way to make sure that the BGP Next Hop is reachable.

The LOCAL_PREF Attribute

This is the Local Preference of the NLRI relative to other routes learned by IBGP within an AS and therefore is not used by EBGP. In contrast to most other routing protocol metrics, with Local Pref, it is the *highest* value that is better. When routes are advertised with IBGP, traffic will flow toward the AS exit point (border router) that advertised the highest Local Preference for the route. For example, if the routing policy for an AS is to use ISP 1 first and only use ISP 2 if ISP 1 is unreachable, this can be easily accomplished by advertising routes with IBGP received from ISP 1 with a higher Local Pref than routes received from ISP 2.

The MULTI_EXIT_DISC (MED) Attribute

The Multi-Exit Discriminator (MED) attribute is the way that one AS tries to influence another when it goes to choosing among multiple exit points (border routers) that link to the AS. This makes sense when a route lies much closer to one border router than another. Why not have the other AS just send the traffic for that network to that border router instead of another?

A MED is the closest thing to a purely IGP metric that BGP has. Manipulating MEDs is one of the most common ways that one ISP tries to make another ISP use the links it wants between the ISPs, such as higher-speed links. However, since the MED is optional, there is no guarantee that the other ISP will comply with the MED settings. Once inside another AS, the MED might be modified or ignored.

The MED only really makes sense when (1) there are multiple links between ASs and (2) the links are between a pair of ASs. The first condition is more or less by definition, but the second condition is subtle. Because the AS that originates the MED has no idea what other external links the other AS maintains, there is no point in trying to influence traffic beyond the neighboring AS. All traffic from beyond the neighboring AS must pass through that AS anyway, and the MED does its job there, not anywhere else. So why pass a MED along?

Also, MED values are totally arbitrary. A high MED in one AS might actually be a relatively low value in another AS. Lack of defined values makes coordination between the two ASs crucial. The local aspect of MED values and operation means comparing MEDs received from two different ASs—which is not recommended or even wise. The "AS in the middle" would usually end up comparing apples to oranges, although most BGP implementation allow some sort of "always compare MEDs" operation, regardless of whether or not the NLRIs were received from the same AS.

The ATOMIC_AGGREGATE and AGGREGATOR Attributes

These two attributes work together. Both are used when routing information is aggregated for BGP. A common goal on the Internet today is to represent as many networks (routes) with as few routing table entries as possible. So as routing information makes its way through the Internet, each AS often tries to condense (aggregate) the routing information as much as possible with as short a VLSM as can be properly contrived.

In BGP, routers frequently advertise *overlapping* routes. Overlapping routes are not identical but point to the same destination and one route is contained within the other. For example, the routes 192.168.192.0/19 and 192.168.128.0/17 are overlapping in the sense that the first route is also contained in the second. Of course, many more routes are covered by 192.168.128.0/17 than the more specific route, so why not just advertise the /17 route to another AS?

In fact, the range of possibilities presented to a BGP router confronted with overlapping routes to deal with is quite broad. The router can:

- Advertise both routes, more specific and less specific alike.
- Advertise only the less specific route.
- Aggregate even further and advertise only that aggregate.

It is even possible for the BGP router to advertise only the more specific route, advertise only the nonoverlapping portion of the route, or even ignore the routes and advertise neither. But it is more common to advertise only the less specific route.

This is when a problem arises. What should the BGP attributes be on the route (NLRI) advertised? The /17 and /19 could have originated in two different ASs, each with its own value for AS Path, Origin, MED, and so on. Aggregation always results in a loss of routing information. The Atomic Aggregate is used to alert other routers that some attribute information has been lost as a result of BGP aggregation. Any other router that receives an NLRI with the Atomic Attribute set cannot make the information about that route more specific, since the details have been lost. When that route is advertised further, the Atomic Aggregate attribute must remain attached to the route.

Whenever the Atomic Aggregate attribute is set, the BGP router can also attach the Aggregator attribute, which is optional. This attribute gives the AS number and Router ID of the router that performed the aggregation. The use of the ATOMIC_AGGREGATE and AGGREGATOR attributes is shown in Figure 13.5.

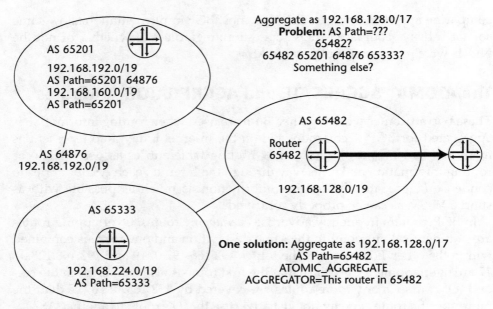

Figure 13.5   Aggregation and loss of path information.

It is possible to attempt to preserve all information about routes by making the aggregated attributes the *union* of all attributes under the aggregate address. An AS Path does not have to be an ordered list of ASs. The list can be unordered and so at least include all ASs along the path. Similar arguments can be made for other BGP attributes.

The COMMUNITY Attribute

Think of the BGP Community attribute as clubs for routes. For instance, in the United States people can belong to social and community organizations like the Elks Club, the Lions Club, and the Rotary Club. Rather than dealing with gatherings of the whole town name-by-name, it is easier to say something like "all members of the Elks Club over here." And just as people can belong to more than one club (and so follow more than one set of directions when they gather), routes can belong to more than one BGP Community and so might have more than one policy applied when they arrive at or leave a router.

Communities make it easier to apply policies to routes as a group. There might be a community that applies to an ISP's customers. In that case, it is not necessary to list every customer's IP address in a policy to set Local Pref or MED, for example, as long as they all are assigned to a unique "customer" community value. Community values are often used today as a way for one

ISP to inform a peer ISP of the value of the Local Pref for the route inside the originating ISP's AS (Local Pref is not present in EBGP).

The Community attribute was originally Cisco-specific but was standardized in RFC 1997. Unfortunately, the use of the Community fields was changed in the process. Cisco defined the 32 bits of the Community attribute in the form NN:AA, where NN was the 16-bit *Community value* (0-65535) and AA was the 16-bit AS number that set the Community value. RFC 1997 reverses these fields into AA:NN and Cisco routers must be configured to recognize the "new format."

RFC 1997 reserves some values for the Community attribute, which can be written as AA:NN (for humans) or as decimal or hexadecimal values. Values (NN) from 0x00000000 to 0x0000FFFF (Community values from 0 to 65535) are reserved, as are combined values for AA:NN from 0xFFFF0000 through 0xFFFFFFFF (the range 65535:0 through 65535:65535). All routes not reserved belong to the INTERNET community, which is defined as *well known* (supported by all BGP implementations that support the Community attribute).

There are three other *well-known communities* with global significance established in RFC 1997. These meanings must be respected in any BGP implementation that supports the Community attribute:

NO_EXPORT (0xFFFFFF01).   These routes cannot be advertised to EBGP peers, but are advertised within a BGP confederation (discussed later in the chapter).

NO_ADVERTISE (0xFFFFFF02).   These routes cannot be advertised at all, either with IBGP or EBGP.

LOCAL_AS (0xFFFFFF03).   This was defined as NO_EXPORT_ SUBCONFED in RFC 1997. These routes cannot be advertised by EBGP, even when the EBGP peers belonging to the same confederation (discussed discussed later in the chapter).

The ORIGINATOR_ID and CLUSTER_LIST Attributes

These attributes are used by BGP *route reflectors*, also discussed in full later in this chapter. Both of these attributes are used to prevent routing loops when route reflectors are in use. The Originator ID is a 32-bit value created by the route reflector and is the originator of the route within the local AS. If the originator router sees its own ID is a received route, a loop has occurred and the route is ignored.

The Cluster List is a list of the route reflection Cluster IDs of the clusters through which the route has passed. If a route reflector sees it own Cluster ID in the Cluster List, a loop has occurred and the route is ignored.

BGP Route Selection

In the interconnected ISP world that is the Internet, it is not unusual for a route to a particular prefix to be reachable through *every* router with a link to another AS. The AS paths might be different, but might be the same length. In terms of the IGP world, the link-state database might contain routes with equal cost metrics out more than one interface on the router. In BGP this applies now to the entire AS. The simplest solution with an IGP is just to pick one next hop at random to install in the forwarding table.

This "just pick one" approach could be used with BGP. But BGP might present not two or three choices, but 10 or more, depending on the size of the AS in question. And BGP has more than just a simple metric available to choose a route to be used for packet forwarding. In fact, there is a whole procedure in the BGP specification that should be followed before a router selects a BGP route to use for a prefix.

This is a good time to introduce the Routing Information Base (RIB) tables that BGP uses. BGP is not a link-state protocol and not an IGP, so BGP has no link-state database to hold routing information while running the route selection process and deciding what to do with the routes inside a particular update.

Three parts (tables) are defined for the BGP database: Adj-RIBs-in (often just called RIB-in), Loc-RIB (RIB-local), and Adj-RIBs-out (RIB-out). The RIB-in table contains the routing information from all received BGP update messages. This is the raw material for the BGP route selection process. The RIB-local table has the routing information that is locally available to the router once all local routing policies have been applied to the attributes of the route. The RIB-out table stores the information that will potentially be advertised to the router's BGP peers.

So the content of a BGP Update message is stored in RIB-in. A route selection process installs the best route to a prefix into RIB-local, where it is available to the router's forwarding table. This route, the active route to the destination, is now added to the RIB-out table for advertisement to BGP peers. This means that BGP will advertise only *active* routes, routes that are currently being used by the local router to reach a destination. Why take up bandwidth advertising routes that are not being used?

This also has implications for BGP troubleshooting. A router with many BGP peers can receive many ways to reach a particular prefix. Yet the router only advertises *one* way to its own peers. There is nothing wrong and the routing information is not being "swallowed up" by the router. It is just that BGP will only advertise the route it is actually using to reach the destination prefix: the active route.

This also means that if a route becomes unreachable because of router or link failure, the route must be explicitly *withdrawn* by BGP. This fact is advertised to all peers through the RIB-out table, and another active route can be selected from the RIB-in table (and advertised in turn). If the router or link is restored, the same criteria that made this path preferable to the new active route now makes the original route active again. So the active route is withdrawn and the original route active again.

When intermittently failing links go up and down rapidly, this causes a BGP phenomenon known as *route flapping*. Since many IP prefixes could be reachable through one link, the resulting BGP Update and Withdrawn messages can cause tremendous traffic bursts on the network, but usually only in very large collections of BGP routers. The solution to the route flapping problem, called *route damping*, is discussed in the section of this chapter covering BGP scaling issues.

Once BGP routes are safely in the RIB-in table, a route selection Decision Process determines which routes should end up in the routing and forwarding tables to direct packets to these destinations. Since BGP collects routing information from many sources, it is common to find the RIB-in table packed with contenders each claiming to be the best way to reach a prefix. So BGP employs a very elaborate selection process to pick one way to reach a particular prefix.

Each router vendor has its own interpretation of how the rules outlined in RFC 1771 should be used to elect a BGP route. There can be added constraints (Cisco adds a proprietary *administrative weight*) or internal procedures (Juniper Networks adds details for routes stored in different routing tables). But generally, the BGP route selection process is as follows with regard to BGP attributes:

1. Make sure the BGP Next Hop is reachable through the IGP, or ignore the route.

2. Prefer the route with the *highest* Local Pref.

3. If the Local Prefs are the same (or absent, as on EBGP routes), prefer the route with the shortest AS Path.

4. If the AS Path lengths are the same, prefer the route with the lower Origin code.

5. If the Origin codes are the same, prefer the route with lowest MED value. There are several other considerations here, depending on whether the router should "always compare MEDs" from different ASs or not.

6. If the MED values are the same, prefer EBGP routes over confederation EBGP routes, and prefer confederation routes over IBGP routes. The point here is that EBGP routes have better loop prevention (the AS Path) than confederation BGP or IBGP routes.

7. If everything is still the same, prefer the BGP route with the lowest IGP metric for its BGP Next Hop.

8. When all else fails to distinguish the route, prefer the route with the lowest BGP Router ID.

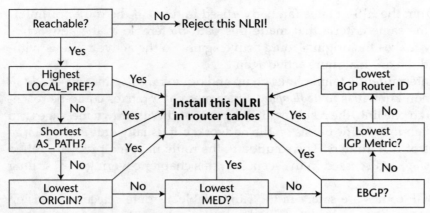

Figure 13.6 BGP attributes and the route selection process.

Router vendors often vary these listed steps a lot, adding substeps and additional situations, especially toward the bottom of the route selection process. There are allowances for multiple paths and load balancing. The sequence of BGP attributes used in the route selection process is shown in Figure 13.6.

This outline emphasizes the precedence of the BGP attributes themselves and the role of the IGP.

BGP as a Policy-Driven Routing Protocol

If BGP is not like an IGP and does not bootstrap itself into existence by advertising the local topology and addressing to adjacent routers, then how does routing information get into BGP in the first place? How are the contents of the BGP attributes other than the defaults determined and adjusted? How can some routes advertised by BGP end up being ignored by routers that would ordinarily seem to find the routes very attractive?

The answer to each of these questions is the same: through the use of routing policy. BGP is nothing if not a *policy-driven* protocol. What BGP does and how BGP does it can be almost totally determined by routing policy. It is difficult to make BGP do exactly what an ISP wants without judicious use of routing policies.

Want BGP to advertise customers on static routes or running OSPF, IS-IS or RIP? Redistribute statics, OSPF, IS-IS and RIP into BGP. Want to artificially extend an AS path to make an AS look very unattractive for transit traffic? Write a routing policy to prepend the AS multiple times. Want to change the community attribute to add or subtract information? Use a routing policy. Concerned about the sheer amount of routes advertised? Write a routing policy to aggregate the routes any way that makes sense. Want to advertise a more specific route along with a more general aggregate (called "punching a hole" in the advertised address space)? Write a routing policy. And so on.

More than any other protocol in use today, BGP depends on routing policy to behave the way it should. The majority of the routing policies considered in the later chapters of this book will be concerned with BGP attribute manipulation.

BGP Scaling

When BGP4 was first standardized, the Internet consisted of about 20,000 routes and many companies, even large ones, had national networks with fewer than 10 routers on the backbone. Full mesh IBGP requirements were not burdensome in this environment, although 10 routers required 45 IBGP sessions to fully mesh the network (the formula is $N(N-1)/2$). Adding an IBGP router required 10 more sessions, one to each of the other routers, but this was still not too bad. The update messages needed to keep the BGP information current was manageable as well.

But consider an AS with 100,000 routes to maintain, even with aggregation. A global corporation today might have 3,000 routers large and small spread around the world. Even with multiple ASs, there could be 1,000 routers within an AS that might all need IBGP information, no matter how the routes have been aggregated. To fully mesh 1,000 IBGP routers within an AS requires 499,500 IBGP sessions! A network 100 times larger than the 10 router network of 1995 requires more than 10,000 times more IBGP sessions. Adding one router adds 1,000 additional IBGP sessions to be configured to the network.

This problem with the exponential growth of IBGP sessions is the main BGP scaling issue. There are two major ways to deal with this issue, the use of router reflectors (RR) and confederations. Both are discussed in this section.

What is the difference between route reflectors and confederations? At the risk of offending BGP purists, it can be loosely stated that route reflectors are a way of grouping BGP routers inside an AS and running IBGP between the RR clusters, and confederations are a way of grouping BGP routers inside an AS and running EBGP between the confederation sub-ASs. Because of the differences between RR and confederations, it is even possible to have *both* configured at the same time in the same AS, and this is frequently done.

This section ends with a look at BGP *route damping*, which is not a way of dealing with BGP scaling directly but rather a way to deal with the *effects* of BGP scaling in terms of the amount of routing information that needs to be distributed to IBGP and EBGP peers when a router or link fails.

Route Reflectors

When there are a large number of IBGP inside an AS, route reflectors, described in RFC 2796, can be a real help in cutting down on the number of IBGP sessions needed. Unless all external routes are redistributed with the IGP (rarely done in order the keep the link-state database sizes manageable), IBGP peers inside the AS must be fully meshed. Adding a new router means peering with all current IBGP speakers, and configurations must all be modified.

The basic idea behind route reflectors (RR) is to relax the IBGP rule that an IBGP router never advertises routes learned from IBPG peers. The rule relaxation applies only to the RR itself to minimize the risk of routing loops. The RR has a group of *clients* in a *cluster*. Any routing update sent to the RR by its client are sent to all other clients of the RR, and to any other routers that the RR peers with but are not members of the cluster (called *non-clients*). So routes from on RR IBGP client are *reflected* to the other IBGP clients. The RR cannot change any of the attributes of the received routes it readvertises. This is another routing loops prevention mechanism.

A client of an RR can run EBGP to external peers but can only run IBGP to the RR or other clients in the cluster. The RR itself can peer to other IBGP peers and run EBGP as well. So an RR client needs only one IBGP session—to the RR—instead of many. All BGP information can be sent to and received from the RR.

The routers that the RR advertises routes to depends on the source of the routing information:

- Routes learned from non-client IBGP peers are reflected to clients only.
- Routes learned from clients are reflected to all clients and non-clients (except back to the originating client in most cases).
- Routes learned through EBGP are reflected to all clients and non-clients.

The basic principles of route reflectors are shown in Figure 13.7.

Naturally, depending on a single RR for a large number of routers introduces a single point of failure risk into the network. So a cluster is allowed to have more than one RR. The clients usually have a direct connection to each of the RRs, so if one fails, there is always a direct link to the other RR.

It is common for a large AS to have multiple RR clusters. The more direct connections there are among the routers within a cluster, and the route reflectors themselves, the better. Because only the RR itself has anything other than a typical IBGP configuration, an RR can be a client in another RR cluster. A whole hierarchy of router reflectors can be built up in this fashion, forming a set of *nested* clusters and RR devices.

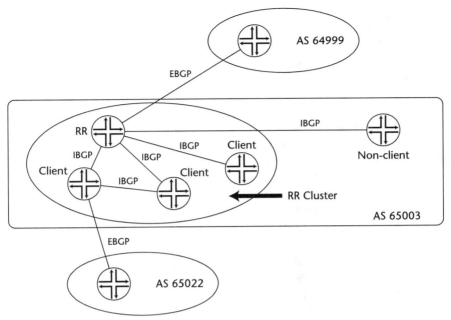

Figure 13.7 A BGP route reflector (RR).

RR clients can peer with each other as well as the RR. However, RR clients cannot peer with routers outside their cluster. In a fully meshed RR cluster, since all clients have a direct link to each other, the RR is configured only to reflect routes for the cluster from clients to non-client peers and from non-clients to client peers.

Because the AS Path does not change inside an AS, use of the Originator ID and Cluster List attributes prevent BGP RR loops. The Originator ID is created by the RR and used to detect if a routing Update has looped around and returned to its originating cluster's RR (this is not supposed to happen).

The Cluster List attribute is almost like an AS Path for RRs. Each RR cluster also has a Cluster ID, usually the 32-bit Router ID of the RR. If the cluster has more than one RR, the Cluster ID must be configured on each RR. When the RR reflects a route from client to non-client, the Cluster ID is prepended to the Cluster List. If an RR ever receives a BGP Update with its own Cluster ID in the Cluster List, a loop has occurred and the RR ignores the information in the Update.

Confederations

If route reflectors are a way of grouping BGP routers and running IBGP between them, then confederations are a way of grouping BGP routers and running EBGP between them, all in the name of requiring fewer IBGP peering sessions per AS. Some documentation refers to *subconfederations*, but this book uses the more common term.

Confederations are described in RFC 3065. A confederation is built by dividing an AS into a number of *member autonomous systems*, or sub-autonomous systems. These sub-ASs have special AS numbers called *confederation IDs*, almost always taken from the private AS number range (64512-65535), and the routers inside run IBGP to their peers inside the confederation and run EBGP to their peers in other confederations.

Between confederations, a special type of EBGP often called *confederation BGP*, or CBGP, is used. CBGP peering sessions only modify the AS Path attribute and keep all other BGP attributes such as MED or Local Pref unchanged. CBGP sessions can also traverse multiple hops, but only if multihop is configured, as in EBGP. Routers running IBGP inside a confederation must still be fully meshed, unless route reflectors are used.

When a confederation is configured, in addition to the AS Path types of ordered list (AS_SEQUENCE) and unordered collection of AS numbers (AS_SET), the AS Path also uses AS_CONFED_SEQUENCE to indicate that the AS Path ordered list now contains AS numbers used within the confederation and AS_CONFED_SET to indicate that the list of confederation AS numbers is now unordered.

The rest of the Internet (that is, other ASs) only sees the confederation as a single AS. The private AS numbers are removed from the AS Path attribute before the route is advertised outside of the AS. The sub-AS numbers in the AS Path appear inside the confederation, but all other BGP routers outside the confederated AS see only a single AS number.

When A BGP Update is sent out of the confederation to another AS with EBGP, the AS_CONFED_SEQUENCE and AS_CONFED_SET values are removed from the AS Path attribute and the confederation ID (the "real" AS number) is prepended to the AS Path. The only use of the sub-AS numbers is for loop prevention inside the confederation.

As an example, consider a group of ASs using the AS numbers 64555 and 64777 (it is difficult to show an example mixing public and private AS numbers when books should really only use private AS numbers). Another AS, number 64999, uses a confederation with three sub-ASs numbers 65001, 65002, and 65003. Inside AS 64999, BGP routes might have AS Paths like (65002 65003) 64777 64555 or (65001) 64777 64999. But when passed on to another AS, the BGP routes that have traversed AS 64999 will show up as 64999 64777 64555.

Figure 13.8 shows a typical confederation for an AS.

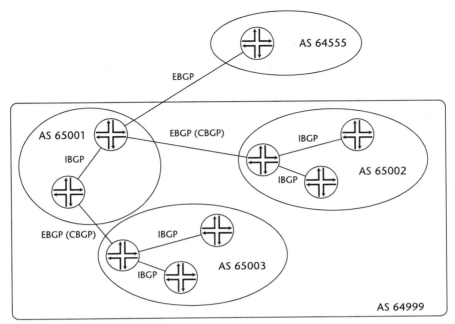

Figure 13.8 A BGP confederation.

When confederations are used, the BGP Next Hop and MED can be sent unchanged, and the Local Pref, usually not present on EBGP sessions, can be sent between confederation sub-ASs. In contrast the route reflectors, configuration is required on all members of a confederation.

Route Damping

A standard form of *route damping* (also often called *route dampening*) for BGP is described in RFC 2439. Although not really a BGP scaling mechanism, as ASs grow to include more and more routers running IBGP, the issues raised by unstable routes become more and more challenging. Route damping addresses those issues. There are other forms of route damping, but this section describes the RFC 2439 mechanism.

Route damping is needed mainly because only active routes are advertised with BGP. When a link or router fails, BGP Update messages must be sent to inform other BGP routers that the route is no longer active and the destination cannot be reached. A physical link that is intermittently failing rapidly can force BGP to withdraw and reestablish an active route every few minutes as the link fails and restores itself. This is called *route flapping*. Since many routes can map to the same physical link in BGP, route flapping can add a great deal of traffic to a network.

Ironically, many route flaps are caused by network administrators innocently trying to reconfigure and optimize a production router by adding routes, shutting down some interfaces, and so on. In a worst-case scenario, this activity might overload the ISP's edge router, causing it to fail. Subsequent BGP route Withdraw message Updates fail other routers, and so on across the Internet.

Aggregation helps control route flapping effects because even if more specific routes become unreachable, the aggregate remains in place. But aggregation is not always possible when customers have IP addresses independent of the ISP's address space, when customers are multihomed, and so on. Aggregation might help control flapping in another AS, but with the local AS, the flaps can be a real problem.

Route damping assigns to each route a numerical value, called a *figure of merit*. In this case, *figure* means number, not a drawing. When a route flaps, either withdrawn or reestablished, a numeric *penalty* is added to the figure of merit, which is in most cases initially zero. The number is reduced over time through a *half-life* decay formula. This is a curve that reduces the figure of merit in half in a given time period, assuming no more penalties from flaps are assessed. The figure of merit also has a preconfigured *ceiling* value.

If the penalties accumulate faster than they can decay, the figure of merit will exceed the preconfigured *suppress limit* and the route is suppressed (no longer advertised). Once the figure of merit has decayed through the half-life formula to a value below another preconfigured value, the *reuse limit*, the route is advertised again.

The figure of merit can be cleared manually, and there is a *maximum suppress time* that allows the route to be advertised again even if penalties have been added while the route was suppressed. The relationship between all of these route damping parameters is shown in Figure 13.9.

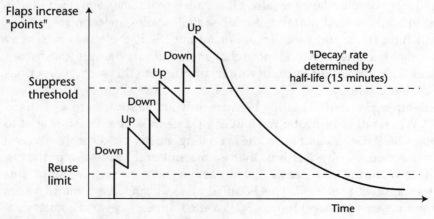

Figure 13.9 Route damping figure of merit.

Router vendors use slightly different default values for damping parameters, but all can be changed by a routing policy of configuration. The most common values are:

Penalty. 1,000 per flap up or down; Juniper Networks also adds 500 for a BGP attribute change.

Suppress Limit. 2,000 for Cisco; or 3,000 for Juniper Networks.

Reuse Limit. 750.

Half-Life. 15 minutes.

Maximum Suppress Time. 60 minutes (four times the half-life).

IGP links must be allowed to come and go, or else IBGP sessions that depend on the IGP might drop, so damping is ignored on IBGP routes. Damping only applies to EBGP sessions. The status of a link in another AS is hardly of vital importance to local routers.

Different damping *profiles* can be applied to different EBGP sessions. For example, a customer's route might have no damping applied to it at all, a peer AS might be subjected to default damping for its routes that flap, and the rest of the Internet might get very aggressive damping with a low suppress limit because the likelihood of a flapping link somewhere on the Internet almost anytime is quite high.

BGP Message Types

BGP messages types are much simpler than those used by OSPF and IS-IS because of the presence of TCP. TCP handles all of the details, and before a BGP peering session is established, the routers perform the usual TCP three-way handshake using TCP Port 179 on one router. The other router uses a non-well-known port, and the router whose TCP SYN message arrives first determines which BGP peer is technically the server. All BGP messages are then unicast over the TCP connection.

There are only four BGP message types:

Open. Used to exchange version numbers (usually 4, but two routers can agree on an earlier version), AS numbers (same for IBGP, different for EBGP), hold time until a Keepalive or Update is received (the smaller value is used if they differ), the BGP identifier (Router ID, usually the loopback interface address), and options such as authentication method, if used.

Keepalive. Keepalive messages are used to maintain the TCP session when there are no Updates to send. The default time is one-third of the hold time established in the Open message exchange.

Update. This advertises or withdraws routes. The Update has fields for the NLRI (both prefix and VLSM length), path attributes, and withdrawn routes by prefix and length.

Notification. These are for errors and always close a BGP connection. For example, a version mismatch in the Open message closes the connection, which must then be reopened when one router or the other adjusts its version support.

The maximum TCP segment size for a BGP message is 4,096 bytes, and the minimum is 19 bytes. All BGP messages have a common header, as shown in Figure 13.10.

The Marker is a 16-byte field used for synchronize BGP connections and in authentication. If no authentication is used and the message is an Open, this field is set to all one-bits. The Length is a 16-bit field that contains the length of the message, including the header, including the header, in bytes. Finally, the Type is an 8-bit field set to either 1 (Open), 2 (Update), 3 (Notification), or 4 (Keepalive).

BGP Message Formats

A data portion follows the header in all but the Keepalive messages. Keepalives consist of only the BGP message headers and so need not be discussed further in this section.

The Open Message

Once a TCP connection has been established between two BGP speakers, Open messages are exchanged between the BGP peers. If the Open is acceptable to a router, a Keepalive is sent to confirm the Open. Once Keepalives are exchanged, the peers can exchange Updates, further Keepalives, and Notification messages.

The format of the Open message is shown in Figure 13.11.

The Open message has an 8-bit Version field, a 2-byte My Autonomous System field, a 2-byte Hold Time value (either 0 or at least 3 seconds), a 32-bit BGP Identifier (Router ID), an 8-bit Optional Parameters Length field (set to 0 if no options are present), and the Optional Parameters themselves in the familiar TLV format. BGP options are not discussed in this book.

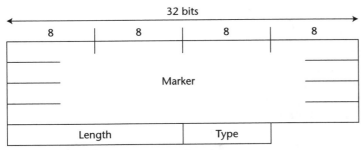

Figure 13.10   The BGP message header.

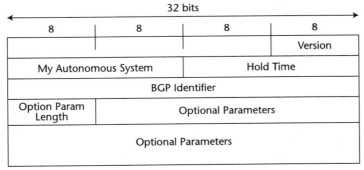

Figure 13.11   The BGP Open message.

The Update Message

The Update message is used to advertise NLRIs to a BGP peer, to withdraw multiple routes that are now unreachable (or *unfeasible*), or both. The format of the Update message is shown in Figure 13.12. Because of the peculiar skew the 19-byte BGP header puts on subsequent fields, this message is shown in a different format than the other headers. The two distinct sections in the Update message are used to Withdraw and Advertise routes.

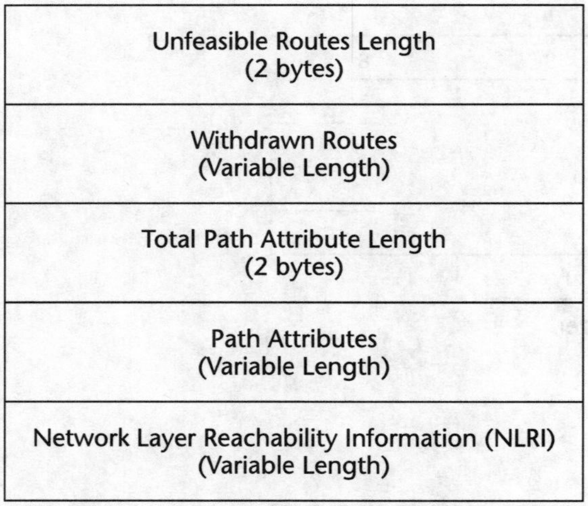

```
┌─────────────────────────────────────────────┐
│         Unfeasible Routes Length             │
│              (2 bytes)                        │
├─────────────────────────────────────────────┤
│            Withdrawn Routes                  │
│            (Variable Length)                 │
├─────────────────────────────────────────────┤
│        Total Path Attribute Length           │
│              (2 bytes)                        │
├─────────────────────────────────────────────┤
│            Path Attributes                   │
│            (Variable Length)                 │
├─────────────────────────────────────────────┤
│  Network Layer Reachability Information (NLRI)│
│            (Variable Length)                 │
└─────────────────────────────────────────────┘
```

Figure 13.12   The BGP Update message format.

The Update message starts off with a 20-byte field indicating the total length of the Withdrawn Routes field in bytes. If there are no Withdrawn Routes, this field is set to zero. If there are Withdrawn Routes, the routes follow in a variable-length field with the list of Withdrawn Routes. Each route is a Length/Prefix pair. The length indicates the number of bits that are significant in the following prefix and form a mask/prefix pair.

The next field is a 2-byte Total Path Attribute Length. This is the length in bytes of the Path Attributes field that follows. A value of zero means that nothing follows.

The variable-length Path Attributes field lists the attributes associated with the NRLIs that follow. Each Path attribute is a TLV of varying length, the first part of which if the 2-byte Attribute Type. There is a structure to the Attribute Type field, as shown in Figure 13.13. There are four flag bits, for unused bits, and then an 8-bit Attribute Type code.

The Attribute Type codes are shown in Table 13.2.

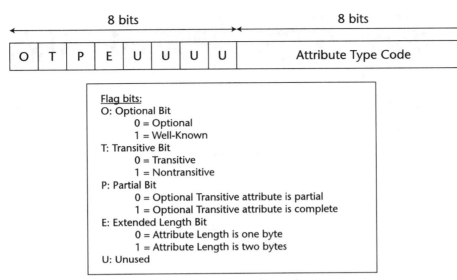

Figure 13.13   The Attribute Type structure and meanings.

Table 13.2   BGP Attribute Types and Values

TYPE CODE	ATTRIBUTE	ATTRIBUTE VALUE CODE	ATTRIBUTE VALUE
1	ORIGIN	0	IGP
		1	EGP
		2	Incomplete
2	AS_PATH	1	AS_SET
		2	AS_SEQUENCE
		3	AS_CONFED_SET
		4	AS_CONFED_SEQUENCE

(continues)

Table 13.2 BGP Attribute Types and Values *(Continued)*

TYPE CODE	ATTRIBUTE	ATTRIBUTE VALUE CODE	ATTRIBUTE VALUE
3	NEXT_HOP	0	Next Hop IP Address
4	MULTI_EXIT_DISC	0	4-byte MED
5	LOCAL_PREF	0	4-byte LOCAL_PREF
6	ATOMIC_AGGREGATOR	0	None
7	AGGREGATOR	0	AS number and IP address of aggregator
8	COMMUNITY	0	4-byte community identifier (AA:NN)
9	ORIGINATOR_ID	0	4-byte router ID of RR originator
10	CLUSTER_ID	0	Variable-length list of RR Cluster IDs

There are other attribute codes in use with BGP that are not discussed in this book. One of the most important of these other attributes is the Extended Community attribute used in VPNs.

The Update message ends with a variable-length NLRI field. Each NLRI is a Length/Prefix pair. The length indicates the number of bits that are significant in the following prefix. There is no length field for this list that ends the Update message. The number of NLRIs present is derived from the known length of all of the other fields.

So instead of saying "here's a route and these are its attributes..." for each and every NLRI advertised, the Update message basically says "here's a bunch of path attributes and here are the routes that these apply to..." This cuts down on the number of messages that need to be sent across the network. In this way, each Update message forms a unit of its own and has no further fragmentation concerns.

The Notification Message

Error messages in BGP have an 8-bit Error Code, an 8-bit Subcode, and a variable-length Data field determined by the Error Code and Subcode. The format of the BGP Notification message is shown in Figure 13.14.

A full discussion of BGP Notification codes and subcodes is beyond the scope of this chapter. The major Error Codes are Message Header Error (1), Open Message Error (2), Update Message Error (3), Hold Timer Expired (4), Finite State Machine Error (5, used when the BGP implementation gets hopelessly confused about what it should be doing next), and Cease (6).

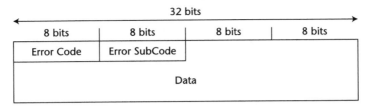

Error Code	Error	Error SubCode	Error SubCode Detail
1	Message Header Error	1	Connection not synchronized
		2	Bad Message Length
		3	Bad Message Type
2	Open Message Error	1	Unsupported Version Number
		2	Bad Peer AS
		3	Bad BGP Identifier
		4	Unsupported Optional Parameter
		5	Authentication Failure
		6	Unacceptable Hold Time
3	Update Message Error	1	Malformed Attribute List
		2	Unrecognized Well-Known Attribute
		3	Missing Well-Known Attribute
		4	Attribute Flags Error
		5	Attribute Length Error
		6	Invalid Origin Attribute
		7	AS Routing Loop
		8	Invalid Next-Hop Attribute
		9	Optional Attribute Error
		10	Invalid Network Field
		11	Malformed AS Path
4	Hold Timer Expired	0	–
5	Finite State Machine Error	0	–
6	Malformed AS Path	0	–

Figure 13.14   The BGP Notification message.

Configuring BGP

Configuring BGP can be deceptively simple. Set up internal and external peers, redistribute some routes from the IGP or some static routes into BGP, and just sit back and watch as the routing tables grow across the network. The growth of the routing tables, of course, is one of the main issues in BGP. Some of the first decisions to be made with BGP concern just which routes BGP should advertise and how specific the masks should be. And even simple BGP configurations can have annoying instances of routes that *should* be there, or *must* be there, not showing up in the routing tables on the intended routers. Next Hop Self can go a long way in making many of these absent routes appear in the right places.

Scaling is also an issue with BGP, especially with the usual practice of fully meshing IBGP across an entire AS. In this chapter we are not able to use the numbers of routers as in a real ISP to demonstrate realistic IBGP scaling issues. Space limitations impose boundaries on the number of routers we can use in the example network. But there are route reflectors and confederations on a modest scale. Once appreciated on a smaller scale, larger or hierarchical collections of route reflector clusters and confederations seem much less of a mystery.

Nevertheless, this chapter on configuring BGP is not as elaborate or complex as the IGP chapters on OSPF or IS-IS. This might sound surprising, but there are two reasons for this. First, BGP does not have multiple area types, as

does OSPF, or special addressing needs, as does IS-IS. Even adding route reflectors or confederations to BGP does not radically change the basic operation of
IBGP or EBGP. The second reason has to do with routing policy. As mentioned
in the previous chapter, BGP is nothing if not a policy-driven routing protocol.
But only the most basic routing policies are applied to BGP in this chapter. A
full discussion of routing policies to manipulate BGP attributes such as Local
Pref, AS Path, MED, and Community appear in later chapters. Even damping
is considered later. This chapter employs BGP defaults for all attributes, except
for changing the BGP Next Hop with Next Hop Self when necessary.

As usual, the size of the chapter was a concern in preparing it. This chapter,
just to remain manageable and readable, does not show many of the configuration step details, typically detailing them only for a new feature. In other
cases, only the results of the configuration are shown. Details are reserved for
BGP specifics. Configurations shown are limited in scope to the sections that
affect BGP operation. Again, all of the links in the example in this chapter are
point-to-point Ethernet links using crossover cables, even though BGP would
be more realistic in a serial link environment. However, some ISPs have POPs
that link routers with Ethernet, although the main reason for using Ethernet
here is just as a result of the lab environment used to produce this book.

Another way of limiting the amount of information presented here is by
assuming that all of the routers inside the main AS are configured properly
and running OSPF. The only OSPF area in this chapter is Area 0, the OSPF
backbone area. This is not done to suggest IS-IS is somehow not worthy of IGP
use with BGP, but just to cut down on the configuration steps needed to bring
the network up. The use of one OSPF area is done to avoid any chance of taking the focus of the chapter away from BGP. OSPF is the IGP, but the OSPF
used is the simplest form possible. There are only a pair of ASBRs to complicate the OSPF configuration.

This chapter first places eight Juniper Networks routers inside an AS. Two
EGP sessions connect to other border routers in other ASs using EBGP. The
routers in the main AS peer with IBGP in a full mesh, and no BGP routes are
injected into the OSPF link-state database, which is the way that the relationship between BGP and the IGP are typically configured. (Earlier chapters on
the IGPs did inject a single BGP route into the IGP, but only because IBGP had
not been discussed yet.) Once the basic AS has been configured, a Cisco router
replaces one of the Juniper Networks routers running IBGP and EBGP.

Then two of the routers in the main AS become BGP route reflectors with
both client and non-client routers in the AS. Once we have investigated this
configuration with Juniper Networks routers, we replace one of the route
reflectors with a Cisco router and compare and contrast the configurations.
There are no hierarchical route reflectors in this chapter.

Finally, the main AS becomes a confederation with two sub-ASs, keeping the route reflectors in place to show the relationship between the two BGP scaling strategies. There is one route reflector in each sub-AS. Naturally, once we have investigated this configuration with Juniper Networks routers, we replace one of the confederation routers with a Cisco router and compare and contrast the configurations.

Just to show where all this configuration activity is heading, Figure 14.1 shows the final state of the network when all area types have been explored.

Naming for the routers was challenging, since calling a router something like Route Reflector 1 would be confusing because this router only becomes a route reflector later in the chapter. After some thought, I decided to give the routers the names of planets rather than cities, composers, writers, or other common naming conventions in many other router books. This is hardly unique, but it does furnish enough names to go around. Loopbacks are assigned in order (176.16.0.1=Mercury, etc.).

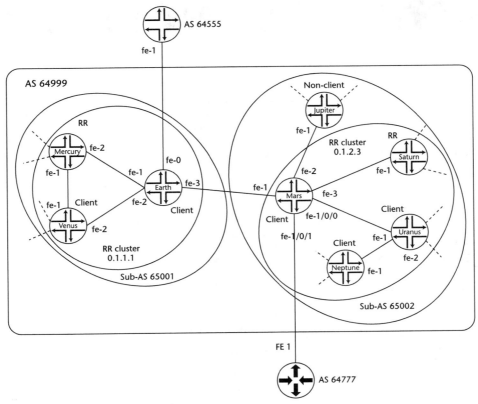

Figure 14.1 The main AS and BGP.

This time, rather than clutter up the figure with all the details of the interface names and IP addresses used for loopback addresses and static routes, these details are presented separately. The router reflector clusters and confederation Sub-AS regions are enough information to present in the figure. The interfaces are abbreviated as fe-1 for fe-0/0/1, fe-2 for fe-0/0/2, and so on. The only exceptions are FE 1 on the Cisco AS64777_router and the fe-1/0/0 and fe-1/0/1 interfaces on the Mars router, which is spelled out in full. The details on the interfaces and addresses are shown in Table 14.1. The external links are again given distinctive addresses. To help with seeing the static address assignment patterns inside AS 64999, the binary equivalents of the third byte (192.168.x.0) of the static route ranges on each router are given. No subnet zero addresses are assigned in this example network. All masks are /24.

Table 14.1 Interfaces and Addresses of Routers

ROUTER	INTERFACE(S)	IP ADDRESS	THIRD BYTE IN BINARY
Mercury	fe-0/0/1	10.0.2.1/24	
	fe-0/0/2	10.0.3.2/24	
	lo0	172.16.0.1	
	static range	192.168.0.0/24 to 196.168.15.0/24	0000 0000-0000 1111
Venus	fe-0/0/1	10.0.2.2/24	
	fe-0/0/2	10.0.4.2/24	
	lo0	172.16.0.2	
	static range	192.168.16.0/24 to 192.168.31.0/24	0001 0000-0001 1111
Earth	fe-0/0/1	10.0.3.1/24	
	fe-0/0/2	10.0.4.1/24	
	fe-0/0/3	10.0.8.1/24	
	fe-0/0/0	10.100.100.99/24	
	lo0	172.16.0.3	
	static range	192.168.32.0/24 to 192.168.63.0/24	0010 0000-0011 1111
Mars	fe-0/0/1	10.0.8.2/24	
	fe-0/0/2	10.0.9.1/24	

Table 14.1   *(Continued)*

ROUTER	INTERFACE(S)	IP ADDRESS	THIRD BYTE IN BINARY
	fe-0/0/3	10.0.10.1/24	
	fe-0/0/0	10.0.11.1/24	
	fe-1/0/1	10.200.200.199/24	
	lo0	172.16.0.4	
	static range	192.168.128.0/24 to 192.168.175.0/24	1000 0000-1010 1111
Jupiter	fe-0/0/1	10.0.9.2/24	
	lo0	172.16.0.5	
	static range	192.168.176.0/24 to 192.168.191.0/24	1011 0000-1011 1111
Saturn	fe-0/0/1		10.0.10.2/24
	lo0	172.16.0.6	
	static range	192.168.192.0/24 to 192.168.207.0/24	1100 0000-1100 1111
Uranus	fe-0/0/1		10.0.11.2/24
	e-0/0/2	10.0.12.2/24	
	lo0	172.16.0.7	
	static range	192.168.208.0/24 to 192.168.215.0/24	1101 0000-1101 1111
Neptune	fe-0/0/1	10.0.12.1/24	
	lo0	172.16.0.8	
	static range	192.168.216.0/24 to 192.168.223.0/24	1101 1000-1101 1111
AS64555	fe-0/0/1	10.100.100.100/24	
	lo0	172.20.55.5	
	static range	10.100.0.0/24 to 10.100.255.0/24	
AS64777	FE 1	10.200.200.200/24	
	lo0	172.30.77.7	
	static range	10.200.0.0/24 to 10.200.255.0/24	

All of the information needed for the configurations is shown in the figure and table. A range of static routes representing customer sites is given for each router. This chapter only distributes the first and last static route IP address in the assigned range, to show how quickly the number of routes that must be maintained grows, even for the modest number of routers used here. Aggregates to represent these static routes and cut down on the amount of routes exchanged are configured and applied in a later chapter. However, since the same static routes are used later, they are introduced here to give a more realistic feel to the example network.

The AS numbers used are from the private AS numbering range. The main AS is AS 64999, and the other two AS numbers are AS 64555 and 64777. All of the routers shown in the main AS 64999 are initially Juniper Networks routers. The external router in the lower portion of the figure in AS 64777 is a Cisco router, and this router runs BGP to AS 64999. The router in AS 64555 is a Juniper Networks router, but this has little to do with the points of this chapter.

This collection of routers really just forms the backbone of an AS. Some of the routers have dashed lines attached to them. This is done to represent other routers in the AS that might be present but not running IBGP. These other routers could easily be OSPF ABRs and attach to various OSPF stub areas. All these routers would need is a default route out of the stub. It is assumed that the IP address assignments within the main AS have been done rationally and that the address ranges employed on the routers to represent the IP addresses around the AS are accurate and correct (not always a valid assumption in the real world).

The eventual router reflectors and clients are indicated, as is the non-client router, but initially all routers are meshed with IBGP. The confederations Sub-AS numbers are also indicated, but these are added to the network last of all.

This chapter uses only LAN links, as mentioned, mainly because of the actual lab environment where this network was built. All LAN links are 100-Mbps Ethernet having an OSPF metric of 1. The links are used as point-to-point links by employing simple crossover cables between the interfaces. WAN links such as T1 or E1 links will have higher IGP metrics and just complicate the routing tables in the examples.

In terms of the real world, each of these routers could be seen as a *POP (point-of-presence) router* and the routers outside of the backbone area (the dashed lines) could easily be *access routers*. The routers running EBGP are the *border routers* that link this OSPF routing domain (AS 64999) to others on the Internet, a role played by the routers in AS 64555 and AS 64777 in this example.

Basic BGP Configuration

In this section we configure EBGP on the Earth and AS6555 routers. Both are initially Juniper Networks routers. The only major difference between the configurations is in the remote AS number, so only one router's configuration need be detailed.

It is not even necessary to run an IGP to get the BGP link between Earth and the AS64555 router up and running. A full IGP should not run on links outside an AS, and this example does not consider an IGP passive interface yet. Looking at EBGP in isolation has the added benefit of not having routing tables filled with IGP routes.

This is the only step-by-step EBGP configuration presented. All Juniper Networks BGP configurations must include a peer group, and the name of this peer group is significant only in the configuration on the local router. In this case the group name is ebgp-as64555. The remote AS number must be different than the local AS number for EBGP, and the type statement establishes this group as EBGP (the group name is just a variable and could have easily been something like Rabbit).

```
[edit protocols]
lab@Earth# edit bgp group ebgp-as64555
[edit protocols bgp group ebgp-as64555]
lab@Earth# set type external
lab@Earth# set peer-as 64555
lab@Earth# set neighbor 10.100.100.100
```

Note the use of the remote physical interface address for the sole peer in this BGP group. In most cases, this link would be a point-to-point WAN link, and if the link were down, the peer router (and AS) would be unreachable anyway. Of course, this is a risky single-point-of-failure situation. Using a redundant link between these two routers is beyond the scope of this chapter and is not discussed further, mostly to limit the size of the chapter.

The remote AS number must be different than the local AS number configured on the Earth router. But where is the local AS number? It is not in the BGP configuration. The AS number is considered to be a *protocol-independent* property on Juniper Networks routers. Like all protocol-independent properties such as statics or aggregates, which do not have to be configured in many cases or, once set, depend on particular routing protocol used to be useful, the AS number is set in the routing-options section of the configuration:

```
[edit routing-options]
lab@Earth# set autonomous-system 64999
```

Except for the AS numbers, which are reversed, and the interface address, the configuration is the same on the Neptune router and need not be detailed. On Earth, the EBGP looks like the following:

```
[edit protocols bgp]
lab@Earth# show
group ebgp-AS64555 {
```

```
        type external;
        peer-as 64555;
        neighbor 10.100.100.100;
}
```

Once these two initial routers have been configured and the configurations committed, one essential operational command shows the state of the BGP sessions on the router:

```
lab@Earth> show bgp summary
Groups: 1 Peers: 1 Down peers: 0
Table    Tot Paths  Act Paths Suppressed History Damp State    Pending
inet.0        2          2         0        0       0            0
Peer            AS   InPkt OutPkt OutQ  Flaps Last Up/Dwn State|
#Active/Received/Damped...
10.100.100.100  64555 47      49    0     0   22:34       0/0/0
0/0/0
```

The output of this command is a little awkward to read because of the line wrap, but all of the information will be explained. The output shows the number of groups configured and peers that are up (1), but never shows that the BGP session is actually established. Instead, if all is well at the BGP level, the `#Active/Received/Damped` column shows three numbers separated by a slash. In this case, the numbers are `0/0/0`. Somewhat confusingly, the `active` status is *bad* as far as BGP is concerned. This means that the TCP connection has been established over the link, but BGP is not up and running. The most likely reason is a simple typo in the AS number or IP address. BGP is quite forgiving when it comes to option matching.

The command output shows that there are no active routes, and in fact no routes have been received by the Earth router from AS 64555 . This is what the first two 0s means. No routes have been damped, so the state of the peering is "0/0/0" as far as routes are concerned. The "extra" 0/0/0 appears as the previous state of the EBGP session.

Viewing the Routing Table

Once BGP is up and running, a look at the routing table on Earth should show if any routes are being exchanged by EBGP. The command `show route protocol bgp` only shows the routes in the routing table that are learned from BGP:

```
lab@Earth> show route protocol bgp
inet.0: 6 destinations, 6 routes (6 active, 0 holddown, 0 hidden)
```

Where are the BGP routes? EBGP is up and running, and there are some static routes around.

Similar to previous chapters on the IGPs, an explicit but simple routing policy is needed to redistribute the desired information from AS 6455 into AS 64999 using EBGP. (Earlier, in the IGP chapters, it was the *BGP* route that was redistributed into the IGP.) The routing policy required on `AS64555_router` to send the static routes defined there to Earth is the same `send-statics` policy used in AS 64999 for OSPF:

```
policy-statement send-statics {
        term 1 {
            from protocol static;
            then accept;
        }
    }
```

This policy will only send the static routing information from AS 64555 to AS 64999, and nothing is yet going to AS 64555 from Earth. In practice, the exchange of routes over EBGP would be mutual. But the `send-statics` policy applied to Earth would only send Earth's statics to AS 64555, not all of the statics on all routers in AS 64999. Routing policies to focus on the routes to send to AS 64555 are covered in a later chapter. For now, this `send-static` routing policy is applied as an export (output) policy to the EBGP group on the AS64555_router, although AS64555 has only two static routes to share right now:

```
[edit protocols bgp]
lab@AS64555_router# show
group ebgp-to-AS64999 {
    type external;
    export send-statics;
    neighbor 10.100.100.99;
    peer-as 64999;
}
```

The export policy is applied to the EBGP group. On Juniper Networks routers, it is possible to apply an import and export policy at the BGP, group, or individual neighbor level. An import or export policy set at a lower level overrides any import or export policy set at the higher level. A neighbor policy always overrides a group policy, and a group policy always overrides a BGP policy. For example, if another export policy (such as `send-aggregate`) was defined and applied to neighbor 10.100.100.99, then the group export policy `send-statics` would never be executed at all. Care is needed when applying multiple policies to BGP.

Now the routing table on Earth looks much better:

```
lab@Earth> show route protocols bgp
inet.0: 8 destinations, 8 routes (8 active, 0 holddown, 0 hidden)
+ = Active Route, - = Last Active, * = Both

10.100.1.0/24      *[BGP/170] 00:00:12, MED 0, localpref 100
                      AS path: 64555 I
                    > to 10.100.100.100 via fe-0/0/0.0
10.100.254.0/24    *[BGP/170] 00:00:12, MED 0, localpref 100
                      AS path: 64555 I
                    > to 10.100.100.100 via fe-0/0/0.0
```

The default routing protocol preference for BGP routes, EBGP or IBGP, is 170, higher than any IGP. Note that the metric (MED) and on the routes from AS 64555 route is 0. This is default MED value and must be set to another value with a routing policy. The default value of the Local Preference BGP attribute is 100 (the range is 0 to 255).

If the router in AS 64555 had many routes to advertise to Earth, EBGP would be better off only advertising the aggregate for the static address range instead of each and every static route. The statics represent customer sites in all of these examples. With Juniper Networks routers, a fairly complex routing policy is needed to advertise the aggregate and suppress the more specific routes. This is covered in Chapter 17 "EGP Routing Policies."

Before tackling the configuration to turn on OSPF as an IGP and build a full IBGP mesh in AS 64999 to advertise the routes from AS 64555 to all other routers, in the next section, we look at configuring EBGP on a Cisco router.

Earth Cisco Configuration

This section gives the configuration for a Cisco router instead of a Juniper Networks router as the Earth router. There is only one interface to worry about, and there is not yet any aggregate addressing to concern ourselves with.

Although this router will also run OSPF, only the BGP configuration for Cisco_Earth is shown here:

```
Cisco_Earth#conf t
Enter configuration commands, one per line.  End with CNTL/Z.
Cisco_Earth(config)#router bgp 64999
Cisco_Earth(config-router)#redistribute static
Cisco_Earth(config-router)#neighbor 10.100.100.100 remote-as 64555
Cisco_Earth(config-router)# no auto-summary
```

The router bgp 64999 configuration command ends with the AS number. The other configuration statements redistribute the static routes to AS 64555, establish the router in AS 64555 at an EBGP neighbor, and turn off summarization of advertised addresses along classful boundaries (more flexibility is needed).

The following are the relevant portions of the configuration:

```
hostname Cisco_Earth
!
autonomous-system 64999
!
router bgp 64999
 redistribute static
 neighbor 10.100.100.100 remote-as 64555
 no auto-summary
!
```

The Cisco_Earth routing table now looks like the following:

```
Cisco_Earth#sh ip route

Codes:C - connected,S - static,I - IGRP R - RIP,M - mobile,B - BGP
      D - EIGRP,EX - EIGRP external,O - OSPF,IA - OSPF inter area
      E1 - OSPF external type 1,E2 - OSPF external type 2,E - EGP
      i - IS-IS,L1 - IS-IS level-1,L2 - IS-IS level-2,* - candidate
default

Gateway of last resort is not set

     10.0.0.0 255.255.255.0 is subnetted, 3 subnets
C       10.100.100.0 is directly connected, FastEthernet0
B       10.100.1.0 [20/0] via 10.100.100.100, 00:08:44
B       10.100.254.0 [20/0] via 10.100.100.100, 00:08:45
S    192.168.32.0 is directly connected, Null0
S    192.168.63.0 is directly connected, Null0
     172.16.0.0 255.255.255.255 is subnetted, 1 subnets
C       172.16.0.3 is directly connected, Loopback0
```

The BGP routes are the static routes from AS 64555, as before. The default protocol preference for BGP routes is 20, and the MED is not set (0), as might be expected. The following are some other helpful BGP commands:

```
Cisco_Earth#sh ip bgp
BGP table version is 7, local router ID is 172.16.0.3
Status codes:s suppressed,d damped,h history,*valid,>best,i internal

Origin codes: i - IGP, e - EGP, ? - incomplete

   Network          Next Hop         Metric LocPrf Weight Path
*> 10.100.1.0/24    10.100.100.100        0             0 64555 i
*> 10.100.254.0/24  10.100.100.100        0             0 64555 i
*> 192.168.32.0     0.0.0.0               0         32768 ?
*> 192.168.63.0     0.0.0.0               0         32768 ?
```

The code shows the route associated with BGP. The two routes learned from AS 64555 are there, with a MED of 0, but with no Local Preference at all. Cisco routers assign an *administrative weight* of 32768 internally (the weight is not sent to other routers) to the routes originating on Cisco_Earth, but of course there is no weight associated with the routes received from other routers because none has been assigned. The default weight is 32,768, and the range is 0 to 65,535.

```
Cisco_Earth#sh ip bgp summ
BGP table version is 7, main routing table version 7
4 network entries (4/8 paths) using 688 bytes of memory
2 BGP path attribute entries using 164 bytes of memory
0 BGP route-map cache entries using 0 bytes of memory
0 BGP filter-list cache entries using 0 bytes of memory

Neighbor      V  AS  MsgRcvd MsgSent TblVer InQ OutQ Up/Down  State
10.100.100.100 4 64555    24      24       7   0    0 0:09:36
```

The output shows some details about the BGP routing table (no database is used because BGP is not a link-state protocol). Memory is closely watched, and the neighbor status is also given.

The routing table on the Juniper Networks router in AS 64555 is identical to what it was before, even though Cisco_Earth is now a Cisco router.

As with the other Juniper Networks configurations, the rest of this chapter does not go into the configuration details of EBGP configuration further. The steps are simple and straightforward. Only the results of the configuration steps are shown.

IBGP Mesh Configuration

Before an IBGP is configured inside AS 64999, OSPF must be configured as the IGP on all of the routers Although EBGP peering to immediate and adjacent neighbor's physical interfaces did not require an IGP, IBGP full-mesh peering addresses would be impossible without an active IGP. All routers will be configured in OSPF Area 0, the backbone. Showing the configuration details on all of the routers in AS 64999 is not necessary. Instead, we just show that OSPF has been configured properly and that the static routes, which represent customer links, have been advertised into OSPF through the use of a simple send-statics policy along the lines of the policy applied to EBGP on the AS 64555 router in the EBGP section. All of the statics, as usual, have a next hop of reject, since there are no real interfaces on the router to send packets to. The policy is as follows:

```
policy-statement send-statics {
      term 1 {
          from protocol static;
          then accept;
      }
   }
```

This `send-statics` routing policy is applied as an export (output) policy to OSPF on Earth and all other routers in AS 64999:

```
[edit protocols]
lab@Earth# show
ospf {
    export send-statics;
    area 0.0.0.0 {
        interface fe-0/0/1.0;
        interface fe-0/0/2.0;
        interface fe-0/0/3.0;
        interface lo0 passive;
    }
}
```

With the IGP up and running, the full routing table on Earth has 40 destinations and looks as follows:

```
lab@Earth> show route
inet.0: 40 destinations, 40 routes (40 active, 0 holddown, 0 hidden)
+ = Active Route, - = Last Active, * = Both

10.0.2.0/24        *[OSPF/10] 00:03:53, metric 2
                      to 10.0.3.2 via fe-0/0/1.0
                    > to 10.0.4.2 via fe-0/0/2.0
10.0.3.0/24        *[Direct/0] 00:05:50
                    > via fe-0/0/1.0
10.0.3.1/32        *[Local/0] 00:05:50
                      Local via fe-0/0/1.0
10.0.4.0/24        *[Direct/0] 00:05:50
                    > via fe-0/0/2.0
10.0.4.1/32        *[Local/0] 00:05:50
                      Local via fe-0/0/2.0
10.0.8.0/24        *[Direct/0] 00:05:50
                    > via fe-0/0/3.0
10.0.8.1/32        *[Local/0] 00:05:50
                      Local via fe-0/0/3.0
10.0.9.0/24        *[OSPF/10] 00:03:53, metric 2
                    > to 10.0.8.2 via fe-0/0/3.0
10.0.10.0/24       *[OSPF/10] 00:03:43, metric 2
                    > to 10.0.8.2 via fe-0/0/3.0
```

```
10.0.11.0/24          *[OSPF/10] 00:03:23, metric 2
                       > to 10.0.8.2 via fe-0/0/3.0
10.0.12.0/24          *[OSPF/10] 00:03:23, metric 3
                       > to 10.0.8.2 via fe-0/0/3.0
10.100.1.0/24         *[BGP/170] 00:05:46, MED 0, localpref 100
                          AS path: 64555 I
                       > to 10.100.100.100 via fe-0/0/0.0
10.100.100.0/24       *[Direct/0] 00:05:50
                       > via fe-0/0/0.0
10.100.100.99/32      *[Local/0] 00:05:50
                          Local via fe-0/0/0.0
10.100.254.0/24       *[BGP/170] 00:05:46, MED 0, localpref 100
                          AS path: 64555 I
                       > to 10.100.100.100 via fe-0/0/0.0
172.16.0.1/32         *[OSPF/10] 00:05:35, metric 1
                       > to 10.0.3.2 via fe-0/0/1.0
172.16.0.2/32         *[OSPF/10] 00:05:30, metric 1
                       > to 10.0.4.2 via fe-0/0/2.0
172.16.0.3/32         *[Direct/0] 00:05:50
                       > via lo0.0
172.16.0.4/32         *[OSPF/10] 00:03:53, metric 1
                       > to 10.0.8.2 via fe-0/0/3.0
172.16.0.5/32         *[OSPF/10] 00:03:53, metric 2
                       > to 10.0.8.2 via fe-0/0/3.0
172.16.0.6/32         *[OSPF/10] 00:03:43, metric 2
                       > to 10.0.8.2 via fe-0/0/3.0
172.16.0.7/32         *[OSPF/10] 00:03:23, metric 2
                       > to 10.0.8.2 via fe-0/0/3.0
172.16.0.8/32         *[OSPF/10] 00:03:23, metric 3
                       > to 10.0.8.2 via fe-0/0/3.0
192.168.1.0/24        *[OSPF/150] 00:05:35, metric 0, tag 0
                       > to 10.0.3.2 via fe-0/0/1.0
192.168.15.0/24       *[OSPF/150] 00:05:35, metric 0, tag 0
                       > to 10.0.3.2 via fe-0/0/1.0
192.168.16.0/24       *[OSPF/150] 00:05:30, metric 0, tag 0
                       > to 10.0.4.2 via fe-0/0/2.0
192.168.31.0/24       *[OSPF/150] 00:05:30, metric 0, tag 0
                       > to 10.0.4.2 via fe-0/0/2.0
192.168.32.0/24       *[Static/5] 00:05:50, metric 0
                          Reject
192.168.63.0/24       *[Static/5] 00:05:50, metric 0
                          Reject
192.168.128.0/24      *[OSPF/150] 00:03:53, metric 0, tag 0
                       > to 10.0.8.2 via fe-0/0/3.0
192.168.175.0/24      *[OSPF/150] 00:03:53, metric 0, tag 0
                       > to 10.0.8.2 via fe-0/0/3.0
192.168.176.0/24      *[OSPF/150] 00:03:53, metric 0, tag 0
                       > to 10.0.8.2 via fe-0/0/3.0
192.168.191.0/24      *[OSPF/150] 00:03:53, metric 0, tag 0
                       > to 10.0.8.2 via fe-0/0/3.0
```

```
192.168.192.0/24      *[OSPF/150] 00:03:43, metric 0, tag 0
                      > to 10.0.8.2 via fe-0/0/3.0
192.168.207.0/24      *[OSPF/150] 00:03:43, metric 0, tag 0
                      > to 10.0.8.2 via fe-0/0/3.0
192.168.208.0/24      *[OSPF/150] 00:03:23, metric 0, tag 0
                      > to 10.0.8.2 via fe-0/0/3.0
192.168.215.0/24      *[OSPF/150] 00:03:23, metric 0, tag 0
                      > to 10.0.8.2 via fe-0/0/3.0
192.168.216.0/24      *[OSPF/150] 00:03:23, metric 0, tag 0
                      > to 10.0.8.2 via fe-0/0/3.0
192.168.223.0/24      *[OSPF/150] 00:03:23, metric 0, tag 0
                      > to 10.0.8.2 via fe-0/0/3.0
224.0.0.5/32          *[OSPF/10] 00:05:50, metric 1
```

Most importantly, all of the link, loopback, and static addresses are in the table, all with the expected OSPF metrics and tags (the static routes are *external* to OSPF, and so have a preference of 150). Even with only two static routes for each router, the routing table is quite long already.

From now on in this chapter, since the emphasis is on BGP, it is not necessary to give the full routing table in all cases. The main object of the routing tables from now on is the status of the static routes and loopback addresses. For example, the routes to the other routers in AS 64999 are shown by the following:

```
lab@Earth> show route 172.16/16
inet.0: 40 destinations, 40 routes (40 active, 0 holddown, 0 hidden)
+ = Active Route, - = Last Active, * = Both

172.16.0.1/32         *[OSPF/10] 00:07:31, metric 1
                      > to 10.0.3.2 via fe-0/0/1.0
172.16.0.2/32         *[OSPF/10] 00:07:26, metric 1
                      > to 10.0.4.2 via fe-0/0/2.0
172.16.0.3/32         *[Direct/0] 00:07:46
                      > via lo0.0
172.16.0.4/32         *[OSPF/10] 00:05:49, metric 1
                      > to 10.0.8.2 via fe-0/0/3.0
172.16.0.5/32         *[OSPF/10] 00:05:49, metric 2
                      > to 10.0.8.2 via fe-0/0/3.0
172.16.0.6/32         *[OSPF/10] 00:05:39, metric 2
                      > to 10.0.8.2 via fe-0/0/3.0
172.16.0.7/32         *[OSPF/10] 00:05:19, metric 2
                      > to 10.0.8.2 via fe-0/0/3.0
172.16.0.8/32         *[OSPF/10] 00:05:19, metric 3
                      > to 10.0.8.2 via fe-0/0/3.0
```

As already shown, the routes from AS 64555 have made their way to AS 64999 and the Earth router. All of the other routers should be able to use these routes to send packets to AS 64555 if that is their destination. But looking at the routing table on any other router in AS 64999 shows disappointing results.

There is no sign of the routes from AS 64555, as this result from a search for them on the Mars router shows:

```
lab@Mars> show route 10.100/16
lab@Mars>
```

Relying on a default static route for external routes outside of the AS will not work for AS 64999. There will be other routes arriving from the router in AS 64777 through EBGP once that router is fully configured. It seems hardly wise to send all packets for any destination outside of AS 64999 to AS 64555, especially if they are bound for addresses that should be reached through AS 64777. If the router in AS 64555 is doing what is obvious, the packets would probably just flow back to AS 64999 and a routing loop would result, as the default in AS 64999 sent them right back to AS 64555 again.

All of the other routers in AS 64999 would know about the routes in AS 64555 learned through EBGP in two ways. Both have been explained in the previous chapter. The first way is by simply redistributing the EBGP routes with OSPF. In the chapters on IGPs—Chapter 8 "Configuring RIP," Chapter 10 "Configuring OSPF," and Chapter 12 "Configuring IS-IS"—this was exactly what was done. However, when the Internet routing tables hover around 100,000 routes, this flood of external routes would easily overwhelm the link-state databases on a lot of routers. The second way is by fully meshing the routers in AS 64999 with IBGP. This is what we do in this section, and this is the way it is done in the real world today. The RIB-in BGP table is a lot more elastic than an IGP link-state database. And instead of using only one metric to select routes, BGP comes armed with a whole range of attributes to assist routers in picking just the right path to a destination, from a very IGP-like metric (MED) to a count of ASs on the way to a destination (AS Path) to a measure of confidence (Origin) and beyond.

To mesh the routers in AS 64999 with IBGP, which are now back to all Juniper Networks routers, we must create an internal peer group running IBGP to all seven other routers in AS 64999, since BGP will not flood and pass information learned through IBGP on to IBGP. The steps are similar to those used to create the EBGP group, and the final result, again from the Earth router, is as follows:

```
[edit protocols]
lab@Earth# show bgp
bgp {
    group ebgp {
        type external;
        export send-statics;
```

```
        peer-as 64555;
        neighbor 10.100.100.100;
    }
    group ibgp-mesh {
        type internal;
        local-address 172.16.0.3;
        neighbor 172.16.0.1;
        neighbor 172.16.0.2;
        neighbor 172.16.0.4;
        neighbor 172.16.0.5;
        neighbor 172.16.0.6;
        neighbor 172.16.0.7;
        neighbor 172.16.0.8;
    }
}
```

Note that the type this time is internal, meaning that the AS number at the other end of the TCP connection must match the AS number configured on the local router. The neighbor is now not the physical interface address but the loopback address of the other router. This is common practice with IBGP, so even if the interface is down, the router might still be reachable through the IGP. For example, if the direct link to Mercury fails, that router can still be an IBGP peer of Earth through Venus. Finally, the local-address statement sets the local loopback address as the source address of the IP packets sent by the BGP routing protocol to the destination router. This strategy avoids the risk of BGP sessions failing because packets cannot return to a down physical interface. If Earth can reach Mercury directly or through Venus, it makes no sense to source the BGP packets from the physical interface leading to Mercury.

Once all of the routers in AS 64999 have been configured for an IBGP mesh, the show bgp summary on the Earth router reveals that all of the IBGP sessions are up and running:

```
lab@Earth> show bgp summary
Groups: 2 Peers: 8 Down peers: 0

Table      Tot Paths Act Paths Suppressed History Damp State     Pending
inet.0         2         2         0        0       0            0
Peer          AS  InPkt  OutPkt  OutQ Flaps Last Up/Dwn State|
#Active/Received/Damped...
172.16.0.1 64999    21     23      0     0     9:37 0/0/0      0/0/0
172.16.0.2 64999    18     20      0     0     8:29 0/0/0      0/0/0
172.16.0.4 64999    13     15      0     0     5:32 0/0/0      0/0/0
172.16.0.5 64999    10     12      0     0     4:23 0/0/0      0/0/0
172.16.0.6 64999     8     10      0     0     3:13 0/0/0      0/0/0
```

```
172.16.0.7 64999      6        8      0      0      2:05 0/0/0      0/0/0
172.16.0.8 64999      2        5      0      0      1:00 0/0/0      0/0/0
10.100.100.100 64555 58      60      0      0     27:45 2/2/0      0/0/0
```

Even though all of the routers are linked directly with an IBGP mesh, the routers do not have to be directly connected with a *physical* mesh. Mercury is three hops away from Saturn. But because BGP uses TCP to connect routers, the BGP messages inside the TCP segments and IP packets are simply routed hop by hop through the AS like any other type of application traffic. If IGP were not running beneath BGP, then the routers would *have* to be physically fully meshed to run IBGP successfully. This would be impractical today, and an IGP is always used with BGP.

The Earth router is not *receiving* any BGP routes from its IBGP neighbors, so all of the internal BGP sessions show 0/0/0. Only the external group shows the two routes arriving from AS 64555.

Now the routing tables on all of the routers in AS 64999 should show the external routes from AS 64555. The following is the routing table search for those routers from Mars:

```
lab@Mars> show route 10.100/16
inet.0: 40 destinations, 40 routes (38 active, 0 holddown, 2 hidden)
lab@Mars>
```

What's wrong now? No routing policy is needed to redistribute routes received by EBGP into IBGP; that is the default BGP behavior. The response shows that among the 40 routes, there are two *hidden routes*. Could these be the two routes from AS 64555? Another command shows that these routes are indeed hidden on Mars:

```
lab@Mars> show route hidden
inet.0: 40 destinations, 40 routes (38 active, 0 holddown, 2 hidden)
+ = Active Route, - = Last Active, * = Both

10.100.1.0/24     [BGP/170] 00:11:23, MED 0, localpref 100, from 172.16.0.3
                      AS path: 64555 I
                      Unusable
10.100.254.0/24   [BGP/170] 00:11:23, MED 0, localpref 100, from 172.16.0.3
                      AS path: 64555 I
                      Unusable
```

Juniper Networks routers will mark routes that are received fine by the routing protocol but cannot be used as the active route and installed in the forwarding table for packet forwarding as hidden routes. The only clue as to why these routes are hidden is the `unusable` term in the entry. The real reason behind the unusable (hidden) routes is revealed by examining one of the hidden routes in detail:

```
lab@Mars> show route hidden 10.100.1.0/24 extensive
inet.0: 40 destinations, 40 routes (38 active, 0 holddown, 2 hidden)
10.100.1.0/24 (1 entry, 0 announced)
          BGP     Preference: 170/-101
                  Next hop type: Unusable
                  State: <Hidden Int Ext>
                  Local AS: 64999 Peer AS: 64999
                  Age: 14:47      Metric: 0
                  Task: BGP_64999.172.16.0.3+179
                  AS path: 64555 I
                  Localpref: 100
                  Router ID: 172.16.0.3
                  Indirect nexthops: 1
                      Protocol Nexthop: 10.100.100.100 Indirect nexthop: 0
```

BGP will never consider a route feasible for forwarding packets unless the BGP next hop is reachable. The value of the BGP Next Hop attribute (the last line's `Protocol Nexthop`) for these routes is the *physical interface address* on the router in AS 64555. The use of this address as a BGP next hop is hardly AS 64555's fault. How can AS 64555 be expected to know what address to use inside another AS for the BGP Next Hop? The physical interface address facing AS 64999 is the farthest outpost of AS 64555, so this is the address used by the AS64555_router.

BGP resolves routes by recursively searching the routing table (actually, the forwarding table) for a physical interface on the router to forward the packet. So the longest match lookup on the BGP route in the IGP table produces the BGP Next Hop, which must in turn be found through a longest match lookup in the IGP routing table, and so on until a next hop maps to a physical interface on the router. If the BGP Next Hop cannot be found in the IGP routing table, the BGP Next Hop is unreachable and the BGP route is unfeasible. The hidden route is no longer even eligible to be readvertised through EBGP or the IGP, since the BGP route is not active. If the EBGP link to AS 64777 were configured and active at this point, no routes to AS 64555 would pass through AS 64999 and ever be advertised to AS 64777. This is one way that external BGP routes seem to disappear inside an AS, swallowed up as if they never existed.

If the external BGP routes were redistributed on the border router (Earth) into the IGP, as was done in the OSPF and IS-IS chapters, the problem would disappear. Once injected into the IGP, the BGP Next Hop is irrelevant once the route becomes an IGP route inside AS 64999 (and external IGP route to be sure, but an IGP route nonetheless). When this redistribution of BGP routes into the IGP was the default behavior of routers, and the Internet routing tables had fewer than 10,000 entries, this was not a problem. No one worried about making BGP change the Next Hop attribute when a route arrived with EBGP and was redistributed into IBGP. The IGP had taken over anyway. So the BGP Next Hop stayed the same. This is called the BGP Next Hop issue. What can be done about it to make the EBGP routes in AS 64555 reachable and useful to all the routers in AS 64999?

Solving the BGP Next Hop Issue

There are five ways to solve the BGP Next Hop issue. The Next Hop issue just means that the value of the BGP Next Hop attribute is not changed when a route arriving from another AS through EBGP is redistributed into the AS through IBGP. The first three of these solutions will work as well as the last two but are not recommended or used much today. The last two are used today, and the last one—Next Hop Self —is the more common solution.

The following are the five solutions to the BGP Next Hop issue:

Static routes.   A static route to the physical interface address used by EBGP can be defined and distributed to the other routers along with the EBGP routes. Then the BGP Next Hop would be found in the IGP routing table. However, this relies on manual configuration, and if AS 64555 ever changes its interface address, the packet arriving at the border router would be undeliverable even though the link to AS 64555 was up and running.

Network connected.   This is a Cisco term. Juniper Networks calls this approach "from protocol direct," but the effect is the same. This means is that the network address on the interface on the Earth router facing AS 64555 is exported into EBGP and so is known to the IGP and available for the EBGP routes in AS 64999 for Next Hop resolution. But again this method is dependent on addressing determined in part outside of the local AS.

Full IGP.   The IGP can also be run on the link to the other AS. For example, if OSPF is running on the link to the AS64555 router, then the physical interface address would be in every router's routing table in AS 64999 just waiting for BGP to find it. However, this completely violates every rule regarding IGPs (*inside* the AS only) and ASs (independent of each other).

IGP passive. The IGP does not have to form an adjacency with the AS 64555 router. Running an IGP *passively* just means that routing protocol packets are exchanged, and the interface address is advertised by the IGP (as with the loopback address), but the routers never form a full adjacency over the inter-AS link. The address is now known to the IGP, but no IGP rules are broken. This method is very common and widely used.

Next Hop Self. Often abbreviated NHS, this is just the practice of putting a local routing policy in place on the border router (Earth) to change the value of the BGP Next Hop attribute to the border router's address (Self). This address is usually the loopback interface address of the border router, again for reachability purposes if a physical interface is down. Use of NHS allows the IGP to be run only on internal AS links and lets the ASs only run BGP between them, as intended. This chapter uses Next Hop Self.

Next Hop Self on Juniper Networks Router

On a Juniper Networks router, Next Hop Self is an *export* policy applied to routes advertised by BGP. The policy could be applied globally to all BGP groups, but it is only needed on IBGP groups. The following is the policy and its application to BGP:

```
[edit policy-options]
lab@Earth# show
policy-statement next-hop-self {
    term 1 {
        from protocol bgp;
        then {
            next-hop self;
        }
    }
}
```

Actually, only the then clause is needed, since only BGP has a Next Hop attribute to set. A visualization of the IBGP Next Hop issue and its resolution through Next Hop Self is shown in Figure 14.2.

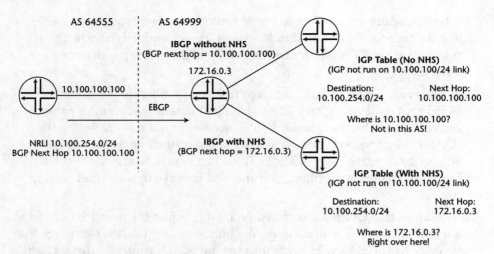

Figure 14.2 Use of Next Hop Self in IBGP.

This policy is applied as an export policy only to the IBGP group on Earth. This policy will not apply to the routes sent to AS 64555 at all:

```
[edit protocols bgp]
lab@Earth# show
group ebgp {
    type external;
    export send-statics;
    peer-as 64555;
    neighbor 10.100.100.100;
}
group ibgp-mesh {
    type internal;
    local-address 172.16.0.3;
    export next-hop-self;
    neighbor 172.16.0.1;
    neighbor 172.16.0.2;
    neighbor 172.16.0.4;
    neighbor 172.16.0.5;
    neighbor 172.16.0.6;
    neighbor 172.16.0.7;
    neighbor 172.16.0.8;
}
```

Now all of the routers in AS 64999 can reach the two routes from AS 64555, as this view from Neptune shows:

```
lab@Neptune> show route protocol bgp
inet.0: 36 destinations, 36 routes (36 active, 0 holddown, 0 hidden)
+ = Active Route, - = Last Active, * = Both

10.100.1.0/24        *[BGP/170] 00:27:46, MED 0, localpref 100,
                       from 172.16.0.3, AS path: 64555 I
                     > to 10.0.12.1 via fe-0/0/1.0
10.100.254.0/24      *[BGP/170] 00:27:46, MED 0, localpref 100,
                       from 172.16.0.3, AS path: 64555 I
                     > to 10.0.12.1 via fe-0/0/1.0
```

All the routers running IBGP are Juniper Networks routers. The time has come to replace one of them with a Cisco router performing the same task.

Cisco IBGP Configuration

In this section we configure a Cisco router as the Mercury router. The Mercury router links directly to Venus and Earth and peers to all of the other routers in AS 64999 with IBGP.

The Cisco configuration for the static routes and to run OSPF need not be repeated. The IBGP portion of the configuration on Cisco_Mercury is:

```
!
router bgp 64999
 no synchronization
 neighbor 172.16.0.2 remote-as 64999
 neighbor 172.16.0.2 update-source Loopback0
 neighbor 172.16.0.3 remote-as 64999
 neighbor 172.16.0.3 update-source Loopback0
 neighbor 172.16.0.4 remote-as 64999
 neighbor 172.16.0.4 update-source Loopback0
 neighbor 172.16.0.5 remote-as 64999
 neighbor 172.16.0.5 update-source Loopback0
 neighbor 172.16.0.6 remote-as 64999
 neighbor 172.16.0.6 update-source Loopback0
 neighbor 172.16.0.7 remote-as 64999
 neighbor 172.16.0.7 update-source Loopback0
 neighbor 172.16.0.8 remote-as 64999
 neighbor 172.16.0.8 update-source Loopback0
 no auto-summary
!
```

For each IBGP neighbor, the `remote-as` number matches the BGP AS, so these are IBGP neighbors. Instead of the *local-address* statement to set the source address on BGP packets to the local loopback address, Cisco repeats the neighbor address using the `update-source` statement to accomplish the same thing. The `no auto-summary`, also used with EBGP, prevents the router from summarizing along classful lines. The `no synchronization`, which was not needed in EBGP, is necessary in IBGP so that the routes from AS 64555 will be installed as active routes even though the routes are not known to the IGP. Without `no synchronization`, the AS 64555 routes will reach Cisco_Mercury from Earth but never appear in the main routing table.

Successful peering is now achieved to all of the other Juniper Networks routers in AS 64999. The Earth router sees Cisco_Mercury (172.16.0.1) no different than before:

```
lab@Earth> show bgp summary
Groups: 2 Peers: 8 Down peers: 0

Table     Tot Paths Act Paths Suppressed History Damp State   Pending
inet.0        2         2         0         0        0          0
Peer          AS InPkt  OutPkt    OutQ    Flaps Last Up/Dwn State|
#Active/Received/Damped...
172.16.0.1    64999 33      35       0       0    15:54 0/0/0   0/0/0
172.16.0.2    64999 109     112      0       0    54:14 0/0/0   0/0/0
172.16.0.4    64999 109     111      0       0    53:44 0/0/0   0/0/0
172.16.0.5    64999 109     111      0       0    53:38 0/0/0   0/0/0
172.16.0.6    64999 109     111      0       0    53:38 0/0/0   0/0/0
172.16.0.7    64999 109     111      0       0    53:38 0/0/0   0/0/0
172.16.0.8    64999 109     111      0       0    53:38 0/0/0   0/0/0
10.100.100.100 64555 111    113      0       0    54:27 2/2/0   0/0/0
```

On Cisco_Mercury, all IBGP peers are running fine:

```
Cisco_Mercury#sh ip bgp summ
BGP router identifier 172.16.0.1, local AS number 64999
BGP table version is 1, main routing table version 1
2 network entries and 2 paths using 268 bytes of memory
1 BGP path attribute entries using 52 bytes of memory
1 BGP AS-PATH entries using 24 bytes of memory
0 BGP route-map cache entries using 0 bytes of memory
0 BGP filter-list cache entries using 0 bytes of memory
BGP activity 2/0 prefixes, 2/0 paths
Neighbor        V    AS MsgRcvd MsgSent   TblVer  InQ OutQ Up/Down
State/PfxRcd
```

```
172.16.0.2        4 64999      39        38        1      0      0 00:17:05
          0
172.16.0.3        4 64999      42        41        1      0      0 00:19:13
          2
172.16.0.4        4 64999      36        36        1      0      0 00:16:52
          0
172.16.0.5        4 64999      36        36        1      0      0 00:16:43
          0
172.16.0.6        4 64999      36        36        1      0      0 00:16:39
          0
172.16.0.7        4 64999      36        36        1      0      0 00:16:36
          0
172.16.0.8        4 64999      35        35        1      0      0 00:16:18
          0
```

As expected, there are only the two routes from AS 64555, received from the Earth router (172.16.0.3), in the routing table of Cisco_Mercury:

```
Cisco_Mercury#show ip route bgp
     10.0.0.0/24 is subnetted, 10 subnets
B       10.100.1.0 [200/0] via 172.16.0.3, 00:04:25
B       10.100.254.0 [200/0] via 172.16.0.3, 00:04:25
```

The 10 subnets reflect the fact that the 10.0.x/24 subnet is also used for physical interfaces in AS 64999. The Cisco administrative distance for routes learned through IBGP is 200 (EBGP routes were only 20). These routes can also be seen in isolation, along with some of their BGP attributes:

```
Cisco_Mercury#sh ip bgp
BGP table version is 3, local router ID is 172.16.0.1

Status codes:s suppressed,d damped,h history,*valid,>best,i internal

Origin codes: i - IGP, e - EGP, ? - incomplete

   Network          Next Hop          Metric LocPrf Weight Path
*>i10.100.1.0/24    172.16.0.3             0    100      0 64555 i
*>i10.100.254.0/24  172.16.0.3             0    100      0 64555 i
```

The routes are valid (*), meaning the Next Hop Self on Earth is working, and the best way (>) to reach the destination, so the routes appear in the routing table. Note the MED (Metric) of 0 and Local Preference of 100, the defaults used by the Earth router, a Juniper Networks router (Cisco's default values are the same). But there is no Weight for the routes: weight is only a Cisco-internal BGP attribute and is not sent to or received from other routers.

Adding the AS 64777 Router

The only thing we need to complete the basic AS is to add the Cisco router in AS 64777 to communicate with EBGP to AS 64999. We do this by adding an EBGP group to Mars (the IBGP group is not shown):

```
[edit protocols bgp]
lab@Mars> show
group ebgp-to-AS64777 {
    type external;
    peer-as 64777;
    neighbor 10.200.200.200;
}
```

Naturally, something must be done about Next Hop Self with regard to the routes arriving from AS 64777. To show that running an IGP passively on the inter-AS link is just as capable a way of solving the Next Hop issue, this router will run OSPF passively on the link to AS 64777 and show the result. IGP passive solutions must communicate using the IGP, even though no neighbor adjacency is formed with the IGP. The passive configuration is done in OSPF itself. Mars, as all the AS 64999 routers in this chapter, is in the OSPF backbone Area 0 (a good assumption for an ASBR like Mars). The Mars configuration looks like this:

```
[edit protocols ospf]
lab@Mars# show
area 0.0.0.0
    interface fe-0/0/0.0;
    interface fe-0/0/1.0;
    interface fe-0/0/2.0;
    interface fe-0/0/3.0;
    interface fe-1/0/1.0 {
        passive;
    }
```

Only the interface to the other AS is running OSPF passive. The other interfaces internal to AS 64999 run complete OSPF and form full adjacencies. On the Cisco router in AS 64777, the statement to run OSPF passive on the link to AS 64999 is `passive-interface FastEthernet0`. Passive interfaces (in this case, fe-1/0/1.0) will not find neighbors but do exchange OSPF packets:

```
lab@Mars> show ospf interface

Interface  State   Area       DR ID      BDR ID     Nbrs
fe-1/0/1.0 DRother 0.0.0.0    0.0.0.0    0.0.0.0       0
```

```
fe-0/0/0.0 DR      0.0.0.0      172.16.0.4      172.16.0.3      1
fe-0/0/1.0 BDR     0.0.0.0      172.16.0.5      172.16.0.4      1
fe-0/0/2.0 BDR     0.0.0.0      172.16.0.6      172.16.0.4      1
fe-0/0/3.0 BDR     0.0.0.0      172.16.0.7      172.16.0.4      1
```

A look at the routing table on any other router in AS 64999 shows that the routes from the two other ASs are present and active. The external routes are reachable and point to the proper border routers. Here is the view from Jupiter:

```
lab@Jupiter> show route 10.100/16
inet.0: 39 destinations, 39 routes (39 active, 0 holddown, 0 hidden)
+ = Active Route, - = Last Active, * = Both

10.100.1.0/24       *[BGP/170] 00:28:22, MED 0, localpref 100,
                      from 172.16.0.3, AS path: 64555 I
                    > to 10.0.9.1 via fe-0/0/1.0
10.100.254.0/24     *[BGP/170] 00:28:22, MED 0, localpref 100,
                      from 172.16.0.3, AS path: 64555 I
                    > to 10.0.9.1 via fe-0/0/1.0

lab@Jupiter> show route 10.200/16
inet.0: 39 destinations, 39 routes (39 active, 0 holddown, 0 hidden)
+ = Active Route, - = Last Active, * = Both

10.200.1.0/24       *[BGP/170] 00:11:50, MED 0, localpref 100,
                      from 172.16.0.4, AS path: 64777 ?
                    > to 10.0.9.1 via fe-0/0/1.0
10.200.200.0/24     *[OSPF/10] 00:12:14, metric 2
                    > to 10.0.9.1 via fe-0/0/1.0
10.200.254.0/24     *[BGP/170] 00:11:50, MED 0, localpref 100,
                      from 172.16.0.4, AS path: 64777 ?
                    > to 10.0.9.1 via fe-0/0/1.0
```

Note the presence of the 10.200.200.0 network for the physical interface to AS 64777 learned from OSPF. The protocol next hop (the BGP Next Hop attribute value) for the 10.200/16 routes is still the physical interface to AS 64777, but it is now resolvable in the IGP table on Jupiter:

```
lab@Jupiter> show route 10.200.1.0/24 extensive
inet.0: 39 destinations, 39 routes (39 active, 0 holddown, 0 hidden)
10.200.1.0/24 (1 entry, 1 announced)
TSI:
KRT in-kernel 10.200.1.0/24 -> {indirect(30)}
     *BGP    Preference: 170/-101
             Source: 172.16.0.4
             Nexthop: 10.0.9.1 via fe-0/0/1.0, selected
             Protocol Nexthop: 10.200.200.200 Indirect nexthop: 8428088 30
             State: <Active Int Ext>
```

```
           Local AS: 64999 Peer AS: 64999
           Age: 14:06       Metric: 0        Metric2: 2
           Task: BGP_64999.172.16.0.4+179
           Announcement bits (2): 0-KRT 4-Resolve inet.0
           AS path: 64777 ?
           Localpref: 100
           Router ID: 172.16.0.4
           Indirect nexthops: 1
                   Protocol Nexthop: 10.200.200.200 Metric: 2 Indirect
nexthop: 8428088 30
                       Indirect path forwarding nexthops: 1
                           Nexthop: 10.0.9.1 via fe-0/0/1.0
```

The output is fuller than in the previous "extensive" look at a BGP route because this route is now active. The `Metric` value is the MED (0) and `Metric2` value is the IGP metric of the BGP Next Hop (2). The network now appears as in Figure 14.3.

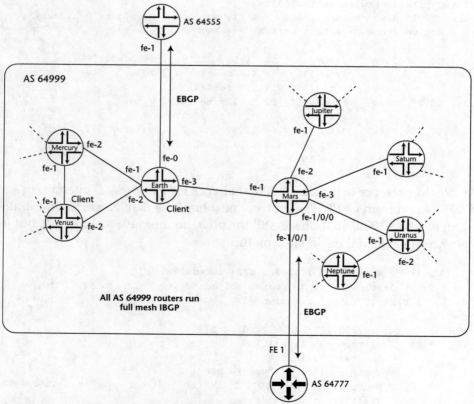

Figure 14.3   AS 64999 running EBGP and IBGP.

It is not necessary to configure a Cisco router to replace Mars. Both EBGP and IBGP have already been configured on Cisco routers. It is more important to do something about the BGP scaling issue as AS 64999 presumably prospers and grows.

BGP Route Reflectors

Even this simple AS with eight routers has 28 IBGP sessions that must be up and running at all times if routing within and without the AS is to perform properly. But because all of the IBGP mesh groups must be individually configured and maintained on each and every router, the IBGP mesh requirement quickly becomes a crushing burden when there might be hundreds of routers in an AS.

In this section we look at *route reflectors* (RR) as a way to deal with the BGP scaling issue. Two RR *clusters* are formed, one with three routers and the other with four (one router will be a *non-client*). Cluster 0.1.1.1 comprises the Mercury, Venus, and Earth routers. Mercury is the route reflector, and the other two are *clients*. Cluster 0.1.2.3 comprises the Mars, Saturn, Uranus, and Neptune routers. Saturn is the router reflector, and the other three are clients. Jupiter is a non-client router in the AS, just to show the behavior of the non-client routers and to demonstrate that there is no requirement for a router to belong to a route reflector cluster when clusters are established in an AS. Direct connection to a route reflector is always nice, but this is only an example.

BGP Route Reflectors on Juniper Networks

Juniper Networks routers use 32-bit numbers in the form of IP addresses as Cluster IDs, similar to the format used in OSPF areas. The Cluster ID can even *be* an IP address, although this is not required and no one ever routes packets to a Cluster ID. The Cluster ID is just for loop prevention within the AS. The Cluster ID used in these examples was chosen especially for multivendor environments, as is explained in the next section when a Cisco router becomes the route reflector. When only Juniper Networks routers are used within an AS as route reflectors, it is common to see the router's loopback address used as the Cluster ID. This instantly identifies the route reflector and makes troubleshooting easier. But translating loopback addresses to the Cisco Cluster ID format can be awkward, so simpler Cluster IDs are used here.

The route reflectors are not routers that happen to have the inter-AS links, and there is no requirement that route reflectors be border routers or the other way around. To the contrary, there are good arguments *against* making border routers the route reflectors. Today route reflectors have a lot to do, and it is common to see routers dedicated to the route reflector task. The selection of

Mercury and Saturn as route reflectors is designed to demonstrate this philosophy of having a router "one step back" from the border router as a route reflector. If a route reflector *does* have EBGP peers, routes received from the border router in the other AS are treated no differently than if the border router were not a router reflector. That is, no Cluster ID or Originator ID is attached to the route received from the EBGP peer. Route reflection only applies to IBGP routes. There is also no requirement to connect each client router directly to its route reflector, as is shown by the Uranus router, although this is routinely done.

The addition of the route reflectors causes AS 64999 to look as shown in Figure 14.4. The route reflectors represent the cluster to other IBGP routers and route reflectors, sending BGP updates from non-clients (and other route reflectors) to their clients and sending BGP updates from client to non-clients (and other route reflectors) and to all clients except the client that originated the BGP update. BGP updates can be generated by clients when new static routes (customers) are defined or other changes are made.

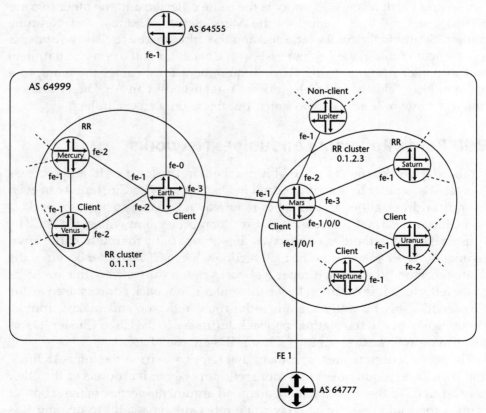

Figure 14.4 AS 64999 with two route reflector clusters.

Once route reflectors and clients are established, the client routers will have a simpler IBGP configuration. It is only necessary for Earth and Venus to peer with Mercury instead of six other routers as before. No matter how many other routers are added to the AS or Cluster 0.1.1.1, Earth and Venus are configured for IBGP, once and for all.

Although not done in this configuration, Earth and Venus, since they have a direct link, could retain their IBGP session. Then the route reflector would not have to reflect any client routes, but only forward the BGP updates to non-client routers.

Only a simple statement has to be added to the IBGP configuration on Mercury and Saturn to make the routers into the route reflector for the cluster. Basically, only the Cluster ID needs to be added. The following is the configuration from Saturn:

```
[edit protocols bgp]
lab@Saturn# show
group ibgp-mesh {
    type internal;
    local-address 172.16.0.6;
    cluster 0.1.2.3;
    neighbor 172.16.0.4;
    neighbor 172.16.0.5;
    neighbor 172.16.0.7;
    neighbor 172.16.0.8;
    neighbor 172.16.0.1;
}
```

Saturn can drop IBGP peering sessions with Venus and Earth but must retain IBGP peering with its clients, the other route reflector (172.16.0.1), and Jupiter (172.16.0.5), the non-client. This does not seem like much of a savings, but the route reflector is special. On a client router, only an IBGP session to the route reflector is needed:

```
[edit protocols]
lab@Neptune# show
bgp {
    group ibgp-mesh {
        type internal;
        local-address 172.16.0.8;
        neighbor 172.16.0.6;
    }
}
```

This is lot easier, and no changes are made if routers are added to the cluster. And even distant Neptune, and the far end of the AS, still knows how to reach routes in AS 64555 and AS 64777:

```
lab@Neptune> show route 10.100/16
inet.0: 39 destinations, 39 routes (39 active, 0 holddown, 0 hidden)
+ = Active Route, - = Last Active, * = Both

10.100.1.0/24       *[BGP/170] 00:12:05, MED 0, localpref 100,
                      from 172.16.0.6, AS path: 64555 I
                      > to 10.0.12.1 via fe-0/0/1.0
10.100.254.0/24     *[BGP/170] 00:12:05, MED 0, localpref 100,
                      from 172.16.0.6, AS path: 64555 I
                      > to 10.0.12.1 via fe-0/0/1.0

lab@Neptune> show route 10.200/16
inet.0: 39 destinations, 39 routes (39 active, 0 holddown, 0 hidden)
+ = Active Route, - = Last Active, * = Both

10.200.1.0/24       *[BGP/170] 00:12:14, MED 0, localpref 100,
                      from 172.16.0.6, AS path: 64777 ?
                      > to 10.0.12.1 via fe-0/0/1.0
10.200.200.0/24     *[OSPF/10] 00:15:26, metric 12
                      > to 10.0.12.1 via fe-0/0/1.0
10.200.254.0/24     *[BGP/170] 00:12:14, MED 0, localpref 100,
                      from 172.16.0.6, AS path: 64777 ?
                      > to 10.0.12.1 via fe-0/0/1.0
```

Notice that the routes are now learned from the route reflector (Saturn, 172.16.0.6) and not directly from the Earth and Mars routers with the links to AS 64555 and AS 64777. Juniper, the only non-client, finds out about the routes from Saturn, its only needed IBGP peer. The non-client status only influences the route reflector's behavior regarding client routes.

A detailed look at one of the external routes (this time on Mars) shows the presence of the route reflector attributes Cluster List and Originator ID. Even though the route originates on Earth (172.16.0.3), the route is learned from Mars's route reflector, Saturn (172.16.0.6):

```
lab@Mars> show route 10.100.1.0/24 extensive
inet.0: 43 destinations, 43 routes (43 active, 0 holddown, 0 hidden)
10.100.1.0/24 (1 entry, 1 announced)
TSI:
KRT in-kernel 10.100.1.0/24 -> {indirect(50)}
Page 0 idx 1 Type 1 val 83c6dc8
    Nexthop: 172.16.0.3
    AS path: 64555 I (Originator)
    Cluster list: 0.1.2.3 0.1.1.1
    Originator ID: 172.16.0.3
    Communities:
Path 10.100.1.0 from 172.16.0.6 Vector len 4.  Val: 1
(more lines deleted...)
```

Route reflectors can introduce a single-point-of-failure risk into IBGP configurations. If the route reflector is down, the client routers have no IBGP peer to rely on for BGP routing information. This is not as much a problem as it might seem at first. Although not attempted here with this modest collection of routers, it is common to configure *two* router reflectors per cluster, so that if one fails, the other can carry on.

In the real world, route reflectors within a cluster are often deployed as in Figure 14.5.

A lively debate revolves around the "correct" Cluster ID for redundant route reflectors. Should the route reflectors have unique Cluster IDs, or should they be the same? In either case, there could be a problem with unreachable destinations if just the right IBGP session fails. This risk is inherent in IBGP. When different Cluster IDs are used, some feel there is less of a risk of unreachable routes at the cost of larger routing tables. But when multiple clients peer to route reflectors with different Cluster IDs, the clean boundary between clusters is lost and some feel that the whole concept of a cluster is compromised. Using the same Cluster ID saves the cluster boundary, but others feel the cluster is preserved at the cost of a greater risk of unreachable destinations. There is no absolutely correct answer at this time, and both approaches are commonly used today.

Clients remain unaffected by such Cluster ID debates. Clients view the route reflectors as just simple peers for their IBGP sessions. Only the route reflector, configured with the Cluster ID, need change its default IBGP operation. The redundant route reflectors can peer with each other as usual. When one route reflector sees a BGP route with its own Cluster ID as an attribute, the update is simply dropped and routing loops are always prevented. However, it is actually better for one of the route reflectors to fail outright than for an IBGP session to drop and perhaps render some routes unreachable.

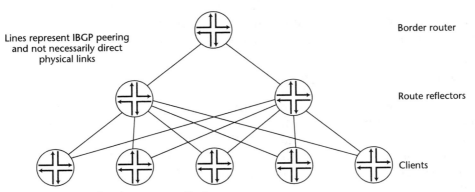

Lines represent IBGP peering
and not necessarily direct
physical links

Border router

Route reflectors

Clients

Figure 14.5 Redundant route reflectors.

There is no debate about having multiple route reflectors in a cluster if over-lapping clients are avoided. There can be as many route reflectors as desired, each with their own set of clients. An AS can surround a border router with as many route reflectors as there are direct links to other routers inside the AS. The border router is a non-client of the cluster and now peers only with the set of route reflectors. These front-line route reflectors have their own clients and control the number of IBGP peering sessions required on the border router(s). The border router is still used as the Originator ID for routes outside the AS, and the Cluster ID prevents loops. Another benefit is that only active routes are considered eligible for route reflector advertisement. Instead of having a border router send a complete set of routing information to every other router and letting each router figure out the active route, the route reflectors act as screens that only propagate the active routes to their clients. This lets the clients deal with far less routing information than they ordinarily would have to consider.

There are even ISPs that deploy route reflectors in a hierarchical fashion. That is, a client of one route reflector can be the route reflector for another client. This cuts down even further on the number of IBGP peering sessions and routing information distributed. It is best not to be dogmatic about the proper reason to select and configure route reflectors and clients. It all depends on what the ISP is trying to accomplish. Route reflectors are almost like establishing a routing policy in hardware. So a firm definition of the goal and evaluation of the router reflectors' performance are much more important than the route reflectors' configuration or application.

The full routing tables on all of the routers do not have to be shown to know that the route reflectors are doing their jobs. OSPF takes care of the IGP routes, and the route reflectors take care of the BGP routes, as has been shown. Only details regarding the routes from AS 64555 and AS 64777 have changed, and only minimally at that.

A route reflector client does not have to be replaced with a Cisco router. Only the peering changes. But configuring a Cisco router to work as a route reflector with Juniper Networks clients is worth a look.

A Cisco Route Reflector

In this section we now replace the Juniper Networks Saturn route reflector in Cluster 0.1.2.3 with a Cisco router. Since Cisco routers comply with all of the usual route reflector rules, such a substitution should be relatively painless. However, there is a complication right away, even before the configuration begins. The complication has to do with the way Juniper Networks and Cisco routers configure the Cluster ID.

Both Cisco and Juniper Networks routers represent the Cluster ID as a 32-bit number. So far so good, and that's in the RFC. But the two router vendors differ in how they configure this number, which can be larger than 4,000,000,000 (4 thousand million, or 4 billion) in decimal. Juniper Networks routers, as has already been shown, configure the 32 bits in four parts as decimal numbers between 0 and 255, just like an IP address (and the Cluster ID can even be an IP address). In contrast, Cisco routers configure the same 32-bit Cluster ID as a large, unstructured decimal number.

If the Cluster ID is allowed to be anything at any time, there is no problem in the AS. But if a Juniper Networks route reflector already has a Cluster ID of, for example, 0.0.2.255 and a Cisco route reflector needs to have a *different* Cluster ID, then the Cisco route reflector cannot use 767 as its Cluster ID. Both 0.0.2.255 and 767 represent the same 32-bit number, although this is not immediately obvious. So some rule for converting Juniper Networks format to Cisco format, and back, should be given, especially since this example keeps the same Cluster ID as configured on the Juniper Networks route reflector.

To convert Cluster ID 0.1.2.3 to Cisco format, do the following:

1. Multiply the first number by 16,777,216 (0 x 16,777,216 = 0).

2. Multiply the second number by 65,536 (1 x 65,636 = 65,536).

3. Multiply the third number by 256 (2 x 256 = 512).

4. Add the fourth number to the other three (0 + 65,536 + 512 + 3 = 66,051).

So the Cisco router will have Cluster ID 66051. Cluster ID 0.1.1.1 converts to 65793. This was one reason why the loopback addresses in the form of 172.16.10.1 were *not* used in the Juniper Networks route reflectors. In the other direction, to convert the number 66051 back to Juniper Networks format, do the following:

1. Divide the number by 256 and note the remainder (66,051 / 256 = 258 with 3 left over).

2. Divide the whole result by 256 and note the remainder (258 / 256 = 1 with 2 left over).

3. The remainder is less than 256, so form the Juniper Networks format as 0.1.2.3.

Note that the Cisco to Juniper Networks conversion builds up the dotted decimal from right to left. It is possible to build up the Juniper Networks format from left to right, but this requires division by numbers much larger than 256.

Once the conversion (if desired) is made, the configuration of the Cisco_ Mercury router as a route reflector is as follows:

```
router bgp 64999
 no synchronization
 bgp cluster-id 65793
 neighbor 172.16.0.2 remote-as 64999
```

```
neighbor 172.16.0.2 update-source Loopback0
neighbor 172.16.0.2 route-reflector-client
neighbor 172.16.0.3 remote-as 64999
neighbor 172.16.0.3 update-source Loopback0
neighbor 172.16.0.3 route-reflector-client
neighbor 172.16.0.6 remote-as 64999
neighbor 172.16.0.6 update-source Loopback0
no auto-summary
```

Note that it is necessary to distinguish between route reflector clients and non-client with the use of the `route-reflector-client` statement.

As long as the Cluster ID is the same, the swapping of the Mercury route reflector for a Cisco router is transparent to the Juniper Networks clients. The Cisco_Mercury router reflects the same BGP routes as before:

```
Cisco_Merciry#sh ip bgp
BGP table version is 9, local router ID is 172.16.0.1

Status codes:s suppressed,d damped,h history,*valid,>best,i internal

Origin codes: i - IGP, e - EGP, ? - incomplete

    Network          Next Hop         Metric LocPrf Weight Path
*>i10.100.1.0/24     172.16.0.3            0    100      0 64555 i
*>i10.100.254.0/24   172.16.0.3            0    100      0 64555 i
*>i10.200.1.0/24     10.200.200.200       0    100      0 64777 ?
*>i10.200.254.0/24   10.200.200.200       0    100      0 64777 ?
```

Although not shown here, the rest of the Juniper Networks routers do not see the Cluster ID as 65793, but as 0.1.1.1, just as before.

BGP Confederations

The use of route reflectors goes a long way toward easing the IBGP mesh scalability issue. But route reflectors are often used with BGP confederations to cut down on IBGP mesh requirements even further. For example, the route reflectors still need to mesh with each other to distribute BGP routing information correctly.

In this section we add confederations to the route reflectors already configured. The confederations are established as shown in Figure 14.6. Each route reflector cluster fits nicely inside each Sub-AS and their behavior is unchanged, except that there is no longer any IBGP peering between Mercury and Saturn, since these route reflectors are now in different Sub-ASs.

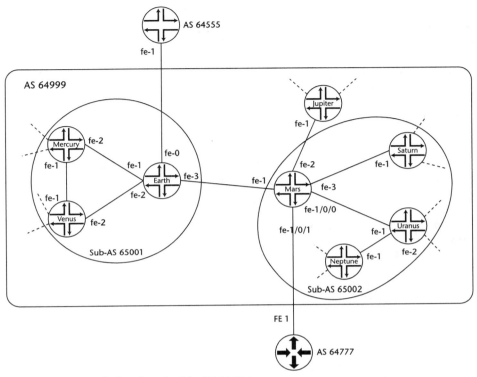

Figure 14.6 Confederations inside AS 64999.

All the details of every router in AS 64999 do not have to be examined to investigate confederations. Routers such as Earth and Mars occupy the key positions in the confederation, so we examine these routers extensively.

To make a Juniper Networks router into a member of a confederation Sub-AS, two statements must be set correctly in the routing-options section of the configuration. The AS number is now the Sub-AS number to which the router belongs, and the confederation statement identifies the *global AS* (public AS number seen outside the confederation) along with the Sub-AS numbers of all of the members of the confederation. There are only two Sub-ASs in AS 64999. The two statements must be configured on each router.

Normally, OSPF would only run within an AS, but each Sub-AS is really a member of the global AS, so the Earth and Mars routers will *not* remove OSPF from the interface to each other. It is possible to configure a Sub-AS within a confederation to run BGP only (with direct links), an IGP only within the Sub-AS, or even different IGPs inside the Sub-AS, as long as routes are distributed as required. This example leaves OSPF in place and simply addresses IBGP peering issues. The following is how the routing options for the confederation will look on Earth:

```
[edit routing-options]
lab@Earth# show
(static routes not shown)
autonomous-system 65001;
confederation 64999 members [ 65001 65002 ];
```

All other routers will mimic these two statements, with their own Sub-AS number for the autonomous-system. On Earth, the protocols configuration looks as follows:

```
lab@Earth# show protocols
bgp {
    group ebgp {
        type external;
        export send-statics;
        peer-as 64555;
        neighbor 10.100.100.100;
    }
    group ibgp-mesh {
        type internal;
        local-address 172.16.0.3;
        export next-hop-self;
        neighbor 172.16.0.1;
    }
    group cbgpto-subas65002 {
        type external;
        peer-as 65002;
        export next-hop-self;
        neighbor 10.0.8.2;
    }
}
ospf {
    export send-statics;
    area 0.0.0.0 {
        interface fe-0/0/2.0;
        interface fe-0/0/1.0;
        interface fe-0/0/3.0;
        interface lo0 {
            passive;
        }
    }
}
```

The new BGP group, cbgp-to-subas65002, is very similar to any other EBGP configuration, except now the peer-as is 65002. Even the export policy next-hop-self is needed or else the 10.100/16 routes will be hidden on Mars and never be advertised to AS 64777. (Next Hop Self is not needed on the Mars router because IGP passive is used there instead.)

The BGP routes learned from AS 64777 through Mars in Sub-AS 65002 show the change in their AS path, listing the SUB-AS:

```
lab@Earth> show route 10.200/16
inet.0: 43 destinations, 43 routes (43 active, 0 holddown, 0 hidden)
+ = Active Route, - = Last Active, * = Both

10.200.1.0/24       *[BGP/170] 00:04:12, MED 0, localpref 100
                       AS path: (65002) 64777 ?
                     > to 10.0.8.2 via fe-0/0/3.0
10.200.200.0/24     *[OSPF/10] 00:05:22, metric 11
                     > to 10.0.8.2 via fe-0/0/3.0
10.200.254.0/24     *[BGP/170] 00:04:12, MED 0, localpref 100
                       AS path: (65002) 64777 ?
                     > to 10.0.8.2 via fe-0/0/3.0
```

Juniper Networks routers use parentheses to delimit Sub-AS (private) numbers from global AS numbers assigned to the entire AS. On Mars, of course, routes from 10.100/16 show Sub-AS 65001 in the path. These Sub-AS numbers are removed from the routes advertised to AS 64555 and AS 64777, as shown by a look at a route on the AS 64555 router (a Juniper Networks router) that originated in AS 64777:

```
lab@AS64555_router> show route 10.200.254.0/24 extensive
inet.0: 9 destinations, 9 routes (9 active, 0 holddown, 0 hidden)
10.200.254.0/24 (1 entry, 1 announced)
TSI:
KRT in-kernel 10.200.254.0/24 -> {10.100.100.99}
Page 0 idx 0 Type 1 val 83c5cb0
    Nexthop: 10.100.100.99
    AS path: 64999 64777 ?
    Communities:
(more lines not shown...)
```

Only the path through AS 64999 shows up outside the confederation. Confederations can be complicated by multiple links (such as a link from Neptune to Earth or Venus). This chapter has only explored the basics of confederations.

A Cisco Confederation Router

This final section simply demonstrates how to configure a confederation with a mix of Juniper Networks and Cisco routers. Only the use of a private AS number instead of a public AS number really distinguishes confederation BGP configurations from EBGP configurations. This section returns to the Earth router and makes the Cisco_Earth router into a router with the AS_64555 router as an EBGP peer, Mercury as a route reflector, and Mars as a confederation BGP peer.

For the first time, this Cisco configuration establishes BGP *peer groups*, which have been used all along on the Juniper networks routers because they are required. Once a Cisco router is configured with mixed BGP types, such as IBGP, EBGP, and CBGP, it is easier to keep peers straight with peer groups.

A peer group is established on a Cisco router by simply assigning a neighbor BGP router to a peer group, for example using `neighbor 10.0.8.1 peer-group IBGP-peer`. Then other BGP statements can be applied to the peer-group instead of each neighbor, such as `neighbor IBGP-peer update-source Loopback0`.

Unlike Juniper Networks routers, Cisco routers use the confederation Sub-AS number to identify the BGP process. The `bgp confederation identifier` statement gives the public global AS number (AS 64999 in this example) and the `bgp confederation peers` statement lists the Sub-AS numbers (65001 and 65002 in this example). Cisco routers also apply Next Hop Self directly to the BGP configuration.

The confederation configuration on Cisco_Earth looks like the following:

```
!
 router bgp 65001
 no synchronization
 bgp confederation identifer 64999
 bgp confederation peers 65001 65002
 neighbor Confed peer-group
 neighbor Confed remote-as 65002
 neighbor Confed next-hop-self
 neighbor IBGP peer-group
 neighbor IBGP remote-as 65001
 neighbor IBGP update-source Loopback0
 neighbor IBGP next-hop-self
 neighbor EBGP peer-group
 neighbor EBGP remote-as 64555
 neighbor EBGP redistribute static
 neighbor 10.0.8.2 peer-group Confed
 neighbor 172.16.0.1 peer-group IBGP
 neighbor 10.100.100.100 peer-group EBGP
 no auto-summary
!
```

Everything elsewhere inside and outside of the AS is still the same, as might be expected. Here is the view of the BGP routes from AS 64777, which is also a Cisco router:

```
Cisco_AS64777#sh ip bgp
BGP table version is 30, local router ID is 172.30.77.7

Status codes:s suppressed,d damped,h history,*valid,>best,i internal

Origin codes: i - IGP, e - EGP, ? - incomplete
    Network          Next Hop      Metric LocPrf Weight Path
*> 10.100.1.0/24    10.200.200.199                    0 64999 64555 i
*> 10.100.254.0/24 10.200.200.199                     0 64999 64555 i
*> 10.200.1.0/24     0.0.0.0          0          32768 ?
*> 10.200.254.0/24   0.0.0.0          0          32768 ?
```

Summary

We could discuss many more topics with regard to BGP. This chapter has explored only the most basic of BGP attributes and how Juniper Networks and Cisco routers treat them. Later chapters focus on the use of aggregates to advertise the entire static range used in these examples, the setting and use of the MED, communities, and so on. This same network is used again to explore more advanced routing policies later on in this book.

PART

Four

IGP Routing Policies

This part of the book contains two chapters. Up to this point, the emphasis has been on just getting the IGP routing protocols up and running in a multivendor environment. Not much discussion was spent on the role of routing policies in the operation of the IGPs such as OSPF and IS-IS, but that will change now. Our emphasis shifts to routing policies and the IGPs. Specifically, we look at creating and implementing routing policies to make the routing protocols interact so that traffic is shuttled as needed around the network.

Nothing is said about RIP, either RIPv1 or RIPv2, in these chapters. This is not to slight RIP in any way as a routing protocol, just to acknowledge the limitations of RIP and its use in the real world. RIPv1, lacking IP address mask information and therefore limited to classful application, is really immune to all but the simplest routing policy manipulations of hop counts. RIPv2 is a better subject for routing policy application, but even so, the positioning of RIP far from the AS core and ISP backbone means that little done with RIP routing policies will have a major effect on the flow of packets through the Internet.

The emphasis here is on OSPF and IS-IS. Even without consideration of routing policies for these IGPs in their respective chapters, a few simple routing policies were necessary just to make the routing protocols function as needed in the example networks. However, there was little discussion of all of the implications of these routing policies, including application of routing policies between OSPF areas and IS-IS levels, and there was no attempt to develop more complex routing policies to modify the default behaviors of OSPF and IS-IS.

In these chapters we explore more complicated routing policies with regard to OSPF and IS-IS. To be sure, there is much more to do with routing policy with an EGP such as BGP than there is with IGPs. But no one should imagine that IGPs are not a worthwhile arena to investigate the application of routing policies.

Before we look at applying routing policies to OSPF and IS-IS, we start off with a crucial chapter on the routing policies themselves: Chapter 15, "Routing Policy." There is a world of difference between how routing policies are configured and applied in Cisco and Juniper Networks routers. Cisco routing policies, as might be expected in a product line that stretches all the way back to the dawn of routers, have accumulated in the IOS software over the years and are almost organic in their relationship to the routing protocols that the policies modify. That is, the configuration of the routing policy is intimately tied up with the routing protocol. On the other hand, Juniper Networks routers treat routing policies as almost a separate entity altogether. JUNOS software routing policies tend to look a lot like C language programs, complete with `from` (if) conditions, `then` actions, and `default` (else) behavior. This should be perhaps expected in a young company seeking a unified framework for routing policy applications. This is not to say that one approach is inherently better than the other, but that they are radically and vastly different.

Once the basics of both Cisco and Juniper Networks routing policy structures have been outlined, in Chapter 16, "IGP Routing Policies," we configure and apply routing policies to OSPF and IS-IS. Here we apply policies to summarize IP address spaces inside of areas and manipulate external Type 1 (E1) and Type 2 (E2) metrics, tag routes, and so on. With regard to IS-IS, Chapter 16 mainly addresses *route leaking* between Level 2 and Level 1, but it also investigates other relationships between IS-IS levels and areas.

Routing Policy

Routing policy is a *toolkit* for working on routing protocols. Like all tools, routing policies in the hands of a master can produce wonders of the craft, sending packets in just the right ways through a maze of routers and links. But if a careless apprentice rummages through the toolkit and uses all the wrong tools, the end result might be a haphazard product that bears little resemblance to the fine structure intended.

No one would blame the hammer or the screw for a cabinet with doors that do not mesh properly or praise the saw and nail for the table with sturdy legs. So it is with routing policy. Some may prefer the integrated Cisco approach or the define-and-apply approach of Juniper Networks, but the fact remains that the same things can be done with both toolkits, and the results will be identical as long as the level of knowledge and expertise are the same to start with.

Before we plunge into how Cisco and Juniper Networks establish the ground rules for their routing policies, this might be a good time to review the definition of a routing policy as used in this book. The informal definition of *routing policy* in this book has been relatively narrow. Some apply the term *policy routing* to methods of deploying quality of service (QoS) levels and enforcing these service-level parameters across an AS. There is nothing wrong with this definition, and indeed it would mesh nicely with the definition of routing policy used here. But IP QoS considerations are worthy of a book-length treatment of their own and remain outside the scope of this book. This book defines a *routing policy*, or *policy framework*, or whatever other term a vendor might use to describe the technique, as a *plan that determines exactly which routes and in what form are accepted by a router and which routes and in what form are advertised by a router*.

The term *form* in this definition applies not only to the IP prefix or mask length but also to whatever metrics, tags, or attributes are associated with the route. That is all the routing policy is really for: to determine what routing information goes into a router and what routing information comes out of a router. This might be a rather narrow definition, but it is workable and consistent.

Routing policies therefore have an *inbound* and *outbound* application on a router. This can be called *import* or *export*, but the point is the same. An *import* routing policy filters and modifies routes *before* they are placed in the routing table or considered for the active route installed in the forwarding table. An *export* policy filters and modifies routes that are usually selected for advertisement to other routers, typically because they are the active routes used to reach a destination prefix. The action of a routing policy on routes is shown in Figure 15.1.

Note that you can even apply a routing policy to routes that are to be installed in the forwarding table. This is one way that you can install multiple routes in the forwarding table for load balancing or eliminate routes that would otherwise be active routes, for example. However, no routing policies in this book are applied in this fashion.

In a very real sense, the configuring of routers with their correct addressing schemes and routing protocols is just the *beginning* of the process of creating a network. Routers with basic routing protocols just forward packets as they see fit and make no allowance for the service providers' wishes with regard to security, performance, or just business. Sending a packet over *here* can end up costing money, while sending a packet over *there* can guarantee making money. Routing policy is a way of imposing the service provider's wishes and intentions on the decisions the routing protocols would ordinarily make on their own.

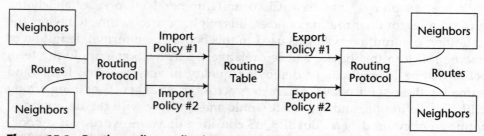

Figure 15.1 Routing policy application to routing information.

There are at least three major occasions that a router's default routing protocol behavior might need to be modified with respect to routes accepted and advertised:

- To control the route that a routing protocol places into the routing table
- To control the active routes that a routing protocol advertises from the routing table
- To change the route's characteristics as the routing protocol places the route into the routing tables or as the routing protocol advertises the route from the routing table

Changing a route's characteristics such as the metric can influence which route is selected from the routing table as the active route. Active routes are used for forwarding traffic that passes through the router. Generally, the active route is advertised to the router's neighbors.

A multivendor environment requires a certain level of abstraction regarding routing policy. When only a single router vendor is involved, people responsible for routing policy tend to think in terms of the specifics of the router vendor's syntax: "Hmmm. Need a route map here . . ." or "I have to add a term to export directs . . ." When it is not a given that a routing policy will be implemented on one platform or another, you need to take one step back and define the routing policy in more vendor-neutral terms.

There should be five steps to creating any routing policy:

Definition. In human terms, define exactly what the routing policy should do.

Configuration. Translate the routing policy is into vendor-specific language.

Application. Apply the routing policy to a test environment, then a working environment.

Evaluation. Determine whether the routing policy is producing the desired results.

Refinement. Finding a better or more efficient way to produce the results.

Naturally, the last step could lead right back to the first step. This is fine; networks change and evolve, and so must their routing policies.

Unfortunately, this book cannot describe all aspects of Cisco and Juniper Networks routing policy configuration. This would require a small volume all its own. The main consideration in this book is the *application* of routing policy in a multivendor environment. For example, not all of the details of regular expressions (regex, or RE) are covered in this chapter. Explaining the essentials of regular expressions and showing some examples of their use in routing policies should be sufficient.

This chapter examines the Cisco routing policy framework first and then ends with an investigation of the Juniper Networks routing policy framework.

Cisco Routing Policy

Cisco routers were revolutionary devices around 1990. Instead of linking LANs with bridges, it was now possible to use a *router* (previously called a *firewall* or *gateway*) to link LANs together over WAN links. But Cisco's Internetwork Operating System (IOS) did not spring fully formed into existence. IOS evolved and added features from release to release. One key area where functionality has been added to Cisco's IOS is in the method of controlling routing information shared among routing protocols, accepted into a router, and advertised to other routers. This is just routing policy, of course, but although it is common to talk about routing policy as a unified approach to routing information control, as IOS evolved, different aspects of routing policy were added wherever it made the most sense at the time. So Cisco routing policy implementation can be a considerable undertaking and may require many different sections of the configuration to be manipulated, coordinated, and adjusted.

The general application of routing policy on a Cisco router is often called *route filtering*. But route filtering is not a unified tool, just an overall concept. The main methods used to implement routing policies on a Cisco router are as follows:

Redistribution.   A fundamental tool, but the main way that one routing protocol learns about routes from another source. The source can be a routing protocol, interface, static route, or many other things. The only real policies in this book so far have been simple redistributions of routing information. A key concept is what Cisco calls the *administrative distance* of the route and what Juniper Networks calls the *protocol preference*.

Route maps.   A kind of access lists for routes. Route maps are the primary way that a Cisco router finds certain packets (through match criteria) and permit, deny, or set attributes of the routing information found. Route maps are important enough to have their own section of the Cisco configuration. Route maps are often used with redistribution or *policy routing* (special handling of packets, such as for quality of service, based on source address). Route maps are not used in this book for quality of service.

Distribution lists.   A special type of access list applied to the routing process, often used in BGP. This is a very powerful tool for filtering BGP routes. Used in conjunction with access lists.

Prefix list.   Yet another special type of access list applied to routing in BGP. The only match allowed in a prefix list is an IP network address prefix such as 192.168.14/24. The prefix list offers very precise control over routing updates.

Access lists.   Access lists are used for a lot more than just implementing routing policies. Anytime a Cisco router needs to permit or deny traffic based on the source IP address (standard), or even higher-layer header information (extended), an access list can be used. It is hard to talk about Cisco routing policy, especially distribution lists, without mentioning access lists, although access lists are primarily used to filter user traffic. Only access list concepts that apply to routing policies are discussed in this chapter.

Miscellaneous tools.   This category includes things like the use of passive interfaces and `network connected` to solve next-hop reachability in BGP, static and default routes to avoid dynamic routing instabilities and uncertainties, and the use of the null interface as a next hop. No special section is dedicated to these routing policy tools.

Of all the concepts, the most fundamental is the use of the route map. Many books and papers even mention route maps and route filtering to lump everything else used to control routing information into a separate category. But they are all related. This section can only discuss the basics of each tool, but this will be enough for the routing policies used in the rest of this book.

When a Cisco router learns about a prefix from multiple sources (for example, OSPF and BGP), the router applies a default *administrative distance* to the source of the routing information and prefers the lower value. The administrative distances for the routing protocols discussed earlier in this book have been mentioned but not emphasized. The default administrative distances are shown in Table 15.1.

So routes learned through OSPF are preferred over routes learned through IBGP, static routes are preferred to IS-IS routes, and so on. The administrative distance values are not often changed on an individual router, since this can bring curious results to other routers on the network. But the administrative distance can be used in a coordinated fashion to ease IGP transitions, as we will see in the next chapter.

Table 15.1 Default Cisco Administrative Distances

SOURCE OF ROUTING INFORMATION	DEFAULT ADMINISTRATIVE DISTANCE
Connected network interface	0
Static route	1
EIGRP summary route	5
EBGP	20
EIGRP internal	90
IGRP	100
OSPF (all types)	110
IS-IS (all types)	115
RIP	120
EGP	140
IBGP	200
Unknown (not trusted: ignored)	255

Redistribution

Some Cisco routing protocols automatically share what they know with other routing protocols, but usually they do not. The default redistribution behavior for Cisco routing protocols is shown in Table 15.2.

As the table shows, automatic redistribution is limited to Cisco-specific protocols. To get the standard routing protocols used in this book to redistribute what they know to other routing protocols, you must manually configure and apply a routing policy. We have already done this several times before with static routes. For example, a simple `redistribute static` line in the OSPF configuration exports all that the router knows about its static routes (the source) to OSPF neighbors (the target).

The `redistribute` command has many additional optional fields that you can use to control the routes actually shared with the target protocol. These options form a type of *match condition* that must be met in order for the route to be shared. In this respect, `redistribute` *is* a routing policy, although a very simple one. In addition, metrics and other parameters of the source route can be adjusted.

Table 15.2 Cisco's Default Redistributions

ROUTING INFORMATION SOURCE	REDISTRIBUTION POLICY
Static routes	Manual redistribution required.
Connected network interface	Manual redistribution required unless included in the `network` command for the routing process.
RIP	Manual redistribution required.
OSPF	Manual redistribution required for different process IDs.
IS-IS	Manual redistribution required.
BGP	Manual redistribution required.
IGRP	Automatic to EIGRP if same AS; otherwise, manual redistribution required.
EIGRP	Automatic to IGRP if same AS; otherwise, manual redistribution required. Special rules for AppleTalk and IPX.

The full syntax of the `redistribute` command is as follows:

```
redistribute protocol [process id] {level-1 | level-2 | level-1-2}
[metric metric-value] [metric-type type-value] [match {internal |
external 1 | external 2}] [tag tag-value] [route-map map-tag] [weight
weight] [subnets]
```

The `protocol` is the protocol that is providing the routes. In its simplest form, used so far in this book, the command looks like `redistribute static` or similar routing sources such as `connected` (direct interfaces), `bgp`, `isis`, `ospf`, `rip`, and others. The `process id` is an AS for BGP, but for OSPF this is the OSPF process ID. The levels apply to IS-IS, and the optional `metric` should be consistent with the target routing protocol (if the value is not set here or specified with `default-metric` elsewhere in the configuration, the route might not be advertised). The `metric-type` applies to OSPF and is used to set external Type 1 routes (metric type = 1) or external Type 2 (metric type = 2). `Match` also applies to OSPF, but matches internal, Type 1, or Type 2 OSPF routes. The `tag` value defaults to the remote AS for BGP and EGP, but to 0 for all other protocols. A `route map` can match specific routes (explained in the next section), `weight` is Cisco-specific for BGP, and `subnets` is used to distribute subnets into OSPF.

Route Maps

The `redistribute` command can reference a `route-map` to help filter the routes imported into the target protocol. If there is no `route-map`, all eligible routes are redistributed from source to target.

Route maps are used in two major places on a Cisco router: with redistribution and to implement *policy routing* (not the same as general routing policy). Cisco's policy routing is a method of using special static routes to give preferential treatment to some packets based on source address or other characteristics. Although this policy-routing aspect of route maps is certainly a valid application of routing policy, this section only addresses the use of route maps with regard to routing information redistribution. This is done both to limit the size of this section and to focus on the actual routing policies used in this book, which emphasize the effects of policy on routing information, not user traffic.

Route maps are configured in a special section of the Cisco router configuration (`config-route-map`). Each route map consists of name, action (permit or deny), and a sequence number on one line. This is followed by a series of `match` conditions, then a series of `set` statements. The match and set commands that can be used with redistribution are shown in Table 15.3.

Table 15.3 Match and Set Commands for Redistribution

COMMAND	COMMENT
match interface *type number* [*...type number*]	Matches routes with that interface as next hop(s).
match ip address {*access-list-number/name*}	Matches routes with destination address in one access list [*...access-list-number/name*].
match ip next-hop {*access-list-number/name*}	Matches routes with route next hop in one access list [*...access-list-number/name*].
match ip route-source {access-list-number/name}	Matches routes advertised by router in one access list [*...access-list-number/name*].
match metric *metric value*	Matches routes with that metric value.
match route-type {*internal*	*external* {*type-1*	*type-2*]	*level-1*	*level-2*}	Matches OSPF, IS-IS, or EIGRP routes of that type.

Table 15.3 *(Continued)*

COMMAND	COMMENT
match tag *tag-value* [...tag-value]	Matches routes with that tag value(s).
set level {*level-1*	*level-2*	*level-1-2*	*stub-area*	*backbone*}	Sets IS-IS level or OSPF area type into which matched route is to be redistributed.
set metric {*metric-value*	*bandwidth delay reliability loading mtu*}	Sets the metric value for the matched route.
set metric-type {*internal*	*external*	*type-1*	*type-2*}	Sets the OSPF or IS-IS metric type for matched route.
set next-hop *next-hop*	Sets next-hop router for the matched route.
set tag *tag-value*	Sets tag value for the matched route.

Route maps have a default action of permit and default sequence number of 10, but they are commonly included anyway, since multiple route maps are the rule. When multiple match conditions are used with a set command, all of the match conditions must be true in order for the set command to be executed. Route maps do nothing until they are referenced in a redistribute or explicit ip policy route-map command applied to an interface. The following is an example of a route map and its application:

```
router ospf 10
 redistribute isis route-map Level-1-20s
 network 10.0.15.1 0.0.0.0 area 0
 ...
!
route-map Level-1-20s permit 10
 match route-type level-1
 match metric 20
 set metric 2
 set level stub-area
!
```

This route map finds IS-IS Level 1 routes with a metric of 20 and advertise them through OSPF with a metric of 2 and as if they were from an OSPF stub area. This type of route and metric is much more suitable for OSPF routes. Other kinds of IS-IS routes, such as Level 2 backbone routes, are "permitted" by the route map.

Distribution Lists

A powerful method to perform route filtering on a Cisco router is to use a distribution list. Distribution lists are really just access lists applied to routes. Distribution lists can filter routes inbound (routes arriving for the routing protocol from neighbors) or outbound (routes to be advertised to neighbors). So a distribution list can have a finer degree of control over a route than a redistribution or route map. Like most of the other policy tools on a Cisco router, the distribution list acts in concert with an access list, referenced by access list number. A distribution list can be defined for routes arriving at the router (in) or to be advertised by the router (out). For example, the configuration fragment:

```
...
neighbor 10.0.32.1 distribute-list 1 in
...
access-list 1 permit 0.0.0.0
...
```

allows (permits) only a default route (0.0.0.0) in from the neighbor at 10.0.32.1. And the configuration fragment:

```
...
neighbor 10.0.64.2 distribute-list 2 out
...
access-list 2 deny 10.0.30.0
access-list 2 deny 192.168.24.0
access-list 2 deny 172.16.0.0
...
```

suppresses (denies) any routes that would ordinarily be advertised (out) to the router on the 10.0.64.2 interface if they are the prefixes in the access list.

The general form of the `distribute-list in` command is:

distribute-list {access-list-number | name} **in** [type number]

where the access list can be referenced by name or number, and the optional `type number` gives the interface type and number (such as Serial0) to which the distribution list is applied.

The general form of the `distribute-list out` command is:

distribute-list {access-list-number | name} **out** [interface-name | routing-process | autonomous-system-number]

where the access list can be referenced by name or number, and the optional fields describe the interface, routing process (`static` or `connected` can be used as well as `ospf`, `isis`, and so on), or AS number (for BGP) to which the distribution list is applied.

Prefix Lists

Prefix lists, like route maps, are also defined and then applied. Each line in the prefix list has a sequence number, and prefix lists can be edited by referencing these numbers (unlike access lists, which must be entirely rewritten when modified unless ported into a text editor and back). Although similar in many ways to access lists, prefix lists can be used to match more than just a specific prefix in a single statement. For this reason, prefix lists are much better suited for ISPs that must examine many routes and address ranges to implement routing policy.

The general form of the prefix list is:

```
ip prefix-list list-name [seq seq-value] {deny | permit} network/len [ge
ge-value] [le le-value]
```

where the prefix list is given a `list-name` (such as `trial`) and an optional sequence number (`seq`). The prefix list can deny or permit routes that fit the network address and mask given, and other routes either "greater than" (`ge`) or "less than" (`le`) the address and mask specified.

The prefix list does nothing until it is applied to a routing protocol for import (in) or potentially advertised routes (out), such as in `neighbor 10.0.21.2 prefix-list trial in`. If the `trial` prefix list is defined as:

```
ip prefix-list trial permit 172.16/16 ge 16 le 24
ip prefix-list trial permit 10.0/8 ge 24 le 30
```

then the routes arriving on the 10.0.21.2 interface will be accepted (permitted) if they are in the range from 172.16.0.0/16 to 172.16.0.0/24 or the range 10.0.0.0/24 to 10.0.0.0/30. All other routes will be rejected (denied).

There are a number of rules that apply to prefix list evaluation:

- If a route is explicitly permitted, it is accepted for import or export (advertising).

- If a route is explicitly denied, it is not used for import or export.

- If the prefix list is empty, all routes are permitted.

- If a route does not match any prefix, the route is denied. In other words, there is an implicit "deny all" at the end of each prefix list.

- If multiple entries match the route, the entry with the *smallest* sequence number is used.

- Multiple prefix list entries are examined from top to bottom. When a match is made, all further evaluation stops.

- The sequence numbers are either generated by default (as in the preceding example) or set manually with `seq`. The sequence number does not have to be referenced to delete an entry.

If explicit matches are needed in a prefix list, the `ge` and `le` can be omitted. Both match routes equal to their values as well as greater or less. If only `ge` is used, then the range extends to /32. If only `le` is used, the range is from the supplied prefix length to the `le` value. For example, 172.16/16 le /24 matches routes from 172.16.0.0/16 up to and including 172.16.0.0/24.

Access Lists

Most of the routing policy techniques described already have mentioned access lists. Cisco access lists are a huge, sprawling topic that would require a chapter of their own to explore in full. This brief section only examines the use of access lists to implement routing policies for IP routes.

Access lists normally permit or deny packets. Ordinarily, even if the packet is a routing protocol update, the access list will not look at the routes inside the update but only at the packet header fields. Only when the access list is part of a distribution list is the access list applied to the routes (prefixes) inside the routing protocol update.

With routing policy, IP access lists with names are used most often. This is because named IP access lists can be edited by clearing specific lines, while numbered access lists must be cleared and reentered if changed. Standard IP access lists (number range 1 to 99 and 1300 to 1999) match on source address or source address range, while extended IP access lists (number range 100 to 199 and 2000 to 2699) can match on destination address, protocol, and other packet header fields.

The general form of a standard named IP access list is:

```
ip access-list standard name
{permit | deny} source [source-mask] [log]
...
```

where the permit/deny lines can be repeated as many times as needed to accomplish the task required. The source and source mask are in the form of an IP prefix and inverted mask. We have discussed inverted mask (also often called *wildcard mask*) notation before in this book, most notably with OSPF. For example, 172.16.22.0 0.0.0.255 is the same as 172.16.22/24, and 192.168.77.8 0.0.0.0 is the same as 192.168.77.8/32. Logging can also used with access lists for routing policies.

Like prefix lists, access lists form a ordered set that also ends in an implicit (and unseen) deny any, which discards anything not matching a source prefix and mask in the access list. A match results in an immediate permit or deny for the route, so order can be important, just as in a prefix list.

Here is an example of a named access list used with a distribution list applied to a routing process (such as BGP):

```
...
neighbor 10.0.31.1 distribute-list blocksome out
...
ip access-list standard blocksome
deny 172.16.0.0 0.0.255.255
deny 192.168.0.0 0.0.255.255
permit 0.0.0.0 255.255.255.255
...
```

This access list is applied as an export policy to prevent the advertising of any routes that fit the 172.16/16 and 192.168/16 address ranges. The third line permits the advertisement of all other routes. Without the third line, no routes at all would be advertised by that protocol on that interface because of the implicit deny any at the end of every access list.

There is much more that we could discuss about access lists, even when limiting the discussion to routing policy. However, this section is enough to give you a feel for how access lists are applied to routing policies in the Cisco environment. It is more important to provide some examples of how all of these tools are used on a Cisco router to implement routing policy.

A Few Routing Policy Examples

Cisco router configurations often have to deal with a wide array of choices with regard to routing policy. Will a simple redistribute do? Use a distribute-list with access list? A prefix list above all? Generally, BGP (the most policy-driven routing protocol) uses redistribution to gather routing information to advertise, route maps and access lists to match AS paths and set BGP attributes, and prefix lists and distribution lists for filtering routes. But like any tool, any method that does what needs to be accomplished can be used by someone who knows what he or she is doing.

As an example of redistribution, consider this router configuration fragment:

```
router isis
 ...
 redistribute rip metric 20 metric-type internal level-2
 ...
router rip
 redistribute isis level-2 metric 1
 ...
```

This advertises Routing Information Protocol (RIP) routes into IS-IS with a metric of 20 and as internal Level 2 IS-IS routes. And RIP redistributes IS-IS Level 2 routes with a metric of 1.

Distributions lists deserve more elaborate examples. In this first example of distribution lists, two routers are exchanging RIP routing updates over the Serial0 interfaces. The network address of the link is 10.8.0.0/24. Router A is learning about network 172.16.0.0/16 from a source on the Ethernet 0 interface. For reasons that are not important, the network administrator does not want Router B to learn about network 172.16.0.0/16. This routing policy can be accomplished by using a distribution list. The distribution list could be applied either outbound on Router A or inbound on Router B. In either case the distribution list would use the same access list.

Consider implementing the routing policy on Router A first (only relevant configuration fragments shown):

```
router rip
 network 10.8.0.0
 distribute list 10 out serial 0

access-list 10 deny 172.16.0.0 0.0.255.255
access-list 10 permit any
```

Before Router A sends a RIP update out on the Serial 0 link, the router checks to see what networks are permitted by the distribution list and advertises only those networks that are allowed by access list 10. In this case, prefix 172.16/16 is not advertised.

Now consider the implementation of exactly the same routing policy on Router B:

```
router rip
 network 10.8.0.0
 distribute-list 10 in serial 0

access-list 10 deny 172.16.0.0 0.0.255.255
access-list 10 permit any
```

The result is the same: All routes but 172.16/16 enter Router B.

In the next example, the OSPF routing process accepts only two routes: the default 0.0.0.0 and network 192.168.108.0/24:

```
router ospf 10
 network 10.0.21.1 0.0.0.0 area 0
 distribute-list 20 in

access-list 20 permit 0.0.0.0
access-list 20 permit 192.168.108.0 0.0.0.255
access-list 20 deny 0.0.0.0 255.255.255.255
```

All routes but these two are denied by the last line of the access list.

Distribution lists can be combined with redistribution to produce the desired results. This last example redistributes only OSPF route 192.168.100.0/ 24 into IS-IS.

```
router isis
 redistribute ospf 10
 distribute-list 10 out

access-list 10 permit 192.168.100.0 0.0.0.255
```

As already mentioned, a route map is often used with redistribution. This configuration fragment redistributes only the loopback0 address into OSPF and sets the metric to 5.

```
router ospf 10
 redistribute connected subnets route-map only_loopback0
 ...
route-map only_loopback0 permit 10
 match interface Loopback0
 set metric 5
 ...
```

Prefix lists are most often used with BGP. This configuration fragment suppresses advertisement of 10.0.8.0/24 and 192.168.12/24 or longer routes to BGP neighbor 10.0.32.1 and allows all other routes:

```
router bgp 64333
 neighbor 10.0.21.2 prefix-list denial out
 ...
ip prefix-list denial deny 10.0.8.0/24
ip prefix-list denial deny 192.168.12/24 ge
ip prefix-list denial permit any
```

The `permit` any is a shorthand way of allowing any routes not denied already and overriding the implicit and unseen deny any at the end of all prefix lists.

Juniper Networks Routing Policy

In contrast to Cisco routers, whose approach to routing policy has evolved over many years and so pops up in various places and forms throughout the router configuration, Juniper Networks routers have a more unified approach. Juniper Networks routing policies closely resemble C language programs, even more than the Juniper Networks router configuration itself. Almost every aspect of routing protocol operation other than the default behavior can be controlled through the programlike routing policy. Some like the look and feel of this approach and find the syntax more comfortable than more arbitrary formats, while others do not like to be reminded of programming at all, especially when configuring a router. All are free to consider this approach better or worse than Cisco's, but all must agree that it is certainly different.

Juniper Networks calls its approach to routing policy the *JUNOS software routing policy framework*. Some routing policy framework behavior is built into the operation of each and every routing protocol. This default routing policy established for each of the major routing protocols is essentially what will be modified by the routing policy. Naturally, if the default routing policy does exactly what is desired, no routing policy is needed.

You should keep one very important point about the default Juniper Networks routing policies for each of the routing protocols. If a route (IP prefix) that is subjected to a routing policy either is not accepted or is rejected for import into the routing table or export from the forwarding table, then the *route is still subjected to the default routing policy for that routing protocol*. Overlooking the effects of the default routing policy for a protocol can result in a number of odd side effects when JUNOS software routing policies are in use. For example, routes that seem to pass through a routing policy with ease will not show up in the routing table or be advertised because the routes do not pass the default policy for the routing policy. In extreme cases, the advertising router might not even be reachable through the routing protocol, again because of the default routing policy.

The default routing protocol for each of the major routing protocols discussed in this book is shown in Table 15.4.

Table 15.4   Default Routing Protocol for Major Routing Protocols

PROTOCOL	DEFAULT IMPORT POLICY	DEFAULT EXPORT POLICY
RIP	Import all RIP routes	No export without explicit policy
OSPF	Import all OSPF routes (cannot be changed)	Export active OSPF routes
		Export directs with OSPF configured
IS-IS	Import all IS-IS routes (cannot be changed)	Export active IS-IS routes
		Export directs with IS-IS configured
BGP	Import all BGP routes	Export active BGP routes

Keep in mind that the table does not take into account the native behavior of the routing protocol. For instance, no mention is made of OSPF stub area behavior, IS-IS Level 2 default advertising, or IBGP's nonflooding behavior. This is a generalized representation of the default routing policy behavior. We have already encountered most of these behaviors. For example, a routing policy was needed in the RIP configuration chapter to get the Juniper Networks router to advertise anything with RIP at all.

Ordinarily, all of the routing protocols accept any routes they learn from their neighbors running the same protocol and place the routes in the routing table. With OSPF and IS-IS, this default import policy *cannot* be changed. Although some documentation mentions that blocking routes advertised in good faith by other link-state routers could compromise the integrity of the link-state databases, which must be identical in an area, and might result in unsynchronized link-state databases in an area, this no-import-policy behavior for OSPF and IS-IS was really just an arbitrary implementation decision. By default, both OSPF and IS-IS advertise their own active routes and all interfaces addresses (directs) on which OSPF or IS-IS is configured. So only export policies can be applied to OSPF and IS-IS.

BGP ordinarily accepts all BGP routes and exports all active BGP routes. BGP attributes are all given default values, including the BGP Next Hop attribute. The BGP Next Hop could be an interface address, but this is not the same as an IGP next hop, and so it cannot be said that BGP somehow exports "directs."

If the route does not match any of the conditions set up in a routing policy, the JUNOS software applies the default policy to the route and always either accepts or rejects the route based on the default criteria.

You might need to modify a Juniper Networks router's behavior with respect to routes accepted and advertised on any of the following occasions:

- When a route learned from another router should not be considered eligible to be the active route to a destination in the forwarding table.

- When an active route in the forwarding table should not be advertised to other routers.

- When routes learned by one routing protocol should be shared with another routing protocol (route redistribution).

- When the properties associated with a route (for example, the metric) should be modified as the route information enters or leaves the router.

- When BGP route damping needs to be employed.

- When performing load balancing is essential.

- When enabling quality of service categories is crucial.

In this book, we explore all but the last two reasons to use routing policy. Although the last two topics are important, load balancing applies policy to the forwarding table and a full discussion of quality of service is beyond the scope of this book.

What happens when a router learns about routes to the same destination from two different protocols? What should happen, say, when a router knows about the same prefix (for example, 192.168.14/24) through RIP, OPSF, and BGP? The default *protocol preference* (Cisco calls this the *administrative distance*) is applied to determine which route source is preferred over another. Lower preference is better. We have discussed protocol preference default values for individual routing protocols previously, but here we bring all of the defaults together, even for sources of routing information not covered in this book. The default protocol preferences used by the JUNOS software are shown in Table 15.5.

Table 15.5 Juniper Networks Default Protocol Preferences

SOURCE OF ROUTING INFORMATION	DEFAULT PREFERENCE
Direct (connected network interface)	0
Static route	5
RSVP (MPLS)	7
LDP (MPLS)	9
OSPF internal	10
IS-IS Level 1 internal	15
IS-IS Level 2 internal	18
Redirects	30
RIP	100
Point-to-point interface	110
Aggregate/generated routes	130
OSPF external	150
IS-IS Level 1 external	160
IS-IS Level 2 external	165
BGP	170

All of the default preferences can be changed with a routing policy or through explicit configuration. For example, the configuration command

```
[edit protocols]
lab@Router1# set ospf external-preference 180
```

sets the protocol preference for all OSPF external routes (*only on this particular router*) to 180 instead of 150. So on this particular router, IS-IS external routes and BGP routes would be preferred to OSPF external routes.

Structure of a Juniper Networks Routing Policy

All Juniper Networks routing policies share a common structure, shown in Figure 15.2. Although multiple policies are shown and can be configured, applied, and used, a better practice is to use only a single import or export routing policy configured with multiple terms to enforce routing policy whenever possible.

Nevertheless, multiple policies are still used. The routes referred to in Figure 15.2 are just prefixes such as 172.16/16, 192.168.50/24. An arriving route considered for inclusion in the routing table, or an active route considered for export (advertisement to other routers) by a routing protocol, is subjected to whatever routing policies have been applied for the routing protocol. The outcome of a policy can be a *terminating action* of accept or reject, in which case the policy evaluation is terminated and the route is accepted or rejected for import or export depending on where the policy is applied. If there is no terminating action for the route or the conditions in the policy do not apply to the route, then the next policy is considered based on simple sequence or more complex logical relations between the policies.

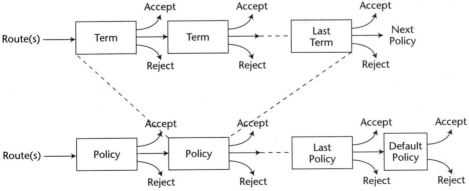

Figure 15.2 Juniper Networks routing policy structure.

At the end of the chain of applied policies, if there is still a terminating action for the route, the default policy for the routing protocols given previously is evaluated for the route. The outcome of the default policy is always a final accept or reject.

Each routing policy itself can consist of multiple *terms*. The terms act almost exactly like a chain of individual routing policies, with a possible accept or reject outcome for each term (ending further evaluation of subsequent terms), or evaluation of the next term when no terminating action applies to the route. If there are no more terms in the policy, the evaluation moves on to the next policy (which might be the default policy for the routing protocol). In all cases, there is a final accept or reject decision made on the route.

A routing policy with only a single term can omit the `term` keyword and variable to label the term. But it is considered best practice to include term labels even in single-term policies. Term labels can make it easier to add other terms to the policy, or reorder the terms, since new terms are *always* simply added to the end of the policy, regardless or where the term really belongs in the policy. There is an `insert` command that is used to reorder the terms within a policy.

This book, in keeping with current thinking on routing policies, will always use terms, even for single-term policies. We will also use only a single routing policy, usually with multiple terms, for all import or export applications. Just as in programming, it is usually possible to make one larger program (routing policy) to do exactly the same thing as a lot of smaller programs (routing policies). The routing policies used in this book are not so complex as to demand the modular approach of separate policies. The smallest policies, again like programs, are often the most powerful. Keeping all of the conditions that apply to a route in one place in the configuration for ease of maintenance usually outweighs considerations of using multiple policies in most cases anyway.

The routing policy terms consist of *match condition* and *action* pairs. Match conditions are typically identified with the `from` keyword, similar in function to the `if` clause in a program. For example, `from protocol static` essentially means "there will be a match if the route is a static route . . . " That is all there is to it. If a term has no `from` clause, then *all* routes match the implied condition.

If the match condition is true (produces a match), the actions following the `then` clause are executed. The simple routing policy in this book to export static routes into many of the routing protocols used a basic `then accept` clause. This terminating action immediately accepts the route for import or export and effectively bypasses what the default policy for the routing protocol would ordinarily do with that route. That is how all types of route redistribution are done on a Juniper Networks router, of course. The same policy (`send-statics`) can be used to inject static routes into any routing protocol that is running on the router.

Term labels are just user-selected variables with only a few rules. Most routing policy terms are just labeled `Term A`, `Term B`, or `Term 1`, `Term 2`, and so on. The policy name is also a user-selected variable but must be unique for that policy on that router. Words are usually connected with a dash (`send-statics`), but an underscore (`send_statics`) works fine as well.

Match Conditions

A routing policy term can produce a match on a route's properties (metrics and several internal tags like color or preference), interface name, neighbor or next-hop address, protocol (really the source of the route information), and many other characteristics that apply to a certain routing protocol only. For example, OSPF routes can be matched on Area ID or Tag values, IS-IS routes can be matched by Level, and BGP routes can be matched on almost any BGP attribute value. If the route characteristic is unique to the protocol, the routing protocol does not even have to be explicitly named. So `from as-path 64555` will only produce a match on BGP routes, since only BGP has an AS Path attribute.

There are four other special types of match conditions in addition to basic route characteristics. In generic form, these are as follows:

`route-filter` *`destination-prefix match-type <actions>`*. The `route-filter` is possibly the most common of the alternate match conditions. The destination prefix is the route mask itself, such as 172.16/16. The `match-type` can be one of six kinds and is discussed in full shortly. The `<action>` is optional but often used. When an action follows a `route-filter`, this action is called an *immediate action* and can be used to instantly accept or reject a route. When an immediate action is taken, *no further actions specified in any* `then` *clause that follows in the term will be executed*. This is an important point and the source of many unwanted side effects.

`source-address-filter` *`destination-prefix match-type <actions>`*. The `source-address-filter` differs from the `route-filter` in that this condition matches on the *source* of the routing information rather than the route destination. The `match-type` and `<actions>` are the same.

`policy` *`subroutine-policy-name`*. Policies can be nested, one inside another. Only one level of nesting is supported, so the "subroutine" policy cannot reference another policy, and so on, through many levels. At times a policy subroutine might be helpful, but almost anything done with a policy subroutine can be done in a simple routing policy. Nested or policy subroutines are not used in this book.

`prefix-list` *name.* The `prefix-list` is used to gather a series of prefixes into a separate place and refer to the whole by a unique `name`. So instead of placing a long list of prefixes into each term match condition, you can reference the list by its `name` and maintain it separately. A `prefix-list` is *not* a `route-filter`, just a list of prefixes without `match-type` that must match routes considered *exactly*. Prefix lists are often used to match an ISP's customers.

A `to` clause can also be configured along with the `from`. The `to` clause applies to routes that are being advertised to a particular destination or some protocol-specific place where the route is being advertised, such as to IS-IS Level 2.

Not all match conditions apply to routing protocols and route characteristics. The match conditions that do apply to routing directly are shown in Table 15.6.

Table 15.6 Match Conditions for Route Characteristics

MATCH	COMMENT
area *area-id*	OSPF only. Match a route learned from a specific OSPF area.
as-path *name*	BGP only. Match an AS Path string specified by a regular expression.
community *[names]*	BGP only. Match one or more named communities (OR'd together).
external [type *metric-type*]	OSPF only. Match all externals or only E1 or E2 as specified.
interface *interface* | *address*	Not for IBGP. Match route `from` or advertised `to` interface name or address.
level *level*	IS-IS only. Match route arriving `from` or advertised `to` specified level, 1 or 2.
local-preference *value*	BGP only. Match a route with the specified Local Preference.
metric *metric*, metric2 *metric*	Match metric or metric2 value. For BGP, `metric` is MED and `metric2` is IGP metric of BGP Next Hop.
neighbor *address*	Match route arriving `from` or advertised `to` specified neighbor address.
next-hop *address*	Match route's next-hop address (more than one can be specified).
origin *value*	BGP only. Match the BGP Origin as igp, egp, or incomplete.

Table 15.6 *(Continued)*

MATCH	COMMENT
preference *preference*	Match the preference of the route on the local.
protocol *protocol*	Match aggregate, bgp, direct, dvrmp, isis, local, ospf, pim-dense, pim-sparse, rip, rip-ng, or static.
tag *tag*, tag2 *tag*	Match OSPF `tag` or `tag2` values in external LSAs. Other protocols use internally.

If multiple conditions are defined in the `from` and `to` clauses of a term, then *all* of the conditions must be true for the match conditions as a whole to produce a TRUE. So, for example, the match conditions:

```
from {
    protocol isis;
    metric 10;
    }
to level 2;
```

only produce a TRUE when the route considered is an IS-IS route *and* the metric is 10 *and* the route is being sent on an interface to a Level 2 IS-IS router (IS-IS routes cannot have an `import` policy). All three conditions must be met. If any one is not true (for instance, if the IS-IS route is going to a Level 2 router with a metric of 40), then there is no match. Multiple match conditions are like a logical AND in this regard.

Actions

Each term can include a `then` clause with a set of actions that are executed if the match conditions in the term are all true. The `then` clause is optional, because the default policy will always apply and accept or reject a route. The following are the three types of actions:

Flow-control actions. These actions affect the evaluation sequence of the policy. `Next term` and `next policy` are obvious flow-control actions, but `accept` and `reject` are also considered flow-control actions because they end policy evaluation.

Actions that change a route's characteristics. For example `as-path-prepend`... places the specified AS numbers that follow in front of the AS Path attribute of a BGP route.

Trace action. This action logs route matches and so helps with assessing the policy's effectiveness and correctness.

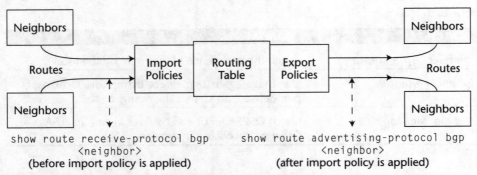

Figure 15.3 Viewing the before and after of a routing policy.

Actions that change a route's characteristics do not directly change the routing information itself. So the changes to the route made by an import policy are not visible in the link-state database, for example, but in the routing table. The command show route receive-protocol... always shows the route characteristics exactly as they were when the route was received by the router and before the policy was applied. Changes made by an export policy are not visible in the routing table but only as the routes travel across the link to the other router. The command show route advertised-protocol... always shows the route characteristics exactly as they were after the policy was applied and when the route left the router. These two commands can be a powerful troubleshooting aid, as shown in Figure 15.3 with BGP.

The actions that change a route's characteristics are quite numerous. Some apply only to MPLS, internal Juniper Networks router operation, or class of service (CoS) and so are not considered here. The actions that directly affect the routing protocols discussed in this book are listed in Table 15.7.

Table 15.7 Actions to Change Route Characteristics

ACTION	COMMENT
As-path-prepend *as-path*	BGP only. Prepends one or more AS numbers to AS Path after local AS has been added. Enclose more than one in double quotes. Special rules apply to confederations.
as-path-expand *last-as count n*	BGP only. Prepends last AS number to AS Path before local AS has been added. *Count n* is between 1 and 32. Special rules apply to confederations.

Table 15.7 *(Continued)*

ACTION	COMMENT
community (+ | add) *[names]*	BGP only. Adds named communities to the set of BGP communities.
community (− | delete) *[names]*	BGP only. Deletes named communities from the set of BGP communities.
community (= | set) *[names]*	BGP only. Sets BGP Community attribute to these named communities.
damping *name*	BGP import only. Applies parameters defined in *name* to route damping.
external type *metric-type*	OSPF export only. Sets the external metric Type 1 or 2 for exported OSPF routes.
local-preference *value*	BGP only. Sets the BGP Local Preference to the specified value.
local-preference (add | subtract)	BGP only. Adds or subtracts the specified number to current Local Preference.
Number	Allowed range of result is 0 to 4294967295 ($2^{32} - 1$). Must begin as nonzero.
metric *metric*, metric2 *metric*	Sets metric or metric2 to value. BGP metric is MED and metric2 is IGP metric of BGP Next Hop. Addition and subtract is also allowed on nonzero metrics.
metric (igp | minimum-igp)	EBGP export only. Changes the MED by the positive or negative offset value.
site-offset next-hop (*address* | peer-address)	Sets the protocol's next hop to the specified address, which can be self. Complex rules apply when `peer-address` is used.
origin *value*	BGP only. Sets the BGP Origin to igp, egp, or incomplete.
preference *preference*	Sets the preference for use on local router to the specified value (0 to 255 valid).
tag *tag*, tag2 *tag*	Sets OSPF `tag` or `tag2` values in external LSAs. Other protocols used internally.
tag (add | subtract) number	Adds or subtracts from `tag` or `tag2` values, but only OSPF advertises these.
tag2 (add | subtract) number	Allowed range of result is 0 to 4294967295 ($2^{32} - 1$). Must begin as nonzero.

Trace actions log routing policy events to a file. For example, a file called policy-log could be established to record information about the flow of the policy through a series of terms. Although quite important for routing policy evaluation and troubleshooting, trace actions do not directly impact the actions of the routing policy and are not discussed further.

An optional *final action* can be configured in a Juniper Networks routing policy. The final action is configured in an unnamed term at the very end of the routing policy. The final action acts as the set of actions for any terms in the policy that do not have a then specified, yet produce a match in the from section of the term.

Route Filter Match Types

An important concept and powerful tool in routing policy is the combination of route-filter and match-type as a match condition. Many routing policies contain long lists of route filters (to use the generic form), and some match conditions consist of nothing but router filters and their associated match types (also in generic form).

Route filter consist of prefix and match type pairs and are often accompanied by an immediate accept or reject action. There are six match types, defined in Table 15.8.

These match types can most easily be understood with relation to the binary tree representation on the IPv4 address space introduced in Chapter 4. Although the same type of tree applies equally to IPv6, only the IPv4 address space is considered here. An example of the IP address space expressed as a binary tree and used in this section is shown in Figure 15.4.

Table 15.8 Route Filter Match Types

MATCH TYPE	WILL MATCH IF THE...
Exact	route's prefix and length is *equal to* the filter's prefix and length (only one match).
Orlonger	route's prefix and length is *equal to or longer* than the filter's prefix and length.
Longer	route's prefix and length is *longer than* the filter's prefix and length.
Upto	route's prefix and length is *bounded by* the filter's prefix and lengths.
prefix-length-range	route's prefix and length falls *between* filter's prefix and length range.
Through	route's prefix and length falls on *exact match path* from first prefix and length to the second prefix and length (a series of exact matches in a shorthand notation).

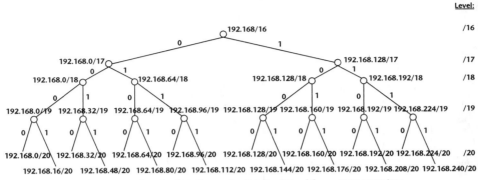

Figure 15.4   Binary tree levels /16 through /20 for IP address 192.168/16.

The only difficult match type to grasp is `through`. This is just a shorthand way to express a series of `exact` matches. The best way to figure out the exact IP addresses that match a route filter using `through` is find the point on the binary tree preceding the `through`, then find the point on the binary tree following the `through`. Then you "connect the dots" from bottom to top to find the series of exact matches that satisfy the route filter and produce a TRUE condition.

Table 15.9 shows an example of the six different match types used in six route filters applied to the 192.168/16 address space. The table also shows a series of routes and whether the route produces a match for one match type or another.

Every one of these example route filters can be used in the same term of a routing policy. A long list of very similar route filters can be challenging to interpret before unleashing the policy on a live network. A special set of rules is used to determine which route filter best applies to a given IP route. Assuming there are only route filters to consider, the rules are as follows:

- When multiple route filters appear in a term, only *one* of them must match a route for any immediate actions associated with the route filter to be executed. This is like a logical OR on the route filters.

- Ignore the match type and just perform a longest-match lookup on the candidate route in the list of route filters. Remember that ranges and "through" match types are really just lists of exact matches in shorthand form.

- If there is no longest match for the candidate route, then the route filter produces no match and the other conditions in the term cannot produce a match (by virtue of the AND requirement for other conditions).

Tables 15.9 Route Filter Examples

PREFIX	EXACTLY 192.168/16	192.168/16 OR LONGER	192.168/16 OR LONGER	192.168/16 UP TO 24	192.168/16 PREFIX-LENGTH-RANGE /18-/20	192.168/16 THROUGH 192.168.16/20
192.0.0.0/8						
192.168.0.0/16	Passes	Passes		Passes		Passes
192.168.0.0/17		Passes	Passes	Passes		Passes
192.168.0.0/18		Passes	Passes	Passes	Passes	Passes
192.168.0.0/19		Passes	Passes	Passes	Passes	
192.168.4.0/24		Passes	Passes	Passes		
192.168.5.4/30		Passes	Passes			
192.168.12.4/30		Passes	Passes			
192.168.12.128/32		Passes	Passes			
192.168.16.0/20		Passes	Passes	Passes	Passes	Passes
192.168.192.0/18		Passes	Passes	Passes	Passes	
192.168.224.0/19		Passes	Passes	Passes	Passes	
192.169.1.0/24						
192.170.0.0/16						

- Apply the match type of the longest match to the route. If the route conforms to the match type condition, this is a match. If the route does not conform to the match type condition, there is no match for the route anywhere in the route filter list.

- If the match type produces a match, apply any immediate actions to the route and ignore any then actions associated with the term. If there are no immediate actions, perform any then actions associated with the term.

Keep in mind that if there are other match conditions besides route filters in the term and no immediate action, all other match conditions and *one* route filter must be true to produce a match. So any route filter match must still be combined with the other conditions (such as protocol BGP in a logical AND operation) to produce a match and perform the actions associated with the term.

A few examples should clarify this somewhat complex set of rules for route filter interpretation. Consider the following policy:

```
[edit] show policy-options
policy-statement policy-testing
    term one {
        from {
            route-filter 192.168.10.0/24 exact accept;
            route-filter 192.168.20.0/24 orlonger accept;
            route-filter 192.168.30.0/24 longer reject;
            route-filter 192.168.00.0/24 orlonger reject;
        }
        then accept;
    }
}
```

The match type does not count until the longest match has been found. Appreciating this rule can avoid many surprises with route filters. For example, route 192.168.30.0/24 will be neither accepted nor rejected by this policy, perhaps unexpectedly. This is because the third line is the longest match for 192.168.30.0/24, but the match type (longer) does not match the route 192.168.30.0/24 itself. But because there is a longest match for the route, the then is bypassed and the next policy invoked.

There is only one chance to match a route in a series of route filters. Even though 192.168.0.0/24 orlonger would apply to 192.168.30.0/24 in both respects, match and match type, this route has had its longest-match chance and failed to pass its longest-match route filter and match type.

The operational command test policy policy-testing 0/0 can be used to test this policy against the entire contents of the routing tables. If the route 192.168.30.0/24 is in the table as an active route, the test will show the result of the policy evaluation in terms of routes accepted and rejected. However, an "accepted" result does not necessarily mean that the route was accepted by the *policy*, because accept is the default action of the policy test itself. This result could mean that the route did not match the route filters and so is "accepted" for further evaluation by other policies or by the final default policy.

The simple policy test will not evaluate all aspects of policy match conditions, but it is effective for policies containing many complex route filters. Note that the test cannot completely determine the fate of all routes, since there is always the default policy and possibly other policies as well that apply to the route.

Generally, the order in which route filters are listed does not matter because a longest-match lookup is performed on the whole list regardless of match type. However, it is possible that identical prefixes might appear in a list of route filters, since different match types can be configured. So `10.8.0.0/16 exact accept;` is not the same as `10.8.0.0/16 orlonger reject;`. If the `exact` is listed first, the route 10.8.0.0/16 is accepted. But if the `orlonger` appears first, the 10.8.0.0/16 route is rejected. You can use the `insert` JUNOS software command to shuffle route filters into their desired order.

Routing Policy Notes

As you might gather from the preceding section, Juniper Networks routing policies have a formal structure and yet many variations on the basic theme. In general, the routing policies actually used in the rest of this book have simple formats. But we should at least outline some of the more complex structures that Juniper Networks routing policies can take part in.

On a Juniper Networks router, policies are defined in the `policy-options` section of the configuration. But configured policies do nothing until they are applied to a routing protocol as either an `import` policy (not allowed in IS-IS or OSPF) or as an `export` policy. IS-IS and OSPF have only a *global* export policy for each instance of the routing protocol. That is, an export policy applied to IS-IS or OSPF must be applied to every neighbor router and cannot be used to selectively filter advertised routes to one router but not another. This maintains the consistency of the link-state database.

But multiple policies can be applied in an `import` or `export` statement. In their simplest form, multiple policy statements just take the form `import [ policy1 policy2 ... ]` or `export [ policy1 policy2 ... ]`, a form called the *policy chain*. In this form, the policies are simply applied to the routes from left to right until a terminating action is encountered or the policy chain ends with the default policy for the routing protocol. The default policy never appears in the policy chain, but it is there nonetheless. The order in which the policies appear in an `import` and `export` statement can be quite important to the final outcome of the policy chain.

The sequential application of multiple policies can be altered with a *policy expression*. A policy expression is an application of Boolean (logical, or truth table) arithmetic applied to the policy chain. The policies form the *arguments* of the policy expression, and logical operators are used to govern the application of the policies in the chain. The Boolean operators used are ! (logical NOT), && (logical AND), and || (logical OR).

The Boolean operators can be combined with policy chains to produce very powerful logical combinations of import and export policies. Parentheses must be used to group the policies into policy expressions. Forms such as export (policy1 && policy2) or import (!policy1 || policy2) or even export [(policy1 || policy2) && policy3] can be used. A full discussion of routing policy chains using Boolean expressions is beyond the scope of this book. No policies used in this book are used to formulate policy expressions. It should be noted that policy expressions are not necessary in the Juniper Networks routing policy framework. They are just other tools that may be used (or avoided) to accomplish the desired routing policy goals.

Special adaptations on UNIX regular expressions can be used, and often are, when looking for special patterns of BGP route AS Path and Community attribute values. These are *very* important for formulating BGP policies, and they are discussed in detail in Chapters 17, 18, and 19, where we apply routing policies to BGP.

Some Routing Policy Examples

Before we configure and apply routing policies to routing protocols, we need to look at some sample routing policies and how they can be used to influence the acceptance or advertisement of routes. These examples are intended to be realistic but at the same time distinct from the routing policies used in the rest of this book.

Each set of policy goals plays a role in what pieces of the routing policy framework are used and how to best use them. Some administrators might find a need for multiple policies in the network, especially for BGP routers at the edge of the network. Each individual policy accomplishes a specific task. These policies can then be combined together on an as-needed basis to accomplish a larger policy goal in the network. While not used in every AS, these policies (or variations) are quite popular:

- Guard against *martian routes*, which are defined in RFC 1812 and were detailed in the section *Private and Martian IP Addresses* in Chapter 3. Martian routes should never appear on an Internet router and "might as well be on Mars" as the story about their origin goes. (Actually, Juniper Networks routers have a built-in "sanity check" against accepting martian routes, but common practice is to formulate an

explicit policy to exclude martians anyway.) Also, there should be no
0.0.0.0/0 exact route accepted from another AS. Finally, neither loopbacks nor reserved blocks (RFC 1918) nor multicast addresses (Class D)
nor Class E (experimental) addresses should be in a unicast routing
table on any router.

- Note that routers should never accept routes to their own local IP
  address space. How could another router or ISP have a better route
  to a network that is local or a customer?

- Do not accept many long prefix routes (just what is "long" is left up to
  the network, but /19 was for some time the longest acceptable Internet
  mask length). Aggregation to shorter prefixes saves bandwidth for
  updates and space in the routing tables. So a routing policy might reject
  any routes more specific, or longer, than a /19.

These defined policies are shown in Figure 15.5. The policies are applied by
AS 64512 to routes arriving from AS 65111 through EBGP.

These routing policies could be formulated as one routing policy with multiple terms. But if the policies are written as three separate policies, they can be
applied separately as needed on other interfaces and other routers (not
directly, but instead of defining and debugging a whole new policy on another
router, this prototype can be used in other routers' configurations).

The following is what the three policies might look like on the border router
of AS 64512:

```
[edit policy-options]
policy-statement no-unwanted {
  term find-unwanted {
    from {
      route-filter 0/0 exact;
      route-filter 127/8 orlonger;
      route-filter 224/3 orlonger;
      route-filter 240/4 orlonger;
    }
    then reject;
  }
}
policy-statement not-mine {
  term find-mine {
    from route-filter 192.168.14/24 orlonger;
    then reject;
  }
}
policy-statement no-specifics {
  term find-specifics {
    from route-filter 172.16.77/19 longer;
    then reject;
  }
}
```

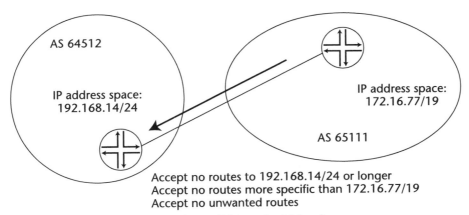

Figure 15.5 Some sample routing policies at the AS border.

When applied as `import [no-specifics not-mine no-unwanted]` to the EBGP link on the AS 64512 router, what will happen if routes 0/0 (the default), 127.0.0.0/8 (a loopback), 192.168.14.0/24 (AS 64512's address block), 172.16.77.192/26 (a *very* specific route for inter-AS advertising), and 192.168.128/19 show up at the border router of AS 64512?

- The 0.0.0.0/0 default route is rejected by the `no-unwanted` policy.

- The 127.0.0.0/8 route is rejected by the `no-unwanted` policy.

- The 192.168.14/24 route is rejected by the `not-mine` policy.

- The 172.16.77.192/26 is rejected by the `no-specifics` policy.

- The 192.168.128/19 route does not match any of the defined policies, so it gets evaluated by the BGP default policy. The default policy for BGP accepts the route.

Regular Expressions and Routing Policy

Both Cisco and Juniper Networks routers allow for the use of UNIX-based regular expressions (regex or REs) in routing policies. These regular expressions are used to match the BGP AS Path and Community attributes, which can be quite long and complicated attributes to filter and modify. We discuss the details of regular expressions applied to AS Paths and Communities in Chapter 18, "AS Path and Local Preference," and Chapter 19, "BGP Community and Route Damping."

IGP Routing Policies

Even interior gateway protocols (IGPs) occasionally need routing policies to tune their operation and achieve the level of routing optimization required within a routing domain (AS). Most of the time, you can leave IGPs pretty much alone and rely on their own internal system of metrics and routing information to find the best paths through AS to destinations. Routes to destinations that lie beyond the local AS are not usually the concern of the IGP, so the IGP is free to concentrate on internal routes. IGPs attempt optimization through a system of hop counts (RIP), bandwidth-related metrics (OSPF), or assumptions about links (IS-IS). Whatever the method, the default behavior of the routing protocol and the characteristics of the routes can be modified. To perform this modification beyond the simple act of changing the default from one value to another (usually a trivial configuration exercise), you typically need a routing policy.

In this chapter we explore many aspects of routing policies applied to IGPs, most notably OSPF and IS-IS. This chapter discusses redistribution as a type of basic routing policy, but because many of the earlier chapters on the IGP routing protocols themselves used redistribution frequently for static routes (and sometimes even BGP routes), redistribution is not a focal point here. Rather, we emphasize the modification of IGP routing information parameters such as metrics and investigate some of the more interesting aspects of IS-IS with regard to routing policy.

The IGP arena is somewhat limited with regard to the application of routing policies. Internal routing information is not usually suppressed. But aggregation with suppression of more specific routes is common, as these types of policies always exist in a multivendor networking environment. As part of the continued attempt in this book to apply routing policy to real-world situations, in this chapter we put each of the routing policies in context, showing just what the issue is and how a routing policy applied to the IGP can help the situation.

We begin with a consideration of routing policies applied to OSPF. After some brief discussion of redistribution metrics, we address the differences between External type 1 (E1) and External type 2 (E2) OSPF routes in the major OSPF routing policy application, as well as the routing policies needed to change the default router behavior regarding E1 and E2 routes. Then a simple policy is given to aid in conversion of an AS running OSPF as an IGP to IS-IS as an IGP (this method could easily be applied in the reverse direction to convert IS-IS to OSPF). Then we apply routing policies to IS-IS itself, most notably to accomplish L2 to L1 route leaking. Route leaking itself is investigated more fully, and an example network again is introduced to demonstrate why route leaking is helpful.

OSPF Routing Policies

There are trivial applications of routing policies to IGPs that need not be considered in this chapter in detail. We have covered basic redistribution of static routes into OSPF or IS-IS several times already and need not investigate it further. To assign a meaningful OSPF metric to a static route, in most cases, all you need is a simple statement such as `metric 10`. But since there are differences in the way that Cisco and Juniper Networks routers can do this, we should start out with a few examples of changing OSPF route metrics.

There is no need to reinvent a sample OSPF network to explore the application of routing policies to OSPF. The example OSPF network used in Chapter 10 is more than adequate for this purpose. The complete network is shown in Figure 16.1.

This same principle is followed later in the chapter with regard to IS-IS. In that section, the example IS-IS network from Chapter 12 is presented and used.

Setting Metrics on Redistributed Routes

When routes are redistributed into a target routing protocol, it is always possible to set the metric that will be advertised with the route in the "new" protocol. This is always a good idea, since the originating protocol will have metrics

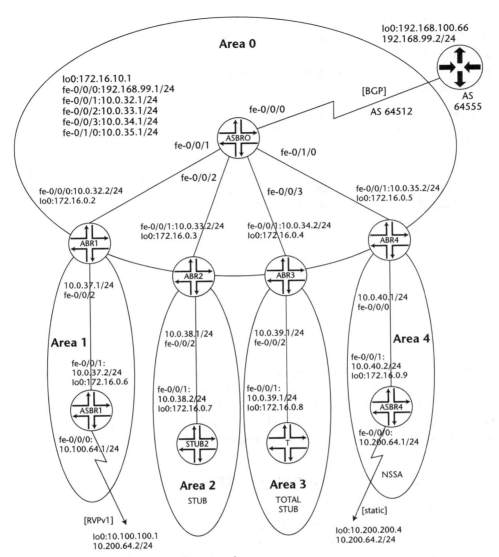

Figure 16.1   The OSPF example network.

that are independent of the target protocol's metrics. RIP hop counts, for example, are totally different than OSPF's bandwidth-based metrics at lower speeds or at high reference bandwidths.

Area 1 of the example OSPF network has an ASBR (ASBR1) introducing a RIP route into OSPF. Suppose that the ASBR link running RIP is a T1 running at 1.5 Mbps. This makes no difference to RIP, since a hop is a hop. But if the network administrator would like to map the OSPF metric scheme to this RIP link, it is possible to assign an OSPF metric of 67 (100 Mbps divided by 1.5 Mbps = 66.666 . . .) to the route.

This is done on a Cisco router directly in the target routing protocol's configuration:

```
Cisco_ASBR1(config)#router ospf 10
Cisco_ASBR1(config-router)#redistribute rip
Cisco_ASBR1(config-router)#default-metric 67
```

This metric setting for redistributed routes is accomplished on a Juniper Networks router with a routing policy, of course. This is how the routing policy applied to ASBR1 in Chapter 10 would be look now:

```
policy-statement from_ripv1 {
      term 1 {
          from protocol rip;
          then {
              metric 67;
              accept;
          }
      }
   }
```

This new policy is still applied as an OSPF export policy. In both cases, Cisco and Juniper Networks, the original RIP metric is replaced by the 67 value.

More elaborate changes to redistributed metrics can be configured. To change route metrics on a per-route basis, Cisco redistribution can reference a route map and Juniper Network's routers can configure a series of route filters.

Type 1 and Type 2 External Routes

OSPF routes are advertised as one of two major types, internal and external. Internal routes are those learned within the AS by the OSPF routing protocol itself, while external routes are those learned from some other source, such as static routes, RIP (usually inside the AS, but external to OSPF), or BGP (usually outside the AS altogether).

Cisco routers assign a default administrative distance of 110 to all OSPF routes and rely on "extra" information in the routing table to identify internal and external routes. For example, O IA is used in the routing table to identify inter-area OSPF routes that are within the AS but outside the area of the router. A plain O identifies intra-area routes in the same areas and AS. Juniper Networks routers, on the other hand, assign a different default protocol preference to OSPF internal and external routes. OSPF internals get a 10 (making these routes very attractive) and OSPF externals get a 150 (higher than any other IGP source of routing information).

However, there are really no interoperability issues involved in these differences because these values are purely for local use on each individual router. Usually, changing the default protocol preference or administrative distance of a routing protocol is done consistently across an AS or area, as we do later in this chapter, but this is not really required.

OSPF external routes fall into one of two categories. As explained in Chapter 9, "Open Shortest Path First (OSPF)," there are OSPF Type 1 external paths (E1) and OPSF Type 2 external paths (E2). Both are still external routes, but the OSPF path type determines the way that the metric for the route is represented when the route is distributed as an OSPF external within the AS by OSPF. The default metric type is Type 2 external. Both types of external are initially distributed by an ASBR (by definition, any router that introduces non-OSPF routing information into OSPF, even a static route, becomes an ASBR). The external route must have a metric that is meaningful to OSPF, and it is the job of the ASBR to set the metric on the external route.

Type 1 external paths simply take the existing metric of the redistributed route and use it for OSPF. All of the other OSPF routers just add their own computed metric to the route when it is flooded all around the AS. But since OSPF metrics by default are tied to a reference bandwidth (usually 100 Mbps), the external route's metric normally has nothing to do with the OSPF metrics added and can lead to some very strange OSPF metrics when the two are combined. For example, RIP metrics are hop counts less than 15, BGP metrics are MEDs that can be in the 100 and higher range, IS-IS links use a metric of 10 for each link, and so on. In OSPF, a T1 link can have an OSPF metric of 64, a 10-Mbps Ethernet can have an OSPF metric 10, and so forth. The low metric becomes the active route when there is a choice, so a high metric assigned to a Type 1 external path by an ASBR can have an influence far out of proportion to its actual desirability within the OSPF AS.

If the metric between OSPF internally and the source routing protocol are essentially incompatible and independent, why make each OSPF router compute an internal cost to reach the ASBR for that route anyway? So an ASBR by default makes the external route an OSPF Type 2 external path. Type 2 external paths only use the inherited metric from the external route and do *not* consider the internal OSPF cost of reaching the ASBR that can reach that destination. The packet has to reach the ASBR one way or another anyway. Why have OSPF optimize on route metrics that have no relation to OSPF?

The choice of advertising OSPF external routes as E1 (Type 1 including OSPF cost with the external cost) or E2 (Type 2 with only the external cost) is strictly up to the network administrator of the border routers (ASBRs). However, this should be done consistently, since mixing E1 and E2 externals inside an AS can change the paths and links used to reach the ASBR. There are times when it *does* matter which way a router uses to reach an ASBR. Consider the situation shown in Figure 16.2.

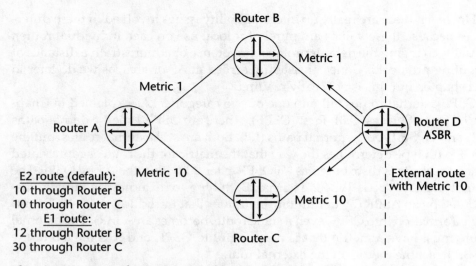

Figure 16.2 External Type 1 (E1) and Type 2 (E2) OSPF paths.

There are three internal OSPF routers linked to an ASBR router, as shown. The links through Router B with an OSPF metric of 1 for each hop are 100-Mbps (or faster) links and the links through Router C with an OSPF metric of 10 for each hop are 10-Mbps Ethernet links (the links could be much slower than that; this is only an example). The ASBR is advertising an external route with a metric of 10 into the OSPF AS.

If the external route is advertised as an OSPF Type 2 external (the ASBR default behavior) then Router A will see the cost to this route to be equal through either Router B or Router C (both will just be 10). Since these are equal-cost paths, it is just as likely that routers will send traffic to the destination on the slower links than on the faster ones. In fact, Cisco's OSPF implementation will automatically load-balance over these two equal-cost paths. But this still leaves half of the traffic on the slower links through Router C.

However, if the external route is advertised as an OSPF Type 1 external (changed with a routing policy), more control is possible over the path taken by the traffic. Router A will see the cost of sending traffic to the destination through the ASBR as 12 through Router B (1 + 1 + 10) and 30 through Router C (10 + 10 + 10). So Router A should pick the faster path through Router B as the active route to reach the ASBR and the destination. This is also shown in the figure.

How can the ASBR change the default external metric type for the advertised external route? Different methods are used on Cisco and Juniper Networks routers.

Cisco OSPF External Types

The easiest time on the ASBR to change from the default OSPF Type 2 external (E2) to a Type 1 external (E1) is when the route is redistributed by OSPF in the first place. With regard to OSPF, the syntax of the configuration command is:

```
metric-type { type-1 | type-2 }
```

Note that the same syntax is used to change an E1 to an E2 as to change an E2 to an E1. This configuration command should be used on the ASBR when redistributing BGP routes (for example) using OSPF. Using the example configuration for Cisco_ASBR0 in Chapter 10, the following shows how this would be done:

```
Cisco_ASBR0(config)#router ospf 10
Cisco_ASBR0(config-router)#redistribute bgp 64512
Cisco_ASBR0(config-router)#metric-type type-1
Cisco_ASBR0(config-router)#network 10.0.32.1 0.0.0.0 area 0
Cisco_ASBR0(config-router)#network 172.16.10.1 0.0.0.0 area 0
```

As an E2, the route to 192.168.100.66 (the AS 64555 router's loopback address) showed up on the Cisco_ABR1 router with a metric of 0 (the default metric assigned to the external loopback—other routes would inherit a more meaningful metric):

```
O E2 192.168.100.0 [110/0] via 10.0.32.1, 00:01:21, FastEthernet0
```

The 0 metric reflects the fact that ASBR0 is now a Juniper Networks router. When the ASBR0 router was Cisco_ASBR0, the default metric assigned to the 192.168.100.0 route was 1, and the OSPF Tag value was 64555 (the remote AS).

Once the metric has been set to E1, the Cisco_ABR1 will see the route with the added internal cost to reach the ASBR:

```
O E1 192.168.100.0 [110/1] via 10.0.32.1, 00:01:21, FastEthernet0
```

As the 192.168.100.0 route was redistributed throughout the AS by OSPF, the metric associated with the route now reflects the cost of getting to ASBR0 as well as the metric to 192.168.100.0 from the other routing protocol.

Setting a `default-metric` for all routes advertised by OSPF is not the same. This will change the metric associated with 192.168.100.0 to something else, but it will not change the OSPF Type to E1.

Juniper Networks OSPF External Types

As you might expect, a Juniper Networks router changes the OSPF external Type from E2 to E1 with a routing policy. The policy on ASBR0:

```
policy-statement from_bgp {
     term 1 {
          from protocol bgp;
          then accept;
     }
}
```

was applied as an *export* policy for OSPF (only export policies are allowed in the JUNOS software for OSPF). On ABR1, the route showed up as:

```
192.168.100.0/24    *[OSPF/150] 00:12:52, metric 0, tag 0

                    > to 10.0.32.1 via fe-0/0/0.0
```

To change the OSPF metric type and make the route look exactly as it would on ABR1 if the ASBR0 were really a Cisco router, you would use this policy:

```
policy-statement from_bgp {
     term 1 {
          from protocol bgp;
          then {
               external type 1;
               metric 1;
               tag 64555;
               accept;
          }
     }
}
```

If a number of routes are to be advertised from a Juniper Networks ASBR to other Cisco routers with different metrics, these routes can be found with a series of route filters (or by matching BGP Communities) and changed as desired.

OSPF Area Range

A very convenient "routing policy" used in OSPF is the Area Range configuration statement. Although technically a routing policy because it changes the behavior of the routing protocol in terms of the usual routes advertised, on both Cisco and Juniper Networks routers the use of the Area Range statement is configured directly in the OSPF configuration. This is unusual in the case of Juniper Networks routers, which always try to gather routing policies into the policy-options section of the configuration. But Area Range is an intimate part of OSPF, and it makes no sense to try to split off this behavior from OSPF itself.

An Area Range is configured only on the ABR between the backbone area 0 and the other area. It allows the entire IP address space used in the nonbackbone area to be advertised on the backbone (and into other areas if appropriate) as a single aggregate (summary) route. When done consistently throughout an AS, the use of Area Range can greatly reduce the size and complexity of the OSPF link-state database, the routing tables, and the overhead and bandwidth needed on each router to advertise OSPF information. Since OSPF Area 0 is special in the sense that the Area 0 link-state database links all of the other areas, some optimization of Area 0 link-state databases and routing tables may be important.

However, care is needed when assigning IP addresses to networks so that the Area Range does indeed reflect the actual use of the IP address space within an OSPF area and throughout the AS. You can have multiple ranges in an OSPF area (for example, one for the 172.16/16 address space and one for the 192.168.14/24 address space, and so on. But the more Area Ranges there are, the less effective the operation of this feature.

Rational use of the IP address space inside an AS is assumed here. The OSPF Area Range is configured on the ABR when OSPF itself is configured. In a lot of older documentation, especially when classful IP is considered, this is also called OSPF *Area Summarization*. This is still a quite useful term for this practice, since the resulting OSPF LSA is a single Type 3 Summary LSA.

The example OSPF network is so simple that it is hard to find address ranges that should be summarized to the backbone. But suppose Area 1 (a nonstub, nonbackbone area), in addition to the IP addresses assigned to the links and loopbacks, also had routes in the range 192.168.32/24 and 192.168.63.0/24.

This address space can easily be consolidated as 192.168.32/19, since 32 is 0010 0000 and 63 is 0011 1111. All of the essential points about IP address ranges and masks were discussed in Chapter 4 and need not be repeated here. The main point is that the /19 mask covers all of the bits that remain the same between the address ending in 0s and the one ending in 1s.

If there is another range from, for instance, 192.168.0/24 to 192.168.7/24 that appears only within Area 1, this can be summarized as 192.168.0/21. Both the /19 and the /21 summary can be used in an OSPF Area Range configuration statement. Of course, networks in these address ranges should only be assigned in OSPF Area 1. You can also use the area range configuration command with the `restrict` option, in which case the routes with the area range remain in the nonbackbone area and are not advertised onto OSPF Area 0.

Cisco Area Range

Cisco routers use this general form of the Area Range statement:

```
area area-id range ip-address mask [advertise | not-advertise ]
```

The *area-id* is the OSPF area to be summarized, the *ip-address* is the base address to be summarized, and the *mask* is, well, the mask is the usually 255 notation. Optionally, the summary can be advertised or not. This on-off switch can be useful to enable or disable the area range as desired, and if the *not-advertise* knob is used, then those routes remain forever hidden outside of that OSPF area. This is a kind of built-in route filter that can be used to suppress route advertisements if desired.

The configuration on Cisco_ABR1 would look as follows:

```
hostname Cisco_ABR1
!
router ospf 10
 network 10.0.32.2 0.0.0.0 area 0
 network 10.0.37.1 0.0.0.0 area 1
 area 1 range 192.168.0.0 255.255.248.0
 area 1 range 192.168.32.0 255.255.224.0
!
```

As long as the intention is to advertise the summary, there is no need to include the optional advertise statement. The Area 0 link-state database and routing tables will reflect the presence of these new routes.

Juniper Networks Area Range

Juniper Networks routers use this general form of the Area Range statement in the [edit protocols ospf area] level of the configuration hierarchy:

```
area-range network/masklength <restrict>;
```

The summary is applied to the OPSF area for which it is configured. The *network/mask-length* is the base address to be summarized with its "slash" format mask. The summary can be advertised or not within the *restrict* knob. This on-off switch can be useful to enable or disable the area range as desired and is used to hide those routes outside that OSPF area. This is a built-in route filter that can be used to suppress route advertisements if desired.

The configuration on ABR1 would look as follows:

```
[edit protocols]
lab@ASBR0# show
ospf {
    area 0.0.0.0 {
        area-range 192.168.32/19;
        area-range 192.168.0/21;
        interface fe-0/0/1.0;
    }
}
```

Note that the *order* in which the ranges appear is not significant, since they do not (and should not) overlap. The Area 0 link-state database and routing tables will reflect the presence of these new routes.

Changing OSPF Administrative Distance/ Protocol Preference

Before we move on to consider IS-IS routing policies, in this final section on OSPF routing policies we change the Cisco default OSPF administrative distance (110) and the Juniper Networks default OSPF protocol preference (10 for internal OSPF routes, 150 for external OSPF routes) with a "routing policy." This change of internal importance is not strictly a routing policy at all, but since this action is usually used in conjunction with a major change to the IGP routes and routing protocol used in the AS, in a broad sense this is certainly affecting the default behavior of the routing protocols.

Why would anyone want to change the default administrative distance or protocol preference in the first place? This transitional section between OSPF and IS-IS is a perfect place to put this very real-world example. The best occasion to alter the default administrative distance or protocol preference is when transitioning an area or entire AS from one IGP to another.

Networks, like much else with computers in general, are potential places where *lock-in* can occur. There is no formal term for the situation where a network becomes so dependent on a particular vendor or routing protocol that the use of an alternative becomes unthinkable to contemplate and nearly impossible to implement. Lock-in limits flexibility in current deployment, the ability to adapt to changing circumstances, and just overall freedom of choice. It's a little like buying a certain type of car and forever after being branded a "Ford person" or "Chevy user" because that is the only type of car that can be bought and driven. Some differences can be annoying and alternatives preferred, but how hard is it really to find the gas tank or trunk switch? (There are those who refuse to seek help through documentation and feel everything should be intuitive.) But once the difference is noted and dealt with, the new way quickly becomes the everyday way.

In this book we have emphasized interoperability between major router vendors, in particular Cisco and Juniper Networks. But the same arguments can be extended to routing protocols as well. There is absolutely no need to feel trapped in an OSPF world when IS-IS would be a better IGP solution. Without repeating all the details, IS-IS can be more forgiving than OSPF with regard to backbone deployment and inter-area routing, as pointed out in Chapter 11, "Intermediate System–Intermediate System (IS-IS)," and Chapter 12, "Configuring IS-IS." Perhaps OSPF made perfect sense when the ISP was small, but after a few years of successful growth, Area 0 is becoming congested and it is becoming harder and harder to justify the need to link to Area 0 in the first place, even when OSPF virtual links are allowed.

This section shows how to migrate from OSPF to IS-IS as an IGP. The section is in no way an endorsement of IS-IS over OSPF, and it could just as easily have shown IS-IS conversion to OSPF. The argument then might be along the lines of "nobody does ISO stuff anymore. Let's junk that silly IS-IS and its funny NET addressing and get into good old OSPF. At least when links are misconfigured, you don't get a routing adjacency over them . . . " Since OSPF was featured first, this section merely transitions to IS-IS.

Gracefully Cutover OSPF to IS-IS

The simplest way to transition OSPF to IS-IS is area by area, leaving the OSPF backbone area for last. The ABR routers still run OSPF on their backbone-facing interfaces and eventually become IS-IS Level 1 and Level 2 (L1/L2) routers. This section assumes that this has already been done, and now all that is needed is to gracefully and nondisruptively transition the OSPF backbone to a collection of IS-IS L2–only routers. The same procedure outlined here will work on a smaller scale in each of the OSPF areas.

In preparation for the cutover, we need to configure Level 2 IS-IS to run on all of the interfaces that are also running OSPF. The basic configurations for OSPF and IS-IS for both Cisco and Juniper Networks were given in Chapters 10 and 12, respectively, and need not be repeated. There is no collision of routing protocols or information at this point; each link will form both OSPF and IS-IS adjacencies if the routing protocols are configured properly. The backbone might look something like the one shown in Figure 16.3.

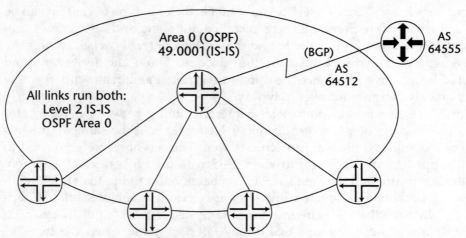

Figure 16.3   OSPF to IS-IS transition on the backbone.

All of the routers will now have both an OSPF and IS-IS link state database. This is not really a great idea, since only one is needed and link-state databases can be large and database maintenance can be a real burden on routers and links. But the OSPF link state database will soon be gone.

The key to making this plan work is the knowledge that all of the routing tables now contain *both* OSPF and IS-IS routes. Of course, by default only one route to each destination will be active. When the same route is learned from two different routing protocols and reachable, the first tiebreaker is the overall Cisco administrative distance or Juniper Networks protocol preference for the routing protocol the route was learned from. The lower number associated with the route becomes the active route used for packet forwarding.

Table 16.1 shows the default numbers associated with OSPF and IS-IS routes, internal and external, on Cisco and Juniper Networks routers.

It is not important that there are more values for Juniper Networks routers or for Cisco, or even what the specific values are. What is important is that by default, all forms of OSPF routes are lower than their IS-IS counterparts. So whenever a route is learned through both OSPF and IS-IS, internal or external, the OSPF route becomes the active route.

To change this behavior in a nondisruptive manner, all we need to do is make the IS-IS routes more attractive than the OSPF routes on all of the backbone routers, Cisco or Juniper Networks. This effectively replaces the OSPF routes in the routing and forwarding tables with IS-IS routes. Once the area has stabilized, we can remove the OSPF routing protocol from each configuration at leisure.

Table 16.1   Default OSPF and IS-IS Administrative Distances/Protocol Preferences

TYPE OF ROUTE PREFERENCE	CISCO ADMINISTRATIVE DISTANCE	JUNIPER NETWORKS PROTOCOL
OSPF internal	110	10
IS-IS L1 internal	115	15
L2 internal	115	18
OSPF AS external	110	150
IS-IS L1 external	115	160
L2 external	115	165

Cisco OSPF to IS-IS Cutover

On a Cisco router, the OSPF configuration allows the default administrative distance of 110 for all forms of OSPF routes to be changed with the `distance` statement. The general form is as follows:

```
distance ospf {[ intra-area dist ] [inter-area dist2 ] [ external dist3 ]}
```

Cisco routers make a distinction between *intra*-area internal routes entirely in a single area and *inter*-area internal routes between areas. In this transition example, both should be set higher than IS-IS (115), 116 is the simplest case. This is done in a single line at the `(config-router)` level of the configuration:

```
!
distance ospf intra-area 116 inter-area 116 external 116
!
```

Once we have performed this configuration change on each router, the IS-IS routes become active and are advertised throughout the former OSPF area. Once connectivity has been verified through IS-IS, the OSPF configuration can be deleted from each router.

However, a strong word of caution is needed at this point. Since the *metrics* used in Cisco's IS-IS are simple 10-per-link cost metrics and the Cisco OSPF metrics use the more sophisticated *reference bandwidth* method mentioned earlier in this chapter, the new IS-IS-based active routes might be radically different than the former OSPF paths, especially in an area or AS with many high-speed/low-speed links. If almost all of the links in the area or AS are the same or speeds are higher than the OSPF reference bandwidth, these OSPF/IS-IS active path differences should not be radical. But in some cases, this might be a problem. How can the OSPF metrics be translated into IS-IS to preserve the OSPF flow of packets?

Unfortunately, there is no easy way on a Cisco router to make IS-IS metric "OSPF-like," but it *can* be done. Each OSPF interface, on every router, would have to also have a configured IS-IS metric that corresponds to the calculated OSPF metric, as long as the IS-IS metric is less than 63 in the default IS-IS metric scheme. This is done using the following:

```
isis metric default-metric { level-1 | level-2 }
```

When IS-IS *wide metrics* (mentioned in Chapter 12 and later in this chapter) are configured on the Cisco router, OSPF metrics can be translated directly to IS-IS metrics for the interface. However, these mappings are static, and if the interface speed changes, the IS-IS metric for the interface must be changed in the configuration.

Juniper Networks OSPF to IS-IS Cutover

On a Juniper Networks router, the OSPF internal routes can be given a preference of 19, which makes the IS-IS internal routes (15 and 18) more attractive than OSPF routes (although this example assumes only L2 routes). Likewise, setting the preference for OSPF external routes to 166 favors IS-IS external routes. Actually, any value is the range 19 to 30 will work for internal (redirects are at protocol preference 30) and 166–169 for external (BGP is at 170). These are just the simplest values that will work.

The preference for OSPF internal routes is set with the `preference` configuration statement and external routes use the `external-preference` statement. The configuration used on each router in the OSPF backbone Area 0 is now as follows :

```
[edit protocols]
lab@ASBR0# show
ospf {
    external-preference 166;
    preference 19;
    area 0.0.0.0 {
        interface fe-0/0/1.0;
    }
}
```

Once this configuration has been performed and committed on each router, the IS-IS routes become active and are advertised throughout the former OSPF area. Once connectivity has been verified through IS-IS, the OSPF configuration can be deleted.

IS-IS Routing Policies

Routing policies applied to IS-IS are not more sophisticated than those applied to OSPF, but they are different. The only major difference is that IS-IS Level 1 routers will not pass along redistributed ("injected") routes to Level 2 routers by default. An explicit routing policy is needed to accomplish this. There is no need to repeat the simple example from the previous section on OSPF regarding metric settings for redistribution. Default metrics can be set on routes redistributed into IS-IS as easily as into OSPF. This section concentrates on more IS-IS-specific application of routing policies (even though many things are built into the IS-IS configuration statements in many cases, as was the case with OSPF).

Juniper Networks Router IS-IS Metrics

The first consideration with regard to IS-IS involves the situation just covered at the end of the OSPF section. As mentioned, when administrative distances were changed on a Cisco router to transition from OSPF to IS-IS, the new paths for traffic through the area and AS might be very different under IS-IS. This is because IS-IS and OSPF metrics are different, as might be expected whenever routing protocols are compared. The IS-IS default of assigning a more or less arbitrary metric of 10 to each and every interface is very different than OSPF's use of the reference bandwidth.

On a Cisco router, little could be done. The Cisco router's IS-IS interface metrics can be changed, but only through configuration. When and if the link speed changes, so must the configured metric. This can be a real concern in an area or AS with many mixed high-speed and low-speed links, or when link speeds are below the configured OSPF reference bandwidth.

But with Juniper Networks routers, things are different. It is possible, and even in a sense trivial, to make IS-IS use the same system of reference bandwidth metrics as OSPF. The result is a totally stable cutover from OSPF active paths to IS-IS active paths, even when and if link speeds change.

This is because Juniper Networks routers support the use of the OSPF reference bandwidth metric calculations for IS-IS. With a Juniper Networks router, support for IS-IS wide metrics is enabled by default (in fact, the use of wide metrics solely can be enabled with the `wide-metrics-only` knob applied to an IS-IS level), so the default IS-IS 63 maximum metric does not apply.

To make IS-IS metrics look like OSPF metrics, the general statement:

```
reference-bandwidth reference-bandwidth
```

is applied to the `[edit protocols isis]` level of the configuration hierarchy. If the default OSPF value of 100 Mbps is to be used, this can be entered as 100m or 100000000. Once this is done, the result shows up as follows:

```
[edit protocols]
lab@L2_Only# show isis
isis {
    export for_bgp;
    level 1 disable;
    reference-bandwidth 100m;
    interface fe-0/0/1.0;
    interface fe-0/0/2.0;
    interface lo0.0 {
        passive;
    }
}
```

If no specific reference bandwidth is added to the keyword, the default reference bandwidth used is 10 Mbps. So 100-Mbps Ethernet links show up with a metric of 10 and so on. Before the cutover, all the OSPF active routes should have the same metrics as the new IS-IS routes:

```
lab@ABR1> show route 172.16.0.2
inet.0: 12 destinations, 12 routes (12 active, 0 holddown, 0 hidden)
+ = Active Route, - = Last Active, * = Both

172.16.0.2/32       *[OSPF/10] 00:34:13, metric 10
                    > to 10.0.32.2 via fe-0/0/1.0
                    [IS-IS/18] 00:57:45, metric 10, tag 2
                       to 10.0.32.2 via fe-0/0/1.0
```

The ability to use the same metrics in IS-IS as in OSPF is a real advantage when transitioning from one IGP to the other. When the transition is from IS-IS to OSPF, Juniper Networks routers can give OSPF metrics to IS-IS routes before the final cutover. This will reveal if there are any radically different routes resulting from OSPF use. With Cisco routers, the same effect can be accomplished with interface metrics or route maps, but with considerably more difficulty.

IS-IS Route Leaking

The most critical application of routing policy to change the default behavior of IS-IS is called *route leaking*. Although mentioned in Chapter 11 on the IS-IS routing protocol, very little detail about route leaking was presented there at that time. In this chapter we explore route leaking in full.

Route leaking is not any easy concept to grasp, so a little background is needed to understand exactly what the policy of route leaking is trying to accomplish. Then the actual mechanisms of route leaking are presented for both Cisco and Juniper Networks routers.

Large ISPs, as has been mentioned several times already in this book, consist of the following: site routers (Cisco often calls them *remote* site routers) on the customer premises; edge routers or access routers (both terms are used) gathered at ISP locations called points of presence, or POPs (a term borrowed from telephone networks); and core routers or backbone routers (again both terms are common). The core exists to link the POPs, and this architecture lends itself easily to OSPF backbone Area 0/other areas and IS-IS Level 1 and Level 2 routing protocol configurations.

Large Tier 1 ISPs in the United States were initially drawn to IS-IS for its ease and flexibility of inter-area routing without requiring virtual links (officially tolerated) or backdoor links (officially forbidden) as OSPF does. But ISPs were at first unfamiliar with most of the subtleties of IS-IS, so many ISPs simply ran Level 1-only IS-IS in their POPs and on their backbone routers. All of the routers were in one IS-IS area and this produced a totally flat network with only a single L1 link-state database on each router. But any change in topology (a new route or new links) required flooding and running the SPF computation on each and every router.

Before route leaking was available, this all made sense. Having all L1 routers eliminated the need for two link-state databases (L1 and L2), and since many of the routers at the time were Cisco AGS+ or 7000 series routers, L1_only was the best solution for these platforms. L1 link-state databases have the minimum information, since the RFC that applied IS-IS to IP, RFC 1195, defined all L1 routers as stub routers.

By the later 1990s, router memory and speed, as well as backbone link bandwidths, had progressed to the point where most large Tier 1 ISPs were now running L2_only routers at both the POPs and in the core. These L2_only routers could have all POPs in the same area as the backbone, or each POP could be in an IS-IS area of its own (IS-IS is much more fluid with regard to areas than OSPF). The result was the same with a single area or with multiple areas: L2_only IS-IS ran on all routers. It just made more sense to extend the IS-IS backbone to the POPs; the routers could take it, and L2 was intended to be the core/backbone level IS-IS all along. All of the ISP routers had a full link-state database for the entire AS (routing domain), but only an L2 link-state database.

But once the POPs and core had grown to about 1,000 routers, or even more in some cases, SPF computation times grew in proportion. Not only that, but all of the L2 routers had all of the LSPs, and these chewed up considerable bandwidth to flood even simple changes in network topology throughout the ISP network.

The obvious solution was to run the POPs as L1_only routers in their own areas, L2_only on the backbone core routers, and use L1/L2 IS-IS routers as the ABRs connecting POPs to the core. The POPs track only their own changes, and SPF computations are limited to each area and the core. Flooding bandwidth is at a minimum because all the L1_only routers need is a single default route to an L1/L2 router, as was shown in Chapter 12. There are now two link-state databases to maintain, L1 and L2, but IS-IS, unlike OSPF, is able to optimize routing not only within an area (L1) but also between areas (L2). All OSPF knows is that a route is outside of the area and therefore reachable somehow through the backbone Area 0. This migration to L1 POPs and L2 cores began around 2000 and continues. This evolution of large ISP's use of IS-IS is shown in Figure 16.4.

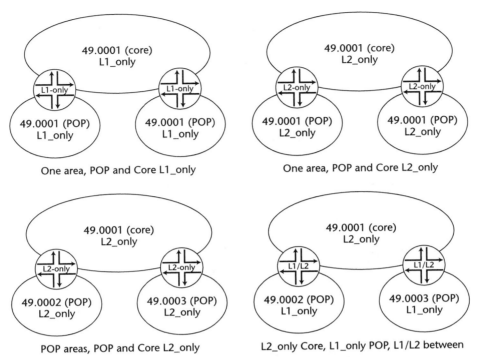

Figure 16.4   Evolution of large ISP's use of IS-IS.

Unfortunately, once ISPs started mixing L1 and L2 IS-IS, the limitations of L1 stubs as defined in RFC 1195 became painfully obvious. All L1–only routers know is that some other router within their area is setting the attached (ATT) bit in their LSPs, and so this router is able to reach other IS-IS areas (it is an L1/L2 router). When faced with different LSPs from different routers with the ATT bit set, the IS-IS router has no choice but to pick the nearest (in terms of intra-area metrics) L1/L2 router to forward packets to and hope that this default is a good way to reach destinations.

As an example, Figure 16.5 shows a slightly modified version of the IS-IS network created at the end of Chapter 12. The L1_only router at the lower right is presented with two ATT bits from two L1/L2 routers. Which potential area exit should be used as the default route to reach all other destinations inside (and outside) the AS?

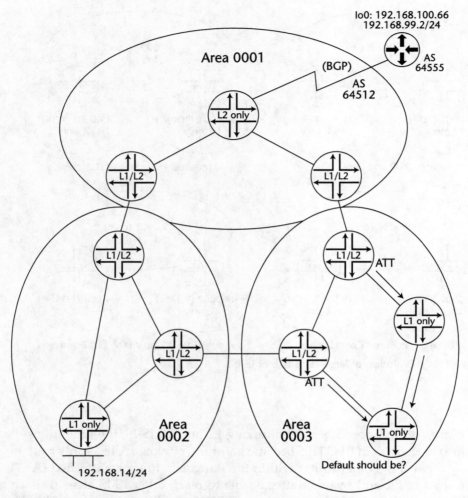

Figure 16.5 Multiple IS-IS area exit points.

It seems clear that the L1/L2 route facing the core would be the best exit to reach all other destinations in and beyond the AS. After all, the core links all other areas, probably has most of the links to other ASs (the ASBRs), and most likely has most of the high-speed links as well. Yet based on the internal metrics, the L1/L2 router to the other area will become the default next-hop router for that area. Packets will still get where they are going, but the lack of any L2 network knowledge at all on the L1–only stub routers often leads to exactly the suboptimal (silly) routing shown in the figure.

And what about 192.168.14.0/24 in Area 0002? Changing the metrics to make the default route face the core forces traffic to this destination to take a very long route to a place that is really close by. And why add this traffic to the backbone anyway?

Route leaking fixes these limitations by allowing L1/L2 routers at the POP exits to "leak" L2 information to the L1 routers. The leaked information is in the form of the routes (prefixes), along with their metrics, as they exist of the L1/L2 router. The intent is to make the L1–only routers smart enough to know which POP exit to use to reach destinations outside of the POP.

In a nutshell, IS-IS areas with L1–only router are much the same as OSPF total stub areas. L1–only routers use default routes to forward packets to L1/L2 routers, but without any detailed knowledge of where the L1/L2 router sits in relation to the whole AS. What is needed is a way to make an L1–only area into a kind of OSPF nonbackbone, nonstub area, so that more details about the whole AS in the form of summary (other area) and external (outside the AS) routes can be relayed to the L1–only routers.

If that was all there was to route leaking, then this section could go right into configuration examples. But things are not so simple. Once L2 routes find their way into an L1 area with route leaking, there has to be a loop prevention mechanism to prevent these routes from being advertised back into L2 through another exit point. This loop prevention is accomplished by setting an Up/Down bit in the IS-IS LSPs.

This route leaking discussion has already grown rather complex and abstract. It is time for a more concrete example.

Route Leaking Mechanisms

Haphazard route leaking can easily lead to routing loops, much in the same way that undisciplined advertisement of BGP routes would lead to routing loops if not for the AS Path attribute. Route leaking is controlled by a number of mechanisms, all designed to prevent a small L1–only area from seeming to be a great way to reach the IS-IS backbone when all the L1–only area can do is pass traffic right back to another L1/L2 router.

An example network designed to illustrate many of the IS-IS mechanisms is shown in Figure 16.6. The mechanisms discussed include the preference of L1 over L2 routing information, the restriction that route leaking only occur if the route being leaked in present on the L1/L2 router's L2 routing table, and the use of the Up/Down bit to prevent routes from being readvertised from L1 back into the L2 core.

The normal situation that occurs when a route to 192.168.14/24 is advertised as an L1 route by Router E is shown in the figure. This L1 LSP reaches Router D, where it is advertised outside the area as an L2 route (intra-area) to Router G. Router G passes this LSP along to all other L2 or L1-L2 routers, but only sends LSPs with the ATT bit set to Router I, an L1–only router. The same applies to Router H, of course. These two routers can only reach 192.168.14/24 through their default routes, which must use either Router F or Router G as a next-hop router.

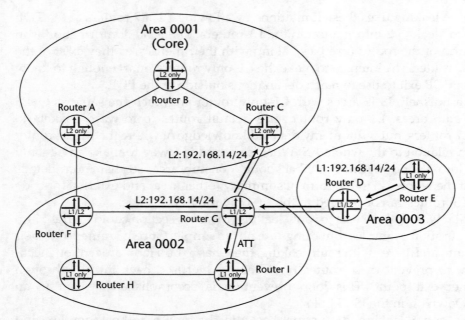

Figure 16.6 An example network for route leaking.

Only the intra-area metric is used on the L1–only routers to choose between Router F or Router G as an area exit point. So, all things being equal, Router H chooses Router F (one "hop" instead of two) and Router I chooses Router G (for the same reason) for their default next hops for all destinations outside their area, including 192.168.14/24.

What's the big deal? So what if Router H sends packets for 192.168.14/24 to Router F instead of Router G? That's only one more hop. But what if the link between Router F and Router G does not exist or has failed? In a small network of nine routers, it is always obvious where physical links should be installed. But many ASs running IS-IS have up to 1,000 routers, as mentioned. Not every helpful link is immediately obvious or economically feasible, especially as networks grow and evolve over time.

The point is that now there is a radical difference between the paths packets take to 192.168.14/24 when there is no link (or a failed link) between Router F and Router G. Router I can still reach Router E in three hops, but poor Router H is loading the whole core with traffic that must pass through seven hops to reach 192.168.14/24. A four-hop path through Router I is available, but Router H, stuck in an IS-IS stub with only a default, cannot find it. Again, three more hops might not sound like much, but if a path almost doubles in this simple network, in a collection of 1,000 routers, the path might be even longer. And no one makes money by allowing packets to take the scenic route through their network.

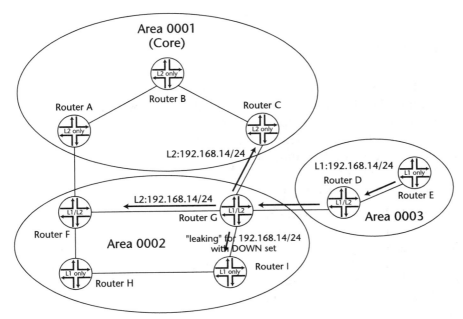

Figure 16.7 L1/L2 route leaking.

Figure 16.7 shows what happens when all of the L1/L2 routers in the AS are configured with route leaking. The configurations of the L1–only area routers and L2–only core routers stay the same, only the L1/L2 routers need to be configured for route leaking.

As before, Router E sends an L1 LSP to Router D for 192.168.14/24. This router passes the information on in an L2 LSP to Router G (route leaking will not change the rules for advertisements of L1 information into L2 in any way, at least not yet). But since Router G is configured with route leaking, Router G will advertise in route to 192.168.14/24 to Router I, but only because of the following:

- The 192.168.14/24 route is present in the L2 routing table. This makes sure that route leaking is strictly from L2 to L1 and that only IS-IS routes are leaked. Route leaking is for inter-area (L2) routes only.

- Router G will advertise 192.168.14/24 to Router I, the L1 router, with the Down bit set so that other L1/L2 routers know that this route has been sent from the L2 backbone "down" to L1 areas. Now, the L1–only area that originated the route might receive the leaked information from an L1/L2 router. It is obvious that no L1/L2 router would have a better way to reach an L1–only route inside the area itself. The default preference for favoring L1 routes over L2 routes prevents the situation where, for example, Router E might actually prefer to send packets for the 192.168.14/24 address space to Router D. Only other areas need to know about an L1/L2 way to the prefix; Router D and Router E know about 192.168.14/24 already through L1 LSPs.

- Since Router I has only an L1 link-state database, the information about 192.168.14/24 will be advertised to Router H as an L1 route, and Router H will pass this L1 LSP right along to Router F. At this point, the Down bit setting prevents Router F from reintroducing the route to 192.168.14/24 into the backbone as reachable through Router H. A potential routing loop from Router F to Router H to Router I to Router G back to Router F has been prevented through this simple one-bit technique.

Even when IS-IS is used to route packets other than IP, route leaking applies to IP information only. Route leaking has its basic application in optimal IS-IS inter-area routing, but it also helps BGP because BGP uses the IGP to resolve next hops, so BGP and MEDs map to the closest AS exit point, and MPLS-based VPNs, so that it is easy to find Provider Edge (PE) routers. All in all, route leaking is a simple change that has many benefits.

With route leaking in place throughout the AS on L1/L2 routers, Router H will know that the best way to reach network 192.168.14/24 in Router E is through Router G.

Route Leaking, TLVs, and Metrics

As touched on in Chapter 11, "Intermediate System–Intermediate System," route leaking involves the use of certain IS-IS TLVs (Type/Length/Value LSP units) and metric types. Because route leaking is an add-on to the original IS-IS for IP (integrated IS-IS), the original form and use of the IS-IS TLVs had to be changed in order to make route leaking work as intended. This section describes those changes.

Route leaking is described in RFC 2622, in which route leaking uses traditional IS-IS narrow metrics (0 to 63 range) and TLV Types 128 and 130 (for internal and external routes, respectively). A newer document, "IS-IS Extensions for Traffic Engineering," describes how to do route leaking with wide metrics (32 bits wide, as wide as OSPF) and TLV Type 135 (used for traffic engineering). The structure of these three TLVs was presented in Chapter 11 but is repeated here in Figure 16.8 for easy reference.

The key change for route leaking is the presence of the Up/Down bit in the TLVs. The Up/Down bit lets routers know whether or not the route has been leaked. If the Up/Down bit is 0 (the Up bit), the L1/L2 router receiving the LSP with that TLV knows that the route came from that L1 area. If this bit is set to 1 (the Down bit), then the L1/L2 router knows that the route is an L2 route

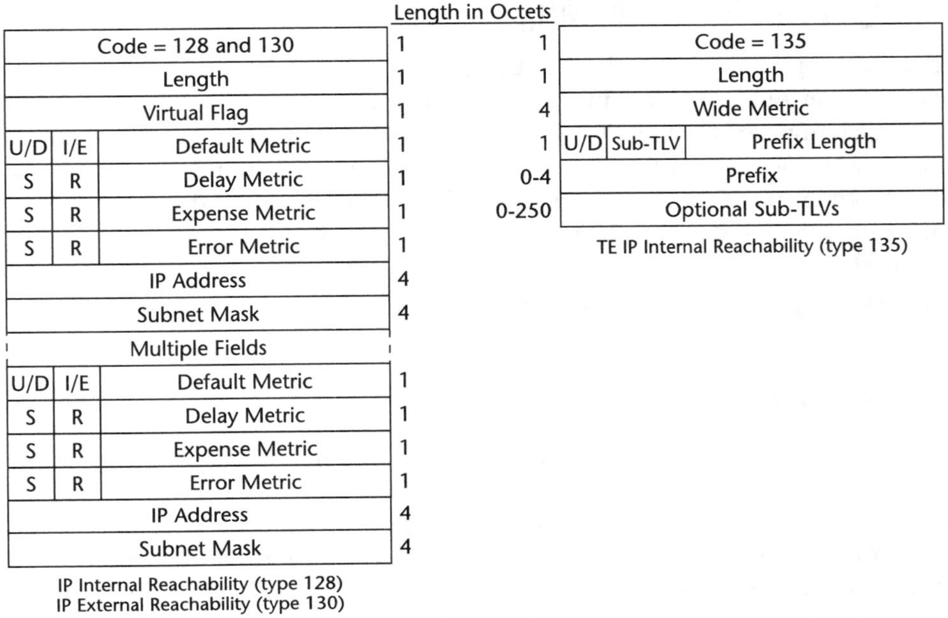

Length in Octets

			Octets
Code = 128 and 130			1
Length			1
Virtual Flag			1
U/D	I/E	Default Metric	1
S	R	Delay Metric	1
S	R	Expense Metric	1
S	R	Error Metric	1
IP Address			4
Subnet Mask			4
Multiple Fields			
U/D	I/E	Default Metric	1
S	R	Delay Metric	1
S	R	Expense Metric	1
S	R	Error Metric	1
IP Address			4
Subnet Mask			4

IP Internal Reachability (type 128)
IP External Reachability (type 130)

Octets			
1	Code = 135		
1	Length		
4	Wide Metric		
1	U/D	Sub-TLV	Prefix Length
0-4	Prefix		
0-250	Optional Sub-TLVs		

TE IP Internal Reachability (type 135)

Figure 16.8   TLV Types 128 and 130, and Type 135.

that has been redistributed into the area by an L1/L2 router. As already mentioned, this bit prevents routing and forwarding loops. An L1/L2 router will not advertise into L2- and L1-learned routes that have the Up/Down bit set to 1.

It is always a good idea to use TLV Type 135 when configuring route leaking. This in turn means that support for wide metrics must be enabled, if not used by default, on the routers. This avoids the need to use TLV Types 128 and 130 for route leaking. But what's wrong with using TLV Types 128 and 130 for route leaking?

The problem is with older routers that have no idea what route leaking is and does and that handle the older format for TLVs Type 128 and 130. In the older, pre-route-leaking format, the metric fields were the same but there was no Up/Down bit. This bit position was reserved and had to be set to 0. This bit position is now the Up/Down bit and can now be set to 1 to indicate route leaking from L2.

So backward compatibility is an issue with older IS-IS implementations when the Up/Down bit position was reserved and had to be set to 0. To avoid any issues, use wide metrics and TLV Type 135 for route leaking.

Configuring Route Leaking

Route leaking is performed by L1/L2 routers, and only those routers need to be able to perform route leaking. However, in many case, especially with Cisco routers, changes might have to be made on other routers because these routers might only understand the older form of TLV Types 128 and 130 where the Up/Down bit position was reserved and had to be set to 0. If this is a concern, only wide metrics and TLV Type 135 should be used.

This should not be an issue on Juniper Networks routers, since the sending and receiving of wide metrics is enabled by default.

Cisco Route Leaking

Confusingly, Cisco routers use different statement syntax for configuring route leaking in different IOS versions. Route leaking is supported in IOS 12.0S, 12.0T, and 12.1. In 12.0S, the commands to configure route leaking are entered in the router's IS-IS configuration. IOS 12.0S only supports route leaking with both wide metrics enabled (to turn on TLV Type 135) and through an extended IP access list to determine the routes to be leaked. Without wide metrics, no route leaking will occur. IOS 12.0T and 12.1 support route leaking with either wide or narrow IS-IS metrics, but the use of wide metrics is recommended to avoid backward-compatibility issues, as described in the previous section. IOS 12.0T and 12.1 use a distribute list to determine the routes advertised. In both cases, the prefixes specified must be in the L2 routing table, of course.

The following is the general syntax to configure route leaking with IOS 12.0S:

```
advertise ip 12-to-11 <100-199>
metric-style wide
```

The bracketed numbers refer to the extended access list. The wide metric-style knob is required. The general syntax to enable route leaking with IOS 12.0T and 12.1 is:

```
redistribute isis ip level-2 into level-1 distribute list <100-199>
metric-style wide
```

This time the wide metric-style knob is optional but recommended. Oddly, the older "advertise" syntax can be used, but it is converted to the newer "redistribute" syntax if entered and shows up that way.

Leaked routes appear as inter-area (ia) routes in the routing table and IS-IS link-state database. (The capital IA is used for OSPF inter-area routes, again leaving only lowercase for IS-IS.)

Consider the example IS-IS network already introduced in this chapter. Suppose that Router E is advertising two different prefixes to the L1/L2 router, Router D. To make these routes stand out, this example uses 192.168.14/24 and 192.168.67/24, and only this area will have 192.168 routes. On Router F, which gets the L2 LSP and will leak these routes to L1–only Router H, the configuration would be:

```
!
router isis
 redistribute isis ip level-2 into level-1 distribute list 120
 metric-style wide
 net 49.0002.0172.0016.0004.00
!
...
ip classless
access-list 120 permit 192.168.14.0 0.0.0.255
access-list 120 permit 192.168.67.0 0.0.0.255
...
```

As long as the two prefixes are present in Router F and Router G's routing table as L2 routes, these prefixes will be leaked to Router H and Router I. This example uses 172.17.0/24 for other internal IS-IS routes and 10.0.x/24 notation for links, as has been done consistently throughout this book. So the routing table on Router H might look something like:

```
Router_H#sh ip route
Codes:C - connected,S - static,I - IGRP,R - RIP,M - mobile,B - BGP
      D - EIGRP,EX - EIGRP external,O - OSPF,IA - OSPF inter area
      N1 - OSPF NSSA external type 1 N2 - OSPF NSSA external type 2
      E1 - OSPF external type 1,E2 - OSPF external type 2,E - EGP
      i - IS-IS,L1 - IS-IS level-1,L2 - IS-IS level-2,ia - IS-IS inter-
area

      * - candidate default, U - per-user static route, o - ODR
      P - periodic downloaded static route

Gateway of last resort is 10.0.41.1 to network 0.0.0.0

     10.0.0.0 255.255.255.0 is subnetted, 4 subnets
C        10.0.42.0 is directly connected, FastEthernet0
i L1     10.0.40.0 [115/20] via 10.0.41.1, FastEthernet1
                   [115/20] via 10.0.42.1, FastEthernet0
C        10.0.41.0 is directly connected, FastEthernet1
i L1     10.0.35.0 [115/20] via 10.0.41.1, FastEthernet1
     172.16.0.0 255.255.255.255 is subnetted, 3 subnets
i L1     172.16.0.8 [115/10] via 10.0.42.1, FastEthernet0
C        172.16.0.9 is directly connected, Loopback0
```

```
 i L1    172.16.0.5 [115/10] via 10.0.41.1, FastEthernet1
  iia      192.168.14.0 [115/40] via 10.0.42.1, FastEthernet0
  iia      192.168.67.0 [115/40] via 10.0.42.1, FastEthernet0
 i*L1 0.0.0.0 0.0.0.0 [115/10] via 10.0.41.1, FastEthernet1
```

The main point here is that Router H now has a longer match in its routing table for packets sent to the 192.168.14/24 and 192.168.67/24 address spaces and will send these packet toward Router I, the shorter path to Router E if Routers F and G are not directly linked, and will avoid the longer path through Router F, even through the default router is closer. Note that the next-hop interface for the 192.168 networks is different than the next hop for the default 0.0.0.0 route. Routers H and I now have acquired some L2 intelligence thanks to route leaking.

However, IOS 12.0T and 12.1 support both wide and narrow metric types. If another Cisco L1 or L1/L2 router is not running 12.0T or 12.1, the Up/Down bit is still what it used to be: a route with a metric type of external. So these routers will send routes that are using metric type external with this bit position set to 1, and any 12.0T or 12.1 L1/L2 routers will incorrectly see this as a route with the Up/Down bit set to 1 (route has been leaked) and not propagate the route properly to all the routers that it should.

The same risk occurs from a route leaking L1/L2 to non-12.0T or non-12.1 routers. This bit position is set to 1 by the L1/L2 router ("I have leaked this route to L1"). But the other non-12.0T or non-12.1 L1/L2 routers will treat the route as a metric type internal route and readvertise the route when it perhaps shouldn't be. In this case the result might be a routing loop.

The whole situation is shown in Figure 16.9. In this very simple example, only two routers are shown, an L1/L2 Router A running IOS 12.1 (or 12.0T) leaking routes into L1 and an L1–only Router B running 12.0S (or older) redistributing routes with metric type external. Router A incorrectly sees in the figure, Router B's routes as inter-area routes, and Router B incorrectly sees Router A's routes as external routes.

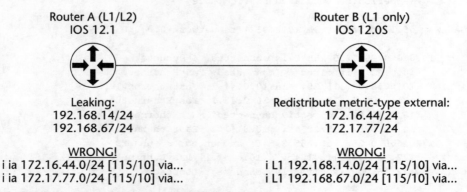

Router A (L1/L2)
IOS 12.1

Router B (L1 only)
IOS 12.0S

Leaking:
192.168.14/24
192.168.67/24

Redistribute metric-type external:
172.16.44/24
172.17.77/24

WRONG!
i ia 172.16.44.0/24 [115/10] via...
i ia 172.17.77.0/24 [115/10] via...

WRONG!
i L1 192.168.14.0/24 [115/10] via...
i L1 192.168.67.0/24 [115/10] via...

Figure 16.9   Route leaking incompatibilities.

There are two workarounds for this situation. First, have all non-12.0T and non-12.1 routes stop using redistribution with `metric-type external`. Second, use wide metrics. Wide-style metrics is the preferred solution because of the inherent limitations of narrow metrics.

Juniper Networks Route Leaking

Juniper Networks routers accomplish route leaking through the application of a routing policy to IS-IS. This should come as no surprise and shows the versatility of Juniper Networks define-and-apply approach to routing policy. Route leaking can be added to the basic IS-IS configuration in the JUNOS software not by adding special configuration commands or sets of commands but just by writing a policy that does what is needed.

The policy to perform route leaking on the two prefixes established already looks like this:

```
policy-statement L2_route_leaking {
        term 1 {
            from {
                protocol isis;
                level 2;
                route-filter 192.168.14.0/24 exact;
                route-filter 192.168.67.0/24 exact;
            }
            to {
                protocol isis;
                level 1;
            }
            then accept;
        }
    }
```

The route filters can be adjusted or augmented to match any routes desired. This policy is applied as an `export` policy to the IS-IS protocol on the L1/L2 routers. No wide metrics statement is needed, since by default Juniper Networks routers understand both. But the knob for L2 `wide-metrics-only` might be configured if there are compatibility issues with older versions of IOS running on Cisco routers in the area and any confusion is possible.

```
isis {
    export L2_route_leaking;
    level 2 wide-metrics-only
    interface fe-0/0/0.0;
    interface fe-0/0/1.0;
    interface fe-0/0/2.0;
    interface lo0.0 {
        passive;
    }

}
```

As expected, the leaked routes shows up in the L1 link-state database and in the routing table as internal routes.

Here's Router_H as a Juniper Networks router:

```
lab@Router_H> show route
inet.0: 12 destinations, 12 routes (12 active, 0 holddown, 0 hidden)
+ = Active Route, - = Last Active, * = Both

0.0.0.0/0          *[IS-IS/15] 00:06:21, metric 10, tag 1
                    > to 10.0.41.1 via fe-0/0/1.0
10.0.35.0/24       *[IS-IS/15] 00:06:33, metric 20, tag 1
                    > to 10.0.41.1 via fe-0/0/1.0
10.0.40.0/24       *[IS-IS/15] 00:19:30, metric 20, tag 1
                    > to 10.0.41.1 via fe-0/0/1.0
                      to 10.0.42.1 via fe-0/0/2.0
10.0.41.0/24       *[Direct/0] 00:20:04
                    > via fe-0/0/1.0
10.0.41.2/32       *[Local/0] 00:20:04
                      Local via fe-0/0/1.0
10.0.42.0/24       *[Direct/0] 00:19:50
                    > via fe-0/0/2.0
10.0.42.2/32       *[Local/0] 00:20:04
                      Local via fe-0/0/2.0
172.16.0.5/32      *[IS-IS/15] 00:19:30, metric 10, tag 1
                    > to 10.0.41.1 via fe-0/0/1.0
172.16.0.8/32      *[IS-IS/15] 00:19:30, metric 10, tag 1
                    > to 10.0.41.1 via fe-0/0/1.0
172.16.0.9/32      *[Direct/0] 00:20:04
                    > via lo0.0
192.168.14.0/24    *[IS-IS/15] 00:16:21, metric 40, tag 1
                    > to 10.0.42.1 via fe-0/0/2.0
192.168.67.0/24    *[IS-IS/15] 00:16:21, metric 40, tag 1
                    > to 10.0.42.1 via fe-0/0/2.0

iso.0: 1 destinations, 1 routes (1 active, 0 holddown, 0 hidden)
+ = Active Route, - = Last Active, * = Both

49.0002.0172.0016.0006.00/80
                   *[Direct/0] 00:20:04
                    > via lo0.0
```

IS-IS Area Range (Summary Address)

Just as with OSPF, IS-IS can be configured with a "routing policy" to advertise only certain ranges of IP addresses from Level 1 to Level 2 (the backbone). This can be done on a Cisco router by using the summary-address configuration command in the IS-IS configuration on the L1/L2 router.

There are some rules to follow. Internal IS-IS routes can be summarized (aggregated) from Level 1 to Level 2, but IS-IS forbids summarizing Level 1 internal routes. However, if external routes are redistributed into Level 1, these can be summarized with the `summary-address` command, which immediately follows the `redistribute` command. This section only considers Level 1 to Level 2 summarization.

Configuring the `summary-address` automatically suppresses more specific routes in the L1 area and advertises only the aggregate to Level 2. So care is needed when assigning IP address spaces. If a more specific route reaches the core from another L1/L2 router not using the `summary-address`, then backbone traffic will all flow to this router because of the longest-match rule. So `summary-address` should be configured on all L1/L2 routers.

To use the `summary-address` command for the two prefixes used earlier for route leaking, Router D would include this is the IS-IS configuration:

```
!
router isis
 metric-style wide
 net 49.0002.0172.0016.0004.00
 summary-address 192.168.14.0 255.255.255.0
 summary-address 192.168.67.0 255.255.255.0
!
```

What about Juniper Networks routers? Juniper Networks routers have no special IS-IS command for IS-IS address summarization, but consider this just to be another application of IP address aggregation.

Little has been said about aggregation as a routing policy at all to this point. The time has come to remedy this situation, since aggregation is most often applied to BGP routes. Routing policies for BGP (or EGPs in general) are the topic of the rest of this book. So we begin the next chapter with a more complete look at aggregation.

PART

Five

EGP Routing Policies

The last section of this book takes a look at routing polices and the only exterior gateway protocol (EGP) that really matters today: the Border Gateway Protocol (BGP). As revealed in the previous part of this book, IGP routing policies are limited and work in very restricted environments, because there are only a few aspects of IGPs beyond redistribution and metrics that affect IGP behavior. In contrast to applying routing policies to IGPs such as OSPF and IS-IS, routing policies for BGP have a very wide range of parameters (attributes) and behaviors to play with.

BGP is above all else a policy-driven protocol. Where in IGPs the details of their operation are spelled out so that interoperability and coordination of effort is all but assured, BGP has fewer absolutes to deal with and many more attributes that can be manipulated to affect BGP operation and performance. As a simple example, if the OSPF Hello interval default of 10 seconds is changed to 5 seconds, the OSPF neighbor will not form an adjacency unless the neighbor router's Hello interval is also set to 5 seconds. It is assumed that OSPF, running within a single routing domain with a single entity in charge (at least in theory), should be able to handle such a change in configuration in a coordinated manner. But if BGP Hello intervals are changed on one end of an EBGP and differ from the other, BGP simply picks the lower interval of the two and carries on.

The BGP environment is much faster and looser than the IGP arena. BGP determines how an ISP deals with its peers and customers. Paying customers should get what they pay for. Peers should at least be treated fairly, but a lot of BGP attribute manipulation is done to try and influence the behavior of other peers and third parties. The cheapest packet to route is the one that exits the AS fastest, enters the AS closest to the destination, or never shows up inside the AS in the first place. The trick is to adjust BGP attributes to make the surrounding ASs cooperate without being obnoxious about it (severing links, for example, would be an obnoxious way to limit transit traffic).

So this part of the book, even though it deals only with BGP, requires three chapters. Chapter 17, "Basic BGP Routing Policies," examines IP address space aggregation in more detail, and the two most fundamental BGP attributes used for BGP route selection, the Origin and Multi-Exit Discriminator (MED) attribute. MED is the closest thing that BGP has to a pure IGP metric, but it is used between ASs rather than inside an AS.

Chapter 18, "AS Path and Local Preference," covers the use of AS Path and Local Preference attributes in routing policies. More than any other attributes, the AS Path and Local Preference control the flow of packets through the Internet from ISP to ISP. AS Path regular expressions are covered here as well.

Chapter 19, "BGP Community and Route Damping," deals with the BGP Community attribute and BGP route damping. Routing policies to adjust Community strings and Community use is discussed, and the book closes with a look at how routing policies can control route damping for different links between ASs and ISPs.

CHAPTER 17

Basic BGP Routing Policies

This book has mentioned the basic idea and goal of route aggregation several times, most recently in the previous chapter in the section on OSPF area summaries. As convenient as route aggregation is for an IGP like OSPF, that is how essential aggregation is for an EGP like BGP. With the full Internet routing table hovering around 100,000 routes (prefixes), it is absolutely essential that even as the Internet grows and more and more routes are added as IP address spaces for LANs, the overall size of the full Internet routing table does not grow as dramatically as it did when the Web became a part of everyone's life in the mid-1990s.

Fortunately, as long as IP addresses are assigned rationally and consistently within an autonomous system (AS), aggregation is a relatively routine operation. Aggregation and the suppression of more specific routes within the aggregation range are controlled with a routing policy. The routing policy to control aggregation might be more or less built in to the routing protocol syntax as it is in Cisco, or appear as almost an independent program as it does in Juniper Networks routers, but it is a routing policy nonetheless. As routing policies go, aggregation is very simple and well understood. So aggregation is a good place to start this exploration of BGP routing policies.

The examples in this chapter frequently reference the same basic BGP configuration introduced in Chapter 14, "Configuring BGP." For ease of reference, the basic network is shown here as Figure 17.1. Addressing for this network was complex and was shown in Table in 14.1.

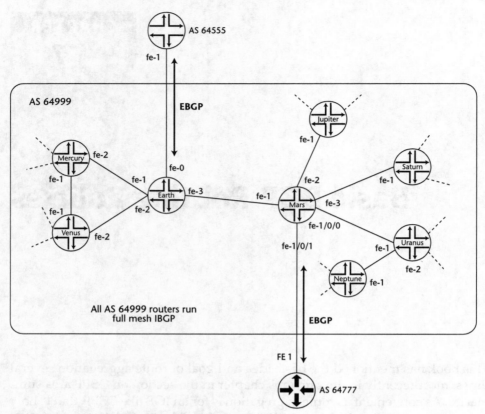

Figure 17.1 The basic BGP network.

Aggregation

In Chapter 14, which covered basic BGP configuration and use, a lot of static routes were configured as virtual customer networks. Virtual customer networks, introduced in the IGP chapters on OSPF and IS-IS, are represented as static routes with a next hop of "reject" to allow configuration and advertising of these non-existent customers. In a real network, these routes would lead to real interfaces, but in this example network, the next hops for these routes were all set so that packets sent to these destinations are simply discarded because there are no real customers on any of the routers in this example network. The only real difference is in how the next hop shows up in the routing tables.

In a real network, there would be no need to advertise all of these static routes outside of the AS as specific /24 routes. The time has come to aggregate the routes for BGP in particular and show how a routing policy can be used to control the advertising of the aggregate and the more specific routes. Table 17.1 repeats the static address ranges and bits in the third byte that were used in AS 64999, which contained routers Mercury through Neptune. Now the aggregate for the range is also shown.

Some of the masks can be longer than others, depending on the number of networks assigned and possible for each router. Each of these address ranges was carefully assigned to make sure that aggregation is simple and easy. Haphazard assignment of addresses makes the whole process much more difficult.

For the whole AS, the entire 192.168/16 address range is assumed to be allocated for use. This is just an example, but such Class B-size allocations in the past were routine for ISPs and large corporations. So for AS 64999, all of 192.168/16 is used.

Table 17.1   Aggregates for the Example Network

ROUTER	IP ADDRESS	THIRD BYTE IN BINARY	AGGREGATE
Mercury	192.168.0.0/24 to 196.168.15.0/24	0000 0000-0000 1111	192.168.0/20
Venus	192.168.16.0/24 to 192.168.31.0/24	0001 0000-0001 1111	192.168.16/20
Earth	192.168.32.0/24 to 192.168.63.0/24	0010 0000-0011 1111	192.168.32/19
Mars	192.168.128.0/24 to 192.168.175.0/24	1000 0000-1011 1111	192.168.128/17
Jupiter	192.168.176.0/24 to 192.168.191.0/24	1011 0000-1011 1111	192.168.176/20
Saturn	192.168.192.0/24 to 192.168.207.0/24	1100 0000-1100 1111	192.168.192/20
Uranus	192.168.208.0/24 to 192.168.215.0/24	1101 0000-1101 1111	192.168.208/20
Neptune	192.168.216.0/24 to 192.168.223.0/24	1101 1000-1101 1111	192.168.216/21

Some of the fundamentals of aggregation have been discussed in Chapters 5, "Cisco Router Configuration," and Chapter 6, " Juniper Networks Router Configuration." In those chapters, Cisco routers are shown to generally view aggregation as something that is intimately tied up with routing protocol configuration. So OSPF and IS-IS have their own summary configuration statements in Cisco's IOS configuration language. But Juniper Networks routers view aggregation as a protocol-independent property of the router, regardless of routing protocol used. OSPF had its own area range statement, but IS-IS lacked such a statement in the JUNOS software, as was pointed out at the end of Chapter 16, "IGP Routing Policies."

In most cases, aggregation on a Juniper Networks router is controlled with a routing policy and applied to whatever routing protocol as required. There is no need to repeat all the details, but in brief an aggregate on a Juniper Networks router can be configured for any address space. The default next hop is `reject`, so that an ICMP message is sent back to the source if a more specific route does not exist (real next hops are what *generated* routes are for). An aggregate becomes active (in this context, eligible for advertisement) whenever one or more *contributing* (more specific) routes become active. The aggregate is advertised with the source router as the next hop, and all should be well.

However, by default the Juniper Networks router continues to advertise the more specific routes under the aggregate if the policy tells the router to do so. For example, `from protocol static...accept` in a policy advertises static routes regardless of the presence of absence of an aggregate. The routing policy controls the entire process.

In this section we create and advertise an aggregate route for the static routes in the example network, first for each router, then for the entire AS. Although the emphasis in this chapter is on aggregation for BGP, router aggregation is good preparation for aggregation over the entire AS. This aggregation is done for Cisco routers and then for Juniper Networks routers.

Cisco Aggregation

Each router in the example network can aggregate its own static routes when they are advertised by OSPF. To do so, the aggregate must first be created. Chapter 16, "IGP Routing Policies," discussed the case where OSPF area routes are advertised to the backbone Area 0 as summaries with Area Range. But this is only for ABRs and so cannot be used in this example where all routers are in OSPF Area 0.

This section considers the redistribution of the static routes into OSPF on each router as an aggregate with an OSPF metric of 1. For this purpose, the OSPF `summary-address` configuration command is used to create the aggregates. Here are the informal configuration statements for Mercury:

```
!
router ospf 10
 redistribute static metric 1
 summary-address 192.168.0.0 255.255.240
...
!
```

On the other routers, this informal configuration would look as follows:

Venus: summary-address 192.168.16.0 255.255.240.0

Earth: summary-address 192.168.32.0 255.255.224.0

Mars: summary-address 192.168.128.0 255.255.128.0

Jupiter: summary-address 192.168.176.0 255.255.240.0

Saturn: summary-address 192.168.192.0 255.255.240.0

Uranus: summary-address 192.168.192.0 255.255.240.0

Neptune: summary-address 192.168.216.0 255.255.248.0

A static route for the summary address itself should be added with a next hop of Null 0. For example, Earth would have an `ip route 192.168.32.0 255.255.224.0 Null 0` static and Mars would have `ip route 192.168.128.0 255.255.128.0 Null 0`. This is so that packets without a more specific match on the router will not loop around the network (this is the same as Juniper Networks discard next hop for aggregates).

Creating a single aggregate for the entire AS is more appropriate for this chapter. To do this on a Cisco border router, we just need to configure a single statement for the BGP process running on the EBGP interface. The general form of the statement is as follows:

```
aggregate-address address mask [as-set] [summary-only]
[suppress-map route-map-name] [advertise-map route-map-name]
[attribute-map route-map-name]
```

The *address* and *mask* fields are the same as used many times in this book. By default, both the aggregate and more specific routes are advertised. To suppress the specifics, use the `summary-only` knob. The `as-set` keyword is used when the border router is advertising aggregates from more than one AS. This causes the set of AS numbers to be advertised as well. Route maps (`route-map-name`) offer even greater control, and `as-set` uses the `advertise-map` route map if configured. Route maps can be created to match conditions for the aggregate route to be suppressed (`suppress-map`) or generated (`advertise-map`). The BGP attributes for the aggregate can also be modified (`attribute-map`). For example, the route map for an aggregate can add a BGP Community of 64999:200 to the aggregate with a simple `set community 64999:200 additive` statement in the route map. (The router must also configure `ip bgp-community new-format` to comply with RFC 1997 format.)

The two border routers in the example network are Earth and Mars. Assuming that these routers are now Cisco routers, the following is the configuration for the aggregate route advertised to AS 64555:

```
hostname Cisco_Earth
!
autonomous-system 64999
!
router bgp 64999
 aggregate-address 192.168.0.0 255.255.0.0 summary-only
 neighbor 10.100.100.100 remote-as 64555
!
```

The following is the configuration for the aggregate route advertised to AS 64777:

```
hostname Cisco_Mars
!
autonomous-system 64999
!
router bgp 64999
 aggregate-address 192.168.0.0 255.255.0.0 summary-only
 neighbor 10.200.200.200 remote-as 64777
!
```

The next section considers how this aggregation would be done on a Juniper Networks router.

Juniper Networks Aggregation

Although not technically an EGP routing policy, the following is how each OSPF router would summarize its static routes into an aggregate and advertise the aggregate only in OSPF. The aggregate route must first be configured in the `routing-options` section of the configuration hierarchy as, for example, `aggregate route 192.168.0/24 discard` on Mercury (`reject` is the default):

```
[policy-options policy-statement ospf-aggregate]
lab@Mercury# show
term 1
    from {
        protocol aggregate;
```

```
            route-filter 192.168.0/20 exact;
        }
        then accept;
    }
```

This policy is then applied as an export policy to OSPF. Since the specifics (statics) are not advertised by OPSF by default, it is not necessary to filter out the specifics. The route filters used on the other routers can easily be derived from Table 17.1 and need not be repeated here.

But what if there was also a 172.16/16 route or some other static not from the 192.168.0/20 space configured on the router? Then it we would need to rewrite the policy to advertise statics, but suppress the more specifics under 192.168.0/20. This is done when applying the aggregate policy to BGP.

Assume that Earth has other static routes, perhaps 172.25.55/24 and 172.27.77/24, that need to be advertised to AS 64555. Obviously, the policy just used for OSPF will not work, since only aggregates are accepted. It might be possible to contrive an aggregate to cover the range, but unless it is absolutely certain that this space is only used locally, it is better to just advertise the specifics in this case.

The policy used on Earth to only advertise those two static routes would be as follows:

```
[policy-options policy-statement ebgp-aggregate]
lab@Earth# show
term 1 {
    from {
        protocol aggregate;
        route-filter 192.168.0/20 exact;
    }
    then accept;
}
term 2 {
    from {
        protocol static;
        route-filter 172.25.55/24 exact;
        route-filter 172.27.77/24 exact;
    }
    then accept;
}
```

All that is needed now is to apply policy to BGP. But where? In the JUNOS software, OSPF and IS-IS have only a single place to apply an export policy: globally. It's all or nothing.

It turns out that Juniper Networks routers applying a BGP routing policy have three possible *policy application points* in the BGP configuration. These are, from highest to lowest configuration level, the *global, group,* and *neighbor* level.

These levels are *not* hierarchical in the sense that a policy (or multiple policies) defined at group level is evaluated as well as a policy or policies defined at the global level. Rather, the levels are exclusive. That is, any policies applied at the neighbor level *override* any policies that might be defined at the group or global level, and these other policies are not evaluated. In the same way, group polices override any global policies.

Import and export policies operate independently. An import policy defined at the group level has nothing whatsoever to do with export policies defined anywhere. This is more difficult to talk about than to show, so a single, unified example should suffice to show the interplay of BGP global, group, and neighbor policies:

```
bgp {
    export all-my-customers;
    import sanity-check;
    group ebgp {
        type external;
        export send-statics;
        import [ AS-64555-policy no-19-plus ];
        peer-as 64555;
        neighbor 10.100.100.100;
    }
    group ibgp-mesh {
        type internal;
        export internal-info;
        local-address 172.16.0.3;
        neighbor 172.16.0.1;
        neighbor 172.16.0.2;
            export send-the-special-route;
        neighbor 172.16.0.4;
        neighbor 172.16.0.5;
        neighbor 172.16.0.6;
        neighbor 172.16.0.7;
        neighbor 172.16.0.8;
    }
}
```

This example BGP configuration has policies applied in many places. When will each policy be used? Keep in mind that this is just an example and has little to do with real routing policies or application points.

`send-the-special-route` is applied to all routes advertised to neighbor 172.16.0.2. No other export polices (`internal-info` and `all-my-customers`) are evaluated. If these policies are desired for this neighbor, they must be repeated as [`all-my-customers internal-info send-the-special-route`] but *in the order required* to produce the desired result.

`internal-info` is applied to all routes advertised to IBGP neighbors, except 172.16.0.2. The export policy `all-my-customers` is not be applied, which is perhaps for the best since the IGP should be advertising these routes inside the AS.

`AS-64555-policy` and the `no-19-plus` policy is applied to all routes arriving from the AS 64555 neighbor. The import `sanity-check` policy will *not* be applied.

`send-statics` is applied to all routes exported to EBGP neighbors.

`all-my-customers` will *never* be applied at all. The group-level IBGP and EBGP export policies essentially override this policy. Only if a new group without an export policy is added will the global export policy apply to advertised routes. Care is needed when applying routing policies to BGP.

Global BGP policies can save configuration steps, but they must be appropriate for all BGP session types and peers. Group BGP policies are most often used to apply different policies to IBGP and EBGP peers. Finally, neighbor BGP policies are usually used when one set of BGP routing information with certain attribute values is to be sent to one EBGP peer but not another (IBGP peers can have differing neighbor policies also, but IBGP policies are usually applied consistently by IBGP group).

With these guidelines in mind, the `ebgp-aggregate` policy should be applied at the EBGP group level for the `ebgp` group on Earth. IBGP peers will not need the aggregate information; OSPF will handle that if needed.

```
[edit protocols]
lab@Earth# show bgp
bgp {
    group ebgp {
        type external;
        export ebgp-aggregates;
        peer-as 64555;
        neighbor 10.100.100.100;
    }
    group ibgp-mesh {
        type internal;
        local-address 172.16.0.3;
        neighbor 172.16.0.1;
        neighbor 172.16.0.2;
        neighbor 172.16.0.4;
        neighbor 172.16.0.5;
        neighbor 172.16.0.6;
        neighbor 172.16.0.7;
        neighbor 172.16.0.8;
    }
}
```

All of the BGP routing policies in the rest of this book could conceivably be applied at many different levels of the Juniper Networks BGP configuration. Only one policy application level is shown, however. This discussion should make the placement of each policy understandable.

The Origin and MED Attributes

BGP routing policies are so important because the BGP route selection is much more complicated in BGP than in IGP. Routers running BGP tend to learn about routes to a particular destination from more than one source over more than one interface. By default, only one route from among those alternatives can become the active route or path to a destination. So BGP has a fairly elaborate series of decisions to guide the path selection process. Four BGP attributes are considered as part of this decision process. In order, the attributes are *Local Preference*, *AS Path*, *Origin*, and *Multi-Exit Discriminator (MED)*. There are many more considerations for BGP route selection if all of these values are equal, but these are the direct BGP attributes used.

Both the Origin and the MED BGP attributes are relatively high in the path selection process used to choose active routes from among BGP alternatives. Origin and MED fall only behind Local Preference and the AS Path in order of BGP attribute importance. This chapter explores routing polices to manipulate the BGP Origin and MED attributes, and the next chapter considers policies to change the AS Path and Local Preference attributes.

The most fundamental BGP routing policies (besides the indispensable policy to adjust Next Hop Self) set the Origin of routing information and associate a MED (metric) with a BGP route. Unlike IGPs, which more or less bootstrap themselves into existence and have their information right at hand in the form of locally attached interfaces, BGP essentially redistributes the information given to it through one means or another. So the BGP Origin attribute is one way that BGP peers can measure the trustworthiness of the routing information passed along by BGP. Routing information learned by BGP from a IGP (Origin = 0) is better than information learned from another AS using EGP (Origin = 1) which is better than information whose source is suspect (Origin = 3, or ?). The lower value for the origin is preferred in BGP route selection.

The MED is the basic BGP metric, but since BGP has no direct knowledge of the underlying network, the MED is only used to allow ASs connected by more than link to favor the use of one link or another for a given route to reach the other AS. A MED is added to a route only when the route is advertised across an inter-AS link with EBGP, because the IGP metrics used within the AS are more than adequate to find efficient paths through a single AS. The MED can reflect the value of the IGP metric of the route in the originating AS at the border router, but that is not a requirement. The lower value for the MED is preferred in BGP route selection.

Both Origin and MED can be set by using various configuration statements and both can be modified by using a routing policy. The modification of these two attributes is most often applied as a way to influence the path that user traffic takes as it returns to the autonomous system through the Internet. That is, the Origin and MED are modified on routes sent (exported) to another AS, where it is hoped that these attributes will influence the path that traffic takes *inbound* to the original AS.

Both Origin and MED attempt to do this by making some routes leading back to the original AS look less attractive than others when considered by the remote AS. Rather than making one route appear *better* than another, Origin and MED alterations are used to make one link back to the originating AS look *worse* than another. As such, both Origin and MED are said to exert a *negative bias* (negative influence) on routes exported to remote AS.

The Origin Attribute

The Origin attribute is set on a BGP Network Layer Reachability Information (NLRI) prefix (route) by the *first* router to inject the route into BGP. Other routers can change this value, of course, as the route makes its way through an AS and on to other ASs. The intent of the Origin code is to provide a measure of the believability as to the origin of the routing information. In other words, the intent was to provide a kind of "where did you get this from?" clue for other routers seeing the route.

As already mentioned in Chapter 13, "Border Gateway Protocol (BGP)," the Origin code is a well-known, mandatory BGP attribute (the attribute Type Code is 1), meaning that each route associated with BGP must have an Origin code assigned to it. The values available for origins include internal, external, or incomplete. The internal (abbreviated as I) origin was designated for all routes learned through a traditional interior gateway protocol (IGP) such as OSPF, IS-IS, or RIP. These types of routes were typically seen as best sources of information because of their stability and use in the IGP. The external (abbreviated E) origin was a tag designated for routes learned from other ASs through the original Exterior Gateway Protocol (EGP). This precursor to BGP was not as robust as BGP and generally provided less reliable information than the IGP within an AS. The last origin of Incomplete (abbreviated as ?) was a tag designated for all routes that did not fall into either the internal or external categories. For example, Cisco uses Incomplete when statics are redistributed into BGP and reserves the I for routes explicitly advertised by BGP with the `network` configuration command. Even though the interface is up, a static route might not have been used to reach a destination for quite some time, while other IGP routes are constantly validated by the local routing protocol.

Each of the Origin tags has a value used when transmitting the attribute to other BGP speakers. The values are 0 for internal origin (I), 1 for external origin (E), and 2 for unknown (incomplete) origin (?). A lower value is better, so routes learned internally are preferred over routes learned from EGP. EGP routes are better than incomplete routes. Cisco uses all of these values depending on the source of the BGP route. So routes advertised with the `network` BGP command have an I Origin, EGP routes from another AS get an E for Origin, and redistributed routes from any source get a ? for Incomplete (meaning "they could have come from anywhere . . . who knows?").

In contrast to Cisco, Juniper Networks routers see all possible routes as "internal" and ultimately sourced from an IGP somewhere. These internal routes all receive a BGP Origin code of Internal (I) when placed into BGP. If consistency is required, then a routing policy must be used to either change all Cisco received BGP Origin codes to I or change Juniper Networks router Origin codes to ? (2) for statics injected into BGP on routes advertised to Cisco routers.

Figure 17.2 shows the difference in Origin behavior with regard to Cisco and Juniper Networks routers.

Inside the AS, there is a redistributed route of 10.0.8.0/24. The 172.31.0.0/24 route arrives from another AS using EGP (at least on the Cisco side of the figure). These routes have been placed into BGP by a routing policy. There is a network address of 192.168.14.0/24 that has been placed into BGP with the `network` command. The lower right of each side of the figure shows the Origin attribute for each route as it is advertised to other ASs through a BGP border router.

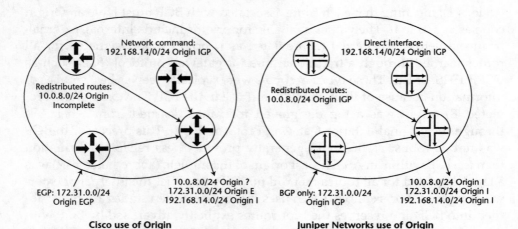

Figure 17.2   Cisco and Juniper Networks routers and BGP Origin.

It does not matter to the Juniper Networks router when these routes are advertised to another AS using EBGP. The BGP Origin code is the same for all of these routes: redistributed routes, direct, IGP, and so on. All are set to Internal. Cisco routers, on the other hand, distinguishes between these route origins, as shown in the figure. Cisco supports EGP, while Juniper Networks routers do not. Routes that arrive at an AS with EBGP with Origin codes set to I or E or ? just pass through the AS with their Origins unchanged. Oddly, the BGP RFCs are very vague about whether only routes learned from the EGP protocol itself should have an EGP Origin, or whether routes learned from *any* EGP (such as EBGP) could also have an EGP Origin.

The main point is that any routers receiving these routes with EBGP will see them coming from a Juniper Networks router with an Origin of I. Naturally, if the other router is a Cisco router, a routing policy can be written and applied on the Juniper Networks border router to make the Origin Attribute codes into the expected values for each route or type of route.

Using the Origin Attribute

The Origin attribute might seem to be too broad to be of much use in affecting inter-AS traffic between ISPs on the Internet. But there are cases where the Origin attribute can be of use, especially since many ISPs more or less ignore the possibilities of Origin affecting Inter-AS traffic and therefore leave the Origin attribute more or less alone. Consider the collection of ASs (probably individual ISPs) connected by direct links as shown in Figure 17.3. The Origin is the highest BGP route selection attribute that allows an originating AS to reach out across the Internet and influence other ASs with respect to how packets reach the originating AS.

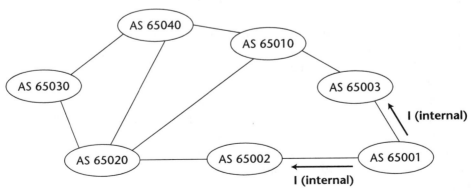

Figure 17.3   Use of the Origin attribute.

Assume that all routes originated by AS 65001 at the lower right of the figure have the BGP Origin value set to Internal. This is a good enough assumption, since most BGP routes are learned from an IGP in the first place. These routes from AS 65001 have been distributed through EBGP to the other ASs in the figure.

Consider the position of AS 65040 in the figure. How will AS 65040 send traffic to AS 65001? Should the traffic flow through AS 65030, AS 65020, or AS 65010? The order of the BGP attributes considered before the Origin attribute is Local Preference, AS Path length, and then Origin. The Local Preference set by AS 65001 is of no help here, since the Local Preference is not sent over EBGP sessions. AS 65040 might set its own value for Local Preference for the AS 65001 route, but since AS 65001 is several hops away, there is little information for AS 65040 to go on to set a realistic Local Preference for routes to AS 65001. Chances are the Local Preference for all of the routes in AS 65001 learned on all three of AS 65040's inter-AS links are the same.

Furthermore, assume that the AS Path BGP attribute accurately reflects the actual path for the route. This is not as firm an assumption as the equal-Local-Preference assumption, since many ASs routinely alter the BGP AS Path as routes leave an AS. But suppose that even if the AS Paths to AS 65001 routes have been changed by the other ASs on their way to AS 65040, the AS Paths for AS 65001 have been altered equally in terms of AS Path *length*, if not in terms of path content (usually, the more remote the AS, the more likely their AS Paths are equal in length). That is, AS 65002 could prepend its own AS number three times to the AS 65001 routes and AS 65020 could prepend its own AS Path number twice, while AS 65003 could prepend its own AS number two times to the AS 65001 routes and AS 65010 could prepend its own AS Path number three times. Once the routes get to AS 65040, the AS Paths are still the same (artificial) length.

The routers in AS 65040 see the AS 65001 routes advertised by AS 65030, AS 65020, and AS 65010. On the AS 65001 routes from AS 65020 and AS 65030, the Local Preference values and AS Path lengths are the same. (AS Path eliminates AS 65030 as a viable way to reach AS 65001 at this point.) So for both sets of AS 65001 routes, the Origin attribute is examined.

In most cases, the Origin value is the same for both sets of routes as well (I = learned through IGP). Some other method must be used to determine which path the AS 65040 routers use to reach AS 65001 destinations. The ultimate determination of how AS 65040 reaches AS 65001 is not really important. What is important is that AS 65001 has no real way to control how the AS 65040 routers reach the AS 65001 destinations, based on this value (I) of the Origin alone.

Note that AS 65040 is the only AS that cannot decide on a path to AS 65001 before the Origin is reached. The routers in AS 65030 will use AS 65020 to reach

AS 65001 routes because of the shorter AS Path through AS 65020. The routers in AS 64020 will use AS 65002 to reach the networks in AS 65001 because of a shorter AS Path as well, and AS Path length will also be the reason that AS 65010 will use AS 65003 to reach AS 65001.

Why should it matter to AS 65001 whether traffic from AS 65040 flows through AS 65002 or AS 65003? This is vitally important if one of the ISPs running the ASs is a peer or not. AS 65001 might have to pay AS 65002 for all packets that flow through it and are delivered to AS 65001. If one of the other ASs is a peer of AS 65001 and the other is not, there might be a concern that traffic flows be more balanced between the two peers. Perhaps AS 65003 is handling far too many packets outbound from AS 65001 and AS 65001 is seeking to make more inbound packets use AS 65003 than AS 65002. (The MED is not really useful here because there are two different ASs involved.)

In any case, something can be done about influencing remote traffic bound for AS 65001 by adjusting the Origin. This is shown in Figure 17.4.

By using a routing policy, AS 65001 has altered the BGP Origin code to Incomplete (?) on all routes advertised to AS 65002. Consider the effect of this routing policy on AS 65040, unable to use the AS Path to decide how to reach AS 65001.

The routers in AS 65040 will still see the AS 65001 routes advertised from both AS 65020 and AS 65010, of course. The Local Preference and AS Path lengths will still be the same for both sets of routes, so the value of the BGP Origin attribute is examined. The AS 65001 routes received by AS 65040 from AS 65010 have an Origin of Internal (0), while the AS 65001 routes received from AS 65020 have an Origin of Incomplete (2). Internal is better (lower) than Incomplete, so the routes from AS 65010 are used to reach the networks in AS 65001. By altering the Origin code, AS 65001 now has a way to influence the routing decisions in AS 65040, three ASs away.

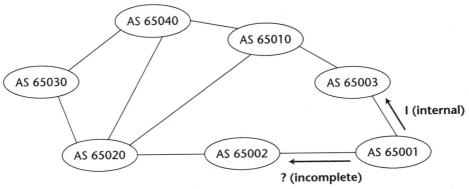

Figure 17.4 The Origin attribute and routing policy.

Notice that this involved AS 65001 making the path through AS 65020 look less desirable than the route through AS 65010, and not making the AS 65010 path look better than the Path through AS 65020. This reflects the negative bias of Origin adjustments.

Setting the BGP Origin is not equally effective for all ASs. The routers in AS 65030 will still use AS 65020 to reach the networks in AS 65001 because of the shorter AS Path length, the routers in AS 65020 will still use AS 65002 to reach the networks in AS 65001 because of shorter AS Path length, and the routers in AS 65010 will still use AS 65003 to reach the networks in AS 65001 because of a shorter AS Path length. So all of the other ASs still use AS Path length for BGP route selection to reach AS 65001. The Origin attribute is really only effective when the AS Path lengths are equal. However, the more remote an AS is from AS 65001, the more likely this is to be true.

Once the Origin attribute for a route has been set, it is always possible to change it. Naturally, only the AS that "owns" the route should set the value of the Origin attribute, but there is no read-only bit in the BGP update message that protects the value of any BGP attribute. There is nothing to stop any router from configuring a router to change the Origin attribute value. For instance, a Juniper Networks router can find all BGP routes being advertised by the router and change the Origin value from internal IGP (0) to Incomplete (2).

Routing Policies for the Origin Attribute

In this section we address the potential issue of differing types of Origin attribute values when a Juniper Networks router is linked to a Cisco router. There is no real interoperability or compatibility issue, since all Origin codes are valid. But if a Cisco router is expecting to see a ? (Incomplete) on any routes coming from a Juniper Networks route, this will not happen.

Cisco routers set the value of the BGP Origin attribute automatically, depending on the source of the route. We can change this by matching the route with a route map and using the `set origin` command.

The general form of this command is as follows:

```
set origin { igp | egp autonomous-system | incomplete }
```

So if a Cisco router is replaced with a Juniper Networks router, either router can find and set the Origin values so that the Cisco-Juniper Networks exchange of BGP information is still what is desired. This assumes, of course, that the value of the Origin attribute is even important to the other routers.

The next two sections configure Origin routing policies. In the first case, a Juniper Networks routing policy finds all BGP routes and changes their Origin codes to I (internal), presumably for advertisement to other Juniper Networks routers. Then the same is done with a Cisco route map. The section after that sets the Origin code of redistributed static routes to ? (Incomplete). Presumably this is done because the neighbor router is a Cisco router and is expecting to see this Origin for redistributed routes. Again the Cisco example follows.

There is no magic here. The example of the use of the Origin attribute to influence BGP path selection is not enormously effective. But much better ways of influencing BGP path selection are explored later in this book.

Cisco to Juniper Networks

This policy just sets all of the Origin attribute values to I as routes arrive from a Cisco router. The JUNOS software has specific keywords that are used to represent the different BGP Origin values, which are as follows:

igp = Internal (value 0)

egp = External (value 1)

incomplete = Incomplete (value 2)

Notice how one of these keywords is used to set the value of the Origin attribute in the routing policy ebgp-aggregate:

```
[policy-options policy-statement ebgp-aggregate]
lab@Earth# show
term 1 {
    from protocol bgp;
    then {
        origin igp;
        accept;
    }
```

The from protocol bgp statement is not strictly needed, since only BGP has an Origin attribute, but it is included here for clarity. This policy will most likely be applied as an import policy at the neighbor level for BGP (Cisco neighbors). However, since neighbor policies override any other import policies configured at the group or global BGP level, if there are any other actions to be taken, these must either be added policy by policy or as other terms in this policy.

To make the same type of change to the Origin on a Cisco router, this configuration fragment can be used on the redistributed routes to be sent to the Juniper Networks router. This example uses static routes:

```
!
router bgp 64999
 redistribute static route-map set-origin
 ...
!
```

```
...
route-map set-origin permit 10
 set origin igp
...
```

This changes the Origin on the routes advertised to the Juniper Networks router.

Juniper Networks to Cisco

When routes are advertised to a Cisco router, the Cisco router expects to see redistributed routes with an Origin of Incomplete (?) and only direct interfaces with the `network` command with an Origin of I (IGP, or internal). This is not the default behavior of the Juniper Networks routers, which set all BGP advertised routes to an Origin of I for IGP. This policy sets the Origin attribute on redistributed statics to Incomplete (?):

```
[policy-options policy-statement ebgp-aggregate]
lab@Earth# show
term 1 {
    from protocol static;
    then {
        origin incomplete;
        accept;
    }
```

The `from protocol static` statement is needed to find the static routes (if aggregates were used, they would have to be found as well). This policy will most likely be applied as an `export` policy at the neighbor level for BGP (Cisco neighbors). However, since neighbor policies override any other export policies configured at the group or global BGP level, if there are any other actions to be taken, these must either be added policy by policy or as other terms in this policy.

On a Cisco router receiving routes from a Juniper Networks router, the following routing policy could be used to set all of the Origins to Incomplete (?):

```
!
router bgp 64999
 ...
 neighbor 10.100.100.100 route-map set-origin in
 ...
!
...
route-map set-origin permit 10
 set origin incomplete
...
```

It would be more complex to detect and set the Origin to incomplete on some arriving routes but not on others. For instance, the network routes might be left to Origin IGP. But it can be done using the match ip address statement in the route map.

The Policy for AS 65001

In this section we examine how Juniper Networks routers create and apply a routing policy to find and change the Origin attribute for the routes to be advertised by AS 65001. As before, this policy is only needed on the border routers facing AS 65002 and AS 65003. Other routers continue to set the value of the Origin attribute as usual.

The match criteria for the routing policy are "all active BGP routes" (protocol bgp) that "currently have an Origin code of Internal" (origin igp) expressed in a from statement. The action for the policy is to change the Origin code to Incomplete. Once applied as a BGP export policy and committed, this policy starts altering the origin code for all BGP routes advertised to all BGP peers.

Here is the routing policy in full. This would be applied as an export policy to the neighbor routers in AS 65002 (if these routers are in the same EBGP group, the policy could be applied at the group level).

```
[edit policy-options]
policy-statement change-all-igps {
    term igp-to-incomplete {
        from {
            protocol bgp;
            origin igp;
        }
        then origin incomplete;
    }
}
```

As before, since neighbor policies will override any other export policies configured at the group or global BGP level, if there are any other actions to be taken, these must either be added policy by policy or as other terms in this policy.

On a Cisco router, the change would be more likely be from advertising redistributed routes with an Origin of Incomplete (?) to an Origin of Internal (I) instead of the other way around:

```
!
router bgp 65003
 redistribute static route-map set-origin
 ...
```

```
!
...
route-map set-origin permit 10
 set origin igp
...
```

This policy would be applied to the neighbors in AS 65003 instead of AS 65002, of course.

The MED Attribute

The BGP Multi-Exit Discriminator (MED) attribute is the BGP equivalent of an IGP metric. However, because BGP is an EGP, the use of this metric is different than in an IGP such as OSPF and IS-IS. An IGP metric is used to represent the total cost of the destination as computed link -by link (hop -by hop) across the AS. This is least-cost routing in action. But the IGP metrics can be a simple hop count (RIP), a link-speed weight (OSPF), or a rather arbitrary number (IS-IS). Since a single AS should be under the ultimate control at some level of a single administrator, at least in title, these IGP metrics can be changed as long as the change is consistent and understood by all of the routers in the AS.

But the same is not true for BGP. One AS has no control at all over the IGP metric system employed by another AS. Unless there is a close understanding between remote ASs (there could be), a route advertised from three ASs away with a metric of 10 remains a mystery as to the underlying system of metric computation. This number could represent 10 RIP hops, one 10-Mbps Ethernet link with default OSPF reference bandwidth metrics, or a single IS-IS link of any speed.

So BGP defined its metric (the MED) as meaningful only between two adjacent ASs connected by more than one link (multiple exits). If there is only one way to reach another AS, there is only a single exit, and the MED is interesting but not really helpful. The MED is added to routes arriving through IBGP and advertised to another AS through EBGP. The other AS circulate the MED value through IBGP to all other routers but do not pass this MED value on to any other ASs.

Even when meaningful, MEDs are often respected between a customer's AS and the service provider but are often ignored between peers ASs. Why should that be the case? Paying customers should be allowed to have some degree of influence over the routers used to send traffic to their AS. Peers, on the other hand, should remain as independent as possible with regard to choosing exit routers on their AS.

As an example, consider two ASs run by two national ISPs. They link in New York and in Las Vegas, and their customers can exchange traffic, naturally. One ISP could use the MED to make the other ISP carry an unfair amount of traffic. The following explains how.

ISP 1 ignores MEDs (MEDs are optional) but always sets MEDs on routes sent to ISP 2. Now suppose an ISP 1 customer in Las Vegas wants to connect to a Web site (or do an FTP transfer) with an ISP 2 customer in New York. ISP 1 hands off the traffic to ISP 2 in Las Vegas as soon as possible, as is normal. ISP 2 takes the packets across the country. But on the way *back*, ISP 2, being up-to-date on all the latest routing techniques, checks the MED that ISP 1 put on the route for the path back to the source in ISP 1. Not surprisingly, the preferred exit point as determined by ISP 1 for that address is Las Vegas. So instead of handing off the return packets to ISP 1 in New York, ISP 2 is stuck with the burden of carrying traffic in *both* directions across the country on their backbone.

Note that no intentional deception on the part of ISP 1 is implied. They are just doing what makes sense. The point is that either *both* peers use and respect MEDs, or both should not even bother with MEDs. Naturally, if paying customers are setting the MEDs, the ISP should respect them. But there are no real guarantees unless things are spelled out in detail.

The MED is an optional, nontransitive attribute of BGP. This means that a BGP implementation does not have to understand or use MEDs at all and that a MED is not sent through one AS and on to another AS. MEDs are only exchanged between pairs of directly connected ASs. The MED travels no further without some intervention by means of a routing policy or alternate configuration.

Unlike an IGP metric, the function of the MED is to assist a neighboring AS to pick which of multiple links connecting the remote AS to the local AS (ingress paths) should be used for traffic to a particular route (prefix). MEDs are an attempt by the local AS to influence the routing decisions in the adjacent AS for traffic *inbound* to the local AS, just as the Origin attribute. And just like Origin, MEDs are a negative bias mechanism to make some paths look worse than others. However, unlike the Origin, MEDs are really only effective when compared to the *same* destination AS (although it is possible to "always compare MEDs" even when they arrive from different ASs).

The received MED values can be used to perform some form of primitive load balancing between ASs with multiple links between them. But the use of MEDs for load balancing is neither efficient nor particularly effective compared to the more sophisticated load-balancing mechanisms available in BGP.

MED values can be set by multiple mechanisms in a router, including router configuration or IGP metrics as well as a routing policy. However, it is very common just to take MED values from the metric values in the IGP. Usually, the MED value is 0 by default.

Despite the best efforts on the part of a local AS to manipulate MEDs to influence inbound traffic flows to the local AS, other ASs can always preempt, or even ignore, the MED. This is not only because the MED is an optional BGP attribute but also because there are several other BGP attributes more important than MED in the BGP route selection process. For example, a properly altered Local Preference attribute will always override the MED.

Figure 17.5 shows a basic example in the use of the BGP MED attribute to influence inter-AS traffic flows. In the figure, AS 65001 has assigned its IP address spaces so that it can aggregate (summarize) its network into two major segments. Furthermore, AS 65001 is relatively cleanly divided into networks that are near the leftmost router (10.10.0.0/16 networks are nearby) and networks that are near the rightmost router (10.200.0.0/16 networks are nearby). Perhaps the split is between Eastern and Western operations, but there are many other alternatives.

AS 65001 has two EBGP sessions to AS 65002 and will be advertising both the 10.10.0.0/16 and the 10.200.0.0/16 networks to AS 65002 on each EBGP session, as shown in the figure. To make the most efficient use of its internal links and obtain lower delays, AS 65001 would like AS 65002 to send traffic to the closest point in the AS 65001 network. Ordinarily, AS 65001 would have no real way to convey this desire to AS 65002, and AS 65002 would simply send traffic to AS 65001 over whichever router and link AS 65002 decided to use based on its own routing policies.

But the MED offers a way for AS 65001 to try and influence the routing policy on AS 65002 for traffic sent to AS 65001. To try and accomplish this closest-point goal, AS 65001 has altered the MED values on the routes that it advertises to AS 65002 with a BGP export routing policy.

Both of the prefixes in AS 65001 are advertised across both of the links for redundancy. All things being equal, the routers in AS 65002 will still see multiple network paths to the routes in AS 65001 as the AS 65001 routes are passed along throughout AS 65002. But the AS 65002 routers will use the MED values of 110 and 120 (110 being preferred) to choose the BGP path to install in their local routing tables.

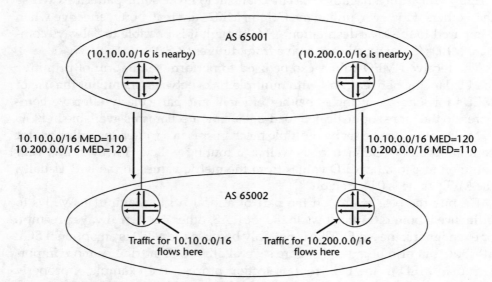

Figure 17.5 Example use of the MED attribute.

So within AS2, traffic to 10.10.0.0/16 networks flows to the leftmost router and out to AS 65001, while traffic to 10.200.0.0/16 networks flows to the rightmost router and out to AS 65001. AS65001 has influenced AS65002 and at the same time achieved a primitive type of load balancing.

This use of the MED attribute is straightforward when adjacent pairs of ASs are considered. The use of the MED attribute becomes a little more complicated when more than one AS is involved. Consider the situation in Figure 17.6.

Both AS 65002 and AS 65003 are advertising the 192.168.77.0/24 route to AS 65001 and want to influence the way that AS 65001 sends traffic to 192.168.77.0/24. All three of the advertisements have identical BGP Local Preferences, AS Path lengths and Origin codes. The other IP addresses in the figure represent the Router IDs of the three routers in New York, Phoenix, and Los Angeles.

The MED value from the AS 65002 router is the lowest (100) among the three advertisements. Yet when the router in AS 65001 chooses the BGP path to use in its local routing table, the AS 65001 router most likely chooses Los Angeles in AS 65003. Why should this be?

The problem in this scenario is that the default evaluation of the MED attribute only happens when route advertisements come from the *same* neighboring AS. In this scenario, only two of the three advertisements come from the same AS; those from Los Angeles and San Francisco. Between those two advertisements, the route from San Francisco is the best because of its lower MED. There is no choice in how to reach the New York router in AS 65002, so the MED here is more or less useless.

The route from New York in AS 65002 cannot be compared to the two routes from AS 65003, since it is from a different AS. At this point, AS 65001 is left with the Los Angeles and the New York routes as possibilities. The Los Angeles route will most likely be selected as the active path because this router has a lower BGP Router ID than New York (172.16.0.2 compared to 172.16.0.4), although other factors might be involved.

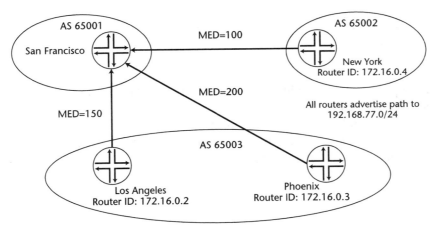

Figure 17.6 Comparing MEDs from different ASs.

There is a way around this. The routers in AS 65001 can compare the MED values for all three of these routes with the use of the "always compare MEDs" configuration statement appropriate for the vendor's configuration language. Once this is configured, the path to 192.168.77.0/24 through New York should be chosen based on the lowest MED.

When "always compare MEDs" is configured, all routes that have the shortest AS Path length are compared to each other to determine the route with the smallest MED value, not just routes from the same AS. The route with the lowest MED value is then selected as the active BGP path regardless of the AS the route came from. The lowest MED value is selected as long as other path selection values for the route, such as Local Preference, are the same.

However, you should use caution when comparing MEDs from different ASs. This is because every autonomous system in the Internet can set their own "good" and "bad" values for MEDs. So one AS may consider a MED of 150 as the best, while another AS might consider a MED of 15 to be good. To complicate matters, some AS networks may not set the MED value at all (MEDs are optional), which essentially sets the MED value to 0, and in many cases the default MED value *is* 0.

Cisco MED Routing Policy

The following is how a Cisco router would find and change the MED attribute for routes to be advertised:

```
!
router bgp 64999
 neighbor 10.100.100.100 route-map set-med out
...
route-map set-med permit 10
 match ip address 172.31.25.0 255.255.255.0
 set metric 50
route-map set-med permit 20
 match ip address 192.168.32.0 255.255.240.0
 set metric 150
...
```

This routing policy sets the MED on route 172.31.25.0/24 to 50 and the MED on route 192.168.32.0/20 to 150.

MED values can be taken from the IGP metric of the route now redistributed with BGP. To set the MED value on the routes advertised to EBGP neighbors to that of the IGP metric on the route's next hop, use:

```
metric-type internal
```

To make BGP routes always compare MEDs, you use the `bgp always-compare-med` knob.

Juniper Networks MED Routing Policy

A Juniper Networks router can use the BGP MED attribute as both a match condition and as an action in a routing policy. The `metric` statement applied to BGP is used to indicate the MED value. That is, a policy can match on a certain MED value, or it can set the MED value to a certain value as an action. Moreover, the MED value can be set not only to a specific value but manipulated mathematically ("add 100 to MED" or "subtract 50 from MED").

The example that follows shows the MED attribute being modified for certain routes. As mentioned, the `metric` statement represents the MED value. Within a policy, the metric can be set to a value, it can have its current value added to, or it can have its current value subtracted from.

```
[edit policy-options]
policy-statement change-the-MED {
    term set-med {
        from route-filter 172.31.25.0/24 exact;
        then metric 50;
    }
    term add-med {
        from route-filter 192.168.32.0/20 orlonger;
        then metric add 50;
    }
    term subtract-med {
        from route-filter 10.124.0.0/16 upto /24;
        then metric subtract 50;
    }
}
```

In this policy:

- The 172.31.25.0/24 route will have its MED set to 50.

- All routes within the 192.168.32.0/20 network will have their current MED value increased by 50.

- All routes within the 10.124.0.0/16 network with a mask shorter than /24 will have their current MED value decreased by 50. Should the current value be less than 50, the result of this policy action will be a MED value of 0.

MED values do not have to be arbitrary. In many cases, the MED values are coordinated with the metric values used by an IGP. So BGP can set the MED value on routes that are advertised based on the IGP metric leading to the BGP peer that the route was received from. For example:

```
[edit protocols bgp]
group as-100-peers {
   type external;
   peer-as 100;
   neighbor 192.168.2.2 metric-out 10;
   neighbor 192.168.3.3 metric-out igp;

   neighbor 192.168.4.4 metric-out minimum-igp;
   neighbor 192.168.5.5 metric-out igp 5;
}
```

In addition to using a policy to alter the MED values, the JUNOS software also allows you to configure a MED value for all BGP routes to an individual neighbor, group, or all peers. The configuration statement used the keyword `metric-out` and has several optional parameters.

To set the MED to a static numeric value, use the `metric-out <value>` statement. This option, setting the MED to 10, can be seen for the 192.168.2.2 peer in the preceding code.

By using the `metric-out igp` statement, you can set the MED to match the internal IGP metric to reach the IBGP that advertised the route. As the IGP metric to this BGP peer changes, the MED value associated with these routes also changes. This option can be seen on the 192.168.3.3 peer in the preceding code.

The MED will then change every time the IGP metric to the peer changes. If this is undesirable, the MED can be associated to the lowest-possible IGP metric ever known for the specific IBGP peer. The MED may decrease if the IGP metric lowers, but a network failure that increases the IGP cost will not increase the MED value. You use the `metric-out minimum-igp` command to do this. This option can be seen on the 192.168.4.4 peer in the preceding code.

Lastly, you can use the addition and subtraction functions from the policy framework in conjunction with both the `igp` and `minimum-igp` options. To alter the MED in this fashion, use the `metric-out igp <offset>` command. This option can be seen on the 192.168.5.5 peer in the preceding code, which adds 5 to the MED based on the IGP metric. To subtract 5, use -5.

MEDs and Aggregates

MED values have, by default, a limited scope of operation. For example, MEDs are not propagated through one AS and on to another AS by default (nontransitive). This limiting concept also applies when route aggregation is examined.

When a new aggregate route is created, any MED values currently assigned to any of the contributing routes remain only with those routes. The aggregate route has no MED assigned to it, which is a MED of 0. While at first this might seem to be a contradiction, since 0 is an actual MED value, the aggregate route has no method for determining which single MED value to choose, so MED = 0 is used.

There is really no alternative. Since a BGP route can have only one MED value, the aggregate would need to choose what that value should be. Should the aggregate take the worst MED value from the contributors and be conservative? Should the aggregate take the best MED value to not "penalize" that contributing route? Should the aggregate average the contributors' MED values together? None of these would adequately represent all of the contributing information, so the aggregate route takes the ultimate conservative approach: MED = 0, or no MED at all.

Figure 17.7 shows the default MED behavior regarding aggregate routes. The router receives the 172.17.1.0/24 route with a MED of 5. The router has a locally defined aggregate route that is being injected into BGP by means of a policy (the policy is not shown).

Both the aggregate route and the more specific received BGP route are advertised (unless the routing policy changes this). The 172.17.1.0/24 route maintains its MED of 5, while the aggregate route of 172.17.0.0/16 has no MED value (MED = 0) assigned. Of course, the MED on the aggregate can always be changed with a routing policy, but this lack of an aggregate MED value is the default behavior.

So it is ironic that MEDs, which are most useful between AS pairs, are all but useless by default on aggregates, which are exactly the types of routes that are most often sent between AS pairs.

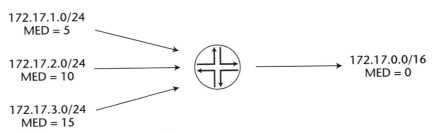

172.17.1.0/24
MED = 5

172.17.2.0/24
MED = 10

172.17.3.0/24
MED = 15

172.17.0.0/16
MED = 0

Figure 17.7   Aggregates and the MED.

AS Path and Local Preference

When BGP attributes are used for BGP route selection to decide the active route to a destination address space, the AS Path and the Local Preference are the twin giants. As important as the MED and Origin attributes are, the two attributes discussed in this chapter overshadow them both. The two attributes, AS Path and Local Preference, can even work together, although Local Preference has the highest priority when BGP routes are chosen. This is because the AS Path remains the same within an AS and changes between ASs, while the Local Preference rules absolutely within the AS but is not sent to another AS at all (it is, after all, the *local* preference).

The AS Path BGP attribute is used as a method of loop prevention among the ASs that make up the Internet. A border router that receives an EBGP route advertisement with its own AS number in the AS Path attribute field rejects the route immediately. No AS should ever have to loop a packet through the Internet to reach a destination. The presence of one's own AS number in a received BGP route is always an error condition.

Oddly enough, this happens all the time. A border router commonly sees its own AS number in the AS Path, and these routes are simply dropped. But EBGP has no concept at all of split horizon, as described in this book with regard to RIP. An IGP's split horizon rule prevents the router from advertising routes back out the interface that they were received on to prevent routing loops. EBGP sessions lack this feature, so border routers frequently just bounce active routes right back to the source AS with the source AS on the path. It would be hard for a router to screen a long AS Path list for every route sent to every AS anyway. This way, each AS watches out for itself and EBGP needs no split horizon rule.

As an aside, IBGP does not need a split horizon rule, since IBGP routers do not flood information from one interface out another (so an IBGP mesh is needed). Some form of split horizon is needed for EBGP-to-IBGP advertisements, however, as we see the section *The Local Preference Attribute* later in this chapter.

In any case, the whole point of the AS Path attribute is that this attribute carries the entire history of a route from the adjacent AS that advertises the route with EBGP right back to the AS that first injected the route into BGP. So an AS Path associated with a route such as 192.168.46.0/24 received at a border router in AS 65222 might look like this:

```
64555 65001 64768 I
```

What this means to the router in AS 65222 is "if you send me a packet to a destination within the IP address space 192.168.47.0/24, I will send it through AS 64555, which is my own AS, then on to AS 65001, which will pass it to AS 64768, where the packet will be delivered internally by the IGP in AS 64768." By convention, the AS Path list is read from left to right and ends with the Origin code for the route, so it possible to also see AS Paths like this:

```
65414 65341 ?
```

However, the I for IGP is so common that some network administrators seem to think that the appearance of the ? indicates some kind of error or path-unknown situation. It is even possible to see the same AS number more than once along the AS Path:

```
64599 65001 65777 65777 65777 64567 I
```

The reasons for prepending an AS number more than once to a route have been mentioned several times already in this book. Prepending is an attempt for an AS to make itself look very unattractive as a transit AS to all other ASs downstream from the AS. All of the implications of AS Path prepending are discussed in this chapter.

The Local Preference attribute should not be confused with a routing protocol preference, or any other use of the term *preference* on the router. Just as the BGP Next Hop is for use of BGP alone, the BGP Local Preference only applies to BGP.

In this chapter we first consider the use and setting of the AS Path first and then Local Preference. The AS Path section is complicated by the fact that routing policies applied to AS Paths can use UNIX-like regular expressions (REs or regex) to find just the right AS. Both Cisco and Juniper Networks routers employ REs for this purpose, but with differences. All of those differences are discussed in this chapter.

The AS Path Attribute

The BGP AS Path attribute contains the information that all BGP routers use to find a route back to a route's source. As a route passes through each AS, the BGP routers add path information in the form of their AS number to this attribute. This AS number is *prepended*, or added at the beginning of the AS Path attribute. So each AS basically counts as a single hop from the perspective of the BGP AS Path attribute.

By default, the total amount of information in the AS Path attribute gives each router the entire list of AS numbers (the path) that the user data must pass through to reach a particular destination. Note that when the AS Path is changed beyond the mandated modification by a routing policy, the AS Path information in the BGP AS Path attribute can be added to, but a existing individual AS number should never actually be changed or deleted, unless it is a private AS number. The basic idea behind the AS Path is shown in Figure 18.1.

The AS Path attribute can be used as a single object, or the string of AS numbers can be parsed by a router (using some form of UNIX-based regular expression) to find specific AS information. For example, a router creates a policy that does something like "find all of the routes that have passed through AS 64999" or "find all routes that have just come from AS 65001." There can be even more complex examples.

In the figure, AS 65222 is originating the route 192.168.77.0/24. AS 65222 advertises that route to both AS 64777 and AS 65001. In turn, each of those AS systems advertises the same route to AS 64678. The BGP routers in AS 64678 see this route as having two possible paths through the Internet, as shown in the figure. The routers can use the AS Path attribute to determine the shortest path back to the route's source. (In this simple example, the paths are of equal length, but this will not always be the case.)

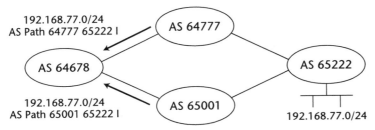

Figure 18.1   The use of the AS Path attribute.

When the AS Path attribute is changed through prepending before the route is readvertised to other BGP routers, this can make a route through the local AS look *less* attractive to another AS. Note that it should not really be possible to make the route more attractive by *shortening* the AS Path. But the path can be lengthened to make the AS Path attribute another type of negative bias path selection mechanism in the sense that "unlengthened" paths will look more attractive for other AS networks to use than artificially lengthened AS Paths.

The only standard way to alter the AS Path attribute is to add information to it by prepending. BGP routers, according to the RFC, are *not* allowed to remove or change information from or in the AS Path attribute. But a routing policy can be used to artificially extend (by prepending) AS information onto an existing AS Path. This type of a policy is often to attempt to influence traffic coming *into* an AS from another AS. In this respect, AS Path is similar in function to MED.

But since the AS Path is higher in the BGP route selection process than MED or Origin attribute, changing the AS Path can make a huge difference in the chain of ASs used to reach a particular destination. Although AS Path still ranks behind the Local Preference in the BGP route selection process, the Local Preference is for IBGP only and never sent between EBGP peers. So when it comes to one AS trying to influence other AS's behaviors, AS Path is essentially the best mechanism to use.

Consider the same network of ASs used in the previous chapter to discuss the BGP Origin attribute. But this example explores the use of the AS Path to influence the ASs used to reach AS 65001. The network is shown in Figure 18.2.

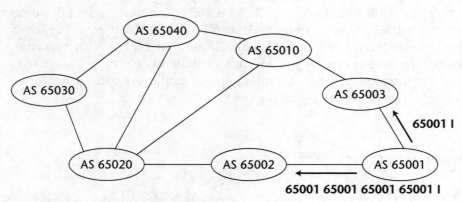

Figure 18.2 Use of the AS Path attribute.

In Figure 18.2 , AS 65001 is announcing its routes to both AS 65002 and AS 65003. Using a routing policy, AS 65001 is prepending its own AS number an extra three times (shown as 65001 65001 65001 65001 in the figure) onto all route announcements to AS 65002. But the routes announced to AS 65003 have the basic 65001 AS Path on the announced routes. This causes the following to occur:

- AS 65002 will use AS 65020 to forward packets to AS 65001.
- AS 65010 will use AS 65003 to forward packets to AS 65001.
- AS 65020 will use AS 65010 to forward packets to AS 65001.
- AS 65030 will use AS 65040 to forward packets to AS 65001.
- AS 65040 will use AS 65010 to forward packets to AS 65001.

All of this is caused by the increased AS Path to reach AS 65001 through AS 65002. The behavior on the part of AS 65002 (using AS 65020 instead of sending directly to AS 65001) is unexpected and would not occur without the routing policy. This behavior is extended to AS 65020 as well, since AS 65002 cannot shorten the AS Path advertised by AS 65001 even if AS 65002 would like to. Increased AS Paths are sticky and changing the AS Path is popular for this very reason.

Removing Private AS Numbers

The BGP RFC prohibits removing information from the AS Path attribute. Despite the wording in the BGP RFC, many vendors have included configuration options in their BGP implementations to actually remove information from the AS Path, which is technically not allowed. This removal, however, only operates on specific information in the AS Path attribute and does not apply to making arbitrary changes to the actual AS Path. Typically, the information removed was placed there by the AS itself or by other routers within the administrative control of the AS. So it is not a question of one AS trampling on the path information another AS has put into the AS Path.

One example of this type of configuration option is the `remove-private` configuration statement. This keyword allows an ISP to remove private AS numbers from paths received from BGP customers when those customers are using private AS numbers. Since the customers are effectively within the administrative scope of the ISP, the provider is allowed to remove the private AS numbers from the path. This is shown in Figure 18.3 with the changed AS numbers.

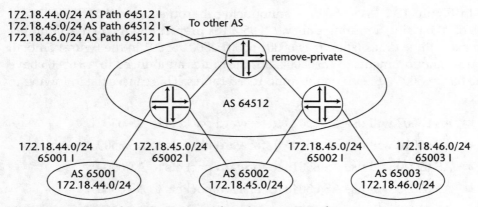

172.18.44.0/24 AS Path 64512 I
172.18.45.0/24 AS Path 64512 I
172.18.46.0/24 AS Path 64512 I

Figure 18.3 Removing private AS numbers from an AS Path.

In the figure, AS 64512 connects to three different customers using BGP. The customers are using private AS 65001, AS 65002, and AS 65003 for the BGP peer communications. Within AS 64512 (also private, but used here for consistency throughout the book), each of the BGP routers see the private AS numbers within the path.

The `remove-private` option is enabled on the edge router in AS 64512 that faces the Internet or other EBGP peers. As the routes from the customer AS systems are advertised from AS 64512, the private AS numbers are removed from the AS Path attribute. In this case, all customer networks are seen to have originated within AS 64512. This is fine, since no one need know what AS numbers AS 64512's customers are using, and, much more importantly, private AS numbers are not unique and might be used by any number of other ASs on the Internet.

Another option for removing AS Path information is when one AS is merged into another, usually through a merger of the ISPs running the ASs. This example assumes all of the AS numbers are really public AS numbers, not private AS numbers as they ordinarily would be. So suppose AS 65412 with two customers, AS 65417 and 65418, merges with an ISP using AS 64777. This situation and the final result are shown in Figure 18.4.

Now suppose the resulting merged organization decides to use AS 64777 as the official AS to represent both AS 65412 and AS 64777 on the Internet (as in most cases, this is more of an acquisition than a merger). To ease in the migration of the customer BGP configurations from AS 65412 to AS 64777, the edge routers can use an option to set the local AS to 65412.

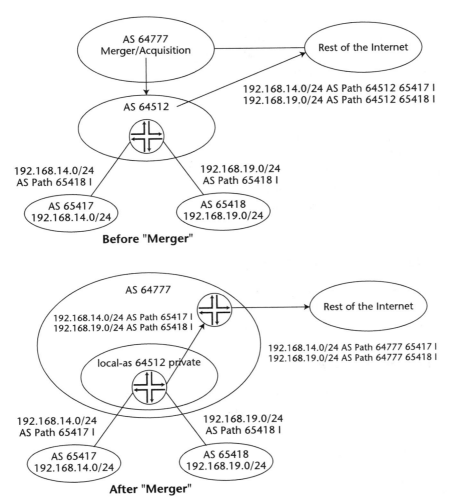

Figure 18.4 Making a merged AS disappear.

The effect of this option is that the customer routes within AS 64777 see *both* AS 65412 and the customer AS numbers (AS 65417 and AS 65418). But as AS 64777 advertises those routes to the Internet, it prepends its own value of AS 64777 onto each of the routes, retaining the "private" AS 64512 on the path, as 192.168.14.0/24 AS Path 64777 64512 65417 I, for example. (This is not shown in the figure.)

The point is that even though AS 64512 has been merged into AS 64777, AS 64512 still shows up on the paths sent to the Internet. So far, this is still just prepending AS numbers to the BGP AS Path attribute. How does AS Path information get *removed*?

In many routers' BGP implementations, an optional parameter can be used that actually does remove AS Path information from the BGP AS Path attribute. This optional parameter restricts knowledge of AS 65412 to the edge router connected to the customer (AS 65417 and AS 65418) only.

In the lower part of the figure, the edge router in the formerly independent AS 64512 is configured with the option to remove AS 65412 as a *private* AS, even if it is not. As the customer routes are advertised into AS 64777 by the edge router facing the customers, AS 65412 information is removed from the AS Path attribute, as shown in the lower part of the figure. At this point the AS 64777 routers, as well as the Internet, have no knowledge of AS 64512.

Again, this AS Path removal applies to a type of special case and should not be used to arbitrarily attempt to change AS Path information received from another AS.

Routing Policy for the AS Path

All router vendors use some form of an AS Path prepend policy to extend the number of values in the AS Path attribute. This section shows a Cisco router example first, and then a Juniper Networks router example.

The Cisco AS Path Routing Policy

Here is how a Cisco router would create and apply the routing policy used by AS 65001 in the example network in this chapter:

```
!
autonomous-system 64999
!
router bgp 64999
 redistribute static
 neighbor 10.100.100.100 remote-as 64555
 neighbor 10.100.100.100 route-map Longer-AS-Path out
 no auto-summary
!
...
!
route-map Longer-AS-Path permit 10
 set as-path prepend 65001 65001 65001
...
```

A route map called Longer-AS-Path has been created on the AS 65001 router. The set action taken on all of the routes will be to add AS 65001 to each route three times. This is done with the set as-path prepend statement.

This routing policy then is applied for routes exported by BGP to the external BGP peer in AS 65002. Note that the router also adds a fourth 65001 to the AS Path as part of its normal route advertisement process.

The Juniper Networks AS Path Routing Policy

Here is how a Juniper Networks router would create and apply the routing policy used by AS 65001 in the example network in this chapter.

```
[edit routing-options]
autonomous-system 65001;



[edit protocols]
bgp {
    group peer-AS65002 {
        type external;
        export longer-as-path;
        peer-as 65002;
        neighbor 10.0.2.2;
    }
}

[edit policy-options]
policy-statement longer-as-path {
    then as-path-prepend "65001 65001 65001";
}
```

A policy called `longer-as-path` has been created on the AS 65001 router. Since there is no `from` statement, all candidate routes will match the policy. The action taken on all of the matched routes will be to add AS 65001 to each route three times. This is done with the `as-path-prepend` statement.

This routing policy then is applied for routes exported by BGP to the external BGP peer in AS 65002. Note that the router also adds a fourth 65001 to the AS Path as part of its normal route advertisement process.

AS Path Regular Expressions

In many cases, it is useful for a network administrator to create BGP routing policies that require route announcements or prefixes be found and acted on based on the information contained within the AS Path attribute. This might be required to enforce some administrative policy regarding other AS networks, peer or customer. Sometimes it is just easier to find routes based on some aspect of their AS Path than by looking for many specific prefixes and routes (or entire AS Paths) individually.

The following are some examples of the types of information that need to be found in the AS Path attribute:

- All routes that originated from a specific AS
- All routes that have transited a specific AS
- All routes that were announced by a specific neighbor AS
- All of the routes that have originated from within the local AS

This type of information can be found quite easily in the AS Path attribute through the use some form of *regular expression*.

A regular expression (often seen as Regex or RE) is a powerful *pattern-matching* tool that can be applied in a routing policy to act on AS Path strings. Widely used on all UNIX-based systems, this pattern-matching engine can find specific strings of text or textual patterns.

When used in a routing policy, regular expressions work not only on fixed strings like wildcard operators such as *, but they act on variable patterns of text. This is done through the combination of basic text patterns and special operators. This combination of basic text patterns and special operators are what make up the regular expression itself. Regular expressions allow information in a string to be found within a specific context, not just in isolated instances. The use of regular expressions in conjunction with the BGP AS Path attribute can be used to match routes within a policy based on their AS Path values.

In general, the regular expressions used by router vendors, just as all regular expressions, have two main components to them: the term and the operator. These take the form `term<operator>`.

The regular expression *term* is the basic matching component to be found by the pattern-matching engine. The term is a mandatory object, and each regular expression must have at least one term. When used with an AS Path, terms identify the AS number. This AS could be a single number (65001), a complete AS Path (65001 64777 64222), or a wildcard character (the dot, or .) representing any single AS number (65001 . 64222).

Use of the term is mandatory. However, the regular expression *<operator>* is an optional component of the pattern-matching engine. An operator can be associated with a single regular expression term. If used, the operator appears immediately after the term it is operating on.

Two special regular expression operators can appear between regular expression terms. Those special characters are the pipe (|) and the dash (-). The pipe operator is used between terms to indicate OR ("65001 OR 64555" is "65001 | 64555"). The dash operator is used between terms to indicate range ("65001 through 65333" is "65001-65333"). An individual regular expression can contain multiple term-operator pairs.

The Null AS Path

The concept of the Null AS Path is quite important for the Internet. Routes that have been originated within a particular AS have yet to prepend any value for the BGP AS Path attribute. Therefore, there is no information contained in the AS Path attribute for routes originating within the AS, and the AS Path is assumed to be null (empty).

So how are routes originating within the AS that have been advertised with BGP to be found with a routing policy using an `as-path` policy? By creating a match condition based on the Null AS Path.

The Null AS Path can be used to find routes advertised by BGP that originated within the local AS. When would this be helpful? Usually when one AS does not want to carry transit traffic for another AS. Remember, just because an AS happens to be the peer for two (or more) other ASs, this does not mean that the AS in the middle is available for transit between other ASs.

Consider the collection of ASs shown in Figure 18.5. The Null AS Path can be used to halt BGP transit traffic from AS 65001 through AS 65002.

In this case, for whatever reason, AS 65002 does not want to readvertise the routes from AS 65001 to AS 65004. That could lead to the possibility that AS 65004 would route traffic for AS 65001 through AS 65002. However, AS 65002 still has to advertise its own routes to AS 65004 so that these prefixes are reachable by the peer AS.

So AS 65002 defines a BGP export policy toward AS 65004 that rejects all routes except those with a Null AS Path. The use of the Null AS Path requires the use of *regular expressions* applied to the AS Path. We follow this section with an investigation of the use of Cisco and Juniper Networks routers regular expression syntax for AS Paths.

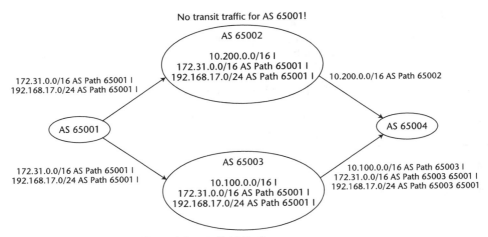

Figure 18.5 Transit traffic and the Null AS Path.

Cisco AS Path Regular Expressions

Cisco routers implement a full, UNIX-based (a version called POSIX) implementation of regular expressions for AS Paths. These expressions can be used to find particular AS Path patterns in a show command and greatly reduce the amount of information presented. Or the regular expressions can be used in the routing policies themselves to find the precise AS Path pattern of interest. The same syntax is used for BGP Community pattern matching (this is not true of Juniper Networks routers, which employ slightly different syntax for AS Paths and Communities).

Cisco routers employ the special characters (also often called *metacharacters*) listed in Table 18.1 for regular expressions, whatever their use.

Examples are always the best way to understand the use of these special characters. Table 18.2 shows some common examples of the use of these special characters for AS Path pattern matching.

Table 18.1 Cisco Regular Expression Special Characters

CHARACTER	MEANING
. (dot)	Match any single character, including white space.
*	Match zero or more sequences (instances) of the pattern.
+	Match one or more sequences (instances) of the pattern.
?	Match zero or one occurrence of the pattern.
^ (caret)	Match the beginning of the string.
$ (dollar sign)	Match the end of the string.
- (hyphen)	Match a range of literal values.
_ (underscore)	Match comma [,] , left brace [{], right brace [}], left parenthesis [(], right parenthesis [)], beginning of a string, end of a string, or a space.
{}	Match any of the AS number within the braces.
()	Match the confederation peer within the parentheses.
[]	Match any character within the brackets.

Table 18.2 Regular Expressions for Use with the AS Path

REGULAR EXPRESSION	AS PATHS MATCHED
^$	Routes originating in this AS (Null AS Path).
^65001_	All routes that came directly from AS 65001 (start of AS Path).
^65002$	All routes that originated in AS 65002 and came directly here.
_65003_	All routes that passed through AS 65003 at some point.
{65001 65002}	Used in the as-set aggregate option. Finds routes from AS 65001 and AS 65002.
(64555)	Used to find confederation peer. This peer is in sub-AS 64555.

Cisco AS Path regular expressions are most often used in special AS Path access lists. As already mentioned, the syntax is ip as-path access-list and identifies the AS numbers that the router is interested in. The AS Path access list is then applied to a BGP neighbor by the neighbor filter-list command. Route maps can also be used, but this initial example uses a filter list.

Suppose AS 64999, which sits between AS 64777 and AS 64555 (as in the example BGP network used in this book), does not want to pass along any BGP routes (NLRIs) from AS 64777 to AS 64555. There are a number of reasons to do this, most simply because AS 64999 does not want to be a transit AS to AS 64777. What AS 64555 does not see, it cannot use.

In the example BGP network, it is the Earth router that borders on AS 64555. What is needed is a way to find and suppress (deny) advertisements to AS 64555 if the AS Path on the route contains AS 64777. All other routes can be advertised. This could always be done by a series of route maps to find specific IP addresses, but this method does not care what addresses came through AS 64777, only the AS Path on the route. Earth is a good place to do this, because there might be many other border routers accepting routes from other ASs with AS 64777 on the path.

The following is what the configuration on Cisco_Earth would look like to accomplish this:

```
hostname Cisco_Earth
...
!
router bgp 64999
 redistribute static
 neighbor 10.100.100.100 remote-as 64555
 neighbor 10.100.100.100 filter-list 1 out
 no auto-summary
!
...
ip as-path access-list 1 deny _65777_
ip as-path access-list 1 permit .*
...
```

The first line in the access list finds all BGP routes that have AS 65777 anywhere in their AS Path attribute field and denies their advertisement. The use of the special characters makes the match specific. For example, if the expression used were just deny 77, the expression would match 77, 777, 64777, and any other combinations of 77 in the AS Path. The second line permits (advertises) all other NLRIs.

A route map could have been used to accomplish the same goal. In this case, the same ip as-path access-list could have been invoked by this configuration, although the way to the access list is more indirect than when the filter-list is used:

```
hostname Cisco_Earth
...
!
router bgp 64999
 redistribute static
 neighbor 10.100.100.100 remote-as 64555
 neighbor 10.100.100.100 route-map No-AS64777 out
 no auto-summary
!
...
ip as-path access-list 1 deny _65777_
ip as-path access-list 1 permit .*
...
!
route-map No-AS64777 permit 10
 match as-path 1
...
```

The basics for AS Path regular expression pattern matching can be extended in many ways. Here are just a few examples:

```
ip as-path access-list 30 permit 22
ip as-path access-list 31 permit ^65001$
ip as-path access-list 32 permit _65001_
ip as-path access-list 33 permit ^$
ip as-path access-list 34 permit ^6500[0123789]$
ip as-path access-list 30 permit ^6500[^4-6]$
ip as-path access-list 30 permit _6500.$
ip as-path access-list 30 permit ^(65001 | 65002 | 65003)$
ip as-path access-list 30 permit ^(65001)?$
ip as-path access-list 30 permit ^(65005)*$
ip as-path access-list 30 permit ^(65005)+$
ip as-path access-list 30 permit ^65001_65002$
ip as-path access-list 30 permit _65001_65002$
```

where

22   Matches any AS Path that contains the digits 22 anywhere. So 65022 matches, 64522, 65222, and so on.

^65001$ Matches only an AS Path of 65001. There can be no other ASs in the AS Path.

_65001_   Matches AS 65001 if it occurs anywhere in the AS Path attribute.

^$ Matches internal routes (Null AS Path) only. These routes originate in this AS.

^6500[0123789]$ Matches AS numbers 65000, 65001, 65002, 65003, 65007, 65008, and 65009 only. Only one AS number can be in the AS Path, but it must be one of these.

^6500[^4-6]$ Matches every AS starting with 6500 and having a last digit that is "not 4 through 6." Only one AS number can be in the AS Path. This expression is the same as the previous one.

_6500.$ Matches every AS number that is in the range 65000 through 65009 anywhere in the AS Path.

^(65001 | 65002 | 65003)$ Matches a single AS Path number, and the AS number must be either 65001, 65002, or 65003.

^(65001)?$ Matches the Null AS Path or an AS Path with only 65001.

^(65005)*$ Matches the Null AS Path and any number of repeated 65005 AS numbers. No numbers beside AS 65005 can be in the AS Path.

^(65005)+$ Matches the same as the previous expression, except for the Null AS Path.

^65001_65002$ Matches AS Path 65001 65002 only.

_65001_65002$ Matches the AS Path pair 65001 65002 appearing anywhere in the AS Path.

More elaborate examples could be constructed, but this is a good sampling. The more complex the regular expression, the more likely it is that there will be patterns that should match but do not, or patterns that do match but should not. It is always best to keep things simple.

Finally, to close this section on Cisco AS Path regular expressions, the following is an example of Null AS Path in action, based on the Null AS Path example introduced previously:

```
!
router bgp 65002
 redistribute static
 neighbor 10.100.100.100 remote-as 65004
 neighbor 10.100.100.100 filter-list 1 out
 no auto-summary
!
...
ip as-path access-list 1 permit ^$
...
```

The same thing could have been done with a route map, of course. The routing policy is applied as a filter list toward an EBGP peer. The policy has an access list that matches on BGP routes with an as-path regular expression of ^&, which is the Null AS Path. All other routes are rejected by the fact that all access lists have an implicit "deny all" term at their end.

Juniper Networks AS Path Regular Expressions

Within the JUNOS software implementation of the AS Path regular expression syntax, unlike the Cisco implementation, the term is a complete AS value. The wildcard character of the dot (.) can be used to represent a single AS number as well. This means that an AS number of 65001, for example, is seen by the JUNOS software not as the five character text string of 6, 5, 0, 0, 1, but as the single *entity* of 65001. To the JUNOS software, AS numbers are not sequences of characters, but a single *integer*.

Table 18.3 shows a subset of the possible regular expression operators that can be used with routing policies on a Juniper Networks router. Some operators are a kind of shorthand for their longer equivalents.

Table 18.3   Juniper Networks AS Path Regular Expressions

SPECIAL CHARACTERS	MEANING
{m,n}	Match at least *m* and at most *n* repetitions of the term.
{m}	Match exactly *m* repetitions of the term.
{m,}	Match *m* or more repetitions of the term.
. (dot)	Match any single instance of any term.
*	Match zero or more repetitions of the term.
+	Match one or more repetitions of the term (same as {0,}).
?	Match zero or one repetitions of the term (same as {1,}).
|	Match one of the terms on either side of the pipe.
- (hyphen)	Used to represent a range.
(...), ()	Used to group terms, or indicate the Null AS Path with an enclosed space: ( ).

Of special note is the use of the parentheses. Typically, the (...) operator is used to group multiple terms together in conjunction with an operator. For example, the regular expression of "(65001 | 65002)?" is translated as "either AS 65001 or AS 65002 can be present in the AS Path zero (absent) or at most one time" (this is what the ? operator means).

The parenthesis operator has another special use. When used with no spaces in between, parentheses represent the Null AS Path value. Table 18.4 shows some examples of regular expression AS Path pattern matching on a Juniper Networks router.

The table shows some examples of regular expression pattern matching as applied to AS Paths. The second column shows the regular expression used, along with examples of values of the BGP AS Path attribute that the regular expression will match. In some cases the list is not exhaustive, so there are more AS Paths that will match the pattern than listed.

Table 18.5 shows a few more-complicated examples. Now the first column shows the pattern to be matched, the second column shows the regular expression to find the pattern, and the last column shows some examples.

Table 18.4 Regular Expressions for Use with the AS Path

REGULAR EXPRESSION	AS PATHS MATCHED
65001	Exactly one instance, which must be 65001, in the AS Path.
65001*	Matches 65001, 65001 65001, and so on, or the Null AS Path (0 or more).
65001+	Matches 65001 or Null AS Path (0 or 1).
65001{1,3}	Matches AS Paths 65001, 65001 65001, or 65001 65001 65001.
"65001{1,3} 65002"	Matches one to three instances of 65001 followed by one instance of 65002.
"65001-65004"	Matches 65001 or 65002 or 65003 or 65004.

Table 18.5 Regular Expression Examples

PATTERN TO MATCH	REGULAR EXPRESSION	EXAMPLE MATCHES (NOT EXHAUSTIVE)
Second AS *must* be 65002 or 65003	". (65002 | 65003)"	65001 65002, 65002 65003, 65002 65002, etc.
Second AS *might* be 65002 or 65003	". (65002 | 65003)?"	65001, 65001 65002, 65003 65003, etc.
All paths from neighbor 65005 followed by *one* AS	"65005 ."	65005 65001, 65005 65003, 65005 65005, etc.
65001 followed by 65002, then etc.	"65001 65002 65003+"	65001 65002 65003, 65001 65002 65003 65003, one or more 65003
Any path containing 65007 anywhere	".* 65007 .*"	65001 65007 65002, 65007, 65002 65007, etc.

The whole point in this regular expression exercise is that AS Path regular expressions can be used as the match criteria within a routing policy. This application of the regular expression is similar in concept to the application of a policy. As such, AS Path regular expressions follow the JUNOS software abstraction concept of first defining the entity and then applying the entity.

A regular expression is used with an AS Path in the `policy-options` section of the Juniper Networks router configuration hierarchy. The general syntax is as follows:

```
[edit policy-options]
user@host# set as-path name regular-expression
```

Both the definition and application of the AS_Path regular expressions occurs within the `policy-options` configuration hierarchy. The regular expression in proper `term<operator>` format is given a name with the `as-path` statement.

That regular expression name can then be referenced within a policy. The name can be up to 255 characters long and can even include spaces, as long as the name is enclosed in double quotation marks. In practice, this is rarely done.

Once defined, the AS Path regular expression can be applied as a policy match condition. For example:

```
[edit policy-options]
as-path digits-route "65234 65156 65178 65009"

policy-statement from-digits-route {
    term A {
        from as-path digits-route;
        then accept;
    }
    term reject-others {
        then reject;
    }
}

[edit protocols]
bgp {
    import from-digits-route;
...
}
```

The example shows an AS Path regular expression being used as a policy match condition. The goal is to have a BGP routing policy that accepts only routes with the exact AS Path of 65234 65156 65178 65009.

An `as-path` called `digits-route` has been defined within the double quotation marks. The `as-path` contains only *terms* (no *operators*) and defines an exact AS Path match of "65234 65156 65178 65009".

The `digits-route` path definition is then used within the `from-digits-route` policy to match routes and accept them. A second term in the policy rejects all other routes. When this policy is applied as an import BGP policy, only routes matching the AS Path defined in `digits-route` are. All other routes seen by BGP are rejected.

The following is more complex routing policy example using varying definitions for the `as-path`:

```
policy-statement testing-as-paths {
    term as-paths {
        from as-path testing-1-2-3;
        then accept;
    }
    then reject;
}
```

When applied as an import policy for BGP, will the router accept a route with the path "65024 65044 65044 64685," given the following as-path statements?

```
set as-path testing-1-2-3 ".* 65024"
set as-path testing-1-2-3 "65024 .*"
set as-path testing-1-2-3 ".* 65024 .*"
set as-path testing-1-2-3 ".* 65044{1,2} .*"
set as-path testing-1-2-3 "64685 65044{1,3} 65024"
set as-path testing-1-2-3 "65024 65044{1,3} 64685"
```

Using the different `as-path` definitions in order within the `testing-as-paths` policy gives the following results:

".* 65024" Starts with any AS zero or more times, followed by 65024. The route will not match the term `as-paths`. This definition does not allow for AS numbers after 65024. Therefore, it will be *rejected* by the final action.

"65024 .*" Starts with 65024, followed by zero or more AS numbers. The route does match the term `as-paths`. It will be *accepted*.

".* 65024 .*" Starts with any AS zero or more times, followed by 65024, followed by zero or more AS numbers. The route does match the term `as-paths`. It will be *accepted*.

".* 65044{1,2} .*" Starts with any AS zero or more times, followed by 65044 once or twice, followed by zero or more AS numbers. The route does match the term `as-paths`. It will be *accepted*.

"64685 65044{1,3} 65024" Start with AS 64685, followed by 65044 one to three times, followed by 65024. The route will not match the term `as-paths`. Therefore, it will be *rejected* by the final action.

"64024 65044{1,3} 64685" Start with AS 64024, followed by 65044 one to three times, followed by 64685. The route does match the term `as-paths`. It will be *accepted*.

Finally, to close this section on Juniper Networks AS Path regular expressions, here is an example of Null AS Path in action, also based on the earlier example:

```
policy-options {
    policy-statement not-a-transit {
        term accept-my-as {
            from {
                protocol bgp;
                as-path my-own-as;
            }
            then accept;
        }
        term reject-all-else {
            then reject;
        }
    }
}
as-path my-own-as "()";
...
```

The `not-a-transit` policy is applied as an export policy towards an EBGP peer in AS 65004. The policy has a term called `accept-my-as` that matches on BGP routes with an `as-path` regular expression of `"()"`. All other routes are rejected by the `reject-all-else` term.

The Local Preference Attribute

The BGP attribute of Local Preference is the highest tiebreaker in the standard BGP path selection process. If a BGP Next Hop is found to be reachable, and there are multiple routes known to BGP, the route with the highest Local Preference is always chosen. So Local Preference is the first BGP attribute that is used to favor one path over another.

Because of the position of the BGP Local Preference attribute, it does not matter what the AS Path length is for the route, or the Origin code, or the MED. The route with the highest Local Preference value will always be chosen as the exit point of the AS at the end.

By default, the Local Preference value is transmitted between all IBGP peers in an AS. The default Local Preference value is usually 100, but there are advantages to using and setting Local Preference values within an AS. Local Preference is used primarily as a method for defining the *exit point* outbound from the AS. Since the Local Preference value is evaluated first during the path selection process, the Local Preference will override the values set in any other BGP attributes.

For example, a route with an AS Path length of five AS numbers and a Local Preference value of 200 will be chosen over a route with an AS Path length of two AS numbers and a Local Preference value of 100. In fact, no matter how the AS Path is manipulated, the Local Preference will always override the AS Path.

Local Preference is unique in many respects as a BGP attribute. The AS Path and many other BGP attributes such as Origin or MED, in many cases, form what are known as *negative bias* path selection mechanisms. This means that these attributes function mainly by making some routes look worse than others. In contrast, Local Preference is a *positive bias* path selection mechanism. That is, there is a default value and a maximum value to assign, and there is no question about how desirable the route looks. The route with the highest Local Preference is always chosen, period.

The Local Preference of a route is always distributed to all IBGP peers within an AS. The Local Preference value can be changed by any router by means of a routing policy.

Using Local Preference to try and influence BGP path selection does have some drawbacks. The biggest is that it is *local* to the AS. The Local Preference value is distributed to IBGP peers, but only to IBGP peers inside the AS.

The Local Preference, being local, does not get transmitted to adjacent neighbors with EBGP. The Local Preference attribute is well known (all BGP implementations must understand Local Preference), but *discretionary*. Discretionary BGP attributes are only used and understood by one BGP configuration or another (for instance, IBGP or EBGP, but not both). Local Preference applies to IBGP. So while Local Preference is very effective at controlling routing decisions within the AS, Local Preference does not assist in affecting routing decisions in other networks. How other AS systems handle the route is still up to them.

To influence traffic *inbound* to an AS from other ASs, other BGP attributes of AS Path, Origin, and MED must be used. Local Preference is used to influence *outbound* AS traffic. The values of the Local Preference BGP attribute is exchanged by IBGP peers only. EBGP peers never see a Local Preference set on route information sent between AS networks.

The Local Preference is typically used to set the preferred *exit point* for a particular route from an AS. This can be important when there are several links between two ASs. Once the Local Preference for a route is set, IBGP propagates that information throughout the entire AS. The basic use of Local Preference is shown in Figure 18.6.

The figure shows the concept of how Local Preference affects traffic leaving an AS. The administrators of AS 65001 on the left have knowledge that Router B should always be used to reach the 172.17.2.0/24 network in AS 65002 on the right. Therefore, the administrators of AS 65001 can configure their border

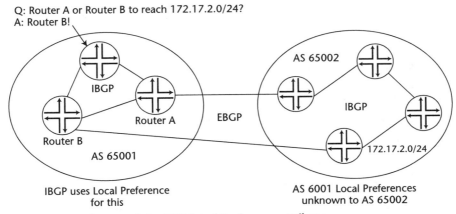

Figure 18.6 The use of the BGP Local Preference attribute.

routers to set the Local Preference value higher on the copy of the route received on Router B than the copy received on Router A. IBGP will make sure that every router in the AS knows that the preferred exit point for this route is Router B. Note that AS 65002 neither knows nor cares about the value of the Local Preference assigned to the route by Router A or Router B.

AS 65001 still has failover capability since it is receiving the route from AS 65002 through both routers. Although Router B is the primary exit point for the route, user traffic can use Router A to reach AS 65002 in the event of a failure of the Router B link to AS 65002.

Here is a more realistic example of how Local Preference is used within an AS. Consider the collection of ISPs shown in Figure 18.7.

As shown in the figure, the network administrators in MyISPnet have decided that the routers in MyISPnet should use the New York router to reach the 192.168.27.0/24 network in ISP9net. This is because of the greater bandwidth capacity available on that link: An OC-12c runs at 622 Mbps, while an OC-3c runs at 155 Mbps.

To do this, the MyISPnet network administrators set the Local Preference on the route to 192.168.27.0/24 advertised to the Los Angeles router from ISP2net to 200, and set the Local Preference on the route to 192.168.27.0/24 advertised to the New York router from ISP3net to 300.

In contrast to almost every other metric associated with routing protocols, the *highest* Local Preference is better. So for this route, the exit point of the AS is through New York. IBGP makes these values known to all other routers in MyISPnet.

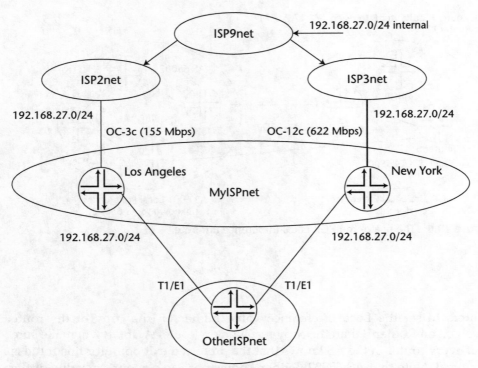

Figure 18.7 Example of BGP Local Preference attribute use.

The link on the Los Angeles router can still be used for inbound traffic flows from ISP9net and for outbound failover traffic if the OC-12c is not usable because of a router or link failure.

We can extended the example further to point out the local nature of Local Preference. Consider another AS called OtherISPnet linked by two lower, but equal, speed links to MyISPnet. Which link should OtherISPnet use to reach 192.168.27.0/24 in ISP9net?

Since the Local Preference values used inside MyISPnet are not propagated by EBGP, the OtherISPnet AS has no knowledge of the Local Preference routing decisions made within MyISPnet with regard to the 192.168.27.0/24 route. MyISPnet, of course, would still like to have traffic from OtherISPnet flow toward the New York router to avoid shuttling all of this traffic across its backbone. However, there is no way for MyISPnet to do this with Local Preference. To accomplish this goal, MyISPnet must use other BGP attributes instead of Local Preference such as AS Path, Origin, or MED to try and influence OtherISPnet's flow of traffic to MyISPnet. This is because of the strictly local nature of the Local Preference attribute.

One concern with Local Preference is the lack of a loop prevention mechanism. For example, consider the situation shown in Figure 18.8.

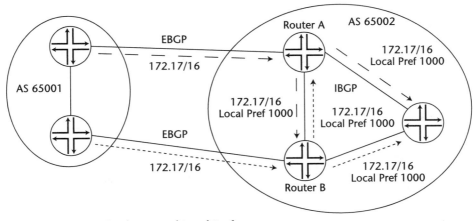

Figure 18.8 Routing loops and Local Preference.

Since the Local Preference attribute overrides all other BGP attributes in the path selection process, is it possible to set up a routing loop? Routing loops are especially bad since the destination is technically reachable, but some or even all routers within an AS cannot find the proper path to the destination.

In this example, both Router A and Router B have a policy in place that takes received EBGP routes and sets the Local Preference to 1000 as the routes are then advertised to IBGP peers, which include each other. So Router A advertises the route to Router B, and Router B advertises the route to Router A.

Theoretically, both Router A and Router B will see the value of 1000 from the other and realize that it is better than the *local* copy of the route received directly from EBGP, which still has the default Local Preference. This is because the Local Preference on the copy of the route within the router is still set to 100.

Therefore, Router A and Router B will see *each other* as the best route to 172.17.0.0/16, and a routing loop will occur as the two routers shuttle traffic back and forth. Right?

It turns out that BGP is a little too smart in this case. The following chain of events assumes that Router B received the EBGP route of 172.17.0.0/16 first and advertises the route with a Local Preference of 1000 to its IBGP peers. (If Router A accomplishes this first, the roles are easily reversed, but the point is the same.) What actually happens is shown in Figure 18.9.

First, Router B receives the EBGP route of 172.17.0.0/16 from its peer in the other AS. Since Router B sees this route as the current best, Router B installs the route in its routing table.

Then Router B alters the Local Preference to 1000 and advertises this route to its IBGP peers with this Local Preference value. At this point, both Router A and the other router in AS 65002 receive the 172.17.0.0/16 route through IBGP.

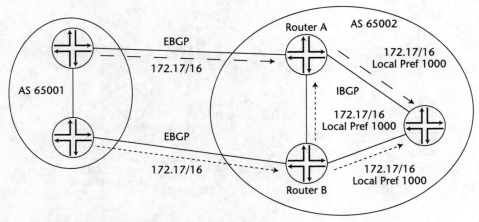

Figure 18.9   Local Preference loop prevention.

Router A then also receives the EBGP route for 172.17.0.0/16 from the other AS. Router A finds at this point that it already has a route to 172.17.0.0/16 from Router B received through IBGP with a Local Preference of 1000. The presence of this route to Router B overrides the EBGP received route.

Because the current version of the route on Router A is from Router B, and since IBGP does implement split horizon, the routing loop never forms in this case. Router A just sends traffic for 172.17.0.0/16 to Router B. And because only active BGP routes are advertised, there is no confusion on the third router in AS 65002 with regard to the best path to reach 172.17.0.0/16; Router B is the choice.

The important points with regard to the Local Preference attribute are as follows:

- It is a guarantee of *outbound* traffic flows. In fact, there is little else that can be done with BGP to establish an exit point for an AS.

- It is the most powerful BGP path selector and is commonly used to override other BGP attributes in the path selection process. This means that Local Preference will select a BGP route regardless of the values of AS Path, Origin, or MED.

- It is very commonly used within an AS but is local to the AS only. So the Local Preference is never sent to another AS with EBGP.

- It should be applied consistently at the edge of the AS for maximum efficiency. That is, the Local Preference should be set on a route advertised from another AS at the border router and not changed haphazardly within the AS.

Cisco Routers and Local Preference

If the value of the BGP Local Preference attribute is not altered with a routing policy, the default Local Preference for any route is set to 100. This default Local Preference value can be altered with a `bgp default local-preference <value>` statement. However, this just alters the Local Preference for every single route advertised within the AS by IBGP. This can be useful, as when the link on this border router is many times faster than any other external link, as was the case in the example given earlier in this chapter.

Consider that network and assume that MyISPnet is AS 64555 and ISP2net is AS 65002 and ISP3net is AS 65003. How should the Los Angeles and New York routers be configured to set the Local Preferences to 200 on routes arriving at Los Angeles (better) from AS 65002 (ISP2net) and the Local Preferences to 300 (best) on routes arriving at New York from AS 65003 (ISP3net)? The default Local Preference can be set in the BGP configuration for BGP routers as follows:

```
Los Angeles:
!
router bgp 64555
 redistribute static
 neighbor 10.100.100.100 remote-as 65002
 neighbor 10.0.32.2 remote-as 64555
 bgp default local-preference 200
 no auto-summary
!

New York:
!
router bgp 64555
 redistribute static
 neighbor 10.200.200.200 remote-as 65003
 neighbor 10.0.32.1 remote-as 64555
 bgp default local-preference 300
 no auto-summary
!
```

Now when the BGP update for 192.168.27.0/24 from distant ISP6net arrived from both ISP2net and ISP3net, all of the routers inside AS 64555 (MyISPnet) will use New York as the exit point because of the higher Local Preference for that route inside AS 64555.

This routing policy sends all routes out of AS 64555 to ISP3net (AS 65003) through New York. However, there might be routes closer to AS 64555 (like those inside AS 65002 at ISP2net itself) that should still leave the AS through Los Angeles. And since New York has another EBGP link to another

AS (OtherISPnet), all of *those* received routes will be advertised inside AS 64555 with New York as this preferred exit point. This makes little sense because the links to OtherISPnet from New York and Los Angeles have the same bandwidth. So more flexibility for setting the Local Preference is provided using route maps, as might be expected.

Adding a route map can filter out the routes received from OtherISPnet (perhaps AS 65333). This is how the configuration on New York would look. The Los Angeles configuration would look similar:

```
New York:
!
router bgp 64555
 redistribute static
 neighbor 10.200.200.200 remote-as 65003
 neighbor 10.200.200.200 route-map Set-Local-Pref in
 neighbor 10.0.32.1 remote-as 64555
 ...
ip as-path access-list 5 permit ^65003_
 . . .
!
route-map Set-Local-Pref permit 10
 match as-path 5
 set local-preference 300
...
```

Now EBGP routes arriving from AS 65003 or beyond (controlled by the ^65003_ regular expression) are given an IBGP Local Preference of 300 (as before), but any other routes from another AS (such as OtherISPnet) will still get the default Local Preference of 100.

Juniper Networks Routers and Local Preference

The BGP attribute of Local Preference should not be confused with the JUNOS software concept of routing protocol preference. The JUNOS software *preference* is local to an individual router and assists the routing table in choosing the active route among many possible paths.

The BGP Local Preference attribute is used only within BGP itself. The Local Preference value gets transmitted among the BGP routers within an AS. If a value for Local Preference is not explicitly configured, the default value used on BGP routes is 100.

This value can be changed on a per-peer basis using the local-preference command within the [edit protocols bgp] configuration hierarchy directory. In addition, the value can be altered via a policy on a per-route basis. The policy action also uses the local-preference command to alter the attribute value.

The default Local Preference applied to a BGP route is 100, but the default *routing protocol preference* applied to BGP itself is 170. The JUNOS software preference applies to the entire routing protocol. Preference is also set in the [edit protocols bgp] configuration hierarchy directory, but as preference, not local-preference, which applies only to BGP.

When configuring routing policies, make sure to change Local Preference on the BGP routes, not the preference of the BGP protocol as a whole!

In many cases, with Local Preference, a routing policy will not consider routes in isolation but will consider other BGP attributes such as the AS Path to select routes for preferred local handling. This can be altered with a routing policy like the following:

```
[edit policy-options]
as-path look-for-path "65003 .*"
policy-statement check-the-path {
    term got-path {
        from as-path look-for-path;
        then {
            local-preference 300;
            accept;
        }
    }
}
```

This example changes the Local Preference value for all received routes that match the AS Path of look-for-path. Within the term got-path, an action of local-preference 300 is specified. This action changes the Local Preference attribute value for those routes to 300. The BGP Next Hop border router for this route will be the exit point of the AS for packets sent to this destination address space that enter the local AS. No other received BGP routes will be affected by this routing policy.

This policy could easily be configured and applied on the New York router in the Local Preference example used in this chapter. When applied as an EBGP group import policy on New York, the policy matches only routes from AS 65003 (ISP3net) because the AS Path must begin with AS 65003. These routes get a Local Preference of 300, while all other EBGP routes (such as from OtherISPnet) still get the default Local Preference of 100.

BGP Community and Route Damping

This last chapter on the application of routing policy to BGP considers the BGP Community attribute and route damping. As explained earlier in this book, BGP communities are like clubs for routes and do not play a standard role in the BGP route selection process. Instead, BGP communities act as a convenient shorthand notation for finding routes that share a common community value. Although route damping is definitely not a BGP attribute, route damping implementation can involve some fairly sophisticated routing policies to get just right. So consider both of these subjects a kind of BGP miscellany of topics that are very important but do not really fit in well anywhere else.

BGP communities started out as a Cisco method of tagging BGP routes (NLRIs) for identification. This method was eventually standardized, but the Community attribute took on a new format that differed from Cisco's original style. The Community attribute is often an ever-increasing string of values, much like the AS Path, although the Community attribute does not enjoy that same protection as the AS Path. That is, the community value can be added to, deleted from, or explicitly set as a BGP route makes it way from AS to AS across the Internet. Recently, a form of BGP Community called the Extended Community has taken on considerable importance in the area of IP-based virtual private networks (VPNs). This role for the Extended Community attribute is well beyond the scope of this book, and only the standard BGP Community format and use are investigated in this chapter.

Mentioned earlier in the book, route damping is a method of countering BGP *route flapping*. Route flapping occurs for a number of reasons, most often because of an intermittently failing link between two BGP routers. The link might fail and restore itself several times an hour, or even within minutes. One moment it's up and can carry 1,000 routes as a next hop; the next it's down and the 1,000 routes are rerouted. This up-and-down quality is where the flapping notion comes from. Flapping causes massive re-routing of traffic and a related flooding (in the sense of "a huge amount") and reflooding of BGP routing updates to all BGP peers not only within the AS, which is understandable and probably unavoidable, but outside of the AS with the bad link as well. But since other ASs only know and care that the destination lies in or through the AS with the flapping route, the other ASs have little choice but simply to keep routing the traffic to the AS anyway. Route damping (also often called route *dampening*) is just a way to give other ASs some peace and not be alarmed about a failing link that is beyond their control to fix in any case.

Both BGP communities and route damping are not overly complex, but they can be used in complex fashions. Communities often use the same type of complicated regular expressions (in some ways, even more complicated) as AS Paths. And route damping can be varied and applied differently for customer links, peer connections, and internal networks. Since the BGP Community is still a BGP attribute, this is a good place to start and close the whole BGP attribute discussion.

The BGP Community Attribute

As was just pointed out, the BGP Community attribute is not complex. The main role of the BGP Community attribute is to make it easy to group routes that should be treated the same with a routing policy. BGP communities are very flexible; a BGP route can belong to many BGP communities.

The BGP Community attribute is an optional attribute, so not all implementations of BGP must recognize and use communities. However, if BGP communities are associated with a BGP route, then the BGP Community attribute must be passed along to all other BGP peers, both within an AS and between AS networks (it is a transitive attribute).

The BGP Community attribute is an administrative *tag* that network administrators can use to associate routes together that share common properties. The nice thing about using BGP communities to group routes is that the communities are globally known, even in other AS networks, and so are not bounded by network, AS, or any other physical constraint. However, communities are not protected in any way. Any router that wishes to can erase a long string of communities and set it to something else or just wipe it out entirely.

The attraction of BGP communities is that they can be used to simplify routing policies. BGP communities identify routes based on the logical boundaries established by the network administrator, and not by AS number (too broad in most cases) or individual IP prefix (too granular in most cases). The community attribute can be used within routing policies to accept or reject routes based on the values of the BGP Communities. In addition, the community attribute values can be used with other BGP attributes to implement routing policies that accept, prefer, or advertise BGP routes.

Within an AS, BGP communities are used to establish various logical *categories* for routes (prefixes). It is helpful here once again to think of BGP communities as communities of interest or even clubs for routes. And just as people can belong to more than one club, routes can fit into more than one BGP community. The BGP community attribute value is often used to implement policies for customer networks, such as altering the Local Preference attribute on incoming routes from customers without having to look for each and every customer's address.

The community attribute can be used to assist network administrators in the configuration and maintenance of policies. This cuts down on the time needed for manual reconfiguration and the complexity of the overall maintenance task. As an example, consider the addition of a new prefix for a new customer within an AS. If communities are used to enforce routing for customer networks, and the new prefix can be placed into an existing community, no changes to overall routing policies are needed. When new customers are brought into the network, the new routes only need to be assigned the proper community attribute. Without the use of communities, each policy in the network might need to be updated to include the new customer information.

However, care is required when establishing communities for the first time. If there are too many communities, this defeats the whole purpose. Maintenance of the communities then becomes as tedious as maintaining a whole list of route filters. Network administrators should also avoid having too many overlapping communities. When customer routes belong to multiple communities, so some routes seem to match everything, this too can be a nightmare. With communities, simplicity is always a worthwhile goal.

Well-Known Communities

Certain *well-known communities* have a global meaning and special purposes. All BGP implementations that understand communities (communities are optional, but transitive) must know these well-known communities and respect their functions.

BGP communities that are not well known are for local use. Local-use communities must be defined locally, but since the BGP Community attribute follows the BGP route wherever it goes, even local-use communities are circulated outside the AS. So care is needed in using BGP Community attribute values arriving from other AS networks. BGP communities are best thought of as a category for a group of routes (such as "all customers").

The BGP Community attribute itself is just a list of the individual community attribute values, or tags, associated with the route. Since there is no real limit on the number of tags in the list, a route can belong to many communities. There is no predefined upper limit on the number of communities allowed on a route.

The community attribute values themselves are designed so the values can be uniquely assigned on the global Internet. The BGP Community attribute itself is a 32-bit (four-octet) value that has two parts. The two high-order octets (16 bits) form the first part and are set aside for the AS number of the network that assigned the community to the route in the first place. The two low-order octets (16 bits) form the second part and are set aside for use by the specific AS networks. Since the AS value is included in the community, the value is guaranteed to be unique on the whole Internet.

When written in bits or hex, communities can look very odd. So communities are usually represented in decimal form as AS:number (for example, 65200:777). This is community 777 in AS 65200. One restriction on possible community values is that the AS values of 0 and 65535 are reserved and cannot be assigned to a route. So in combination, this restriction covers values 0x00000000 to 0x0000FFFF (AS 0) and 0xFFFF0000 to 0xFFFFFFFF (AS 65535).

Three community attribute values have been designated as well-known communities. These communities share the AS value of 65535 (0xFFFFxxxx). The three communities are as follows:

- NO_EXPORT (0xFFFFFF01) tells routers to distribute routes with this community tag within the confederation or AS (if no confederation is defined), but no farther.

- NO_ADVERTISE (0xFFFFFF02) tells routers not to advertise these routes to other BGP peers at all. Despite appearances, this BGP Community is quite useful.

- LOCAL_AS (0xFFFFFF03) tells routers not to distribute routes with this community tag to external BGP peers, so they are confined to the sub-AS. LOCAL_AS was originally NO_EXPORT_SUBCONFED in RFC 1997.

The NO_EXPORT community is typically used to make sure that route aggregation is optimal by suppressing more specific routes. The NO_EXPORT_ SUBCONFED just extends this aggregate concept to the sub-AS.

The NO_ADVERTISE community has a very narrow scope. Routes go to a BGP peer and no farther, usually because the routes are known to the BGP peers through other means. This community is often used in a LAN-connected router environment or when two BGP peers have multiple links between them.

The relationship between the three well-known communities is shown in Figure 19.1.

The figure shows an example of the scope of the NO_ADVERTISE community. The arrow at the lower right shows a BGP route with the NO_ADVERTISE community injected into an AS with subconfederations. The well-known community attribute value of NO_ADVERTISE is designed such that a route can be sent to a single BGP peer and be advertised no further. Routes are restricted to the next-hop router.

The figure also shows an example of the scope of the NO_EXPORT_SUBCONFED community. The arrow at the lower right shows a BGP route with the LOCAL_AS or NO_EXPORT_SUBCONFED community injected into an AS with subconfederations. The well-known community attribute value of NO_EXPORT_SUBCONFED is designed such that a route can be sent into a BGP confederation network and have the information remain with a particular sub-AS. The routing information will be advertised no further than the sub-AS, as shown.

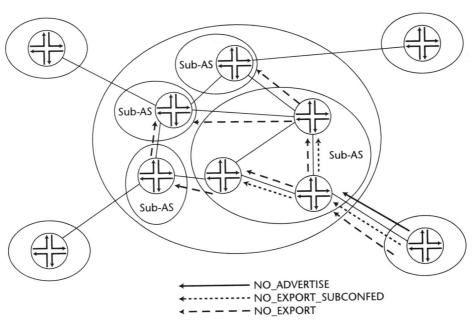

Figure 19.1 Well-known BGP communities.

Finally, the figure shows an example of the scope of the NO_EXPORT community. The arrow at the lower right shows a BGP route with the NO_EXPORT community injected into an AS with subconfederations. The well-known community attribute value of NO_EXPORT is designed such that a route can be sent into a neighboring AS and have the information remain within that neighboring AS. Normally, BGP communities are transitive and are passed from each AS to all others, even if the BGP community option is not supported and used by the router. But the routing information with the NO_EXPORT community tag will not be advertised beyond the AS.

NO_EXPORT can actually be very helpful. Figure 19.2 shows a typical application of this well-known BGP community.

AS 65001 has multiple BGP sessions to its neighbor AS 65002. AS 65001 is also using AS 65002 as a transit AS for connectivity to the Internet. AS 65001 would like to advertise 172.17.0.0/16 to the Internet because AS 65001 owns that entire address space. In addition, AS 65001 would also like to advertise more specific route information (shown as 172.17.0/17 and 172.17.128/17) only to its peer, AS 65002.

Advertising the specifics as well as the aggregate to AS 65002 would assist AS 65002 to more efficiently route user traffic into AS 65001, since *load sharing* could be used on the more specific routes, as shown in the figure. But why should the whole Internet known or care about these specifics?

To assist AS 65002 in finding and rejecting the more specific routes, AS 65001 assigns the NO_EXPORT community to the 172.17.0.0/17 and the 172.17.128.0/17 routes. The BGP edge routers in AS 65002 that connect to the Internet will automatically suppress and not readvertise the /17 routes. Only the /16 route is readvertised to the Internet.

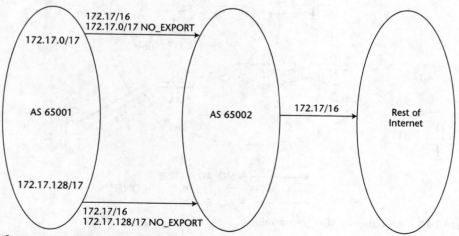

Figure 19.2   NO_EXPORT in action.

Another example of the use of the NO_EXPORT community is shown in Figure 19.3. In the figure, a customer AS 65000 is multihomed to two other ISPs, AS 65001 and AS 65002. In this example, the customer would like to receive Internet traffic through one main ISP (AS 65001) but be able to receive locally originating traffic from the other ISP (perhaps a major trading partner uses AS 65002 as its ISP).

One way to do this is with the BGP NO_EXPORT Community. In this example, the customer has AS 65001 as its main ISP. Customer AS 65000 has address space 172.17.144.0/20, taken from AS 65001's address space of 172.16.0.0/16. The 172.17.144.0/20 route is advertised with BGP to both AS 65001 and AS 65002. Since AS 65002 is not the primary ISP and only traffic originating in AS 65002 should reach AS 65000 directly, the route advertised to AS 65002 is given the BGP NO_EXPORT community. This route goes no farther than AS 65002. AS 65002 will advertise 172.31.0.0/16 to AS 65001 and the Internet, but not 172.17.144.0/20.

AS 65001 covers the 172.17.144/20 address space with aggregate 172.17.0.0/16, as shown in the figure. This is advertised to AS 65002 and the Internet. So AS 65000 is only reachable through AS 65001 from the Internet, but AS 65000 is only reachable by local AS 65002 users. A drawback of this scenario is that if the link from AS 65000 to AS 65001 fails, the 172.17.144.0/20 route is not reachable from the Internet through AS 65002. But since AS 65002 is not the primary ISP for AS 65000 and might not be happy to play transit AS to the Internet, perhaps this is acceptable.

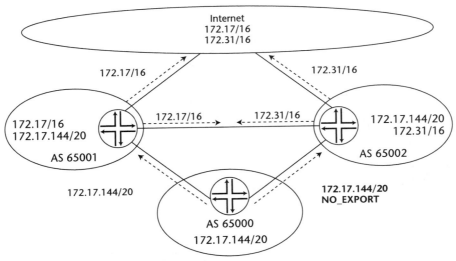

Figure 19.3   An example using NO_EXPORT.

Using Communities to Represent Local Preference

One of the most common uses of the BGP Community attribute addresses one major limitation of the BGP Local Preference attribute. Local Preference is only distributed within an AS, and no Local Preference information is ever sent between two AS networks. Yet Local Preference is a valuable way to establish proper exit points for a route within an AS, especially when the AS has multiple links and the two ISP running the ASs are peers. How can another AS be informed of the Local Preferences of a route learned from another AS? The most popular way is with BGP communities, as shown in Figure 19.4.

This figure might resemble the previous figure, but the addressing is different and the intent different as well. In this example, the customer AS 64999 at the bottom has agreed to provide backup transit service to both AS 65001 and AS 65002 in case their links to each other are lost. The address spaces used are shown in the figure. The customer AS uses 172.17.64.0/18 and 172.20.128.0/18.

What the customer wants to accomplish is to make the 172.20.0.0/16 route sent to AS 65001 to have a *lower* Local Preference than the default of 100, and to make the 172.17.0.0/16 route sent to AS 65002 have a *lower* Local Preference than the default of 100 there as well. This makes other paths look more attractive, but these routes can still be used if the preferred paths on other links are down.

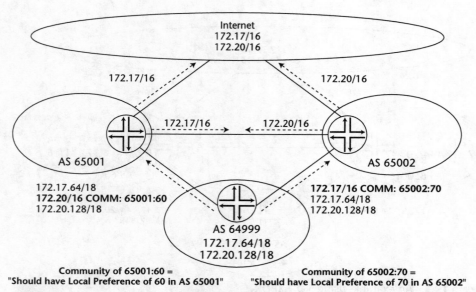

Figure 19.4 Communities and Local Preference.

The key to making this work is with the BGP communities on routes sent to AS 65001 and AS 65002. Route 172.20.0.0/16 sent to AS 65001 is tagged as community 65001:60. This says to AS 65001, "AS 65001, within your AS, this route should have a Local Preference of 60." Naturally, route 172.17.0.0/16 sent to AS 65002 is tagged as Community 65002:70. This says to AS 65002, "AS 65002, within your AS, this route should have a Local Preference of 70." In this example, AS 65001 and AS 65002 only advertise aggregates to each other and the Internet.

If AS 65001 and AS 65002 set the Local Preferences on these routes as requested, the exit points through the customer's AS will only be active when there is no "normal" peering route available (Local Preference = 100). Of course, setting Local Preferences in other AS networks with communities requires that all of the AS administrators play nice and cooperate. Nothing *makes* an AS respect the community attribute value.

This example might seem somewhat complex and contrived. But BGP Communities are routinely used to allow other ASs to determine the Local Preference of the route *within* the AS that has set the Community value. Unless changed or deleted, these values propagate all over the Internet. For example, a Community string such as 65001:200 65002:100 64999:150 might be interpreted as telling an AS that this route (NLRI) has a Local Preference of 200 in AS 65001, a Local Preference of 100 (the default) in AS 65002, and a Local Preference of 150 in AS 64999. Of course, there is nothing to prevent a Community value from using any AS number it pleases.

Even if interpretation of Community as Local Preference were uniform, this says nothing at all about what the current AS should *do* with this information, but at least there is a way to express Local Preference outside of the AS. But any AS can easily use the Community values for their own purposes.

Communities and Transit Traffic

A key area for the application of the BGP Community attribute is with regard to transit and nontransit AS networks. A transit AS carries traffic that neither originates from hosts within the AS nor is destined for hosts within the AS. A nontransit AS only carries traffic that has its own addresses appearing as either the source or the destination. Nontransit AS networks must be careful when advertising BGP routes outside of the AS. Only local routes can be advertised by a nontransit AS.

Routing policies can be used in combination with BGP communities to make an AS appear as a transit AS or a nontransit AS. Communities make it much easier to hold back routes that might be advertised and attract transit traffic. Generally, a small ISP needs to advertise its own local routes, but never be a transit AS for larger ISPs. Such a situation could easily swamp the operation of a small ISP.

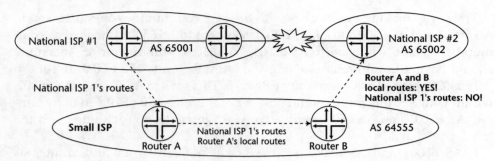

Figure 19.5 Communities and AS transit traffic.

Consider a small ISP linked to two larger, national ISPs: National ISP 1 and National ISP 2. Border Router A links to National ISP 1 and border Router B links to National ISP 2. As an example of what could happen, consider that National ISP 1 advertises all of its BGP routes into border Router A of the small ISP. Router A advertises not only its own local routes to Router B in the small ISP but also National ISP 1's routes so that all users can reach these routes. This situation is shown in Figure 19.5.

But Router B should never, ever advertise National ISP 1's routes to National ISP 2! Router A and Router B's local routes are okay to send to National ISP 2. But if Router B ever advertises the National ISP 1 routes to National ISP 2 and the link (or links) between the two national ISPs ever fail, National ISP 2 will think that a good way to reach National ISP 1 is through the small ISP! Hence, the small ISP has now become a transit network.

The same risk involves Router B's routes sent to Router A. Don't pass along National ISP 2's routes! But which routes are okay and which ones are not? Communities make it easy to find just the right routes. How can communities be added at Router A, the border router, to separate National ISP 1's routes from the small ISP's local routes (and in the real world, the National ISP 2's routes as well) on a Cisco and a Juniper Networks router?

Communities on a Cisco Router

There is a lot of variation in the way BGP Communities are defined and handled on a Cisco router. Cisco was the Community pioneer, and the two initial BGP Community RFCs, RFC 1997 and RFC 1998, were written by Cisco employees. So various versions of Cisco's IOS allow the Community value to be set as a single number in the range 1 to 4294967200 (in the form NN:AA), as the now standard AS:value (*aa:nn*, which Cisco calls the "new format"), or by well-known Community value. To use the new format in older versions of IOS, include the `ip bgp-community new-format` statement in the configuration if necessary.

Cisco replaces the RFC 1997 NO_EXPORT_SUBCONFED well-known Community value with `local-as`. At least `local-as` is simple to understand; it is basically the NO_EXPORT for an AS with sub-ASs because of the presence of a confederation. Cisco uses `no-export` and `no-advertise` for NO_EXPORT and NO_ADVERTISE. All values are unchanged from the RFC, just the name of one well-known Community.

Oddly, Cisco routers will not send BGP advertisements with the BGP Community attribute unless specifically told to do so. This is done for a neighbor or BGP peer group with the `neighbor..send-community` statement. Leaving this statement out will lead to unexpected results. Think of the default Cisco router behavior to assume NO_ADVERTISE for all Communities unless told to advertise them explicitly.

Community values are assigned with the `set community` command, most often in a router map but also with a special *community list*. We investigate both methods in this section. Community values, because of the varied format supported by Cisco, can use the standard form using a colon, hexadecimal form of values, or decimal notation. For example:

```
set community 64512:100
set community 0xFC000064
set community 4227858532
```

All do the same thing: set the 32-bit Community value to the same string of bits. These bits all indicate a decimal value of 64512 in the first 16 bits (the AS) and a decimal value of 100 in the last 16 bits (the Community number or value itself). But however it is entered, the Community will show up in the configuration and with `show` commands as 64512:100.

In the example of Community use introduced earlier in this chapter, Router A should set a Community on BGP routes received from National ISP 1 before advertising them to Router B. This makes it easy for Router B to separate the local routes within AS 64555 when they get to Router B and Router B must be able to easily suppress advertisement of National ISP 1's routes to National ISP 2 (to avoid becoming a transit AS for the two national ISPs if their direct link fails).

Router A will receive routes from the border router in AS 65001 (National ISP 1). The easiest way to find these routes is with a route map and AS Path access list matching on the AS Path of the routes received from AS 65001. These routes all start with AS 65001 and can be found with a regular expression (^65001_). The IP source address of the border router in AS 65001 could be used in an access list as well, but this is more likely to change than the AS number.

These routes can then be given a distinct community value within AS 64512. Perhaps this value has been administratively determined to be 65001 (which makes sense, since these are AS 65001 routes). The AS value will be 64555, of course. Router B will follow similar logic on routes from AS 65002 (National ISP 2), but this example examines Router A.

The first additional consideration is whether Router A will *add* this Community to existing Communities on the routes arriving from AS 65001 or *replace* the existing Communities with one: 64555:65001. The default Cisco behavior is to replace the Communities that exist with the Community in the `set` command. To remove all Communities from a route, use `set community none`. (Router B could use the `set community none` command to remove all of the Communities from all AS 64555 local routes advertised to National ISP 2. After all, why should AS 65002 need to know what Communities a small ISP is using or has seen?)

To add to the existing Communities, use the `additive` knob:

```
set community 64555:65001 additive
```

Router A decides that there might be other Community values on the routes from National ISP 1 that would be of use to other routers in AS 64555 and so decides to add the new Community with `additive`. Here is the way all this would be done with a route map on Router A:

```
autonomous-system 64555
!
router bgp 64555
 neighbor 10.100.100.100 remote-as 65001
 neighbor 10.100.100.100 send-community
 neighbor 10.100.100.100 route-map ISP#1-Comm in
 no auto-summary
!
ip bgp-community new-format
!
ip as-path access-list 1 permit ^65001_
!
route-map ISP#1-Comm permit 10
 match as-path 1
 set community 64555:65001 additive
!
```

Now only routes received from AS 65001 will be advertised within AS 64555 with the 64555:65001 Community attribute on the BGP NLRI routing information.

In addition to using general routing policy tools such as route maps and access lists to find and set Communities, Cisco routers have a special form of the access list for Communities. This is the *community list*, which is used to easily find routes based on their community attributes.

As expected, multiple lines can be in the community list, each with a `permit` or `deny` action. The list is identified with a number between 1 and 99, and there is an explicit `deny any` at the end of the community list. There are also *named community lists*, but these are not discussed in any detail in this section.

Router B can use a Community list to find all of the BGP routes arriving from routers in AS 64555 that have a Community of 64512:65001 on them. All routes with 64512:65001 will be suppressed. Other routes will be advertised to National ISP 2 (AS 65002), but without any Communities at all (no `send-community` is used toward AS 65002).

Here is the configuration on Router B:

```
autonomous-system 64555
!
router bgp 64555
 neighbor 10.200.200.200 remote-as 65002
 neighbor 10.200.200.200 route-map ISP#2-Comm out
 no auto-summary
!
ip bgp-community new-format
!
ip community-list 1 deny 64555:65001
!
route-map ISP#2-Comm permit 10
 match community 1
!
```

Variations on these policies will be used on Router B and Router A to treat the routes from National ISP 2 in a similar fashion.

Communities make it easy to perform operations on groups of routes without needing to know what the addresses are in detail. The ability to extend, erase, or set the list makes the Community attribute a very useful tool.

Cisco Community Regular Expressions

Cisco routers employ exactly the same syntax for regular expressions for BGP Communities as for AS Paths. This is not true for Juniper Networks routers, where regular expressions for AS Paths are a subset of the full regular expression syntax. This is because AS Paths on a Juniper Networks router are stored as integers and not as character strings as they are on a Cisco router. This is only for internal representation and raises no interoperability issues.

For a description of the Cisco regular expression syntax, see the previous chapter on the Cisco regular expression syntax applied the AS Paths. This section just presents a basic example of Community matching with Cisco regular expressions.

Regular expressions applied to BGP Communities most often appear in named Community lists, but of course they can be used wherever a Community value is appropriate. By default, Cisco routers use the old Community format of a single number in the form NN:AA, but in the range 1 to $2^{32} - 1$ (4294967200). So to find and reject any Communities that contain any values at all, the statement:

```
ip community-list 100 deny [0-9]*
```

would be used. Regular expressions are most often used to see if a route contains some Community value or another. For example, to check for the presence of Community 65001:100, the regular expression _4227858532_ will find this value in the Community attribute.

Anytime you use regular expressions to try to find BGP Communities not in the original format of NN:AA (a 32-bit number), but in the standard *aa:nn* format, you must convert the value to a form that the regular expression can work with. In other words, despite the user-friendly aa:nn format, the Community attribute is still really just a 32-bit number, and Cisco routers treat the Community that way.

Communities on a Juniper Networks Router

On a Juniper Networks router, support for BGP Communities is much more elaborate than on a Cisco router. There are new rules, new formats, and new actions in the routing policies when Communities are included. So this section is rather long.

BGP communities are configured in the JUNOS software at the [edit policy-options] CLI hierarchy level. The community is simply given a name and a number of members in the form of the community-id. When multiple community members are defined, it means there is a logical AND between them. So a given name represents Community1 AND Community2 AND Community3 and so on.

The community-id has an as-number:community-value format, with a colon (:) separating the high-order and low-order octets. The keywords no-export, no-advertise, and no-export-subconfed can be used to specify the well-known community values.

When used in a routing policy, the community name can be used as a match condition ("find these BGP communities") or as an action. Actions applied to communities include adding, deleting, or setting community attribute values.

This example routing table snippet and policy shows how to add a community to a BGP route:

```
192.168.0.0/24 (2 entries, 1 announced)
    Communities: 64512:567 65100:20 65050:70 65234:66
```

```
[edit policy-options]
policy-statement community-actions {
    term add-a-community
        then community add test-comm;
    }
}
community test-comm members 65001:1234;
```

```
192.168.0.0/24 (2 entries, 1 announced)
    Communities: 64512:567 65100:20 65050:70 65234:66 65001:1234
```

This policy is used to leave the existing Communities on the route in place but also add the specified community attribute value to the route. Route 192.168.0.0/24 currently has four Communities on the route: 64512:567, 65100:20, 65050:70, and 65234:66.

Since the policy community-actions has no from, all routes are matched. It is not necessary to check for just the BGP routes, since only BGP has a Community attribute to change. (Including a from protocol bgp statement will not change the action of the routing policy. All BGP routes will have the community tag test-comm value of 65001:1234 *added* to the existing Communities on the route.)

After this routing policy has been correctly applied, the 192.168.0.0/24 route now has *five* Communities on the route: 64512:567, 65100:20, 65050:70, 65234:66, and the added 65001:1234.

You can also remove only the specified values of the existing Communities and leave other existing Communities in place. This is done with a then community delete test-comm where test-comm would be defined separately.

With the set command you can also remove *all* of the values of the existing Communities and add the new community tags in place of the old tag values. For example, if test-comm is defined as 64512:1234, the action then community set test-comm replaces the whole original community tag string with community tag 64512:1234.

Consider this policy and community definition:

```
[edit policy-options]
community customers members [64656:2379 64523:46944];
policy-statement from-customers {
        from community customers;
        then {
            metric 20;
            local-preference 200;
            next policy;
        }


}
```

The goal here is create a community named customers. The community is defined as having two members: 64656:2379 AND 64523:46944. When this community is used in a routing policy to find (match) routes, the community will match routes that have *both* 64656:2379 AND 64523:46944 as a community tag value. Once found, these routes are given a MED (the BGP metric) of 20 and a local-preference of 200 (instead of the default 100).

In contrast to other BGP attributes like AS Path, it is perfectly allowable to delete some or all of the community attribute values on a BGP route. In fact, this is very useful at the boundaries of an AS, since there is no guarantee that any other AS will understand or respect the values of the communities established in one AS. If this is not done, by default all BGP communities are sent to all peers inside an AS and outside the AS. Why clutter up the routing updates with useless and potentially harmful information?

To stop the community from being advertised beyond the local AS, you need to delete the community. The wildcard character (*) will match all communities. Note that the wildcard "community" must be applied to *both* "halves" of the community: the AS number as well as the community-value. The syntax is therefore community wild-match members "*:*" to match all communities.

Here is how the same Community actions would be performed on Router A and Router B in Small ISP's AS 64555 to implement the routing policy outlined in the example network in this chapter. Following are the routing policies for Router A and Router B.

Routing policy configuration for Router A:

```
[edit policy-options]
policy-statement ISP#1-inbound {
    term find-routes {
        from {
            protocol bgp;
            as-path AS65001-Path;
        }
        then {
            community add AS64555-Comm;
            accept;
```

```
            }
        }
    }
    as-path AS65001-Comm "65001 .*"
    community AS64555-Comm members 64555:65001;
```

Routing policy configuration for Router B:

```
[edit policy-options]
policy-statement ISP#2-outbound {
    term find-ISP#1-routes {
        from {
            protocol bgp;
            community AS6455-Comm;
        }
        then reject;
    term find-local-routes {
        from {
            protocol bgp;
            as-path Null-AS
        }
        then {
            community delete All-Comms;
            accept;
        }
    }
}
as-path Null-AS "()";
community AS64555-Comm members 64555:65001;
community All-Comms members "*:*";
```

Now Router A adds Community 64555:65001 to the advertised routes when applied as an import policy to the EBGP group facing AS 65001 (National ISP 1). Router B applies its policy as an export policy to the EBGP group for AS 65002 (National ISP 2). Router B detects Community 64555:65001, suppresses these routes, and deletes all Communities from local routes (those with a Null AS Path) advertised to AS 65002.

Variations on these policies will be used on Router B and Router A to treat the routes from National ISP 2 in a similar fashion.

Juniper Networks Community Regular Expressions

A regular expression (regex or RE), also used on Juniper Networks routers for AS Path matching, can be used with BGP communities to produce a powerful pattern-matching system for finding communities that match a given regular expression. Regular expressions used with communities implement the full capabilities of a complete regular expression implementation, unlike the AS Path syntax, which used a subset of full regular expressions.

It will be helpful to describe two forms of regular expressions used with routing policies concerned with BGP communities: *simple* and *complex* regular expressions. These informal terms are defined in this book as follows. Simple community regular expressions contain only the * (asterisk) or . (dot) wildcard characters separately. Complex community regular expressions can use the * (asterisk) and . (dot) in conjunction with each other. Further, the complex regular expression statements can use additional operator syntax characters.

The * (asterisk) matches any single AS number or community-value. The . (dot) matches any single *digit* within the AS number or community value. Note that the combination of these characters (.*) is a complex community regular expression and is considered later in the chapter.

Some examples of simple community regular expression matches include:

`*:1000`   Any possible AS number with a value of 1000.

`65001:*`   AS 65001 with any possible community value.

`65001:100.`   AS 65001 with community values of 1000, 1001, 1002, 1003, 1004, 1005, 1006, 1007, 1008, or 1009.

`651.1:1000`   AS 65101, 65111, 65121, 65131, 65141, 65151, 65161, 65171, 65181, or 65191 with a community value of 1000.

These regular expressions can be used in a routing policy `from` statement or used with the CLI operational command to find BGP routes with the desired communities set. For example, `show route community *:20` will find all BGP routes with a community value of 20 regardless of AS number.

More complex regular expressions can be used with communities. On a Juniper Networks router, a community regular expression is character-based, unlike the regular expressions used with AS Paths, which match entire AS numbers. The format for the community regular expression is still `term<operator>` as in AS Path regular expressions, but the application of the term and operator is different.

When formulated for use with communities, the regular expression *anchors* of ^ (start) and $ (end) are not required, but can be helpful to organize and clearly represent the regular expression. Complex regular expressions can also be used in both the `show route` CLI commands and within a policy as a match condition.

Table 19.1 shows a list of the possible regular expression operators that can be used with BGP communities. Some operators are a kind of shorthand for their longer equivalents. For example, the + (plus) is the same as {1,}. Both will match one or more repetitions of the `term` preceding the operator. The square brackets [] will match a range [2-8] or array [256] of numbers. So the first regular expression in the previous sentence matches 2 through 8, and the second one matches 2 or 5 or 6.

Table 19.1   Regular Expressions for Communities

SPECIAL CHARACTERS	MEANING
{m,n}	Match at least *m* and at most *n* repetitions of the term.
{m}	Match exactly *m* repetitions of the term.
{m,}	Match *m* or more repetitions of the term.
*	Match zero or more repetitions of the term.
+	Match one or more repetitions of the term (same as {0,}).
?	Match zero or one repetitions of the term (same as {1,}).
|	Match one of the terms on either side of the pipe symbol.
^	Match character at the start of the Community.
$	Match character at the end of the Community.
[]	Match range or array of digits.
- (hyphen)	Used to represent a range.
(...), ()	Used to group terms, or indicate the Null AS Path with an enclosed space: ( ).

Of special note is the use of the parentheses. Typically, the (...) operator is used to group multiple terms together in conjunction with an operator. The parenthesis operator also has another special use. When used with no spaces in between, parentheses represent a *null* value.

Table 19.2 shows some examples of quite complex regular expressions that can be used to match communities in routing policies. The first column shows the BGP Community string that the routing policy is trying to match. The second column shows the Community regular expression that is used to match that pattern. The last column shows examples of values of the BGP Community attribute that the regular expression will match.

In some cases the list is not exhaustive, so there are more possible communities that will match the pattern. Note the presence of the : (colon) to separate the AS number of community value sections of the community.

Table 19.2 Community Regular Expression Examples

PATTERN TO MATCH	REGULAR EXPRESSION	EXAMPLE MATCHES (NOT EXHAUSTIVE)
AS is 64556 or 64578	"^((64556)|(64578)):(.*)$"	64556:1000, 64578:63000, etc.
AS is 64556 and value starts with a 2	"^64556:(2.*)$"	64556:2, 64556:255. 64556:2566, etc.
AS can be anything, value ends with a 5, 7, or 9	"^(.*):(.*[579])$"	65001:5, 64512:3357, 64512:65005, etc.
AS is 64556 or 64578, value starts with a 2 and ends with any value 2 through 8	"^((64556)|64578)):(2.*[2-8])$"	64556:22, 64556:21197, 64578:2678, etc.

Route Damping

Route damping is a way to combat *route instabilities* that cause routes to be withdrawn in a series of BGP update messages (often *very many* messages) only to be readvertised as active routes a few minutes when an intermittently failing link restores itself. Route damping gives BGP a memory and enables a BGP router to say "Wait a minute! You can't tell me this link is performing normally. It's been up and down all day . . . " The BGP router then decides to ignore changes to the status of the route for a preconfigured amount of time, usually an hour. Route damping gives a BGP router a way to deal with this phenomenon.

In any real network, routes can appear and disappear rapidly if a link fails and restores itself repeatedly in a short period of time. This is because any routes (and there could the thousands) that use the failed interface as a next hop must respond to the failure and the change in next hop must propagate to all other routers on the network.

Flapping results in a rapid sequence of BGP UPDATE or WITHDRAWN messages. Recall that BGP routers must maintain separate memory tables for inbound and outbound traffic on a per-peer basis. In addition, the BGP routing protocol propagates information on an as-needed basis. These two factors make BGP unstable when confronted with a flapping link.

Every BGP router that receives one of these UPDATE or WITHDRAWN messages has to send this information on to all of its BGP router peers. Much like the link-state IGPs of OSPF and ISIS, BGP must also recalculate its routing tables and databases every time a new update is received. If the new information alters the path selection process, a new route is chosen for the RIB_LOCAL and the new route must be set downstream to all BGP peers. The effect of route flapping quickly cascades and affects router performance. One intermittently failing link can adversely affect a whole network. If this type of update or withdrawal occurs on a very frequent basis, valuable resources in the router such as processing power normally used to forward packets is expended and the bandwidth now needed for routing updates is consumed.

Routes in a network can flap for any number of reasons. Quite possibly, the most frequent reason for a link flap is due to a faulty circuit that is on the brink of outright failure. Any link that rapidly thinks it is okay and then fails is a potential source of route flapping. Route flapping is not totally a BGP phenomenon. IGPs that are unstable because of faulty links can affect BGP when IGP routes are injected into BGP for advertising. BGP stability is always desirable and can be enhanced with careful use of static definitions and aggregates instead of injecting raw IGP routes into BGP.

Normally, links should be very stable, or they should fail outright. But there are other reasons for flapping. Human error can cause route flaps as well. This can happen when an incorrectly configured routing policy causes routes to be first rejected, then accepted because of the change on the route. Link congestion can cause route flaps if the overloaded links drop the BGP sessions. When the sessions reappear, all BGP routes must be readvertised.

In the past, sometimes the routers themselves contributed to the flapping problem. Older routers were filled with software bugs (mostly after an upgrade to a new release), had insufficient power (a busy CPU in a software-based router would drop BGP sessions), and often had insufficient memory (routing tables must be kept in memory). Sometimes just adding equipment for routine network upgrades and maintenance caused route flaps. Newer routers are much more resource-rich, but there are still plenty of older routers around.

Since route flapping can be so harmful to BGP, the protocol was extended to support route damping. Route damping is defined in RFC 2439 "BGP Route Flap Damping" (November 1998).

There is a difference between how damping is applied in BGP for internal and external peers. IBGP sessions should ignore damping and allow routes to flap as they please. This IBGP behavior has a very good reason. IBGP sessions usually peer to loopbacks, so IGP routes must be able to come and go, but IBGP sessions might always have a way to reach the loopback. Recall that BGP has no reachability information of its own and relies on the IGP to resolve next hops.

Route damping is only applied to routes received from an EBGP peer. EBGP sessions can carry information about thousands of routes. Each EBGP session must update or withdraw these routes as required. Route damping seeks to reward route stabilities while penalizing route flapping. Once damping is enabled, the router begins to maintain a database of instability. If an EBGP received route experiences enough flaps, the local BGP process ignores information about that route. This has the effect of *not* including this information in the route selection process and *not* advertising route changes to downstream BGP peers.

The use of BGP routing damping on EBGP is shown in Figure 19.6.

A customer of AS 65001 is connected to the AS by a link running EBGP and is advertising three routes: 172.31.0.0/20, 172.31.64.0/20, and 172.31.128.0/20. AS 65001 is providing transit service for this customer to the Internet, so the three routes are readvertised within AS 65001 and further to the Internet.

But look what happens when the 172.31.64.0/20 route starts to experience stability problems causing multiple update and withdraw message to be sent to AS 65001 (UP/DOWN/UP/DOWN, etc.). Without route damping enabled, this flap action would cause the router in AS 65001 to send new updates to other routers in AS 65001. These IBGP peers would then also send new updates to their Internet peers.

This wave of instability can be halted at the edge of AS 65001 by enabling route damping. Once enabled, the edge router in AS 65001 starts maintaining statistics for the routes received from the customer. Once the 172.31.64.0/20 route has been deemed unstable, the AS 65001 router stops generating new update message to its IBGP peers. The IBGP peers, in turn, also have no need to send updates to the Internet. This makes the Internet as a whole more stable.

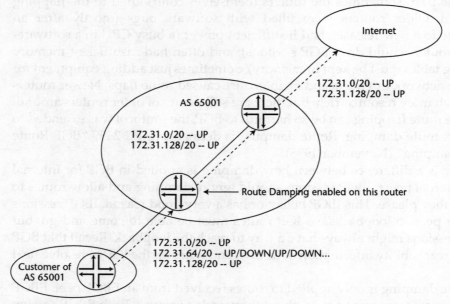

Figure 19.6 EBGP route damping.

How Route Damping Works

The point at which a route is deemed to be too unstable is calculated by the damping *figure of merit*. In this context, the term *figure* means a *number*, not a picture. The figure of merit is a type of "point value" given to a route. The value becomes a "penalty" if the figure of merit exceeds some predetermined value (the route is *suppressed*). It is often said that damping puts a route into a "penalty box" for a given period of time.

Consider how damping works on a Juniper Networks router (Cisco works a little differently). When a previously unknown (new) route arrives at a BGP router that has damping enabled, the new route gets assigned a figure of merit value of 0. Should the route experience any instability, the figure of merit gets incremented according to the following:

- If the route is withdrawn by the EBGP peer, the figure of merit is increased by a value of 1,000.

- If the route is readvertised from the EBGP peer, the figure of merit is increased by a value of 1,000.

- If the BGP attributes for the route change through new update messages from the EBGP peer, the figure of merit is increased by a value of 500.

The points given to a route decay, or reduce in value, at a certain rate, known as the *half-life*. As long as points decay faster than they accumulate, the route is not suppressed. Should the figure of merit value increase beyond a configured cutoff (suppress) threshold, the route is considered unusable and new information about the route from the EBGP peer is ignored. The suppress value is configurable, but must be less than or equal to the merit ceiling value, defined in the text that follows.

The route can once again be considered usable after the figure of merit decreases below a configured threshold. The figure of merit is decreased on a time schedule set by the network administrator. Should the figure of merit not decrease below the bottom threshold in a configured amount of time, the route can automatically be usable again (*reuse*). There is a maximum time that a route can be suppressed. This maximum is established by the configurable *max-suppress* parameter.

Also, the figure of merit can only increase to the maximum value, called the *merit ceiling*. The symbol used for the merit ceiling is ε_c. This maximum value is calculated from a combination of the components listed previously and is determined by the following formula:

$$\varepsilon_i \le \varepsilon_r e \left(\frac{t}{\lambda} \right) (\ln 2)$$

where ε_r is the figure of merit reuse threshold, t is the maximum suppression (hold-down) time in minutes, and λ is the half-life in minutes. However, the mathematics is the least important part of route damping.

The figure of merit value interacts with the damping parameters to produce its results. These parameters are as follows:

- The *suppress* variable is the configured threshold, where a BGP route is considered unstable and will not be used. This represents the value of the penalty that establishes the point at which damping is initiated. When this value is reached, the route is cut off, or suppressed. The usual default value of `suppress` is 3000. If changed, this value must be less than or equal to the merit ceiling ε_c or damping never occurs. The merit ceiling calculation was given earlier.

- The *reuse* variable is the configured threshold where a BGP route is considered usable once again. This is the value the penalty must decay to for the route to go. Then the router will consider the route in its path selection. The usual default value of the reuse is 750.

- The *half-life* variable is the rate at which the figure of merit is decreased to half its value once the value is larger than 0. The usual default value of the half-life is 15 minutes.

- The *max-suppress* variable is the configured maximum amount of time that a BGP route can be deemed unusable. This is the longest time that the route can be suppressed until the route is "given another chance to behave." The usual default value of the `max-suppress` is 60 minutes. At the end of the max-suppress interval, all is forgiven and the route becomes active again.

How these parameters fit in with the figure or merit is shown in Figure 19.7. The figure shows the figure of merit in use for a BGP route. The typical default values for suppress (3000), reuse (750), and half-life (15 minutes) are being used. The important points here are that there is an *exponential decay* (because of the formula used to decrease the value) on the figure of merit, and there is a fixed ceiling on the figure of merit value (the merit ceiling).

After receiving a new BGP route, the figure of merit is 0 for some period of time. As soon as the route is withdrawn, or the link is down, the figure of merit increments to 1,000. As long as the route stays down, the figure of merit decays somewhat. As the route is readvertised, the figure of merit is incremented by another 1,000. Again, the figure of merit starts to decay. Now the route is withdrawn a second time, and again the figure of merit is increased by 1,000. Now when the route is readvertised, the figure of merit is increased by another

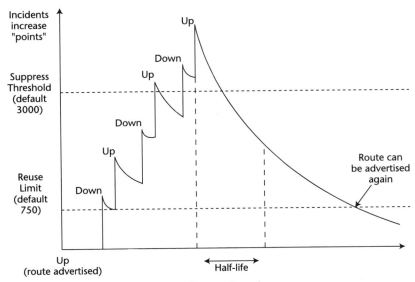

Figure 19.7 The route damping figure of merit.

1,000. This time, since not enough time has elapsed between these events in this example, the route is now over the suppress limit of 3,000 (it is probably closer to 4,000 at this point) and is considered unusable. Shortly after that, the route is withdrawn and readvertised yet again. Each time, the figure of merit increases 1,000 for each action. Notice that the route is still damped and considered unusable, but the figure of merit is still increasing as well as decreasing even while the route is suppressed.

Whenever the figure of merit is greater than 0, the value is constantly and consistently decayed using the configured half-life value. The half-life is always configured in increments of minutes to spare network administrators the chore of computing the formula in detail. The purpose of the half-life is to exponentially decay the figure of merit so that the value at any point in time is *reduced by half* at the end of the configured half-life time period (this half-life behavior is the essence of an exponential decay). The decay is made an exponential process so large that decreases in the figure of merit occur quickly, then taper off, giving rapidly flapping routes almost the same treatment as routes that flap more slowly. Flapping, fast or slow, is always bad.

Here is a fairly sophisticated example of route damping in action. In Figure 19.8, AS 65001 would like to enable damping for all of its EBGP peers based on the following administrative decisions:

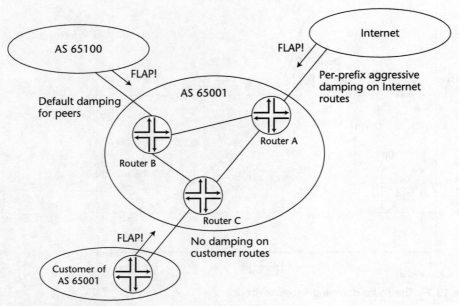

Figure 19.8 Routing damping in the real world.

- AS 65001 would like to use the default damping values for routes received from AS 65100.

- AS 65001 will *not* damp any routes from its customer (it's not wise to ignore customer links).

- AS 65001 would like to aggressively damp all routes from the Internet except for certain prefixes.

How can these route damping profiles be configured and used on a Cisco and a Juniper Networks router?

Cisco Route Damping

Cisco calls it route *dampening*, but it is still the same process and intent: to counter route instabilities due to route flapping. As expected, IBGP routes are not damped, because link-state changes inside the AS are important. Route damping is turned off by default.

Cisco defines four variables that are set with the general command to enable BGP route damping:

```
bgp dampening <half-life-time> <reuse> <suppress> <maximum-suppress-time>
```

- The `half-life-time` variable is the rate at which the figure of merit is decreased to half its value once the value is larger than 0. The default value of the `half-life-time` is 15 minutes. Possible values range from 1 to 45 minutes.

- The `reuse` variable is the configured threshold where a BGP route is considered usable once again. The default value of the `reuse` is 750. Possible values range from 1 to –20000.

- The `suppress` variable is the configured threshold where a BGP route is considered instable and will not be used. The default value of `suppress` is 2000. Possible values range from 1 to –20000. If changed, this value must be less than or equal to the merit ceiling ε_c, or damping never occurs. The merit ceiling calculation was given earlier.

- The `max-suppress-time` variable is the configured maximum amount of time that a BGP route can be deemed unusable. The default value of the `max-suppress-time` is 60 minutes (four times the half-life default). Possible values range from 1 to 255 minutes. At the end of the max-suppress interval, the route becomes active again.

This section configures and applies the appropriate damping parameters to Routers A, B, and C in Figure 19.8. Router C, facing the customer, needs no damping configuration at all, since route damping is disabled by default on Cisco routers.

Router B, the border router facing AS 65100, applies the default damping parameters to routes from this neighbor AS. This is done in the BGP configuration on Router B. Since all the default values for the parameters are accepted, only the main statement is needed:

```
autonomous-system 65001
!
router bgp 65001
 redistribute static
 bgp dampening
 neighbor 10.100.100.100 remote-as 65100
 no auto-summary
!
```

Router A, the border router facing the Internet (AS neighbor is perhaps 64999), applies aggressive damping parameters. These raise the half-life to 30 minutes (from 15), lower the reuse threshold to 200 (from 750), lower the suppress limit to 1500 (from 2000), and increase the maximum suppress time to 120 minutes (from 60). The configuration statement is:

```
bgp dampening 30 200 1500 120
```

Of course, using this on the EBGP configuration for the neighbor in AS 64999 (toward the Internet) would have the result of applying the same damping parameters to *every* route received from AS 64999. This might not be the best thing to do. Perhaps it would be better to allow some routes in AS 64999 to flap "normally," like customer routes, while aggressively damping everything else. The point is not which routes, but that this can be done using a route map and access list, of course.

Assume the address received on Router A facing the Internet (AS 64999) that are *not* to be damped at all are 192.168.10/24, 172.16.240.0/24, 172.27.32.64/26, and 192.168.100.0/24. The configuration on Router A is then as follows:

```
autonomous-system 65001
!
router bgp 65001
 bgp dampening route-map Let-Some-Through
 neighbor 10.200.200.200 remote-as 64999
 no auto-summary
!

!
access-list 1 permit 192.168.10.0 255.255.255.0
access-list 1 permit 172.16.240.0 255.255.255.0
access-list 1 permit 172.27.32.64 255.255.255.192
access-list 1 permit 192.168.100.0 255.255.255.0
access list 2 permit any
!
route-map Let-Some-Through permit 10
 match ip address 1
route-map Let-Some-Through permit 20
 match ip address 2
 set dampening 30 200 1500 120
!
```

For multivendor compatibility, the default Juniper Networks suppress value is 3000, and the maximum suppress time is 720 minutes, not 255 minutes. For Juniper Networks compatibility, these values should be set at:

```
bgp dampening 15 750 3000 60
```

However, this is not all that there is to it. Cisco routers only increment the figure of merit when a route is *withdrawn*. Juniper Networks routers increment the figure of merit *both* when a route is withdrawn (link down) and when the route is readvertised (link up). To get consistent behavior out of the Cisco/ Juniper Networks router collection, it is a good idea to *double* the Juniper Networks route suppress and reuse figures, if the Juniper Networks router defaults remain the same:

```
bgp dampening 15 1500 6000 60
bgp dampening 15 1500 6000 60
```

Do not try to set the value of the maximum-suppress-time above 255. Have the Juniper Networks routers lower theirs if necessary.

Juniper Networks Route Damping

The following are the default values and the ranges used for the four key route damping parameters on a Juniper Networks router:

- The suppress variable is the configured threshold where a BGP route is considered instable and will not be used. The default value of suppress is 3000. Possible values range from 1 to 20000. If changed, this value must be less than or equal to the merit ceiling $\mathcal{E}_c$, or damping never occurs. The merit ceiling calculation was given earlier.
- The reuse variable is the configured threshold where a BGP route is considered usable once again. The default value of the reuse is 750. Possible values range from 1 to 20000.
- The half-life variable is the rate at which the figure of merit is decreased to half its value once the value is larger than 0. The default value of the half-life is 15 minutes. Possible values range from 1 to 45 minutes.
- The max-suppress variable is the configured maximum amount of time that a BGP route can be deemed unusable. The default value of the max-suppress is 60 minutes. Possible values range from 1 to 720 minutes. At the end of the max-suppress interval, all is forgiven and the route becomes active again.

Once damping has been enabled within the BGP portion of the Juniper Networks router configuration, the default values are used for figuring of merit calculations. To alter those default values, a *damping profile* can be created and defined within the [edit policy-options] configuration hierarchy directory.

Much like the AS Path and Community attributes, a damping profile is named and defined first. Then it can be used within a policy as an action. There are five damping parameters that can be specified:

```
[edit policy-options]
damping sample-damping {
    half-life minutes;
    max-suppress minutes;
    reuse number;
    suppress number;
    disable;
}
```

The presence of the `disable` keyword deserves a few words of explanation. The keyword of `disable` can be used within a damping profile to *not* have the figure of merit be calculated for certain routes. This is often useful to exempt certain routes that should never be damped and unusable. One good example of these types of routes is the root DNS servers on the Internet. Should these servers become unreachable because of damping, the ISP and its customers would experience DNS lookup failures. For example, DNS routes could have a damping profile of `no-damping` defined that contains a single statement: `disable`.

The default Cisco suppress value is 2000, and the maximum suppress time is 255 minutes, not 720 minutes. For Cisco compatibility, these values should be set at:

```
half-life 15;
max-suppress 60;
reuse 750;
suppress 2000;
```

However, as noted previously, this is not all that there is to it. Cisco routers only increment the figure of merit when a route is *withdrawn*. Juniper Networks routers increment the figure of merit *both* when a route is withdrawn (link down) and when the route is readvertised (link up). To get consistent behavior out of the Cisco/Juniper Networks router collection, it is a good idea to *double* the Cisco route `suppress` and `reuse` figures, if the Cisco router defaults remain the same:

```
half-life 15;
max-suppress 60;
reuse 1500;
suppress 4000;
```

The damping profiles required for the example network in Figure 19.8 are:

```
[edit policy-options]
policy-statement customer-inbound {
    then damping do-not-damp;
}
[edit policy-options]
policy-statement internet-inbound {
    term let-some-through {
        from {
            route-filter 192.168.10.0/24 exact;
            route-filter 172.16.240.0/24 exact;
            route-filter 172.27.32.64/26 exact;
```

```
            route-filter 192.168.100.0/24 exact;
        }
        then {
            damping do-not-damp;
            accept;
        }
    }
    term damp-all-others {
        then damping aggressive-damp;
    }
}

damping do-not-damp {
    disable;
}
damping aggressive-damp {
    half-life 30;
    reuse 200;
    suppress 1500;
    max-suppress 120;
}
```

The profile do-not-damp has a variable of disable defined so it will never damp any routes. The profile aggressive-damp has defined four variables as suppress 1500, reuse 200, half-life 30, and max-suppress 120 (2 hours). All are much more severe than the defaults.

A policy called customer-inbound has been defined with no from statement, so all possible routes will match the policy. The policy has an action of damping do-not-damp. This action sets the profile of do-not-damp to all routes.

A policy called internet-inbound has been defined with two terms. The let-some-through term has several route-filter statements with actions defined of damping do-not-damp. This term further lists an action of then accept. A second term of damp-all-others has no from statement defined, so all remaining routes are subjected to the damping aggressive-damp action.

These policies are applied to BGP on each of the three routers as follows:

```
Router B:
[edit protocols]
bgp {
    damping;
}
Router C:
[edit protocols]
bgp {
```

```
    damping;
    import customer-inbound;
}
Router A:
[edit protocols]
bgp {
    damping;
    import internet-inbound;
}
```

Router B needs no profile, just `damping`, because all of the defaults are used on the routes from AS 65100. These damping profiles have the same result as the ones applied in the preceding section on Cisco route damping.

Acronym List

ABR	Area border router
ACK	Acknowledgement
AFI	Address Family Identifier (RIP)
AFI	Authority and Format Identifier (IS-IS)
AfriNIC	African Network Information Center
ANS	Advanced Network Systems
AOL	America Online
APNIC	Asian Pacific Network Information Center
APPN	Advanced Peer-to-Peer Networking
ARIN	American Registry for Internet Numbers
ARP	Address Resolution Protocol
ARPA	Advanced Research Project Agency
ARPANET	Advanced Research Project Agency Network
AS	Autonomous system
ASBR	Autonomous system boundary router

ASCII	American Standard Code for Information Interchange
ASIC	Application-specific integrated circuit
ATM	Asynchronous Transfer Mode
ATT	Attached
AUP	Acceptable Use Policy
AUX	Auxiliary
BBN	Bolt, Beranek, and Newman
BBS	Bulletin board system
BDR	Backup designated router
BGP	Border Gateway Protocol
BOOTP	Boot Protocol
BSD	Berkeley Systems (or Software) Distribution
CBGP	Confederation Border Gateway Protocol
CDPD	Cellular Digital Packetized Data
CERN	European Particle Physics Institute (English)
CIDR	Classless interdomain routing
CIP	Connector Interface Panel
CIX	Commercial Internet Exchange
CLI	Command-line interface
CLNP	Connectionless Network Protocol
CLNS	Connectionless Network Service
CLV	Code/Length/Value
CPU	Central processing unit
CSMA/CD	Carrier Sense Multiple Access with Collision Detection
CSNP	Complete Sequence Number PDU
DC	Demand circuit
DD	Database description
DF	Don't Fragment
DHCP	Dynamic Host Configuration Protocol
DIS	Designated Intermediate System
DLCI	Data Link Connection Identifier
DNS	Domain Name System

DR	Designated router
DRAM	Dynamic random access memory
DSL	Digital Subscriber Line
EA	External attributes
EBGP	Exterior Border Gateway Protocol
EGP	Exterior Gateway Protocol; exterior gateway protocol
EIGRP	Enhanced Interior Gateway Routing Protocol
ES	End system
EUI	Extended Unique Identifier
EXEC	Executive (mode)
FDDI	Fiber Distributed Data Interface
FE	Fast Ethernet
FEB	Forwarding Engine Board (M5/M10)
FEIP	Fast Ethernet Interface Processor
FIN	Final
FIX	Federal Internet Exchange
FPC	Flexible PIC Concentrator
FQDN	Fully qualified domain name
FT	Forwarding table
FTP	File Transfer Protocol
GBE	Gigabit Ethernet
GE	Gigabit Ethernet
GGP	Gateway-to-Gateway Protocol
GIF	Graphical Interface Format
GIP	Gateway Information Protocol
GUI	Graphical User Interface
HTML	Hypertext Markup Language
IA	Inter-area
IANA	Internet Assigned Numbers Authority
IBGP	Interior Border Gateway Protocol
ICANN	Internet Corporation for Assigned Names and Numbers
ICMP	Internet Control Message Protocol

IDRP	Inter-Domain Routing Protocol
IEEE	Institute of Electrical and Electronics Engineers
IETF	Internet Engineering Task Force
IGP	Interior gateway protocol
IGRP	Interior Gateway Routing Protocol
IOS	Internetwork Operating System
IP	Internet Protocol
IMP	Interface Message Processor
IRR	Internet Routing Registry
ISDN	Integrated Services Digital Network
IS	Intermediate system
IS-IS	Intermediate System–Intermediate System
ISO	International Organization for Standardization
ISP	Internet service provider
ITU	International Telecommunication Union
JPEG	Joint Photographic Experts Group
LAN	Local area network
LSA	Link-state advertisement
LSP	Link-State PDU (protocol data unit)
MAC	Media Access Control
MAU	Media attachment unit
MBGP	Multiprotocol Border Gateway Protocol
MBone	Multicast backbone
MC	Multicast
MCS	Miscellaneous Control System
MD5	Message Digest 5
MED	Multi-Exit Discriminator
MF	More Fragments
MIB	Management Information Base
MIME	Multipurpose Internet Mail Extensions
MOSPF	Multicast OSPF
MP-BGP	Multiprotocol BGP (sometimes)

MPLS	Multiprotocol Label Switching
MTU	Maximum transmission unit
NAP	Network access point
NAT	Network address translation
NBMA	Non-Broadcast, Multi-Access
NCP	Network Control Protocol
NCSA	National Center for Supercomputing Applications
NET	Network Entity Title
NFS	Network File System
NIC	Network interface card
NLRI	Network Layer Reachability Information
NOC	Network operations center
NSAP	Network service attachment point
NSF	National Science Foundation
NSP	Network service provider
NSSA	Not-so-stubby-area
NVRAM	Nonvolatile random access memory
NVT	Network virtual terminal
OAM&P	Operations, Administration, Maintenance & Provisioning
OC	Optical carrier
OL	Overload
ONC	Open Network Computing
OSI	Open Systems Interconnection
OSI-RM	Open Systems Interconnection Reference Model
OSPF	Open Shortest Path First
PARC	Palo Alto Research Center
PC	Personal computer
PCG	PFE Clock Generator
PCI	Peripheral Component Interconnect
PD	Packet director
PDU	Protocol data unit
PFE	Packet Forwarding Engine

PIC	Physical interface card
POP	Point of presence or Post Office Protocol
POS	Packet over SONET/SDH
PPP	Point-to-Point Protocol
PSH	Push
PSNP	Partial Sequence Number PDU
QoS	Quality of service
RA	Routing arbiter
RADIUS	Remote Access Dial-In User Service
RAM	Random access memory
RARP	Reverse Address Resolution Protocol
RE	Routing Engine or regular expression
RFC	Request for Comment
RIB	Routing Information Base
RIP	Routing Information Protocol
RIPE NCC	Reseaux IP Europeens Network Coordination Center
ROMMON	Read-Only Memory Monitor
RPC	Remote procedure call
RR	Route reflector
RST	Reset
RT	Routing table
RTMP	Routing Table Maintenance Protocol
RTP	Real-time Protocol or Reliable Transport Protocol (Cisco)
SCB	System Control Board (M40)
SDH	Synchronous Digital Hierarchy
SDLC	Synchronous Data Link Control
SFM	Switching and Forwarding Module (M160)
SGML	Standard Generalized Markup Language
SKA	Sender Keeps All
SLIP	Serial Line Interface Protocol
SMTP	Simple Mail Transfer Protocol

SNA	Systems Network Architecture
SNMP	Simple Network Management Protocol
SNP	Sequence Number PDU
SNPA	Subnetwork point of attachment
SOHO	Small office/home office
SONET	Synchronous Optical Network
SPF	Shortest Path First
SSB	System Switching Board (M20)
SSH	Secure shell
SYN	Synchronize
TACACS+	Terminal Access Controller Access Control Systems Plus
TCP	Transmission Control Protocol
TFTP	Trivial File Transfer Protocol
TGZ	tar and gzip
TLV	Type/Length/Value
ToS	Type of Service
TTL	Time To Live
TTY	Teletype
UDP	User Datagram Protocol
URG	Urgent
URL	Universal (or Uniform) Resource Locator
UTP	Unshielded twisted pair
VLAN	Virtual local area network
VLSM	Variable-length subnet masking
VoIP	Voice over IP
VPN	Virtual private network
VTY	Virtual Teletype
WAN	Wide area network
XDR	External Data Representation
XML	Extended Markup Language

Bibliography

No one knows everything, and this is especially true when it comes to the Internet and routing policies. As much as people can learn from hands-on experience and talking with others, there is still a need for good old-fashioned research. This means books and RFCs. And even if you understand something (or think you do), this does not necessarily mean you automatically know the best way to write about something so that others can understand it too. And good examples, I have found, are difficult to contrive on the spur of the moment.

I do not generally recommend anyone try to learn by reading RFCs, so there is no listing of those here. I occasionally check RFCs when sources conflict on a point, but with very few exceptions I do not find RFCs a valuable reading or learning experience. The main RFCs for the routing protocols are mentioned in the text, and each of these sources references the relevant RFCs as well. The only exception to my general rule is with regard to collections of RFCs in book form, and these are valuable mainly for the comprehensive *index* they offer. (How else would you quickly find every BGP RFC that mentions Local Preference?)

I should also mention that the Web sites for each of the vendors in this book, Cisco and Juniper Networks, have complete, current, and historical documentation available on their Web sites. There are valuable white papers and examples as well. Cisco is at www.cisco.com, and Juniper Networks is at www.juniper.net.

The following is a list of the most helpful sources for writing this book. I have included a few comments about just how helpful each of the volumes was.

Abbate, Janet. *Inventing the Internet.* Cambridge, Mass.: MIT Press, 1999. A complete look at the early days of the Internet.

Cerruzzi, Paul E. *A History of Modern Computing.* Cambridge, Mass.: MIT Press, 1998. Yes, there were computers before the Internet. This is for serious students only.

Comer, Douglas. *The Internet Book.* Upper Saddle River, N.J.: Prentice-Hall, 1997. Good Internet background, but for real beginners. Showing its age, so use it as a history book.

Doyle, Jeff. *Routing TCP/IP. Vol. I.* Indianapolis: Cisco Press, 1998. If you only read one book on routing basics, read this one for the IGPs.

Doyle, Jeff, and Jennifer DeHaven Carroll. *Routing TCP/IP. Vol. II.* Indianapolis: Cisco Press, 2001. Covers BGP, multicast, IPv6, and much more. Also essential.

Doyle, Jeff, and Matt Kolon, eds. *Juniper Networks Routers.* Berkeley, Calif.: McGraw-Hill/Osborne, 2002. A truly gigantic book covering all of the basics of Juniper Networks routers.

Feit, Dr. Sidnie. *TCP/IP.* New York: McGraw-Hill, 1999. Excellent perspective on TCP/IP from the user point of view. Despite the title, this book contains a lot about routers and routing.

Gillies, James, and Robert Cailliau. *How the Web was Born.* New York: Oxford University Press, 2000. The most complete history of the development of the Web at CERN by one of the principals (Cailliau).

Halabi, Sam, with Danny McPherson. *Internet Routing Architectures, 2nd ed.* Indianapolis: Cisco Press, 2000. Update of an old classic. This has always been just "the BGP book."

Hucaby, David, and Steve McQuerry. *Cisco Field Manual: Router Configuration.* Indianapolis: Cisco Press, 2002. A very good reference for checking command syntax, etc. Not long on explanation. But I found myself looking up command syntax again and again. The most used of all my Cisco books.

Huitema, Christian. *Routing in the Internet, 2nd ed.* Upper Saddle River, N.J.: Prentice-Hall, 2000. Very good book on IGP/EGP issues and answers. Vendor-neutral, which is almost a rare thing today.

Huston, Geoff. *ISP Survival Guide.* New York: John Wiley and Sons, 1999. Many of the labs in this book were based on issues raised by this fine book on real-world ISP situations.

Leinwand, Allan, and Bruce Pinsky. *Cisco Router Configuration, 2nd ed.* Indianapolis: Cisco Press, 2001. For beginners. Useful for edge or site router configuration, but not much else.

Lewis, Chris. *Cisco TCP/IP Routing Professional Reference.* New York: McGraw-Hill, 1998. Not very useful beyond RIP and the usual basics.

Lohr, Steve. *Go To.* New York: Basic Books, 2001. Nice look at what all those Internet routers are hooking up and carrying. A history of software ending with the Web, Java, UNIX, Linux, and so on.

Loshin, Pete. *Big Book of Border Gateway Protocol (BGP) RFCs.* San Francisco: Morgan-Kaufmann, 2000. What a book! Just having a complete index to all of these RFCs is worth the price. This is one of a whole series that includes other networking and routing concepts as well.

Moy, John. *OSPF.* Reading, Mass.: Addison-Wesley, 1998. OSPF from the man who wrote the RFCs. Sometimes the going gets heavy, but it's all there.

Naugle, Matthew. *Illustrated TCP/IP.* New York: John Wiley and Sons, 1999. I keep going back to this book when I need a quick look at the essentials of one TCP/IP feature or another. Very valuable.

Paquet, Catherine, and Diane Teare. *Building Scaleable Cisco Networks.* Indianapolis: Cisco Press, 2002. Very good for practical examples of OSPF and BGP configurations.

Parkhurst, William R. *Cisco BGP-4 Command and Configuration Handbook.* Indianapolis: Cisco Press, 2002. Very helpful, but the numerous example configurations and show commands tend to clutter up the text and break up the flow. However, for the total amount of BGP information, there is none better.

Perlman, Radia. *Interconnections, 2d ed.* Reading, Mass.: Addison-Wesley, 2000. Updated classic. Read Perlman not only for IS-IS, but for LANs, bridging, and her wry take on the entire industry.

Randall Neil. *The Soul of the Internet.* Boston, Mass.: International Thompson Computer Press, 1997. I have many other books on Internet history, but this is the one I use the most.

Sackett, George C. *Cisco Router Handbook, 2nd ed.* New York: McGraw-Hill, 2001. Very broad in range, it covers everything a router can do. Very light on configuration details.

Sportak, Mark A. *IP Routing Fundamentals.* Indianapolis: Cisco Press, 1999. Sound book on routing basics, especially RIP.

Stevens, W. Richard. *The Protocols. Vol. I of TCP/IP Illustrated.* Reading, Mass.: Addison-Wesley, 1994. Simply the classic book on TCP/IP. The late Stevens' approach to TCP/IP, which was to do the same thing on different platforms and see what happened, inspired my own approach to do the same with routers in this book. Still the best for all but the latest tweaks and features.

Stewart, John W., III. *BGP4.* Reading, Mass.: Addison-Wesley, 1999. Do not underestimate the importance of this slim volume. I found myself drawn to it again and again.

Velte, Toby, and Anthony Velte. *Cisco: A Beginner's Guide, 2nd ed.* Berkeley, Calif.: McGraw-Hill/Osborne, 2001. This is for real beginners; it assumes no knowledge even of Cisco as a company.

Wright, Robert. *IP Routing Primer.* Indianapolis: Cisco Press/Macmillan Technical Publishing, 1998. An absolute beginners guide to Cisco routers. Covers static routing and default routing in detail, but not much else.

On a budget, if the goal is router understanding only, I'd recommend Sportak for real beginners new to IP and routing (most will not need this level), both Doyle volumes for Cisco protocol and policy basics, Hucaby and McQuerry as a Cisco command reference, and Doyle and Kolon for Juniper Networks router details. If the goal includes TCP/IP understanding also, I'd go with Stevens for basic TCP/IP, and Naugle for the latest on TCP/IP. The rest are luxuries.

If you can only afford a couple of books, you can't go wrong buying anything with Jeff Doyle's name on it.

Index

SYMBOLS AND NUMERICS

* (asterisk), 672, 674
: (colon), 675
- (dash) operator, 636
. (dot) operator, 642, 674
$ (end), 674
/ (forward slash), 129
( ) (parenthesis) operator, 643, 675
| (pipe) operator, 636
^ (start), 674
10Base-T LAN, 85
10/100Base-T LAN port (Juniper
   Networks), 206
100-Mbps Fast Ethernet. *See* Ethernet

A

acceptable use policy, 22, 118
access charge, 27
accessing Cisco configuration file, 172
access layer
   Cisco, 168
   TCP/IP, 36, 38–40
access link, 117
access list (Cisco), 535, 542–543
access router, 166, 169, 581. *See also*
   aggregation
account name, 56
action pairs, 550, 553–556
active open, 37

active RIP, 259
active route, 230, 470, 533
`additive` knob (Cisco), 668
Address Resolution Protocols
   (ARPs), 41, 70–73
administrative distance (Cisco), 281,
   534, 535–536, 575–578
advanced distance-vector routing
   protocol, 272
Advanced Network Systems
   (ANS), 13, 25
Advanced Research Project Agency
   Network. *See* ARPANET
AfriNIC (African Network Information
   Center), 122
aggregation
   BGP and, 467–468
   BGP MED attribute and, 624–625
   Cisco router and, 602–604
   Internet and, 142–148
   IPv6 and, 152
   Juniper Networks router and,
      602, 604–608
   overview of, 132–134, 140–142,
      143, 599–602
   routing policy and, 148–150
   setting for Cisco router, 188–191
   setting for Juniper Networks
      router, 228–231

701